KU-305-896

HUMAN RIGHTS LAW

General Editors

Bríd Moriarty and Eva Massa

DBS Library
19-22 Dame Street
Dublin 2.
Phone: 01-4178745

OXFORD

UNIVERSITY PRESS

OXFORD

UNIVERSITY PRESS

Great Clarendon Street, Oxford OX2 6DP

Oxford University Press is a department of the University of Oxford.
It furthers the University's objective of excellence in research, scholarship,
and education by publishing worldwide in

Oxford New York

Auckland Bangkok Buenos Aires Cape Town Chennai Dar es Salaam
Delhi Hong Kong Istanbul Karachi Kolkata Kuala Lumpur Madrid
Melbourne Mexico City Mumbai Nairobi São Paulo Shanghai
Taipei Tokyo Toronto

With offices in

Argentina Austria Brazil Chile Czech Republic France Greece
Guatemala Hungary Italy Japan Poland Portugal Singapore
South Korea Switzerland Thailand Turkey Ukraine Vietnam

Oxford is a registered trademark of Oxford University Press
in the UK and in certain other countries

Published in the United States
by Oxford University Press Inc., New York

© Law Society of Ireland 2011

The moral rights of the authors have been asserted
Database right Oxford University Press (maker)

Crown Copyright material reproduced with the permission of the Controller,
HMSO (under the terms of the Click Use licence)

First edition 2004
Second edition 2008

All rights reserved. No part of this publication may be reproduced,
stored in a retrieval system, or transmitted, in any form or by any means,
without the prior permission in writing of Oxford University Press,
or as expressly permitted by law, or under terms agreed with the appropriate
reprographics rights organization. Enquiries concerning reproduction
outside the scope of the above should be sent to the Rights Department,
Oxford University Press, at the address above

You must not circulate this book in any other binding or cover
and you must impose the same condition on any acquirer

British Library Cataloguing in Publication Data

Data available

Library of Congress Cataloging in Publication Data

Data available

Typeset by Laserwords Private Ltd, Chennai, India
Printed in Great Britain
on acid-free paper by
Ashford Colour Press Ltd, Gosport, Hampshire

ISBN 978–0–19–957619–7

10 9 8 7 6 5 4 3 2 1

Disclaimer

While every care has been taken in the production of this book,
no legal responsibility or liability is accepted, warranted or implied by the
authors, editors, publishers or the Law Society in respect of any
errors, omissions or mis-statements.

341.48
MOR
€ 50.59
65973
3 day loan
6/11

PREFACE

DBS Library
19-22 Dame Street
Dublin 2.
Phone: 01-4178745

This text is designed to support the teaching of human rights law on the Law Society's Professional Practice Course. It provides an introduction to human rights law in Ireland. The text is divided into three parts: Part I provides an overview of the sources of human rights protection in Ireland; Part II is concerned with substantive human rights law and discusses key human rights; and Part III comprises two chapters devoted to refugee and immigration law and practice.

The book covers:
Chapter 1: Foundations of Human Rights Law (Elaine Dewhurst); Chapter 2: Three Spheres of Human Rights Protection in Ireland: An Overview of the Hierarchy (Bríd Moriarty); Chapter 3: Human Rights Protection in Ireland (Andrew Fergus); Chapter 4: The European Convention on Human Rights (Gráinne Mullan); Chapter 5: Incorporation of the ECHR in Irish Law (Gráinne Mullan); Chapter 6: International Human Rights Law (Gráinne Mullan); Chapter 7: The Role of the UN Today: Response to Serious Violations of Human Rights (Eva Massa); Chapter 8: Human Rights in EU Law (Bríd Moriarty); Chapter 9: Family and Child Law (Geoffrey Shannon); Chapter 10: The Right to Life and the Right to Bodily Integrity (Asim A. Sheikh); Chapter 11: Equality (Conor Power); Chapter 12: Due Process and the Right to a Fair Trial (Dara Robinson); Chapter 13: Freedom of Expression (Michael Kealey); Chapter 14: Liberty (Conor Power); Chapter 15: International Protection and Refugee Law (John Stanley & Gráinne Brophy); Chapter 16: Immigration and Citizenship Law (Hilkka Becker).

The authors of Chapter 15 would like to acknowledge the assistance of Caoimhe Sheridan, Enda O'Neill B.L, James Buckley B.L, Jacki Kelly, Bernadette McGonigle, Nuala Egan B.L, Conor Power B.L, Robert Fitzpatrick B.L, Gillian Cahill B.L, Colin O'Dwyer, Noeline Blackwell and Moira Shipsey.

The author of Chapter 16 would like to thank her colleague Catherine Cosgrave, Senior Solicitor with the Immigrant Council of Ireland Independent Law Centre, for her very helpful comments on the chapter.

We wish to thank Gill Clack who proofread the text. We also wish to thank Heather Smyth, Helen Davis, Olivia Rowland and Camille Poiré at OUP for their courtesy, professionalism and hard work on this text.

While every effort has been made to ensure the text is accurate neither the authors, the editors, nor the Law Society of Ireland accept legal liability for any errors, omissions or mis-statements of law. Any comments or queries on this book should be sent to the general editors at the Law Society.

Bríd Moriarty and Eva Massa
March 2010

DES Library
19-22 Dame Street
Dublin 2.
Phone: 01-4179745

AUTHORS

Hilkka Becker is a senior solicitor with the Immigrant Council of Ireland—Independent Law Centre. A graduate of law of the University of Hamburg, she is also qualified to practise law in Germany since 1998. Hilkka is a member of the European Immigration Lawyers' Network and has worked as a trainer and legal consultant with the International Organization for Migration (IOM) and Council of Europe. She is a board member of AkiDwA and a member of the Law Society's Human Rights Committee. She wrote chapter 16.

Gráinne Brophy is a solicitor with a BCL degree from UCD and a Diploma in Public Relations. She has worked in the area of asylum law with the Refugee Legal Service since 1999. She is a former board member of the Vicentian Refugee Service and she is currently a member of the Law Society's Human Rights Committee. She co-wrote chapter 15.

Dr Elaine Dewhurst is a lecturer in International Human Rights Law and Advanced Constitutional Law at Dublin City University. Elaine has a PhD and a First Class Honours BCL degree from University College Cork. In 2006, she successfully completed the EJ Phelan Fellowship in International Law awarded by the National University of Ireland. She has previously worked at the Law Society of Ireland as a Course Executive and as the Parliamentary and Law Reform Executive. She wrote chapter 1.

Andrew Fergus is a practising barrister working mainly in the areas of human rights and European law. He has a Masters Degree in European Communities Law and has tutored regularly in the Law Society on these topics, as well as on negotiation skills and professional conduct. In 2009 he participated as tutor in a training programme at the China University of Political Science and Law, Beijing, sponsored by the European Commission, on 'China in International Law' which included a module on human rights. He wrote chapter 3.

Michael Kealey is a solicitor with an established reputation in defamation, privacy and media law. He advises Associated Newspapers. He has written and lectured extensively on media law and Article 10 of the European Convention on Human Rights. He is a member of the Law Society's European Convention on Human Rights Task Force. He wrote chapter 13.

Eva Massa is a Spanish lawyer and Course Manager at the Law Society with responsibility for the design and management of courses in European Law, Human Rights Law, Professional Conduct, Interviewing and Negotiation skills. She is also Secretary to the EU and International Affairs Committee of the Law Society. She has a Masters Degree in

AUTHORS

International Relations from DCU and wrote a thesis on *'Universal Jurisdiction: Determining complicity in crimes against humanity'*. She wrote chapter 7.

Bríd Moriarty is a practising barrister and lecturer in EU Law at King's Inns. She previously worked as Course Co-ordinator for the Law Society where she was in charge of the European Law and Human Rights Law courses. Prior to joining the Law Society she worked as Senior Judicial Research Assistant in the Judges' Library. Previously she taught at Portobello College and the University of Limerick, where she completed an LL.M. in European Law. She wrote chapters 2 and 8.

Gráinne Mullan is a practising barrister and part-time lecturer in the Law School, Trinity College Dublin, where she lectures on human rights on the LL.M. course. She also lectures on human rights in the Law Society of Ireland and has written a number of articles in the areas of human rights and criminal procedure. She wrote chapters 4, 5 and 6.

Conor Power is a barrister, who practises in the areas of human rights and employment law. He is also a contributor to the Law Society on these topics. He wrote chapters 11 and 14.

Dara Robinson was admitted as a solicitor in London in 1988. He has practised in Dublin since 1992, and is a partner with the firm of Garrett Sheehan and Partners. He is Chairman of the Criminal Law Committee, and a member of the Council, of the Law Society. He regularly writes and lectures on criminal law, human rights and mental health law. He wrote chapter 12.

Geoffrey Shannon is a solicitor and deputy director of education at the Law Society of Ireland. He has been selected by the European Expert Organising Committee as the Irish expert member of the Commission on European Family Law. Geoffrey is Chairman of the Adoption Board and has been appointed by the Irish Economic and Social Research Institute as the child law expert to the longitudinal study of children, which is the most ambitious project of its kind ever to have been commissioned in Ireland. He has recently been re-appointed by the Irish government as a Special Rapporteur on Child Protection in March 2010. Geoffrey was appointed by the government to a two person review group to examine the deaths of children in State care over a ten year period. He wrote chapter 9.

Asim A. Sheikh is a practising barrister, and lecturer in legal medicine with Forensic and Legal Medicine, School of Medicine and Medical Science, UCD. He lectures and has published widely on aspects of medical law, legal medicine and genetics and law. He also lectures in the RCSI and the Law Society. He is Vice-Chair and member of the Irish Council for Bioethics. He is currently Editor-in-Chief of the *Medico-Legal Journal of Ireland*. He wrote chapter 10.

John Stanley is a practising barrister who works in the areas of human rights and refugee law. He is also the Chairman of the Irish Refugee Council. He co-wrote chapter 15.

CONTENTS

CONTENTS

CONTENTS

CONTENTS

CONTENTS

CONTENTS

TABLE OF CASES

TABLE OF CASES

TABLE OF CASES

TABLE OF CASES

TABLE OF CASES

TABLE OF LEGISLATION

TABLE OF LEGISLATION

TABLE OF LEGISLATION

TABLE OF LEGISLATION

TABLE OF LEGISLATION

CHAPTER 1

FOUNDATIONS OF HUMAN RIGHTS LAW

1.1   Introduction

A sound and practical education in human rights law is the aim of this Human Rights Law manual. From this chapter, where the foundations of human rights law are elucidated, to the substantive chapters on individual rights and remedies, the manual deals with all aspects of both domestic and international human rights law that a legal practitioner in Ireland will come across in their work. It will provide a 'one-stop shop' where legal principles are explained, new developments are highlighted and sources of law and additional resources are clearly identified.

The aim of this chapter is to explain what human rights are, as defined at an international level, and what their characteristics are. Specific attention will be given to the protection of human rights in Irish domestic law under the Constitution, the European Convention on Human Rights Act, 2003 and EU law. This will be achieved by demonstrating the manner in which human rights claims can be dealt with in legal practice. A case example will be outlined and a practical approach to identifying, researching and applying human rights law in Ireland to the case will be provided. Finally, the chapter will conclude by briefly noting the role of lawyers in relation to human rights and the professional obligations that flow from that role. This chapter should provide a sound basis upon which students of human rights law can develop their skills in taking human rights cases and can learn about the substantive and procedural aspects of human rights law.

1.2   What are Human Rights?

'Human rights' as a concept is difficult to define and, some academics argue, has roots in natural law, that is, it has its origins in nature and as such possesses 'general validity transcending place and time' (Halstead, *Unlocking Human Rights*, 2009, Hodder, at p. 5). This pre-dates the formalisation of human rights law by international treaties and conventions. However, other academics such as Smith, note that the term 'human rights' dates back to the advent of the United Nations and the ratification of the Universal Declaration on Human Rights in 1948 (Smith, *International Human Rights*, 3rd edn, 2007, OUP, 5). Whatever their origin, the concept of 'human rights' is firmly secured in our national, regional and international legal systems. Yet a comprehensive definition of 'human rights' is no closer to being formulated.

The most common definition of human rights is that formulated by the United Nations Office of the High Commissioner for Human Rights, who has defined 'human rights' as 'basic rights and freedoms that all people are entitled to regardless of nationality, sex, national or ethnic origin, race, religion, language, or other status'. Examining this definition, two distinct issues can be highlighted:

(1) The 'human' in 'human rights' refers to all human beings regardless of nationality, place of residence, sex, national or ethnic origin, colour, religion, language, or any other status. This implies that 'human rights' belong to all humans and can be enforced by all humans. However, humans require knowledge and capacity to seek the enforcement of their human rights. Indeed, other human beings have responsibilities to protect these 'human rights' such as the lawyer who has to identify a violation of human rights, who has to mount challenges to the current legal regime and who has to defend human rights; the court, who through the work of judges, has to vindicate human rights and the State who has to ensure the enforcement of human rights. Human rights are so called not only because they belong to every human being, but also because they require identification, acknowledgement and enforcement by all human beings.

(2) The 'rights' aspect of 'human rights' refers to the 'basic rights and freedoms', as codified in documents such as the Universal Declaration on Human Rights, 1948 and other international, regional and national instruments, that are vital to both those who are tasked to protect them (the addressee) and those who enjoy them (the holder). These rights and freedoms protect human beings from abuse by the political, economic, legal and social systems in operation in the State. In many cases, these rights are essential to survival as human beings.

Therefore, human rights refer to the fundamental rights and freedoms that belong to every human being in an equal manner and require the interaction of other human beings to ensure their protection, enforcement and vindication.

1.2.1 WHAT ARE THE CHARACTERISTICS OF HUMAN RIGHTS?

Human rights at an international level have been shown to possess certain basic characteristics that are important to their survival. These include:

(a) Universality and inalienability

The principles of universality and inalienability are often considered the cornerstone of human rights law. Such characteristics imply that human rights belong to all human beings regardless of the political, social or legal systems within which these humans live. It is important to be aware that there are some who would argue ('cultural relativists') that human rights are not universal but should differ according to the legal, political and social systems in the State in which the holder of the right resides. Cultural relativists would argue that as various standards and ideas operate all over the globe, it is impossible to suggest that one standard of norms (often a 'Western' standard) can apply to all those human beings. Universality is also threatened by the use of terms such as 'citizenship' in national and regional documents. Such terms exclude non-citizens from the scope and protection of the rights guaranteed. However, universality is intended to be an ideal that all nations will work together to achieve. In some areas of human rights law, this ideal has been very successful such as in the prohibition on slavery and the prohibition against torture. However, there is a great deal more to be achieved if universality is to continue to thrive.

The inalienability of human rights provides that human rights should not be taken away or interfered with by the political, social or legal systems. Inalienability does not mean that all human rights are absolute and operate without restriction. There are exceptions in certain cases where a human right can be superseded by an overriding consideration such as the public interest. For example, a person's right to liberty can be restricted in cases where they are imprisoned for a crime they have committed. As long as due process is maintained, these restrictions are permissible under human rights law.

(b) Interdependent and indivisible

An undisputed characteristic of human rights is the fact that such rights are indivisible and interdependent. This means that the deprivation of one right adversely affects the enjoyment of other rights. A good example is the failure of the State to provide adequate educational opportunities for its citizens. Without the protection of the right to education, rights, such as the right to express one's opinion or the right to work, are adversely affected as human beings are unable to enjoy their rights fully.

However, there are situations where rights conflict with one another and where the courts will necessarily have to involve themselves in a balancing exercise to ensure the protection of the rights in conflict, eg in the case of the *Jyllands-Posten* Muhammad cartoons where 12 editorial cartoons, many of which depicted the Islamic prophet Muhammad, were published in the Danish newspaper *Jyllands-Posten* on 30 September 2005, the right to freedom of expression and the right to free practice and expression of religion without discrimination came into direct conflict.

The Irish courts have dealt with this issue on a number of occasions. The initial view was that the role of the courts in such cases was one of balancing (harmonising) the rights in question. In the case of *Quinn's Supermarket v Attorney General* [1972] IR 1 a conflict arose between the right to the free practice of religion and the guarantee against discrimination. The Supreme Court held that the correct approach of the courts in such cases was to balance/harmonise the rights in question and, on the facts of the case, a discrimination, provided it went no further than was necessary, did not infringe the guarantee if its object was to further the practice of religion.

A different approach was adopted in *The People (DPP) v Shaw* [1982] IR 1, a case involving a conflict between the right to liberty (detention in custody excessive) and the right to life (excessive detention considered necessary to save the life of a girl the man had allegedly abducted where there was a slim chance of finding her alive). The Supreme Court held that where there is a conflict between two rights, the one that ranks higher prevails and, in the circumstances of this case, the right to life outranked the right to liberty. However, the case of *Attorney General v X* [1992] 1 IR 1 saw the Supreme Court revert to the harmonious approach to conflicts of rights. The tragic facts of the X case involved the Supreme Court in a balancing act between the right to life of the mother and the right of the mother to travel and the right to life of the foetus. The Supreme Court held that courts, in making determinations in cases where a conflict between rights arises, should in all cases firstly attempt to harmonise the rights. Only if this was not possible should a hierarchy of rights be established. The Court recognised the mother's right to travel to terminate her pregnancy in order to avert a real and substantial risk to her own life. (see Doyle, *Constitutional Law Texts, Cases and Materials*, 2008, Clarus Press, Dublin.)

(c) Equal and non-discriminatory

As previously mentioned human rights belong to all people regardless of their status. The principle of equality and non-discrimination permeates all international human rights treaties, regional agreements and national constitutions and in many ways is the cornerstone of human rights law. Without the characteristic of non-discrimination, human beings could not enjoy the universality or inalienability of human rights fully.

1.2.2   TYPES OF HUMAN RIGHTS

- Civil and political rights: These rights are often referred to as 'first generation rights', are generally characterised by the term 'freedom' and are designed to protect citizens against State interference. Civil and political rights include the right to property, life, equality and liberty and further encompass the fundamental freedoms of movement, thought, conscience and religion, opinion and expression, assembly and association and freedom from slavery, torture or cruel, inhuman and degrading treatment and from arbitrary arrest and detention. These rights require a guarantee of non-interference by the State but rarely require any positive action on the part of the State. Both international law (most notably the International Covenant on Civil and Political Rights 1966) and domestic law (including Bunreacht na hÉireann, the Irish Constitution, and domestic legislation such as the European Convention on Human Rights Act, 2003 protect and provide redress for a breach of civil and political rights in Ireland.

- Economic, social and cultural rights: These rights are often referred to as 'second generation rights', are characterised by the term 'equality' and in many cases require some action on the part of the State to ensure their enforcement and protection. These rights encompass the right to social security, to rest and leisure, to an adequate standard of living, to education, housing, and healthcare, and to freely participate in the cultural life of the community as well as rights to inherit, development rights and rights to protection of personal data and food. Employment rights are also considered to fall among this category of rights. While such rights are protected at an international level (most notably by the International Covenant on Economic, Social and Cultural Rights 1966), economic, social and cultural rights are not normally included in laws protecting human rights in Ireland. The Irish Constitution Bunreacht na hÉireann expressly refers to economic, social and cultural rights in Article 45 dealing with the Directive Principles of Social Policy which essentially means that such rights are non-justiciable (see **chapter 3**). The main legislation in Ireland dealing with human rights, the European Convention on Human Rights Act, 2003, does not refer to economic, social and cultural rights (see **chapter 5**). However, some economic, social and cultural rights, such as employment rights and data protection rights, are protected in domestic law. Increased protection of such rights will also be brought about through the European Union Charter of Fundamental Rights which came into force as a result of the Lisbon Treaty (see **chapter 8**).

- Group rights: These are often referred to as 'third generation rights', are characterised by the term 'solidarity' and include rights of a group or collective to seek self-determination and protection. These are not generally recognised in traditional human rights instruments or in domestic law but are becoming increasingly prevalent at an international level. For example, the rights of migrant workers are protected at an international level by the United Nations Convention on the Rights of Migrant Workers and Members of Their Families 1990. However, this Convention has not yet been incorporated into domestic law.

1.3   Human Rights in Irish Law

There are three main spheres of human rights protection in Irish law (see **chapter 2**). These three spheres operate in conjunction with one another to provide a wide range of protection for all human rights in Ireland. The diagram below represents the protection of human rights law in Ireland.

1.3.1   DOMESTIC LAW

Human rights are protected in Ireland by two main sources of law:

(1)   The Irish Constitution, Bunreacht na hÉireann

(2)   Legislation

(1)   The Constitution provides for human rights protection in Articles 40—44 and includes the protection of rights that are both enumerated and unenumerated (these rights are not expressly mentioned in the Constitution but have been read into the Constitution by the decisions of the courts in Ireland eg the right to bodily integrity (see **chapter 10**) is not expressly mentioned in the Constitution but the courts have held that it is protected as one of the personal rights under Article 40.3.2° of the Constitution (see *Ryan v Attorney General* [1965] IR 294, 313)). The Constitution also prevents the State from enacting laws that are repugnant to the Constitution (Article 15.4)

(2)   The European Convention on Human Rights Act, 2003 is the most important piece of legislation relating to human rights in Ireland. The main purpose of the legislation is to incorporate the European Convention for the Protection of Human Rights and Fundamental Freedoms (ECHR) into Irish law. The ECHR protects a wide range of civil and political rights from the right to life and freedom of expression to the protection of the peaceful enjoyment of possessions. Section 2 of the Act requires that subject to the existing rules of statutory interpretation the courts should apply both common law rules and statutory provisions so that they are compatible with the European Convention on Human Rights. Section 3 requires that 'organs of state' must perform their duties in a manner compatible with the ECHR. Any person who suffers injury, loss or damage as a result of such a body's failure to do this is entitled to damages. Section 1 defines an organ of state as a tribunal or any other body established or any body through which the

powers of the State are exercised. Finally, s 5 of the Act grants to the courts the power to make a declaration that a statutory provision or common law rule is incompatible with the Convention. Such a declaration does not render the law in question invalid; rather the Taoiseach is obliged to bring any such declaration to the attention of both Dáil and Seanad Éireann within 21 days. A litigant who has been granted a declaration of incompatibility may receive monetary compensation in accordance with the principles of just satisfaction under Article 41 ECHR, but the award of such compensation is entirely within the discretion of the Government (see also **chapters 2**, **3** and **5**).

1.3.2   EU LAW

While the founding treaties of the EU did not refer specifically to human rights, such rights were inferred into the treaties by the European Court of Justice (ECJ) in a manner similar to the development of unenumerated rights in Ireland. Subsequent Treaty amendments have recognised the rights guaranteed by the ECHR (Article 6(3) Treaty on European Union (TEU)) as general principles of Community Law. Political sanctions (such as a reduction in voting rights) for states guilty of serious and persistent breaches of fundamental rights and the making of recommendations in cases where there is a clear risk of a serious breach by a Member State of fundamental rights can be implemented (Article 7 TEU). The Lisbon Treaty gives effect to the European Union Charter of Fundamental Rights which sets out in a single text, for the first time in the EU's history, the whole range of civil, political, economic and social rights of European citizens and all persons resident in the EU (Protocol No 30, Lisbon Treaty). These rights are divided into six sections: Dignity, Freedoms, Equality, Solidarity, Citizens' Rights and Justice. These rights are based on the fundamental rights and freedoms recognised by the ECHR, the constitutional traditions of the EU Member States, the Council of Europe's Social Charter, the Community Charter of Fundamental Social Rights of Workers and other international conventions to which the EU or its Member States are parties (see also **chapters 2**, **5**, **6** and **8**).

1.3.3   INTERNATIONAL LAW

If there is no protection of a particular right in Irish law or at a regional level, there may be protection available at an international level. However, international law is not automatically legally binding in Ireland and as such is not justiciable before the Irish courts.

In order for an international law treaty to be binding in Ireland it must be incorporated into the domestic legal system, either as an amendment to the Constitution or by an Act of the Oireachtas. This is due to the fact that Ireland is a dualist state (Article 29 of the Constitution) which means that if Ireland wants to be bound by an international treaty, not only must Ireland sign and ratify the treaty at an international level but it must also incorporate it into the domestic law of the State (see **chapter 2** and **5.2**).

So why should a lawyer be concerned with the provisions of international law? International law has persuasive effect and can be of great assistance to a court and to lawyers in interpreting rights that are protected under national law. It can also be very valuable in situations where rights are currently not recognised in the domestic context. In such cases it may be argued before a court that a right should be recognised and enforced in the domestic legal system because of the fact that it exists at an international level and is protected internationally. International law is therefore aspirational in that it provides a standard of human rights which states should aspire to protect (see **chapters 2**, **6** and **7**).

1.4   The Steps in Dealing with a Human Rights Claim: A Case Study

An interesting recent human rights case (*In the Matter of an Application for Judicial Review by C, A, W, M and McE* [2007] NIQB 101 and *In re McE, In re M, In re C and another* [2009] UKIIL 15) arose in Northern Ireland and involved the arrest of the applicants under anti-terror legislation in April 2006. The applicants were taken after their arrest to the Serious Crime Suite at Antrim Police Station where each of them nominated a solicitor that they wished to represent them. In each case the nominated solicitor asserted their client's right to a private consultation and asked for an assurance from the police that those consultations would not be monitored. The police refused to provide the assurances that the solicitors had sought for the applicants. They said that it was their practice 'not to comment' on such issues. This was because the Regulation of Investigatory Powers Act, 2000 (UK) allowed for direct surveillance in terror cases. The applicants sought declaratory relief to the effect that they were entitled to the guarantee of freedom from covert surveillance. They asserted that the failure to provide them with assurances was incompatible with Articles 6 and 8 ECHR. (Please note that the case and analysis in this section is taken from an article by the author entitled Dewhurst E., 'Bugging Solicitor/Client Consultations', April 2008, Law Society Gazette 18).

A student of law or a lawyer tasked with this case, whether in the UK or in Ireland, would have to ask a number of questions at this juncture. Is such a claim relevant? Would it be successful? What are the guarantees under the ECHR? How do they apply in this context or do they even apply? What are the relevant tests? Have there been similar cases to this case? Are there alternative claims? If such a case arose in the Irish context, would there be a constitutional claim?

So how does a lawyer make a determination that human rights law may have been breached or that he/she will be successful in any resultant claim? The above case demonstrates both the insecurity and the uncertainty that come with practising human rights law in Ireland and navigating unchartered territory may seem discouraging. However, this does not mean that the lawyer is unaided in this task. There are four simple steps that can be followed that can assist a lawyer in taking a human rights claim.

(1)   Identify the human rights issue.

(2)   Research the relevant human rights law.

(3)   Apply the human rights law to the facts of the case.

(4)   Conclude with reference to the remedies and methods of enforcement that are relevant to the case.

1.4.1   IDENTIFYING THE HUMAN RIGHTS ISSUE

It is intended to provide an overview of each of these steps and then to demonstrate how each of the steps would be applied in this jurisdiction in the context of a case similar to the one discussed above.

There is rarely a legal case that fits neatly within one legal subject area. One of the great skills that lawyers offer is the ability to identify disparate issues from a complicated fact scenario. When presented with a case that may engender a potential human rights claim, legal professionals have to be able to identify the type of right that has been affected. It is necessary at this stage to refer to the protection of human rights under of crime was necessary (*Norris v Attorney General* [1984] IR 36) such interferences could be considered legitimate in the circumstances. However, adequate justification would have to exist before the courts would consider that a legitimate interference had occurred. The courts will look at all the circumstances of a particular case and the nature and importance of the particular police duty being discharged before coming to this decision (*Kane v Governor of Mountjoy Prison* [1988] IR 757). Therefore, it would appear that unless the Garda Síochána had a specific justification, surveillance of this type may infringe the constitutionally protected right to privacy and right to a trial in the due course of law.

• ECHR: Article 6 has been interpreted to mean that while the right to consult with a legal adviser in private is an important one, it is not absolute. It will depend on the impact the restriction had on the fairness of the hearing and will be justifiable only where there is good cause to interfere. A consideration of the position of the applicants in this case should involve an analysis of these justifications. As was held in the case of *In the Matter of an Application for Judicial Review by C, A, W, M and McE* [2007] NIQB 101, there was no evidence adduced by the applicants that their consultations had been tapped or that their trials would be prejudiced as a result. Even if they had been tapped, there was no evidence to suggest that a violation of Article 6 would have occurred. Therefore, proving a violation of Article 6 in a case similar to this one may be difficult.

• ECHR: In relation to Article 8, the essential question is whether this interference could be justified under Article 8(2). The interference would be justified only if it was in accordance with law, pursued a legitimate aim and was necessary in a democratic society. The High Court of Justice in Northern Ireland, Queen's Bench Division in *In the Matter of an Application for Judicial Review by C, A, W, M and McE* [2007] NIQB 101 found that the tapping of private consultations between a legal adviser and a client was in accordance with the law as set out in the Regulation of Investigatory Powers Act, 2000 (UK). However, in the UK the Act was held not to be proportionate as the interference could take place on the authorisation of the police. Interference with this right cannot be justified where there is no demonstrable measure of independence on the part of the authorising agency. The confidence that a legal adviser and his client can have in giving advice and providing information would be increased by the knowledge that no monitoring of their consultations will take place unless this has been shown to the satisfaction of an independent person to be strictly necessary. In the absence of this independent monitoring, surveillance of a consultation between a legal adviser and their client could not be justified. As the applicants in this case had not received assurances that their consultations would not be monitored, the privacy to which they were entitled under Article 8 may have been interfered with without justification.

1.4.4   CONCLUDING A LEGAL ANALYSIS

When concluding a legal analysis such as this it is important to make a determination as to whether the client has met the legal tests imposed along with a statement as to the likelihood of success of the client. Reference to the remedies available and the method of enforcement should also be included.

For the applicants in the case study outlined above, it is clear that there are potential avenues of redress both under the Constitution and under the ECHR. It is possible that the legislation, as outlined, if part of Irish domestic legislation may be incompatible with the Constitution and the ECHR.

At a national level, there are remedies for breach of Constitutional rights, remedies for breach of the ECHR and remedies under EU Law. In terms of the ECHR, it is important to be aware of the provisions in the European Convention on Human Rights Act, 2003 for damages where 'organs of state' do not perform their duties in a manner compatible with the Convention under s 3 and the right to request a declaration that a statutory provision or common law rule is incompatible with the Convention under s 5 (see **chapter 5**). This manual, in later chapters, will provide an analysis of the rights and remedies under the Constitution, the ECHR and EU Law.

It is also important to be aware of the rights of litigants to bring proceedings before international courts and relevant UN treaty bodies. In this respect, the book also highlights the various alternative avenues for a litigant who has a serious human rights claim that cannot be dealt with adequately under national law.

1.5   Conclusion

This book has been developed with the legal practitioner and student of law in mind. It highlights both the primary and secondary sources of human rights law in Ireland, discusses the substantive provisions and their interpretations and demonstrates the procedural and remedial avenues available to potential litigants.

This chapter seeks to provide a general overview or foundation of human rights law as utilised by the practitioner in Ireland. The UN Basic Principles on the Role of Lawyers (1990) provides that lawyers, in their education (both initial and continuing), should be made aware of human rights and fundamental freedoms recognised by national and international law (Principle 9). This book aims to increase the awareness of human rights law issues among practitioners and to assist practitioners in taking human rights cases.

The UN Basic Principles on the Role of Lawyers (1990) also provides for a special role for lawyers in the protection of the 'rights of their clients and in promoting the cause of justice' and calls on lawyers to 'uphold human rights and fundamental freedoms recognised by national and international law' (Principle 14). Indeed, many lawyers in Ireland have embraced this role and lawyers play an important part in developing a human rights law culture in Ireland. Lawyers in Ireland who embrace human rights law play a critical role in assisting the courts in the administration of justice and the legislature in developing human rights compliant legislation. It is hoped that this chapter and this book will meet the needs of students and lawyers and assist them in this important function.

THREE SPHERES OF HUMAN RIGHTS PROTECTION IN IRELAND: AN OVERVIEW OF THE HIERARCHY

2.1   Introduction

There are three spheres of human rights law in Ireland: Irish domestic law, European Union (EU) law and international law and all contain guarantees of human rights that Ireland seeks to uphold. In Irish domestic law, Bunreacht na hÉireann, the Irish Constitution is the chief source of such guarantees. Other sources include legislation and case-law.

As Ireland is a strict dualist state, international human rights obligations that are not incorporated into domestic law only bind the State under international law and do not create rights or duties that are enforceable in domestic courts. The European Union, of which Ireland is a member, is increasingly concerned with human rights protection and EU law is enforceable in domestic courts. The rights that are protected in each of these spheres are discussed in the following chapters.

This chapter is concerned with the relationship between domestic and international law and between domestic and EU law. The relationship between international law and EU law is beyond the scope of this text, although the relationship between EU law and the European Convention on Human Rights and Fundamental Freedoms (the ECHR) is discussed in **chapter 8**.

2.2   The First Sphere of Human Rights Protection: The Constitution and Domestic Legislation

The Constitution, Bunreacht na hÉireann, contains a catalogue of human rights protections. These rights are at the apex of domestic human rights protection and are discussed in **chapter 3**. Domestic legislation concerning human rights is also considered in **chapter 3**.

The Constitution prohibits the Irish legislature from enacting laws which conflict with the provisions of the Constitution, including its human rights guarantees.

Article 15.4 of Bunreacht na hÉireann provides:

1°   The Oireachtas shall not enact any law which is in any respect repugnant to the Constitution or any provision thereof.
2°   Every law enacted by the Oireachtas which is in any respect repugnant to this Constitution or any provision thereof, shall but to the extent only of the repugnancy, be invalid.'

In the case of a conflict between constitutionally protected rights, it is the responsibility of the courts to balance those rights. In the *People (DPP) v Shaw* [1982] IR 1, the Supreme Court held that because of 'extraordinary excusing circumstances' evidence obtained in deliberate violation of an accused's constitutional rights was admissible in a murder trial. The police had detained the accused beyond the permissible period but had been motivated by the possibility of saving the victim's life. The Court held that the right to life ranked higher than the right to liberty.

2.3 The Second Sphere of Human Rights Protection: International Law

The domestic impact of international treaties has traditionally been a subject determined in accordance with the constitutional law of the signatory state. In international law there are two theories of incorporation of international obligations into the legal systems of states. These are the monist and the dualist theories. When monist obligations are assumed by a monist state they automatically become part of the legal system of that state, individuals can plead provisions of international law in their domestic courts and international law is considered superior. Dualism binds the State in the international sphere but international treaties do not become part of domestic law on ratification. There must be the additional step of incorporation. Without incorporation, individuals cannot rely on provisions of international law in the domestic courts of dualist states. Difficulties arise when international obligations conflict with domestic legal rules.

Many human rights protections stem from international treaties (see **chapters 4** and **6**). For that reason, it is necessary to consider the relationship between international law and Irish law when considering the hierarchy of human rights norms in this jurisdiction.

2.3.1 BUNREACHT NA HÉIREANN'S APPROACH TO INTERNATIONAL LAW

The Constitution adopts a rigid dualist stance to international law. Article 29.6 of Bunreacht na hÉireann provides:

> *'No international agreement shall be part of the domestic law of the State save as may be determined by the Oireachtas.'*

International laws that are ratified by the Irish State are binding on the State under international law and enforceable by other states in accordance with their terms. However they only become binding on the State under domestic law following incorporation into domestic law as determined by the Oireachtas. This stance has a significant impact on the practice of human rights law as many human rights protections originate as international treaties. It has been noted that this approach is a political choice:

> 'This facility [for the incorporation of international treaties into domestic law] for harmonising or enabling a dialogue between international and domestic standards in the area of human rights has been under-used. . . . Those reasons are, however, political and not legal as the law provides for the integration of international standards within domestic law. It is by reason of political choice—whether in the form of political act or omission—that international standards have remained largely unincorporated in any direct manner.' (O' Connell, *ECHR Act, 2003: A Preliminary Assessment of Impact*, 2006, Dublin Solicitors Bar Association/Law Society of Ireland, 12.)

2.3.2 DUALISM AND THE ECHR PRIOR TO THE EUROPEAN CONVENTION ON HUMAN RIGHTS ACT, 2003

The most significant international human rights treaty from an Irish perspective is the ECHR. Ireland ratified the ECHR in the early 1950s but it has only been incorporated into Irish law as a consequence of the European Convention on Human Rights Act, 2003 (see **2.3.3** and **chapter 5**)

It is proposed to look at the status of the ECHR in Irish domestic law prior to the European Convention on Human Rights Act, 2003. Initially, the Irish courts adopted a rigid dualist approach to the ECHR. Subsequently, they seem to have accepted that the ECHR had some persuasive value. In *Re Ó Laighléis* [1960] IR 93, the Supreme Court stated *per* Maguire CJ:

> 'The insuperable obstacle to importing the provisions of the convention...into the domestic law of Ireland—if they be at variance with that law—is, however the terms of the constitution of Ireland....
>
> The Oireachtas has not determined that the Convention for the Protection of Human Rights and Fundamental Freedoms is part of the domestic law of the State, and accordingly this Court cannot give effect to the convention if it be contrary to domestic law or purports to grant rights or impose obligations additional to those of domestic law.
>
> No argument can prevail against the express command of s 6 of Article 29 of the Constitution before judges whose declared duty it is to uphold the Constitution and the laws.
>
> The Court accordingly cannot accept the idea that the primacy of domestic legislation is displaced by the State becoming party to the Convention for the Protection of Human Rights and Fundamental Freedoms....'

This stance severely limited the individual's ability to rely on the ECHR in domestic courts. In *Norris v AG* [1984] IR 36, the plaintiff challenged legislative provisions which criminalised homosexual activities on two principal grounds: (i) the legislation was inconsistent with the ECHR and (ii) as Ireland had ratified the ECHR there was a presumption of compatibility of the Constitution with the ECHR. The European Court of Human Rights (ECt.HR) in *Dudgeon v UK* (1982) 4 EHRR 149 had previously held that the legislation at issue in *Norris* was incompatible with Article 8 ECHR (the privacy guarantee). Norris also sought to rely on this judgment before the Irish courts. The Supreme Court rejected these arguments on the basis of the Irish dualist stance. *Per* O'Higgins CJ:

> '...acceptance of [counsel's] view would be contrary to the provisions of the Constitution itself and would accord to the government the power, by an executive act, to change both the Constitution and the law. The [ECHR] is an international agreement to which Ireland is a subscribing party. As such, however it does not and cannot form part of our domestic law nor affect in any way questions which arise thereunder. This is made quite clear by Article 29, s. 6, of the Constitution....'

Per Henchy J:

> '...the constitutional question that calls for resolution is unaffected by the fact that the precise statutory provisions in this case were held by the European Court of Human Rights in *Dudgeon v United Kingdom* (1982) 4 EHRR 149 to be in breach of article 8 of the European Convention for the Protection of Human Rights and Fundamental Freedoms. That Convention, as has been held by this Court, although it has by its terms a binding force on the Government of this State as one of its signatories, forms no part of the domestic law of the State.'

Pre-incorporation, the ECHR was not however without domestic impact. Judgments of the ECt.HR are binding under international law on the Irish State albeit indirectly and in compliance with the dualist requirements of the Constitution. Where Ireland is found to be in breach of the ECHR, the State is obliged to amend its domestic law. Subsequent to the Supreme Court ruling, Norris took a case (*Norris v Ireland* (1991) 13 EHRR 360) to the ECt.HR which held that the impugned provisions were in breach of Article 8 ECHR. It took five years after that, however, before the Oireachtas enacted legislation giving effect to the judgment (Criminal Law (Sexual Offences) Act, 1993).

There were some judgments before the incorporation of the ECHR where the Irish courts seemed to recognise that the ECHR had some persuasive value. An example is the High Court decision in *Desmond v Glackin* [1992] ILRM 490. At issue in the case was whether comments made during the course of a radio interview by the Minister for Tourism, Transport and Communications concerning judicial review proceedings, amounted to contempt of court. O'Hanlon J, at 513, considered that judgments of the ECt.HR would have persuasive value:

> 'As Ireland has ratified the [ECHR] and is a party to it, and as the law of contempt of court is based ... on public policy, I think it is legitimate to assume that our public policy is in accord with the Convention or at least that the provisions of the Convention can be considered when determining issues of public policy. The Convention itself is not a code of legal principles which are enforceable in the domestic courts, as was made clear in *In re Ó Laighleis* [1960] IR 93, but this does not prevent the judgment of the European Court from having a persuasive effect when considering the common law regarding the contempt of court in the light of constitutional guarantees of freedom of expression contained in our Constitution of 1937. Henchy J expressed the view in *State (Director of Public Prosecutions) v Walsh* [1981] IR 412 at 440, that there was a presumption that our law on contempt is in conformity with the convention, particularly Articles 5 and 10(2).'

The persuasive value of the ECHR is also apparent from the partly dissenting judgment of Denham J in *O'Brien v Mirror Group Newspapers* [2001] 1 IR 1. The facts concerned an appeal against the quantum of damages awarded in a libel case. Keane CJ at page 18 (for the majority) stated that the appeal on quantum should be dealt with on the basis of the law as stated in *de Rossa v Independent Newspapers plc.* [1999] 4 IR 432. Denham J opined that as ECHR jurisprudence was of persuasive value, a cogent argument that there was an error in the interpretation of an ECt.HR judgment, was a compelling reason to reconsider precedent:

> '... In light of the current practice whereby decisions of the European Court of Human Rights may have persuasive authority on issues where the Convention and Constitution are similar, in light of the fact that Ireland was one of the original states which ratified the Convention (with the consequent effect on policy), and in light of the declared intention of the Irish government to incorporate the Convention into the domestic law of Ireland, the law of the Convention has a persuasive relevance. Consequently a cogent argument that there was error in part in its interpretation is significant and a compelling reason to reconsider the issue.'

According to O'Connell, '... it is clear that the prevailing orthodoxy—that the Convention is of no more than persuasive value in domestic proceedings—remains unpenetrated.' (O'Connell 'Ireland' in Blackburn and Polakiewicz (eds) *Fundamental Rights in Europe: The ECHR and its Member States, 1952–2000*, 2001, OUP, 423, 435).

A useful summary of the pre-incorporation position of the ECHR in Irish law may be found in a dicta of Barrington J in *Doyle v Commissioner of An Garda Síochána* [1999] 1 IR 249. The case arose out of the car bomb explosions that took place in Dublin and Monaghan in 1974 which killed thirty-three people including the plaintiff's daughter and two granddaughters. The plaintiff sought discovery of files relating to these atrocities which were in the possession of An Garda Síochána to use them as evidence in proceedings instituted by him before the ECt.HR. The Supreme Court in considering the ECHR guarantee of the right of individual petition held that the duty imposed by this obligation appears to be a negative duty to refrain from frustrating the individual's right of petition. The Supreme Court also held that as the ECHR (prior to incorporation) was an external Treaty obligation, the domestic courts were not in a position to enforce it. In the course of his judgment Barrington J stated at 268:

> 'Ireland is a signatory of the European Convention on Human Rights and accepts the right of individual petition. But Ireland takes the dualistic approach to its international obligations and the European Convention is not part of the domestic law of Ireland. The Convention may overlap with certain provisions of Irish constitutional law and it may be helpful to an Irish court to look at the Convention when it is attempting to identify unspecified rights guaranteed by Article 40.3 of the Constitution. Alternatively, the Convention may, in certain circumstances influence Irish law through European community law. But the Convention is not part of Irish domestic law and the Irish court has no part in its enforcement. So far as Ireland is concerned the institutions to enforce the provisions of the Convention are the European Court of Human Rights and its Commission.'

One issue mentioned by Barrington J in this paragraph, which has not yet been addressed, is the influence of EC law on the impact of the ECHR in Irish law. It is discussed at **2.4.7.**

The lack of binding force of the ECHR in domestic law was of practical concern when advising clients. It was not possible to rely directly on the ECHR guarantees before the Irish courts. Irish courts were however influenced by the persuasive value of the ECHR. Until the ECHR was incorporated, it was necessary to pursue a case to the ECt.HR to secure an ECHR guarantee. Even after incorporation, it will still be necessary in some cases to go to the ECt.HR to secure human rights protections (see **2.3.3** and **chapter 5**).

2.3.3 THE EUROPEAN CONVENTION ON HUMAN RIGHTS ACT, 2003

The European Convention on Human Rights Act, 2003 was signed on 30 June 2003, and came into force on 31 December 2003. The Act incorporates the ECHR into domestic law, making it applicable and enforceable by Irish courts. The incorporation of the ECHR has the potential to alter the human rights protection within this jurisdiction. The provisions of the Act and the effects of incorporation are discussed in **chapter 5**. The ECHR is discussed in **chapter 4**. For the purposes of this chapter it is important to consider the implications of incorporation on the hierarchy of laws in this jurisdiction.

According to the explanatory memorandum which accompanied the European Convention on Human Rights Bill, 2001, the existing position would be fundamentally altered. The Bill was 'designed to facilitate the bringing of cases involving alleged breaches of rights under the Convention in Irish courts. In other words, it will make rights in the Convention enforceable in Irish courts and this means that cases of this type will be able to be processed much more expeditiously than under the present arrangements.'

Irish courts are required to interpret all statutory provisions or rules of law whether they pre-date or post-date the Act, in accordance with the ECHR in *'so far as possible'*. To the extent that it is not possible to apply or interpret a provision in accordance with the State's obligations under the ECHR provisions, the statutory provision or rule of law at issue prevails. The High Court and the Supreme Court, where there is no other adequate or available remedy, may make a declaration that a statutory provision or rule of law is incompatible with the State's obligations under the ECHR. However, the Act does not provide for the striking down of legislation or rules of law on the basis of incompatibility with the ECHR, so the incompatible domestic provision continues in force.

In such circumstances, proceedings against the State in the ECt.HR may still be necessary to bring rules in line with the ECHR provisions, although the Act also provides for an exgratia compensation payment following a declaration of incompatibility.

The ECHR has been incorporated at sub-constitutional level. The explanatory memorandum provides that the Act 'will ensure that there are two complementary systems in place in Ireland for the protection of fundamental rights and freedoms, with the superior rules under the Constitution taking precedence...'. The rationale for incorporating the ECHR at sub-constitutional level is that there is a considerable overlap between the protection of rights in the Constitution, and the ECHR. Consequently, if the ECHR had been incorporated directly into the Constitution it was feared that this would lead to a diminution in some rights as protected in the Constitution (see the Constitutional Review Group Report and the Explanatory Memorandum to the ECHR Bill, 2001). The question of sub-constitutional incorporation has been the subject of much debate in this jurisdiction. It is problematic because while the Irish Constitution might often offer a higher protection of a right than the protection at ECHR level, this is not always the case. This is evidenced by the fact that the ECt.HR has on a number of occasions found Ireland to be in breach of the ECHR standard of human rights protection in situations where the Irish courts had found the law at issue not to be in breach of the Constitution. For example the Supreme Court in *Norris v AG* [1984] IR 36 held that the legislation at issue was not unconstitutional, where the ECt.HR found a breach of the ECHR in *Norris v Ireland* 13 EHRR 360 (see **4.6**).

The co-existence of two systems of human rights leaves open the possibility of complementary or conflicting standards of human rights protections. Given that in the Irish Constitution some rights are protected at a higher standard and that in the ECHR some rights are protected at a higher standard the systems are difficult to reconcile. This is especially true because the protection of human rights often involves a balance of competing rights (a stark example is the balancing of the right to life of the mother and unborn child in Article 40.3.3° of Bunreacht na hÉireann) and a standard which prefers one right, of necessity, diminishes another. For example, while the Irish Constitution prefers the right of the family over the rights of its constituent members, on occasion the rights of individual members may be better protected by the ECHR (see **9.2**, **9.4** and **9.5**). In a case where an unmarried father had not been consulted prior to the placing of his child for adoption, the Irish courts *In Re SW, K v W* [1990] 2 IR 437 found no breach of constitutional rights whereas the ECt.HR in *Keegan v Ireland* (1994) 18 EHRR 342 found that Ireland had breached the applicants' right to respect for family life under the ECHR.

The complementary systems allow the possibility of redress under one system where it is not available under the other. However, this approach is open to the criticism that this very flexibility renders the protection of human rights uncertain. Litigation is required to determine which of the complementary systems applies in a particular factual situation.

Neither *Norris* nor *Keegan* is an example of a direct conflict between the Constitution and the ECHR. Rather, each is an example of a case where legislation found not to breach the Constitution, was found to breach the ECHR. As a result, legislative changes to bring about compliance with the ECHR do not breach the Constitution.

In the case of a direct conflict between the Constitution and the ECHR, Ireland would be in breach of its international obligations under the ECHR. As a matter of domestic law, even after the coming into force of the European Convention on Human Rights Act, 2003 the Constitution is superior. As a matter of international law the ECHR ranks higher. A constitutional amendment would be required to ensure compliance with Ireland's international obligations.

To date, of the Irish cases before the ECt.HR (discussed at **4.6**), there is one example of a direct conflict. In *Attorney General (SPUC) v Open Door Counselling Ltd and Dublin Well Woman Centre Ltd* [1989] ILRM 19, an issue arose as to the constitutionality of non-directive counselling to pregnant women that included information about abortion clinics in another jurisdiction. The Irish courts found that there could be no constitutional right to information about the availability of the service of abortion outside the State, as this would conflict with the constitutional right to life of the unborn child and granted an injunction restraining the defendants from providing this information. In proceedings challenging the injunction, *Open Door Counselling and Dublin Well Woman v Ireland* (1993) 15 EHRR 244, the ECt.HR took a radically contrasting view and held that the injunction breached the freedom of expression guarantee in Article 10 ECHR. A subsequent constitutional referendum brought Ireland into line with its international obligations.

An area of potential conflict concerns the definition of the family. In Irish constitutional terms this is defined as being based on marriage, but the ECt.HR recognises a broader definition of the family (see **9.2**, **9.4** and **9.5** and see *McD v L* [2009] IESC 81 discussed at **5.7**). Another area of potential conflict concerns freedom of expression (see **chapter 13**).

While pointing out that it was too soon to determine the impact of incorporation of the ECHR, O'Connell stated '[i]t is clear that the coming into effect of the [European Convention on Human Rights Act, 2003] is leading to greater resource to the [ECHR] as a source of persuasive authority by the Irish courts even if it and the jurisprudence established thereunder is not always decisive of those cases in which it is pleaded.' (O'Connell, *ECHR Act, 2003: A Preliminary Assessment of Impact*, 2006, Dublin Solicitors Bar Association/Law Society of Ireland, 29.)

Since incorporation of the ECHR, an interesting issue has arisen in relation to the sequence in which the constitutional and ECHR issues would be considered by the courts. Declarations of incompatibility with the ECHR were sought in two High Court cases in which the issue of whether to consider the constitutional issue or the ECHR issue first was considered. In one it was held that the correct approach was to address the ECHR issue first while in the other it was held that the proper approach was to determine the constitutional issue first.

In *Carmody v Minister for Justice, Equality and Law Reform* [2005] 2 ILRM 1, the plaintiff sought a declaration that s 2 of the Civil Legal Aid Act, 1962 was unconstitutional and a declaration that the section was incompatible with the State's obligations under the ECHR. The objection to the legislative provision centred on the absence of a provision to be assisted by counsel in the preparation and conduct of a defence of the plaintiff in summary proceedings where there were many and complex charges. The area of dispute was whether the provision which the District Court was entitled to make for legal aid for the plaintiff, representation by a solicitor alone, was in breach of the State's obligations under the ECHR and whether the lack of parity with the prosecution was consistent with the Constitution. Laffoy J held that the ECHR issue should be addressed first:

'At first sight, the fact that the plaintiff seeks only two remedies, one of which, the declaration of incompatibility, can only be granted where no other legal remedy is adequate and available, and the other, a declaration of constitutional invalidity which, as a matter of constitutional jurisprudence should only be considered if the resolution of an issue of law other than constitutional law is determined first and does not determine the case (the formulation of the self-restraint rule by Finlay C.J. in *Murphy v Roche* [1987] I.R. 106), would seem to present a classic "catch-22" dilemma. However, on an analysis of the relevant principles, in my view, that is not the case. Section 2 of the Act of 1962 is presumed to be constitutional. As a matter of construction of s.5(1) it cannot have been the intention of the Oireachtas that, where a statutory provision enjoys the presumption of constitutionality, the question of its compatibility with the State's obligations under the Convention provisions which are invoked should be postponed until determination of its constitutional validity. Such a construction would be at variance with the approach adopted by the courts in judicially reviewing legislation under the Constitution from the outset. It would also be at variance with the express purpose of the Act of 2003 as stated in the long title, which expressly subordinates the effect given to the Convention in domestic law to the provisions of the Constitution.'

In *Law Society v The Competition Authority* [2005] IEHC 455 the respondents had published a notice to give guidance to businesses and legal advisers on the Competition Authority's policy in relation to legal representation of persons appearing before the Competition Authority which effectively sought to restrict a lawyer to appearing on behalf of only one party/witness to an investigation. The applicants by means of judicial review, sought *inter alia* a declaration that in purporting to veto a choice of lawyer by a party/witness to an investigation that the respondent had infringed the rights of such persons to a lawyer of their choice and to basic fairness and procedures guaranteed by Article 40.3 of Bunreacht na hÉireann and a declaration that the notice infringed the rights of such persons to a fair hearing as guaranteed by Article 6(1) ECHR. In the alternative the applicant sought a declaration pursuant to s 5 of the European Convention on Human Rights Act, 2003 that the notice was incompatible with the State's obligations under Article 6(1) ECHR. O'Neill J examined the constitutional issue first and having held that the impugned notice infringed Article 40.3 of Bunreacht na hÉireann and granted an order of *certiorari*, went on to state that it was impermissible to make the declaration of incompatibility envisaged in s 5 as another legal remedy was available.

On appeal, in *Carmody v The Minister for Justice Equality and Law Reform* [2009] IESC 71, the Supreme Court determined that it was appropriate to consider the constitutional issue first (see **5.7**).

2.3.4 DUALISM AND OTHER INTERNATIONAL HUMAN RIGHTS INSTRUMENTS TO WHICH IRELAND IS PARTY

The dualist stance set out in Article 29.6 applies to all international agreements and not just the ECHR. In *Application of Woods* [1970] IR 154, a *habeas corpus* application, the applicant argued that his sentence of penal servitude was contrary to Article 4(1) of the Universal Declaration of Human Rights, 1948, ratified by the Irish government in 1953. The Supreme Court held *per* Ó Dálaigh CJ at 161 that:

> '...the United Nations' Universal Declaration of Human Rights is not part of the domestic law of Ireland: see Article 29, s. 6 of the Constitution and the judgment of this Court in *In Re Ó Laighléis* [1960] IR 93.'

More recently, a novel argument concerning the application of international human rights provisions was put forward in *Kavanagh v Governor of Mountjoy Prison* [2002] 3 IR 112. The facts involved an appeal against a refusal to grant leave for judicial review related to the applicant's conviction by the Special Criminal Court. He sought to rely on the UN International Covenant on Civil and Political Rights (ICCPR) and in particular a communication from the Human Rights Committee (HRC), the complaints mechanism established under the ICCPR, which stated that the applicant's trial was in violation of the ICCPR. The Director of Public Prosecutions had certified that the ordinary courts were inadequate to secure the effective administration of justice and consequently the applicant had been tried in the Special Criminal Court and not by the ordinary courts. Inequality of treatment, in that he was tried by a non-jury court, was at the core of his complaint.

The applicant argued that Article 29 'constitutionalises' general principles of international law including the principle of equal treatment and could be invoked in the domestic courts to invalidate a conviction or to render repugnant a statutory provision. The Supreme Court held that the applicant was not entitled to rely on the provisions of the ICCPR as the acceptance in Article 29.3 of the generally recognised obligations of international law only applied in the State's 'rule of conduct with other States' and did not confer, and could not be interpreted as expressing an intention to confer, rights capable of being invoked by individuals. Further, the Court opined *obiter* that to rely on the decision of the HRC which was not a legally binding decision in preference to the judgment of the Special Criminal Court would conflict with Article 34.1 of the Constitution which provides:

> *'Justice shall be administered in courts established by law by judges appointed in the manner provided by the Constitution, and, save in such special and limited cases as may be prescribed by law, shall be administered in public.'*

As already emphasised international law instruments are not automatically binding internally within the State. To determine the status of an international law instrument under Irish domestic law, it is first necessary to check whether it has been incorporated. If it has not been incorporated it is not binding internally within the State and cannot be enforced in the Irish courts. However, the courts might look to the persuasive value of the international law instrument. Irish courts will interpret domestic law in light of the State's international obligations—*Ó Domhnaill v Merrick* [1984] IR 151.

International law instruments are incorporated into domestic law by means of legislation which is also subject to the Constitution. According to the hierarchy of norms laid down by the Constitution, provisions of the Constitution trump provisions of international law that have been incorporated into domestic law by means of legislation, including provisions of human rights treaties.

This point may be more readily understood if one considers the UN Convention on the Rights of the Child, 1989, discussed at **9.3.2**. Ireland ratified this Convention but it has not yet been incorporated into domestic law. Even if it were to be incorporated by means of a legislative enactment, the Constitution would continue to trump the Convention. In domestic law, the Constitution prevails but in international law, the Convention prevails, leaving open the possibility in a case of conflict in standards of protection that, by complying with the constitutional standard the State breaches such international obligations. In domestic law also, legislation prevails over unincorporated international law instruments. Even if an international law instrument were implemented by means of ordinary domestic legislation, later domestic legislation would prevail in the case of conflict. Contrast however the position of the ECHR since incorporation. The ECHR Act, 2003 requires statutory provisions and rules of law to be applied and interpreted in accordance with the State's obligations under the Convention provisions 'in as far as possible'.

Like the pre-incorporation position of the ECHR, other international law instruments rank higher than domestic laws under international law. However, unlike the ECHR most international law instruments do not have a court structure to secure their enforcement (see **chapter 6**). These instruments are largely dependent on political embarrassment to secure change. Individuals can be disappointed to find that grand-sounding commitments in international agreements may be of little effect in securing the protection of rights.

2.4 The Third Sphere of Human Rights Protection: EC/EU Law

Human Rights are protected in a third legal sphere in this jurisdiction, the EU legal order. The evolution of human rights protection in the EU is discussed in **chapter 8**. For now, it is sufficient to note that although the founding Treaties of the European Communities contained no reference to human rights law, the European Court of Justice (ECJ)

the member state may be so circumscribed by Community law that the entire of any legislative measure taken by it or the exercise of such discretion is "necessitated". This could arise where the exercise of a discretion conferred by Community law was required to be exercised exclusively having regard to the policy considerations and objectives of the Community measure and where considerations of national law would distort the proper exercise of such a discretion.

On the other hand, the discretion conferred by Community law on the State when implementing legislative measures may be sufficiently wide to permit the State to have full regards to the constitutional protection afforded to fundamental rights without impinging on the full effect and uniform application of Community law. In such circumstances the State, in the exercise of such discretion, would be bound to respect personal and fundamental rights as guaranteed by the Constitution.'

This safeguard extends to judicial interpretations so that Irish courts interpreting EU obligations will interpret those obligations where possible in compliance with fundamental rights as guaranteed by the Constitution. This safeguard will not apply where there is a direct conflict between EU law and a constitutionally protected right.

2.4.6.4 Disapplication of a constitutional right, where there is a direct conflict between the right and EU law

By virtue of the doctrine of supremacy, EU law may require a national court to dissapply a human rights protection if it is in direct conflict with EU law within the scope of EC law. In doing so the national courts are bound by the EU standard of human rights protection, which standard has proved acceptable to the German Constitutional Court (see **2.4.6.1**).

The potential conflict is not just one of human rights standards. There is also the possibility that protection of a human right may be limited by another objective of EU law (see **8.8.1**). This is apparent from the issues arising in Case C-159/90 *SPUC v Grogan* [1991] ECR I-4685 (see **2.4.6.2**). The issue, which fell outside the scope of EC law, was a conflict between freedom to provide services and a right to life of the unborn child. If the matter had fallen within the scope of EC law, the ECJ would have considered other rights which are protected in EC law such as freedom of expression and the freedom to receive and impart information.

In the case of a direct conflict between EU law and a constitutionally protected right, the Irish courts are required to dissapply a constitutional protection, to comply with their EU law obligations. This differs from a situation of conflict between international law and an Irish constitutional provision where in the Irish courts the constitutional provision will trump the international right and the Irish courts have no authority to dissapply a constitutional provision in favour of an international law.

2.4.7 WHETHER THE ECHR IS PART OF IRISH DOMESTIC LAW BY VIRTUE OF EU LAW

The ECHR is a source of the general principles of EU human rights protections. As EU law is binding in domestic law a question arose as to whether the ECHR, prior to its incorporation, had been indirectly incorporated into Irish law via EU law.

The decision in *Kavanagh v Governor of Mountjoy Prison* [2002] 3 IR 112 was discussed above. The decision to try the applicant before the Special Criminal Court had previously been judicially reviewed unsuccessfully on different grounds in *Kavanagh v The Government of Ireland* [1996] 1 IR 348. On that occasion one of the arguments made by the applicant was that provisions of the ECHR formed part of the domestic law by virtue of the ECHR's status within EC law. The applicant submitted that in considering the thrust of Article

40.1, Bunreacht na hÉireann, which guarantees equality before the law, account must be taken of the obligations of the State under the ECHR. The applicant argued that the ECHR was part of the domestic law of the State by virtue of what was Article 29.4.4, which enabled Ireland to ratify the TEU, and Article F(2) (later Article 6(2), now as amended Article 6(3)) TEU which provided:

> 'The Union shall respect fundamental rights, as guaranteed by the European Convention for the Protection of Human Rights and Fundamental Freedoms signed in Rome on 4 November 1950 and as they result from the constitutional traditions common to the Member States as general principles of Community law.'

The respondents argued, relying on *In Re Ó Laighléis*, that the ECHR is not part of the domestic law. Further, they argued that no essential change was effected by the TEU, that the subject matter of the proceedings was not a matter coming within the scope, operation or competence of the EU and that the TEU did not change the essential adherence by the EC, reflected in the jurisprudence of the ECJ, to the basic rights reflected in the ECHR in the application and interpretation of EC law.

Laffoy J, at 345, considered it unnecessary to determine whether the ECHR had become part of domestic law (as a result of the ECHR's status in EC law) as the applicant had not established any breach of the ECHR or Article 40.1 of the Constitution.

> 'In my opinion the respondent's view is the better one and ex Article F(2) (Now Article 6(2)) merely confirms the jurisprudence of the ECJ, that the ECJ will protect human rights as general principles of EU law, that the ECHR is one source of these general principles and that Member States are only bound by the EU standard of human rights protection when acting within the scope of EU law.'

This view is consistent with the views of Barrington J in *Doyle v Commissioner of An Garda Síochána* [1999] 1 IR 249, 268. He emphasised that the ECHR in contrast to the EC Treaties, is not part of Irish domestic law but stated that 'the ECHR may in certain circumstances influence Irish law through European Community law'. One commentator has provided the following explanation. 'The [ECJ] has stressed that such general principles can be discerned from the [ECHR]. However, this is not a back door incorporation of the [ECHR] into national law since the [ECJ] has been keen to state that the national court can use these general principles of Community law only in matters where Community law is at issue. These general principles cannot be applied to matters which fall solely within the ambit of the national legislator...' (Burrows, 'The European Union and the European Convention', in Dickson (ed), *Human Rights and the European Convention: The Effects of the Convention on the United Kingdom and Ireland*, 1997, Sweet and Maxwell). Within the scope of EU law the ECHR may be applied by the Irish courts.

2.5 Conclusion

There are three spheres of human rights protections in this jurisdiction. The first sphere encompasses the constitutional protection of fundamental rights which is at the apex of domestic law within the scope of national law. Within the domestic sphere, constitutional rights rank above all domestic legislation. However, constitutional rights do have to be balanced against one another.

The second sphere is the international sphere. These international and domestic spheres are entirely separate unless an international law instrument is incorporated into domestic law. Where there is a conflict between a right as protected by the Constitution and by an international instrument, the constitutional protection ranks higher in domestic law while the international obligation ranks higher in international law. A domestic court will apply the constitutional right over the international right and will not be required to dissapply a constitutional protection. An international court will apply an international right over a domestic provision. In the instance of a constitutional/international law clash of rights, Ireland would be required as a matter of international law to amend the Constitution to comply with the international obligation. If the clash is between a domestic legislative provision and an international law instrument arises, the situation will follow the constitutional/international clash scenario apart from the fact that it is only domestic legislation which will be required to bring Ireland into line with its international law obligations.

Where an international human rights obligation is incorporated into domestic law, its status will depend on how it has been incorporated. If it is incorporated as an ordinary statute it will have the status of legislation and will rank below the Constitution and later legislation. If it is incorporated on the basis of an interpretative model, courts will be required to interpret national law in accordance with it. If it is incorporated by constitutional amendment then it will have constitutional status and will rank above legislation. The ECHR has been incorporated on the basis of an interpretative model at sub-constitutional level.

The third sphere is the EU law sphere. At EU level, the ECJ will apply EU law, balancing rights against one another. The EU sphere and the domestic sphere apply concurrently in the Irish legal system, as there can be no dualist approach to EU law. EU law is superior to all domestic law, including the human rights protections in the Constitution within the scope of EU law. In the case of a conflict within the scope of EU law between EU law and a constitutional protection of a human right, EU law will prevail at both ECJ level and at domestic court level, although the ECJ and the domestic courts will be required to take account of the EU law standard of human rights protection. In the case of a direct conflict, national courts would have to dissapply national laws, including constitutionally protected human rights in favour of EU law. It is apparent from **8.8.1** that EU human rights protection can be limited by reference to other European law objectives such as the organisation of the common market.

However, it must be emphasised that the doctrine of supremacy of EU law operates only within the scope of EU law and in any case without an EU law dimension, it is the constitutional protection which is at the top of the hierarchy. In addition, where there is a conflict between EU law and Irish law which is capable of being resolved in accordance with the Constitution this method will take precedence.

Within a sphere it is for the courts to balance rights with one another. Across the spheres it is a question of hierarchy of laws rather than a balancing of rights.

CHAPTER 3

HUMAN RIGHTS PROTECTION IN IRELAND

3.1 Introduction

This chapter explores the development of human rights protections in Irish law, both under the Constitution (Bunreacht na hÉireann), and through legislation. It analyses the sources of human rights protection under the Constitution and the methods of interpretation used by the Irish courts. The chapter also examines the evolution of the law in certain key areas, with particular emphasis on those rights which receive express mention in the Constitution as well as those which have evolved through the Doctrine of Unenumerated Rights. It will also look at how judicial discussion and elucidation of these rights has been influenced by broader European and global trends and will analyse the impact of the European Convention of Human Rights (ECHR) in Irish law. Finally it will look at how the legal landscape may change since the entry into force of the Lisbon Treaty and the incorporation of the Charter of Fundamental Rights of the EU into 'hard' European law, as well as briefly examining Irish legislation with a human rights focus.

When first promulgated, Bunreacht na hÉireann was ahead of its time in relation to protecting the rights of citizens. It also sought to define the State as one which placed Catholicism at its core. The preamble for example is in striking contrast to those of other Western nations, or indeed contemporaneous constitutions. Whilst this was a perhaps understandable reaction to the events of the previous century, and the degree to which the Catholic Church was both a symbol of and driving force behind nationalism, the ramifications are felt to this day. In an increasingly secular and diverse society, it raises the question as to what extent certain elements of the Constitution should be jettisoned or modified to accommodate our changed and more diverse society.

3.2 Sources of Human Rights as Identified by the Courts

Numerous sources have been identified as grounding human rights. First and foremost are those identified specifically in the Constitution, in Articles 40–44, headed 'Fundamental Rights'. The preamble has also been noted as assisting in the elucidation of these protections. International instruments such as the ECHR have also provided inspiration. The courts, and indeed the Constitution itself, also declare natural law as a source of rights.

3.2.1 ARTICLES 40–44 OF THE CONSTITUTION: FUNDAMENTAL RIGHTS

There is clear provision made in the Constitution for what are now called human rights protections in these provisions, headed 'Fundamental Rights'. (See **3.5.**)

3.2.2 NATURAL LAW

A further source of human rights is natural law, as is explicitly stated in some of Fundamental Rights' Articles, where they are declared to be 'antecedent and superior to all positive law'. As was noted in *McGee v Attorney General* [1974] IR 284, these rights are not created by the Constitution, rather they are merely recognised by it:

> 'Articles 41, 42 and 43 emphatically reject the theory that there are no rights without laws, no rights contrary to the law and no rights anterior to the law. They indicate that justice is placed above the law and acknowledge that natural rights, or human rights, are not created by law but that the Constitution confirms their existence and gives them protection. The individual has natural and human rights over which the State has no authority; and the family as the natural primary and fundamental unit group of society, has rights as such which the State cannot control'.

This is by no means a concept unique to the Irish constitutional tradition; such venerated documents as the French Declaration of the Rights of Man and the Citizen 1789 speak of the 'natural and imprescriptible rights of man'. However, as Walsh J recognised later in the judgment, what constitutes natural law is not a subject upon which there is agreement. Clearly, and as envisaged by the Constitution, specifically the Preamble, the Christian faith and the central tenets of democracy are guides as to what is meant by natural law. The 'Christian and Democratic nature of the State' is one of the grounds that was used to stake out the (qualified) right to privacy in *Kennedy v Ireland* [1987] IR 587 and *Cogley v Radio Telefís Éireann* [2005] 4 IR 79 amongst numerous other cases. The Doctrine of Unenumerated Rights as discussed below (see **3.5.4**) is also an important source of human rights protection. Indeed the analysis of this doctrine reveals many of the sources of human rights in the Constitution.

3.2.3 INTERNATIONAL INSTRUMENTS

Other sources of human/fundamental rights which aided the courts in identifying the scope of human rights protections as laid out in the Constitution are international human rights provisions as arise from the UN system of law, the European Union and the European Convention on Human Rights (ECHR). The extent to which such treaties may be relied upon is however somewhat constrained by the Irish dualist system which means that without the incorporation of an international treaty into domestic law—as for example has happened with the European Convention of Human Rights Act, 2003—such treaties do not form part of the law of Ireland (see **2.3**). Furthermore, the ratification (without incorporation) by the State of such a treaty does not mean that it can be relied on by an individual against the State; it is merely binding in international law; *Kavanagh v Governor of Mountjoy Prison* [2002] 3 IR 97, *per* Fennelly J (see **2.3.4**). However, the courts have accepted in some cases that international treaties such as the ECHR and decisions of the European Court of Human Rights (ECt.HR) can be of persuasive value. The Supreme Court has relied on the jurisprudence of the ECt.HR in *inter alia, O'Brien v Mirror Group Newspaper Ltd* [2000] 1 IR 1.

The High Court stated in *O'Domhnaill v Merrick* [1984] IR 151 that unincorporated international instruments may have indirect legal effect in that there can be a presumption of compatibility of domestic legislation with such instruments. This was subsequently cited with approval by O'Hanlon J in *Desmond v Glackin (No. 1)* [1993] 3 IR 1, in reading the common law principles of contempt of court in light of the ECHR Article 10 freedom of expression guarantee. Similarly, prior to incorporation of the ECHR, the Supreme Court in *Doyle v Commissioner of An Garda Síochána* [1999] 1 IR 249 stated that the ECHR may be useful as a source for an Irish judge attempting to identify unspecified rights guaranteed by Article 40.3.

Non-incorporation does, however, greatly reduce the efficacy, from the individual's rights perspective, of many of the international human rights treaties to which the State is a party, such as the UN Conventions on the Rights of the Child (see **chapter 9**), the Rights of Persons with Disabilities and the Universal Declaration of Human Rights.

3.3   Christianity as a Basis of the Constitution and its Application to Human Rights

One feature which looms larger in the Irish Constitution than in its western counterparts is the explicit references to religion. The Preamble sets the tone for this:

> *'In the Name of the Most Holy Trinity, from Whom all authority and to Whom, as our final end, all actions both of men and States must be referred, We, the people of Éire, Humbly acknowledging all our obligations to our Divine Lord, Jesus Christ, Who sustained our fathers through centuries of trial, Gratefully remembering their heroic and unremitting struggle to regain the rightful independence of our Nation, And seeking to promote the common good, with due observance of Prudence, Justice and Charity, so that the dignity and freedom of the individual may be assured, true social order attained, the unity of our country restored, and concord established with other nations, Do hereby adopt, enact and give to ourselves this Constitution.'*

Article 6 of the Constitution continues this theme of subservience to God in stating that *'all powers, of government, legislative and judicial, derive under God, from the People'*. Similarly, by Article 44.1 *'The State acknowledges that the homage of public worship is due to Almighty God. It shall hold His Name in reverence, and shall respect and honour religion.'*

There are a great many reasons why the Christian nature of the State should have been given such strong prominence in the Constitution. First and foremost, it reflected the will of the people. It was also recognition of the role played by the [Catholic] Christian Church in development of [Nationalist] Irish culture, and indeed as a force, moral and logistical, in the fight for independence down through the centuries. Similarly, Catholicism was seen as one of the features which defined a person as either, of what may be termed native stock, or nationalist bent, notwithstanding the vital and often leadership roles played by Protestant Irish men and women in the various national struggles.

The Preamble to the Constitution has been referred to in numerous cases and whilst no decision could be said to have been based solely on it, it has proved useful as a guide to the 'spirit' of the Constitution. An example of how it has been used can be seen in *Attorney General v Southern Industrial Trust* [1960] 94 ILTR 61, where the Supreme Court, *per* Lavery J said:

> *'The declaration in the Preamble, made in general terms, may add little to the more precise terms of the relevant Articles. Nevertheless, the words of the Preamble declaring the purpose of the people in adopting, enacting and giving to themselves the Constitution may help in determining the meaning of and effect to be given to particular provisions.'*

The Preamble has been used as a basis for securing basic and essential human rights not otherwise mentioned in the Constitution and to provide a basis for the Doctrine of Unenumerated Rights, discussed below. As Hogan and Whyte note in *JM Kelly: The Irish*

Constitution, 4th edn, 2.1.11, the Preamble has been invoked to justify judicial activism in the construction of the Constitution. In *McGee v Attorney General* [1974] IR 284, Walsh J noted:

'According to the Preamble, the people gave themselves the Constitution to promote the common good with due observance of prudence, justice and charity so that the dignity and freedom of the individual might be assured. The judge must, therefore, as best they can from their training and their experience interpret these rights in accordance with their ideas of prudence, justice and charity. It is but natural that from time to time the prevailing ideas of these virtues may be conditioned by the passage of time; no interpretation of the Constitution is intended to be final for all time.'

3.4 Constitutional Interpretation

Before looking at how the courts have interpreted the Constitution, we must first look at the various ways in which it may be interpreted. The Constitution contains numerous general principles and rules, prescriptions and prohibitions. Should a dispute arise as to whether a particular action or course of conduct is required or is prohibited, the answer may not be obvious. In this case, it is for a court to decide what the Constitution intends. Over the years, the courts have developed general principles regarding the interpretation of laws. A simple textual reading of the Articles would not suffice to deal with the diverse multitude of issues which can arise.

A constitution is written for the coming decades and centuries; it must be flexible enough to deal with issues of morality and law which cannot even have occurred to us yet; however, it must be robust enough to still impart a guiding light to those who seek to adapt it to the circumstances of today, and indeed tomorrow. A constitution must be a living document, which remains relevant to contemporary society. However, it should be noted that although the Constitution is a living document as identified in *Sinnott v Minister of Education* [2001] 2 IR 545 and *McGee v Attorney General* [1974] IR 284 this does not give free rein for each succeeding generation to re-examine all issues as social mores evolve. As was pointed out by Dunne J in *Zappone v Revenue Commissioners* [2008] 2 IR 417, the process of considering the Constitution as a living instrument is not one which is available to the interpretation of the Constitution itself, as opposed to the interpretation of legislation. However, the door is never completely closed; the Supreme Court has ruled that it may depart from its former decisions (eg *McGlimpsey v Ireland* [1990] 1 IR 110), but only for compelling reasons, and not simply because the current Supreme Court favours a different conclusion.

Clearly, a starting point for interpreting the Constitution is the words used in the document. In *Sinnott v Minister for Education* [2001] 2 IR 545 Murray J, as he then was, stated:

'It is axiomatic that the point of departure in the interpretation of a legal instrument, be it a constitution or otherwise, is the text of that instrument, albeit having regard to the nature of the instrument and in the context of the instrument as a whole.'

The most important principle of interpretation is the elementary rule that the ordinary meaning of the Constitution's words override all other considerations. However, very often these words can be open-ended or capable of multiple inferences, requiring taking into account the context, the provenance of any particular provision and the overall objectives and structure of the Constitution.

Generally speaking, six separate approaches to the interpretation of the Constitution have been developed: the literal approach, the purposive approach, the doctrine of harmonious interpretation, the hierarchical approach, the historical approach, and the natural law approach. However, there is no particular consistency as to which approach is taken.

3.4.1   LITERAL APPROACH

A clear example of this can be seen in *The People (Director of Public Prosecutions) v O'Shea* [1982] IR 384, where O'Higgins CJ stated:

> 'The Constitution, as the fundamental law of the State, must be accepted, interpreted and construed according to the words which are used; and these words, where the meaning is plain and unambiguous, must be given their literal meaning. Of course, the Constitution must be construed as a whole and not merely in parts and, where doubts or ambiguity exists, regard may be had to other provision of the Constitution and to the situation which obtained and the laws which were in force when it was enacted. Plain words must, however, be given their plain meaning unless qualified or restricted by the Constitution itself.'

The advantage of this approach is that it vastly reduces the scope for what has been termed 'judicial activism', inherent in other approaches to the Constitutional interpretation. However, this activism, or rather judicial subjectivity, is what is required to ensure that a constitution does not become frozen in time at the point of its inception. It is also arguably not appropriate when dealing with some of the more general principles enunciated in the Constitution; however, it is suitable for technical constitutional provisions.

3.4.2   THE PURPOSIVE APPROACH

This approach is based on the reasoning that a constitution is not analogous to merely some piece of super legislation, but is rather a political document, expressing the will of the people, and as such must be read as a whole. Such an approach is best characterised by rejecting the excessive literalism outlined above. It seeks to construe the text of the Constitution in a broad purposeful manner which best advances the intentions of the people. Costello J expressed this view in *Attorney General v Paperlink Ltd* [1984] ILRM 373, a case concerning the right to communicate.

> 'The Constitution is a political document as well as a legal document and in its interpretation the courts should not place the same significance on differences of language used in two succeeding sub-paragraphs as would, for example, be placed on differently drafted subsections of the Finance Act. A purposive rather than a strictly literal approach to the interpretation of the sub-paragraphs is appropriate.'

This sees a judicial focus on intention and purpose rather than a strict literal approach. Such an approach can be seen again in *Murray v Ireland* [1985] IR 532 where the High Court found that the correct approach to interpretation was one which would look at the whole text of the Constitution and identify its purpose and objective in protecting human rights.

3.4.3   THE DOCTRINE OF HARMONIOUS INTERPRETATION

This principle states that a constitutional provision should not be construed in isolation from all other parts of the Constitution among which it is embedded, but should be read so as to harmonise with them. The doctrine was first expressed in *Dillane v Ireland* [1980] ILRM 167 in the context of a challenge to a rule of court that prevented the plaintiff recovering his costs against the Gardaí, which he argued was an unjust attack on his property rights (and thus covered by Article 40.3.2 of the Constitution) and was an unjustified discrimination in favour of the police (prohibited under Article 40.1). Henchy J stated in his judgment:

'Under the doctrine of harmonious interpretation, which requires, where possible, the relevant constitutional provisions to be construed and applied so that each will be given due weight in the circumstances of the case, it would not be a valid constitutional interpretation to rule that the immunity given to a Garda by Rule 67 is necessarily permitted by Article 40.1, and in the same breath to hold that it is proscribed by [Article 40.3.2] ... What happened when the Plaintiff was denied his costs ... was categorically permitted by Article 40.1, so it cannot be part of the injustice which Article 40.3.2 was designed to prevent.'

As can be seen in the case of *The State (Director of Public Prosecutions) v Walsh* [1981] IR 412, the doctrine allows the modification of the absoluteness of particular provisions. The case was an attempt to reconcile Article 38.5 (prescribing trial by jury for all offences other than minor ones) with the need of the courts to be able to protect their own process and independence by punishing criminal contempts summarily. O'Higgins CJ said:

'This result seems to follow logically and inevitably from a consideration of Article 38.5 in isolation and apart from the other Articles and the general scheme of the Constitution. However, to do so is erroneous. Article 38.5 may not be so considered. It must be construed and considered as part of the Constitution and it should be given, if possible a meaning and application which does not lead to conflict with other Articles and which conforms with the Constitution's general scheme.'

However, certain provisions are to be considered absolute and not amenable to modification. This can be seen in the decision of Geoghegan J in *Attorney General v Hamilton (No. 2)* [1993] 3 IR 227 regarding the question of whether parliamentary privilege had to give way to the right to a good name (as protected by Article 40.3).

'... privilege and non-amenability [are] absolute and intended by the Constitution to be absolute in the sense that [they] cannot be sacrificed to protect other constitutional rights.'

A problem with this form of interpretation, and indeed any interpretation which strays from a strict reading of the text of the Constitution, is that it arguably interferes with the democratic will of the people as expressed through the text of the Constitution. In the case of *The People (Director of Public Prosecutions) v O'Shea* [1984] IR 384 Henchy J gave a dissenting judgment which advocated an even broader approach to harmonious interpretation than that which had been accepted. He sought to expand it to encompass the harmonious interpretation of a constitutional provision not just with other such Articles, but also to other more general principles of law. The case concerned an attempt by the Director of Public Prosecutions (DPP) to appeal an acquittal in a criminal case, and whether a provision of the Constitution which seemingly allowed this was overridden by the principle of *autrefois acquit* (ie the person had already been acquitted of the charge, and so could not be re-tried), an accepted cornerstone of the legal system, but one which was without constitutional basis.

'I agree that if the relevant subsection of the Constitution is looked at in isolation and is given a literal reading, it would lend itself to that interpretation. But I do not agree that such an approach is a correct method of constitutional interpretation. Any single constitutional right or power is but a component in an ensemble of interconnected and interacting provisions which must be brought into play as part of a larger composition, and which must be given such an integrated interpretations as will fit it harmoniously into the general constitutional order and modulation. It may be said of a constitution, more than any other legal instrument, that "the letter killeth, but the spirit giveth life". No single constitutional provision (particularly one designed to safeguard personal liberty or social order) may be isolated and construed with undeviating literalness'.

The above passage, notwithstanding it was a dissenting judgment, has been cited with approval in the High and Supreme Courts on many occasions, eg in *The People (Director of Public Prosecutions) v MS* [2003] 1 IR 606 where Keane CJ added:

'Even if a literal reading did lend support to that decision, however, I am satisfied that the reading having results which cannot have been within the contemplation of the framers of the Constitution should be avoided, unless only that construction is open.'

The doctrine is a reasonable and rational response to the issue of competing constitutionally protected rights. However, where such reconciliation is not possible, the courts will take into account the view that there is a hierarchy of rights.

3.4.4 HIERARCHY OF CONSTITUTIONAL RIGHTS

The question can be asked whether some rights are more important than others. Whilst initially the courts rejected this notion, such an approach did begin to emerge over time. It was finally recognised in *The People v Shaw* [1982] IR 1 where Kenny J declared:

'There is a hierarchy of constitutional rights and, when a conflict arises between them, that which ranks higher must prevail . . . The decision on priority of constitutional rights is to be made by the High Court and, on appeal by this Court. When a conflict of constitutional rights arises, it must be resolved by having regard to (a) the terms of the Constitution, (b) the ethical values which all Christians living in the State acknowledge and accept and (c) the main tenets of our system of constitutional parliamentary democracy'.

3.4.5 THE HISTORICAL APPROACH

Another approach which the courts have taken is to look at the state of affairs in 1937 when the Constitution was enacted. This approach was taken by Lavery J in *Melling v Ó'Mathghamhna* [1962] IR 1 where he asserted 'that in construing a provision of a statute or of the Constitution, it is proper to consider how the law stood when the statute was passed'. The utility of this approach was seen again in *Sinnott v Minister for Education* [2001] 2 IR 545 where Murray J said that while the Constitution is a living document, that did not mean that it can be divorced from its historical context. There can of course be difficulties identifying what exactly the state of affairs was in 1937, and in this regard, it would seem that this approach is best suited to what might be termed technical issues. Certainly it would seem that for interpreting fundamental concepts, the doctrine is inappropriate. Indeed, many of these concepts were left deliberately vague (such as equality before the law and personal liberty) so as to have the inherent flexibility to allow the provisions to adapt to a changing world.

3.4.6 THE NATURAL LAW APPROACH

The clearest application of this method can be seen in the development of the Doctrine of Unenumerated Rights, which is discussed below. Hogan and White in *JM Kelly: The Irish Constitution*, 4th edn, 1.1.55, note that the use of this technique has declined since the 1980s:

'probably as a result of an increasing judicial awareness that an express reliance on this approach is open to the objections that it permits reliance on standards which, in the words of Budd J in the High Court in *Riordan v An Tánaiste* [1995] 3 IR 62, "are often subjective and nebulous and which may not give reliable guidelines in dealing with actual constitutional problems'''.

However, natural law is acknowledged by Fennelly J in the Supreme Court case of *AO & DL v Minister of Justice* [2003] 1 IR 1 as being deeply influential on the common law.

All of the above approaches have their advantages and disadvantages, and none has been marked out as having primacy over the others. The approach to be chosen will depend on both the circumstances of the case, and on the inclinations of the presiding judge.

3.5   Overview of Human Rights Protections Under the Constitution

3.5.1   FUNDAMENTAL RIGHTS: ARTICLES 40–44

Article 40 of the Constitution is entitled 'Personal Rights'. The Article highlights such issues as equality, right to life, good name, property and person, personal liberty and freedom of expression, assembly and association. Article 41 concerns the family, which is recognised as the 'natural, primary and fundamental unit group of society, and as a moral institution possessing inalienable and imprescriptible rights, antecedent and superior to all positive law'. The Article also deals with the position of women (principally as homemakers) and marriage. Article 42 is headed 'Education', and concerns the State's duty to provide primary education, and the freedom of parents to choose the type of education which they prefer for their child. The Article also allows for the State to supply the place of the parents, should they fail in their duty to their children for physical or moral reasons. Article 43 deals with the property rights, guaranteeing private property. Article 44 is entitled 'Religion'. It acknowledges the 'homage of public worship is due to Almighty God', and determines that the State shall 'hold his name in reverence and shall respect and honour religion'. The Article goes onto set out the broad terms of the State's interaction with the religious. Some of these provisions are addressed to citizens, whereas others make no mention as to whom they apply. Questions have arisen as to the extent to which non-nationals may benefit from such protections. Not all of these questions have yet been answered. Whilst it is accepted that non-citizens have broadly the same rights regarding access to justice (*Re Illegal Immigrants Trafficking Bill 1999* [2000] 2 IR 360) the position is not clear with respect to other protections.

It is not proposed to go into any detailed analysis of the jurisprudence of the Court in relation to the rights protected, as these topics are covered elsewhere in the book. However, a general overview of the protections provided by the Constitution follows.

3.5.2   EQUALITY

Article 40.1 of the Constitution proclaims:

> *'All citizens shall, as human persons, be held equal before the law. This shall not be held to mean that the State shall not in its enactments have due regard to individual differences of capacity, physical and moral, and of social function.'*

This guarantee of equality is somewhat more constrained than that to be found in for example, the Fourteenth Amendment to the United States Constitution which stipulates that: '*[n]o State shall . . . deny to any person within its jurisdiction the equal protection of the laws'.* Similarly Article 14 ECHR states that *'the enjoyment of the rights and freedoms set forth in this Convention shall be secured without discrimination on any ground such as sex, race, colour, language, religion, minority, property, birth or other status.'.* The Supreme Court noted in *Re*

The Employment Equality Bill 1996 [1997] 2 IR 321 that '[t]he forms of discrimination which are, presumptively at least, proscribed by Article 40.1 are not particularised; manifestly they would extend to classifications based on sex, race, language, religious or political opinions'.

However, it should be recognised that equality is not the same as uniformity. The second limb of the guarantee explicitly authorises distinctions to be made between different classes of people. The law may differentiate between different classes of citizens, and indeed justice may require it do so.

Essentially, the guarantee of equality can be read in a number of ways. One is as a strictly formal requirement that a rule or law be applied equally to all to whom it is stated to apply—this limits any analysis of whether the distinctions drawn by the rule or law itself are permissible. An example of this can be seen in *People (DPP) v Quilligan (No. 3)* [1993] 2 IR 305 where Finlay CJ affirmed:

> 'The mere fact that a law discriminates as between one group or category of persons and another does not, of itself, render it constitutionally invalid. What is necessary to establish such invalidity is the existence of invidious discrimination.'

This clearly raises the issue of what constitutes invidious discrimination as opposed to discrimination simpliciter. The Supreme Court has identified invidious discrimination as that which is *'unreasonable, arbitrary or unjust'* (*Breathnach v Ireland* [2003] 3 IR 230). However, this definition does not greatly expand our understanding of the term and most judgments concerning this term have tended to offer synonyms rather than definitions.

The courts have also adopted what has been termed a 'rationality test' to identify whether there has been an infringement of the guarantee of equality, which examines whether the basis for the distinction is in itself permissible. This was first enunciated by Barrington J in *Brennan v Attorney General* [1983] ILRM 449 when he said that 'the classification must be for a legitimate legislative purpose...it must be relevant to that purpose, and...each class must be treated fairly.'

As is clear from the wording of the Article, the concept of equality applies only to 'human persons'; bodies corporate cannot seek protection under this provision. The courts have however clarified that non-citizens are protected. Equality is considered further in **chapter 11**.

3.5.3   PERSONAL RIGHTS

By Article 40.3.1 of the Constitution the State *'guarantees in its laws to respect, and as far as practicable, by its law to defend and vindicate the personal rights of the citizen'*. Article 40.3.2 goes on to say *'The State shall, in particular, by its laws protect as best it may from unjust attack and, in the case of injustice done, vindicate the life, person, good name and property rights of every citizen.'*

3.5.3.1   Right to life

The right to life aspect of this provision has been considered in cases relating to the unborn, rights to contraception and the right to a natural death. This last right does not however currently extend to a right to die—in other words through assisted suicide—it is confined to natural death. This point was made explicit by Denham J in *Re a Ward of Court (withholding medical treatment) (No. 2)* [1996] 2 IR 79: 'This right, as so defined, does not include the right to have life terminated or death accelerated and is confined to the natural process of dying. No person has the right to terminate or have terminated his or her life or to accelerate or have accelerated his or her death.' Clearly decisions such as these involve balancing the right to life with rights to privacy and autonomy (see **chapter 10**).

3.5.3.2 Right to a good name

The right to one's good name is also given Constitutional recognition. The Supreme Court has identified four minimum protections arising out of this right in the context of public inquiries, namely:

> '(a) the person accused should be furnished with a copy of the evidence which reflected on his good name; (b) he should be allowed to cross-examine, by counsel, his accuser; (c) he should be allowed to give rebutting evidence; and (d) he should be permitted to address the tribunal, again by counsel, in his own defence.' (*In re Haughey* [1971] IR 217).

The Supreme Court has also held on the basis of this provision that the Oireachtas has no power to conduct an inquiry liable to affect adversely a non-member's name unless that person was, by virtue of his or her appointment to a particular office, answerable to the Houses of the Oireachtas (*Maguire v Ardagh* [2002] 1 IR 419). In that same judgment the Court noted that the express inclusions of the right to a good name in the Constitution was unusual by international standards, there being no equivalent for example in the US Constitution or the ECHR.

3.5.3.3 Right to life of the unborn

Article 40.3.3 deals specifically with the case of the right to life of the unborn and was introduced into the Constitution by the eighth amendment in 1983 following a referendum (see **chapter 10**). It states: *'The State acknowledges the right to life of the unborn and, with due regard to the equal right to life of the mother, guarantees in its laws to respect, and, as far as practicable, by its laws to defend and vindicate that right.'* The referendum was proposed on the basis that as there was no constitutional prohibition in respect of abortion, and with the US Supreme Court's legalisation of abortion on the grounds of privacy in *Roe v Wade* 410 U.S. 113 (1973), such an argument might find favour in an Irish court given the constitutional protection of a right to privacy in *McGee v Attorney General* [1974] IR 284. Following the *'X' case (Attorney General v X* [1992] 1 IR 1), in which an injunction was initially granted to prevent a 14-year-old rape victim travelling to the UK to seek an abortion and then lifted by the Supreme Court, further referenda expanded the scope of Article 40.3.3:

> *'This subsection shall not limit the freedom to travel between the State and another State. This subsection shall not limit the freedom to obtain or make available, in the State, subject to such conditions as may be laid down by law, information relating to services lawfully available in another State.'*

The right to life of the unborn has also been examined in the context of the unimplanted embryos as a result of in vitro fertilisation. The Supreme Court decided in *Roche v Roche & Ors* [2009] IESC 82, that such unused embryos did not constitute the 'unborn' for the purposes of Article 40.3.3 on the basis of the context of the amendment, the fact that the Article refers to a situation where the rights of the mother *and* the unborn child are engaged, and the harmonious interpretation of this Article with Article 41.1.2 regarding the rights of the family.

3.5.3.4 Right to property

The guarantee of property rights in Article 40.3.2 tends to arise in the same context as the specific property rights guarantees of Article 43.

3.5.4   UNENUMERATED RIGHTS DOCTRINE

Article 40.3.1 and Article 40.3.2 of the Constitution state:

'1. The State guarantees in its laws to respect, and, as far as practicable, by its laws to defend and vindicate the personal rights of the citizen. 2. The State shall in particular, by its laws protect as best it may from unjust attack, and in the case of injustice done, vindicate the life, person, good name and property rights of every citizen.'

The basis for the doctrine lies in the phrase 'in particular' in Article 40.3.2 implying as it does that there are other, unenumerated, rights protected by Article 40.3.1. The doctrine was first propounded by Kenny J in *Ryan v Attorney General* [1965] IR 294:

'[T]he personal rights which may be involved to invalidate legislation are not confined to those specified in Article 40, but include all those rights which result from the Christian and Democratic nature of the State . . . . A number of factors indicate that the guarantee is not confined to the rights specified in Article 40 but extends to other personal rights of the citizen. Firstly there is subsection 2 of section 3 of Article 40. It reads: "The State shall, in particular, by its laws protect as best it may from unjust attack and, in the case of injustice done, vindicate the life, person, good name, and property rights of every citizen". The words "in particular" show that sub-s. 2 is a detailed statement of something which is already contained in sub-s.1 which is the general guarantee. But sub-s. 2 refers to rights in connection with life and good name and there are no rights in connection with these two matters specified in Article 40. It follows I think that the general guarantee in sub-s. 1 must extend to rights not specified in Article 40. Secondly there are many rights which follow from the Christian and Democratic nature of the State, which are not mentioned in Article 40 at all.'

Since that decision, various sources have been identified as grounding these unenumerated rights. The 'Christian and democratic nature of the State' was expressly noted by Finaly P in *State (M) v Attorney General* [1979] IR 73 in concluding that they formed the basis of a *prima facie* right to travel. The 'Human Personality' was identified by Henchy J in *McGee v Attorney General* [1974] IR 284 as a basis for the protection of a personal right to privacy protected by Article 40.3.1:

'[T]he unspecified personal rights guaranteed by sub-s.1 of s.3 of Article 40 are not confined to those specified in sub-s.2 of that section. It is for the Courts to decide in a particular case whether the right relied on comes within the constitutional guarantee. To do so, it must be shown that it is a right that inheres in the citizen in question by virtue of his human personality. The lack of precision in this test is reduced when Article 40.3.1 is read (as it must be) in the light of the Constitution as a whole and, in particular, in the light of what the Constitution, expressly or by necessary implication, deems to be fundamental to the personal standing of the individual in question in the context of the social order envisaged by the Constitution. The infinite variety in the relationships between the citizen and his fellows and between the citizen and the State makes an exhaustive enumeration of the guaranteed rights difficult, if not impossible.'

It could be argued that this decision does not necessarily clarify the scope of the doctrine. While it does seek to offer some precision in its application, it does so by speaking of what is fundamental to the person, and the social order envisaged by the Constitution. It could be argued that this is no clearer than the Christian and democratic nature of the State, as not much further guidance can be found in the Constitution as to the social order envisaged; the Preamble and Article 45 regarding social policy speak to largely Christian and democratic values. There is also a problem in that very often these sources can be in conflict; for example in the *Norris* case (*Norris v Attorney General* [1984] IR 23) regarding the criminalisation of homosexual acts, the Court found against the plaintiff (who was later successful before the ECt.HR in *Norris v Ireland* (1991) 13 EHRR 186 (see **4.6**)), partly on the basis of the Christian character of the nation; Henchy J dissented on the basis of inherent rights, one of which was the right to privacy.

An appeal to natural law has also formed the basis of these unenumerated rights. Walsh J stated in *State (Nicolaou) v An Bord Úchtala* [1966] IR 567 that 'It is abundantly clear that the rights referred to in s 3 of Article 40 are those which may be called the natural personal rights and the very words of sub-section 1, by the reference therein to "laws", exclude such rights as are dependent only upon law.' Further illumination as to the nature of such natural laws was given by the same judge in *McGee v Attorney General* [1974] IR 284 where he stated:

> 'Articles 41, 42, 43 emphatically reject the theory that there are no rights without laws, no rights contrary to the law and no rights anterior to the law. They indicate that justice is placed above the law and acknowledge natural rights, or human rights, are not created by law but that the Constitution confirms their existence and gives them protection.... Both in its preamble and in Article 6, the Constitution acknowledges God as the ultimate source of all authority. The natural or human rights to which I have referred...are part of what is generally called the natural law...What natural law is and what precisely it import is a question which has exercised the minds of theologians for many centuries and on which they are not yet agreed...I do not feel it necessary to enter upon an inquiry as to their extent or, indeed, as to their nature. It is sufficient for the Court to examine and to search for the rights which may be discoverable in the particular case before the court in which these rights are invoked.'

However, unanimity is not found in the case-law regarding the higher status of the natural law: the Supreme Court in *Re Article 26 and the Regulation of Information (Services outside the State for Termination of Pregnancies) Bill 1995* [1995] 1 IR 1 stated that the court in *McGee v Attorney General* had merely 'recognised the Constitution as the fundamental law of the State to which the organs of the State were subject and at no stage recognised the provision of natural law as superior to the Constitution'.

Rights have also been implied from other constitutional provisions. For instance in *Macauley v Minister for Posts and Telegraphs* [1966] IR 345, Kenny J held that Article 34.1 providing that justice shall be administered in courts established by law, implied a right of access to the courts, which was protected by Article 40.3.1.

One of the major difficulties associated with the doctrine of unenumerated rights is the scope of manoeuvre it affords to judges—it is inherently vague and subjective. Appeals to natural law, the Christian and democratic nature of the State and the social order envisaged by the Constitution are not what one could consider concrete principles. A very great deal of uncertainty as to how these may be applied exists; and it is arguable that the outcome of any particular matter depends to an enormous extent on the personality of the court in cases where the doctrine is deployed. However, the very nature of a constitution is such that a great deal of latitude is allowed to those judges who pronounce upon its meaning; this is the case the world over. In these circumstances, and particularly given the wording of Article 40, such judicial creativity is not only necessary, and to be welcomed, but was specifically envisaged.

Unenumerated rights, which like all other rights in the Constitution are not absolute, have been held to include: the right to bodily integrity (*Ryan v Attorney General* [1965] IR 294, 345); the right to work and earn a livelihood (*Re Article 26 and the Employment Equality Bill* [1997] 2 IR 321); the right to privacy (marital—*McGee v Attorney General* [1974] IR 284 and individual—*Kennedy v Ireland* [1987] IR 587); the right of autonomy (*Re A Ward of Court (withholding medical treatment) (No. 2)* [1996] 2 IR 79); the right to travel (*The State (M) v Attorney General* [1979] IR 73); the right to marry (*Ryan v Attorney General*), although this right is not absolute, and does not apply to same sex couples (*Zappone v Revenue Commissioners* [2008] 2 IR 417); the right to procreate (*Murray v Ireland* [1985] IR 532);

the right to independent domicile, in the context of common law rules determining that the domicile of a wife was that of her husband (*CM v TM (No. 2)* [1990] 2 IR 52); and the right to maintenance (*CM v TM (No. 2)*). The doctrine of unenumerated rights has also been used to protect non-marital family rights, which are excluded from the protections of Article 41. They have not however extended so far as to grant constitutional protection to the rights of unmarried fathers to guardianship (see **9.2**).

3.5.5   LIBERTY

The remaining sections of Article 40 of the Constitution deal broadly with the issue of liberty, namely: personal liberty; the *habeas corpus* procedure; the defence forces not being amenable to *habeas corpus* in times of war and armed rebellion; the refusal of bail, and; the inviolability of the dwelling (see **chapter 14**). Article 40.4.1 acknowledges that *'no citizen shall be deprived of his personal liberty save in accordance with law'*. The courts have clarified that in accordance with the law 'means without stooping to methods which ignore the fundamental norms of the legal order postulated by the Constitution' (*King v Attorney General* [1981] IR 233). This provision has arisen in numerous contexts, most obviously powers of arrest, detention and imprisonment, but also in the context of what may be termed police measures curtailing liberty in the interest of State security, public order or health, for example to facilitate deportation or extradition, or by judicial order, for example regarding contempt of court.

The *habeas corpus* procedure set out in Article 40.4.2–4 is considered in **chapter 14** (see **14.4**). That regarding, the defence forces and *habeas corpus* in time of war or rebellion (Article 40.4.5) has never arisen. Article 40.4.6 regarding the refusal of bail states:

> *'Provision may be made by law for the refusal of bail by a court to a person charged with a serious offence where it is reasonably considered necessary to prevent the commission of a serious offence by that person.'*

It was introduced as a result of a referendum following two Supreme Court decisions holding that the above could only happen in the most extraordinary circumstances to secure public peace and order or public safety or the preservation of the State. The consequent Bail Act 1997 is considered at **14.4.4**.

Article 40.5 deals with the inviolability of the dwelling and affirms: *'The dwelling of every citizen is inviolable and shall not be forcibly entered save in accordance with the law.'* The courts have concluded that this inviolability only applies to that part of a premises used as a dwelling and only in respect of the person whose dwelling it is. This guarantee only applies to the actual structure itself and not to the surrounding area such as a garden or driveway.

3.5.6   FREEDOM OF EXPRESSION, ASSEMBLY AND ASSOCIATION

Article 40.6.1 concerns the protection of the freedoms of expression, assembly and association. The matter is dealt with more fully in **chapter 13**. These rights are primarily designed to ensure that people are free to express their political views and preserve their autonomy, though are of course of far broader application. However, the constitutional protections contain an explicit caveat, namely, that they are subject to public order and morality.

3.5.6.1   Freedom of expression

The freedom of expression is further fettered by firstly, expressly allowing censorship for the 'education of public opinion', and secondly, stating that the utterance of blasphemous, seditious or indecent matter is an offence. Blasphemy was first defined in the 2009 Defamation Act as the publication or utterance of a material that is grossly abusive or insulting to matters held sacred by any religion, thereby causing outrage amongst a substantial number of the adherents of that religion and it is intended to cause such outrage. A defence exists if a reasonable person would find genuine literary, artistic, political, scientific or academic value in the matter.

The courts have also held that freedom of expression is distinct from freedom to communicate information. This is protected as an unenumerated right under Article 40.3, as identified by Costello J in *Attorney General v Paperlink* [1984] ILRM 373, and confirmed by the Supreme Court in *Murphy v The Independent Radio and Television Commission* [1999] 1 IR 12, *per* Barrington J. The distinction however, will often be artificial, and the courts are less concerned with the question of under which provision a statement or communication is protected, and more with whether it is in fact protected. Generally speaking the constitutional protection of freedom of expression is more limited than that outlined in the ECHR. The Constitutional Review Group, established by the government in 1995, recommended in its 1996 report that Article 40.6.1.i be replaced with the Article 10 ECHR text, but to date no such steps have yet been taken.

There are restrictions on freedom of expression beyond just those identified in the texts, such as, in the interests of the right to life, for example in the regulation of the provision of information about abortion services; in the interests of state security and official secrets, and regarding publications about illegal organisations. Generally speaking in Ireland, the courts have been slow to restrict freedom of expression. One of the major issues which arises in this context is the balancing of a right to freedom of expression, with that of the right to privacy. The matter has been dealt with in a recent judgment of Dunne J in the High Court in *Herrity v Associated Newspapers (Ireland) Ltd* [2009] 1 IR 316 (see **13.8.5**). In that case the Court made clear that the freedom of expression:

'is subject to clearly defined exceptions laid down by the common law or statute. It is in that context that the constitutional right to privacy comes into the equation. Accordingly, it seems to me that there is a balancing exercise engaged in circumstances where the right to freedom of expression conflicts with the right to privacy. It is clear that newspapers are free to publish all sorts of matters regardless of the public interest and questions of good taste but, as with the right to privacy, the right to freedom of expression is not an unqualified right...There is a hierarchy of constitutional rights and as a general proposition, I think that cases in which the right to privacy will prevail over the right to freedom of expression may well be few and far between. However, this may not always be the case.'

The judge also confirmed in that case that an action for damages for breach of a constitutional right to privacy will not be confined to actions against the State or state bodies, but could also be maintained against a private person or entity.

3.5.6.2 Freedom of assembly

Article 40.6.1.ii concerns the right of citizens to assembly peaceably and without arms. This too is subject to public order and morality. There is also provision to prevent or control meetings which are determined, in accordance with law, to be calculated to cause a breach of the peace or to be a danger or nuisance to the general public, and to prevent or control meetings in the vicinity of either House of the Oireachtas. There are, as with all protections under the Constitution, limitations on the freedom of assembly. Firstly, such a freedom does not override private property rights and an assembly held on private property and without the owner's permission can constitute trespass. The Article does not protect non-peaceable meetings, and there are statutory prohibitions on meetings in support of unlawful organisations. There is further statutory regulation of public meetings and assemblies under the Criminal Justice (Public Order) Acts 1994 and 2003.

3.5.6.3   Freedom of association

Article 40.6.1.iii guarantees citizens liberty for the exercise, subject to public order and morality, of the right to form associations and unions. The Article is explicit in recognising that law may be enacted for the regulation and control of same in the public interest. The primary focus of case-law on this Article has been in the context of the role of trade unions. The courts have interpreted the guarantee as a right to form a trade union, though not necessarily to join one, and there is judicial recognition of the right of a trade union to refuse new members. A necessary corollary to the freedom of association is the freedom of dissociation and courts have also recognised that there is freedom to abstain from membership. It is important to note there is no obligation on an employer to recognise and negotiate with a union.

3.5.7   ARTICLES 41 AND 42: FAMILY AND EDUCATION

The family is specifically recognised as the natural, primary and fundamental unit group of society by Article 41.1 and as a moral institution possessing inalienable and imprescriptible rights, antecedent and superior to all positive law. (see **chapter 9**) The State further guarantees to protect the family *'in its constitution and authority as the necessary basis of social order and as indispensable to the welfare of the Nation and State'*. Article 41.2 goes on to recognise the importance to the State of women as homemakers, and endeavours to ensure that a mother shall not be obliged by economic necessity to engage in labour, to the neglect of her duties in the home. By subsection 3 of Article 41, the State pledges to guard with special care the institution of marriage, and to protect it from attack. Divorce is permitted by Article 41.3.2 following the referendum on the fifteenth amendment to the Constitution, which was signed into law on 17 June 1996.

The provisions in relation to education are set out in Article 42. Therein, the State acknowledges that the primary and natural educator of the child is the family, and guarantees to respect the inalienable right and duty of parents to provide, according to their means, for the religious and moral, intellectual, physical and social education of their children. It goes on to clarify that parents are free to home-school their children, or send them to private or state schools. The third section of the Article asserts that the State shall not oblige parents to send children to any particular type of school, but that the State is mandated to secure particular minimum levels of moral, intellectual and social education. Article 42.4 provides that the State shall provide free primary education and shall endeavour to:

> *'supplement and give reasonable aid to private and corporate educational initiatives, and, when the public good requires it, provide other educational facilities or institutions with due regard however for the rights of parents, especially in the matter of religious and moral formation'*.

Finally, Article 42.5 states that:

> *'in exceptional cases, where the parents fail in their duty towards their children, the State as guardian of the common good, by appropriate means shall endeavour to supply the place of the parents, but always with due regard for the natural and imprescriptible rights of the child.'*

It has been argued that the provisions relating to the family and education reflect the strong influence of Catholic teachings on the framers of the Constitution. This is not a view with universal support however, and in a recent decision Hardiman J declared that he did not 'regard . . . Articles 41 and 42 as reflecting uniquely any confessional view' (*North Western Health Board v HW* [2001] 3 IR 622). Whatever the truth of this it seems clear that Article 42 was designed as much to respect and secure the rights of the Protestant minority, as much as to reflect any Catholic ideology. In any event, the increased secularisation of society, and the change in attitudes to the Church, allied to the different roles played by women in society, and indeed society's different views on what constitutes a family have placed an increasing strain on these initially innovative provisions.

The courts have limited the definition of family to that founded on marriage, and restricted the impact of Article 41 in relation to non-marital families (*State (Nicolau) v An Bord Uchtála* [1966] IR 567. Marriage has been defined as between a man and a woman, and a right to marry has been recognised (*Zappone v Revenue Commissioners* [2008] 2 IR 417, *per* Dunne J). Article 41.2 has been used to provide far stronger rights to non-marital mothers as against non-marital fathers, an example of these provisions trumping the right to equality. The rights guaranteed under these Articles can be relied on by non-nationals, not just citizens, but they can be applied more restrictively. One criticism of these Articles is that they do not place enough emphasis on the rights of children, and to this end a constitutional amendment is being prepared to be put before the people which will more expressly protect their rights. Clearly, further criticism can be made of the paternalistic attitude towards women enunciated, which could not be said to reflect current values of society. Family and child law is discussed further in **chapter 9**.

3.5.8 RIGHT TO PROPERTY

Article 43 of the Constitution concerns the right to private property which is recognised as being a natural right, antecedent to positive law, which the State will protect from unjust attack. This is not an untrammelled right however, and the State may regulate the exercise of this right by the principle of social justice and in accordance with the exigencies of the common good. This provision is complementary to that contained in the more general personal rights in Article 40.3. To assess whether any attack on private property rights is unjust, and therefore unconstitutional, the courts have developed a proportionality test. In *Heaney v Ireland* [1994] 3 IR 593 Costello J set out the test:

> 'The objective of the impugned provision must be of sufficient importance to warrant overriding a constitutionally protected right. It must relate to concerns pressing and substantial in a free and democratic society. The means chosen must pass a proportionality test. They must: (a) be rationally connected to the objective and not be arbitrary, unfair or based on irrational considerations; (b) impair the right to title as little as possible, and; (c) be such that their effects on rights are proportional to the objective.'.

It is considered by such eminent scholars as Gerard Hogan that the courts have focused more on the individual property rights aspect of Article 43, rather than the wider social obligations noted in the provision (Hogan G., The Constitution, Property Rights and Proportionality, 1997, 32 *Irish Jurist* 373).

3.5.9 RELIGION

Article 44.1 of the Constitution concerns religion, wherein the State *'acknowledges that the homage of public worship is due to Almighty God. It shall hold his name in reverence, and shall respect and honour religion'*. There has been very little judicial reflection on this Article but one example is the comment by Walsh J in *Quinn's Supermarket v Attorney General* [1972] IR 1 that it 'reflects a firm conviction that we are a religious people . . . [and] acknowledges that the homage of public worship is due to Almighty God but it does so in terms which do not confine the benefit of that acknowledgment to members of the Christian faith.'

Article 44.2.1 states that: *'[f]reedom of conscience and the free profession and practice of religion are, subject to public order and morality, guaranteed to every citizen'*. As noted above, this freedom is not restricted to the Christian religion. However, the freedom of conscience aspect of the Article is limited to that of religious conscience (*McGee v Attorney General* [1974] IR 284). This right, as explicitly stated in the Article, is subject to public order and morality.

By Article 44.2.2 the State guarantees not to endow any religion. Article 44.2.3 asserts that the State shall not impose any disabilities or make any discrimination on the ground of religious profession, belief or status. This constitutional guarantee is binding only on the State, and does not extend to bodies which receive public moneys from the State: *McGrath v Trustees of Maynooth College* [1979] ILRM 166, *per* Kenny J. However, the courts have held that the guarantee of non-discrimination is subordinate to the provision guaranteeing free practice of religion, and that the State may discriminate where necessary to give full effect to the free practice clause (*Re Article 26 and the Employment Equality Bill 1996* [1997] 2 IR 321).

3.5.10 SOCIAL POLICY

Article 45 of the Constitution is entitled 'Directive Principles of Social Policy' and demands that the State strive to promote the welfare of the whole people and secure a social order characterised by justice and charity. Its themes are those of social justice, an equitable division of the wealth of society and the value of private enterprise. This Article is very much influenced by the social Catholic teaching of the time, which was in turn influenced by the need to counteract the threat of socialism/communism and to deal with widespread poverty. The Article specifically declares that it shall not be cognisable by any court under any of the provisions of the Constitution, although it has been referred to as an interpretive instrument.

3.6 The European Convention on Human Rights (ECHR) Act, 2003

The European Convention of Human Rights Act became law on 31 December 2003 (see **chapter 5**). Pursuant to this legislation Ireland finally incorporated the ECHR despite having been one of the original signatories to the ECHR. Delayed incorporation is all the more remarkable when one considers that Ireland was one of only two states to allow the right of petition to the ECHR to its citizens upon the entry into force of the Convention in September 1953.

So why the delay? The Constitutional Review Group mentioned above, submitted a report to the government in 1996 which spells out some of the reasons for the time lag in incorporation of the ECHR into Irish law. The group noted that in many areas, such as the protections of personal liberty, the provisions of the Constitution go further than those of the Convention. They also considered that incorporation would not, as such, fill any gaps at constitutional level, since every substantive right afforded by the ECHR is either expressly protected by the Constitution, or has been recognised by the courts as an unenumerated right under Article 40.3. They also observed that incorporation into the Constitution by replacement would lead to new gaps in areas such as the right to a jury trial (not part of the civil law tradition, and in fact the subject of a current challenge before the ECt.HR), and the guarantee that the State not endow any religion. They also felt that a replacement of the fundamental rights provisions of the Irish Constitution by the text of the ECHR would represent too great a change in the legal system, which was not warranted by any existing flaws in those provisions. The Review Group also argued that such incorporation would mean the jettisoning of almost 60 years of well-established case-law. A further reason why such incorporation was unnecessary was by virtue of the Irish system of judicial review of legislation.

This report, whilst not without its flaws, principally that it only seemed to consider the disadvantages of incorporation from the perspective of replacing Article 40–44, and not from say the addition of an Article that no law may be enacted which would conflict with Ireland's obligations as flow from the ECHR, does illustrate some of the reasons why incorporation took so long. There are many more: that the ECHR jurisprudence would not reflect the wishes of what was for many years a more conservative society than that of many of the ECHR's signatories. There was also the fact that most of the judges on the ECt.HR came from a civil law background, and so may not have fully appreciated the subtleties and nuances of the common law position. This was a fear which receded over time through Ireland's participation in the European Union, and indeed the Council of Europe. A further argument against such incorporation arose from the case of Northern Ireland and the State's attempts to deal with the crises of the Troubles.

Further reasons can also be seen from the nature of the small number of cases involving the State which came before the ECt.HR, all of which are discussed at **4.6**. They have mostly arisen either in the context of the Troubles (*Lawless v Ireland; Quinn v Ireland*) or in the context of what could be termed social issues which arose owing to the conservative nature of the State (*Norris v Ireland*, criminalisation of homosexual acts; *Johnston v Ireland*, divorce; *Open Door and Well Woman v Ireland*, provision of information on abortion; *Keegan v Ireland*, adoption laws). It could be argued that in the context of the Troubles, the State did not want their actions fettered by the judgments of a European Court which may not have had quite the appreciation of the circumstances as an Irish court. Similarly, it could be said that the socially conservative nature of the State, and it must be said the populace, meant that there was a fear that social change, for which the majority were unprepared and had no desire, would be foisted upon the country by a foreign court. However, underpinning all of this was a justifiable pride in the operation of the Constitution and its protection of human rights through many turbulent decades, which can be seen in the very low number of cases involving Ireland in the ECt.HR.

The ECHR was enacted into Irish law in 2003. The impetus for this step was the Belfast Agreement, by which the United Kingdom and Ireland both agreed to take steps to improve the position of human rights in their respective jurisdictions. The provisions of the ECHR and of the ECHR Act are considered in **chapters 4** and **5**.

3.7 European Union: Post Lisbon and the Charter of Fundamental Rights

The Treaty of Lisbon came into force on 1 December 2009. One of the innovations of the Treaty of Lisbon is that Article 6(1) of the amended Treaty on European Union (TEU) grants the Charter of Fundamental Rights the same legal value as the Treaties (the TEU as amended and the Treaty on the Functioning of the European Union (TFEU)) and as a result the Charter is now legally binding. Article 6(1) TEU makes clear however, that this incorporation in no way extends the competences of the Union. Article 6(2) TEU as amended by the Treaty of Lisbon, provides for EU accession to the ECHR but accession has not yet taken place (see **chapter 8**). The Charter's 55 Articles list political, social and economic rights. Article 51 of the Charter itself addresses the Charter to the EU institutions, bodies, offices and agencies of the EU, and, when in the course of implementing EU law, the Member States. The provisions of the Charter are considered in **chapter 8**.

3.8 Legislation in the Area of Human Rights

There are myriad pieces of legislation which deal with human rights issues. Some are obviously identifiable as such, for example the Equality Act, 2004, which amended the Equal Status Act 2000, and the Employment Equality Act 1998 (see **chapter 10**). Others in this vein include the European Convention of Human Rights Act, 2003 and the Human Rights Commission Acts, 2000 and 2001. The Human Rights Commission is mandated to protect and promote:

> '*The rights, liberties and freedoms conferred on, or guaranteed to, persons by the Constitution, and . . . any agreement, treaty or convention to which the State is a party.*'

International agreements relating to human rights have also been incorporated into Irish law, notably in the Geneva Convention Acts, 1962 and 1998, the International Criminal Court Act, 2006, and the Cluster Munitions and Anti-Personnel Mines Act, 2001. Many of these pieces of legislation are inspired by EU directives, which have to be implemented into Irish law, or as a result of the Belfast Agreement, by which both the United Kingdom and Northern Ireland pledged to improve human rights protections in both jurisdictions.

However, it is important to always bear in mind that human rights arise in a great many other areas of legislation. Clearly, the Defamation Act, 2009 has an impact on both freedom of expression and the right to privacy. The various Child Care Acts, 1991–2007 affect both the personal rights of children and the rights of families protected under Article 8 of the ECHR and Article 41 of the Constitution. The National Assets Management Agency Act, 2009 has implications for property rights protections. Human rights is not a discrete topic; rather it pervades every aspect of law.

3.9 Conclusion

Human rights have long been at the core of Irish law. The constitutional protections afforded, and the courts' mostly robust defence of these provisions have played a part in shaping Irish society for generations. A considerable body of jurisprudence has developed since the foundation of the State concerning human rights. The influence of European law, whether of the EU or the ECHR, has added to the weight of our established constitutional guarantees. This will be enhanced in years to come with the accession of the EU to the ECHR, and the addition of the Charter of Fundamental Rights to the body of EU law. These developments should not distract our attention from the substantial protections which have emerged from the domestic field.

CHAPTER 4

THE EUROPEAN CONVENTION ON HUMAN RIGHTS

4.1 Introduction

In 1949, a group of nations, appalled by the atrocities of the Second World War and concerned about the rise of Communism in central and eastern Europe, came together to form an organisation named the Council of Europe. In the statute establishing this organisation, the founding members pledged to uphold the principles of the rule of law and to protect the human rights and fundamental freedoms of all persons within their jurisdiction. However, it was recognised that to make this political promise a legal reality something more was needed: a document which would set out the minimum content of these protected rights and freedoms and, perhaps even more importantly, establish mechanisms to ensure the enforcement of these guarantees.

Hence, in 1950, the Council of Europe adopted the European Convention for the Protection of Human Rights and Fundamental Freedoms (usually known as the European Convention on Human Rights or the 'ECHR') although it did not in fact come into force until 3 September 1953. From that time onwards, the ECHR has become increasingly significant, to the extent that today it is often described as the single most successful international human rights instrument. Its influence can be seen from the fact that it is now a precondition to membership of the European Union (EU) that the applicant country has signed and ratified the ECHR, and indeed one of the measures contained in the Lisbon Treaty is the provision of a legal basis for the EU itself to accede to the ECHR, thus making the EU a potential respondent before the European Court of Human Rights. (ECt.HR) (see **chapter 8**).

The major achievement of the ECHR lies in the fact that it provides a mechanism whereby both *individuals* and *states* can make a complaint to the institutions established under the ECHR. Individuals can complain if they feel that their rights have been infringed by their own governments and states can complain if they feel that another state within the Council of Europe is abusing the rights of those within its own jurisdiction. A contracting state can therefore be held to account by both an individual from within its jurisdiction and also another state concerned by its actions. As will be seen however, the ECHR has become something of a victim of its own success, in that increasing support for the ECHR has led to increasing strains being placed on its institutions (there are currently 47 states parties to the ECHR). Radical procedural reform was introduced in 1998 in an attempt to remedy this, but it would appear that further reform may be needed to keep pace with the ever-growing number of new applications made under the ECHR. It should also be noted that there has not always been universal approval of the decisions of the institutions of the ECHR, with some arguing that these have been on the whole too conservative, others arguing they have been too liberal.

Ireland was one of the original signatory states to the ECHR but has only recently, over 50 years later, passed legislation to bring it into domestic law. This issue will be examined further in **chapter 5**.

4.2 The Scope of the ECHR

4.2.1 TYPE OF RIGHTS PROTECTED

The ECHR primarily covers what are sometimes referred to as 'first generation rights', ie civil and political rights. It does not, on the whole, protect 'second generation' or economic and social rights. The reason for this was essentially pragmatic. The original founding states knew that it would be much more difficult to get agreement on a text that included both types of rights. Instead, they pursued a short and non-controversial text which states could and would immediately accept, and agreed to consider at a later date the issue of economic and social rights.

The ECHR, as originally drafted, has since been supplemented by a number of protocols, some of which contain further substantive rights guarantees, and others which deal with procedural matters. The protocols are separate treaties meaning that each individual state has a discretion whether or not to adopt them and that, with one exception, they bind only those states that have adopted them (the exception is Protocol 11 which we shall look at later). The protocol mechanism has therefore been used for those most controversial issues such as the death penalty on which it was unlikely that there would be unanimous agreement.

4.2.2 TYPE OF PERSONS COVERED

In Article 1 ECHR, the State parties agree 'to secure to *everyone within their jurisdiction* the rights and freedoms defined in the ECHR and its substantive protocols'. It can be seen therefore that the rights contained in the ECHR are not confined to the citizens only of contracting states. Instead, these states agree to protect the ECHR rights of all those within their jurisdiction, regardless of whether they are nationals or non-nationals. This can be contrasted with the position under the Irish Constitution where it remains unclear to what extent non-nationals enjoy the guarantees contained in the fundamental rights provisions.

4.2.3 TEMPORAL SCOPE OF THE ECHR

The ECHR binds states only from the moment of ratification. It is not retrospective in its effect. Therefore, as a general rule, a complaint can only be made in relation to an event that occurred after the State concerned ratified the ECHR, although where it is alleged that there has been a continuing abuse of rights, so that events prior to ratification are so closely bound up with events post-ratification that the two cannot be divorced, the ECHR institutions may consider matters that arose before the State involved had ratified the ECHR. However, such cases are highly unusual.

4.2.4 RESERVATIONS AND DEROGATIONS

Any state, when it signs up to the ECHR, can agree to be bound by all of its provisions. However, most of the contracting states have taken advantage of a concession in the ECHR that allows states at the time of signature or ratification to enter a *reservation* in respect of a provision of the ECHR if it considers that any law then in force in its jurisdiction is not in conformity with that particular provision. This prevents claims against that law being brought on the basis that it infringes the rights guaranteed by the particular provision. In other words, the law is given a certain immunity from challenge on ECHR grounds. However, such reservations cannot be vague, over-broad or of a general character. Although states can make these reservations, it must be clear to what they relate and they must be limited in nature.

A further type of restriction that can be made on the scope and application of the ECHR is the *derogation*. Article 15 of the ECHR allows states to derogate or opt out of its obligations under the ECHR but only in time of war or other public emergency and only to the extent strictly required to meet the exigencies of the situation. A number of states have invoked Article 15. For example, in the early 1990s, the United Kingdom government derogated from its obligations under the ECHR in relation to the length of time persons can be kept in custody without trial in respect of the holding of suspects in Northern Ireland. This derogation was challenged but the ECt.HR accepted that the situation in Northern Ireland at the time did constitute a public emergency so that Article 15 could be invoked. There is some scope for abuse of the Article 15 procedure but this is tempered by the requirement that states keep its use under review and the ability of the European Court of Human Rights to declare that the particular circumstances no longer justify derogation under Article 15.

4.3   Structures of the ECHR

As noted above, the ECHR has been very successful in terms of the number of state signatories and the number of important decisions it has generated. However, as time went on it became clear that the structures initially established by the ECHR did not have the time, money or other resources to deal with the increasing number of applications being made to them. A certain amount of piecemeal structural reform was achieved in an attempt to alleviate the situation, but by the late 1980s it was clear that nothing short of wholesale structural change would have the required effect. Therefore, the states embarked on an ambitious drafting project that eventually resulted in Protocol 11. Protocol 11 was opened for signature in 1994 and came into force on 1 November 1998.

Under the system before Protocol 11, there had been a two-tier system for applications, with the initial application being dealt with by a body known as the European Commission of Human Rights, which was composed of experts in the area. If the Commission did not consider that the case was admissible, the application would be dismissed at this stage. If the Commission considered that the application was admissible, it would form an opinion on the substantive merits of the case which would be sent on to the ECt.HR, a body composed of judges. The Court would then give a determinative decision as to whether any or all of the complaints set out in the application were valid. However, both the Court and the Commission were part-time bodies and this two-tier system inevitably led to delay, particularly as the number of state signatories increased and knowledge of the ECHR became more widespread. Indeed, by the time Protocol 11 came into force there was a backlog of over 6,700 cases before the Court. The need for fundamental reform was evident, the aim being to produce a system that was relatively quick and cheap yet which would operate in a way that would produce quality case-law and maintain the confidence of all the participants in the system.

Protocol 11 attempted to achieve this primarily by abolishing the old Court and Commission and replacing these by a single, full-time court. This Court would deal with *all* applications, at least to some extent, which has the merit that all applications will receive some level of judicial scrutiny.

The structures which now exist under Protocol 11 are as follows.

4.3.1 THE EUROPEAN COURT OF HUMAN RIGHTS (ECT.HR)

This newer body, unlike its predecessor, is full-time and permanent. All contracting states *must* accept the jurisdiction of the ECt.HR in all cases and so it is an institution to which all individuals wishing to make a complaint will have access. The ECt.HR is now the first international court to which individuals (over 800 million of them) have automatic direct access for alleged breaches of a state's international obligations. The ECt.HR is composed of judges who are elected by the Parliamentary Assembly of the Council of Europe from a list of three candidates supplied by the relevant state, although there is no necessity that such judges be nationals of the State nominating them. To make its operations more efficient, the ECt.HR has been divided into five *sections*, which are designed to be balanced in terms of regional and gender representation. These sections can then be subdivided into the following:

4.3.1.1 Committees

These are composed of three judges who sift through the initial individual applications made to the ECt.HR and weed out any clearly unfounded cases at an early stage. The committees perform the 'filtering' role previously carried out by the old Commission, except for inter-state complaints, the admissibility of which must be considered by a chamber. However Protocol 14 allows for admissibility decisions to be made by single judges in respect of applications which are plainly inadmissible, and also allows committees to make decisions on the merits of so-called 'repetitive cases' (see **4.3.13**). Judges on committees are appointed for a 12-month period.

4.3.1.2 Chambers

Chambers are the bodies which will decide the majority of cases and are composed of seven rotating judges. When a case is assigned to a particular section, the President of that section and the judge from the country against which the complaint has been made will always sit on the Chamber. Chambers can consider both the admissibility of a case and the merits of a case.

4.3.1.3 Grand Chamber

This is composed of 17 judges and will decide the most important cases: namely those which raise a question of interpretation or application of the ECHR or those which raise a 'question of general importance'. Cases can end up before the Grand Chamber in two ways. First, a chamber may decide that a case before it raises a question of interpretation of the ECHR or that the case is likely to prompt a departure from existing case-law, and so relinquish jurisdiction to the Grand Chamber. Second, if a chamber has given judgment in a case, any party to the case may in exceptional circumstances request that the case be referred to the Grand Chamber for rehearing. The Grand Chamber shall accept the request if the case raises a serious question affecting the interpretation or application of the ECHR or a serious issue of general importance. Since 2004 the Grand Chamber has also engaged in a process known as the pilot judgment procedure, which was introduced to try and reduce the burden of the case load before the ECt.HR. This mechanism is used where numerous very similar applications are received which indicate to the Court that a systemic problem exists in the respondent state; effectively where the Court receives a large number of well-founded but repetitive cases. Typically under this procedure the Court singles out one or a small number of applications for priority treatment and adjourns all other applications until the pilot case has been decided. In its judgment in the pilot case the Court gives the national authorities advice as to how to cure the systemic problem and when implementing the judgment the relevant national authorities should in particular address the situations of persons who have cases pending before the Court. The idea is that the Court will not then be required to decide the remaining applications pending before it as these will be satisfactorily dealt with by the national authorities. The first pilot judgment was delivered in 2004. Although this judgment was successful in ensuring the particular systemic problem involved was addressed (relating to a compensation scheme for Polish citizens displaced after World War II) in fact the pilot judgment process has not been used as often as first predicted.

The Grand Chamber will always contain the President of the ECt.HR, the two Vice-Presidents (who are also Presidents of sections), the Presidents of the other sections and the judge of the respondent state. This requirement that certain judges always sit on the Grand Chamber is designed to ensure that there is consistency in the decisions of the Grand Chamber, which is particularly desirable given that the Grand Chamber decides the most important cases.

4.3.1.4 Plenary court

Unlike under the old system, the full ECt.HR will only rarely sit and when it does, it decides purely procedural matters such as the composition of chambers, the appointment of Presidents of the Chambers and the adoption of rules of procedure. The plenary ECt.HR sits only in an administrative capacity. It no longer sits in a judicial capacity.

4.3.2 THE COMMITTEE OF MINISTERS

This is the executive or political arm of the Council of Europe and is composed of the foreign ministers of each of the contracting states (although in fact the day-to-day business of the Committee of Ministers is performed by career diplomats who are the permanent representatives of the contracting states in Strasbourg). The principal role now of the Committee of Ministers is to ensure the enforcement of the judgments of the Court. For example, it can discuss cases on a six-monthly basis and the relevant national representative on the Committee must explain what steps have been taken by his or her government to enforce the particular decision. Given the importance of rapid execution of judgments, especially in cases concerning structural problems, Protocol 14 now also allows the Committee of Ministers to decide, in exceptional circumstances and with a two-thirds majority, to initiate proceedings of non-compliance in the Grand Chamber in order to make the state concerned execute the Court's initial judgment. The Committee of Ministers however has lost the power it had under the old system to decide whether there had been a violation of the ECHR in those non-contentious cases that were not referred to the ECt.HR by the Commission. The now limited role of the Committee of Ministers is seen to enhance the credibility of the system as a *judicial* rather than political process.

4.3.3 SECRETARIAT OF THE COUNCIL OF EUROPE

Under the old system this was in fact the only full-time body. It remains a full-time body and is composed of nationals of all of the contracting states. The Secretariat has a supervisory role in relation to reservations made by states and in relation to the ratification of the ECHR by potential contracting states. It also has the power to request reports from states to explain how their domestic law reflects the provisions of the ECHR.

4.3.4 PARLIAMENTARY ASSEMBLY OF THE COUNCIL OF EUROPE

This institution is composed of members of each of the national parliaments of the Member States of the Council of Europe who are appointed by these parliaments to sit on the assembly. The main function of the parliamentary assembly is to examine whether the domestic law of countries applying for membership of the Council of Europe complies with the ECHR and to recommend individual states to the Committee of Ministers for membership of the Council of Europe.

4.4 Taking a Case to Strasbourg

There are two types of applications that can be made to the ECt.HR. These are individual applications and inter-state applications.

Previously, states had a discretion as to whether to accept the jurisdiction of the ECt.HR to hear individual petitions brought against them but since the entry into force of Protocol 11 all present and future parties to the ECHR must accept the right of individual application to the ECt.HR. The jurisdiction of the ECt.HR to hear inter-state complaints, ie a complaint brought by one state against another on the basis of the latter state's treatment of those within its borders, has always been compulsory.

Each of these forms of application will be examined in turn, followed by an examination of the admissibility criteria in respect of these applications.

4.4.1 INDIVIDUAL APPLICATIONS

Article 34 ECHR now provides that not only individuals but also groups of individuals and also non-governmental organisations (NGOs) claiming to be the victim of a violation of the ECHR can make an application to the ECt.HR. States are obliged to ensure that they do not hinder in any effective way the exercise of this right, so that for example, applicants and potential applicants must be able to communicate freely with the Strasbourg authorities in relation to their application. As mentioned earlier, this ability on the part of an individual to make a complaint against their government to an international court has been critical to the success of the Strasbourg system, not only in terms of public confidence in the process but also in producing a body of case-law which has been influential not just in the domestic legal systems of Europe but in other domestic legal systems and in international human rights jurisprudence generally.

4.4.2 INTER-STATE APPLICATIONS

Article 33 ECHR enables any state party to the ECHR to make a complaint against any other state party to the ECHR. This is an immediate right, ie all states enjoy this right and it is not dependent on any other act by any of the parties involved. The thinking behind such a mechanism is that every state party is one of the collective guarantors of the ECHR rights, so that every state party can take action designed to ensure the implementation of the ECHR and the protection of the public order of Europe generally. For this reason, the right is not limited to cases involving nationals of the State bringing the action. Hence, a number of Scandinavian countries brought a case against Greece in the 1960s in relation to the treatment by the Greek government of its own nationals. In fact, for an application to be brought, there does not even have to be a threat to any particular individual, merely a danger that the ECHR is about to be breached.

However, this procedure has not been used very often, perhaps because states are aware of the political risks in bringing an action against another state. In fact under the old system, while approximately 15 inter-state complaints were made to the Commission, only one made it as far as the Court, this being the case brought by Ireland against the United Kingdom government in respect of the treatment of prisoners in Northern Ireland under emergency legislation introduced in the early 1970s (discussed below). Under the new procedure of course, all such applications are now dealt with by at least a chamber of the ECt.HR, but this does not yet appear to have had the effect of increasing the number of such applications.

4.4.3   MAKING AN APPLICATION

It is very easy to make an initial application to the Strasbourg authorities. All that is required is some sort of written complaint setting out the name of the applicant, the nature of the claim the person or state is making and the ECHR Articles the applicant considers relevant. This complaint should be sent to the Registrar of the ECt.HR who will then forward an official application form to the applicant. When the official application form is returned, the application will be assigned to a section whose President then appoints a 'judge-rapporteur' (unless the application is clearly one to be dealt with by a single judge under Protocol 14; in such cases the single judge will be assisted by a non-judicial rapporteur). The judge-rapporteur then decides whether the application will be dealt with by a committee or a chamber (or whether it can in fact be dealt with by a single judge). The committee, chamber, or single judge will then decide whether the application should get past this first stage in the process. To do so, it must satisfy a number of criteria known as 'admissibility criteria'.

4.4.3.1   Admissibility criteria

It is in fact quite difficult to get over the hurdle of admissibility and the vast majority of claims fall at this first stage. (Prior to the coming into force of Protocol 11 less than 2% of claims were ultimately held to be admissible and today on average 90% of applications each year are deemed inadmissible.) The first two admissibility criteria relate to both individual and inter-state applications, the remaining four relate only to individual applications.

Exhaustion of local remedies

It is a cardinal procedural rule of international law that before a claim can be brought before an international court, all domestic remedies must be exhausted and this requirement is reiterated in Article 35 ECHR. This is consistent with the idea that domestic law, rather than international law, should be at the forefront in the protection of human rights. As a general rule therefore, potential Irish applicants must take their case to the highest possible court (which will usually be the Supreme Court) and lose there, before they can apply to Strasbourg. However, the ECt.HR has put something of a gloss on this requirement. It has held that Article 35 requires to be exhausted only those remedies which *relate to the breach alleged* and are *available and effective*. For example, in an Irish context, if the Supreme Court has already given judgment in a practically identical case and that judgment is unfavourable to a person who believes that their ECHR rights have been violated, that person will not be required to go all the way to the Supreme Court before they apply to Strasbourg if such domestic proceedings would clearly be in vain.

Six-month rule

A complaint can only be considered by the ECt.HR if brought within six months of the date on which the final domestic decision is made. The reason for such a time limit is three-fold. First, it ensures a degree of legal certainty; second, it ensures that cases raising an ECHR point are examined within a reasonable time; and third, it ensures that the facts of the case can be established. The rule is usually strictly applied in relation to individual complaints (except for example in cases of ill-health) but there is more flexibility in relation to inter-state complaints, as these tend to relate to ongoing situations of abuse and hence it is more difficult to identify an act or decision from which time should run. This six-month period is a relatively short period of time but the potential harshness of this rule is alleviated by the fact that any sort of communication with the Strasbourg authorities within this time frame will be enough to satisfy this condition.

Applicant must be a victim of the complained violation

As noted earlier, this criterion relates only to individual complaints. It does not relate to inter-state applications as the entire purpose of such applications is to enable claims to be brought on behalf of all the peoples of Europe. The Strasbourg authorities have drawn a distinction between those who are 'directly affected' and those who are 'indirectly affected' by a violation. As a general rule, only the former can claim to be 'victims' so as to satisfy this criterion. This distinction can be particularly important where a group claims that its rights have been violated. For tactical reasons it is advisable to submit both a group application and an application on behalf of an individual member of the group as the latter is more likely to be able to show he or she has been directly affected. In any case, what needs to be demonstrated is a clear link between the applicant and the treatment complained of, so that complaints of a very general nature from individuals who object simply to the existence of a law or government action will not satisfy this condition. Again however, the Strasbourg authorities have shown some flexibility here, for example allowing family members to lodge a complaint where the person most directly affected is physically not able to do so.

Application must not be anonymous

This requirement is designed to weed out frivolous or sinister claims. However, the condition relates only to the application when it is sent to Strasbourg; the Strasbourg authorities can decide to conceal the identity of an applicant from the public at large for reasons of security or confidentiality.

Matter must not have been examined already by the Strasbourg court or submitted to another international procedure

This condition ensures that there is no duplication of complaints either within the Strasbourg system or between the Strasbourg system and another international procedure. An applicant cannot continuously apply to the ECt.HR to rehear a complaint it has already decided upon. Likewise the complaint cannot already have been submitted to another international human rights body for consideration. However, if circumstances have fundamentally altered since the matter was previously examined, the ECt.HR may decide that it will look afresh at the application.

Complaint must not be manifestly ill-founded, an abuse of the right of petition or incompatible with the convention

Again this condition is designed to eliminate entirely unmeritorious complaints. The ECt.HR is always concerned to ensure that its procedures are used in the manner intended. So for example, a complaint cannot be made if it is not in fact directed at the State or an arm of the State, because to allow such claims would be incompatible with the ECHR which is designed to protect individuals from the actions of the State. Further, the ECHR should not be used for political or propaganda reasons, so that applications which are made purely for these purposes will be inadmissible as an abuse of the right of petition.

If the complaint is declared inadmissible, it will go no further. If it is declared admissible by a committee, it will then be sent to a chamber for a determination as to the merits of the case. As mentioned earlier, the Chamber can relinquish jurisdiction to the Grand Chamber if the case raises a serious question of interpretation of the ECHR or it may prompt a departure from existing case-law. If the Chamber does not relinquish jurisdiction, it will make a decision as to the merits of the case. Once it gives its decision, the parties have three months within which to request a referral of the case to the Grand Chamber. The Grand Chamber will only consider such a referral in cases of grave importance. If the parties do not make such a request within this three-month period, the decision of the Chamber becomes final.

4.4.4   REFORM: PROTOCOL 14

As mentioned earlier, the ECHR is sometimes said to be a victim of its own success in that the ECt.HR's workload rises every year causing delays in the processing of individual cases. This is due to the fact that new countries (particularly populous countries, such as Russia) continue to sign up to the ECHR, thus increasing the number of potential applicants to the ECt.HR, whilst at the same time the number of applications from existing contracting parties continues to rise. Therefore, even though radical procedural reform was introduced in 1998 to try and deal with this situation, the number of pending cases (ie the backlog) before the ECt.HR has continued to grow at an exponential rate. Thus in 2009 over 57,000 new applications were allocated to a formation of the ECt.HR and although 35,000 cases were 'disposed of' during that year, this resulted in an extra 20,000 new cases being added to the existing backlog before the ECt.HR. The number of cases pending before the ECt.HR at the beginning of 2010 was over 117,000.

In response to this administrative difficulty a new protocol, Protocol 14, was drafted which came into force on 1 June 2010, and which introduces significant procedural change. Protocol 14 contains three main reforms:

(a) it allows a single judge to declare individual applications inadmissible rather than the existing three-member committee. However this will only occur where inadmissibility is obvious from the outset; if this is not the case the decision as to admissibility will still be made by a committee.

(b) it allows the merits of 'repetitive cases', ie those cases where the issue involved is already the subject of well-established case-law from the ECt.HR, to be decided by a committee rather than a chamber, thus giving committees, for the first time, the power to determine the merits of a case rather than simply deciding the admissibility issue. Such 'repetitive cases' currently comprise 70% of the ECt.HR's caseload and it is hoped that the introduction of this measure will allow these cases to be dealt with more efficiently by the smaller, three-member committees rather than the seven-member chambers.

(c) it introduces a new admissibility criterion in respect of individual applications. Under Article 12 of Protocol 14 the ECt.HR will be able to declare inadmissible those cases where the applicant has not suffered any significant disadvantage and which, in terms of respect for human rights, do not otherwise require an examination of the merits of the case by the ECt.HR. This is in fact the most controversial aspect of Protocol 14 as many feel that it will result in cases being deemed inadmissible which would otherwise have been examined by the ECt.HR, simply because in the ECt.HR's view the applicant has not suffered a 'significant' disadvantage even where such cases raise important points of law. However in order to safeguard against any such potential injustices, Protocol 14 allows the ECt.HR to continue examining the case if it considers that respect for human rights requires this, and further provides that an application cannot be declared inadmissible on this ground if the case has not been duly considered by a domestic court. There is also a two-year transition period in which this admissibility criterion can only be used by a chamber or grand chamber so that jurisprudence in relation to how terms such as 'significant disadvantage' will be obtained from these more senior sections of the ECt.HR before the criterion can be used by a committee or single judge.

It is hoped that by introducing these changes, Protocol 14 will allow the ECt.HR the procedural means and flexibility it needs to process all applications in a timely manner while allowing it to concentrate on the most important cases which require in-depth examination. However critics of the measure are concerned that it may result in a more summary form of examination of applications so that the quality of decision-making, especially in relation to admissibility, which as we have seen results in 90% of cases being dismissed at the first hurdle, will be diminished.

Protocol 14 came into force on 1 June 2010. Until the beginning of 2010, Russia (which currently accounts for approximately 25% of applications made to the Court), had steadfastly refused to ratify the Protocol and this effective vetoing of the measure had resulted in an even greater backlog of cases before the Court and increasing frustration on the part of those charged with ensuring the ECt.HR acts as efficiently and effectively as possible. In response to this situation an interim measure, Protocol 14*bis*, was opened for signature in May 2009 and came into force on 1 October 2009 following its ratification by the requisite number of countries (including Ireland). As it was designed to be a provisional measure only, Protocol 14*bis* was deliberately limited to the introduction of two procedural elements taken from Protocol 14 which it was felt would have the greatest and most immediate impact on the ECt.HR's case-processing capacity, namely:

• The introduction of the single-judge formation of the ECt.HR with the power to declare individual applications inadmissible;

• The extended competence of the three-judge committees to decide on the merits of so-called repetitive cases.

Along with those states that adopted Protocol 14*bis* a number of other countries made a declaration that the corresponding procedures contained in Protocol 14 be provisionally applied to applications filed against them and the ECt.HR delivered a number of decisions applying the new procedures in 2009. However, with the entry into force of Protocol 14 on 1 June 2010, the rationale for Protocol 14*bis* no longer exists and its terms have no further effect from that date. The cases that were dealt with under Protocol 14*bis* however may give some early indication whether the criticisms outlined above in relation to Protocol 14 have any merit. Finally, although it is hoped that Protocol 14 will increase the efficiency of the Court, it is recognised by all concerned that further reform of the Court is necessary to deal effectively with the backlog of cases before the Court. To that end, a ministerial conference on the future of the ECt.HR was held in February 2010 which resulted in the drafting of an Action Plan containing short and medium-term measures as well as an agenda for their implementation. Some proposals relate to the filtering of applications, the supervision of execution of judgments or the implementation of the ECHR at national level (for example, states parties are called to inform the Committee of Ministers before the end of 2011 of the measures taken). The Committee of Ministers should evaluate, between 2012 and 2015, to what extent the implementation of Protocol 14 and the Action Plan has improved the situation of the Court, and the Committee of Ministers should decide, before the end of 2019, whether more profound changes are necessary.

4.4.5 PROCEDURES BEFORE THE ECT.HR

As a general rule, the admissibility stage is conducted on paper. However there is provision whereby oral hearings as to admissibility can take place but if this occurs the hearing as to the merits of the case will usually be conducted simultaneously.

If the application is declared admissible, the parties will be encouraged to reach a friendly settlement. If this cannot be achieved, then a date for the oral hearing will be set. Each side will submit written submissions before the hearing and the ECt.HR may also direct that briefs (known as *amicus curiae* or 'friends of the court' briefs) may be submitted by NGOs or other groups having expertise in the particular area involved.

The hearing itself is open to the public (unless the parties and the ECt.HR agree otherwise). It is adversarial in nature but is more informal than proceedings before an Irish court. For this reason, applicants often represent themselves, though respondent states will always have legal representation. It is possible for an applicant to get *legal aid* but Council of Europe legal aid is low compared to domestic legal aid systems and usually consists only of a contribution to the travel and subsistence expenses of the applicant, together with a flat rate contribution to legal costs. It is most unlikely therefore that a lawyer would decide to represent an applicant for purely financial reasons. It also often occurs that legal academics rather than practitioners appear before the ECt.HR. The ECt.HR will decide on the order of oral submissions and usually prescribes a time frame within which these are to be presented. Given the backlog of cases before it, the ECt.HR is always keen to ensure that hearings proceed in as speedy and efficient a manner as possible.

4.4.6   REMEDIES

The ECt.HR is limited in terms of the orders it can make. It cannot for example strike down a piece of legislation or order that the State take a particular course of action, such as reforming legislation or reviewing administrative practice.

However, it can:

(a)   declare that a violation of the applicant's ECHR rights has occurred;

(b)   award compensation (although this tends not to be a huge sum);

(c)   order interim measures pursuant to a procedure known as a Rule 39 indication, which can be used in emergency situations where the applicant faces an immediate risk of irreparable harm, usually where the applicant's life is at risk or where there is a substantial risk of serious ill-treatment (including where that risk arises as a result of an immigration measure);

(d)   award costs of the case to the applicant. Again these may not represent the full measure of an applicant's costs.

As we have seen, the execution of the ECt.HR's decision will be policed by the Committee of Ministers who may take certain measures to ensure that the decision is given effect to. The ultimate sanction for failure to comply with a ECt.HR decision is, however, political rather than legal in nature in that the non-compliant state may be ordered to leave the Council of Europe, although this has never been done.

4.5   Rights Protected by the ECHR

As mentioned earlier, the rights covered by the ECHR are primarily civil and political rights, as no consensus existed at the time of the drafting of the ECHR as to either the content or the justiciability of economic and social rights. Any such rights as have been included in the ECHR have been introduced by means of an additional protocol rather than a substantive amendment to the main ECHR, leaving the decision to accept such rights to the individual contracting parties.

However, this is not to detract from the success of the ECHR system in respect of those rights which do come within its scope, although it must be acknowledged that some provisions have been more successful than others. For example, Article 14, the non-discrimination provision, has yielded little in terms of increased human rights protection. This is primarily due to the way in which the Article is drafted, providing as it does that the right not to be discriminated against can only be claimed in conjunction with another Article in the ECHR. In other words, there is no free-standing freedom from discrimination, let alone right to equality, provided by the ECHR. In this regard, the Irish Constitution can be said to offer more protection that the ECHR. This should change with the coming into force of Protocol 12 to the ECHR, which introduces a much stronger equality guarantee. However, Ireland has not, at the time of writing, ratified this Protocol, and therefore is not yet bound by it.

Other rights protected by the ECHR include:

4.5.1   RIGHT TO LIFE

Article 2 ECHR provides that persons should not be intentionally deprived of their right to life by the forces of the State. However, this right will not be violated where death occurs as a result of the use of force in self-defence, to effect an arrest or to quell a riot or insurrection. Further, Article 2 does not prohibit the use of the death penalty. This is the subject of two separate protocols, Protocol 6, which provides, in respect of those states which have signed and ratified it, that the death penalty shall be abolished save in times of war, and Protocol 13 which provides for the abolition of the death penalty in all circumstances, even for crimes committed in times of war or imminent threat of war. The issue of abortion has only tentatively been dealt with by the ECt.HR which has held that it is neither desirable, nor even possible, to answer in the abstract the question of whether the unborn child is a person for the purposes of Article 2 (*Vo v France* (2005) 40 EHRR 259). Further, even if it could be said that the unborn do have a 'right' to 'life' this right is implicitly limited by the mother's rights and interests, and this is an area where national authorities must enjoy a certain discretion, given the controversial nature of such an issue (*Paton v UK* (1981) 3 EHRR 408). Whilst the ECt.HR has not ruled out the possibility that in certain circumstances safeguards may be extended to the unborn child the issue will be determined by weighing up the various (often conflicting) interests involved (*Boso v Italy*, Application No 50490/99, judgment of 5 September 2002). In the *Vo v France* case the ECt.HR found that even if Article 2 was applicable it had not been violated where French law did not allow for the criminal prosecution of a doctor for the unintentional destruction of a foetus in circumstances where the doctor's negligence had caused the applicant to have to undergo a therapeutic abortion. The ECt.HR held that the rights of the unborn child and those of the mother coincided so that the unborn child's rights could be protected through the mother, and French law did allow for criminal proceedings in respect of unintentional injury to her. Further the applicant could have taken an action in damages against the doctor for medical negligence. Therefore French law provided an adequate remedy to the applicant in respect of her injuries and there was no violation of Article 2.

4.5.2   FREEDOM FROM TORTURE

Article 3 provides that all persons are to be free from torture and inhuman or degrading treatment or punishment. No definition of these terms is given but the ECt.HR has made it clear that a 'sliding scale' of prohibited treatment is covered by the Article, with torture being seen as the most serious form of such treatment but with other 'lesser' types of treatment covered too, including the use of corporal punishment in state schools in the UK (*Campbell and Cosans v UK* (1982) 4 EHRR 293). After a long period in which the ECt.HR failed to find that any state had committed torture contrary to Article 3, in a number of cases it found Turkey guilty of a breach of the ECHR in this regard (see eg *Aksoy v Turkey* (1997) 23 EHRR 533). Article 3 will also be violated if a state fails adequately to investigate allegations of ill-treatment contrary to the Article. Article 3 is also one of only a very small number of substantive rights provision in the ECHR from which no derogation is allowed, indicating the seriousness with which this type of treatment was regarded by the drafters of the ECHR. For this reason also a state will be held to be in violation of Article 3 if it removes a person to a country where they face a real risk of ill-treatment of a type that would constitute a breach of the Article, regardless of whether that state is a contracting party to the ECHR (*Soering v UK* (1989) 11 ECHR 439).

4.5.3   RIGHT TO LIBERTY

Article 5 provides that no one shall be deprived of their liberty save in certain specified circumstances and even then this can only be done if the law in the individual country clearly provides for it. The type of circumstance in which deprivation of liberty can lawfully occur includes detention:

(a)   of a person after conviction of an offence;

(b)   for the purposes of bringing a person before a court; and

(c)   for the purposes of preventing unlawful entry into a country or of facilitating lawful deportation from a country.

Article 5 also provides that persons who are deprived of their liberty by state authorities must be able to challenge the lawfulness of that detention and be released if such challenge is successful.

4.5.4   RIGHT TO A FAIR TRIAL

Article 6 provides that persons are entitled to a fair trial before an independent and impartial tribunal. This right applies to both civil and criminal proceedings. Article 6 also provides that proceedings are to take place within a reasonable time and in fact the bulk of cases under this Article have related to the length of time which has elapsed before a final domestic decision has been given. It also enshrines the principle that persons shall be presumed innocent until proven guilty, a provision which has been the subject of some litigation relating to domestic laws which penalise persons for or allow adverse inferences to be drawn from their failure to answer questions or to produce documents. Certain other specific guarantees are provided for persons charged with criminal offences, such as the right to free legal aid if a person is not in a financial position to secure legal assistance.

4.5.5   RIGHT TO RESPECT FOR PRIVATE AND FAMILY LIFE

Article 8 ECHR has been one of the most successful provisions, not least because of the expansive view adopted by the ECt.HR towards its interpretation. It provides that persons are entitled to a right to respect for their private and family life, and home and correspondence, although such rights may lawfully be interfered with in certain specified circumstances, such as where this is necessary to prevent crime or protect the rights of others. Article 8 has been held to cover a wide range of interests, including:

(a)   freedom from criminal prosecution for consenting adult homosexuals (*Dudgeon v UK* (1982) 4 EHRR 149);

(b)   non-discrimination in succession laws as between marital and non-marital children (*Marckx v Belgium* (1979–80) 2 EHRR 330);

(c) freedom from unwarranted surveillance from state security forces (*Klass v Germany* (1979–80) 2 EHRR 214);

(d) freedom from deportation where to do so would result in the break-up of the family unit (*Moustaquim v Belgium* (1991) 13 EHRR 802);

(e) positive obligations on a state to safeguard the physical integrity of a pregnant woman in the context of a controversy as to whether she was entitled to a therapeutic abortion (*Tysiac v Poland*, Application No. 5410/03, judgment of 20 March 2007);

(f) positive obligations on a state to provide adequate procedural safeguards to those facing eviction from local authority accommodation (*Connors v UK* (2004) 40 EHRR 189).

Indeed, it is in relation to the concept of 'family life' that the ECt.HR has been most expansive. From very early on, the ECt.HR indicated that the protection afforded by Article 8 did not depend on the existence of formal legal ties between the individuals involved. Instead, the ECt.HR would examine whether real and close personal ties exist between the parties and if they do, the ECt.HR will hold that this is 'family life' within the meaning of Article 8. Family life has been held to exist between:

(a) engaged couples provided their relationship is sufficiently established (*Wakefield v UK*, Application No. 15817/89);

(b) non-marital fathers and their children (*Keegan v Ireland* (1994) 18 EHRR 342);

(c) children and parents who are no longer cohabiting and whose relationship has broken down (*Berrehab v Netherlands* (1989) 11 EHRR 322); and

(d) a transsexual, his female partner and her child born as a result of artificial insemination in circumstances where the male transsexual had been fully involved throughout the process and had acted as the child's 'father' since its birth (*X, Y and Z v United Kingdom* (1997) 27 EHRR 143).

This broad view of the notion of family life is in marked contrast to that traditionally taken by the Irish courts (see **chapter 9**) and it is not surprising that Article 8 has featured prominently in the Irish cases which have come before the ECt.HR.

4.5.6 FREEDOM OF THOUGHT, CONSCIENCE AND RELIGION

Article 9 protects the right to freedom of thought, conscience and religion which is stated to include the right to change one's religion etc, and to manifest one's religion in worship, teaching and practice. The exercise of this right to manifest one's religion is however, subject to certain restrictions if these are necessary for the protection of public safety, order, health or morals and the protection of the rights of others. Again, it is possible for states to prohibit public displays of worship if it can be objectively shown that this is required for example to prevent public disorder.

4.5.7 FREEDOM OF EXPRESSION

Article 10 has been one of the most significant Articles of the ECHR, protecting as it does everyone's freedom of expression, which is stated to include the freedom to hold opinions and receive and impart information. Again however this freedom may be restricted if this is necessary to further some specified objective, such as the protection of the reputation or rights of others or the protection of morals. For example, a number of cases have come before the ECt.HR in which controversial books, paintings and films have been banned or subject to restrictions and these restrictions have been upheld by the ECt.HR on the grounds they were necessary to protect morals or the rights of others, especially young persons (see, eg *Muller v Switzerland* (1991) 13 EHRR 212). Also, Article 10 is unusual in that it stresses that the exercise of the right to freedom of expression carries with it duties and responsibilities. However, there is no doubt that this Article has on the whole been interpreted in a way which is beneficial to the press, although some recent decisions have indicated that a more restrictive view may be emerging (see, for example, *Independent News and Media plc and Others v Ireland* (2006) 42 EHRR 1024, see **4.6** and *Von Hannover v Germany*, Application No. 59320/00, judgment of 24 June 2004) (see **13.8.3**). The ECt.HR has also stressed that comment on particular types of persons, especially those in politics and government, is vital in the interests of a democratic society and will receive a high degree of protection (see, eg *Lingens v Austria* (1986) 8 EHRR 407).

These are just some of the rights protected by the ECHR and include those most likely to be of relevance within the Irish system. We turn now to the cases which have come before the ECt.HR involving the Irish government.

4.6   Irish Cases before the European Court of Human Rights

At the time of writing, the merits of 19 cases involving the Irish government have been heard and determined by the ECt.HR (other cases have been dismissed by the ECHR authorities at the admissibility stage). Eighteen of these were taken by persons exercising the right of individual petition under the ECHR (a right, incidentally, that the Irish government was the first government to accept), and in 13 of these the government was found to have been in breach of the ECHR. One case was taken by the Irish government itself against another state party to the ECHR, using the inter-state application mechanism.

There have of course been other cases which have been accepted as admissible by the ECHR authorities but which have been settled by the government before any decision was handed down by the ECt.HR. Some cases have even been settled before a decision as to admissibility has been made by the Strasbourg authorities. The advantages of such 'friendly settlements' can include, for the applicant, a greater financial award than he or she was likely to receive from the ECt.HR and for the State, the benefits of confidentiality and of avoiding a finding by an international court that it is in default of its human rights obligations. Usually, such settlements will involve some sort of undertaking on the part of the government to introduce legislation to amend the law in question.

The cases which have reached the ECt.HR do not by any means tell the whole story of the Irish government's compliance with its international human rights obligations under the ECHR. They do however give an idea of the areas of most concern relating to the observance of these guarantees on a domestic level.

Lawless v Ireland (1979) 1 EHRR 15—This was in fact the first ever case to be decided by the ECt.HR and involved a claim by the applicant that his rights under Article 5 had been breached by the Irish government when he had been interned as a suspected member of the IRA pursuant to emergency legislation introduced in the late 1950s. The ECt.HR however, found that the Irish government had lawfully derogated from its obligations under Article 5 due to the existence of a public emergency threatening the life of the nation (due to increased IRA activity at the time) and hence it could not conduct any further investigation of the applicant's claims.

Airey v Ireland (1979–80) 2 EHRR 305—The applicant complained that the lack of legal aid in judicial separation proceedings violated her right of effective access to the courts under Article 6 and her right to private and family life under Article 8 (Mrs Airey argued that a judicial separation from her husband was necessary to ensure the peaceful enjoyment of the family life she enjoyed with her children). The ECt.HR agreed with her contentions and approved terms of compensation to be awarded to the applicant. The government subsequently introduced a restricted, non-statutory scheme of civil legal aid and advice in 1980 (this being later replaced by the Civil Legal Aid Act, 1995).

Johnston v Ireland ((1987) 9 EHRR 203)—The applicants in this case were a couple who lived together but were unable to marry as one of them was already married and divorce was at that time prohibited in Ireland. They complained that their rights to private and family life under Article 8 and their right to marry and found a family under Article 12 of the ECHR had been breached by the prohibition on divorce in Irish law and the legal treatment of their child, especially for the purposes of succession rights. The Court found that there had been a violation of their family rights in respect of the inferior status given in Irish law to children born outside of marriage, but rejected their claims based on the prohibition on divorce. Following this decision, the government introduced the Status of Children Act, 1987 which effectively abolished the legal status of illegitimacy.

Norris v Ireland ((1991) 13 EHRR 186)—The applicant was a practising homosexual who claimed that his right to respect for private life under Article 8 had been violated by the continued existence on the statute books of legislation criminalising homosexual activity between consenting male adults, even though the evidence indicated that it was unlikely this legislation would be invoked against the applicant. The ECt.HR found that the fact that the legislation existed and could in theory be used against the applicant constituted an interference with his right to respect for private life for which the government had not forwarded any sufficient justification. The ECt.HR rejected the government's contention that such legislation was necessary for the protection of health and morals (arguments which had met with some success before the Supreme Court which rejected Mr Norris's constitutional challenge to the legislation). This decision of the Court caused some controversy and it took five years for Irish law to be amended so as to be in line with the judgment in *Norris*, when the Criminal Law (Sexual Offences) Act, 1995 was passed, which decriminalised most forms of homosexual activity and provided for the same age of consent as for heterosexuals.

Pine Valley Developments Ltd v Ireland ((1992) 14 EHRR 319)—This case arose out of a complicated series of cases and legislative amendments relating to the granting of planning permission. The net result was that the first applicant company was not entitled to the benefit of legislation retrospectively validating decisions to grant planning permission which the Supreme Court had found to be void. (The first applicant company had sold on the relevant property to another company which was owned by one individual and this company and individual also were applicants to the case.) The applicants claimed that their property rights under Article 1 of Protocol 1 had been breached and also that they had been discriminated against in the exercise of these property rights, contrary to Article 14. The ECt.HR upheld this latter claim and awarded substantial damages, in excess of £1m, to the applicants.

Open Door Counselling Ltd v Ireland ((1993) 15 EHRR 244)—This case related to an injunction which had been granted against the applicants prohibiting them from distributing information to pregnant women about the availability of abortion services in the United Kingdom. The ECt.HR found that the extensive nature of the injunction constituted an unwarranted interference with the freedom of expression of the applicants under Article 10 and damages were awarded to the applicants. While the injunction was not immediately lifted, a subsequent constitutional referendum took place which resulted in an amendment to the Constitution allowing for such information to be distributed within the State.

Keegan v Ireland ((1994) 18 EHRR 342)—The applicant was the father of a non-marital child whose mother attempted to place the child for adoption without the consent of the applicant. The ECt.HR agreed with the applicant's claim that the Irish legislation which allowed this to occur was contrary to his right to respect for family life under Article 8.

The ECt.HR also upheld his claim that the lack of procedures allowing him to challenge the mother's decision was a violation of his right of access to the courts pursuant to Article 6. As a result of this judgment the Adoption Act, 1998 was introduced which provides consultation procedures for natural fathers in the adoption process and sets out the circumstances in which such procedures do not need to be followed.

Heaney, McGuinness v Ireland and *Quinn v Ireland* (2001) 33 EHRR 264—The applicants complained that s 52 of the Offences Against the State Act, 1939 which provides for the punishment or imprisonment of persons who fail to give certain information to the Gardaí constituted a breach of their right to silence pursuant to Article 6 and of their freedom not to express themselves pursuant to Article 10 of the ECHR. The ECt.HR found that there had been a violation of Article 6 (both of the right to silence and the presumption of innocence) and having held in this way, found that no separate issue arose under Article 10.

McElhinney v Ireland (2002) 34 EHRR 322—The applicant was involved in an accident at the border between Derry and Donegal during which the car he was driving was shot at by a member of the British Armed Forces. The applicant instituted proceedings against the individual soldier and the Secretary of State for Northern Ireland but the latter succeeded in getting the summons set aside on the basis that the applicant was not entitled to bring proceedings in an Irish court against a member of a foreign sovereign government. The applicant claimed the doctrine of sovereign immunity was a breach of his right to a judicial determination of his compensation claim under Article 6. The ECt.HR however held that this right is not absolute and that the grant of sovereign immunity to a State in civil proceedings pursued the legitimate aim of complying with international law to promote good relations between States. Further, the measure was not disproportionate as it reflected generally recognised rules of international law and the applicant could have pursued his claims in the courts in Northern Ireland. There was therefore no violation of Article 6(1).

DG v Ireland (2002) 35 EHRR 1153—The applicant who was a minor at the time of the impugned action, was the subject of High Court proceedings taken to vindicate his constitutional and statutory rights. In the course of these proceedings, the High Court ordered that he should be placed in St. Patrick's Institution, a juvenile detention centre, even though he had not committed a crime, because his welfare and safety required him to be placed in secure accommodation, thus outweighing his right to liberty and there was no other secure facility in which he could be placed. The High Court also ordered that, while in St. Patrick's Institution, he should be subject to a different regime from that experienced by juveniles detained there as a result of the criminal justice system. This action was upheld by the Supreme Court and the applicant applied to the ECt.HR on the basis that his right to liberty under Article 5 ECHR had been infringed. The ECt.HR found that while Article 5(1)(d) permits the detention of children *for the purpose of* educational supervision, on the facts of this case it could not be said that the detention of the applicant in St. Patrick's Institution was sufficiently connected to the provision of education supervision. The ECt.HR found first that St. Patrick's Institution did not of itself constitute 'educational supervision' for the purposes of the ECHR. It then noted that when the relevant detention orders were made no specific proposal for the secure and supervised education of the applicant was in place and even though the applicant was eventually placed in an educationally appropriate facility this did not occur until six months after his release from St. Patrick's. Therefore, it could not be said that his detention in St. Patrick's Institution constituted an 'interim custody' measure 'for the purpose' of an educational supervisory regime, which was followed speedily by the application of such a regime and a violation of the applicant's right to liberty had occurred.

Murphy v Ireland (2004) 38 EHRR 212—The applicant was a pastor with the Irish Faith Centre, a Christian ministry based in Dublin which sought to have an advertisement aired on a local radio station. However, the advertisement was prohibited pursuant to s 10(3) of the Radio and Television Act, 1988 which outlawed the broadcast of any advertisement directed towards any religious or political end. The applicant claimed that this ban violated his rights under Article 9 and 10 ECHR, although the ECt.HR examined his complaint under Article 10 only. The ECt.HR held that there were relevant and sufficient reasons for the measure, especially bearing in mind the religious sensitivities of the Irish people and that religion had been extremely divisive in Irish society in the past. The ECt.HR also noted that, other than advertisements in the broadcast media, the applicant's religious expression was not restricted. Further, the ECt.HR accepted the government's contention that to allow some form of religious advertising could result in unequal treatment between particular religions, or particular religious views could benefit a dominant religion and could result in unequal consequences for national and independent broadcasters. In all the circumstances the ECt.HR found there was no violation of Article 10.

Doran v Ireland (2006) 42 EHRR 232—This case related to the length of civil proceedings instituted by the applicants against a number of defendants, including two firms of solicitors, claiming, *inter alia*, negligence in relation to the purchase of a plot of land. The proceedings, which went all the way to the Supreme Court, were begun in July 1991 but did not finally end until December 1999 when the issue of costs was determined. The applicants claimed that their right to a fair hearing within a reasonable time under Article 6, and their right to an effective remedy under Article 13 ECHR had been violated. The ECt.HR found that despite the fact that the proceedings had not been administratively or factually complex they had lasted almost eight-and-a-half years and that the delay in the proceedings had been caused largely by the relevant authorities and had placed strain on the applicants. Therefore there had been a breach of Article 6. The ECt.HR also rejected the government's argument that the applicants could have taken a constitutional action in relation to the delay as the government had not cited a single example of a case where this had been successfully done. The ECt.HR found that no effective, adequate or accessible remedy had been available to the applicants and that accordingly Article 13 ECHR had also been violated. The ECt.HR awarded the applicants €25,000 in damages.

O'Reilly and Others v Ireland (2005) 40 EHRR 929—The applicants had premises on a public road and challenged the local authority's failure to repair the road. Proceedings began in July 1994 and ended in June 1999, although the road was repaired in the interim. The applicants complained that the length of proceedings violated their rights under Article 6. The ECt.HR noted that the case was neither procedurally nor factually complex and that the applicants had not contributed to the delay. On the other hand the domestic authorities had contributed to the delay in the length of time between the High Court hearing and the delivery of its judgment and the delay in the hearing of the appeal to the Supreme Court. Further the matter remained important to the applicants because, even though the road had been repaired in the interim, the issue of costs had to be determined. The ECt.HR therefore found that the proceedings were not dealt with within a 'reasonable time' under Article 6(1). There had also been a violation of Article 13 as there was no evidence before the court to indicate that the applicants had an effective, adequate or accessible domestic remedy in relation to this delay. The applicants were awarded €1,400 each in damages.

McMullen v Ireland Application No. 42297/98, judgment of 29 July 2004—The applicant was involved in a lengthy set of proceedings which was ongoing at the time of his application to the ECt.HR. The proceedings began in June 1988 as a negligence action and led to bankruptcy and taxation of costs proceedings. The ECt.HR concluded that the relevant length of proceedings was 16 years, and that they had initially concerned the issue of whether the applicant's solicitor had given him negligent advice. Furthermore since January 1998 they had concerned only the issue of taxation of costs. The proceedings were therefore not significantly complex from a procedural, factual or legal perspective. While the applicant had contributed to the delay this did not absolve the State from complying with the requirement to deal with the case within a reasonable time. The ECt.HR noted that a number of lengthy delays in the proceedings were attributable to the domestic authorities for which no explanation had been given. Therefore there had been a breach of Article 6(1) of the Convention and the applicant was awarded €8,000 in damages.

Independent News and Media plc and Others v Ireland (2006) 42 EHRR 1024—A newspaper owned by the applicants published an article about a prominent politician, alleging he had engaged in activities of a criminal nature. The politician instituted libel proceedings and was awarded £300,000 damages by a jury. The Supreme Court upheld the award which was three times the highest libel award previously approved by it. The applicants claimed that the award was disproportionately high and that there were no adequate and effective domestic safeguards in Irish law against such awards. The ECt.HR considered that the trial judge had given the jury concrete guidance in relation to the size of award to be made and that the Supreme Court had considered the issue of proportionality as well as a number of other relevant factors, including the gravity of the libel and the timing of the publication. It concluded that the libel involved was serious and grave and the award made was not disproportionate to the injury suffered by the politician. In light of this and the measure of appellate control exercised by the Supreme Court it could not be said that Irish law contained inadequate or ineffective safeguards against a disproportionate award of damages. Therefore there was no violation of Article 10.

Bosphorous Hava Yolari Turizm ve Ticaret AS v Ireland (2006) 42 EHRR 1—The applicant airline had leased an aircraft from the national airline of the former Yugoslavia (FRY), a country against whom the EU had implemented a series of sanctions, including one calling on Member States to impound aircraft in their territories in which a controlling interest was held by an undertaking in the FRY. The applicant's aircraft had come to Ireland for maintenance work and was impounded by the Minister for Transport pursuant to the relevant EU regulation. The applicant instituted judicial review proceedings and the matter was referred to the European Court of Justice (ECJ) which confirmed that the regulation did apply. The Supreme Court, applying this decision, found in favour of the State. The applicant complained that the manner in which Ireland had implemented the sanctions regime was a reviewable exercise of discretion within the meaning of Article 1 of the Convention and a violation of Article 1 of Protocol 1. The ECt.HR found that the applicant did come within the jurisdiction of the Irish State so that it could examine the claim under Article 1 of Protocol 1. In relation to this the ECt.HR found that once the EU regulation was adopted it was generally applicable and binding in its entirety meaning no Member State could depart from its provisions. It had become part of Irish law prior to the impoundment and it was entirely foreseeable that a Minister for Transport would implement the powers contained therein. The ECt.HR found that the Irish authorities had rightly considered themselves obliged to impound any aircraft to which the regulation applied. The impugned interference was therefore not an exercise of discretion by the Irish authorities but rather amounted to compliance by Ireland with its legal obligations flowing from EU law. The ECt.HR then considered whether the impoundment was justified and found that the protection of fundamental rights by EU law could have been considered, at the relevant time, to be 'equivalent' to that of the ECHR system. Consequently a presumption arose that Ireland did not depart from the requirements of the ECHR when it implemented legal obligations flowing from its membership of the EU. This presumption could be rebutted if it was considered that the protection of ECHR rights was manifestly deficient, in which case the interest of international co-operation could be outweighed by the ECHR's role as a 'constitutional instrument of European public order' in the field of human rights. Here however the ECt.HR held that it could not be said that the protection of the applicant's ECHR rights was manifestly deficient and the presumption of ECHR compliance had not been rebutted. Therefore there was no violation of Article 1 of Protocol 1.

Barry v Ireland Application No. 18273/04, judgment of 15 December 2005—The applicant was a doctor against whom a number of allegations were made in 1994 and criminal proceedings were instituted against him in April 1996. These initial charges were struck out but further criminal proceedings were instituted in October 1997. The applicant began judicial review proceedings and the prosecution against him was stayed pending the determination of these proceedings. These proceedings were finally determined in December 2003 and the applicant was informed in December 2004 that the prosecution against him would continue. The applicant complained about the excessive length of the criminal proceedings against him and the lack of an effective remedy in that regard. The ECt.HR held the relevant delay was over ten years and although the case was somewhat complex, this alone could not explain the delay in bringing the charges to trial. Further, while the applicant had contributed to some of the delay in the processing of his judicial review action, several periods of delay were attributable to the domestic authorities. The ECt.HR noted that the allegations against the applicant were grave, and that the applicant, who by then was in his eighties, had had to bear the weight of these charges for over ten years as well as being concerned about a possible prison sentence. He had also during this time been denied the possibility of pursuing his medical career and been subjected to fairly strict bail conditions. Therefore the ECt.HR found that the length of time involved had not been reasonable and that Article 6 had been violated. Further there had been a breach of Article 13 in that the applicant's judicial review proceedings were not capable of remedying the matter of which he complained, namely the delay in the prosecution, since the judicial review proceedings could only stay the prosecution not expedite it. Nor could these proceedings be said to be preventative of future delay, given the length of time taken to determine them. Further they were not capable of providing adequate redress for the delays that had already occurred as there was no evidence that damages would have been available and the Supreme Court had stated that it would only take into account delay caused by the DPP rather than the judicial authorities. Therefore the judicial review mechanism could not be considered an effective remedy.

Ireland v United Kingdom (1979–80) 2 EHRR 25—This was in fact the first inter-state application to be decided by the ECt.HR. The Irish government complained about the treatment of detainees in detention centres in the North, primarily that the use of certain interrogation techniques known as the 'five techniques' constituted a violation of the prohibition on torture and inhuman or degrading treatment. The ECt.HR found that the treatment involved did constitute inhuman and degrading treatment but did not amount to torture. Interestingly the United Kingdom government had, prior to this decision being handed down, stated that it had ceased to use such methods in the North and that it would not use them again in the future. The case was significant not only in relation to its particular facts but also because it highlighted the impact which the threat of international scrutiny could have. However, it must be said that it has not been followed by a flurry of inter-state applications, presumably for the reasons given earlier.

So we can see that the number of cases in which the Irish government has appeared before the ECt.HR is relatively small. As stated earlier, this does not give the full picture of the level of compliance on the part of the Irish government with its obligations under the ECHR. A number of cases involving the Irish government have been settled before they reached the ECt.HR. Many cases have also been declared inadmissible on procedural grounds without a substantive examination of the actual merits of the case (for example, in *Panevskii v Ireland*, Application No.2453/03, decision of 13 October 2005, the Court declared inadmissible a complaint by failed asylum seekers in relation to their proposed expulsion to Moldova on the basis that no deportation order had yet been made and therefore the applicants could not claim to be 'victims' of any violation of the ECHR; thus interesting arguments as to whether, *inter alia*, judicial review was an adequate domestic remedy in such circumstances were not addressed). Also a number of cases are currently making their way through the Strasbourg procedures or are pending before the ECt.HR, and of course there must be a number of legitimate cases which never reach Strasbourg at all, due to lack of awareness of the remedies offered there.

and ECHR rights. The High Court agreed that there had been an unreasonable delay in the processing of charges against the applicant and held this amounted to a violation of his constitutional right to a reasonably expeditious trial. Having made this finding in favour of the applicant the Court did not find it necessary to go on and consider the ECHR-based arguments. (Note the Supreme Court judgment in this case which, while deciding the case on 'traditional' judicial review grounds, contains some interesting *obiter* remarks on the relevance and import of decisions of the ECt.HR, particularly in relation to the availability of certain remedies; *TH v DPP* [2006] 3 IR 520.) On the other hand there have been cases where the courts have gone to some lengths to discuss ECHR arguments in order to show that domestic law provides as much, if not more, protection than the ECHR. For example, in *JF v DPP* [2005] 2 IR 174 the applicant argued that the refusal of the complainant in a sexual abuse case to be examined by an independent psychological expert was inconsistent with his right to call evidence rebutting the accusations made against him. The court agreed and found that this amounted to a breach of his constitutional right to a fair trial. Interestingly, however, having already found in the applicant's favour, Hardiman J went on to examine the ECHR-based arguments that had been made, partly he said because of the aptness of some of the citations. He explicitly stated however that he did not believe 'that the [ECHR] in this instance supplies rights lacking in the constitutional regime of trial in due course of law . . . . I am quite satisfied that the same rights are afforded by domestic law.' Likewise in *Meadows v Minister for Justice, Equality and Law Reform*, 21 January 2010, Supreme Court (unreported), although Fennelly J referred in his judgment to Article 13 ECHR and the right to an effective remedy provided for therein (along with the obligation on decision-makers under s 3 of the European Convention of Human Rights Act, 2003 to act in a manner compatible with the ECHR) in considering the test to be applied in judicial review applications, the other judges of the majority used 'traditional' principles of reasonableness and implied constitutional limitation of jurisdiction in declaring that the principle of proportionality did indeed form part of the relevant test.

In terms of subject-matter of cases in which the ECHR has been cited, we can see that the reach of the obligations imposed by the Act is quite wide. As might be expected the Act has been pleaded in a wide range of cases relating to criminal proceedings, for example, extradition proceedings, court martial, delay in prosecutions, detention of a minor, prison conditions and revocation of a temporary release order. But it has also been relied on in proceedings relating to civil law matters such as the seizure of assets by the Revenue Commissioners, a determination of the Labour Court, security for costs orders, family law proceedings, the rights of unmarried fathers in the adoption process, a decision of the Broadcasting Commission of Ireland not to renew a radio licence, summary eviction proceedings, the failure to provide adequate housing for local authority tenants with disabilities, dismissal from employment, procedures in the Coroner's Court, decisions of a Tribunal of Inquiry and educational provision for minors.

However it does seem that the Act is being cited more extensively in some areas of law than others. For example the 2003 Act is regularly discussed in asylum and immigration cases and a brief review of some of these cases indicates the potential scope of application of the Act. In *Makumbi v Minister for Justice, Equality and Law Reform* [2005] IEHC 403, the High Court considered Article 2 ECHR (the right to life provision) in deciding whether the respondent Minister would be acting unlawfully in transferring an allegedly suicidal person out of the country. Finlay Geoghegan J held that the Minister could be said to have a discretion not to implement a transfer order where to do so would be in breach of the State's obligations under Article 2. In *Gashi v Minister for Justice, Equality and Law Reform*, Clarke J, 3 December 2003, High Court (unreported) the applicants had been living together as a couple when the second-named applicant was deported. The applicants subsequently married and the second-named applicant sought to have the deportation order revoked. This was refused on the basis that the applicants had not lived together as a family unit for an appreciable length of time. Clarke J held in granting leave to seek judicial review that while the time that the applicants had lived together prior to getting married would not be considered to constitute family life under the Constitution, it could be deemed to be family life under the ECHR, which, arguably, the State must weigh in the balance when making decisions which affect that family life. That a balancing exercise is involved was confirmed by the Supreme Court in *Dimbo v Minister for Justice, Equality and Law Reform*, 1 May 2008, a case which contained quite a detailed analysis of the relevant ECHR jurisprudence. The Supreme Court held that what was required in this case where the parents of an Irish child had been served with deportation orders, was a fair balance to be struck between the right to respect for family life of the parents and child (particularly the rights of the Irish child) and the relevant public policy issues of the State. It found that in the circumstances of the case the respondent minister had failed to give specific consideration to the ECHR (and constitutional) rights of the Irish child and thus had acted in breach of his obligations under s 3 of the Act. On the other hand, in *Moldovan v Minister for Justice, Equality and Law Reform*, Gilligan J, 29 April 2005, High Court (unreported), the High Court refused to grant leave to an applicant who claimed that her rights to a fair trial had been breached through the failure of the Refugee Appeals Tribunal (RAT) to call her husband as a witness at the hearing to determine whether she was entitled to refugee status. The High Court held that the rights claimed by the applicant applied only in relation to criminal proceedings and not to proceedings such as those before the RAT which were essentially inquisitorial in nature.

These cases indicate that the 2003 Act can, in an appropriate case, be used to generate both substantive and procedural rights for individuals in the immigration area.

It had also been thought that the Act might have an impact in the area of freedom of expression (see **chapter 13**) and some recent decisions of the Supreme Court would appear to bear this out. *Mahon v Post Publications Limited* [2007] 3 IR 338 concerned an appeal by the Mahon Tribunal against a refusal by the High Court to grant it an injunction restraining the defendant from publishing certain material which the Tribunal considered confidential prior to the material being disclosed at a public hearing of the Tribunal. The Supreme Court stated that the right at issue was freedom of expression, as protected both by the Constitution and Article 10 ECHR, and further stated that the approach of the Irish courts in relation to this right was 'closely comparable' to the approach of the ECt.HR when interpreting the ECHR. However, Fennelly J, delivering the judgment of the majority of the Supreme Court, then stated that not only must the Tribunal seek to justify the restriction of this right on the basis of some exception recognised by law, as required by the Constitution, it must *also* seek to justify this restriction by reference to one of the interests listed in Article 10(2) ECHR. Potentially this involves an additional burden on those seeking to restrict freedom of speech in that it may not be sufficient to point to some pre-existing exception in common law or constitutional jurisprudence which would justify such a restriction; if the restriction does not also meet one of the aims set out in Article 10(2) it will be deemed unlawful, despite the fact that pre-2003 Act it would have been justified. This extra layer of scrutiny and analysis may therefore result in an increased level of protection of freedom of expression as a result of the introduction of the 2003 Act. In *Mahon Tribunal v Keena and Others*, 31 July 2009, Supreme Court (unreported) the Supreme Court considered whether the High Court had been correct in directing a journalist and editor of a national newspaper to answer questions posed by the Mahon Tribunal intended to unveil the source of certain documents that had been published by the newspaper. In its decision the Supreme Court followed closely the reasoning of the ECt.HR in a similar case (*Goodwin v UK* (1996) EHRR 123) and held that an order compelling the appellants to answer questions for the purpose of identifying their source could only be justified by an 'overriding requirement in the public interest'. It found that the High Court had not struck this balance properly, both because it severely devalued journalistic privilege and because the value to the Tribunal of information sought was limited.

There have also been a handful of cases on the interpretation and operation of the 2003 Act itself. The first significant such case was *Dublin City Council v Fennell* [2005] 2 ILRM 288. The appellant, Ms Fennell, was a tenant of Dublin Corporation who was served with a notice to quit in July 2003. However she had remained in possession of the premises and Dublin Corporation commenced proceedings for possession, which proceedings were heard in the District Court on 12 December 2003 and determined in favour of Dublin Corporation. Ms Fennell then appealed this decision to the Circuit Court and the case came on for hearing in June 2004. Ms Fennell attempted to argue that the relevant legislation, the Housing Act, 1966, was inconsistent with the ECHR, in particular Articles 6, 8, 13 and Article 1, Protocol 1. However the respondent argued that she could not rely on the ECHR in this way as the proceedings in being had commenced prior to the coming into force of the ECHR Act 2003 and the Act was not retrospective in effect. The Circuit Court stated a case to the Supreme Court, asking firstly whether the provisions of the 2003 Act applied to proceedings begun before 31 December 2003. The Supreme Court held that they did not, and that the Act in general had no retrospective effect. Kearns J, delivering the judgment of the court, accepted that if the 2003 Act did apply important issues would arise in relation to the compatibility of the Housing Act, 1966 with the ECHR. However he held that given the constitutional imperative against retrospective legislation and given that there was nothing in the 2003 Act to suggest that the legislature had intended it to have any retrospective effect, the Act could not be said to apply retrospectively. The Court further rejected an argument that the proceedings in the Circuit Court, which commenced after the Act came into force, could be considered separately from those in the District Court and that they could therefore be subject to the 2003 Act even if the District Court proceedings were not. Kearns J held that the 'proceedings' at issue in the case began when the notice to quit was served, prior to the Act coming into force, and that the District Court proceedings could not be divorced from the subsequent appeal to the Circuit Court. Therefore although the Circuit Court hearing did not take place until after the Act had come into force, the Act did not apply to the proceedings before that Court. Therefore as the Act did not apply no further consideration of the issues involved was possible. In an interesting *dictum*, however, Kearns J stated that his conclusion as to non-retrospectivity related to a need to protect the respective rights of those involved and that this requirement was all the greater where vested rights were involved 'and where the changes proposed by the 2003 Act are agreed to be substantive rather than procedural'. This would seem to reject implicitly an argument made at the time the Act was being introduced to the effect that it would only be of procedural rather than substantive assistance to individuals.

Therefore the *Fennell* case has settled the issue as to whether the Act applies to proceedings initiated before the Act came into force even if those proceedings do not come on for hearing until after the Act was in force (it may however be possible to persuade a court that the relevant 'proceedings' did not begin until after 31 December 2003). Because of this finding the Supreme Court made no further comment on the substantive issues in the case, although it did state that the issues involved were important and that it was clearly arguable that the relevant provisions of the Act did infringe ECHR rights.

In light of these last comments it is perhaps not surprising therefore that s 62 of the Housing Act, 1966 (see **12.1**) has since been found to be incompatible with the ECHR. In *Donegan v Dublin City Council* [2008] IEHC 288 Laffoy J granted a declaration under s 5 of the ECHR Act to the effect that s 62 was incompatible with Article 8 ECHR insofar as it authorises the District Court to grant a warrant for possession where there is a factual dispute as to whether the tenant has breached the tenancy agreement and there is no mechanism for an independent review of this dispute. This has since been followed by *Dublin City Council v Gallagher* [2008] IEHC 354 in which O'Neill J granted a declaration of incompatibility insofar as s 62 did not provide a mechanism whereby a factual dispute as to the applicant's entitlement to succeed to his mother's tenancy of a local authority house could be determined. O'Neill J proceeded to grant the declaration even though one had been granted in the *Donegan* case, because without it, he held, the applicant would not be able to apply for an *ex gratia* payment under s 5(4) of the 2003 Act. These cases were then followed by *Pullen v Dublin City Council* [2009] 2 ILRM 484 where Irvine J held that the respondent in performing its functions as an organ of the State failed to have sufficient regard to the plaintiffs' rights under Article 6(1) (right to a fair hearing) and Article 8 ECHR and thus was in breach of s 3 of European Convention on Human Rights Act, 2003 which requires organs of the State to perform their functions in accordance with the ECHR as there was an alternative legal mechanism available to the local authority to seek possession of a local authority dwelling, under s 14 of the Conveyancing Act, 1881. According to the Court this would have allowed the District Court to examine the merits of the application for possession, and given the plaintiffs a full opportunity to defend the allegations of anti-social behaviour.

The *Donegan* case was only the second case in which a declaration of incompatibility was granted by the courts. The first instance in which a s 5 declaration was made was the case of *Foy v An t-Ard Chlaraitheoir and Others*, 19 October 2007, High Court (unreported). The applicant was a male to female transsexual who argued that certain provisions of the Civil Registration Act 2004 were incompatible with the ECHR insofar as they did not allow for changes to be made to entries on birth certificates to reflect a person's acquired gender. An interesting aspect of the case was the fact that proceedings relating to an earlier request by the applicant to have her birth certificate altered were originally commenced before the 2003 Act came into force, and the applicant initially lost her case in the High Court. She then appealed to the Supreme Court and in the time between the High Court decision and the Supreme Court hearing three significant events occurred; first the 2003 Act came into force, secondly the ECt.HR gave judgment in favour of an applicant in circumstances very similar to those of Ms Foy (*Goodwin v UK* (2002) 35 EHRR 18), and thirdly the Civil Registration Act 2004 was passed. As a result the applicant wished to raise new issues before the Supreme Court, but it held that as these issues had not (and indeed could not have) been addressed by the High Court the case should be sent back there for a decision to be made on them at first instance. Hence the proceedings were remitted back to the High Court where the applicant argued that the relevant legislation breached her rights to private life under Article 8, to marry a person of the opposite sex under Article 12 and to be free from discrimination before the law under Article 14 ECHR. The applicant also tried to repeat the constitutional law arguments she had made previously in the first High Court case but which had been rejected by the Court. McKechnie J held that he was bound by these earlier findings and in any event, even if he could look again at this issue in light of the *Goodwin* decision which had subsequently been delivered by the ECt.HR, this would still not affect these findings, since the 2003 Act was incorporated at a sub-constitutional level (in other words, the Convention case could not disturb the constitutional law decision). However, in relation to the Convention arguments the court found that the State had failed in its positive obligations under Article 8 to have in place a scheme which would allow for the acquired identity of the applicant to be recognised. (The Court made no decision in relation to the Article 12 right to marry argument in view of the fact that the applicant had not yet been granted a divorce from her spouse, and the Court also held that no separate issue arose under Article 14 ECHR and hence made no finding in relation to the non-discrimination argument.) McKechnie J granted a declaration under s 5 of the 2003 Act.

The *Foy* decision also examined the meaning of s 2 of the European Convention on Human Rights Act, 2003 and how courts were to fulfil the obligation therein to interpret statutory provisions and rules of law 'insofar as is possible' in accordance with the ECHR. McKechnie J held that since the Oireachtas used the word 'possible' rather than less wide-ranging phrases such as 'reasonable' or 'practicable' it clearly intended the courts to go much further than applying traditional criteria such as, for example, the purposeful rule or giving ambiguous words a meaning which accords with Convention rights. However he said it was equally clear that the section cannot extend to producing a meaning which is fundamentally at variance with a key feature of a statutory provision nor can it permit the destruction of a scheme or its replacement with a remodelled one. If the court were to find itself so restricted, then the only remedy available is the declaration of incompatibility. Indeed that was the position in the *Foy* case itself where McKechnie J held that the practice and legal position in the case were so well established that they could not be interpreted, pursuant to s 2 of the 2003 Act, in a manner compatible with the ECHR, as to do so would involve the creation of a fundamentally altered scheme. Hence the court went on to issue the declaration of incompatibility. However, in *Dublin City Council v Gallagher* O'Neill J stressed the fact that the interpretative obligation in s 2 is said to be 'subject to the rules of law relating to such interpretation'. Therefore, he held, the courts are required to adhere to existing rules of interpretation meaning that the relevant dominant rule of statutory construction must still prevail (unlike for example in the UK where the equivalent interpretative obligation is not subject to the same qualification).

Another important point discussed in *Foy* was the question of whether a court can make findings in relation to whether the applicant's rights under the ECHR have been breached or make a declaration of incompatibility where the 'Convention-unfriendly' aspect of Irish law is not some positive piece of legislation or rule of common law, but rather the fact that there is no such legislation or rule in the first place. In *Foy* the State respondents argued that no findings could be made as regards Articles 8 and 12 of the Convention since there the applicant could not identify any particular provision which prohibited the exercise of these rights and therefore no declaration of incompatibility could be made. It argued that since the applicant's case was firmly based on the State's failure to enact appropriate legislation, rather than in condemning an existing piece of legislation, she could not successfully seek these said remedies. The Court rejected this argument as to hold otherwise would mean that the State, purely by inactivity, could circumvent virtually at will, any and all ECHR rights (and indeed constitutional rights). The Court held that the failure by the State, through the absence of having any measures to honour the ECHR rights of its citizens, was every bit as much a breach of its responsibility as if it had enacted a piece of prohibited legislation. The courts regularly made findings of unconstitutionality in respect of the State's failure to put in place certain measures and likewise the ECt.HR has often found states to be in breach of the ECHR as regards their failure to observe their positive obligations under the Convention. In relation to the s 5 argument the court agreed with the applicant that the relevant provisions of the Civil Registration Act 2004 were the only substantive provisions dealing with the power to vary an original entry in a birth certificate since they did not permit a variation in the applicant's case, they constituted an obstacle to the legal recognition of her rights under Article 8 ECHR and as such came within the scope of s 5 of the 2003 Act.

Therefore it is arguable that this aspect of the *Foy* case suggests that s 5 may be available as a remedy not just to those who can point to specific statutory provisions which they claim are in breach of the ECHR but also to those who complain of gaps in statutory schemes as a result of which their Convention rights are not respected (although the remarks of Murray CJJ and Fennelly J in *McD v L* (see **5.5.1**) on the question of domestic law silence on an issue and available remedies under the 2003 Act may hint at a different view). Since the State has now abandoned its appeal in the *Foy* case, this issue remains to be resolved.

The State also argued in *Foy* that a declaration of incompatibility should not be issued because, as a result of s 5(2) (pursuant to which a declaration of incompatibility does not affect the continuing validity of the relevant statutory provision) such a declaration would be of no value to the applicant. However McKechnie J rejected this argument, holding that the granting of a s 5 declaration may indeed have consequences which would be of value to the applicant—specifically the requirement that the Taoiseach must bring the declaration to the attention of the Oireacthas, the fact that there must be a reasonable expectation that the other branches of government would not ignore a declaration made by the superior courts, the ability of the successful applicant to apply to the Attorney General for an *ex gratia* payment under the 2003 Act and finally the fact that the making of such a declaration may have consequences in relation to the issue of the costs of the legal proceedings concerned.

One further issue which has now been definitively resolved is the correct sequence in which the courts should consider constitutional and ECHR arguments when both are raised in the same case. In *Carmody v Minister for Justice* [2005] 2 ILRM 1, Laffoy J had held that the correct approach was to address the ECHR issue first and the constitutional question last as this conformed with the general judicial rule of practice that constitutional issues should be addressed last in any given case. However in *Law Society of Ireland v Competition Authority* [2005] IECH 455, O'Neill J took the opposite view, and addressed the constitutional issue first (and, having granted *certiorari* on this basis, did not feel it necessary to examine the ECHR argument). The latter approach seemed to accord with the wording of s 5 of the Act which states that a declaration of incompatibility should only be granted if no other remedy is available, which O'Neill J took to include constitutional remedies (although it must be noted that the *Carmody* case was not referred to in the *Law Society* case). Moreover it is likely that in practice applicants would want their constitutional arguments heard in any event as these, if successful, would give them a much more effective remedy than a declaration of incompatibility, so that it makes more practical sense for the constitutional issue to be considered first. It was also argued that if the sequence approved by the High Court in *Carmody* were to be adopted it would give rise to the possibility that examination of constitutional arguments would become the exception rather than the norm, and that the ECHR might in some way surpass the Constitution as the primary source of protection of fundamental rights in Ireland, and, it was argued, given that the Act expressly subordinates the ECHR to the Constitution such an outcome would not have reflected parliamentary intention.

The *Carmody* case was appealed to the Supreme Court and it determined that constitutional rather than ECHR arguments in any given case should be addressed first (see *Carmody v Minister for Justice* [2009] IESC 71 (discussed further at **12.3.2**)). Indeed the Supreme Court was of the view that '[i]t hardly needs to be said that the provisions of the Act of 2003 cannot compromise in any way the interpretation or application of the Constitution', a principle the Court said was acknowledged in the long title to the 2003 Act where it states that the effect of the Act is 'subject to the Constitution'. Therefore the Court held that where a party makes a claim that an Act or any of its provisions is invalid for being repugnant to the Constitution and at the same time makes an application for a declaration of incompatibility of such Act with the State's obligations under the ECHR, the issue of constitutionality must first be decided. If a court concludes that the statutory provisions in issue are incompatible with the Constitution and such a finding will resolve the issues between the parties as regards all the statutory provisions impugned, then, the Supreme Court stated, that is the remedy which the Constitution envisages the party should have. As any such declaration means that the provisions in question are invalid and do not have the force of law, the question of a declaration pursuant to s 5 concerning such provisions could not then arise. If, on the other hand, a court decides that the statutory provisions impugned are not inconsistent with the Constitution then it is open to the Court to consider the application for a declaration pursuant to s 5 if the provisions of that section including the absence of any other legal remedy, are otherwise met.

If the Supreme Court had upheld Laffoy J's approach that ECHR issues should be decided first then the frequency with which the Act was cited and its importance in terms of the outcome of cases would have increased and the Act would have been seen as a primary rather than residual source of human rights protection. As, however, the Supreme Court has decided that constitutional issues are to be considered first then it is likely the Act will be relied on less and certainly it will not receive as much judicial consideration as it might otherwise.

Indeed the limitations of the 2003 Act are quite starkly seen in the recent case of *McD v L*, 10 December 2009, Supreme Court (unreported), [2009] IESC 81 This case concerned the rights of the biological father of a child born as a result of sperm donation. The child's mother was in a long-term same-sex relationship with another woman and difficulties had arisen between the biological father and the mother and her partner. In the High Court *McD v L* [2008] IE HC 96, Hedigan J held that the mother and her partner constituted a *de facto* family which enjoyed rights under Article 8 ECHR which were cognisable under Irish law. The Supreme Court however held that the trial judge had erred in approaching the case in this manner, in that he had failed to identify any provision of Irish law to which the interpretative obligation in s 2 of the 2003 Act could apply (and none of the other remedies under the 2003 Act appear to have been claimed). Rather, the Supreme Court held, the trial judge had sought to apply the ECHR directly into Irish law, something which was not provided for either under Article 29.6 or the terms of the 2003 Act itself. Furthermore the trial judge had been incorrect in his interpretation of the ECt.HR's jurisprudence on the issue of whether the protection of family life under Article 8 extended to same-sex couples, but even if he had been correct, there was no such concept of the *de facto* family under the Irish Constitution. Therefore in this case, because there was no domestic rule or provision which dealt with the issue, the Irish courts could not apply the case-law of the ECHR. Even if they had been able to do so they could only apply the jurisprudence of the ECt.HR to date in relation to the concept of family life; they could not go further and anticipate any development of the ECt.HR's thinking in relation to this issue, no matter how likely such a development was. And finally even if the courts were able to say the concept of family life under the ECHR extended to same-sex couples, this would have been trumped by the notion of the family contained in the Constitution, namely the family based on marriage.

5.8   Conclusion

Although the practical impact of the European Convention on Human Rights Act, 2003 cannot yet be definitively determined, its passage into law does at least seem to have had the effect of increasing popular awareness of the ECHR. It also obliges judges for the first time to listen to arguments based on the ECHR and have due regard to the decisions of the ECt.HR, and this has also resulted in decisions from other legal systems, which have regard to ECHR jurisprudence, being considered by the Irish courts (particularly decisions of the UK courts). Finally, the courts' obligation as far as is possible to interpret legislation in a manner compatible with the ECHR should ensure that points of legislative ambiguity are resolved in a ECHR-friendly manner (provided there are no competing constitutional arguments), meaning that cases that might otherwise have gone to Strasbourg will be satisfactorily resolved before the domestic courts (although in cases where a s 5 declaration of incompatibility is made recourse to Strasbourg may still be necessary if the Oireachtas fails to pass remedial legislation).

Clearly, much still depends on the attitude of judges, lawyers, parliamentarians, administrators and individual litigants as to the effect the legislation will have. It would seem however from the few Supreme Court decisions on the interpretation of the 2003 Act that it will not be a vehicle for radical change. As Fennelly J stated in *McD v L* '[t]he Act of 2003 does not provide an open-ended mechanism for our courts to outpace Strasbourg'. The 2003 Act may in time be viewed as unsatisfactory and new or amending legislation may always be drafted. In this sense, the use of the legislative model offers some flexibility. Ultimately, however, as some have suggested, this issue may have to be revisited on a constitutional level if true, effective incorporation is to occur.

CHAPTER 6

INTERNATIONAL HUMAN RIGHTS LAW

6.1　Introduction

Ireland is a party to many international human rights instruments as well as being a member of a number of international organisations. As a result, it has a wide variety of international obligations in the area of human rights law, obligations which exist at both the regional and global levels. However, as has already been discussed, it has long been held (see *Re Ó Laighléis* [1960] IR 93) that because Ireland is a dualist country these obligations are not binding on a domestic level, meaning that individuals cannot seek to enforce these obligations before national courts (unless of course the particular measure has been incorporated into Irish law, which some treaties have been). The status of international human rights law in Irish law was confirmed in the case of *Kavanagh v Governor of Mountjoy Prison* [2002] 3 IR 97, in which the applicant sought to challenge the validity of his detention on foot of conviction by the Special Criminal Court (SCC) on the basis that his trial before the SCC had been found to be in breach of the International Covenant on Civil and Political Rights (ICCPR) by the UN Human Rights Committee (see **6.2.3.1**). Both the High Court and Supreme Court confirmed that *Re Ó Laighléis* remains the law and that the Constitution is clear and unambiguous in its terms in relation to the status of international agreements. It draws a clear distinction between domestic and international law until such time as the Oireachtas decides to pass legislation incorporating the particular piece of international law into Irish law. Until such incorporating legislation is passed, *neither* the terms of the ICCPR *nor* the views of the Human Rights Committee (HRC) could prevail over the legal effect of a domestic statute or a conviction by a duly constituted domestic court.

However this does not mean that the State's duties under international human rights law have no practical effect in the domestic sphere. A number of developments in domestic law and practice owe their origins to obligations arising by virtue of the State's acceptance of various international human rights measures. It is therefore important to examine the nature of some of these obligations. However, because it is not possible to look at every human rights measure to which Ireland is party, only the more significant of these measures will be discussed in this chapter.

It should be noted at the outset that in terms of deciding whether and when to accede to a human rights treaty, Ireland has stated that its practice is to accede to such a treaty only after it has taken all necessary domestic measures to ensure that the State is in compliance with the obligations set out in the particular treaty. This approach can be questioned from a factual perspective in that it is clear from the instances in which the State has been found to be in violation of a human rights treaty that the State has not in fact taken all necessary compliance measures before acceding to the treaty. Moreover, the approach can be criticised in that it fails to recognise the evolving nature of obligations under international human rights instruments, which generally require states to develop policies and practices designed to change societal attitudes, to promote a culture of human rights and, if necessary, to take positive steps to benefit persons and groups traditionally discriminated against. It is not sufficient for the State simply to say that it only accedes to a human rights treaty after it has taken all necessary steps for compliance, as this fails to understand that the act of accession itself gives rise to these ongoing obligations.

6.2   Universal Human Rights Law

The emergence of the notion that there are certain rights which are universal, ie enjoyed by everyone, no matter where in the world they live, and moreover that these rights might be enforced by international or domestic bodies, was one of the most significant legal developments of the twentieth century. The fact that the existence of such rights is almost taken for granted today belies the controversial beginnings of the concept. However, today, there are a variety of international instruments dealing with general and specific human rights issues and a number of international organisations whose task it is to ensure the implementation of these treaties.

6.2.1   UN CHARTER

The United Nations (UN) was founded in the wake of the Second World War with a view to preventing the sort of devastation wrought in the period before and during that war. Its founding document is the UN Charter of 1945 (the UN Charter), which, it has been said, 'internationalised' human rights. The UN Charter set out the purposes of the UN, one of which was to promote and encourage respect for human rights and fundamental freedoms for all, and required members to pledge that they would take both joint and separate action, in conjunction with the UN, to achieve this purpose. In this way, the State parties to the UN Charter, by signing up to it, accepted that human rights were the subject of *international* and not just domestic concern. Having said this, however, attempts to build more detailed human rights provisions into the UN Charter failed and it was to be some 20 years before such provisions were incorporated into an international treaty. Instead, the focus of the UN Charter was the establishment of institutions which could give effect to the statements of purpose and principle contained in the Charter. Historically the most important body within the UN in terms of the protection of human rights was the Economic and Social Council (ECOSOC), more specifically, the Commission on Human Rights established by ECOSOC in 1946 and its sub-division, the Sub-Commission on the Promotion and Protection of Human Rights, a body supposedly composed of experts in the area of human rights. These two institutions carried out a number of functions in relation to the protection of human rights, including mechanisms known as 'special procedures' established by the Commission to deal with either country-specific situations or thematic issues such as disappearances, extra-judicial executions and child prostitutions. The Commission was also authorised to undertake a thorough study of situations which revealed a consistent pattern of human rights abuse (the 'Resolution 1235 procedure'), although in practice this mechanism was rarely used. The Sub-Commission could also act upon allegations of gross human rights violations through the confidential 'Resolution 1503 procedure'. Under this mechanism the Sub-Commission would investigate the allegations and decide whether to give the State concerned more time or whether to refer the matter to the Commission, which in turn could keep the matter under review, transfer the matter to the public 1235 procedure, make recommendations to ECOSOC or discontinue consideration of the matter. The Sub-Commission also conducted studies on discriminatory practices and made recommendations to ensure minorities were protected under law (for example it established working groups on indigenous populations, on the administration of justice and on contemporary forms of slavery). While undoubtedly much good work was achieved by the Commission and Sub-Commission, particularly in the area of standard-setting, criticism of the system grew over time with allegations being made against the Commission that it lacked impartiality and that some of its choices were politically motivated rather than being based on human rights considerations. The Commission's working methods were also seen to be inconsistent, with some countries more likely to be investigated than others. Finally the Commission met for only six weeks per year, and was seen to be unable or too slow to react to emergency situations. The confidential nature of the 1503 procedure used by the Sub-Commission also caused concern.

Indeed, such was the dissatisfaction with the old system and the mechanisms established thereunder that, rather than attempt to reform this system, the decision was taken to abolish it completely and replace it with a new body, the Human Rights Council (see **6.2.1.1**).

6.2.1.1   Human Rights Council

The Human Rights Council was established under Resolution 60/251 of the General Assembly in March 2006. Initially the Human Rights Council's status is as a subsidiary organ of the General Assembly but this position will be reviewed five years after the establishment of the Council in 2011, with the hope that the Council will then be elevated to a principal organ of the United Nations. If this does happen it will mean that a body dedicated exclusively to the protection of human rights will enjoy the same status in the UN as the Security Council and ECOSOC, a hugely significant potential development, and would serve to confirm that human rights, along with economic and social development and peace and security are the pillars upon which all of the UN's work is built.

Under Resolution 60/251 the functions and powers of the Human Rights Council are set out as follows:

(a)   to promote universal respect for the protection of human rights for all, without distinction and in a fair and equal manner;

(b)   to address situations of violations of human rights, including gross and systematic violations and make recommendations thereon;

(c)   to promote the effective co-ordination and mainstreaming of human rights within the UN system;

(d)   in performing its functions, to be guided by the principles of objectivity, impartiality and non-selectivity, constructive international dialogue and co-operation;

(e)   to promote human rights education as well as advisory services and technical assistance;

(f)   to serve as a forum for dialogue on thematic issues on all human rights;

(g)   to make recommendations to the General Assembly for the further development of international human rights law;

(h)   to undertake a universal periodic review based on objective and reliable information of the fulfilment by each state of its human rights obligations in a manner which ensures equal treatment for all states. This review is to be a co-operative mechanism;

(i)   to contribute through co-operation and dialogue towards the prevention of human rights violations and respond promptly to human rights emergencies;

(j)   to assume, review and where necessary improve the mandates of the Commission on Human Rights;

(k)   to work in close co-operation with national governments, regional organisations, national human rights institutions and civil society;

(l)   to make recommendations for the promotion and protection of human rights;

(m)   to submit an annual report to the UN General Assembly.

There are forty-seven members of the Human Rights Council. Membership of the Council is open to all states who are members of the United Nations, and Members are elected directly by the General Assembly itself rather than ECOSOC, giving the Council more authority whilst at the same time making those appointed more accountable and the Council more representative. Membership is staggered and decided on the basis of equitable geographical distribution (in practice members of the Council are divided into five regional groups: African States, Asian States, Eastern European States, Latin American and Caribbean States, and Western European and Other States). When electing members the General Assembly is required to take into account the contribution made by candidates to the promotion and protection of human rights. The General Assembly may also suspend the rights of membership in the Council of a member of the Council that commits gross and systematic violations of human rights. Members of the Council are also reviewed under the periodic review mechanism during their term of office.

Importantly in the light of criticism that the Commission on Human Rights did not meet regularly or often enough, Resolution 60/251 also directs that the Council is to meet regularly throughout the year, for *at least* three sessions lasting ten weeks. The Council may also sit in special session when needed provided at least one-third of the Council support this. Therefore the Council is a standing body, able to meet regularly and at any time, so that, in theory at least, it should be capable of dealing with emergency situations and give timely and in-depth consideration to human rights issues.

The Human Rights Council sat for the first time in June 2006 and in June 2007 adopted an 'institution-building package' providing guidance as to its future work, the main elements of which are:

(i)   The Universal Periodic Review—this procedure is intended to provide a mechanism whereby the human rights records of each of the 192 members of the United Nations will be reviewed once every four years. This unique procedure should therefore ensure that by 2011 the human rights record of every country in the UN will have been examined, thus confirming the universal nature of human rights and avoiding some of the criticisms of partiality that dogged the old Human Rights Commission (members of the Council itself are to be examined while sitting on the Council and thereafter countries are examined in a manner which respects the principle of equitable geographical allocation, in alphabetical order, which has resulted in Ireland being one of the last countries scheduled to be reviewed, in late 2011). The review is conducted by the UPR Working Group, which in fact consists of the 47 members of the Council, but any UN Member State can take part in the discussions with the State under review. NGOs and national human rights institutions can also contribute to the review. An outcome report is then issued which consists of the comments, questions and recommendations made by states to the country under review, along with that state's response to the same. These outcome reports are then reviewed by the Working Group and the reviewed state may make preliminary comments on the recommendations choosing to either accept or reject them. Both accepted and refused recommendations are included in the report. The report is then adopted at a plenary session of the Human Rights Council, during which the State under review can reply to questions and issues that were not sufficiently addressed during the Working Group and respond to recommendations that were raised by states during the review. Time is also allotted to member and observer states who may wish to express their opinion on the outcome of the review and for NGOs and other stakeholders to make general comments. The State reviewed has the primary responsibility to implement the recommendations contained in the final outcome but when the time comes for the second review of a state they will be required to provide information on what they have done to implement the recommendations made during the first review four years earlier. The Council has stated that it will, if necessary, address cases where states are not co-operating, taking appropriate steps in instances of 'persistent non-co-operation' by a state with the UPR. The procedure is however state-driven, which led to concerns that states would not participate fully or at all with the process. Although it is a little early to judge the success of the procedure the initial signs are positive; the procedure has enjoyed 100% participation by states and appears to have led to an increase in ratifications of international conventions and to improved national human rights institutions. However it remains to be seen exactly how fully states comply with recommendations made by the Council under the UPR.

(ii) The Advisory Committee—this body was established to act as a 'think tank' for the Human Rights Council and work at its direction (in effect the Advisory Committee replaced the old Sub-Commission on the Protection and Promotion of Human Rights). The Advisory Committee provides expertise in the manner and form requested by the Council, focusing mainly on studies and research-based advice, but acts only when asked to by the Council. Although in theory the Advisory Committee cannot adopt resolutions or decisions it has in practice made recommendations arising out of its research into a particular area. For example, at the conclusion of its third session in August 2009 the Committee proposed for the consideration of the Council a set of principles for the elimination of discrimination against persons affected by leprosy and recommended that its Drafting Group on human rights education and training continue its work with a view to submitting a draft declaration on the issue to the fourth session of the Committee. The Committee can also make proposals to the Council as to further research areas it might engage in.

(iii) The Complaints Procedure—the complaints procedure of the Human Rights Council is the successor to the Resolution 1503 procedure discussed above and is designed to address consistent patterns of gross and reliably attested human rights violations occurring in any part of the world and under any circumstances. Like the 1503 procedure it is a confidential procedure, the justification for this being the need to ensure state co-operation. Despite this it is stated to be a victim-oriented process, with the author of a complaint now being kept informed at various stages, including when the communication is deemed inadmissible, when it is taken up for consideration and as to the final outcome. The procedure is also designed to ensure communications are considered in a timely fashion, with the period between transmission of a communication to the State concerned and consideration by the Human Rights Council to be no more than 24 months. When a communication is sent in to the Council it is examined first by the Working Group on Communications which determines whether the complaint merits investigation. If it does, the Working Group on Communications passes the complaint on to the Working Group on Situations which then prepares a report on the allegations for the Human Rights Council and makes recommendations to the Council on the course of action to take. The Council then takes a decision on the final outcome of a case, namely whether to keep a situation under review and ask the State involved to provide further information or appoint an independent expert to monitor the situation and report back, to continue consideration of the matter in public, to recommend that the Office of the High Commissioner for Human Rights provide technical assistance or to discontinue consideration of the case.

(iv) Special Procedures—these procedures are the mechanisms established by the Commission on Human Rights and assumed by the Human Rights Council to address either specific country situations or thematic issues in all parts of the world (at the time of writing there were 30 thematic studies and eight country mandates). Special procedures mandates-holders are either individuals (such as Special Rapporteurs) or working groups. In order to ensure their independence, they act in a personal capacity and receive no compensation for their work. Pursuant to the Human Rights Council's institution building package, a review of these special procedures was conducted in 2007 and 2008. Following this review all existing thematic mandates have been retained and some new thematic mandates have been established, for example a mandate on cultural rights. Most country-specific mandates have also been continued, and a new mandate to investigate the human rights situation in Sudan was created.

The Human Rights Council is a relatively new human rights body and it is too early to judge whether it will be effective in carrying out its mandate. Certainly there are some positive aspects to its work, including the universal periodic review mechanism. However there has also been criticism of the Human Rights Council, in particular allegations that the Council is effectively controlled by some Middle Eastern and Asian countries (supported by other countries) who protect each other from scrutiny, and that the Council has unduly focused on Israel while failing to address adequately situations in places such as Darfur, Tibet and Zimbabwe.

6.2.2   UNIVERSAL DECLARATION ON HUMAN RIGHTS

As mentioned earlier, the UN Charter focused more on the establishment of institutions which could supervise the enforcement of human rights rather than setting out in detail what such rights were. Efforts to draft an instrument which would contain a list of such rights continued, and in 1948 the Universal Declaration on Human Rights (the UN Declaration) was signed. The UN Declaration recognises two broad categories of human rights, civil and political rights and economic, social and cultural rights, and sets out a list of such rights. The rights protected are:

- The right to life, liberty, and security of the person

- Freedom from slavery

- Freedom from torture, inhuman or degrading treatment or punishment

- The right to recognition before the law

- The right to equality before the law and to equal protection from the law

- The right to an effective remedy for acts violating fundamental rights

- Freedom from arbitrary arrest, detention or exile

- The right to a fair trial

- The right to be presumed innocent until proven guilty and protection against retro-activity of the criminal law

- Freedom from arbitrary interference with privacy, family, home and correspondence and from attacks upon honour and reputation

- Freedom of movement within the borders of a state and the right to leave a country and return to one's own country

- The right to seek and enjoy asylum

- The right to a nationality

- The right to marry and found a family

- The right to own property

- Freedom of thought, conscience and religion

- Freedom of opinion and expression

- Freedom of peaceful assembly and association

- The right to participate in government of one's country

- The right to social security

- The right to work, to favourable conditions of work, the right to equal pay for equal remuneration and the right to form and join trade unions

- The right to rest and leisure

- The right to a standard of living adequate for oneself and one's family

- The right to education

- The right to participate freely in the cultural life of the community.

However, the Declaration is not a treaty. It was adopted by the General Assembly as a resolution having no force of law, its purpose being to set a standard, which states would strive in their domestic laws to achieve. However, as time has progressed, and particularly in the absence of binding international human rights treaties of universal effect, the status of the Declaration in international law has changed. It is now generally recognised that the Declaration does have some legal effect and that at least some of its provisions are legally binding. The difficulty lies in identifying which of the rights in the Declaration have this character, and to what extent. What is clear however is that the Declaration has been consistently relied on by the United Nations when applying the human rights provisions of the UN Charter, and by state governments and international organisations when invoking human rights norms. The Declaration has been extremely important in the development of the notion and content of international human rights law.

6.2.3 INTERNATIONAL COVENANT ON CIVIL AND POLITICAL RIGHTS

The International Covenant on Civil and Political Rights (ICCPR) was eventually signed in 1966, after a long period of negotiation, which had originally been designed to produce a single, binding human rights treaty that would have universal effect as opposed to the non-binding Declaration. However, it became clear that agreement on a single treaty would not be achieved and so a compromise was reached that two treaties rather than one would be drawn up, with a clear distinction between civil and political rights on the one hand and economic, social and cultural rights on the other, and with different enforcement mechanisms for each. The products of this process were the ICCPR and the International Covenant on Economic, Social and Cultural Rights (ICESCR) which were both signed in 1966 but which did not come into force for another ten years, in 1976. Ireland signed the ICCPR in 1973 but it did not come into force in this country until December 1989.

The ICCPR contains a broad catalogue of rights, which have been supplemented by a number of additional protocols relating to matters too controversial to be included in the main treaty, for example a prohibition on the death penalty. The rights protected by the ICCPR are:

- The right to life

- Freedom from torture and inhuman treatment

- Freedom from slavery and forced labour
- The right to liberty and security
- The right of detained persons to be treated with humanity
- Freedom from imprisonment from debt
- Freedom of movement and of choice of residence
- Freedom of aliens from arbitrary expulsion
- The right to a fair trial
- Protection against retroactivity of the criminal law
- The right to recognition as a person before the law
- The right to privacy
- Freedom of thought, conscience and religion
- Freedom of expression and opinion
- Prohibition of propaganda for war and of incitement to national, racial or religious hatred
- The right of peaceful assembly
- Freedom of association
- The right to marry and found a family
- The rights of the child
- Political rights
- The right to equality before the law
- The rights of minorities to enjoy their own culture, to profess and practise their own religion or to use their own language.

Protocol 1 is also extremely important in that it provides for a right of *individual petition*; in other words, unlike the 1235 and 1503 procedures, the ICCPR provides a mechanism whereby an individual can complain to an international body about treatment they have received at the hands of the State and seek redress for this. In this way, as well as in relation to the rights enumerated, the ICCPR resembles quite closely the ECHR. However, while complaints under the ECHR are made to a court, under the ICCPR they are made to the Human Rights Committee (HRC).

6.2.3.1 Human Rights Committee (HRC)

The HRC (see **7.7.3**) has a number of functions relating to the supervision and enforcement of human rights in those states which are parties to the ICCPR. It consists of 18 members who are elected by the states parties to the ICCPR, but all members have legal expertise. The HRC meets three times a year and proceedings are held in private.

Again, because of the dualist nature of Irish law, decisions of the HRC do not have the effect of overriding Irish law, but its recommendations are usually implemented by the government, not least because it is keen to avoid embarrassment in the General Assembly. However, since 1990, the HRC has appointed rapporteurs whose duty it is to monitor the progress of individual countries in implementing recommendations of the HRC.

The two main powers of the HRC are to receive individual complaints and to consider state reports.

Individual petitions

As mentioned earlier, the individual complaints procedure is not mandatory under the ICCPR, unlike the ECHR. Individual complaints can only be made against those state parties who have ratified the First Optional Protocol and thereby accepted the jurisdiction of the HRC to hear such complaints. Also, the respondent state must not have entered a reservation in relation to the particular provision relied on. However, the ICCPR procedure for individual complaints does have some advantages over the ECHR procedure, in that primarily the admissibility criteria for making such a complaint are less strict and the length of time for the complaint to be determined has traditionally been much shorter (averaging about two years to the ECHR's five).

Since the entry into force of the Protocol in 1976, the HRC has dealt with quite a large number of individual communications, and in dealing with those communications it considered admissible, the HRC has been able to develop a valuable body of case-law interpreting and applying the ICCPR and Protocol, which is significant given the universal nature of the ICCPR. A number of these cases have involved Ireland, including *Kavanagh v Ireland* (Communication No. 819/1998, decision of 4 April 2001). In this case, the HRC found that the State had failed to demonstrate that the decision to try Mr Kavanagh before the Special Criminal Court, as opposed to the ordinary courts, was based upon reasonable and objective grounds. In these circumstances, the HRC found that the applicant's rights under Article 26 ICCPR to equality before the law and to equal protection from the law had been violated. In the wake of this decision, the government asked the Hederman Committee which had been established to examine the Offences Against the State Act, 1939 to provide it with an interim report to assist the government in its response to the HRC's view in this case. The government also offered the sum of £1,000 to Mr Kavanagh by way of satisfaction of the decision of the HRC, but this sum was refused. In its response to the HRC, the government simply quoted the majority view of the Hederman Committee that the continued existence of the Special Criminal Court was justified in the current circumstances without even citing the existence of a minority, dissenting view.

Admissibility criteria

As mentioned earlier, before an individual can make a complaint to the HRC, the government concerned must have accepted the right of individual petition by ratifying the First Optional Protocol. The individual must also satisfy certain criteria before a complaint can be made, in particular they must have exhausted all domestic remedies available to them before making the complaint to the HRC. The complaint must relate to a 'victim' of an alleged violation of the ICCPR, although this term has been broadly interpreted so that a representative of such a person can make the complaint. Class actions are not allowed. Nor are applications seeking to prevent future events from occurring. A major advantage of the ICCPR system is that there is no time limit for the making of complaints, unlike under the ECHR system where complaints have to be made within six months of the alleged violation. This makes the ICCPR system a very valuable alternative, particularly for persons who cannot make a complaint to Strasbourg because they are outside the six-month time limit. However, as with the ECHR, an application will not be considered by the HRC if it is currently before another international human rights body.

Making a complaint

Complaints are initially sent to the secretariat for the HRC in Geneva which will send out a model form to be filled out concerning the case (although it is not essential that this form be used to make the complaint). The complaint will then be assigned to an officer of the HRC known as the Special Rapporteur on New Applications who will decide whether the complaint should be registered under the Optional Protocol and will issue any pertinent instructions relating to the processing of the complaint. If the case is registered, the HRC's usual course of action, given the large number of complaints received under this procedure, is to consider the admissibility and merits of the case simultaneously. To this end, the state party against whom the complaint is directed has six months to present its submissions on the admissibility and merits of the case. After this is done the complainant will be given two months to comment, following which the case is ready for a decision by the HRC. If the state party fails to respond to the complaint, it will receive two reminders after the six-month deadline has passed and if there is still no reply, the HRC will consider the complaint on the basis of the information initially supplied by the complainant. However if the state party presents submissions after a reminder, these will be transmitted to the complainant who will then have an opportunity to comment. The HRC may also at any stage of the process request that a state takes interim measures to protect the alleged victim, and although such a request has no binding force, the HRC has indicated that a failure to comply with such a request is incompatible with the obligation to respect in good faith the procedure established under the First Protocol.

Occasionally, the HRC adopts a different procedure to maximise the time at its disposal to consider communications and to spare both state parties and complainants needless effort. For example, if a state party, within two months of receiving a complaint, presents submissions relating only to admissibility and the HRC considers that there may indeed be serious doubts relating to this issue, it may invite the complainant to comment only on those submissions. The HRC will then take a preliminary decision on admissibility alone and proceed to the merits stage only if the case is declared admissible. If it is, the state party is given a further six months to present submissions on the merits of the communication and the complainant is in turn requested to comment within two months. The complainant will always be informed of any such departure from the usual practice.

The HRC will decide on the merits of the case at one of its thrice-yearly sessions. Its decision will be based on written submissions and documents only as there is no provision for oral argument before the HRC in respect of individual complaints.

In terms of the burden of proof, the HRC has established that, in cases where allegations of severe abuse have been made, the burden of proof will not fall exclusively on the complainant, so that it will not be enough for the respondent state simply to refute the complaint in general terms.

The HRC will issue a single consensus report, although occasionally dissenting opinions may be included. If the HRC has decided that a violation of the ICCPR has occurred, it will give suggestions as to how the situation may be rectified and may include a suggestion that compensation be paid. Again, however, these suggestions are not legally binding and it is primarily a matter of conscience for the respondent state as to whether to follow these suggestions. The HRC will then appoint a special rapporteur to follow up on the case and observe the manner in which the State gives effect to the decision of the HRC, which may involve the rapporteur meeting with non-governmental organisations (NGOs) and independent lawyers to ascertain their views on the action taken by the State. The HRC will also give information on these follow-up missions in their annual report.

Once the HRC makes its decision, this will be communicated to the parties involved. It will also be published in the HRC's annual report to the UN General Assembly and is generally available to the public. Until this time, however, proceedings are strictly confidential. It should also be noted that there is no provision for legal aid under the ICCPR system.

State reports

Unlike the right of individual petition, the state reporting obligation is mandatory, so that all state parties to the ICCPR must submit such reports to the HRC. Given the optional nature of the individual petition process, the State reporting procedure is very significant, and the HRC has broadened its role in this process to maximum effect to encompass areas that are not likely ever to form the basis of an individual complaint.

Once a state has ratified the ICCPR, it must submit an initial report as to the human rights situation existing in its jurisdiction. This report is then followed up by periodic reports every three to five years. The reports fall into two parts, a general section which details the legal, political and constitutional background of the State and the legal framework within which human rights are protected in the State, followed by a section which examines the ICCPR Article by Article and relates how the State has given effect to the right contained in the particular article. The report should also indicate the manner in which human rights knowledge and in particular knowledge about the ICCPR itself is promoted at every level in the State. Periodic reports must also address the issues raised in previous reports and deal with any findings of the HRC in relation to breaches of the ICCPR.

The process of examining a state report runs across two HRC sessions. Since 2002 the report is assigned to a Country Report Task Force (CRTF) composed of between four and six HRC members, at least one of whom should come from the same region as the state party involved. The CRTF will draw up a List of Issues addressing the most crucial issues relating to the enjoyment of Covenant rights in the State concerned and calling for additional information if necessary. This List of Issues is sent to the State concerned well in advance of the HRC's examination of the report and it is increasingly common for state parties to supply written answers to the List of Issues in advance of or at the start of the HRC's public examination of the report. At the beginning of the session at which the HRC examines the report the HRC hears in private from representatives of specialised agencies and other parts of the UN that wish to provide information. The HRC may also be informally briefed by NGOs at this stage (see below). The HRC will then sit in public session to scrutinise the report with a delegation from the relevant state party. The State representative will introduce the report, including often a response to the List of Issues, and will then be questioned by members of the HRC (usually by members of the relevant CRTF) in respect of the content of the report. This dialogue normally takes place over two to three meetings and there is usually some time after the conclusion of the dialogue for the State representative to supply additional information.

The HRC will then draft detailed written concluding observations in respect of the report. These concluding observations are consensus comments on positive and negative aspects of the state party's implementation of the Covenant. They will also include the HRC's recommendations for remedial action. In almost all concluding observations the HRC will identify a limited number of issues of particular priority. It then asks the State to provide no less than a year thereafter information on the measures it has taken to address these issues. A Special Rapporteur on Follow-up to Concluding Observations will then assess this follow-up information and make a recommendation to the HRC as to any further steps that may be appropriate. The HRC will then examine these findings and decide on any further action. If states do not co-operate with this follow-up procedure this fact will be noted in the HRC's annual report to the General Assembly. The HRC also encourages states to make its concluding observations public and to engage in public debate on the observations. Thereafter the HRC leaves it to national authorities to decide how best to assess and implement whatever measures are necessary to give effect to the concluding observations.

In 2001 the HRC decided, in response to the chronic failure on the part of some states to submit a report on time or at all, or to attend scheduled meetings, that it could examine such a state's record under the Covenant in the absence of a report or even in the absence of a delegation of the relevant state. However in this instance the HRC will adopt confidential, provisional concluding observations.

The role of NGOs and other independent parties

The success of the reporting procedure depends to a large extent on the participation of NGOs or other independent parties who can provide the HRC with alternative sources of information in relation to the human rights situation in a country, and challenge the government's assessment of its compliance with the ICCPR. It is vital that NGOs are made aware of the reporting process, and indeed each state is required to inform such groups that a report is being prepared. However, it appears that some states, including Ireland, have not always fulfilled their obligation to do this, and so many state reports have been submitted without the critical input of such groups. This is significant, because NGOs have no formal right of audience before the HRC, so the major way they can influence the State reporting procedure is in the drafting of the report itself. If NGOs are not involved, it can mean that many issues are not covered by the report and that the State is not questioned on these issues by the HRC.

However, NGOs can still have an impact, even if not consulted in the drafting of the report, as the HRC will accept written submissions from interested parties during the reporting procedure, and NGOs are able to lobby the HRC members during the examination procedure. Members of the pre-sessional working group also tend to be willing to meet informally with NGOs, and these encounters can be important in influencing the questions which are put to the State representatives. It is, therefore, always advisable for NGOs to send representatives to the HRC sessions for this to occur, as experience has shown that direct meetings with members serve to enhance the impact of submissions.

Lawyers can play a role in advising NGOs in preparing these submissions, particularly in challenging the government's analysis of the legal situation pertaining in the State and of its compliance with the Covenant. These submissions should be as clear and simple as possible, and should reflect the State report by dealing with issues on an Article-by-Article basis (sometimes NGOs will prepare what are known as 'shadow reports'). This will make the submissions much easier for the HRC members to use in examining the State report. The submission should also be as concise as possible, as HRC members tend to be very busy during the thrice-yearly sessions and will not have time to read lengthy and elaborate submissions. Submissions should be sent at least seven weeks in advance to the Secretary of the Human Rights Committee, Palais des Nations, Geneva, CH-1211, Switzerland. NGOs should also remember the value of publicity and should use whatever contacts they have to ensure that the reporting process is widely covered by both domestic and international media.

Ireland's record

Ireland's first report to the HRC was submitted in 1992 and covered a number of areas. The HRC questioned the government representatives closely on issues including emergency legislation, lack of divorce legislation, inadequacies in the legal aid system and the treatment of Travellers, areas in which there have since been improvements. It seems clear that the State's obligations under the ICCPR, including the reporting obligation, were significant in bringing about those changes.

The government department responsible for preparing Ireland's reports is the Department of Foreign Affairs, in particular the Human Rights Unit. This unit has a broad range of responsibilities, including overseeing the State's ratification of international human rights treaties and the compilation of reports required under various human rights instruments. In preparing Ireland's report under the ICCPR, the Human Rights Unit will liaise with other government departments responsible for particular areas, for example, the Department of Justice. These departments will also keep the Human Rights Unit up to date in relation to any action taken to implement the HRC's recommendations. Ireland's second periodic report was submitted in 1998 and its third periodic report was due in July 2005 but only submitted in February 2007. Ireland was then reviewed by the Human Rights Committee in July 2008 following which the HRC produced a number of observations and recommendations as to how Ireland should further fulfil its obligations under the Covenant. These include:

• A recommendation that Ireland should ensure that all rights protected under the Covenant are given full effect in domestic law;

- Concern about the limited resources given to the Irish Human Rights Commission;

- A recommendation that Ireland should ensure its legislation is not discriminatory of non-traditional forms of partnership, and that the right of transgendered persons to a change of gender should be recognised by permitting the issuance of new birth certificates;

- Concern that inequalities continue to exist between women and men in many areas and Ireland should thus reinforce the effectiveness of its measures to ensure gender equality by increased funding for the institutions established to promote and protect this aim;

- Concern that Irish law does not contain a definition of 'terrorism' and about allegations that Irish airports have been used as transit points for so-called 'rendition flights' of persons to countries where they risk being subjected to torture or ill-treatment. Ireland should therefore introduce a definition of 'terrorist acts', should carefully monitor how terrorist acts are being investigated and prosecuted, and should establish a regime for the control of suspicious flights and ensure that all allegations of so-called renditions are publicly investigated;

- A recommendation that Ireland should bring its abortion laws into line with the Covenant and take measures to help women avoid unwanted pregnancies so that they do not have to resort to illegal or unsafe abortions that could put their lives at risk or to abortions abroad;

- Concern about the increased levels of incarceration in the State and about the persistence of adverse conditions in a number of Irish prisons, including overcrowding, insufficient personal hygiene conditions, non-segregation of remand prisoners, a shortage of mental health care for detainees and the high level of inter-prisoner violence;

- A recommendation that Ireland should increase its efforts to ensure that non-denominational primary education is widely available in all regions;

- A recommendation that Ireland take steps to recognise Travellers as an ethnic minority group.

The State produced a response to some of these recommendations in June 2009.

Emergency procedures/ad hoc reports

In the 1990s the HRC developed a procedure to respond to what it considered to be emergency situations. The HRC requested that several states facing serious difficulties in the implementation of Covenant rights either present their overdue initial/periodic report without delay or prepare *ad hoc* reports on specific issues. The HRC could then make comments on the emergency report and request the UN Secretary-General to bring the situation to the attention of the competent organs of the UN, including the Security Council. However this mechanism met with only limited success and fell into disuse although consideration has since been given to reviving the urgent procedure/*ad hoc* report procedure.

Inter-state complaints

The ICCPR also provides for an inter-state complaint machinery that allows one state party to bring a complaint against another state that it has violated the ICCPR. However this can only be done if both states have recognised the jurisdiction of the HRC to hear such complaints. The mechanism is further weakened by the fact that the HRC is not entitled to make an adjudication on the complaint, but rather provides only a conciliation process designed to encourage a friendly settlement between the parties. If this is not reached, the HRC will prepare a report setting out the facts and submissions of both parties and may decide to appoint an *ad hoc* conciliation commission. This commission can ultimately suggest its own solution to the dispute but neither party is required to accept this proposal. The inter-state procedure is a very weak mechanism, and has nowhere near the same importance as the individual complaint and state reporting procedures.

6.2.4 OTHER INTERNATIONAL HUMAN RIGHTS INSTRUMENTS

Ireland is a party to a number of other international human rights instruments under which it has a variety of obligations. Some of the most important of these are the International Covenant on Economic, Social and Cultural Rights and the United Nations Convention on the Rights of the Child (discussed in **chapter 9**). As well as having the general obligation to ensure that its laws and practices are in conformity with the rights contained therein, these conventions impose a specific reporting obligation on the State. It appears that participation in the reporting process has been significant in focusing domestic and international attention on areas where Irish law and practice is deficient, and in bringing about change in these areas.

It should also be noted that the State is a party to a variety of regional human rights treaties, including the European Convention on the Prevention of Torture, the European Social Charter as well as of course the European Convention on Human Rights.

6.2.4.1 International Covenant on Economic, Social and Cultural Rights

The sister covenant to the ICCPR, the International Covenant on Economic, Social and Cultural Rights (ICESCR) was also adopted by the United Nations in 1966. It contains a detailed list of economic, social and cultural rights, including the following:

- The right to work

- The right to enjoyment of just and favourable conditions of work

- The right to form and join trade unions

- The right to social security

- The right to the protection of the family

- The right to an adequate standard of living, including adequate food, clothing and housing

- The right to enjoyment of the highest attainable standard of physical and mental health

- The right to education

- The right to partake in cultural life.

The ICESCR in many cases also sets out steps which are to be taken by states to achieve the realisation of these rights. For example, Article 6, which guarantees the right to work, provides that the steps to be taken by states shall include technical and vocational guidance and training programmes, policies and techniques to ensure full and productive employment under conditions safeguarding fundamental political and economic freedoms to the individual. Article 7, which provides the right to the enjoyment of 'just and favourable conditions of work' is even more detailed, stipulating that such conditions should ensure, *inter alia*, fair remuneration for all workers, safe and healthy working conditions and equal opportunity for everyone to be promoted in their employment. However, it is clear that the obligations imposed on states under the ICESCR are *progressive* rather that immediate in nature. States are obliged to take steps 'to the maximum of their available resources' to achieve 'progressively the full realization' of the rights set out in the ICESCR. Unlike the ICCPR, states are not expected to be in a position to implement the ICESCR fully at the time of ratification. The traditional reason given for this difference in

CHAPTER 7

THE ROLE OF THE UN TODAY: RESPONSE TO SERIOUS VIOLATIONS OF HUMAN RIGHTS

7.1 Introduction

When the Second World War could not be averted by the League of Nations, the international community decided to come together to prevent future conflicts and to promote co-operation between nations. To this aim, the United Nations (UN) was created at the San Francisco Conference in 1945, starting its work on 24 October of the same year. The Conference was sponsored by the five main victors of the Second World War: the United States, the United Kingdom, the Soviet Union, France and China. However, an additional 40 countries were present at the Conference and a total of 51 countries signed the Charter of the United Nations (the UN Charter).

The UN replaced the traditional system of unilateral state response and political alliances by establishing a common institution based on mutual collaboration to restore global peace and security. Only a few years after its creation, the Cold War put at risk the stability of the organisation by dividing the international community into two blocs. Luckily, this tension between the two Great Powers came to an end in the 1990s following the disintegration of the Soviet Union. Since then the work of the United Nations has focused on new challenges such as internal conflicts and new emerging states, terrorist threats, nuclear proliferation, violation of human rights and poverty reduction. This has led to an increased demand by Member States on the UN agencies, funds and programmes.

Throughout the years, one of the UN's greatest achievements has been its strong commitment to human rights promotion. At the time of its creation, there was no agreed definition of human rights. Today, we enjoy a large body of human rights treaties, instruments and monitoring bodies, thanks to the tremendous work of the United Nations in this area.

The former Secretary-General of the United Nations, Kofi Annan, stated:

> 'States [. . .] are the servants and instruments of human beings, and not the other way round. Once this fundamental principle is understood and accepted, it becomes easy to see why the three cardinal purposes of the Organisation–development, security and human rights–are so indissolubly interconnected' (*Investing in the UN: For A Stronger Organization Worldwide*, March 2006).

This chapter is divided in two sections. The first section explores the structure and role of the UN; the second section analyses the response to serious violations of human rights.

7.2 An Overview of the UN

7.2.1 MEMBERSHIP AND FINANCING

The UN Charter was signed in 1945 by 51 countries, including the five permanent members of the Security Council: the People's Republic of China, France, Russia, the United Kingdom and the United States. The original number of members increased progressively over the next few years, with a substantive addition of new emerging countries after the Cold War, following the disintegration of the former Soviet Union and the former Yugoslavia. Today, with the admission of Montenegro in June 2006, the UN has 192 members, comprising all internationally recognised independent states. Membership entails acceptance of all the obligations established in its Charter. States such as the Holy See (Vatican City), Taiwan and the Saharawi Arab Democratic Republic (SADR) are not full members of the UN, but have observer status.

Non-state actors frequently enjoy observer status, which allows them to attend and speak at meetings and to submit documents, but does not entail the right to vote. However, the non-representation of repressed people (like the Tibetans), stateless people (such as Palestinians and Kurds) and established minorities (such as the Australian Aborigines) in the UN has long been questioned. International and non-governmental organisations such as the European Union and the International Committee of the Red Cross have similar observer status.

The main source of UN financing is the contribution from Member States. The regular budget is approved by the General Assembly, jointly with a scale of assessment for each Member State. This scale is based on the capacity of countries to pay and it is revised and adapted to current circumstances.

In addition voluntary contributions from Member States constitute an important source to finance special programmes and humanitarian emergencies not included in the regular budget. Nevertheless, the UN will always remain independent from specific members financing its operations.

7.2.2 PURPOSE AND PRINCIPLES

Article 1 of the UN Charter declares that the purposes of the organisation are:

> 'to maintain international peace and security, to develop friendly relations among nations, to achieve international co-operation in solving international problems and to be a centre for harmonising the actions of nations in the attainment of these common ends.'

These purposes are achieved through the acceptance, respect and promotion of six main principles, also recognised in the Charter, each of which is now considered in turn.

The Principle of Sovereign Equality of States

This principle, recognised in Article 2.1 of the UN Charter, involves two aspects: sovereignty, in the sense that each state can exercise exclusive power within its territory; and equality, meaning that all states should have the same status in the international sphere.

The Principle of Non-Intervention in the Affairs of Other States

No state has the right to intervene, directly or indirectly, in the internal or external affairs of any other state. This principle was declared by the General Assembly in Resolution 2625 (XXV) Declaration on Principles of International Law concerning Friendly Relations and Co-operation among States in Accordance with the Charter of the United Nations (24 October 1970).

The term 'intervention' is not limited to armed aggression, but also refers to indirect interference by means of political destabilisation, instigation and financing unrest in a foreign country. (Cassese, *International Law*, 2nd edn, 2005, OUP, 55.)

The Principle of Peaceful Settlement of Disputes

Article 2.3 of the UN Charter establishes: *'in any dispute, states should strive for a peaceful resolution'*. If one of the states party to the conflict does not co-operate in finding a peaceful settlement, the other state involved can take two steps: raising the issue with an international body; and/or taking counter-measures (Cassese, *International Law*, 2nd edn, 2005, OUP, 59.)

The Principle of Prohibition of the Threat or Use of Force

Article 2.4 of the UN Charter bans the threat or use of force against the territorial integrity or political independence of any state. Force is generally understood as an armed attack by one state against another and the UN General Assembly proclaims that *'the threat or use of force against another state constitutes a violation of International law'*. (Resolution 2625 (XXV) Declaration on Principles of International Law concerning Friendly Relations and Co-operation among States in Accordance with the Charter of the United Nations (24 October 1970)). There are, however, some exceptions to this principle, in the way of collective enforcement measures (Ch VII UN Charter), self-defence (Article 51 UN Charter) and enforcement action by regional agencies (Article 53 UN Charter) (see **7.3**).

The Principle of Respect for Human Rights

This principle occupies a privileged position in international law, as it is considered *jus cogens*, a fundamental principle of general customary international law that cannot be ignored or derogated from by any treaties or agreements. Respect for human rights implies that states must refrain from seriously and repeatedly infringing a basic right or rights (see **7.7**).

The Principle of Self-Determination of Peoples

The right to self-determination is recognised in Article 1 of the 1966 International Covenant on Civil and Political Rights, but it also has a long customary tradition. States must refrain from oppressing people under colonial domination, subjected to foreign military occupation and racial groups. This is a right *erga omnes* (of universal interest for the international community).

7.2.3 LEGAL PERSONALITY

The recognition of the legal personality of the UN has been the subject of discussion. The legal personality of an international organisation entails a series of rights, powers, duties and liabilities distinct from its creators and members (White N., *The UN System: Toward International Justice*, 2002, Lynne Rienner Publishers, 28).

Even though the notion of separate legal personality was not acknowledged upon its creation, the actions of the UN actions over the years have generated an increased recognition of its legal capacity, which can almost be compared to that of states. Evidence of this is found in the UN's competence to make and sign international treaties, the privileges and immunities enjoyed by UN personnel, and its ability to bring claims and to create peacekeeping forces. The International Court of Justice (ICJ) has confirmed the legal personality of the UN in numerous occasions, including its Advisory Opinion *Reparation for Injuries Suffered in the Service of the United Nations*, of 11 April 1949. In the '*Reparation*' case, concerning the reparation of damages caused by a State to UN personnel, the Court concluded:

> '...*The organisation has the capacity to bring an international claim against a State (whether a Member or non-member) for damage resulting from a breach by that State of its obligations towards the Organisation...*'

> '...*The UN possesses the international legal personality necessary for discharging its functions and duties on the international plane.*'

Most theorists agree that the legal capacity of the UN is strictly limited to those powers granted under its Charter. However, the Charter does not contain provisions that explicitly address the question of UN responsibility for unlawful acts of its organs and the judicial redress of their consequences (Janev, 'On the UN's legal responsibility for the irregular admission of Macedonia', Feb. 2003, *Macedonian News*, www.MakNews.com).

On the other hand, the legal effects of UN acts are not subjected to any effective judicial control, as the advisory opinions of the ICJ are not legally binding.

7.2.4   INTERNAL STRUCTURE

The United Nations has six principal organs: the General Assembly, the Security Council, the Secretariat, the Economic and Social Council, the Trusteeship Council and the International Court of Justice. As with states, the three powers (executive, legislative and judiciary) are distributed between these organs. Nevertheless, the separation of powers within the UN is imperfect, as explained in this section.

The General Assembly

The General Assembly is a universal deliberative body composed of representatives of all Member States, and the principal legislative organ of the United Nations. The Assembly meets in regular annual session starting each September, but it may also meet in special sessions at the request of the Security Council, of a majority of Member States, or of one Member if the majority of Member States concur. There is a 'one state–one vote' rule in the sessions, where a two-thirds majority is required for decisions on critical matters (peace and security, admission of new members, budget, etc) and a simple majority for decisions on other matters. The work of the Assembly is carried out by six specialised committees, dealing with different matters. They are:

First Committee – Disarmament and International Security

Second Committee – Economic and Financial

Third Committee – Social, Humanitarian and Cultural

Fourth Committee – Special Political and Decolonisation

Fifth Committee – Administrative and Budgetary

Sixth Committee – Legal.

Besides its legislative function, the General Assembly is considered a secondary executive body within the UN, as it is the organ that can convene an international conference to focus global attention on a specific matter. In addition, through its resolutions, the Assembly can initiate studies and make recommendations for military enforcement and can bring claims to the ICJ (Articles 10 to 15).

The Security Council

The Security Council is the primary executive organ of the UN. It has responsibility for the maintenance of international peace and security and has the power to take decisions, which Member States are required to carry out under the Charter.

The Council has five permanent members: China, France, the Russian Federation, the United Kingdom and the United States, and ten non-permanent members elected by the General Assembly for two-year terms and not eligible for immediate re-election. A representative of each of its members must be present at all times at the UN Headquarters, to ensure the continuous function of the Council. Each Council member has one vote. Decisions on procedural matters are made by an affirmative vote of at least nine of the fifteen members. Decisions on substantive matters require nine votes, including the concurring votes of all five permanent members. This is the rule of 'great power unanimity', often referred to as the veto power, though no such term is actually mentioned in the UN Charter. Although the voting system in the Council is seen at times as unrepresentative and as an obstacle to reaching agreement in some vital situations, there is the possibility that by opening the voting to other members, the Council may put at risk its key executive role. A state that is a member of the UN, but not of the Security Council, may participate, without a vote, in its discussions when the Council considers that country's interests are affected.

In dealing with a conflict situation, the Security Council may decide to adopt non-aggressive (non-armed) measures such as mediation by appointed representatives, ceasefire directives and peacekeeping forces in troubled areas. Alternatively, the Council may decide to impose economic sanctions or collective military action.

The Security Council has three basic mechanisms for expressing its opinions. The first is a press release which only has the effect of transmitting the work of the Council to the media. The second is a Presidential Statement, issued at the discretion of the current President, which expresses the President's opinion on a matter before the Council. The third and most powerful option is a Security Council resolution.

The resolutions of the Security Council, unlike those of the General Assembly, are binding upon all UN Member States. In accepting the Charter, all nations agree to accept and carry out Security Council decisions. A Member State who has persistently violated the principles of the Charter may be suspended or even expelled from the United Nations by the Assembly on the Council's recommendation.

The Council works through Standing Committees, of which there are currently three: Security Council Committee of Experts, Security Council Committee on Admission of New Members and Security Council Committee on Council Meetings Away from Headquarters. It also works through *ad hoc* committees which are established as needed and comprise all Council members.

In addition to peacekeeping operations (see **7.3.2**), the Security Council oversees the international *ad hoc* tribunals (see **7.10.3**).

The configuration of the UN permits the concentration of power in the Security Council. In most situations, due to the lack of control of the plenary organ (the Assembly), the Council can make crucial decisions without being held accountable.

The Secretariat

The Secretariat carries out the diverse day-to-day work of the organisation. It services the other principal organs of the UN and administers the programmes and policies laid down by them. It is composed of the Secretary-General and a group of international staff working in duty stations around the world. The Secretary-General is appointed by the General Assembly on the recommendation of the Security Council to a five-year renewable term and, by convention, rotates by geographic region. (Mr Ban Ki-moon from the Republic of Korea is the current Secretary-General and was elected in 2006.) Article 97 of the UN Charter describes this position as the 'chief administrative officer' of the organisation. Although the post was originally conceived as an administrative role, most Secretary-Generals have acted as mediators of disputes and have expressed their opinion on global issues. Secretariat staff are independent and do not seek or receive instructions from any authority other than the UN.

The functions of the Secretariat include: administering peacekeeping operations, mediating international disputes, surveying economic and social trends and problems. The role also involves preparing studies on human rights and sustainable development, communicating to the media about the work of the UN and organising international conferences on issues of worldwide concern. The Secretary-General may bring to the attention of the Security Council any matter that, in his or her opinion, may threaten international peace and security. Two key Secretariat offices are the Office of the Coordinator of Humanitarian Affairs and the Department of Peacekeeping Operations.

The Economic and Social Council

The Economic and Social Council (ECOSOC) (see **6.2.1**) was established by the UN Charter as the principal organ to assist the General Assembly in promoting international economic and social co-operation and development. It does so by co-ordinating the United Nations' specialised agencies, functional commissions and regional commissions and by receiving reports from the UN funds and programmes.

The ECOSOC has 54 member governments elected by the General Assembly for over-lapping three-year terms. Its president is elected for a one-year term. Each member of ECOSOC has one vote, and decisions are made by a majority of voting members present. ECOSOC meets once a year in July for a four-week session. Its Bureau (Bureau of the Economic and Social Council) proposes the agenda, draws up a programme of work and organises the session with the support of the UN Secretariat.

The ECOSOC serves as a forum for international economic and social issues, and for formulating policy recommendations addressed to Member States and the UN system. Some of its aims are: promoting higher standards of living, full employment and economic and social progress. ECOSOC also works in identifying solutions to international economic, social and health problems; facilitating international cultural and educational co-operation; and encouraging universal respect for human rights and fundamental freedoms.

Seventy per cent of the human and financial resources of the entire UN system are allocated to ECOSOC. In carrying out its mandate, ECOSOC consults with academics, business sector representatives and more than 2,100 registered non-governmental organisations (NGOs). At the 2000 Millennium Summit in New York, heads of state adopted the eight Millennium Development Goals (MDGs), to be reached by 2015. The Millennium Development Goals require the international community to:

(1) Eradicate extreme poverty and hunger

(2) Achieve universal primary education

(3) Promote gender equality and empower women

(4) Reduce child mortality

(5) Improve maternal health

(6) Combat HIV/AIDS, malaria and other diseases

(7) Ensure environmental sustainability

(8) Develop a global partnership for development.

The Trusteeship Council

The Trusteeship Council was established to supervise the administration of Trust Territories placed under the Trusteeship System (mandates of the League of Nations and territories from nations defeated in the Second World War). Its task was to help ensure that non-self-governing territories were administered in the best interests of the inhabitants and of international peace and security. The main goals of the system were to promote the advancement of the inhabitants of Trust Territories and their progressive development towards self-government or independence. Palau was the last of these territories to become a member of the UN in December 1994.

The aims of the Council have been fulfilled and its operation was suspended on 1 November 1994. The Council amended its rules of procedure to drop the obligation to meet annually and agreed to meet as the occasion required.

In relation to its future, in 1996, a report from the Commission on Global Governance recommended amending Chapters 12 and 13 of the UN Charter to give the Trusteeship Council authority over the global commons, which consists of oceans, the atmosphere, outer space and Antarctica. However, the former UN Secretary-General, Kofi Annan, proposed the complete elimination of the Trusteeship Council as part of the UN reforms.

The International Court of Justice

The International Court of Justice (ICJ) is the principal judicial organ of the UN. It began work in 1946, replacing the Permanent Court of International Justice. The Court sits in the Peace Palace in The Hague (Netherlands) and has a dual role: firstly, to settle legal disputes submitted to it by states (only states can be parties in contentious cases) and, secondly, to give advisory opinions on legal questions submitted to it by authorised international organs and agencies.

The ICJ's jurisdiction is based on consent and acceptance by the states concerned. In cases of doubt as to whether the ICJ has jurisdiction, it is the Court itself which decides. Article 91 of the UN Charter states that all UN members are automatically parties to the Statute of the International Court of Justice (ICJ Statute). The most frequent matters of dispute refer to territorial sovereignty and boundaries, diplomatic relations, asylum, nationality and non-interference in internal affairs. Concerning its second role, the ICJ delivers advisory opinions to international organisations, the five organs and the specialised agencies of the UN, to help in deciding complex legal issues. In principle, the ICJ's opinions are consultative and not binding. Since 1946, the ICJ has delivered 118 judgments and 25 advisory opinions.

The ICJ is composed of 15 permanent judges elected to nine-year terms by the UN General Assembly and the Security Council. Members of the Court are independent magistrates and do not represent their governments. There may be no more than one judge of any nationality and the composition is required to represent the main forms of civilisation and the principal legal systems of the world (Article 9 ICJ Statute). The ICJ sits as a full Court but, at the request of the parties, it may establish special or smaller chambers. *Ad hoc* judges may sit in contentious cases if requested by the parties. In its decisions, the ICJ applies international law, including international conventions, international custom and the general principles of law recognised by civilised nations (Article 38 ICJ Statute).

The statute of the ICJ contains a controversial issue in Article 94, which establishes the duty of all UN members to comply with decisions of the ICJ concerning them. The failure to do so will result in enforcement action by the Security Council. The controversy lies in that any resolution on enforcement will be vetoed if the judgment is against one of the permanent five members of the Security Council or its allies. This issue was patent in cases like *Nicaragua v United States of America ('Nicaragua Case')*, ICJ, 27 June 1986, in which the ICJ found against the United States for indirect use of force against Nicaragua (see **7.3**). However, the United States used its veto power in the Security Council to block a resolution enforcing the Court's decision.

Specialised Agencies and Programmes

Besides its six principal organs, most of the UN's work is carried out by 15 specialised agencies and several programmes, each devoted to a particular aspect of development. The specialised agencies are separate, independent intergovernmental organisations funded by Member States but they form part of the UN system. The specialised agencies operate in one or various countries through a partnership and their work is related to specific fields such as trade, education, health and agriculture. Their internal structure includes legislative and executive bodies responsible for the appointment of the agencies heads.

Two of these agencies are the two leading international financial institutions: the World Bank and the International Monetary Fund. The remaining agencies focus specifically on social and economic development and their work is directly guided by the Millennium Development Goals and include: FAO (Food and Agriculture Organisation of the UN), ILO (International Labour Organisation), UNESCO (United Nations Educational, Scientific and Cultural Organisation, WHO (World Health Organisation), UNHCR (United Nations High Commissioner for Refugees), etc.

7.3   Maintenance of International Peace and Security

The maintenance of international peace and security constitutes one of the main purposes of the UN, as stated in its Charter. This principle has acquired special relevance in recent years as a result of the new dimension of terrorism since 2001. The role of the UN has been crucial in confronting this and other security challenges through actions such as the disruption of the financing of terrorism, the creation of peacekeeping operations and its long fight to eliminate all weapons of mass destruction.

As recognised in Article 2.4 of the UN Charter and reiterated by the 1970 Declaration on Friendly Relations (*UN Declaration on Principles of International Law, Friendly Relations and Co-Operation among States in Accordance with the Charter of the United Nations, A/5217 (1970), 24 October 1970*):

> *'All members shall refrain in their international relations from the threat or use of force against the territorial integrity or political independence of any state, or in any other manner inconsistent with all the Purposes of the United Nations'.*

There is an ongoing debate on three issues related to the use of force. Firstly, what constitutes threat or use of force? Second, how to determine the international dimension of the use of force? And third, what constitutes self-defence?

What constitutes threat or use of force?

The armed invasion of one nation by another is commonly accepted as use of force and it is explicitly banned. However, other subtle acts could also be included in this category. The Declaration on Friendly Relations differentiates between direct and indirect threat or use of force. Direct use of force refers to an armed attack against the territorial integrity or political independence of a state, (for example, the invasion of Kuwait by Iraq in 1991). Indirect use of force refers to external assistance to insurgent or rebels, by ways of 'organising or encouraging the organisation of irregular forces or armed bands including mercenaries, for incursion into the territory of another State' or 'organising, instigating, assisting or participating in acts of civil strife or terrorist acts in another State'.

An illustration of this indirect use of force can be found in the *Nicaragua Case* where Nicaragua accused the United States of 'conceiving, creating and organising a mercenary army, the contra force' against the Nicaraguan Government. The United States' actions included the President authorising a US government agency to lay mines in Nicaraguan ports without issuing any official warning to international shipping. The ICJ decided that 'the United States in [... those acts of intervention ... which involve the use of force] had acted, against the Republic of Nicaragua, in breach of its obligation under customary international law not to use force against another State.' (Military and Paramilitary Activities in and against Nicaragua *(Nicaragua v United States of America* 1984 ICJ REP 392, 27 June, 1986).

How to determine the international dimension of the use of force?

Most current armed conflicts are internal and there is an imperative on UN members to refrain from interfering in the internal affairs of another state. However, intervention is sometimes justified by the impact that an internal conflict may have in the international sphere. The UN Charter provides for the prevention of inter-state conflict when this conflict has the potential of provoking an international armed conflict between states on a short-medium term. This was the case with the UN's intervention in the former Yugoslavia and in Rhodesia, where internal struggle could have affected other neighbouring nations.

In addition, most internal conflicts involve the violation of humanitarian laws including torture and racial discrimination, in violation of the Fourth Geneva Convention (Geneva Convention on the Protection of Civilian Persons in Time of War, 1949). This justification has also been used in support of intervention, as in the case of NATO's bombing of Serbia in March 1999. Justification for this act rested 'upon the accepted principle that force may be used in extreme circumstances to avert a humanitarian disaster'. However, this action was not authorised by the UN Security Council. One of the challenges facing the United Nations is the issue of the need for humanitarian intervention to avert or to stop mass killings, and of whether regional organisations can act to intervene in this way only with the authorisation of the UN (Thakur, 'The UN and Kosovo's Challenge of "Humanitarian Intervention" ', *International Studies Association (ISA)*, www.isanet.org/archive/kosovoandun.html).

What constitutes self-defence?

One of the exceptions to the prohibition of threat or use of force is self-defence. Self-defence is a right conferred on a state to employ force against another state's attack on its territory or political independence. Self-defence can be individual or collective, but it can only be exercised in response to an armed attack. However, the extensive definition of this concept can lead to abuse from states pursuing their own interests. It is complicated to balance the necessity to act in certain cases, as a pre-emptive measure, with the risk of abuse. In the past, the Security Council has needed flexibility in its actions, for example after the introduction of a massive armament program in Iran or following regional destabilisation in the former Yugoslavia (De Wet, *The Chapter VII Powers of the United Nations Security Council*, 2004, Hart, 140).

Once the threat to peace or use of force has been determined, the United Nations opens the procedure under Chapter VII of the Charter, which involves the following kinds of measures.

7.3.1 NON-ARMED MEASURES

Article 39 of the UN Charter establishes that as a first measure the Security Council *'shall make recommendations ... to maintain or restore international peace and security'*. Article 41 allows the Security Council to 'decide what measures not involving the use of armed force are to be employed to give effect to its decisions'. The UN's non-armed response to breaches of peace and security may be in a number of forms, each of which is set out below.

Non-recognition of an illegal situation that is contrary to certain basic values commonly accepted by the world community

Examples of non-recognition can be found in Resolution ES-10/15 (*On the Legal Consequences of the Construction of a Wall in the Occupied Palestinian Territory, including in and around East Jerusalem*, ICJ, 2 August 2004) where the General Assembly, following the ICJ Advisory Opinion, did not recognise the legality of the construction by Israel of a wall in the occupied Palestinian territory and in Security Council Resolution 541(1983) (Resolution 541, *On Cyprus*, 18 November 1983) that considered the 'attempt to create the Turkish Republic of Northern Cyprus invalid and called for Turkey's withdrawal'.

Condemnation by the Security Council of serious violations of international law

Security Council Resolution S/RES/9679/09 condemned 'in the strongest terms the nuclear test conducted by the Democratic People's Republic of Korea [25 May 2009] in flagrant disregard of its relevant resolutions'. It also demanded 'that the DPRK [shall] not conduct any further nuclear tests and shall suspend all activities related to its ballistic missile programme'.

Public exposure by the General Assembly of gross violations of International principles

In Resolution A/RES/63/191, of 24 February 2009, the General Assembly referred to the human rights situation in the Islamic Republic of Iran expressing 'its deep concern at serious human rights violations' including torture, other inhuman treatment, arrests and violent repression.

Imposition of sanctions

Article 41 of the UN Charter states:

> '... These may include complete or partial interruption of economic relations and of rail, sea, air, postal, telegraphic, radio, and other means of communication, and the severance of diplomatic relations.'

Security Council Resolution S/RES/0661(1990) (*Concerning the Situation between Iraq and Kuwait*, 6 August 1990) imposed economic sanctions on Iraq, including a full trade embargo barring all imports from and exports to Iraq, excepting only medical supplies, foodstuffs, and other items of humanitarian need.

Establishment of International Criminal Tribunals

The Security Council created the ICTY (International Criminal Tribunal for the former Yugoslavia) in 1993 and the ICTR (International Criminal Tribunal for Rwanda) in 1994 and the Special Tribunal for Lebanon in 2006 (see **7.10.3**).

7.3.2   UN PEACEKEEPING OPERATIONS

Peacekeeping operations constitute one of the more visible aspects of UN intervention in international conflicts. Even though the UN Charter does not contain specific provisions on these operations, these can be authorised by the Security Council in exercise of its power and responsibility to order collective action for the maintenance of international peace and security.

Peacekeeping was initially developed during the Cold War era as a means to ease tensions and help resolve conflicts between states by observing the ceasefires or separation of forces. Over the years, peacekeeping has developed to involve more non-military elements to ensure sustainability (UN Department of Peacekeeping Operations, www.un.org/Depts/dpko).

Since its creation in 1945, the UN has accomplished 63 field missions in more than 45 countries. State contribution to these missions is voluntary; 123 countries have provided more than 750,000 military and civilian personnel since 1948. The objectives of peacekeeping missions may vary depending on the conflict, but general peacekeeping duties include rebuilding domestic institutions, mine clearance, assisting in political processes, reforming justice systems, training of law-enforcement and police forces, disarming former combatants and eradicating sexual exploitation and abuse.

There are three kinds of operations that can be identified under the peacekeeping umbrella:

- **Peacemaking**—To bring hostile parties to agreement through diplomatic means. The Secretary-General plays an important role in bringing the situation to the attention of the Security Council and in initiating preventive diplomacy. Peacemaking can be done through negotiation, mediation, conciliation and arbitration, as well as through international courts provided by International law. An example of this action is the Agreement of Good Will and Confidence Building for the Settlement of the Problem in Darfur, signed on 17 February 2009 by the Government of National Unity of the Republic of Sudan (GNU) and the Justice and Equality Movement of the Sudan (JEM) under the UN auspices.

- **Peace-building**—To help countries rebuild administrative, health, educational and other services. Assignments include supervising elections and supporting human rights in countries struggling to deal with the aftermath of conflict. An example of this is the UN's supervised elections in Zimbabwe on 29 March 2008.

- **Peacekeeping**—To maintain peace and international security and it involves military duties, such as observing a ceasefire and establishing a buffer zone, and civilian duties, such as organising elections and monitoring human rights. This action was taken to monitor the ceasefire between Ethiopia and Eritrea (UNMEE).

At present there are 17 UN peacekeeping missions around the world, including: UNMIK (UN Interim Administration Mission in Kosovo), UNMISET (UN Mission of Support in East Timor) and MINUSTAH (UN Mission in Haiti).

7.3.3   ARMED MEASURES UNDER CHAPTER VII

Article 42 of the UN Charter authorises the Security Council to take *'action by air, sea, or land forces as may be necessary to maintain or restore international peace and security'* when measures provided for in Article 41 have proven inadequate. Even though armed measures are usually collective, individual action can also be permitted in certain cases. The Security Council, assisted by the Military Staff Committee, decides on the application of such measures.

Armed measures have been resorted to in a number of different scenarios:

Authorisation of the Security Council after acts of aggression by a state

In 1950, Security Council Resolution 83 (S/1511 (1950) *Complaint of Aggression upon the Republic of Korea*, 27 June 1950) authorised an armed attack to assist the Republic of Korea in defending itself against an armed attack by the forces of North Korea. Equally, in 1990, Security Council Resolution S/RES/678 (*Concerning the Situation between Iraq and Kuwait*, 29 November 1990) authorised Member States to use 'all necessary means to uphold and implement Security Council Resolution S/RES/660 (*Condemning the Invasion of Kuwait by Iraq'*, 2 August 1990).

Authorisation of state in case of threats to peace, such as humanitarian crises, in order to secure the environment for humanitarian relief operations

This was the case of humanitarian crises in Bosnia (1995), Rwanda (1994), Somalia (1993) and Haiti (2004).

Putting into effect economic sanctions imposed by the Security Council

Security Council resolutions S/RES/1737/06, S/RES/1747/07 and S/RES/1803/08 established economic sanctions against the Islamic Republic of Iran including an embargo on nuclear and ballistic equipment, an export ban on arms and individual targets sanctions (freezing assets of designated persons or entities).

Measures taken by regional or other organisations upon authorisation of the Security Council

An example of such actions include the EU intervention in Congo in 2003, in response to the UN request for support. The EU deployed a military force (EUFOR) working in close co-operation with the United Nations Organisation Mission in the Democratic Republic of the Congo (MONUC).

Individual Self-Defence

As described above, self-defence is permitted as a reaction to an armed attack. The right to self-defence allows for a response to an aggression from a state or from individuals (eg terrorists); it can also be used against indirect aggression or infiltration; and it can include the forcible protection of nationals abroad. But this right is also limited by respect of the principles of necessity and proportionality; the requirement to minimise harm to civilians; and the obligation to be ceased as soon as its purpose has been achieved (Cassese, *International Law*, 2nd edn, 2005, OUP, 355).

7.4   International Law

While states do not recognise a legislative power for the UN to pass legally binding norms of international law, Article 13 of the UN Charter confers the General Assembly the power to

> '... *initiate studies and make recommendations for the purpose of: a) promoting international co-operation in the political field and encouraging the progressive development of international law and its codification'.*

In 1946, through Resolution 94 (General Assembly 94(I) on *Progressive Development of International Law and its Codification*, 11 December 1946) the General Assembly established a Committee on the Progressive Development of International Law and its Codification, to assist with this responsibility conferred by the Charter. Following the Committee's recommendation in 1948, General Assembly Resolution 174 (General Assembly Resolution 174(II) on the *Establishment of an International Law Commission*, 21 November 1947) created the International Law Commission (ILC), whose task is the progressive development and codification of international law, in accordance with Article 13(1)(a) of the Charter of the United Nations. The International Law Commission is made up of 34 members, elected for a five-year period, and holds its annual session in Geneva, Switzerland. The Commission's achievements include the Nuremberg Principles (1950) on international criminal law and the draft Code of Crimes against the Peace and Security of Mankind (1996).

Also in 1946, the Office of Legal Affairs was created in order to provide legal advice to the Secretary-General and to act on his behalf in legal matters. The UN Office of Legal Affairs provides a unified central legal service for the Secretariat and the principal and other UN organs and contributes to the progressive development and codification of international public and trade law.

The Office is composed of six departments: Office of the Legal Counsel (OLC), General Legal Division (GLD), Codification Division (COD), Division for Ocean Affairs and the Law of the Sea (DOALOS), International Trade Law Division (ITLD) and Treaty Section (TREATY).

7.4.1   INTERNATIONAL TREATIES

'Treaty' is the term frequently used to refer to legally binding international instruments, concluded between states. There are however, multiple denominations for these instruments, such as Convention, Declaration, Protocol and Covenant, even though they all have similar legal status. The provisions contained in an international treaty frequently originate from the common practice in international relations between states, and are accepted as binding in international customary law.

The 1969 Vienna Convention on the Law of Treaties, which entered into force on 27 January 1980, contains rules for treaties concluded between states. The Convention defines the general steps for the adoption and entering to force of an international treaty. These steps include:

Adoption: Expression of the consent of the states participating in the treaty-making process.

Acceptance or approval: Expression of the consent of a state to be bound by a treaty when, at a national level, constitutional law does not require the treaty to be ratified by the head of state.

Ratification: Act whereby a state indicates its consent to be bound to a treaty if the parties intended to show their consent by such an act. In the case of multilateral treaties the usual procedure is for the depositary to collect the ratifications of all states, keeping all parties informed of the situation.

Accession: Act whereby a state accepts the offer or the opportunity to become a party to a treaty already negotiated and signed by other states. It has the same legal effect as ratification. Accession usually occurs after the treaty has entered into force.

Amendment: Formal alteration of treaty provisions affecting all the parties to the particular agreement.

Authentication: Procedure whereby the text of a treaty is established as authentic and definitive. Once a treaty has been authenticated, states cannot unilaterally change its provisions.

Declaration: Expression of the state's understanding of some matter or as to the interpretation of a particular provision. They merely clarify the state's position and do not purport to exclude or modify the legal effect of a treaty.

Reservation: Declaration made by a state by which it purports to exclude or alter the legal effect of certain provisions of the treaty in their application to that state.

Article 102 of the UN Charter states:

'Every treaty and every international agreement entered into by any Member of the United Nations after the present Charter comes into force shall as soon as possible be registered with the Secretariat

and published by it. Therefore registration, not publication, is the prerequisite for a treaty to be capable of being invoked before the International Court of Justice or any other UN organ'.

At present, the Secretary-General is the depositary for over 500 multilateral treaties.

In relation to the entry in force of a treaty, normally the provisions of the treaty determine the date on which the treaty enters into force. Where the treaty does not specify a date, there is a presumption that the treaty is intended to come into force as soon as all the negotiating states have consented to be bound by the treaty.

In 1986 another Convention was adopted, the Vienna Convention on the Law of Treaties between States and International Organisations or between International Organisations, which added rules for treaties with international organisations as parties. This Convention has not yet entered into force.

7.5 Support for Self-Determination and Democracy

7.5.1 SELF-DETERMINATION

The United Nations aims *'to develop friendly relations among nations based on respect for the principle of equal rights and self-determination of peoples . . .'* (Article 1.2 UN Charter)

The right to self-determination of peoples originated in the decolonisation period following the Second World War and has been recognised in several UN instruments, including the International Covenant of Civil and Political Rights (1966), which ascertains that all peoples have the right of self-determination and that states parties shall promote and respect the realisation of this right.

This right has also been the subject of numerous resolutions (eg General Assembly Resolution A/RES/51/84 *Universal Realisation of the Right of Peoples to Self-Determination* 28 February 1997) and of decisions from the International Court of Justice. In the Case Concerning East Timor (*Portugal v Australia*) of 30 June 1995, the ICJ refused to rule on the validity of the Timor Gap Treaty between Australia and Indonesia due to the absence of Indonesia as a third party by not consenting to the jurisdiction of the Court. However, the Court stated: 'The Court recalls in any event that it has taken note in the present judgment that, for the two parties, the Territory of East Timor remains a non-self-governing territory and its people have the right to self-determination.'

Many have catalogued this case as an example of 'external self-determination', which recognises that people subject to colonisation or foreign occupation have the right to govern their own affairs free from outside interference.

The principle of self-determination of peoples guarantees respect for the wishes and aspirations of peoples and nations by binding states to accept and support it. Cassese writes that self-determination 'appears firmly entrenched in the corpus of international law in only three areas: as an anti-colonialist standard, as a ban on foreign military occupation and as a requirement that all racial groups be given access to government' (Cassese, *International Law*, 2nd edn, 2005, OUP, 63). While in the first two cases the principle has been acknowledged and enforced, the third scenario presents more difficulties. This right is not always recognised in ethnic, national, religious or cultural groups, even though the UN *'shall promote universal respect for, and observance of, human rights and fundamental freedoms for all without distinction as to race, sex, language, or religion'* (Article 55 UN Charter).

In some situations, the concept of self-determination clashes with the concept of territorial integrity. The latter prevails in practice, understanding by 'people entitled to self-determination' those persons living in a particular geographic area within a state, rather than persons sharing a common culture or language.

7.5.2 DEMOCRACY

This principle is not explicitly recognised in any UN instruments and the UN Charter does not require states to be democratic in order to be a member. However, the support for democracy arises from UN recognition of human rights, in particular from the right to self-determination of peoples, and it is implicit in many norms of international law. White identifies the relation between democracy and self-determination by stating that the internal aspect of self-determination may require that governments generally have a democratic base, and that minorities be allowed political autonomy (White, *The UN System: Toward International Justice*, 2002, Lynne Rienner Publishers, 176).

It is established in Article 25 ICCPR that every citizen shall have the right to take part in the conduct of public affairs, to vote and to be elected at genuine periodic elections and to have access to public service in his country.

The UN has endorsed the concept of democracy through different actions orientated particularly around supporting emerging democracies with technical, legal and financial assistance and advice. Some of these activities include: electoral assistance (eg Afghanistan, Palestine and Burundi, formation of the Independent Electoral Commission of Iraq (IECI)), democratic governance (eg Iraq, guiding the process of drafting its first constitution); rule of law (eg East Timor, strengthening its judicial, human rights and police capacities, upon completion of peacekeeping missions); and anti-corruption (eg UN Office on Drugs and Crime in Nigeria and Kenya).

In addition, the General Assembly adopted in 2003 Resolution 58/13 (General Assembly Resolution A/RES/58/13 *Support by the United Nations System of the Efforts of Governments to Promote and Consolidate New or Restored Democracies*, 24 November 2003). This resolution gave confidence to the Secretary-General to keep improving the capacity of the organisation and to strengthen the support to consolidate democracy and good governance. Following this resolution, on 4 July 2005, the then UN Secretary-General Kofi Annan announced the establishment of a UN Democracy Fund, to promote and consolidate new and restored democracies.

7.6 Development

Article 1 of the 1986 UN Declaration on the Right of Development states:

> 'The right to development is an inalienable human right by virtue of which every human person and all peoples are entitled to participate in, contribute to, and enjoy economic, social, cultural and political development, in which all human rights and fundamental freedoms can be fully realized.'

This right is also recognised in the two International Covenants of 1966, the Universal Declaration on Human Rights and the UN Charter: '*The Purposes of the United Nations are . . . To achieve international co-operation in solving international problems of an economic, social, cultural or humanitarian character . . .*' (Article 1.3 UN Charter).

The existence of poverty has been linked to the failure of governments to fulfil their legal human rights obligations (Sengupta, *A Rights-Based Approach to Removing Poverty*, 2006, World Bank Institute). Poverty eradication as an element of respect for human rights has acquired more relevance in international development and programming conducted by the United Nations. A recent example of the importance of this right is the *Common Understanding on a Human Rights-Based Approach to Development Cooperation* issued by UN agencies in May 2003 and incorporated by the UN Development Group (UNDG) into operational guidelines for UN country teams (Ingram and Freestone, *Human Rights and Development*, 2006, World Bank Institute). The intention of this instrument is that all programmes of development co-operation, policies and technical assistance advance the realisation of human rights as dictated by the Universal Declaration of Human Rights and other international human rights instruments.

Many UN institutions and specialised agencies are involved in development and economic welfare. The biggest and more powerful institutions are the so-called Bretton Woods Institutions (the IMF and the World Bank Group), created in 1944. The Bretton Woods Agreements established a set of rules, institutions and procedures to regulate the international monetary system. The IMF and the World Bank were not UN specialised agencies, but entered the UN system by agreement under Article 63 of the UN Charter. Even though they work under the UN system, they have greater autonomy than the other specialised agencies and do not have an obligation to report to ECOSOC (White, *The UN System: Toward International Justice*, 2002, Lynne Rienner Publishers, 267).

The International Monetary Fund (IMF)

The IMF is an international organisation established to promote international monetary co-operation, exchange stability and orderly exchange arrangements; to foster economic growth and high levels of employment; and to provide temporary financial assistance to countries to help ease balance-of-payments adjustment. It operates in three ways: observing exchange rates, observing balance of payments and providing financial and technical assistance. It is composed of 184 members and has its headquarters in Washington DC.

Countries in financial difficulties may request loans in exchange for certain national reforms. The IMF can also create legally binding monetary rules, such as 'conditionalities' (conditions attached to a loan or to debt relief) on structural adjustments that impose changes in the economic policy of developing countries to promote economic growth. These changes may include for example privatisation and reduction of trade barriers.

The World Bank Group

The World Bank Group was created to provide financial and technical assistance to developing countries around the world. It has 124 members and it is composed of five agencies:

> International Bank for Reconstruction and Development (IBRD)
>
> International Finance Corporation (IFC)
>
> International Development Association (IDA)
>
> Multilateral Investment Guarantee Agency (MIGA)
>
> International Centre for Settlement of Investment Disputes (ICSID)

The World Bank acts in the fields of human development, agriculture and rural development, environmental protection, infrastructure and governance. Therefore it has an impact on human rights (eg education, health, work, housing etc). Over the last two decades, the World Bank has been transforming into a development agency.

Both the IMF and the World Bank have experienced an increased criticism from various sectors, especially in relation to their marked political influence and the primacy of macroeconomics over welfare issues. In response to this, both agencies seem to be moving towards a more participatory approach and transparency in decision-making.

Other agencies

The UN has established other agencies and programs dedicated to development, including UNCTAD (UN Conference on Trade and Development), UNIDO (UN Industrial Development Organisation) and WFP (World Food Programme).

In addition, the Commission on Human Rights established in 1998 a Working Group on the Right to Development, to monitor and review progress made in the promotion and implementation of the right to development. In 2004, the Commission created the High-Level Task Force on the Right of Development, to provide the necessary expertise to the Working Group to enable it to make appropriate recommendations to the various actors on the issues identified for the implementation of the right to development.

7.7   Human Rights Protection

The protection and promotion of human rights is a core principle of the UN that influences the work of each UN body and specialised agency. The proclamation of human rights as norms of *jus cogens* (norms of general customary international law that cannot be ignored or derogated by any treaties or agreements) was established after the atrocities of the Second World War, when both victors and other nations and institutions demanded the advancement of international criminal law in order to bring war criminals to justice. They also supported the proclamation of certain basic standards of respect for human rights to avoid future violence between and within states ' . . . to save succeeding generations from the scourge of war . . . ' (UN Charter).

The recognition and protection of human rights was therefore one of the pillars upon which the UN was founded in 1945. The preamble to the UN Charter pronounces the goal of the organisation is: ' . . . *to reaffirm faith in fundamental human rights, in the dignity and worth of the human person, in the equal rights of men and women and of nations large and small* . . . '. In 1948 the Universal Declaration of Human Rights (see **6.2.2**) listed a number of basic human rights and fundamental freedoms, establishing:

> ' . . . *every individual and every organ of society* . . . *shall strive by teaching and education to promote respect for these rights and freedoms and by progressive measures* . . . , *to secure their universal and effective recognition and observance, both among the peoples of Member States themselves and among the peoples of territories under their jurisdiction.' (Preamble, Universal Declaration of Human Rights.)*

Over the years, human rights protection has evolved and developed to a great extent, particularly since the end of the Cold War. Today, 'human rights conditions have become recognised as core indicators of the maintenance of international peace and security' (Mertus, *The United Nations and Human Rights*, 2005, Routledge, 46). The intention is to project domestic bills of rights on to the international stage. 'States are to respect human rights obligations not only on their own territory but also abroad, whether the individuals subject to this authority or power have the state's nationality or are foreigners' (Cassese, *International Law*, 2nd edn, 2005, OUP, 386).

Through the establishment of specialised bodies and mechanisms, the UN works to promote and protect human rights and to assist governments in carrying out their responsibilities. One of its achievements is the creation of a comprehensive body of human rights law.

7.7.1   INTERNATIONAL HUMAN RIGHTS INSTRUMENTS

Beyond the UN Charter, which provides the basis of international human rights regulation, the main international instrument regarding human rights is the Universal Declaration of Human Rights. The Declaration, adopted in 1948, sets out basic rights and freedoms to which all women and men are entitled. It is not legally binding on states, but constitutes a recommendation with a moral impact. Structured in 30 Articles, it appears to give more significance to civil and political rights (such as the right to life, the right to liberty and security and the right to equality) over economic, social and cultural rights (such as the right to work, the right to an adequate standard of living and the right to education). Perhaps it is more difficult to address the violation of economic, social and cultural rights because of their diffuse nature and their general or communal character (Mertus, *The United Nations and Human Rights*, 2005, Routledge, 5).

In 1966 two international instruments were adopted: the International Covenant on Civil and Political Rights (ICCPR) (see **6.2.3**) and the International Covenant on Economic, Social and Cultural Rights (ICESCR) (see **6.2.4.1**). Both Covenants entered in force in 1976 and are legally binding for states parties. The ICCPR contains a list of 'first-generation human rights', dealing essentially with liberty, participation in political life and the protection of the individual from any state abuse. The ICESCR refers to 'second-generation human rights' related to equality on living conditions and treatment. Since the adoption of universal human rights instruments (the Universal Declaration on Human Rights, ICCPR and ICESCR), the UN has increasingly developed specific human rights laws related to the protection of women, children, disabled persons, migrant workers and other vulnerable groups. International treaties possess an extraordinary value as they set standards for state conduct, encouraging governments to implement internal legislation to meet the obligations set up in the treaties. Treaties have also an educational value for the population.

- Together with the two International Covenants, other key international treaties on human rights are: Convention on the Prevention and Punishment of the Crime of Genocide. New York, 9 December 1948

- International Convention on the Elimination of All Forms of Racial Discrimination. New York, 7 March 1966

- Convention on the Elimination of All Forms of Discrimination against Women. New York, 18 December 1979

- Convention against Torture and other Cruel, Inhuman or Degrading Treatment or Punishment. New York, 10 December 1984

- Convention on the Rights of the Child. New York, 20 November 1989

- International Convention on the Protection of the Rights of All Migrant Workers and Members of their Families. New York, 18 December 1990

- Convention on the Rights of Persons with Disabilities, 2006

- International Convention for the Protection of All Persons from Enforced Disappearance, 2006 (not yet in force)

7.7.2   INTERNATIONAL HUMAN RIGHTS PROTECTION: MONITORING BODIES

Subsequent to the recognition of standard human rights, the UN established specialised bodies to monitor and enforce those rights in different areas. Some of these bodies are established by the UN Charter and have a more general role, while other bodies are created by international treaties that focus on specific areas of concern.

7.7.2.1   Charter-based bodies (non-treaty bodies)

These monitoring bodies have not been established by specific human rights treaties, but rather by the UN system; they are Charter-based bodies. The UN Charter assigns responsibility on human rights to:

The General Assembly, with power to initiate studies and make recommendations. Even though its recommendations are not legally binding for states, they have a strong moral and political power and they can become customary law over the years. The General Assembly also monitors the work of all treaty bodies.

The Economic and Social Council (ECOSOC) can also make recommendations and set up commissions for the promotion of human rights. Through this function, The ECOSOC established the UN Commission on Human Rights (now Human Rights Council), the Commission on the Status of Women and the Sub-Commission on the Promotion and Protection of Human Rights (1947).

The Human Rights Council (ex Human Rights Commission), an intergovernmental body whose function it is to examine, monitor and publicly report either on human rights situations in specific countries or territories (country mechanisms or mandates) or on major phenomena of human rights violations worldwide (thematic mechanisms or mandates). The Council has the power to examine gross violations of human rights that come to its attention, as well as to process individual complaints *(ECOSOC Resolution 1503 (XLVIII) Procedure for Dealing with Communications relating to Violations of Human Rights and Fundamental Freedoms, 27 May 1970) and 1235 (ECOSOC Resolution 1235 (XLII) of 6 June 1967).* The monitoring process can be carried out through country-specific *Rapporteurs* (whose task is to report on the full range of human rights in the specific country) or through the thematic mechanism (where the focus is on a specific area of human rights, without necessarily identifying one particular country). In any case, these field missions are only undertaken at the invitation of a government (see **6.2.1.2**).

In addition, there are special procedures dealing directly with governments on specific allegations of violations of human rights that have already occurred, are ongoing or have a high risk of occurring.

The Office of the High Commissioner on Human Rights (OHCRH)

The Office of the High Commissioner on Human Rights (OHCRH), established in 1993 with the aim to protect and promote human rights. It does so by providing technical assistance, creating country offices, carrying out field operations and by monitoring National human rights institutions.

The role of the non-governmental organisations (NGOs)

ECOSOC Resolution 1503 allows information from non-governmental sources to be taken into consideration at Council sessions. NGOs offer their expertise in different areas of human rights, resulting from their work and research on the field.

There are currently 3051 NGOs in consultative status with the ECOSOC. They participate at different levels, depending on their size, background and field of activity. The work and input of human rights NGOs have increased in recent years (see **6.2.3.1**).

The Commission on the Status of Women

The Commission on the Status of Women was established by ECOSOC in 1946. Its main objective is to promote implementation of the principle that men and women shall have equal rights. It is composed of 45 members and it meets once a year. Its function is to prepare recommendations and reports to the Council on promoting women's rights in political, economic, civil, social and educational fields.

The International Court of Justice

'The International Court of Justice may...address human rights issues by interpreting conventions incumbent upon states or by evaluating state conduct implicating human rights concerns' (Mertus, *The United Nations and Human Rights*, 2005, Routledge, 51) (see **6.2.4.7**).

7.7.2.2   Other non-treaty bodies

United Nations High Commissioner for Refugees (UNHCR)

The UNHCR was established by the General Assembly in 1950. The agency is mandated to *'lead and co-ordinate international action to protect refugees and resolve refugee problems worldwide. Its primary purpose is to safeguard the rights and well being of refugees'* (www.unhcr.org). The term 'refugee' includes people displaced as a consequence of a war, conflict or natural disaster.

The UNHCR is a humanitarian not a political organisation, which pursues two objectives: to protect refugees and to seek ways to help them restart their lives in a normal environment. The UNHCR promotes international refugee agreements and monitors government compliance with international refugee law. It also focuses on trying to prevent humanitarian crises by anticipating large population movements from regions worldwide. Such humanitarian initiatives are helpful but nevertheless governments and international political bodies must ultimately make political decisions to solve refugee and other human displacement problems (see **chapter 15**).

United Nations Children's Fund (UNICEF)

UNICEF was created in 1946 to bring humanitarian aid to European children affected by the disasters of the Second World War. At present the Fund aims to 'advocate for the protection of children's rights, to help meet their basic needs and to expand their opportunities to reach their full potential'. Its activities focus on nurturing and caring for children, promoting girls' education, immunising children against common childhood diseases, preventing the spread of HIV/AIDS and creating protective environments for children.

In 1989 the UN adopted the Convention on the Rights of the Child that guides the work of UNICEF by recognising children's rights as enduring ethical principles and international standards of behaviour towards children.

United Nations Development Program (UNDP)

The UNDP is the 'UN's global development network, an organisation advocating for change and connecting countries to knowledge, experience and resources to help people build a better life'. It also helps developing countries attract and use aid effectively. Poverty reduction is currently the principal objective of the UNDP. The UNDP has offices in many countries, where the head person acts as the Resident Co-ordinator of development activities for the UN system as a whole.

7.7.2.3   Treaty bodies

Treaty bodies are committees of independent experts that monitor implementation of the core international human rights treaties. They are created in accordance with the

144

provisions of the treaty that they monitor. There are eight treaty bodies correlated to seven international human rights treaties:

Body	Treaty/Date entered into force
Human Rights Committee	International Covenant on Civil and Political Rights (ICCPR), 1976
Committee on Economic, Social and Cultural Rights	International Covenant on Economic, Social and Cultural Rights (ICESCR), 1976
Committee on the Elimination of Racial Discrimination	Convention on the Elimination of All Forms of Racial Discrimination (CERD), 1969
Committee on the Elimination of Discrimination against Women	Convention on the Elimination of Discrimination Against Women (CEDAW), 1981
Committee against Torture	Convention against Torture and Other Cruel, Inhuman or Degrading Treatment or Punishment (CAT), 1987
Committee on the Rights of the Child	Convention on the Rights of the Child (CRC), 1990
Committee on the Rights of All Migrant Workers and Members of their Families	International Convention on the Protection of the Rights of All Migrant Workers and Members of their Families, 1993
Committee on the Rights of Persons with Disabilities	Convention on the Rights of Persons with Disabilities, 2006

Treaty bodies monitor the compliance of human rights standards through two mechanisms: state reporting (by submission of periodic reports on the implementation of each treaty) and individual complaints (or inter-state communications) (from a state party concerning the violation of a treaty by another state party). NGOs and national human rights institutions should also be involved in monitoring compliance (see **chapter 6**).

7.8 Ireland's Involvement in the United Nations

Ireland's involvement in and contribution to the UN has been remarkable from the outset. In the 1930s the Irish government, led by Eamonn De Valera, was actively involved with the League of Nations. De Valera not only attended meetings as Minister for External Affairs, he was also elected president of the Council of the League of Nations in 1932 and president of the Assembly of the League in 1938, as recognition of his independent stance on international issues.

Prior to joining the UN, Ireland was already a member of some specialised agencies, such as the International Labour Organisation (ILO), the International Civil Aviation Organisation and the Food and Agriculture Organisation (FAO). It participated in the Marshall Plan and joined the Organisation for Economic European Co-operation (Geiger, 'A Belated

Discovery of Internationalism? Ireland, the United Nations and the Reconstruction of Western Europe', in Kennedy and McMahon (eds), *Obligations and Responsibilities: Ireland and the United Nations, 1955–2005*, 2005, Institute of Public Administration, 31).

Ireland, like other nations that were neutral during the Second World War, was excluded from attending the San Francisco Conference, which gave birth to the UN. However, the Irish state saw the organisation as a key forum for international issues and really wished to become a member of it.

Although many countries appreciated Ireland's contribution to the British economy during the war, its application for membership of the UN was rejected on four occasions (July 1946, December 1946, July 1947 and September 1949). The veto to Ireland came mostly from the Soviet Union, in response to Western powers that refused to accept the Soviet satellite countries such as Albania and Outer Mongolia as members (McMahon, 'Our Mendicant Vigil Is Over: Ireland and the United Nations, 1946–55', in Kennedy and McMahon (eds), *Obligations and Responsibilities: Ireland and the United Nations, 1955–2005*, 2005, Institute of Public Administration, 13).

Ireland was finally accepted on 16 December 1955 when Seán McBride was Minister of Foreign Affairs. Since then, Ireland has sought to play an active role in all UN activities and programmes. In fact, its position and input within the organisation has been notable, particularly in the fields of peace and security, human rights, development, decolonisation and setting up a common dialogue.

As expressed in the government's White Paper on foreign policy: 'It is precisely because Ireland is small and hugely dependent on external trade for its well-being that we need an active foreign policy.' (DFA, 1996 *White Paper on Foreign Policy: 'Challenges And Opportunities Abroad'*, para 2.37.)

In 1973, Ireland's admission into the then European Economic Community (EEC) introduced a new set of priorities for the country, as the Irish government had to contemplate the Community's position before making any decisions on international issues. In those years, Irish foreign policy was trending in emphasis from the UN system towards the EEC system. But, as E. Connolly and J. Doyle note, 'Even with an increased emphasis on EU integration, the UN has retained a central place in Irish foreign policy. . . . [there is] . . . support for the organisation as a source of international legitimacy and as the appropriate forum to make major decisions regarding peace and security, international human rights and development.' (Connolly and Doyle, 'The Place of the United Nations in Contemporary Irish Foreign Policy', in Kennedy and McMahon (eds), *Obligations and Responsibilities: Ireland and the United Nations, 1955–2005*, 2005, Institute of Public Administration, 362.)

7.8.1   IRISH DIPLOMACY WITHIN THE UNITED NATIONS

Ireland's independence and neutrality in many issues has translated into the enjoyment of a privileged position within the UN. This is evidenced by the fact that despite being a small country, Ireland has been considered a middle power and it has played a constructive role balancing the powers and influencing important decisions during its first two decades in the organisation. However, with the increase of newly independent states becoming members of the UN, that balance of power seemed to change over the years and the role of small states like Ireland is not as central as it used to be.

Ireland has been elected as one of the ten non-permanent members of the Security Council on three occasions: in 1962, from 1981 to 1982 and from 2001 to 2002. This last term was particularly relevant as the international atmosphere was much more hostile and insecure, following the September 11 attacks. These membership terms in the Security

Council have allowed Ireland to play a part in the analysis of conflictive international issues, while at the same time reviewing its own foreign policy.

The Cold War

During the years of the Cold War, Ireland adopted a close stance to the United States' policies, based on historical links between both countries and on the influence that the United States had in Irish economy. This was made evident when the Irish delegation to the UN did not address issues such as US intervention in the Vietnam War but it did condemn the Soviet invasion of Czechoslovakia. However, it must be noted that the obvious support for US policies generated in the Cold War has not been constant and Ireland's posture on human rights and development has opposed the United States' interests on numerous occasions. Examples of this are the Irish effort to end the arms embargo on Ethiopia and Eritrea in 2001 and Ireland's disagreement with Security Council Resolution S/RES/1422 (12 July 2002) on *United Nations Peacekeeping*, exempting US citizens from the International Criminal Court's mandate (see **7.11**). During the Cold War Ireland stayed neutral from either of the two blocs and instead supported multilateral diplomacy and development of newly independent states.

The Israel-Palestine conflict

Ireland has been very involved in UN efforts to peace and stability in the Middle East (Miller, 'Ireland and the Middle East at the United Nations, 1955–2005', in Kennedy and McMahon (eds), *Obligations and Responsibilities: Ireland and the United Nations, 1955–2005*, 2005, Institute of Public Administration, 54).

With regard to this conflict, Ireland has maintained a neutral position, recognising the rights and obligations of both parties and avoiding highly political decisions that could be interpreted as taking stance for one party.

Ireland recognised the State of Israel in 1963 and has maintained good diplomatic relations with her. However, the Irish government is strongly concerned by the situation of Palestinian refugees in the occupied territories and has advocated the recognition of a Palestinian state.

In general, the main points on Irish vision of the conflict are:

• Recognition of Israel's right to security within recognised borders and to self-defence in accordance to humanitarian law

• Support for the rights of Palestinian people

• Condemnation of terrorism and violence (including Palestinian violence and Israel's excessive response to it).

In 1967 Ireland supported Security Council Resolution 242 claiming '*land for peace*' and in 2001 it also supported a draft resolution by Arab states for the same purpose.

In terms of humanitarian aid in this geographical area, Ireland participated in the UN missions UNOGIL (UN Observation Group in Lebanon) and UNTSO (UN Truce Supervision Organisation) and has been one of the biggest donors to the UN Relief and Works Agency (UNRWA), the main provider of basic services to the refugees.

Decolonisation and self-determination

Because of its history of colonisation by Britain, Ireland has continuously promoted political independence for all states and in particular supported the new African nations emerging in the 1960s and 1970s.

With respect to African colonies, Ireland encouraged the submission to the Security Council of the case of apartheid in South Africa and Namibia. It also strongly supported

General Assembly Resolutions A/RES/2396 (XXIII) *On the Policies of Apartheid of the South African Government* (2 December 1968), condemning the main trading partners of South Africa whose activities were encouraging that government to persist in its racial policies; and A/RES/42/23 (20 November 1987) reaffirming that apartheid is a crime against humanity and a threat to international peace and security. Nevertheless, in the question of Southern Rhodesia, Ireland abstained from resolutions, in support of the British government. As a consequence, a report to the Secretary-General in 1962 found that Southern Rhodesia did not qualify as self-governing territory within the meaning of the UN Charter.

In 1959 during China's invasion of Tibet, Ireland advocated for the fundamental rights of Tibetan people and for the restoration of their civil and religious liberties. It also supported General Assembly Resolution 1353 (XIV) calling for '*respect for the fundamental human rights of the Tibetan people and for their distinctive cultural and religious life'*.

Disarmament

The non-proliferation of nuclear weapons has always been a key issue in Irish policy and Ireland's role in this matter has been internationally recognised. In 1968, the Irish State was the sole sponsor of a Non-Proliferation Treaty (NPT), arguing that negative security provides guarantees to enhance international peace and security (Spelman, 'Ireland at the United Nations, 1965–69: Evolving Policy and Changing Presence', in Kennedy and McMahon (eds), *Obligations and Responsibilities: Ireland and the United Nations, 1955–2005*, 2005, Institute of Public Administration, 229).

In 1998 a group of states including Ireland, Brazil, Mexico, New Zealand, South Africa, Slovenia and Sweden launched the New Agenda Declaration which called for a commitment by nuclear states to eliminate their nuclear weapons by undertaking practical steps and negotiations. This Declaration resulted in the 2000 General Assembly Resolution A/RES/55/34G (20 November 2000) *Convention on the Prohibition of the Use of Nuclear Weapons*.

In addition, Ireland also encouraged the negotiation of the 1997 Convention on the Prohibition of the Use, Stockpiling, Production and Transfer of Anti-Personnel Mines and of their Destruction (Mine Ban Treaty) and it actively participated in the 2001 UN Conference on the Illicit Trade in Small Arms and Light Weapons in All Its Aspects.

Terrorism and the Iraq War

On 11 September 2001 Ireland was a temporary member of the Security Council. Following the US proposal to launch a military operation against Afghanistan, Ireland voted in favour of Resolutions 1368 and 1373, which included the creation of a Counter-Terrorism Committee. In this regard, Ireland strongly supports the inclusion of a human rights and counter-terrorism expert in the Committee, in order to ensure a human rights focus on its work. One year later, the Irish government also supported Resolution 1441 submitting Iraq to aggressive new weapons inspections, but not authorising the use of force.

In contrast, the Irish government remained silent on its position towards the decision of the United States and their allies to invade Iraq. It was assumed that Ireland had taken a neutral stance and was not supporting the United States. However, the Irish government provided overflight, landing and refuelling to US aircraft at Shannon airport.

7.8.2   IRELAND'S ROLE IN HUMAN RIGHTS PROTECTION

Ireland's stance in international relations has been defined by its commitment to the protection and promotion of human rights as a crucial tool for maintaining peace and supporting development. As a result, Irish background in this field is very extensive: from the large contribution of the Irish Army in peacekeeping missions to devoted Irish involvement in UN humanitarian agencies and NGOs. The Irish State has also made use of its temporary membership in the Security Council to emphasise the protection of human rights across different topics.

In 1996 the Irish government published the White Paper on *Irish Aid*, reaffirming the principles of international relations proclaimed in the Irish Constitution and the UN Charter. One of Ireland's former Presidents, Mary Robinson, became UN High Commissioner for Human Rights from 1997 to 2002. During this term, Mrs Robinson gave priority to implementing the reform proposal of Secretary-General Kofi Annan to integrate human rights concerns in all the activities of the UN. Ireland chaired the Commission Session in Geneva in 1999 and in the period 2003–2005, at the end of which it welcomed the replacement of the Human Rights Commission by the Human Rights Council.

In relation to the seven main treaties on human rights, Ireland has ratified six of them. Ratification of the International Convention on the Protection of the Rights of All Migrant Workers and Members of their Families, 1993 remains outstanding.

Treaty	Ratified by Ireland
International Covenant on Civil and Political Rights (ICCPR), 1976	8 December 1989
International Covenant on Economic, Social and Cultural Rights (ICESCR), 1976	8 December 1989
Convention on the Elimination of All Forms of Racial Discrimination (CERD), 1969	29 December 2000
Convention on the Elimination of Discrimination against Women (CEDAW), 1981	3 December 1985
Convention against Torture and Other Cruel, Inhuman or Degrading Treatment or Punishment (CAT), 1987	11 April 2002
Convention on the Rights of the Child (CRC), 1990	28 September 1992
International Convention on the Protection of the Rights of All Migrant Workers and Members of their Families, 1993	Pending ratification
Convention on the Rights of Persons with Disabilities, 2006	Pending ratification

Ireland has been a strong supporter for the creation of an international tribunal to punish the most serious crimes of international concern: genocide, war crimes and crimes against humanity.

'The entry into force of the Rome Statute in July will represent one of the most significant developments in international human rights and humanitarian law since the Second World War. In ratifying the Rome Statute, Ireland once again affirms its commitment to the promotion and protection of human rights and to the rule of law throughout the world. This commitment is felt not alone by the Government, but by the people of Ireland, who directly expressed their support for the International Criminal Court in a referendum held in June last year.' (Statement to the Dáil by the then Minister of Foreign Affairs, Mr Brian Cowen, April 2001, www.iccnow.org/documents/IrelandforMinApril01.pdf.)

Ireland, on the other hand, expressed its disagreement with Security Council Resolution S/RES/1422 (12 July 2002), which sought to prevent the International Criminal Court (ICC), from exercising its jurisdiction over persons involved in operations established or authorised by the UN, if they are nationals of states which have not ratified the Rome Statute of the International Criminal Court (Rome Statute). This Resolution was adopted at the insistence of one state, the United States of America, pursuing impunity for United States' nationals involved in peacekeeping missions. In a 2002 statement at the Security Council, Irish Ambassador Richard Ryan, stated: 'While we understand the concerns of the US, we do not feel that they are well founded. Nor can we agree to the mechanism that it has proposed, hitherto, to allay them...We consider that the Rome Statute of the ICC already contains adequate safeguards against politically inspired investigations or prosecutions before the Court' (Security Council Public Meeting, 10 July 2002).

7.8.2.1 Peacekeeping operations

Ireland has significantly contributed to UN peacekeeping operations since 1958, with Irish troops serving in over 50,000 individual missions, including operations in the African continent, where most Western powers have not participated. These operations confirm Irish commitment to the support and promotion of peace and human rights.

As of 2009 Ireland is contributing 760 defence forces personnel to 14 missions throughout the world, including: EUFOR, TCHAD/RCA and KFOR.

In addition, Ireland has committed 850 defence forces personnel to UN peacekeeping under the UN Standby Agreements System (UNSAS), with the objective of increasing the UN's capacity to respond to emergency situations. In 1993, the UN Training School Ireland (UNTSI) was established with the principal aim of ensuring that the defence forces training for peacekeeping would be of the highest standards.

Beside policy enforcement and maintenance of peace and security, the role of Irish troops in peacekeeping operations include humanitarian and social assistance, such as medical care, restoration of essential services and public facilities and assistance to local enterprises. Ireland's commitment to peacekeeping goes beyond deploying Irish Army personnel; financing of UN peacekeeping operations has always been a priority and Ireland has battled to include this item in the agenda of the General Assembly at every session. In 2005 Ireland also welcomed the agreement to build a Peace-Building Commission.

7.8.2.2 Promoting Development

The 1996 Government's White Paper included a detailed description of Ireland's vision and activity in promoting development: 'Ireland's approach to development reflects our commitment to international justice and fairness and mirrors the ideals and hopes of the Irish people'.

Ireland is also one of the world's principal donors to development aid programmes. In 2005 the government spent 0.4% of gross national income on overseas development aid. And that aid will be €734 million in 2006. This contribution is motivated by the 2000 Millennium Development Goals and focuses on basic needs (health and education, fight against HIV/AIDS etc), as well as on long-term development and investment on rural development and the private sector.

The Irish Aid Department of Foreign Affairs and Development Cooperation Ireland (as the official co-operation programme) ensure co-ordination and efficiency in the provision of emergency and long-term support to developing countries. This support is concentrated on a number of UN programmes and funds with which Ireland has establish partnerships. Irish aid is mainly destined to the UN Development Programme (UNDP), the UN Children's Fund (UNICEF), the Office of the UN High Commissioner for Refugees (UNCHR), the Food and Agriculture Organisation (FAO), the World Health Organisation (WHO) and the UN Educational Scientific and Cultural Organisation (UNESCO).

Geographically, Irish assistance focuses principally on sub-Saharan Africa, in particular Ethiopia, Lesotho, Mozambique, Tanzania, Uganda and Zambia. The main objectives include: basic relief; support for African institutions (such as the African Union); and the creation of regional development programmes. Ireland's aid is also present in Asia (Timor-Leste, Vietnam), Latin America (El Salvador, Honduras, Nicaragua), the Middle East (support for Palestinian refugees), Europe and Central Asia (Partnership Programme for Europe and Central Asia, PPECA)

With regards to debt cancellation, the Irish government has been a strong supporter and has committed to reach the UN target of 0.7% of GNP on official development assistance in 2012.

7.9 Serious Violations of Human Rights: International Crimes

The protection and promotion of international human rights is one of the principal roles of the UN. While specific UN bodies have been established to monitor the compliance with international human rights treaties and conventions, violations of fundamental rights are still rather frequent. Some of these violations are particularly grave because of their nature and dimension, rising to the level of international crimes. The following section looks at three categories of serious international crimes recognised by various treaties that fall under the jurisdiction of the International Criminal Court; namely genocide, crimes against humanity and war crimes. The prohibition of these crimes is a norm of *jus cogens* (superior norm not subject to derogation) and can be subject to universal jurisdiction. This section will also examine the kind of responses to those crimes set up by the UN and by sovereign states.

7.9.1 WAR CRIMES: INTERNATIONAL HUMAN RIGHTS AND INTERNATIONAL HUMANITARIAN LAW

War crimes are defined as serious violations of international humanitarian law committed during international or non-international armed conflicts including: wilful killing of a protected person (eg wounded or sick combatant, prisoner of war, civilian); torture or inhuman treatment of a protected person; wilfully causing great suffering to, or serious injury to the body or health of a protected person; attacking the civilian population; unlawful deportation or transfer; using prohibited weapons or methods of warfare; making improper use of the distinctive red cross or red crescent emblem or other protective signs; killing or wounding perfidiously individuals belonging to a hostile nation or army; pillage of public or private property (*International Committee of the Red Cross, International Humanitarian Law. Answers to your Questions, October 2002*). A detailed definition of war crimes is also expressed in Article 8 of the Rome Statute of the International Criminal Court.

International humanitarian law is the part of public international law that deals with the protection of people in times of armed conflict, who are not (or are no longer) taking part in the hostilities and with the restriction of the methods and means of warfare employed. The Geneva Convention for the Amelioration of the Conditions of the Wounded in Armies in the Field of 1864 constituted the first codified example of international humanitarian law, followed by The Hague Conventions 1899 (Convention with Respect to the Laws and Customs of War on Land) and 1904 (Convention for the Exception of Hospital Ships, in Time of War, From the Payment of All Duties and Taxes Imposed for the Benefit of the State), which limited the means by which belligerent states could conduct warfare. The Geneva Conventions of 1949 extended protection to non-combatants civilians and prisoners of war and, in order to strengthen the protection for the victims, additional protocols to the Conventions were adopted in 1977. International humanitarian law applies to both international and non-international armed conflicts, for instance, to wars of national liberation pursuing self-determination or civil wars (Article 1(1) of the Protocol refers to armed conflicts which

> 'take place within the territory of [a State party to the Protocol] between its armed forces and dissident armed forces or other organised armed groups which, under responsible command, exercise such control over a part of its territory as to enable them to carry out sustained and concerted military operations and to implement this Protocol'. *(Common Article 3 of Geneva Conventions 1949 and Protocol II of 1977.)*

While International humanitarian law and International human rights law are complementary in pursuing the protection of individuals, there are distinctions between them:

(a) The circumstances under which they apply. Humanitarian law applies in times of armed conflict; human rights law applies both in times of war and peace.

(b) The possibility of derogation. Some human rights treaties permit governments to derogate from certain rights in situations of public emergency; however, no derogations are permitted under international humanitarian law because it was conceived for emergency situations.

(c) The individuals they apply to. Humanitarian law aims to protect people who do not or are no longer taking part in hostilities; human rights law applies to everyone.

(d) The implementation mechanisms. States have the duty to implement both humanitarian law and human rights law. Human rights law rights implementing mechanisms include regional systems and supervisory bodies (treaty and non-treaty bodies (see **chapter 6**). The International Committee of the Red Cross (ICRC) acts as monitory body for humanitarian law, having a right of initiative to assist victims of armed conflicts without constituting interference in the internal affairs of the State.

The Geneva Conventions and Protocols set up enforcement mechanisms for states parties to a conflict who breach their duty to prevent and prosecute violations. These include: the enquiry procedure; the International Fact-Finding Commission; the examination procedures concerning the application and interpretation of legal provisions; co-operation with the UN. State parties to the Geneva Conventions are obliged to enact any legislation necessary to punish persons guilty of grave breaches of the Conventions; to prosecute in their own courts any person suspected of having committed a grave breach of the Conventions, or to hand that person over for judgment to another state.

In Ireland, the Geneva Conventions Act, 1962 gave effect to the Conventions. On 19 May 1999, Ireland ratified Additional Protocols I (relating to the Protection of Victims of International Armed Conflicts) and II (relating to the Protection of Victims of Non-International Armed Conflicts).

7.10.5.2 State practice

Some states have included universal jurisdiction in domestic legislation, mostly in reference to war crimes, ordinary crimes, as well as to the crimes or torture and Apartheid.

Some examples of the exercise of universal jurisdiction by national courts are:

- Canada (Crimes Against Humanity and War Crimes Act, 2000) (Case: *Regina v Finta*, 28 CR (4th) 265 (1994)).

- France (French Law 95–1 of 2 January 1995 recognises jurisdiction over crimes committed in the former Yugoslavia since 1991. French Law 96–432 of 22 May 1996 recognises jurisdiction over crimes committed in Rwanda in 1994) (Cases: *Re Javor*, ordonnance, N. Parquet 94052 2002/7 Tribunal de Grande Instance, Paris, 6 May 1994; and *Munyeshyaka, Jugement*, Cour de cassation, Chambre Criminelle, No. 96-82.491 PF, 6 January 1998; *Fedération Nationale des Déportés et Internés Résistants et Patriotes and Others v Klaus Barbie*, Cour de Cassation (Chambre Criminel), judgment, 6 October 1983 (summarising decision of Cour d'Appel), 78 Int'l L Rep 128.)

- Israel. In *Eichmann*, the Supreme Court of Israel established 'this jurisdiction [universal] was automatically vested in the State of Israel on its establishment in 1948 as a sovereign State'. (Cases: *Attorney General of Israel v Eichmann*, 36 Int'l L Rep 18, 50 (Isr Dist Ct—Jerusalem 1961), aff'd, 36 Int'l L Rep 277 (Isr Sup Ct 1962); and *Decision of Israel Supreme Court On Petition Concerning John (Ivan) Demjanuk* (August 18, 1993.)

- Spain. Article 23.4, Ley Orgánica 6/1985, de 1 de julio, del Poder Judicial establishes that Spanish courts should have jurisdiction over crimes of genocide and crimes against humanity. (Cases: *R v Bow Street Metropolitan Stipendiary Magistrate, ex parte Pinochet Ugarte* [1988] 3 WLR 1456 (HL), 37 ILM 1302 (1998); *Sentencia del Tribunal Constitucional español reconociendo el principio de jurisdicción penal universal en los casos de crímenes contra la humanidad*. STC 237/2005, de 26 de septiembre de 2005.)

- Belgium. Loi relative a la repression des violations graves du droit international humanitaire, 10 février 1999, Article 7 allows jurisdiction over people accused of war crimes, crimes against humanity or genocide. (Cases: *Case Concerning the Arrest Warrant* (*Democratic Republic of the Congo v Belgium*) [2002] ICJ Rep 3, judgment of 14 February 2002; *Cour d'Assises de Bruxelles c. Vincent NTEZIMANA, Alphonse HIGANIRO, Consolata MUKANGANGO et Julienne MUKABUTERA*, 8 juin 2001.)

- Germany. Article 6, Penal Code of the Federal Republic of Germany, Völkerstrafgesetzbuch, establishes jurisdiction over war crimes, genocide and crimes against humanity. (Cases: Oberlandesgericht Dusseldorf, '*Public Prosecutor v Jorgic*', 26 September 1997; *Novislav Djajic*, Bayerisches Oberstes Landesgericht, 23 May 1997, re D., 3 St 20/96.)

7.10.5.3 Universal jurisdiction in Irish law

Under Irish law, Irish courts can exercise universal jurisdiction only for war crimes; specifically for grave breaches of the Geneva Conventions of 1949, its first additional protocol and for torture. The concept of universal jurisdiction was introduced by enactment of the Geneva Conventions Acts, 1962 and 1998. The Criminal Justice (United Nations Convention Against Torture) Act, 2000 also contains provisions for the exercise of conditional universal jurisdiction by the Irish courts. The International Criminal Court Act, 2006 provides for universal jurisdiction over the same crimes covered by the *Geneva Conventions Acts* but does not extend such jurisdiction to crimes against humanity and genocide, both of which are criminalised by the 2006 Act. Section 12 of the Act provides:

'(1) An Irish national who does an act outside the State that, if done within it, would constitute an ICC offence or an offence under *section 11 (1)* is guilty of that offence and liable to the penalty provided for it.

(2) *Subsection (1)* also applies in relation to a person of any other nationality who does an act outside the State that, if done within it, would constitute both—

(a) a war crime under subparagraph (*a*) (grave breaches of the Geneva Conventions) or (*b*) (other specified serious violations of the laws and customs applicable in international armed conflict) of Article 8.2, and

(b) an offence under section 3 (grave breaches of the Geneva Conventions and Protocol I thereto) of the Geneva Conventions Act 1962'.

The prosecution of a defendant accused of a serious international crime raises the issue of government consent as a requirement. While prosecutions for grave breaches of the Geneva Conventions and Protocol I do not explicitly require the consent of the executive, the Geneva Conventions Act does specify that the Minister of Foreign Affairs has sole authority to determine whether the Act is applicable to a particular case (Geneva Conventions Act, 1962, as amended by s 5 of the Geneva Conventions (Amendment) Act, 1998). With respect to torture and ancillary offences, the consent of the Director of Public Prosecutions (DPP) is required in order to proceed with a prosecution beyond the initial charge and arrest (Criminal Justice (United Nations Convention Against Torture) Act, 2000, s 5(2)). The DPP has the discretion to decide whether to prosecute an indictable offence, and must make this decision on the basis of the sufficiency of the available evidence and the public interest. The DPP is legally prohibited from explaining its reasons for deciding against a prosecution (Prosecution of Offences Act, 1974, s 6(1)(a)). (The DPP introduced a pilot scheme on 22 October 2008 under which he will give reasons for his decision not to prosecute in some cases where someone has died as a result of an alleged crime.)

In November 2004, a group of Irish lawyers requested the Garda Commissioner to investigate and arrest Mr Huang Ju, the then Chinese Deputy Prime-Minister, on allegations of his involvement in torture against Falun Dafa practitioners. Mr Huang Ju was on a three-day official visit to Ireland. The application for an arrest warrant was refused by Judge Cormac Dunne of the District Court.

7.11 CONCLUSION

The UN was created as a platform for co-operation between peace-loving nations. Its role has been transformed over the years from being a discussion forum to becoming the principal provider of assistance at international level.

With 192 members and working in more than 50 countries, today the UN plays a vital role in setting global standards in the fields of peace and security, human rights, development, democracy and self-determination.

While its aim and purposes are extremely important, the work of the UN is sometimes limited by its own structure. Former Secretary-General Kofi Annan referred to the need for reform of the organisation in terms of administration, financial management, public access to documentation and other areas. But the UN also requires the trust and support of all its members in order to properly perform its duties.

With regard to the UN, the Irish government has traditionally adopted a neutral and independent stance. Nevertheless, it has played a key role in UN negotiations and in human rights promotion. At present, with new larger states becoming members of the

UN, Ireland has seen a change in its role, but its contribution (both financially and with personnel resources) continues to be substantial.

The international community is slowly evolving towards a system of justice and accountability. While the establishment of the *ad hoc* tribunals and the creation of the ICC constitute a huge step, states must make joint efforts to ensure that no perpetrators of human rights violations remain immune to justice.

CHAPTER 8

HUMAN RIGHTS IN EU LAW

8.1   Introduction

This chapter aims to provide an overview of EU human rights law. The history of human rights law in the EC/EU is explored. It will be noted that the method of development which resulted initially from judicial rather than Treaty sources impacts on the system of protection which exists today. The history of human rights law in the EU has significant consequences for issues such as the competence of the political institutions to legislate in the field of human rights, the scope of fundamental rights protection in the EU and the standard of human rights protection.

The human rights *acquis* is explored to indicate what substantive rights are protected. The sources of human rights include the Treaties, secondary legislation and case-law of the ECJ. While the human rights protection has developed on an *ad hoc* basis there now exists a considerable human rights *acquis*.

A Charter of Fundamental Rights for the EU was solemnly proclaimed at the Inter-Governmental Conference (IGC) in Nice in December 2000 (OJ 2000/C364/01 18 December 2000). The text of the Charter was adapted with a view to making it legally binding and this adapted version of the Charter was solemnly proclaimed by the three political institutions of the EU (the European Parliament, the Council and the Commission) on 12 December 2007 (OJ C303/01 14 February, 2007), the eve of the signing of the Lisbon Treaty (a consolidated text of the Treaty on European Union and the Treaty on the Functioning of the European Union, formerly the EC Treaty, post Lisbon are published at OJ C115/01 9 May, 2008).

This chapter provides an overview of the contents of the Charter together with some of the issues concerning it which have arisen for debate. These issues include the sources, scope and legal status of the Charter as well as questions as to who is to benefit from it and its relationship with the European Convention on Human Rights (ECHR).

The Charter of Fundamental Rights is legally binding since the entry into force of the Treaty of Lisbon on 1 December 2009. Article 6(1) TEU provides;

> *'The Union recognises the rights, freedoms and principles set out in the Charter of Fundamental Rights of the European Union of 7 December 2000, as adapted at Strasbourg, on 12 December 2007, which shall have the same legal status as the Treaties.'*

The Treaty of Lisbon also provides a legal basis (Article 6(2) TEU) for EU accession to the ECHR (see **chapter 4**).

The Treaty of Lisbon (OJ C306/01 17 December 2007) contains two substantive clauses amending respectively the Treaty on European Union (TEU) and the Treaty establishing the European Community which was renamed the Treaty on the Functioning of the

Union (TFEU). The Treaty of Lisbon resulted from the failure of the now defunct Treaty establishing a Constitution for Europe (OJ 2004/310/01 16 December, 2004). However many of the reforms proposed in that Treaty are maintained in the Treaty of Lisbon, including two significant proposals in respect of human rights; that the Charter become legally binding and that a legal basis be provided for EU accession to the ECHR. The Treaty establishing a Constitution for Europe had also provided that the text of the Charter would be included in the Treaty. The Treaty of Lisbon did not incorporate the text of the Charter into the text of the Treaties.

The Treaty of Lisbon affords the EU a single legal personality and the word 'Community' is replaced throughout the text of the Treaties by the word 'Union'. Acts adopted under the pre-existing Treaties continue to have effect. Some modifications suggested in the Treaty establishing a Constitution for Europe are maintained. Changes effected by the Treaty of Lisbon include; competences are more clearly delimited, national parliaments are afforded an increased role, the specific nature of common foreign and security policy is maintained, the powers of the European Parliament are increased through the extension of co-decision (now called the Ordinary Legislative Procedure); new posts of the President of the European Council and of High Representative of the Union for Foreign Affairs and Security Policy are created, the system of qualified majority voting in the Council is replaced with a double majority system, the European Court of Justice is renamed the Court of Justice of the European Union, the CFI (Court of First Instance) is renamed the General Court. The right of individuals to bring actions directly before the ECJ is expanded. There are significant changes in the Area of Freedom Security and Justice.

Following a no vote in Ireland, the Irish government commissioned a study which showed that the main reason for voting no among the Irish electorate was a lack of information and knowledge. A number of issues also emerged as significant for Irish voters. These included the composition of the Commission; ethical issues notably abortion, security and defence issues (including conscription) and workers' rights. In June 2009, the European Council agreed a number of legal guarantees covering areas of concern to Irish voters. It was agreed a Commissioner from each Member State would be retained. The legal guarantees confirm that nothing in the Lisbon Treaty makes any change to the EU's competence in taxation, that the Lisbon Treaty does not prejudice Ireland's traditional policy of neutrality, that it does not create a European Army and does not provide for conscription and that nothing in the Lisbon Treaty or the Charter of Fundamental Rights affects in any way the scope and applicability of the provisions of the Irish Constitution relating to the protection of the right to life, family and education. The European Council also agreed a Solemn Declaration on workers' rights. A second Irish referendum took place on 2 October 2009 and on this occasion ratification of the Treaty of Lisbon was approved.

Article 6(1) TEU, post-Lisbon, as set out above contains a cross-reference to the Charter on Fundamental Rights giving it legally binding force. Article 6(1) at indents 2 and 3 also sets out the scope of application providing:

'The provisions of the Charter shall not extend in any way the competences of the Union as defined in the Treaties.

The rights, freedoms and general principles in the Charter shall be interpreted in accordance with the general provisions in Title VII of the Charter governing its interpretation and application and with due regard to the explanations referred to in the Charter, that set out the sources of those provisions.'

In 2002 an EU network of independent experts on fundamental rights was set up by the Commission which monitors human rights protections in the Member States. A European Union Agency for Fundamental Rights was established on 1 March 2007 (Council Regulation 168/2007 of 15 February 2007 establishing a European Union Agency for Fundamental Rights and see **8.11**).

8.2 The History of Human Rights Protection in the EC/EU

8.2.1 EXCLUSION OF A BILL OF RIGHTS FROM THE FOUNDING TREATIES

The Treaties establishing the European Economic Community (EEC), European Coal and Steel Community (ECSC) and the European Atomic Energy Community (EURATOM), as ratified in the 1950s, did not contain a catalogue of human rights. At first glance it may seem surprising that organisations established in the immediate aftermath of the Second World War and with the stated objective of preserving and strengthening peace did not state themselves bound by a bill of rights. This exclusion can be explained by the political failure of the European Defence Community Treaty and the consequent failure of the European Political Community Treaty (which was to include the application of the ECHR) which meant that a more cautious approach was taken when drafting the Community Treaties. Also, it may not have been so readily apparent at the time that a Community predominantly concerned with economics would impact on human rights.

8.2.2 THE EARLY APPROACH BY THE EUROPEAN COURT OF JUSTICE

In a series of early cases, the European Court of Justice (ECJ) declined when invited to take human rights considerations into account. Examples of this former attitude can be seen in Case 1/58 *Stork v High Authority* [1959] ECR 17 and Joined Cases 16, 17 and 18/59 *Ruhr v High Authority* [1960] ECR 47.

In these cases, the ECJ decided that it did not have the competence to review a decision of the High Authority for compatibility with German basic law. The rationale for this decision was that the ECJ is only permitted to apply Community law and is not competent to apply the national laws of Member States.

8.2.3 A NEW APPROACH BY THE ECJ

With the emergence of the EC as a new supranational legal order based on the concepts of supremacy, as espoused by the ECJ in Case 6/64 *Costa v ENEL* [1964] ECR 585 and direct effect, as espoused by the ECJ in Case 26/62 *Van Gend en Loos v Nederlandse Administratie der Belastingen* [1963] ECR 1, it was no longer sufficient to leave the protection of fundamental human rights to the national courts. This was especially true when the ECJ in Case 11/70 *Internationale Handelsgesellschaft* [1970] ECR 1125 declared that Community law was superior even to the constitutional provisions of Member States.

8.2.4 THREAT OF CONSTITUTIONAL REBELLIONS IN THE MEMBER STATES

The ECJ's new approach to human rights may have resulted at least in part from a desire to head off threatened rebellions in certain Member States. The doctrine of supremacy of European law is a key method adopted by the ECJ to ensure the effectiveness and uniformity of EC law. In particular, German and Italian lawyers had difficulties with the possibility that the provisions of a supranational legal order might trump the constitutional provisions, and in particular, the fundamental rights provisions, of their respective legal orders as the EC system lacked *inter alia* a codified catalogue of fundamental human rights.

8.2.5   HUMAN RIGHTS AS GENERAL PRINCIPLES OF EC LAW

The ECJ responded by recognising an unwritten catalogue of fundamental human rights enshrined in the general principles of EC law and by holding that the ECJ had jurisdiction to review acts of the institutions to ensure compatibility with this human rights standard. The protection of fundamental rights in EC law, at least at the outset, was a product of judicial activism. In this section, it is proposed to examine the early case-law of the ECJ in which it espoused a Community concept of human rights protection.

The ECJ first recognised fundamental human rights as general principles of Community law requiring protection by the ECJ in Case 29/69 *Stauder v City of Ulm* [1969] ECR 419. The case concerned a European scheme to provide cheap butter to those on social welfare. The applicant was a social welfare recipient. He objected to the fact that he had to present a coupon bearing his name and address to obtain the cheap butter. He argued that the humiliation of revealing his identity was a breach of his fundamental human rights. He further argued that the Community decision was invalid in that it contained this requirement. The ECJ at para 7 held that on a proper interpretation, the Community provision did not require the beneficiary's identity to appear on the coupon.

> 'Interpreted in this way the provision at issue contains nothing capable of prejudicing the fundamental rights enshrined in the general principles of Community law and protected by the Court.'

This decision is remarkable given the exclusion of the protection of fundamental rights from the ambit of the European Community Treaties by the Member States.

In Case 11/70 *Internationale Handelsgesellschaft* [1970] ECR 1125, the ECJ confirmed its view of human rights as general principles of EC law. The facts of the case concerned the Common Agricultural Policy. A system was in place whereby exporters of certain agricultural products had to obtain an export licence. When applying for such a licence the exporter had to pay a deposit. If he failed to export during the validity of the licence, the sum was forfeit. The applicants argued that the system violated the principle of proportionality and hence the German Constitution.

Consistent with the judgment in *Stork*, the ECJ pointed out at para 3 that the validity of EC law measures could not be judged according to national law rules.

> 'Recourse to the legal rules or concepts of national law in order to judge the validity of measures adopted by the institutions of the Community would have an adverse effect on the uniformity and efficacy of Community law. The validity of such measures can only be judged in the light of Community law. In fact, the law stemming from the Treaty, an independent source of law, cannot because of its very nature be overridden by rules of national law, however framed, without being deprived of its character as Community law and without the legal basis of the Community itself being called into question.'

The ECJ emphasised that the validity of Community measures could not be judged even according to national constitutional provisions protecting human rights:

> 'Therefore the validity of a Community measure or its effect within a Member State cannot be affected by allegations that it runs counter to either fundamental rights as formulated by the constitution of that state or the principles of a national constitutional structure.'

Hence, the doctrine of supremacy of EC law extends to supremacy over the fundamental rights provisions of the Member State Constitutions.

The measures at issue were however subject to review by the ECJ for compatibility with the Community standard of human rights protection. The fundamental human rights which the ECJ found itself obliged to protect could be inspired by the constitutional traditions of the Member States. The ECJ stated at para 4:

> 'However, an examination should be made as to whether or not any analogous guarantee inherent in community law has been disregarded. In fact, respect for fundamental rights forms an integral part of the general principles of law protected by the Court of Justice. The protection of such rights, whilst inspired by the Constitutional traditions common to the Member States, must be ensured within the framework of the structure and objectives of the Community.'

According to Hartley (*Foundations of European Community Law*, 3rd edn, 1994, Clarendon Press, 142) this decision goes beyond that in *Stauder*—the concept of human rights applied by the ECJ while deriving its validity solely from Community law is nevertheless inspired by the Constitutional traditions of the Member States. On the facts, the ECJ concluded that the system did not violate any fundamental human rights.

The ECJ cited another source of inspiration for fundamental human rights in Case 4/73 *Nold v Commission* [1974] ECR 491—International Treaties for the protection of human rights on which the Member States have collaborated or to which they are signatories. However, it is the general principle and not the Treaty, which is the source of law. The facts of this case related to a Commission decision under the ECSC Treaty which provided that coal wholesalers could not buy Ruhr coal unless they agreed to purchase a specific quantity. Nold, who was not in a position to purchase the minimum quantity, claimed the decision was a breach of his fundamental human rights for two reasons. He claimed first, that it was a violation of a property right and second, that it breached his right to the free pursuit of a business activity.

The ECJ seemed to recognise the two rights as general principles of EC law but held that they were not absolute rights. These rights were held to be subject to limitations justified by the overall objectives pursued by the Community. The ECJ held that no infringement had taken place. The ECJ in its judgment made the following pronouncement at para 13:

> 'As the Court has already stated, fundamental rights form an integral part of the general principles of law, the observance of which it ensures.

> In safeguarding these rights, the Court is bound to draw inspiration from constitutional traditions common to Member States, and it cannot therefore uphold measures which are incompatible with fundamental rights recognised and protected by the Constitutions of those states.

> Similarly, international Treaties for the protection of human rights on which the Member States have collaborated or of which they are signatories, can supply guidelines which should be followed within the framework of Community law.'

This judgment is significant in that it makes clear that a Community measure in conflict with fundamental rights will be annulled.

A detailed discussion of human rights by the ECJ may be found in the decision in Case 44/79 *Hauer v Land Rheinland-Pfaltz* [1979] ECR 3727. The facts concerned a Regulation banning new plantings of vines. It was argued on behalf of the applicant that her right to property and her freedom to pursue a profession under German law were infringed. The ECJ rephrased the question asked and analysed the measure at issue in the light of the Community human rights standard. Again, the ECJ accepted these rights as general principles of Community law but pointed out that they were not absolute rights and were subject to the general interest exception.

The judgment is of interest in that the ECJ analysed provisions of the Irish, German and Italian Constitutions and the relevant provision (the First Protocol) of the ECHR in order to establish that, in principle, it was permissible to restrict the rights at issue. The ECJ went on to consider whether the restrictions introduced by the measures at issue in fact corresponded to objectives of general interest pursued by the Community or whether the restrictions constituted a disproportionate and intolerable interference with those rights and found that the restrictions were justified.

The key points of these early judgments may be summarised as follows. It is possible to review the acts of the Community for compatibility with human rights protection but it is a Community standard of human rights protection. This standard is inspired by the constitutional traditions of the Member States and international human rights treaties to which the Member States are party. An act which is in breach of the human rights standard will be annulled. The rights protected are not absolute but subject to restrictions justified by the objectives pursued by the Community. These restrictions must be proportionate and must not constitute an intolerable interference with the right at issue.

In addition, it is worth noting that, in each of these four judgments, the ECJ recognised the existence of rights but went on to hold that the rights had not been violated.

In a recent judgment the ECJ held that non-discrimination on the grounds of age was a general principle of EC law. In Case C-144/04 *Mangold v Helm* [2005] ECR I-9981, the ECJ held in the context of age discrimination in relation to fixed-term contracts that it was the responsibility of the national court to ensure the full effectiveness of the general principle of non-discrimination on the grounds of age, setting aside the provision of national law which conflicts with EC law, specifically Directive 2000/78/EC, even where the period prescribed for transposition of the directive had not yet expired. The ECJ held that Article 6(1) of Directive 2000/78/EC which permits direct discrimination on the grounds of age in specified circumstances precludes a provision of national law which authorises without restriction, unless there is a close connection with an earlier contract of employment with the same employer, the conclusion of fixed-term contracts once the worker has reached the age of fifty-two.

However in a subsequent case the ECJ took a narrower approach and held that sickness was not an additional ground on the basis of which discrimination was prohibited where sickness was not listed as a ground in the relevant directive. In Case C-13/05 *Chacón-Navas v Eurest Colectividades SA* [2006] ECR I-6467, the ECJ held that an individual dismissed on the grounds of sickness does not fall within the general framework for combating discrimination on the grounds of disability covered by Council Directive 2000/78/EC. The ECJ also held that sickness cannot as such be regarded as an extra ground in addition to those in which Directive 2000/78/EC prohibits discrimination. The ECJ stated at para 39 that 'disability is not defined in the Directive', and at para 44 that the two concepts could not be treated the same. The ECJ held at para 56:

'It is true that the fundamental rights which form an integral part of the general principles of Community law include the general principle of non-discrimination. . . . However it does not follow from this that the scope of Directive 2000/78 should be extended by analogy beyond the discrimination in the grounds listed exhaustively in Article 1 thereof.'

8.3   Political Acceptance of Fundamental Human Rights as General Principles of Community Law

The ECJ's elaboration of fundamental human rights as general principles of Community law subsequently gained political acceptance. In 1977, the three political institutions issued a Joint Declaration on Fundamental Human Rights ([1977] OJ C103/1). This Declaration states:

'*1.   The European Parliament, the Council and the Commission stress the prime importance they attach to the protection of fundamental human rights, as derived in particular from the*

> *Constitutions of the Member States and the European Convention on Human Rights and Fundamental Freedoms.*
> 2. *In exercise of their powers and in pursuance of the aims of the European Communities, they respect and continue to respect these rights.'*

The European Council endorsed the Joint Declaration the following year. Since the 1977 joint declaration, there have been a number of political initiatives, including a Joint Declaration by the institutions in 1986, a number of declarations and resolutions on racism and xenophobia by the European Council, a declaration of Fundamental Rights and Freedoms by the European Parliament ([1989] OJ C120/51) and a Charter of Fundamental Social Rights.

8.4   Treaty Amendments

Treaty amendments, subsequent to the ECJ's elaboration of a human rights policy approved the development. The Single European Act, 1987 contains the first explicit Treaty reference to human rights. In the preamble, the Member States determined

> *'to work together to promote democracy on the basis of the fundamental rights recognised in the constitutions and laws of the Member states, in the Convention for the Protection of Human Rights and Fundamental Freedoms and the European Social Charter, notably freedom, equality and social justice.'*

Article F(2) of the Treaty on European Union (TEU) (the Maastricht Treaty) required the European Union to respect fundamental rights as general principles of Community law, as guaranteed by the ECHR and as they result from the constitutional traditions common to the Member States. However, pursuant to Article L TEU, this provision was originally not justiciable before the ECJ. A two-stage evolution was evident in the Treaty of Amsterdam amendments to the TEU. Article 6(1) TEU declared fundamental human rights as one of the basic principles on which the Union was founded and Article 6(2) TEU (ex Article F(2)), pursuant to the newly inserted para (d) in Article 46 TEU (ex Article L), now came within the jurisdiction of the ECJ.

Article 6 TEU after the Treaty of Amsterdam provided:

> *'1.   The Union is founded on the principles of liberty, democracy, respect for human rights and fundamental freedoms and the rule of law, principles which are common to the Member States.*
> 2.   *The Union shall respect fundamental rights, as guaranteed by the European convention for the Protection of Human Rights and Fundamental freedoms signed in Rome on 4 November, 1950 and as they result from the constitutional traditions common to the Member States, as general principles of Community law.'*

Even after the Treaty of Amsterdam, Article 6(2) TEU (ex Article F(2)) did not go further than confirming the jurisprudence of the ECJ, that the ECJ would protect human rights as general principles of Community law. As Hartley has pointed out, '[t]he significance of this is that general principles prevail over Community legislation, but not over the Community Treaties' (Hartley, *European Union Law in a Global Context* 2004, CUP, 313. Rendering Article 6(2) justiciable did mean that the ECJ could review the actions of the EC institutions for compatibility with the human rights standard under provisions of the two intergovernmental pillars in the event that the ECJ has been given jurisdiction (see **8.7.1**). Respect for the fundamental principles set out in Article 6(1) TEU was made a condition of the application for membership of the EU by the Amsterdam Treaty (Article 49 (ex Article O) TEU).

The Maastricht Treaty did introduce one justiciable provision relating to human rights. Article 177(2) EC (ex Article 130u(2) EC) provided that *'Community policy in [the field of development co-operation] shall contribute to the general objective of developing and consolidating democracy and the rule of law, and to that of respecting human rights and fundamental freedoms.'* The ECJ's interpretation of this provision in C-268/94 *Portugal v Council* [1996] ECR I-6177 is discussed at **8.6.2**.

The Treaty of Amsterdam introduced a political mechanism for sanctioning states guilty of a 'serious and persistent breach' of the principles on which the Union is founded, including respect for fundamental rights. Pursuant to Article 7 TEU, a 'serious and persistent breach' of fundamental rights may result in the suspension of rights, including voting rights, derived from the Treaty.

Article 7 TEU was amended by the Nice Treaty. A procedure was added allowing the Council to make recommendations to a Member State where there was a clear risk of a serious breach by a Member State of the principles mentioned in Article 6(1) (the basic principles on which the Union is founded including those of democracy, respect for human rights and fundamental freedoms, and the rule of law). This procedure was designed to allow a more gradual response to a developing situation and the ECJ has jurisdiction over the procedures of Article 7. The Treaty of Lisbon makes minor amendments to Article 7 TEU which now refers to the principles found in Article 2 TEU. The Treaty of Lisbon moved ex Article 6(1) TEU to Article 2 TEU and added a number of values. Article 2 TEU now provides:

> *'The Union is founded on the values of respect for human dignity, freedom, democracy, equality, the rule of law and respect for human rights, including the rights of persons belonging to minorities. These values are common to the Member States in a society in which pluralism, non-discrimination, tolerance, justice, solidarity and equality between men and women prevail.'*

The Treaty of Lisbon replaced the text of Article 6 TEU with the following text:

1. *'The Union recognises the rights, freedoms and principles set out in the Charter of Fundamental Rights of 7 December 2000, as adapted at Strasbourg, on 12 December 2007 , which shall have the same legal value as the Treaties.*
    The provisions of the Charter shall not extend in any way the competences of the Union as defined in the Treaties.
    The rights, freedoms and principles in the Charter shall be interpreted in accordance with the general provisions in Title VII of the Charter governing its interpretation and application and with due regard to the explanations referred to in the Charter, that set out the sources of those provisions.
2. *The Union shall accede to the European Convention for the Protection of Human Rights and Fundamental Freedoms. Such accession shall not affect the Union's competences as defined in the Treaties.*
3. *Fundamental rights, as guaranteed by the European Convention for the Protection of Human Rights and Fundamental Freedoms and as they result from the constitutional traditions common to the Member States, shall constitute general principles of the Union's law.'*

The adapted version of the Charter was solemnly proclaimed by the three political institutions of the EU in December 2007. It is this version which has the same legal status as the Treaties. Thus since the entry into force of the Treaty of Lisbon on 1 December 2009 and pursuant to Article 6(1) TEU the Charter has legally binding status. The Charter now forms part of the body of constitutional rules and principles against which the ECJ can adjudicate. In addition Article 6(2) provides the legal basis for EU accession to the ECHR.

There is a Declaration concerning the Charter annexed to the final conclusions of the IGC which adopted the Treaty (Declaration No.1, see the consolidated text of the Treaties at OJ C115/01 9 May, 2008). It provides:

> *'The Charter of Fundamental Rights of the European Union, which has legally binding force, confirms the fundamental rights guaranteed by the European Convention on the Protection of*

Human Rights and Fundamental Freedoms and as they result from the constitutional traditions common to the Member States.

The Charter does not extend the field of application of Union law beyond the powers of the Union or establish any new power or task for the Union, or modify powers and tasks defined by the Treaties.'

There is a both a Protocol (No. 8) and Declaration (No. 2) (consolidated text of the Treaties at OJ C115/01 9 May, 2008), concerning Article 6(2) TEU on EU Accession to the ECHR. The Protocol contains three articles. Article 1 provides that the accession agreement

'shall make provision for preserving the specific characteristics of the Union and Union law, in particular with regards to:

(a) The specific arrangements for the Union's possible participation in the control bodies of the European Convention;

(b) The mechanisms necessary to ensure that proceedings by non-Member States and individual applications are correctly addressed to Member States and/or the Union as appropriate.'

Article 2 of the Protocol provides:

'The [accession agreement] shall ensure that accession of the Union shall not affect the competences of the Union or the powers of its institutions. It shall ensure that nothing therein affects the situation of the Member States in relation to the Convention, in particular in relation to the Protocols thereto, measures taken by Member States derogating from the European Convention in accordance with Article 15 thereof and reservations to the European Convention made by the Member States in accordance with Article 57 thereof.'

Article 3 provides that nothing in the Accession agreement shall affect Article 344 TFEU (ex Article 292 EC), the provision by which the EU Member States undertake not to submit a dispute concerning the application or interpretation of the EU Treaties to any method of settlement other than those provided in the Treaties.

The Declaration on Article 6(2) provides:

'The [IGC] agrees that the Union's accession to the European Convention on the Protection of Human Rights and Fundamental Freedoms should be arranged in such a way as to preserve the specific features of Union law. In this connection, the [IGC] notes the existence of a regular dialogue between the Court of Justice of the European Union and the European Court of Human Rights; such dialogue could be reinforced when the Union accedes to the Convention.'

The UK and Poland have a derogation from the Charter of Fundamental Rights (See Protocol No. 30 and two Declarations (Nos 61 and 62) by Poland in respect of the Charter) and this derogation is to be extended to the Czech Republic.

8.4.1   HUMAN RIGHTS AND THE FUTURE OF EUROPE

A Declaration on the Future of the Union was agreed at Nice. At Laeken, the European Council decided to convene a Convention on the Future of Europe, modelled on the body which drafted the EU Charter of Fundamental Rights (see **8.10.1** and **8.10.2**), composed of the main parties involved in the debate, to prepare for the next IGC which commenced in 2003 and concluded in 2004 (the 2004 IGC).

The Convention's task was to identify the key issues which would form the basis for the IGC. More specifically, the Convention was charged with preparing a document, which together with national debates on the future of Europe, such as Ireland's National Forum on Europe, would form a basis for the 2004 IGC. The Convention was composed of representatives of the Heads of State or government of the Member States and accession States, members of national parliaments of the Member States and accession States, members of the European Parliament and members of the Commission. In the Nice (December 2000) and Laeken (December 2001) Declarations on the Future of Europe, it was agreed that consideration would be given to the status of the Charter of Fundamental Rights and whether it should be included in the EC Treaty (see **8.10.10**).

The members of the Convention participated in working groups to look into particular issues more fully. In total, there were 11 Working Groups' reports on the following subjects: Subsidiarity, Charter/ECHR, Legal Personality, National Parliaments, Complementary Competencies, Economic Governance, External Action, Defence, Simplification, Freedom, Security and Justice and Social Europe. After the Working Groups submitted their final reports, the Convention moved to the next stage of its work, the drafting of a Constitutional Treaty to replace the existing Treaties. The Working Group reports are available on the Convention website (http://european-convention.eu.int). The Working Group Report on Incorporation of the Charter and Accession of the EU to the ECHR (CONV 354/02 Final report of Working Group II 'Incorporation of the Charter/Accession to the ECHR', Brussels, 22 October 2002) is discussed later (see **8.6.5** and **8.10.10**).

On completion of the work of the Convention a 'Draft Treaty establishing a Constitution for Europe' (a corrected text was published as CONV 820/1/03, Brussels, 27 June 2003) was presented to the European Council. The 2004 IGC commenced its work in October 2003 and the draft Treaty formed the basis for negotiations under the Italian presidency and later the Irish presidency. The work of the 2004 IGC was completed when the Treaty establishing a Constitution for Europe was signed in Rome on 29 October 2004. The Treaty could only come into force if ratified by all of the EU Member States (see **8.1** and **8.10.10**). In May and June 2005 voters in France and the Netherlands rejected the Treaty establishing a Constitution for Europe. Following these 'no' votes the European Council announced a period of reflection on the future of the Constitutional Treaty, after which the European Council decided to convene an IGC with a mandate to draft a Reform Treaty (see **8.1**). The Reform Treaty became the Treaty of Lisbon (see **8.1**). Many of the amendments which were to have been included in the Treaty establishing a Constitution for Europe were maintained in the Treaty of Lisbon. For that reason the work done in preparing the Treaty establishing a Constitution for Europe is of assistance in understanding the amendments in the Treaty of Lisbon.

8.5   The Issue of EU Accession to the ECHR

The idea of EU accession to the ECHR has been mooted consistently since the late 1970s. The principal advantage of accession is that it would remedy an apparent lacuna in EU law. Currently, as the EU is not party to the ECHR, the EU institutions are not answerable to the European Court of Human Rights (ECt.HR) for possible violations of the ECHR.

The ECJ, in *Opinion 2/94* [1996] ECR I-1759, determined that the EU had no competence to accede to the ECHR. As a consequence of this judgment, accession could only be brought about by means of an amendment to the Treaties. Prior to the Treaty of Lisbon, while the Member States were subject to the ECHR they had not amended the EC Treaty to subject the EU institutions to the possibility of review by the ECt.HR.

The Treaty of Lisbon provides a legal basis for accession to the ECHR (see **8.10.10**). However the EU has not yet acceded to the ECHR. Accession of the EU to the ECHR is not without difficulties. Practical issues such as whether there should be an EU judge on the ECt.HR and how the exhaustion of domestic remedies rule in the ECHR (see **chapter 4**) will operate in the context of Member States acting within the scope of EU law will have to be addressed. Also accession is not a unilateral EU decision but is dependent on the Council of Europe and the contracting states to the ECHR who are not Member States of the EU.

8.6 The Nature of EU Human Rights Law

The form of evolution of human rights protection within the EU legal order raises two issues. First, a question arises as to whether the EU political institutions have the competence to legislate in the field of human rights. Second, a question arises as to whether the Member States might be subject to review by an international legal order, specifically the ECt.HR, to ensure that the standard of human rights signed up to by the Member States is maintained. This issue arises in part as the Member States of the EU are all parties to the ECHR and subject to scrutiny by the ECt.HR. Difficulties may result from Member States transferring competences which might then be beyond the review of an international human rights standard to which the Member State is subject.

8.6.1 COMPETENCE

European Union law is distinct from international law. The ECSC was not established as a forum for intergovernmental decision-making. What was unique about the ECSC and the subsequent steps to European integration was the Member States' willingness to hand over their decision-making power to the institutions of these supranational Communities. Within defined areas, the Member States transferred competence to the political institutions of the European Communities. The Treaty of Lisbon affords the EU a single legal personality. Article 5(1) TEU (ex Article 5 EC) provides; 'The limits of Union competence are governed by the principle of conferral.'

Consequently, while individual states clearly have competence to legislate in the domestic sphere and to conclude international agreements which will be binding on the State or both binding on the State and internally within the State, the European Union only has competence where the Member States have chosen to transfer the requisite competence.

European integration is an ongoing process taking place incrementally. The first step was taken with the establishment of the European Coal and Steel Community. The process continued with the establishment of the European Atomic Energy Community and the European Economic Community. Further developments ensued when the Treaty establishing this latter Community was amended by the Single European Act, the Maastricht Treaty, the Treaty of Amsterdam and the Treaty of Nice. With each incremental step, further competences have been transferred from the Member States to the EU. The Treaty of Lisbon provides for a single legal personality of the EU.

Prior to the Treaty of Lisbon, the Treaties did not contain a demarcation of the division of competences between the Member States and the EU. In the pre-Lisbon system of allocation of competences there were three types of competence: exclusive, shared and complementary.

Three types of legislative competence were conferred upon the EC/EU: exclusive, concurrent or shared. These terms were not defined in the Treaties but definitions are given in a discussion paper prepared by the Convention on the Future of Europe. (The European Convention, *Discussion Paper on the Delimitation of Competence between the European Union and Member States*, Brussels 15, May 2002, CONV 47/02, 6 *et seq.*)

The EU enjoys exclusive competence when it alone is able to adopt rules in an area.

There is concurrent (or shared) competence in areas in which Member States may legislate until such time and insofar as the EU has not exercised its powers by adopting rules, which it may do as of right. Once the EU has legislated in such an area, Member States may no longer legislate in the field covered by this legislation, except to the extent necessary to implement it, and the legislative rules adopted have precedence over those of the Member States.

Complementary competence covers areas in which the competence of the EU/EC is limited to supplementing or supporting the action of the Member States, adopting measures of encouragement or co-ordinating the action of the Member States. The bulk of the power to adopt legislative rules in these areas remains in the hands of the Member State and intervention by the EU cannot have the effect of excluding intervention by them.

Areas of Member State competence were not referred to in the Treaty and therefore, as a result of the principle of conferred powers, not within the competence of the EC/EU and remain within the competence of the Member States. There are specific areas where the Treaties expressly exclude competence or expressly recognise the competence of the Member States, and areas in which the Treaty forbids the EU to legislate.

Problems with that system include a lack of clarity in that there were no provisions in the Treaty governing the allocation of competences between the EU and Member States. It was not always clear whether a competence rested with the EU or the Member States. There was a lack of precision with regard to the boundary of some Articles such as Article 308 EC. There were insufficient checks to ensure compliance with the delimitation of competence, in particular very little political monitoring. The EU could be accused of legislating in areas where it does not have competence. The lack of clarity of the delimitation meant that it is difficult for citizens to understand how powers are divided.

In addition, the limit line between EU competence and national competence was changing all the time. The Convention on the Future of Europe looked at establishing a more precise delimitation of competence between the EU and the Member States and a means of monitoring compliance with the delimitation of competence.

The Lisbon Treaty contains provisions concerning the delimitation of competences. In a decision on the Lisbon Treaty, the German Federal Constitution Court on 30 June 2009 considered at para 275:

> 'With a view to the extent of competences that have been transferred and the degree of independence of the decision-making procedures, the level of legitimisation of the European Union still complies with constitutional requirements to the extent that the principle of conferral is safeguarded to an extent which goes beyond the measure provided for in the Treaties (a). The Treaty of Lisbon neither transfers constituent power, which is not amenable to disposition by the constitutional bodies, nor abandons state sovereignty of the Federal Republic of Germany (b). The German *Bundestag* still retains sufficiently weighty responsibilities and competences of its own (c).'

Articles 1–6 TFEU, post-Lisbon determine the delimitation of competences and set out the categories and areas of Union competence;

Article 1 TFEU provides:

> '1. This Treaty organises the functioning of the Union and determines the areas of, delimitation of, and arrangements for exercising its competences.
> 2. This Treaty and the Treaty on European Union constitute the Treaties on which the Union is founded. These two Treaties, which have the same legal value, shall be referred to as "the Treaties".'

Article 2 TFEU sets out the categories of EU competence. The categories of competence are exclusive, shared and supporting, co-ordinating or supplementing. There is specific provision for Common Foreign and Security Policy and for co-ordination of economic and employment policies. Article 3 sets out the areas of exclusive EU competence. They are:

'(a) customs union;
 (b) the establishing of the competition rules necessary for the functioning of the internal market;
 (c) monetary policy for the Member States whose currency is the euro;
 (d) the conservation of marine biological resources under the common fisheries policy;
 (e) common commercial policy'.

There is also provision for exclusive competence in the conclusion of international agreements in circumstances set out (Article 3(2)).

Article 4 TFEU sets out the areas of shared competences. The principal areas are:

'(a) internal market;
 (b) social policy, for the aspects defined in this Treaty;
 (c) economic, social and territorial cohesion;
 (d) agriculture and fisheries, excluding the conservation of marine biological resources;
 (e) environment;
 (f) consumer protection;
 (g) transport;
 (h) trans-European networks;
 (i) energy;
 (j) area of freedom, security and justice;
 (k) common safety concerns in public health matters, for the aspects defined in this Treaty'.

Article 6 TFEU sets out the areas supporting, co-ordinating or supplementing competences:

'(a) protection and improvement of human health;
 (b) industry;
 (c) culture;
 (d) tourism;
 (e) education, vocational training, youth and sport;
 (f) civil protection;
 (g) administrative cooperation.'

There is a specific provision governing co-ordination of economic and employment policies (Article 5 TFEU).

The advantage of delimiting competence is that the EU is less open to the accusation that it is encroaching on powers that have not been transferred by the Member States.

8.6.2 WHAT POWERS DO THE INSTITUTIONS HAVE TO ACT IN THE FIELD OF HUMAN RIGHTS?

In *Opinion 2/94* [1996] ECR I-1759 the ECJ commented on the EC's power to act in the field of human rights. The ECJ examined the issue of whether the EC could accede to the ECHR. The principal change which would be brought about by accession would be that the EC institutions would be subject to scrutiny by the ECt.HR. The ECJ declined to rule on the compatibility of accession with the EC Treaty on the basis that it did not have sufficient information regarding the institutional systems which would operate. The ECJ went on to consider whether the EC had competence to accede to the ECHR. The ECJ, in ruling that the EC lacked competence to accede, opined at para 27:

'No Treaty provision confers on the Community institutions any general power to enact rules on human rights or to conclude international conventions in this field.'

The ECJ went on to consider whether Article 235 EC (later Art 308 and post-Lisbon Article 352 TFEU) could constitute a legal basis for accession. Article 235 is designed to fill a gap where no specific provisions of the Treaty confer on the Community institutions powers to act, if such powers appear necessary to enable the EC to carry out its objectives. The ECJ stated at para 30:

'...Article 235 cannot be used as a basis for the adoption of provisions whose effect would, in substance be to amend the Treaty without following the procedure which it provides for that purpose.'

Craig and de Búrca (*EU Law: Text, Cases and Materials*, 3rd edn, 2003, OUP, 353) have explained the judgment in the following terms:

'In ruling that the Community lacked legislative competence under the Treaties to become a party to the [ECHR], the ECJ gave some indication of the limits of human rights as a legislative foundation for Community action, although without ruling more specifically on the issue of what other, less fundamental kinds of legislation the [EC] might be competent to adopt in the human rights field. Para 27 is particularly relevant in this respect, although it merely denies that the [EC] has any jurisdiction under specific Treaty provisions to enact general rules on human rights.

The opinion however can be read as agreeing that Article 235 (now Article 308) may form a basis for the adoption of specific Community measures for the protection of human rights, so long as they do not amount to an amendment of the Treaty by going beyond the scope of the Community's defined aims and activities.

... What appeared to place accession to the ECHR beyond the scope of [EC] competence was... the fact that the agreement envisaged would bring with it fundamental institutional and constitutional changes which would actually require a Treaty amendment....'

In a later case, the ECJ again discussed the issue of competence, specifically the external competence of the EC, in the field of human rights. In Case C-268/94 *Portugal v Council* [1996] ECR I-6177, Portugal challenged the legal basis of the EC's competence to conclude a development co-operation agreement with India. Portugal argued that that the acceptance of fundamental rights as general principles of Community law did not equate with a competence in the field, whether internal or external. Portugal submitted that the references to human rights in the Treaties were 'programmatic', that they defined a general objective of the EC but did not confer a specific power of action.

The agreement's legal basis was in ex Articles 113 and 130y EC (later Articles 133 and 181 and post-Lisbon Articles 207 and 211 TFEU). In particular, Portugal objected to a provision in the agreement that respect for human rights and democratic principles was the basis for the co-operation and constituted an essential element of the agreement. In Portugal's view, the correct legal basis for the adoption of such human rights provisions was Article 235. The ECJ held that the correct legal basis had been utilised and pointed to the provision in Article 130u (later Article 177, post-Lisbon Article 208 TFEU) which states that EC policy in the sphere of development co-operation shall contribute to respecting human rights and fundamental freedoms. The ECJ notes that the human rights clause in the agreement was an essential element and not a specific field of co-operation. According to Craig and De Búrca (*EU Law: Text, Cases and Materials*, 3rd edn, 2003, OUP, 354), the implication of this judgment is that the EC 'would not have had competence under Article 151 (ex Article 130y, post-Lisbon Article 167 TFEU) to conclude a co-operation agreement principally on the subject of human rights, although it does have the power, under its development policy provisions, to insert a clause such as this one, making respect for human rights an essential element and basis for co-operation.' Article 181a (post-Lisbon Article 212 TFEU), added by the Nice Treaty, provides an express basis for human rights clauses in a co-operation policy.

In Case C-249/96 *Grant v South-West Trains Ltd* [1998] ECR I-621, at para 5, the ECJ explained the limitation on the power to act in the field of human rights in the following terms:

> 'Although respect for the fundamental rights which form an integral part of those general principles of law is a condition of the legality of Community acts, those rights cannot in themselves have the effect of extending the scope of the Treaty provisions beyond the competences of the Community.'

It seems that the EU may act to protect human rights provided it acts within the scope of EU Law. (See Weiler, and Fries, 'A Human Rights Policy for the European Community and Union: The Question of Competences' in Alston (ed), *The EU and Human Rights*, 1999, OUP, 147, 157.) Craig and de Búrca (*EU Law: Text, Cases and Materials*, 3rd edn, 2003, OUP, 357) submit that '[t]he institutional response to *Opinion 2/94* of the Court was a cautious one'. As evidence of this cautious approach, they cite, *inter alia*, Article 13 EC (post-Lisbon Article 19 TFEU), which, while creating a new EC power to combat discrimination, can be adopted only within the limits of the powers conferred on the EC by the Treaty and Article 51 of the Charter of Fundamental Rights, which emphasises that the Charter does not establish any new power for the Community. The Treaty of Lisbon, (see **8.1**) provides for a new Article 6 of the Treaty on European Union. Article 6(1), indent 2, provides '*The provisions of the Charter shall not extend in any way the competences of the Union as defined in the Treaties.*' No new competences will be conferred by virtue of the cross-reference to the Charter in new Article 6 TEU (see **8.4**). Article 6(2) TEU provides an express legal basis for EU accession to the ECHR.

8.6.3   MEMBER STATE COMPETENCE SUBJECT TO REVIEW BY AN INTERNATIONAL COURT

Another issue arises from the nature of EU law and the transferral of competences from the national to the supranational legal order. Member States are the primary protectors of human rights within their own territories but in fact the Member States are not completely independent in their application of human rights law.

All 27 Member States are party to the ECHR, and consequently, have subjected themselves to review by an external international court (the ECt.HR) for compliance with a minimum standard of human rights protection as set out by the ECHR.

The question arises as to whether the Member States can transfer to a supranational legal order, competences that at national level would be subject to review in accordance with human rights norms, when that supranational legal order is not (or at least was not) subject to review for compliance with human rights standards. This question is discussed in this chapter specifically in terms of the relationship between the EU and ECHR legal orders. It should be noted that the ECHR is not the only supervisory mechanism to which the EU Member States are party. A paragraph from the EU Annual Report on Human Rights, 2002, 13 (published on the Europa website (http://europa.eu/) as 12747/02 Rev 1 COHOM 11, Brussels, 16 October 2002) illustrates this point.

> 'Protection and promotion of human rights within the member states of the Union are primarily a concern of the States themselves with due regard to their own judicial systems and international obligations. The member states are parties to a number of international instruments of legally binding as well as political character, and

are therefore obliged to account for their actions within the field of human rights to a number of international organisations, including the Council of Europe, the Organisation for Security and co-operation in Europe and the United Nations.'

8.6.4 ARE EUROPEAN UNION ACTS SUBJECT TO SCRUTINY UNDER THE ECHR MACHINERY?

The Treaty of Lisbon provides a legal basis for EU accession to the ECHR (see **8.1** and **8.4**). Article 6(2) provides: '*The Union shall accede to the European Convention for the Protection of Human Rights and Fundamental Freedoms. Such accession shall not affect the Union's competences as defined in the Treaties.*' There is also a Protocol and a Declaration in respect of Article 6(2) (see **8.4**).

Prior to the Treaty of Lisbon, the EC refused to accede to the ECHR. This was a political decision taken by the Member States. While the Treaty of Lisbon provides a legal basis for accession by the EU to the ECHR, accession has not yet taken place. Pending accession it would seem that the EU institutions are not currently subject to review by the ECt.HR. Ironically, the Member States may find themselves accountable for breaches of the ECHR by the EU institutions. Two ECt.HR decisions illustrate this point.

The facts of *Matthews v United Kingdom* (1999) 28 EHRR 361 involved the applicant alleging a violation of the right to vote provision of the ECHR (Article 3, Protocol 1) by a Council decision and a Treaty. These European laws prevented the applicant, a national of Gibraltar, from voting in the direct elections to the European Parliament (EP). The ECt.HR held that the Community acts at issue were subject to review by the ECt.HR and held the Member States accountable for this breach. The ECt.HR held that the United Kingdom along with the other EU Member States, as contracting parties to the ECHR, could be held responsible for denying the inhabitants of Gibraltar the right to vote in the EP elections.

It should be emphasised however, that the acts at issue in *Matthews*, as primary laws, were not capable of review by the ECJ. The ECt.HR stated at para 33 of the decision in *Matthews*:

'Indeed [the primary law at issue in *Matthews*] cannot be challenged before the European Court of Justice for the very reason that it is not a "normal" act of the Community, but is a Treaty within the Community legal order.'

(ECJ jurisdiction is discussed at **8.7.1**.) *Matthews* cannot be taken as clear authority for the proposition that all Community or Union acts are subject to review by the ECt.HR.

In *Bosphorus Hava Yolari Turizm ve Ticaret AS* (2006) 42 EHRR 1, the measure at issue was an EC Regulation, a form of secondary EC legislation reviewable by the ECJ and which had in fact been reviewed by the ECJ which had held that the measure was not contrary to EC human rights law (see **8.8.1**). The Irish government had impounded an aircraft operated by the applicant pursuant to EC Regulation 990/93 which implemented in the EC UN sanctions against the Federal Republic of Yugoslavia (Serbia and Montenegro). The applicant judicially reviewed the decision to impound and the High Court ordered the release of the aircraft. The High Court decision was appealed to the Supreme Court who referred a question concerning the interpretation of the EC Regulation to the ECJ under the Article 234 (now Article 267 TFEU) preliminary reference procedure. The ECJ held that the EC Regulation applied to the aircraft. The Supreme Court bound by this ruling allowed the appeal. The applicant complained to the ECt.HR under Article 1, Protocol 1 ECHR that the impounding of the aircraft was a disproportionate interference with its peaceful enjoyment of possessions. The ECt.HR held (at paras 147–148) that the impugned interference with the applicant's property rights was not as a result of an exercise of discretion of the Irish authorities but rather amounted to compliance by the Irish State with its legal obligations flowing from the EC Regulation. The ECt.HR (at para 150) accepted that compliance with EC law was a legitimate general interest objective capable as serving as a justification for breaches of property rights. In order to balance the aim with the necessity of ensuring that state parties do not escape their responsibilities under the ECHR the ECt.HR invoked the 'equivalent protection' doctrine at para 155:

> 'In the [ECt.HR's] view, State action taken in compliance with such legal obligations [flowing from membership of an international organisation] is justified as long as the relevant organisation is considered to protect fundamental rights, as regards both the substantive guarantees offered and the mechanisms controlling their observance, in a manner which can be considered at least equivalent to that for which the [ECHR] provides.... By "equivalent" the [ECt.HR] means "comparable".... However any such finding of equivalence could not be final and would be susceptible to review in the light of any change in fundamental rights protection.'

The ECt.HR emphasised that a state would be fully responsible for acts falling outside its strict international obligations. As regards the substantive guarantees offered the ECt.HR noted the development of human rights protection by the ECJ, in particular the special significance afforded the ECHR by the ECJ. On the mechanisms controlling the observance of the ECHR within the EC legal system the ECt.HR noted the role of the ECJ and that of the national courts. Where such equivalent protection is provided by the international organisation a presumption would arise that the State had not departed from its ECHR obligations in fulfilling its obligations of membership of the international organisation. The presumption can be rebutted in a particular case if the protection of the ECHR rights is 'manifestly deficient'. The ECt.HR then went on to consider whether the presumption of ECHR compliance applied in the instant case and concluded that the protection of fundamental rights by EC law can be considered to be equivalent to that of the ECHR system and that the presumption of ECHR compliance had not been rebutted and that there had been no violation of Article 1, Protocol 1, ECHR.

The judgment is a significant one. Costello states:

> 'the "equivalent protection" doctrine depends on an assessment of the level of fundamental rights protection provided. Although this assessment is general in nature, in that the ECtHR looks at the EC judicial system as a whole, and the status of the ECHR as generally reflected in the EC case-law, an inquiry nonetheless did take place... it is a general rather than a specific finding. As such it avoids having to scrutinise the particular findings of the ECJ in its *Bosphorus* ruling and thus a situation in which it would have to review the particular findings of the ECJ. The hierarchy of Strasbourg over Luxembourg on fundamental rights issues is, thus, masked.' (Costello, 'The *Bosphorus* Ruling of the European Court of Human Rights: Fundamental Rights and Blurred Boundaries in Europe', [2006] 6 (1) *Human Rights Law Review*, 87, 100.)

According to Costello the hierarchy is reflected in three aspects of the 'equivalent protection' doctrine. First, the 'equivalent protection' doctrine depends on an assessment from time to time and is not an enduring assumption of compliance by the EU. Second, it is also subject to revision in those areas where the EU does not provide 'equivalent protection' citing *Matthews* and a number of situations where the ECJ does not have jurisdiction as examples. Third, the presumption is rebuttable.

It is clear that an EU Member State may be held accountable by the ECt.HR for a breach of the ECHR flowing from its EU law obligations. This is unlikely to occur on a regular basis given the ECt.HR's general finding that an equivalent measure of protection is currently offered by the EU legal system. An example of where the ECt.HR might hold that equivalent protection is not afforded by the EU legal system is an EU law not subject to the jurisdiction of the ECJ (see **8.7.1**) on the basis that it does not meet the requirement of sufficient mechanisms controlling the observance of the ECHR. Two separate concurring opinions in *Bosphorus*, one signed by six judges, accepted that there was no violation of the ECHR property right but expressed concern in respect of the 'equivalent protection' review approach and submitted that the contracting States to the ECHR could also claim that this abstract approach be applied to them.

8.6.5   THE FUTURE OF EUROPE AND ACCESSION

It is worth looking back at the Future of Europe Working Group's work on accession. The Future of Europe Working Group on the Charter/ECHR was asked to consider the question of whether the European Union should be able to accede to the European Convention on Human Rights.

The Working Group stressed that it was to decide only the issue of whether to introduce into the new Treaty a constitutional authorisation enabling the Union to accede to the ECHR. It would be for the Council of Ministers of the EU to decide unanimously when and how accession might take place.

All members of the Group either strongly supported or were willing to give favourable consideration to the creation of a constitutional authorisation enabling the EU to accede to the ECHR. The Working Group set out the main political and legal arguments in favour of accession:

> 'As the Union reaffirms its own values through its Charter, its accession to the ECHR would give a strong political signal of the coherence between the Union and the 'greater Europe', reflected in the Council of Europe and its pan-European human rights system.
>
> Accession to the ECHR would give citizens an analogous protection *vis à vis* all the Member States. This appears to be a question of credibility, given that Member States have transferred substantial competences to the Union and that adherence to the ECHR has been made a condition for membership of new states in the Union.
>
> Accession would be the ideal tool to ensure a harmonious development of the case law of the two European Courts in human rights matters; for some, this has even greater force in view of a possible incorporation of the Charter into the Treaties. In this connection, mention should also be made of the problems resulting from the present non-participation of the Union in the Strasbourg judicial system in cases where the Strasbourg Court is led to rule indirectly on Union law without the Union being able to defend itself before that Court or to have a judge in the court who would ensure the necessary expertise on Union law.'

The Working Group concluded that a legal basis to authorise accession of the EU to the ECHR should be inserted in the Constitutional Treaty but that accession should be on the basis of a unanimous decision of the Council and with the assent of the European Parliament.

The Working Group emphasised (at page 12) that after accession, the ECt.HR could not be regarded as a superior court but rather as a specialised court exercising external control over the international obligations of the EU resulting from accession to the ECHR. The Working Group indicated that incorporation of the Charter (see **8.10.10**) and accession should be viewed as complementary rather than as alternative steps.

The Working Group also clarified a number of issues surrounding the accession debate. First, accession would have effect only insofar as the law of the EU is concerned; no new EU competences would be created, the EU would not become a member of the Council of Europe, there would be an EU judge at the Strasbourg Court and the positions of the individual Member States with respect to the ECHR would not be affected.

The Treaty establishing a Constitution for Europe (OJ 2004/310/01 16 December 2004) had provided for accession to the ECHR, and an identical provision to that which had been included in that Treaty is included at Article 6(2) TEU, post-Lisbon (see **8.1**, **8.4**, **8.6.2** and **8.6.4**).

8.6.6 IS THERE AN OBLIGATION ON THE ECJ TO ENSURE ADHERENCE TO THE ECHR?

The reference for a preliminary ruling in Case C-466/00 *Kaba v Secretary of State for the Home Department* [2003] ECR I-2219 raises an interesting issue of whether there is an obligation on the ECJ to ensure adherence to the ECHR. The question asked by the UK Immigration Adjudicator was whether the procedure followed in a case before her, which had included an earlier preliminary reference to the ECJ, met the requirements of a fair hearing pursuant to Article 6, ECHR. However the ECJ was able to resolve the matter at issue without specifically answering this question.

8.7 Scope of Fundamental Human Rights Protection in the EU

Two questions arise concerning the scope of application of this EU human rights protection. First, over what activities of the Union does the ECJ have jurisdiction and second, who is bound by the EU standard of human rights protection?

8.7.1 ECJ JURISDICTION

The Maastricht Treaty did not afford the ECJ jurisdiction over all EU activity.

The Maastricht Treaty heralded the establishment of the European Union founded on three pillars. One of these pillars was the European Economic Community which became the European Community and over which the ECJ had jurisdiction. Common Foreign and Security Policy constituted the second pillar and Justice and Home Affairs, the third pillar. These two new pillars were essentially intergovernmental rather than supranational in nature and a provision was included in that Treaty (Article L) limiting the role of the ECJ.

The Treaty of Amsterdam amended certain aspects of the EU's pillar structure. Some elements of the third pillar were incorporated into the European Community (first) pillar. The ECJ was given jurisdiction over certain measures under the third pillar but there were differences in some procedures. ECJ jurisdiction remained excluded from the second pillar. Article 46 TEU defined the scope of the ECJ's jurisdiction after the Amsterdam amendments. The Treaty of Nice did not significantly change the scope of the ECJ's jurisdiction but the procedures of Article 7 TEU were rendered justiciable (see **8.4**).

Certain areas of EU activity were outside the scope of ECJ human rights review as the ECJ did not have jurisdiction. Even after the Nice Treaty, the ECJ had no jurisdiction over the common foreign and security policy (CFSP) and only limited jurisdiction over the third pillar, now called Police and Judicial Co-operation in Criminal Matters (PJCC).

Pursuant to the Treaty of Lisbon the EU is afforded a single legal personality and the EU has acquired the competences previously conferred on the European Community (EC). The pillar structure introduced by the Maastricht Treaty is modified by the Treaty of Lisbon and largely disappears. The jurisdiction of the ECJ now extends to the law of the EU, unless the Treaty provides otherwise.

Even after the Treaty of Lisbon the ECJ has a very limited role in respect of CFSP but its role in respect of PJCC is expanded. Under the Treaty of Lisbon, the CFSP, under Title V of the EU Treaty, remains subject to special rules and specific procedures (Article 24 TEU). The Court of Justice pursuant to Article 275 TFEU shall not have jurisdiction with respect to Common Foreign and Security Policy, subject to two exceptions, namely (1) the Court will have jurisdiction to monitor the delimitation of the Union's competences and the CFSP, the implementation of which must not affect the exercise of the Union's competences or the powers of the institutions in respect of the exercise of the exclusive and shared competences of the Union (Article 275 TFEU and Article 40 TEU), and (2) it will have jurisdiction over actions for annulment brought against decisions providing for restrictive measures against natural or legal persons adopted by the Council in connection, for example, with combating terrorism (freezing of assets) (Article 275 TFEU).

The Court of Justice will acquire general jurisdiction to give preliminary rulings in the area of freedom, security and justice, as a result of the modification of the pillars and the repeal by the Treaty of Lisbon of Article 35 EU and Article 68 EC which had imposed restrictions on the jurisdiction of the Court of Justice.

8.7.2 ARE THE MEMBER STATES SUBJECT TO REVIEW BY THE ECJ FOR COMPLIANCE WITH THE EU HUMAN RIGHTS STANDARD?

It is clear from the case-law discussed above that the ECJ reviews the acts of the institutions for compatibility with human rights, as general principles of EU law. The issue also arises as to whether the Member States are subject to review for compliance with the human rights *acquis*. Are the Member States subject to review by the ECJ for compliance with the EU human rights standard within the field of EU law?

As the EU human rights standard is sourced in the constitutional traditions of the Member States and international human rights instruments to which the Member States are party, it might appear that the Member States would have no objection to complying with the EU human rights *acquis*. However, there are a number of reasons why the Member States might object. Rights protected may vary from Member State to Member State. The standard and/or scope of protection may also vary. Also, the ECJ's jurisdiction to review the acts of Member States is very limited. It is likely, at least at the outset of the European integration project, that the Member States would have been surprised to find themselves subject to review by the ECJ for compliance with a human rights standard to which they had not expressly agreed. The ECJ has however held the Member States subject to review for compliance with the EU human rights *acquis* when the Member States act in the context of EU law.

> '... it should be remembered that the requirements flowing from the protection of fundamental rights in the Community legal order are also binding on Member States when they implement Community rules. (Case C-2/92 *R v Ministry of Agriculture, ex parte Bostock* [1994] ECR I-955, para 16 and Case C-292/97 *Karlsson*, [2000] ECR I- 2737, para 37.)'

The reason why Member States are only subject to review for compliance with the European human rights *acquis* in limited instances results from the division of competences between the EU and the Member States.

A number of specific categories in which the Member States are subject to review by the ECJ for compliance with the EC human rights *acquis* emerge from the case-law (see Craig and De Búrca, *EU Law: Text, Cases and Materials*, 4th edn, 2008, OUP, 395 *et seq*).

First, where Member States were applying provisions of Community law which were based on protection for human rights. A case within this category is the decision in Case 222/84 *Johnston v Chief Constable of the RUC* [1986] ECR 1651. The ECJ recognised the right to an effective remedy as a general principle of EC law. The ECJ held that Member States when applying the Equal Treatment Directive 76/207 were obliged to ensure the right to obtain an effective remedy in a competent court against measures which they consider to be contrary to the principle of equal treatment for men and women.

Second, when Member States are interpreting and enforcing EU provisions and thus acting as agents for the EU. Where the EU measures at issue do not specifically protect the right claimed, the ECJ has required the Member States to protect the right in their implementation processes. An example of a case within this category is the decision in Case 5/88 *Wachauf v Germany* [1989] ECR 2609. The applicant, a tenant farmer sought compensation for the discontinuance of milk production. A Community measure provided for such compensation. The German national implementing measure made the payment of compensation, conditional on the written consent of the lessor. The ECJ held that to deprive the tenant of the fruits of his labour without compensation would be incompatible with the requirement of protection of fundamental rights within the EC legal order. The ECJ held that these requirements were also binding on Member States when they implement EU rules. An example in the Irish courts is the decision in *Maher v Minister for Agriculture* [2001] 2 IR 139. This case involved a challenge to the validity of a statutory instrument implementing an EC Regulation on milk quotas. The Supreme Court was bound by the interpretation of the extent to which a milk quota could be considered a property right in Case C-2/92 *R v Ministry of Agriculture, ex parte Bostock* [1994] ECR I-955.

Third, when Member States derogate from EU Law requirements. An example of a case within this category is Case C-260/89 *Elliniki Radiophonia Tileorassi AE v Dimotiki Etairia Pliroforissis* [1991] ECR-I 2925. The ECJ held that national measures derogating from the freedom to provide services would only be permissible where the derogations were compatible with the protection of fundamental rights, specifically in this case, freedom of expression.

Apart from these specific examples, it is difficult to define precisely the limits of the scope of EU law application and thus difficult to specify the limit of the ECJ's power to review Member State action for compliance with the EC human rights standard.

It is clear that cases which fall within the scope of national law and outside the scope of Community law will not be subject to review by the ECJ. An example is the ECJ decision in Case C-299/95 *Kremzow v Austria* [1997] ECR I-2629. The proceedings leading to Kremzow's conviction for murder were held by the ECt.HR to be in violation of the Article 6 ECHR right to a fair trial. Kremzow argued in the ECJ proceedings that his right to free movement had been infringed by his unlawful imprisonment. The ECJ held that there was no connection between his situation and any of the situations contemplated by the Treaty provisions on free movement of persons. Hence the circumstances of his case fell outside the scope of EU law. As such, the ECJ did not have jurisdiction to review national measures for compatibility with the EC human rights standard.

8.8   The Standard of Human Rights Protection

The ECJ applies an EU standard of human rights protection. The EU interest is different to the Member State interest. The ECJ does not apply the maximum standard of human rights protection, ie it does not impose the highest standard from one state on other Member States. Neither does the ECJ apply a minimum standard. In the *Bosphorus Hava Yolari Turizm ve Ticaret AS* (2006) 42 EHRR 1 decision the ECt.HR made a general finding that the level of human rights protection in the EU legal system is equivalent to that afforded by the ECHR while noting that this assessment depended on review from time to time (see **8.6.4**). '[I]t does not amount to an enduring assumption of compliance' (Costello, 'The *Bosphorus* Ruling of the European Court of Human Rights: Fundamental Rights and Blurred Boundaries in Europe' [2006] 6 (1), *Human Rights Law Review*, 87, 100). Of significance is the manner in which the ECt.HR deals with the restrictive standing rules under Article 230(4) which the CFI, in Case T-177/01 *Jégo-Quére et Cie SA v Commission* [2002] ECR II-2365, had held would in some circumstances deprive an individual of an effective remedy in EC law (see **8.8.1** and **12.7.1**). The ECJ set aside this judgment on appeal Case 263/02 P *Commission v Jégo-Quéré* [2004] ECR I-3425 (see **8.8.1** and **8.10.6**). The ECt.HR in considering the mechanisms controlling the observance of the ECHR within the EU legal system as part of its analysis of whether an equivalent level of protection was offered did not criticise Article 230(4) but did note that access under Article 230(4) was 'restricted'. (at para 163 and see **12.7.1** and Costello, 'The *Bosphorus* Ruling of the European Court of Human Rights: Fundamental Rights and Blurred Boundaries in Europe' [2006] 6 (1), *Human Rights Law Review*, 87, 102). In *Bosphorus Hava Yolari Turizm ve Ticaret AS* (2006) 42 EHRR 1 (see **8.6.4**), Judge Ress (at para 2) in his concurring opinion noted that the ECt.HR 'has not addressed the question of whether limited access is really in accordance with [Article 6(1) ECHR] and whether particular provisions [Article 230(4) EC, ex Article 173] should be interpreted more extensively in light of [Article 6(1) ECHR]'. Judge Ress referred to the CFI judgment in Case T-177/01 *Jégo-Quére et Cie SA v Commission* [2002] ECR II-2365 and the ECJ judgment in Case C-50/00 P *Unión de Pequenos Agricultores v Council* [2002] ECR I- 6677 and stated 'One should not infer from para 162 of the judgment in the present case that the [ECt.HR] accepts that Article 6(1) does not call for more extensive interpretation.' (The decisions referred to by Judge Ress are discussed at **8.8.1**.)

Post-Lisbon, the standing rules have been modified slightly in Article 263(4) TFEU (ex Article 230(4)). *Locus standi* rules for individual applicants have been modified in a limited way. It remains to be seen whether this is sufficient to ensure an effective remedy.

8.8.1   LIMITS OF EU HUMAN RIGHTS PROTECTION

Protection of human rights at EC level is not absolute (see **8.2.5**). To ascertain the standard of human rights protection it is beneficial to analyse some case-law and the limits imposed on the protection of human rights. Human rights are regularly used to challenge EU provisions. While the ECJ has often accepted that, in principle, a right is protected, there are only rare examples of broad Community legislation being struck down on the grounds of a violation of human rights (see Weatherill and Beaumont, *EU Law*, 3rd edn, 1999, Penguin, 287–8 and Craig and de Búrca, *EU Law: Text, Cases and Materials*, 4th edn, 2008 OUP, 390–400). Craig and de Búrca point out that 'there has been a greater degree of success challenging individual administrative acts of the Commission or other EC actors, but that the Court has remained deferential in its review of EU legislation'. According to Weatherill and Beaumont '[o]ne of the reasons that fundamental rights pleas [in EC law] are rarely successful is that that rights are not absolute . . .'.

The approach of the ECJ to broad legislative measures is apparent in Case 4/73 *Nold v Commission* [1974] ECR 491 (see **8.2.5**). The applicant sought to annul a Commission decision authorising new trading rules, on the grounds, *inter alia*, that his fundamental rights had been violated. The applicant submitted that the effect of the decision was to deprive him of direct supplies for his business, thereby endangering both the profitability and the free development of business activity to such an extent as to endanger the existence of the business, thereby violating his proprietary rights and the right to free pursuit of a business. The ECJ stated that it was bound to ensure the observance of fundamental rights before indicating limitations on the protections of rights:

> 'If rights of ownership are protected by the constitutional laws of all the member states
> and if similar guarantees in respect of their right freely to choose and practise their

trade or profession, the rights thereby guaranteed, far from constituting unfettered prerogatives, must be viewed in the light of the social function of the property and activities protected thereunder.

For this reason, rights of this nature are protected by law subject always to limitations laid down in accordance with the public interest.

Within the Community legal order it likewise seems legitimate that these rights should, if necessary, be subject to certain limits justified by the overall objectives pursued by the Community, on condition that the substance of these rights is left untouched.

As regards the guarantees accorded to a particular undertaking, they can in no respect be extended to mere commercial interests or opportunities, the uncertainties of which are part of the very essence of economic activity.

The disadvantages claimed by the applicant are in fact the result of economic change and not of the contested decision.'

In Case 5/88 *Wachauf v Germany* [1989] ECR 2609 (see **8.7.2**), a tenant farmer sought compensation pursuant to an EC regulation for the discontinuance of milk production. The German national implementing measure made the payment of compensation conditional on the written consent of the lessor. The ECJ held that to deprive the tenant of the fruits of his labour, without compensation, was incompatible with the requirement of protection of fundamental rights within the EC legal order. The ECJ stated that fundamental rights recognised by the court are not absolute:

'The fundamental rights recognised by the Court are not absolute, however but must be considered in relation to their social function. Consequently, restrictions may be imposed on the exercise of those rights, in particular in the context of a common organisation of the market, provided that those restrictions in fact correspond to the objectives of general interest, pursued by the Community and do not constitute, with regard to the aim pursued, a disproportionate and intolerable interference, impairing the very substance of those rights.'

The ECJ went on to hold that Regulation at issue did not breach fundamental rights as the Regulation afforded the competent national authority a sufficiently wide margin of appreciation to enable the rules to be applied in accordance with the requirement of fundamental human rights protection.

In Case 44/79 *Hauer v Rheinland-Pfalz* [1979] ECR 3727 (see **8.2.5**), the applicant submitted that a Regulation prohibiting the new planting of vines infringed, *inter alia*, her right to property. The ECJ conducted a survey of limits on the right to property contained in a number of Member State constitutions and in the ECHR, in determining that the Regulation at issue did not entail any undue limitation on the right to property and that the restriction was justified in the interest of the common organisation of the market.

In Case C-280/93 *Germany v Council* [1994] ECR 4973, a case involving the introduction of a quota and rules for its subdivision in the banana market resulting in alleged discrimination against traders in third-country bananas, the ECJ again stated that the rights at issue, the rights to property and freedom to pursue a profession, were not absolute but could be restricted in the context of a common organisation of the market.

The facts of Case C-84/95 *Bosphorus Hava Yolari Turizm ve Ticaret AS v Minister for Transport, Energy and Communications* [1996] ECR I-3953 (see **8.6.4**) involved the impounding, by the Irish government, of an aircraft leased by the applicant, pursuant to EU sanctions against the Federal Republic of Yugoslavia (Serbia and Montenegro). The applicant alleged breaches of its right to peaceful enjoyment of its property and its freedom to pursue a commercial activity and of the principle of proportionality. The ECJ held that the impounding of the aircraft was not contrary to EC human rights law, stating that it was 'settled case-law that the fundamental rights invoked by [the applicant] are not absolute and their exercise may be subject to restrictions justified by objectives of general interest pursued by the Community'. In the view of the ECJ, the measure could not be regarded as disproportionate in light of the objective of the international community to put an end to the state of war.

It is apparent from the cases cited that restrictions can be imposed on human rights protection. In *Wachauf, Hauer* and *Germany v Council* the ECJ justified restrictions on fundamental rights by reference to the common organisation of the market. In *Bosphorus Hava Yolari Turizm ve Ticaret AS* the ECJ justified restrictions by reference to the international situation at the time, namely a state of war.

It seems an interpretation of EU Law flowing from the Treaty may trump the protection of a right.

The facts of Case 263/02 P *Commission v Jégo-Quére et Cie SA*, [2004] ECR I-3425 (see **12.7.1** and **8.8**) involve an appeal against a decision of the Court of First Instance (CFI) (Case T-177/01 *Jégo-Quéré v Commission* [2002] ECR II-2365) in which the CFI had proposed a new interpretation of the test for individual concern. Article 230(4) EC requires natural or legal persons to show direct and individual concern to establish standing to bring an application for annulment. Jégo-Quéré had been unable to show individual concern according to the traditional interpretation. The CFI held that the strictness of the traditional interpretation meant that in some circumstances Community Law would fail to guarantee to individuals access to an effective judicial remedy and went on to propose a new reading of individual concern.

Subsequent to the CFI decision the ECJ in Case C-50/00 P *Unión de Pequeños Agricultores* [2002] ECR I-6677 upheld the traditional interpretation of individual concern as an unavoidable condition for standing under Article 230(4) EC. Advocate General Jacobs in the appeal in Case 263/02 P *Commission v Jégo-Quéré* delivered his opinion in July 2003.

> 'However, it clearly follows from the [ECJ's] judgment in *Unión de Pequeños Agricultores* [Case C-50/00 P [2002] ECR I-6677] that the traditional interpretation of individual concern, because it is understood to flow from the Treaty itself, must be applied regardless of its consequences for the right to an effective judicial remedy.
>
> Such an outcome is to my mind unsatisfactory, but is the unavoidable consequence of the limitations which the current formulation of the fourth para of Article 230 is considered by the Court to impose. As the Court made clear in *Unión de Pequeños Agricultores* [Case C-50/00 P [2002] ECR I-6677], necessary reforms to the Community system of judicial review are therefore dependent upon action by the Member States to amend that provision of the Treaty. In my opinion, there are powerful arguments in favour of introducing a more liberal standing requirement in respect of individuals seeking to challenge generally applicable Community measures in order to ensure that full judicial protection is in all circumstances guaranteed.'

The ECJ in Case 263/02 P *Commission v Jégo-Quéré* [2004] ECR I-3425 followed the decision in Case C-50/00 P *Unión de Pequeños Agricultores* [2002] ECR I-6677, set aside the CFI decision and upheld the traditional interpretation of individual concern (see **12.7.1**).

As noted above (see **8.8**) the Treaty of Lisbon relaxed the standing rules but in a limited way. Ex Article 230(4) EC is now found, as amended at Article 263(4) TFEU.

It is submitted that the real concern for human rights protection within the scope of EU law is that EU law is superior to the human rights protections of the Member State constitutions whether EU law protects human rights or not and regardless of the standard or limits of rights protection. On occasion the ECJ has been criticised for not taking human rights protections seriously (Coppel and O' Neill, 'The European Court of Justice: Taking Rights Seriously?' (1992) 29 *CMLR* 669; but see also Weiler and Lockhart, ' "Taking Rights

Seriously" Seriously: The European Court and its Fundamental Rights Jurisprudence' (1995) 32 *CMLR* 51 and 579.)

8.9 The Human Rights *Acquis*

8.9.1 WHAT RIGHTS ARE PROTECTED?

Whilst the protection of human rights by the ECJ is to be welcomed, it is open to the criticism that it is uncertain. Human rights protection by the ECJ has developed on an *ad hoc* basis in response to the issues raised. There is no guarantee that a right will be afforded protection by the ECJ if it is protected in the Constitutions of the Member States or in an international human rights treaty. The issue of whether a right is protected in European law is only determined when the ECJ makes a pronouncement on that right. This is hardly a satisfactory situation for an aggrieved litigant.

It is proposed to examine some of the rights protected in the European human rights *acquis* under three headings to provide example of the sources of human rights law. This discussion does not contain an exhaustive list of the rights protected nor the sources of rights in European law, but will serve as an indication of the human rights *acquis*.

8.9.2 THE TREATIES AS A SOURCE OF HUMAN RIGHTS

The omission of a bill of rights from the original Community Treaties was mentioned earlier. A number of provisions in the Treaty relate to human rights issues; for example Article 18 TFEU (ex Article 12 EC (ex Article 6)) prohibits discrimination on the grounds of nationality and Article 157 TFEU (ex Article 141 EC (ex Article 119)) provides for equal pay for equal work for men and women.

The Treaty of Amsterdam added two new legal bases in the field of human rights. Article 13 (now Article 19 TFEU) empowered the political institutions to take action to combat discrimination based on sex, racial or ethnic origin, religion or belief, disability, age or sexual orientation. Article 141 EC (now Article 157 TFEU has been widened to apply the principle of equal opportunities and equal treatment of men and women in matters of employment and occupation as well as pay. In addition, Article 141(4) (now Article 157(4) TFEU) allows for affirmative action in favour of the under represented sex.

8.9.3 SECONDARY LEGISLATION AS A SOURCE OF HUMAN RIGHTS

Secondary EC legislation may also act as a source of human rights. It is beyond the ambit of this chapter to analyse all relevant secondary legislation. Instead it examines some important examples of secondary legislation.

On the basis of Article 13 EC (now Article 19 TFEU), as inserted by the Treaty of Amsterdam, two Directives were adopted relating to equal treatment. Council Directive 2000/43 on Race Discrimination is designed to prohibit discrimination on the grounds of race and ethnic origin. (Council Directive 2000/43 [2000] OJ L180/22.) The Directive prohibits any direct or indirect discrimination on the grounds of race or ethnic origin in areas such as access to employment, access to vocational training, working conditions, membership of organisations, social protection, education and access to supply of goods and services. The Directive is applicable to both the public and private sectors. In cases where the facts establish a presumption of discrimination the burden shifts to the respondent to show that there has been no breach of the principle of equal treatment.

Council Directive 2000/78 establishes a general framework to secure equal treatment in employment and occupation and is designed to prohibit discrimination on the grounds of religion, belief, disability, age and sexual orientation (Council Directive 2000/78 [2000] OJ L303/16).

There are also a considerable number of directives relating to workers rights. These include Directive 89/391/EEC on the introduction of measures to encourage improvements in the safety and health of workers at work, Directive 80/987/EEC on the protection of employees in the event of the insolvency of their employer, Directive 93/104/EC concerning certain aspects of the organisation of working time, Directive 94/33/EC on the protection of young people at work and Council Directive 92/85/EEC on the introduction of measures to encourage improvements in the health and safety at work of pregnant workers and workers who have recently given birth or are breastfeeding.

8.9.4   RIGHTS RECOGNISED IN THE CASE-LAW OF THE ECJ

The early development of the protection of human rights by the ECJ was discussed at **8.2.5**. The ECJ indicated that the sources of rights included the constitutional traditions of Member States and international treaties on which the Member States have collaborated.

There is a useful survey of the rights which the ECJ has ruled on in Lenaerts and Van Nuffel (*Constitutional Law of The European Union*, 1999, Sweet and Maxwell, 548). This list gives an indication of the breadth of rights protected by the ECJ. The rights recognised in the case-law of the ECJ are:

- The principle of equal treatment

- The right to a fair hearing and to an effective remedy

- The principle that provisions of criminal law may not have retroactive effect

- Respect for private life, family life, the home and correspondence, in particular respect for a person's physical integrity, the right to keep one's state of health private, medical confidentiality and the right to inviolability of one's home

- Freedom to manifest one's religion

- Freedom of expression

- Freedom of association, in particular the right to be a member of a trade union and to take part in trade union activities

- Rights of ownership or the rights to property

- Freedom to carry on an economic activity (trade or profession)

- The right of everyone lawfully within the territory of a state to liberty of movement therein.

8.10   The Charter of Fundamental Rights of the EU

8.10.1   BACKGROUND TO THE CHARTER

The European Council in Cologne in June 1999 agreed that it was necessary to establish a Charter of Fundamental Rights 'in order to make their overriding importance and relevance more visible to the Union's citizens.' (Conclusions of the European Council, Cologne, 3 and 4 June 1999.) The Council agreed that the Charter should contain the fundamental rights and freedoms as well as the basic procedural rights guaranteed by the ECHR and derived from the constitutional traditions common to the Member States, as general principles of Community law, fundamental rights that pertain only to the Union's citizens and that the Charter should take account of the economic and social rights as contained in the European Social Charter and the Community Charter of the Fundamental Social Rights of Workers (Article 136 TEU, insofar as they do not merely establish objectives for action by the Union). The Cologne European Council set up a timetable and a procedural framework for the drafting of the Charter.

8.10.2   INTRODUCTORY COMMENTS

At the meeting of the European Council in Nice on 7 December 2000, the European Parliament, the Council and the Commission solemnly proclaimed the Charter of Fundamental Rights of the European Union (OJ 2000/C-364/01 18 December 2000).

The stated objective of the Charter was to increase the visibility of human rights protection within the European Union legal order. Consequently, the Charter is confined to cataloguing existing rights. This point requires two clarifications. First (and more obviously) the purpose of the exercise was to increase the visibility of existing rights and not to create new rights. Second, that the task of the Charter is to catalogue existing rights might give rise to the supposition that all rights protected in EU law are to be found in the Charter. The Charter, however, affords a higher standard of protection than is actually protected (ie higher than the standard currently protected by ECJ case-law) but a lower standard than that which the ECJ is capable of protecting by reference to the constitutional traditions of the Member States and/or international human rights treaties to which the Member States are party.

Another interesting aspect of the Charter relates to the unusual manner of its drafting (see de Búrca, 'The Drafting of the European Union Charter of Fundamental Rights' (2001) 26 *European LR* 126). The Charter was drafted by a unique body composed of 62 representatives of the Member State governments, the Commission, the European Parliament and the national parliaments. The openness of the deliberative process stands in marked contrast to the traditional IGC method of EU development. A multitude of submissions were made by other institutions, civil society, non-governmental organisations (NGOs) and applicant countries. Proceedings were generally in public and submissions and drafts were available on the Charter website. The Charter was drafted on a consensus-building basis. At least from the perspective of increased transparency, the process can be regarded as a success. In fact, the Convention for drafting the Charter was the model for the Convention on the Future of Europe which drafted the Draft Treaty establishing a Constitution for Europe (CONV 820/1/03 Brussels, 27 June 2003) (see **8.4.1** and **8.10.10**).

An explanatory text of the Charter was published by the drafting body (*Charter of Fundamental Rights of the EU: Explanations relating to the complete text of the Charter*, Office for Official Publications of the European Communities, Luxembourg, 2001). The purpose of the explanatory text was to clarify the provisions of the Charter and it had no legal status.

It should be noted that there are now two versions of the Charter; the original version proclaimed in December 2000 and an adapted version solemnly proclaimed by the three political institutions of the EU on 12 December 2007 (OJ C303/01 14 December 2007 and see **8.1**). The adapted version the Charter became legally binding on the entry into force of the Treaty of Lisbon on 1 December 2009 pursuant to Article 6(1) TEU. That Treaty Article also states that 'due regard' is to be had to the Explanations to the Charter which were also adapted and updated (see **8.1**, **8.4** and **8.10.5**).

8.10.3 CONTENTS OF THE CHARTER

This section provides an overview of the content of the Charter and the origins of the rights to be protected. The Charter is divided into a preamble and seven Titles: Dignity, Freedoms, Equality, Solidarity, Citizen's Rights, Justice and General Provisions Governing the interpretation and application of the Charter. The Titles are divided into Articles numbered from 1 to 54. This section will largely refer to the Charter in its adapted form. This version of the Charter almost replicates the original Charter but some changes, discussed below, have been incorporated into Title VII: General Provisions Governing the Interpretation and Application of the Charter.

Title I, *Dignity*, affirms the protection of the dignity of the person, the right to life (including freedom from the death penalty), right to integrity of the person, prohibition of torture, inhuman or degrading treatment and punishment and prohibition of slavery and forced labour. The majority of the Articles in this chapter correspond to rights protected by the ECHR but inspiration is also drawn from the Universal Declaration on Human Rights and the Convention on Human Rights and Biomedicine.

Title II, *Freedoms*, assures a right to liberty and security, respect for private and family life, protection of personal data, the right to marry and found a family, freedom of thought, conscience and religion, freedom of expression and information, freedom of assembly and association, freedom of the arts and sciences, a right to education, freedom to choose an occupation and a right to engage in work, freedom to conduct a business, a right to property, a right to asylum and protection in the event of removal, expulsion or extradition. Similarly, the Articles in Title II correspond in large part to the freedoms guaranteed by the ECHR with additional inspiration from the constitutions of EU Member States, Community secondary legislation, case-law of the ECJ and the Geneva Convention on Refugees.

Title III, *Equality*, protects equality before the law, non-discrimination, cultural, religious and linguistic diversity, equality between men and women, rights of the child, rights of the elderly and integration of persons with disabilities. Title III is inspired by European constitutions, case-law of the ECJ, the ECHR, the Convention on Human Rights and Biomedicine, the EC Treaty, Community legislation, the European Social Charter and the New York Convention on the Rights of the Child.

Title IV, *Solidarity*, provides for workers' rights to information and consultation within the undertaking, a right of collective bargaining and action, a right of access to placement services, protection in the event of unjustified dismissal, fair and just working conditions, prohibition of child labour and protection of young people at work, reconciling family and professional life, social security and social assistance, health care, access to services of general economic interest, environmental protection and consumer protection. The rights in Title IV are predominantly drawn from the European Social Charter and the Community Charter on the Rights of Workers with additional inspiration from the ECHR and the TFEU.

Title V, *Citizenship*, assures a right to vote and to stand as a candidate in elections to the European Parliament, a right to vote and to stand as a candidate at municipal elections, a right to good administration, a right of access to documents, a right to refer to the Ombudsman, a right to petition the European Parliament, freedom of movement and of residence, diplomatic and consular protection. Rights accruing to EU citizens are drawn from the TFEU and ECJ case-law.

Title VI, *Justice*, guarantees a right to an effective remedy and a fair trial, presumption of innocence, a right of defence, principles of legality, proportionality of criminal offences and penalties and a right not to be tried or punished twice in criminal proceedings for the same criminal offence. The dominant source of justice rights is the ECHR with further inspiration from the case-law of the ECJ and the ICCPR.

Title VII, *General Provisions governing the interpretation and application of the Charter*, sets out the field of application of the Charter, the scope and interpretation of the rights and principles in the Charter, the level of protection and prohibits an abuse of rights. Title VII includes the 'horizontal clauses' whose objects are to explain the relationship of the Charter with the ECHR and to safeguard the position of the ECHR.

There are a number of changes to Title VII in the adapted 2007 version of the Charter. Article 51 was amended to clarify that the Charter does not extend the field of application of EU law beyond the powers of the EU or establish any new power or task for the EU. A horizontal provision (Article 52(4)) is added to ensure that where the Charter recognises rights which result from the common traditions of the Member States that those rights are interpreted in accordance with those traditions. A provision was added (Article 52(5)) that the provisions of the Charter which contain 'principles' may be implemented by legislative or executive acts of the EU and by acts of the EU when implementing EU law. Thus a distinction is drawn between rights and principles but it is not clear which Charter provisions contain principles. A provision was added (Article 52(6)) to clarify that full account shall be taken of national laws and practices as specified in the Charter. Many of these changes had been suggested by the Working Group on the Incorporation of the Charter. The Working Group emphasised that its suggested amendments were not intended to alter the substance of the Charter but rather to render absolutely clear and legally watertight certain key elements of the overall consensus of the Charter as agreed by the previous Convention (CONV 354/02 Final report of Working Group II 'Incorporation of the Charter/Accession to the ECHR' Brussels, 22 October 2002).

The replacement Article 6 TEU, the text of which is set out at **8.4**, states that the version of the Charter as adapted in 2007 will have the same legal status as the Treaties. Thus since 1 December 2009, the Charter has legally binding status (see **8.1** and **8.4**).

8.10.4 THE LEGAL STATUS OF THE CHARTER

A legally binding Charter required a Treaty amendment. A decision was taken at the 2004 IGC that the Charter would be included in the Treaty establishing a Constitution for Europe and that the Charter would become legally binding (OJ 2004/310/01 16 December 2004 and see **8.1** and **8.10.10**). However, the Treaty establishing a Constitution for Europe was not ratified by all of the Member States and following a period of reflection, the European Council in June 2007 determined to convene an IGC to draft a Reform Treaty (see **8.1**), which became the Treaty of Lisbon. The Treaty of Lisbon contains a provision providing that the Charter shall have the same legal value as the Treaties (Article 6 of the reformed TEU, the text of which is set out at **8.4**). A Protocol giving the United Kingdom and Poland an opt-out of the Charter is annexed to the Treaties (Protocol No. 30, see **8.4**)). It states *inter alia*:

> *'Article 1*
> 1. *The Charter does not extend the ability of the Court of Justice of the European Union, or any court or tribunal of Poland or of the United Kingdom, to find that the laws, regulations or administrative provisions, practices or action of the United Kingdom are inconsistent with the fundamental rights, freedoms and principles that it reaffirms.*
> 2. *In particular, and for the avoidance of doubt, nothing in Title IV of the Charter creates justiciable rights applicable to Poland or the United Kingdom except in so far as Poland or the United Kingdom has provided for such rights in its national law.*
> *Article 2*
> *To the extent that a provision of the Charter refers to national laws and practices, it shall only apply to Poland or the United Kingdom to the extent that the rights or principles that it contains are recognised in the law or practices of the United Kingdom.'*

Previously a decision had been taken by the Member States at the Nice IGC that the Charter was to be declaratory rather than a legally binding text. At that time the Member States decided not to incorporate the Charter into the Treaties, nor to refer to the Charter as a source of general principles of human rights law in Article 6 (ex Article F) TEU. In the Nice (December 2000) and Laeken (December 2001) Declarations on the Future of Europe, it was agreed that consideration would be given to the status of the Charter of Fundamental Rights and whether it would be included in the EC Treaty. A decision was taken at the 2004 IGC that the Charter would be included in the Treaty establishing a Constitution for Europe (OJ 2004/310/01 16 December 2004).

Initially, the Charter was not binding and thus was not a source of rights. However, some of the rights listed in the Charter were already legally binding within the EU legal order. The reason for this was that the Charter had disparate sources. Some of the Charter Articles are based on the Treaties, secondary EU legislation and the case-law of the ECJ while others stemmed from the ECHR, other international human rights instruments to which the EU Member States are party and the national constitutions of the EU Member States. The former were binding on the EU while the latter served as guidelines to the general principles of EU human rights law.

Pre-Lisbon pursuant to Article 6(2) TEU (ex Article F), the ECJ already had jurisdiction to monitor the acts of the institutions to ensure compliance with rights found in the ECHR and constitutional traditions of the Member States.

To determine whether a right was binding it was necessary to look at its source.

8.10.5 WHAT FUNDAMENTAL RIGHTS IN THE CHARTER WERE ALREADY PROTECTED IN EUROPEAN LAW?

An analysis of the Charter will provide us with an overview of which of the rights enumerated in the Charter were previously (ie pre-Charter) protected in EU law. Those rights which have as their source the Treaties, EC secondary legislation or case-law of the ECJ are binding on the EU institutions either in the sense of requiring positive action to protect the rights or in the form of a negative prohibition on the breach of the rights.

However, not every right listed in the table setting out the rights was binding. Some of the sources were more ambiguous. An example is the European Social Charter, a document drafted under the aegis of the Council of Europe but after the Amsterdam Treaty, explicitly referred to in Article 136 EC as a possible source of the Community's Social Policy. The information contained in the table is taken from the Explanations relating to the Charter of Fundamental Rights (2007 C303/02 14 February 2007 and see **8.1, 8.4** and **8.10.10**). Article 6(1) indent 3, TEU post Lisbon provides:

> 'The rights, freedoms and principles in the Charter shall be interpreted in accordance with the general provisions in Title VII of the Charter governing its interpretation and application and with due regard to the explanations referred to in the Charter, that set out the sources of those provisions.'

It seems therefore that the explanations are some sort of interpretative guide to the Charter.

Charter Guarantees Sourced in EC/EU Law

Title	Article	Guarantee	Source
Title I: Dignity	Art 1	Human Dignity	In Case 377/98 *Netherlands v European Parliament and Council* [2001] ECR I-7079, the ECJ confirmed that a fundamental right to human dignity is part of EU law
	Art 3	Right to Integrity of the Person Prohibition on trafficking in human beings	In Case 377/98 *Netherlands v European Parliament and Council* [2001] ECR I-7079, the ECJ confirmed that a fundamental right to human integrity is part of EU law and encompasses, in the context of medicine and biology, the free and informed consent of the donor and the recipient
	Art 5(3)		Sourced in part in Chapter VI of the Convention Implementing the Schengen Agreement, which has been integrated into the *acquis communautaire*, in which the United Kingdom and Ireland participate
Title II: Freedoms	Art 8	Right to protection of personal data	Sourced in part in Art 286 EC (now replaced by Art 16 TFEU and Art 39 TEU) and Directive 95/46/EC on the protection of individuals with regard to the processing of personal data and on the free movement of such data. Reference is also made to Regulation (EC) No 45/2001 of the European Parliament and Council on the protection with regard to the processing of personal data by the Community institutions and bodies and on free movement of such data
	Art 11(2)	Freedom and pluralism of the media shall be respected	Sourced in ECJ case-law regarding television (particularly Case C-288/89 *Schichting Collectieve Antennevoorziening Gouda* [1991] ECR I-4007), the Protocol on the System of Broadcasting in the Member States annexed to the EC Treaty, now to the Treaties and on Council Directive 89/552/EC (particularly its seventeenth recital)

	Art 12(1)	Freedom of Assembly and Association	Sourced in part in point 11 of the Community Charter of the Fundamental Social Rights of Workers
	Art 12(2)	Political parties at Union level contribute to expressing the political will of the citizens of the Union	Corresponds to Art 191 EC, now 10(4) TEU
	Art 14(1)	The extension of the right to education to include access to vocational and continuing training	Sourced in part in point 15 of the Community Charter of the Fundamental Social Rights of Workers
	Art 15(1)	Freedom to choose an occupation	Recognised in the case-law of the ECJ, in *inter alia*, Case 4/73 *Nold* [1974] ECR 491 (paras 12–14), Case 44/79 *Hauer* [1979] ECR 3727 and Case 234/85 *Keller* [1986] ECR 2897 and in Art 1(2) of the European Social Charter and on point 4 of the Community Charter of the Fundamental Social Rights of Workers
	Art 15(2)	Freedom of movement for workers, freedom of establishment and freedom to provide services	Sourced in Arts 39, 43 and 49 *et seq* EC, now Arts 26, 45, 49 and 56 TFEU
	Art 15(3)	Entitles nationals of third countries authorised to work in the territories of the Member States to working conditions equivalent to those of citizens of the Union	Based on Article 153(1)(g) TFEU and on Art 19(4) of the European Social Charter
	Art 16	Freedom to conduct a business	Sourced in ECJ case-law which has recognised a freedom to exercise an economic or commercial activity (Case 4/73 *Nold* [1974] ECR 491 (para 14) and Case 230/78 *SPA*

Title	Article	Guarantee	Source
			Eridiana [1979] ECR 2749 (paras 20 and 31)) and freedom of contract (*inter alia* Case 151/78 *Sukkerfabricken Nykøbing* [1979] ECR 1 (para 19)) and Case C-240/97 *Spain v Commission* [1999] ECR I- 6571 (para 19) (and Art 119 (1) and (3) TFEU) and (2) which recognises free competition
	Art 17(1)	The right to property	Sourced in Art 1 of the Protocol to the ECHR but is a right which has been recognised on numerous occasions by the ECJ, initially in Case 44/79 *Hauer* [1979] ECR 3727
	Art 18	Protects the right to asylum	Based on TEC Art 63, now 78 TEFU. This Article is in line with the Protocol on Asylum annexed to the EC Treaty
Title III: Equality	Art 20	Equality before the law	Recognised as a basic principle of Community law in the case-law of the ECJ (Case 283/83 *Racke* [1984] ECR 3791 and Case 15/95 *EARL* [1997] ECR I-1961 and Case 292/97 *Karlsson* [2000] ECR I-2737)
	Art 21(1)	The prohibition of discrimination on any ground such as sex, race, colour, ethnic or social origin, genetic features, language, religion or belief, political or any other opinion, membership of a national minority, property, birth, disability, age or sexual orientation	Sourced in part in Art 13 of the EC Treaty, now Art 19 TFEU
	Art 21(2)	Prohibits within the scope of application of the EC and EU treaties any discrimination on the grounds of nationality	Corresponds to Art 12 EC, now Art 18 TFEU
	Art 22	Respect for cultural, religious and linguistic diversity	Sourced in Art 6 TEU, Art 151 (1) and (4) EC (now replaced by Art 167 (1) and (4) TFEU concerning culture and respect for cultural and linguistic diversity is also at Art 3(3) TEU) and Declaration No. 11 to the Final Act of

			the Treaty of Amsterdam, now taken over by Art 17 TFEU
	Art 23	The principle of equality between men and women	Sourced in Arts 2 EC, 3(2) EC and 141(3) EC, now Art 4 TEU and Art 8 TFEU and Art 157 TFEU, Art 20 of the revised European Social Charter, point 16 of the Community Charter on the Rights of Workers and Art 2(4) of Council Directive 76/207/EEC. Art 23(2) limits the equality guarantee in that it permits affirmative action in favour of the underrepresented sex in accordance with Art 141(4) EC, Art 157 (4) TFEU
	Art 25	Rights of the elderly	Sourced in Art 23 of the revised Social Charter and points 24 and 25 of the Community Charter of the Fundamental Social Rights of Workers
	Art 26	Promotes the integration of persons with disabilities	Sourced in Art 15 of the European Social Charter, Art 23 of the revised Social Charter and point 26 of the Community Charter of the Fundamental Social Rights of Workers
Title IV: Solidarity	Art 27	Workers' right to information and consultation within the undertaking	Sourced in Art 21 of the revised European Social Charter and in points 17 and 18 of the Community Charter on the Rights of Workers. Arts 154 and 155 TFEU are also relevant together with Directives 2002/14 EC, 98/59/EC, 2001/23/EC and 94/45/EC
	Art 28	A right of collective bargaining and action	Sourced in Art 6 of the European Social Charter and on points 12–14 of the Community Charter of the Fundamental Social Rights of Workers
	Art 29	A right of access to placement services	Based on Art 1(3) of the European Social Charter and point 13 of the Community Charter of the Fundamental Social Rights of Workers
	Art 30	Protection in the event of unjustified dismissal	Sourced in Art 24 of the revised Social Charter and in Directive 2001/23/EC, Directive 80/987 EEC and Directive 2002/74/EC
	Art 31(1)	For fair and just working conditions	Sourced in Directive 89/391/EEC, Art 3 of the Social Charter and point 19 of the Community Charter on the

Title	Article	Guarantee	Source
			Rights of Workers and Art 26 of the revised Social Charter. The expression 'working conditions' must be understood in the sense of Art 140, now Art 156 TFEU
	Art 31(2)	Relates to the organisation of working time	Sourced in Directive 93/104/EC, Art 2 of the European Social Charter and point 8 of the Community Charter on the Rights of Workers
	Art 32	Prohibits child labour and protects young people at work	Based on Directive 94/33/EC, Art 7 of The European Social Charter and points 20–23 of the Community Charter of the Fundamental Social Rights of Workers
	Art 33(1)	Protects family life	Sourced in Art 16 of the European Social Charter
	Art 33(2)	Reconciles family and professional life	Sourced in Council Directive 92/85/EEC, Directive 96/34/EC, Art 8 of the European Social Charter and Art 27 of the revised Social Charter
	Art 34(1)	Recognises the entitlement to social security and social assistance	This principle is sourced in Arts 153 and 156 TFEU, and in Art 12 of the European Social Charter and point 10 of the Community Charter on the Rights of Workers. The Union must respect the principle when exercising the powers conferred on it by Arts 153 and 156 TFEU
	Art 34(2)	Provides that everyone residing and moving legally within the EU is entitled to social security benefits	This principle is sourced in Art 13(4) of the European Social Charter and point 2 of the Community Charter of the Fundamental Social Rights of Workers and reflects the rules arising from Regulation 1408/71 and Regulation 1612/68
	Art 34(3)	The right to social and housing assistance	Sourced in Art 13 of the European Social Charter, Arts 30 and 31 of the revised Social Charter and point 10 of the Community Charter. The Union must respect it in the context of policies based on Art 153 TFEU
	Art 35	A right of access to health care	Sourced in Art 152 EC, now 168 TFEU and Arts 11 and 13 of the European Social Charter
	Art 36	Access to services of general economic interest	Sourced in Art 14 TFEU

	Art 37	Environmental protection	Sourced in Arts 2, 6 and 174 EC, now replaced by Art 3(3) TEU and Arts 11 and 191 TFEU
	Art 38	Consumer protection	Sourced in Art 169 TFEU
Title V: Citizens' rights	Art 39(1)	A right to vote and to stand as a candidate at elections to the European Parliament	Sourced in Art 20(2) TFEU
	Art 39(2)	Provides that members of the European Parliament shall be elected by direct universal suffrage in a free and secret ballot	Sourced in Art 14(3) TEU
	Art 40	A right to vote and stand as a candidate at municipal elections	Sourced in Art 20(2) TFEU
	Art 41(1) and (2)	A right to good administration	Sourced in the case-law of the ECJ. (Case C-255/90 P, *Burban* [1992] ECR I-2253, Case T-167/94 *Nolle* [1995] ECR II-2589, Case T-231/97 *New Europe Consulting* [1999] ECR II-2403) The wording for this right in the first two paragraphs results from the case-law of the ECJ (Case 222/86 *Heylens* [1987] ECR 4097 (para 15), Case 374/87 *Orkem* [1989] ECR 3283, Case C-269/90 *TU Munchen* [1991] ECR I-5469, Case T-450/93 *Lisrestal* [1994] ECR II-1177 and Case T-167/94 *Nolle* [1995] ECR II-2589) and the wording regarding the obligation to give reasons is sourced in Art 296 TFEU
	Art 41(3)	Every person has a right to have the Community make good any damage caused by its institutions	Sourced in Art 340 TFEU
	Art 41(4)	Every person may write to the institutions of the	

Title	Article	Guarantee	Source
		Union in one of the languages of the Treaties	Sourced in Art 20(2)(d) and Art 25 TFEU
	Art 42	Right of access to documents	Sourced in ex Art 255 EC, on the basis of which Regulation 1049/2001 was adopted. See also Art 15(3) TFEU
	Art 43	For a right to refer to the Ombudsman	Sourced in Arts 20 and 228 TFEU
	Art 44	A right to petition the European Parliament	Sourced in Arts 20 and 227 TFEU
	Art 45(1) and (2)	Free movement and residence	Sourced in Art 20(2)(a) TFEU, the decision in Case C-413/99 *Bambaust* [2002] ECR I-7091 and Arts 77, 78 and 79 TFEU
	Art 46	Diplomatic and consular protection	Sourced in Art 20 TFEU
Title VI: Justice	Art 47	A right to an effective remedy and to a fair trial	Sourced in Art 13 of the ECHR. However, in Community law the protection is more extensive since it guarantees the right to an effective remedy before a Court. The ECJ enshrines this principle in its case-law (Case 222/84 *Johnston* [1986] ECR 1651, Case 222/86 *Heylens* [1987] ECR 4097 and Case C-97/91 *Borelli* [1992] ECR I-6313)
	Art 47(2)	Everyone is entitled to a fair and public hearing	Sourced in Art 6(1) ECHR but the Community law right is more extensive as in Community law the right to a fair hearing is not confined to disputes relating to civil law rights and obligations. This is a consequence of the fact that the Community is based on the rule of law (Case 294/83 *Les Verts v European Parliament* [1986] ECR 1339)
	Art 47(3)	Legal aid	It should be noted that there is a system of legal assistance for cases before the ECJ
	Art 50	Right not to be tried or punished twice in criminal proceedings for the same criminal offence	This right is sourced in Art 4 of Protocol 7 ECHR but is also sourced in ECJ case-law (Cases 18/65 and 35/65 *Gutmann v Commission* [1966] ECR 103 and Joined Cases T-305/94 *Limburgse Vinyl Maatschappij NV v Commission* [1999] ECR II-931). This principle applies not only within the jurisdiction of one state but also

			between the jurisdictions of several Member States. This understanding is based on the *acquis* in Union law and sourced also in Arts 54 to 58 of the Schengen Convention and see the decision in Case C-187/01 *Gozutok* [2003] ECR I-1345, Art 7 of the Convention on the Protection of the European Communities' Financial Interests and Art 10 on the Convention on the fight against corruption

It is apparent from this table that in fact many of the rights enumerated in the Charter had legal sources which were legally binding. If the original source was legally binding, the simple restatement of that right in a new document (the Charter), whatever its legal status could not have deprived the underlying right of its binding legal status. The language used by the CFI in some judgments confirms this view. (These cases are discussed in **8.10.6**.) The practitioner was required to conduct an analysis of the source of a particular right to determine its legal status. That the Charter was being regularly pleaded before the ECJ, prior to it having legal status, is evident from the following extract from the *EU Annual Report on Human Rights* (2002, 19):

> 'Lawyers are also invoking the Charter more often before judicial bodies of the Union, and the advocates general at the Court of Justice of the Community regularly refer to it in their conclusions while underlining it must be admitted its lack of binding force.'

The *Annual Report*, at page 19, also makes reference to the increased currency of the Charter among EU citizens:

> 'Although the Charter is not legally binding, citizens are invoking it ever more frequently in their approaches to the institutions of the Union. Complaints, petitions and letters referring to the Charter are addressed in very large numbers to the European Parliament and to the Commission.'

In the wake of the Charter, it is necessary to remember that while the development of human rights protection has been on an *ad hoc* basis that there now exists a considerable human rights *acquis* that can be invoked in the courts.

8.10.6 ENFORCEMENT

Enforcement of the Charter is necessarily dependent on status. A declaratory Charter was not binding on the ECJ or the national courts of the Member States.

There was the possibility that the ECJ would rely on the Charter as a guide to the general principles of human rights. In this manner, the Charter might have been given legally binding effect indirectly in the Member State courts as these courts are bound within the scope of Community law by decisions of the ECJ. Prior to the Treaty of Lisbon, the Charter was not without legal effect (see **8.10.5**).

As Craig and de Búrca (*EU Law: Text, Cases and Materials*, 4th edn, 2008, OUP, 417) observed:

> '...despite the blow dealt to the full legal effect of the Charter by the non-ratification the Constitutional Treaty...the Charter [was] not without current legal effect.'

Further, Craig and de Búrca stated prior to the Treaty of Lisbon, that a range of institutional actors including the Commission (see **8.10.11**) and the European Ombudsman made use of the Charter (*EU Law: Text, Cases and Materials*, 4th edn, 2008, OUP, 417).

During the period in which the Charter did not have full legal effect (2000–2009) it was cited in the Opinions of a number of Advocates General (see *inter alia* Advocate General Alber in Case C340/99 *TNT Traco SpA v Poste Italiane SpA* [2001] ECR I-4109, para 94, Advocate General Tissano in Case C-173/99 *Broadcasting, Entertainment, Cinematographic and Theatre Union (BECTU) v Secretary of State for Trade and Industry* [2001] ECR I-4881, para 28 and Advocate General Léger in Case C-353/99P *Council v Hautala*, [2001] ECR I- 9565, para 80 *et seq*) and in judgments of the CFI (post-Lisbon, renamed the General Court), and more recently by the ECJ (post-Lisbon renamed the Court of Justice of the European Union). The nature of the rights was evident from the language used. Two Advocate General Opinions, two decisions of the CFI and two decisions of the ECJ serve as illustrations. The two CFI decisions have been set aside on appeal by the ECJ.

In a footnote to his Opinion in Case C-466/00 *Kaba v Secretary of State of the Home Department* [2003] ECR I-2219, Advocate General Ruiz-Jarabo Colomer gives examples of how the Charter was being referred to by Advocates General of the ECJ (at footnote 74)

'As regards the Charter of Fundamental Rights of the European Union, proclaimed in Nice on 7 December 2000 (OJ 2000 C 364, p.1) which contains a more extensive and up-to-date list of rights and freedoms than the Convention, some Advocates General, within the Court of Justice and without ignoring the fact that the Charter does not have any *autonomous* binding effect, have nevertheless emphasised its clear purpose of serving as a substantive point of reference for all those concerned in the Community context . . . , point out that it has placed the rights which it recognises at the highest level of the hierarchy of values common to the Member States and necessarily constitutes a privileged instrument for identifying fundamental rights . . . , or argue that it constitutes an invaluable source for the purpose of ascertaining the common denominator of the essential legal values prevailing in the Member States, from which the general principles of Community law in turn emanate . . . .' (Citations of Opinions omitted)

The significance of the Charter, even at its declaratory stage, was also evident from the Opinion of Advocate General Mischo in Joined Cases C-20/00 and C-64/00 *Booker Aquaculture Ltd v The Scottish Ministers* [2003] ECR I-7411. The facts involved a preliminary reference from a Scottish court asking in essence whether the right of property, as recognised by EC Law requires that compensation be paid to farmers whose fish have had to be destroyed under measures imposed by a Council Directive for the control of diseases. In reaching the opinion (at para 132) that the principles of EC Law concerning the protection of fundamental rights, in particular the right of property, are not to be interpreted as meaning that they require the payment of compensation to the owners concerned, Advocate General Mischo stated (at paras 125–6):

'I note, lastly, that the European Union Charter of Fundamental Rights, proclaimed in December 2000 at the European Council of Nice, likewise does not encourage the conclusion that the protection of the right to private property requires that the owners of animals affected by an epidemic, or animal disease, have a right to compensation.

I know that the Charter is not legally binding, but it is worthwhile referring to it given that it constitutes an expression, at the highest level, of a democratically established political consensus on what must today be considered as the catalogue of fundamental rights guaranteed by the Community legal order . . . .'

Case T-54/99 *max.mobil Telekommunikation service GmbH v Commission* [2002] ECR II-313, a case involving competition in the telecommunications sector, involved an action for annulment against a rejection of a complaint. The CFI reasoned that the Charter was a confirmation of existing rights stating at para 48:

'Since the present action is directed against a measure rejecting a complaint, it must be emphasised at the outset that the diligent and impartial treatment of a complaint is associated with the right to sound administration which is one of the general principles that are observed in a state governed by the rule of law and are common to the constitutional traditions of the member States. Article 41(1) of the Charter of Fundamental Rights of the European Union...*confirms* that "[e]very person has the right to have his or her affairs handled impartially, fairly and within a reasonable time by the institutions and bodies of the Union.'" (Emphasis added)

The CFI also stated at para 57:

'Such judicial review is also one of the general principles that are observed in a state governed by the rule of law and are common to the constitutional traditions of the Member States, as is *confirmed* by Article 47 of the Charter of Fundamental Rights, under which any person whose rights guaranteed by the law of the Union are violated has the right to an effective remedy before a tribunal.'

On appeal in C-141/02P *Commission v max.mobil* [2005] ECR I-283 the ECJ set aside the judgment of the CFI in Case T-54/99 *max.mobil Telekommunikation service GmbH v Commission*. The ECJ stated (at para 70) that the letter by which the Commission informed max.mobil that it was not intending to bring proceedings against Austria was not a challengeable measure that is capable of being subject of an action for annulment. The ECJ stated (at para 72) that this finding was not at variance with the principle of sound administration or with any other general principle of Community law.

Case T-177/01 *Jégo-Quére et Cie SA v Commission* [2002] ECR II-2365, a fisheries case, involved an argument that the inadmissibility of an action for annulment would deprive the applicant of a right to an effective remedy (see **8.10.6**). The CFI, in holding (at para 47), that the procedures did not guarantee the right to an effective remedy, relied on Articles 6 and 13 of the ECHR and Article 47 of the EU Charter of Fundamental Rights. The CFI opined at paras 41 and 42:

'...The Court of Justice bases the right to an effective remedy before a court of a competent jurisdiction on the constitutional traditions common to the Member States and on Articles 6 and 13 of the ECHR....

In addition, the right to an effective remedy for everyone whose rights and freedoms guaranteed by the law of the Union are violated has been *reaffirmed* by Article 47 of the Charter of Fundamental Rights of the European Union proclaimed at Nice on 7 December 2000.' (Emphasis added)

On appeal in Case 263/02 P *Commission v Jégo-Quéré* [2004] ECR I-3425 (see **8.8.1** and **12.7.1**) the ECJ set aside the CFI decision in Case T-177/01 *Jégo-Quére et Cie SA v Commission* [2002] ECR II-2365. The ECJ stated, at para 29, that individuals are entitled to effective judicial protection of the rights they derive from the Community legal order, and the right to such protection is one of the general principles of law stemming from the constitutional traditions common to the Member States and enshrined in Articles 6 and 13 of the ECHR. The ECJ stated at para 30 'the Treaty has established a complete system of legal remedies and procedures designed to ensure review of the legality of acts of the institutions'. The ECJ did not refer to the Charter.

In Case C-432/05 *Unibet (London) v Justitiekanslern* [2007] ECR I-2271, a case concerning Swedish legislation which prohibited the advertising of unlawful lotteries or lotteries abroad, the ECJ held that the principle of effective judicial protection of an individual's rights under Community law must be interpreted as meaning that it does not require the national legal order of a Member State to provide for a free-standing action for an examination of whether national provisions are compatible with ex Article 49 EC (the freedom to provide services provision) provided that other effective legal remedies, make it possible for such a question of compatibility to be determined as a preliminary issue, which is a task that falls to the national court. The ECJ stated at para 37:

'It is to be noted at the outset that, according to settled case-law, the principle of effective judicial protection is a general principle of Community law stemming from the constitutional traditions common to the Member States, which has been enshrined in Articles 6 and 13 of the European Convention for the Protection of Human Rights and Fundamental Freedoms . . . . and which has also been *reaffirmed* by Article 47 of the Charter of fundamental rights of the European Union, proclaimed on 7 December 2000 in Nice (OJ 2000 C 364, 1). (Emphasis added)

In Case C-540/03 *European Parliament v Council* [2006] ECR I-5769, in which the European Parliament challenged the Family Reunification Directive, the ECJ stated at para 38:

'The Charter was solemnly proclaimed by the Parliament, the Council and the Commission in Nice on 7 December 2000. While the Charter is not a legally binding instrument, the Community legislature did, however acknowledge its importance by stating, in the second recital to the preamble to the Directive, that the Directive observes the principles recognized not only by Article 8 of the ECHR but also in the Charter. Furthermore, the principal aim of the Charter, as is apparent from its preamble is to *reaffirm* 'rights as they result, in particular from the constitutional traditions of the Member States, the Treaty on the European Union, the Community Treaties, the European Convention on Human Rights and Fundamental Freedoms, the social Charters adopted by the Community and by the Council of Europe and the case-law of the Court . . . and of the ECt.HR.' (Emphasis added)

The ECJ and CFI were unlikely to rely on the Charter as a source of rights given the decision by the Member States at the Nice IGC not to give binding status to the Charter and pending ratification of a treaty containing provision for a legally binding Charter. Now that the Treaty of Lisbon gives legal effect to the Charter (Article 6(1) TEU and see **8.1** and **8.4**), it remains to be seen whether the ECJ and the General Court will treat the Charter differently.

8.10.7 SCOPE OF THE CHARTER

Article 51 deals with the scope of application of the Charter. It is clear from Article 51(1) that the institutions, bodies, offices and agencies of the EU are the primary addressees of the Charter. The Charter is concerned with increasing the visibility of the limits on the actions of the EU institutions. The Charter is also addressed to Member States when implementing Union law. This latter point is both consistent with the case-law of the ECJ (see **8.7.2**) and logical in that when implementing Community law, the Member States are acting as agents of the EU. Post Lisbon Article 6(1), indent 2, provides that 'The provisions of the Charter shall not extend in any way the competences of the Union as defined in the Treaties.' Article 51 of the adapted 2007 Charter was amended to clarify that the Charter does not extend the field of application of EU law beyond the powers of the EU or establish any new power or task for the EU (see **8.10.3**).

It is clear from Article 51(2) that the Charter does not increase the competence of the EU in the field of human rights. Lord Goldsmith answers the objections of some commentators who have criticised the Charter on the basis that the rights contained in the Charter go far beyond the competences transferred to the EU (Lord Goldsmith, 'A Charter of Rights, Freedoms and Principles' 38 *CMLR* (2001) 1201). He states that the Charter must deal with the risk of touching fundamental rights with a side wind when an EU institution is exercising competence in another area. To illustrate this point, he gives the example that while the Charter enshrines the right to freedom of thought, conscience and religion, the EU has no competence to legislate in this field. However, if the EU is considering legislation on slaughterhouses, it cannot ignore the rituals of various religions in the area of animal slaughter as to do so would be to deny respect to religious freedom.

On this question of whether the Charter extends the powers of the Union, Mr Michel Petite, Director General Legal Service, European Commission has explained that

> '[t]he important thing here is to bear in mind the distinction between the powers of the Union (which are limited) and the duty of the institutions to respect fundamental rights when they act. This duty applies equally to rights such as the right to strike or the freedom of religion that the institutions could well affect indirectly by their measures, even if they cannot legislate on them.'

He emphasised that review of Member States for compliance with the EC human rights standard is limited to circumstances where Member States are implementing Community law. He states: 'The fear that the Charter could have an impact on broad fields of the Member States' national legislation and that the slightest indirect link with Community law or powers would suffice to make it applicable therefore strikes me as unfounded.' (Working Document 13 of Working Group II, *Incorporation of the Charter/Accession to the ECHR*, Brussels, 5 September 2002). The Working Group on Incorporation of the Charter emphasised that no modification in the allocation of competences between the EU and the Member States would result from the Charter and stated '[t]he fact that certain Charter rights concern areas in which the Union has little or no competence to act is not in contradiction to it, given that, although the Union's competences are limited, it must respect all fundamental rights wherever it acts and therefore avoid indirect interference also with such fundamental rights on which it would not have competence to legislate' (CONV 354/02 Final report of Working Group II, *Incorporation of the Charter/Accession to the ECHR* Brussels, 22 October 2002, 5). The ECJ has no jurisdiction to review national measures for compatibility with the EU human rights standard (see **8.7.2**).

A final point to note is that the Charter, even in its original declaratory form, was not restricted to the European Community but applied to Union activity under all three pillars. Traditionally the ECJ power of review was largely restricted to the supranational pillar (see **8.7.1**). Now that the Charter has been given legally binding status the scope of Community human rights protection over the intergovernmental pillars will be extended (see **8.4** and **8.7.1**).

The distinction between the pillars has been largely abolished in the Treaty of Lisbon. (see **8.1**, **8.6.1** and **8.7.1**). Article 47 TEU of the Treaty provides '[t]he Union shall have legal personality'. On ratification of the Treaty of Lisbon, the three-pillar structure is almost done away with and the EU's institutions have a single structure. Article 52 of the Charter is concerned with the scope of the rights guaranteed in the Charter. It is accepted that rights are not absolute and that limitations may be imposed on rights but only to the extent that they are provided for by law and respect the essence of the rights and freedoms. Article 52(2) specifies that where a right is sourced in the TEU/TFEU, the right must be exercised under the conditions and within the limits defined by those Treaties. The adapted version of the Charter included a provision in Article 52(4) that:

> 'Insofar as the Charter recognises fundamental rights as they result from the constitutional traditions of the Member States, those rights shall be interpreted in harmony with those provisions.'

Article 52(5) of the adapted version of the Charter draws a distinction between rights and principles contained in the Charter (see **8.10.3**). A provision was added (Article 52(6)) to clarify that full account shall be taken of national laws and practices as specified in the Charter (see **8.10.3**).

8.10.8 RELATIONSHIP OF THE CHARTER AND THE ECHR

Two European Courts applying different human rights codes implies the possibility of different standards.

It is important when considering the Charter to examine the wider picture of human rights in Europe. A key issue in drafting the Charter has been the relationship of the Charter to the ECHR. The rights and freedoms protected by the ECHR and interpreted by the ECt.HR are restated (although not replicated) in the Charter and could be interpreted by the ECJ.

However, it should be noted that the Charter is not the origin of this difficulty as the ECJ has used the ECHR as a source of inspiration for the general principles of EC human rights law since the late 1960s. Already the ECt.HR and the ECJ are both interpreting ECHR rights with the consequent possibility of divergent interpretations.

There is also a possibility of divergence between the case-law of the ECt.HR and the case-law of the Council of Europe Member States in that the latter are entitled to apply a higher standard through the operation of the margin of appreciation doctrine.

However, there are two crucial differences between the possible divergence between the national courts and the ECt.HR and the ECJ and the ECt.HR. First, in the case of the Council of Europe Contracting States, the ECt.HR retains ultimate authority to interpret the ECHR (see Lawson 'Confusion and Conflict? Diverging Interpretations of the European Convention on Human Rights in Strasbourg and Luxembourg' in Lawson and de Bloijs (eds), *The Dynamics of the Protection of Human Rights in Europe: Essays in Honour of Henry G. Schemers*, 1994, Nijhoff, iii, 219, 229–30) while the ECJ does not consider itself bound by the ECt.HR interpretation of an ECHR right. (See the opinion of Advocate General Darmon in Case 374/87 *Orkem v Commission* [1989] ECR 3283, 3337–8.) Second, the Council of Europe Member States through the operation of the margin of appreciation doctrine are obliged to apply the ECHR as a minimum standard. No such obligation rests on the ECJ as the EU is not a party to the ECHR.

Efforts to counteract these concerns are evident in the final Title of the Charter. Article 52 is concerned with the scope of guaranteed rights and Article 53 with the level of human rights protection. Article 52(3), intended as a mechanism to ensure consistency between the Charter and the ECHR, provides:

> *'Insofar as this Charter contains rights which correspond to rights guaranteed by the Convention for the Protection of Human Rights and Fundamental Freedoms, the meaning and scope of those rights shall be the same as those laid down by the said Convention. This provision shall not prevent Union law providing more extensive protection.'*

Article 52(3) is designed to ensure consistency between the ECHR rights and the corresponding rights, in the Charter by stating that the meaning and scope including any limitations must comply with ECHR standards.

According to the explanatory text to the Charter, the reference to the ECHR in Article 52(3) is to be read as including the Protocols to the ECHR and when determining the meaning and scope of those rights, the case-law of both the ECt.HR and the ECJ is to be taken into account.

The explanations provide two lists of Articles in the Charter covered by Article 52(3). One list details the Articles which have both the same meaning and scope as the corresponding Articles of the ECHR. The second list details the Articles which have the same meaning as the corresponding Articles of the ECHR but where their scope is wider.

Article 53 is entitled 'Levels of Protection' and provides:

'Nothing in this Charter shall be interpreted as restricting or adversely affecting human rights and fundamental freedoms as recognised in their respective fields of application, by Union law and international law and by international agreements to which the Union, the Community or all the Member States are party, including the European Convention for the Protection of Human Rights and Fundamental Freedoms, and by the Member States' constitutions.'

Reading Articles 52(3) and 53 together it is apparent that when a right in the Charter corresponds to a right in the ECHR, the ECHR right serves as a minimum standard in determining the meaning and scope of the right but there is nothing to prevent the EU from adopting a more extensive standard.

Some rights are based on a combination of the ECHR and the EU or EC Treaty. Lenaerts and De Smijter ('A "Bill of Rights" for the European Union' 38 *CMLR* 273, 294) have explained the situation with regard to those rights as follows:

'Fundamental rights recognised by the Charter, corresponding to rights guaranteed by the ECHR and based on the EU or EC Treaty, should thus be exercised under the conditions and within the limits defined by the EU or EC Treaty to the extent only that these conditions and limits do not interfere with the meaning and scope of these rights as they are guaranteed by the ECHR. On the basis of a combined reading of Article 52(2) and (3) and Article 53 of the Charter we may thus conclude that the EU or EC Treaty as well as the ECHR (in fact, the norm offering the highest protection) serve as a reference to determine the minimal content of those fundamental rights contained in the Charter that are based on the EU or EC Treaty and correspond to a right guaranteed by the ECHR.'

8.10.9   BENEFICIARIES

The issue of beneficiaries is decided Article by Article. The rights and freedoms set out in Titles I (Dignity), II (Freedoms), III (Equality) and VI (Justice) are for everyone. Within Title IV (Solidarity), some rights such as collective bargaining and the right to fair and just working conditions are for workers while other protections such as reconciliation of family and professional life and health care are for everyone. The title of Title V (Citizens' Rights) would seem to imply that the rights in this chapter accrue only to citizens of the European Union and this is generally true although Article 45(2) provides for a right of movement and residence to nationals of third countries legally resident in the territories of a Member State.

8.10.10   THE CHARTER AND THE FUTURE OF EUROPE

Decisions regarding the status of the Charter and whether it should be included in the Treaty establishing a Constitution were taken at the 2004 IGC. The Treaty establishing a Constitution for Europe (OJ 2004/310/01 16 December 2004) incorporated the text of the Charter. The Treaty establishing a Constitution for Europe did not take effect but it is still instructive to examine the conclusions of the Working Group on the Charter.

The Working Group on the Charter submitted its final report to the Convention on 22 October 2002. (CONV 354/02 Final Report of Working Group II, *Incorporation of the Charter/Accession to the ECHR*, Brussels, 22 October 2002.) The Working Group had been asked to answer the question; 'Should the Charter of Fundamental Rights of the European Union be incorporated into the Treaty?' The Working Group was also asked to consider a second question: 'Should the European Union be able to Accede to the European Convention on Human Rights?' (See **8.6.5**).

The question regarding incorporation of the Charter was answered resoundingly in the affirmative. The members of the Working Group indicated that they either strongly supported the incorporation of the Charter in a form which would make it legally binding and give it constitutional status or would not rule out giving favourable consideration to such incorporation. The Working Group stressed that the political decision on the possible incorporation of the Charter into the Treaty framework is reserved to the Convention.

The Working Group set out three basic incorporation options:

'(a)   insertion of the text of the Charter articles at the beginning of the Constitutional Treaty, in a title or Chapter of that Treaty; or

(b)   insertion of an appropriate reference to the Charter in one article of the Constitutional Treaty; such a reference could be combined with annexing or attaching the Charter to the Constitutional Treaty, either as a specific part of the Constitutional Treaty containing only the Charter or as a separate legal text (e.g. in the form of a Protocol);

(c)   an "indirect reference" to the Charter could be used to make the Charter legally binding without giving it constitutional status.' (See document CONV 116/02, 7.)

The Report indicated that a large majority of the group favoured option (a), a smaller number option (b). Either option would 'serve to make the Charter a legally binding text of constitutional status'.

The Working Group also provided a series of supplementary conclusions and recommendations on legal and technical aspects of the Charter, which would be significant in ensuring the smooth incorporation of the Charter into the new Treaty architecture. The Working Group:

(a)   concluded that the content of the Charter should be respected by the current Convention and should not be re-opened, apart from a number of drafting adjustments which would not alter the substance of the Charter;

(b)   emphasised that no new competences would be conferred on the EU by virtue of incorporation of the Charter;

(c)   proposed that a referral clause should be included in the Charter to ensure full compatibility between those fundamental rights which are already expressly enshrined in the EC Treaty and the Charter articles which restate them;

(d)   reconfirmed Article 52(3) of the Charter and the explanation of this Article in the explanatory text which accompanies the Charter, that the rights in the Charter which correspond to ECIIR have the same meaning as laid down in the ECHR but that the EU is not prevented from guaranteeing a higher level of protection for a particular right;

(e)   proposed the addition of a paragraph to the General Provision on the scope of guaranteed rights (Art 52 EU Charter) to ensure an interpretation of fundamental rights in harmony with the common constitutional traditions of the Member States; and

(f)   proposed the addition of an additional general principle to encapsulate the understanding of the concept of 'principles' as distinct from 'rights'.

While the Treaty establishing a Constitution for Europe is now defunct, many of these recommendations of the Working Group were followed in the adapted version of the Charter.

The Group recommended that the Preamble to the Charter should be preserved in the future Constitutional Treaty framework and that the explanations should be made more accessible to practitioners and should be more widely publicised. These recommendations were also followed. The Preamble is included in the adapted version of the Charter and Article 6(1) TEU refers to having 'due regard' to the explanations referred to in the Charter (see **8.1**, **8.4**, **8.10.2** and **8.10.5**).

The explanations have been updated to take account of amendments to the Charter and developments to EU law.

The Working Group signalled to the Convention that it should consider whether, on incorporation of the Charter, the Constitutional Treaty should also contain a reference to the two external sources of inspiration for fundamental rights, currently found in Article 6(2) TEU, ie the ECHR and the common constitutional traditions of the Member States, and the procedure for the future amendment of the Charter.

Ultimately however, the decision as to whether the Charter would be legally binding was a political decision to be taken by the Member States at the 2004 IGC. The Member States decided to give the Charter legally binding effect by means of including it in the Treaty establishing a Constitution for Europe, but the Treaty also required ratification in accordance with the constitutional traditions of each of the Member States. The Treaty was not ratified by all of the EU Member States (see **8.1**) and the European Council mandated an IGC commencing in July 2007 to draft a Reform Treaty, which became the Treaty of Lisbon and pursuant to which the Charter gained legally binding status (see **8.1** and **8.4**). The UK and Poland negotiated a protocol to opt out of the Charter (see **8.10.4**). The Czech Republic has also opted out of the Charter.

8.10.11 THE CHARTER'S IMPACT ON LEGISLATION

In the EU *Annual Report on Human Rights* (2002, 19), the Commission indicated another significant impact of the Charter:

> 'The Commission also considers that it is necessary to draw practical lessons from the proclamation of the Charter and to guide its conduct by the rights contained in it. With this in mind, any proposal for a legislative or regulatory Act adopted by the Commission will now be subject to an *a priori* compatibility check with the Charter, attested by the inclusion of a standard recital and proposals which have a connection with fundamental rights.'

An example of a recital in a directive referring to the Charter is Council Directive 2003/86/EC of 22 September 2003 on the right to family reunification (OJ 2003 L251, 12). The second recital in the Preamble to the Directive is worded as follows:

> 'Measures concerning family reunification should be adopted in conformity with the obligation to protect the family and respect family life enshrined in many instruments of international law. This Directive respects the fundamental rights and observes the principles recognised in particular in Article 8 of the European Convention for the Protection of Human Rights and Fundamental Freedoms and in the Charter of Fundamental Rights of the European Union.' (OJ 2000 C364, 1.)

It was this Directive which was at issue in Case C-540/03 *European Parliament v Council* [2006] ECR I-5769 (see **8.10.6**).

8.11 The European Union Agency for Fundamental Rights

Another recent development in the protection of fundamental rights at EU level is the establishment, pursuant to Council Regulation (EC) No. 168/2007 of the European Union Agency for Fundamental Rights (FRA), which began its work on 1 March 2007. The FRA is the legal successor of the European Monitoring Centre on Racism and Xenophobia (EUMC). Article 2 of the Regulation sets out the objective of the FRA:

'The objective of the Agency shall be to provide the relevant institutions, bodies, offices and agencies of the Community and its Member States when implementing Community law with assistance and expertise relating to fundamental rights in order to support them when they take measures or formulate courses of action within their respective spheres of competence to fully respect fundamental rights.'

The Regulation also sets out the scope, tasks, areas of activity and working methods of the FRA. The fundamental rights referred to in Article 6(2) TEU, as reflected in the Charter of Fundamental Rights, are the point of reference for the mandate of the agency. The thematic areas of activity will be laid down in a multi-annual framework but must include the fight against racism, xenophobia and related intolerance. Its tasks include information and data collection and analysis, co-operation with civil society, awareness raising, advising EU institutions and Member States when implementing EC law and publishing an annual report on fundamental rights in the EU. The Regulation provides for co-operation *inter alia* with the Council of Europe and Civil Society. The Regulation sets out the structure of the FRA and practical operational matters such as that its seat is in Vienna. From 1 March 2007, the FRA became operational in the field of racism and xenophobia as covered by the previous mandate of the EUMC and it will gradually build up knowledge and expertise with regard to other areas of fundamental rights.

8.12   Conclusion

While the Charter of Fundamental Rights of the EU is a recent initiative human rights have been protected within the European legal order since the 1960s. The key points may be summarised as follows.

The protection of human rights was initially a product of judicial activism but now has a firm basis in the Treaties. The ECJ looks to the human rights provisions in the constitutions of the Member States and international agreements to which the Member States are parties for inspiration. The ECJ is entitled to annul an action which does not comply with the human rights standard.

The EU institutions are bound by the European human rights standard. Member States are also bound but only when acting within the scope of EU law. Originally the Charter of Fundamental Rights of the EU had declaratory status but since the coming into force of the Treaty of Lisbon on 1 December 2009, the Charter has the same status as the Treaties and is legally binding (see Article 6(1) TEU, **8.1** and **8.4**). An adapted version of the Charter was solemnly proclaimed on 12 December 2007 (OJ C303/01 14 December 2007) and it this slightly amended version which has legal effect. The Treaty of Lisbon provides a legal basis for EU accession to the ECHR (Article 6(2) TEU) but accession has not yet taken place.

A new EU Agency for Fundamental Rights (FRA) (see **8.11**) has been established. This is an exciting time for the development of human rights in the EU.

CHAPTER 9

FAMILY AND CHILD LAW

9.1   Introduction

The principal source of fundamental rights in the family law arena in Ireland has been the Constitution. Articles 41 and 42 of the Constitution have had a profound impact on the manner in which family legislation has been enacted and family law judgments delivered.

9.2   The Constitution and the Family

Article 41 of the Irish Constitution of 1937 concerns the family and 'recognises the family as the natural and primary unit group of society' and further guarantees 'to protect the family in its constitution and authority'. It is, however, immediately evident from the terms of Article 41.3.1° itself that the family, which the Constitution contemplates as deserving such protection, is that based on marriage alone. The latter-mentioned section speaks, with a somewhat misguided air of self-evidence, of 'the institution of marriage, on which the family is founded'. The pre-eminence of the family based on marriage, in other words, is not so much asserted as assumed. The institution of marriage enjoys a privileged position in the Irish constitutional order. By virtue of Article 41.3.1° of the Constitution, the State 'pledges to guard with special care the institution of marriage, on which the family is founded, and to protect it against attack'.

The Irish courts have remained steadfast in asserting the exclusivity of the constitutional 'family'. In *State (Nicolaou) v An Bord Uchtála* [1966] IR 567, the Supreme Court definitively affirmed that the family referred to in Article 41 did not include an unmarried couple and their child. The Court, moreover, ruled that the applicant, as unmarried father of the child, had no constitutional rights whatsoever in respect of his child.

The courts cannot be accused of inconsistency in this regard. In the early 1990s the Supreme Court reiterated this position in *In Re SW, K v W* (1990) 2 IR 437. (See also *Keegan v Ireland* (1994) 18 EHRR 342, discussed at **9.5.5**.) The applicant in this case and his partner, although unmarried, had enjoyed a stable relationship for approximately two years. The couple had decided to have a child together, but some time before the child's birth, they became estranged from each other. The applicant's partner placed the child for adoption without the consent, or even the knowledge, of the applicant. At the time, he had no right under Irish law to challenge a decision to place for adoption either before the Adoption Board or before the courts. The applicant argued that this was a breach of his constitutional rights. The Supreme Court, however, concluded that the failure to consult the father of the child was not a breach of any constitutional right, whether of the family or otherwise, again noting that the applicant was not, and had not been, a member of the family in the sense understood by the Constitution. (See also *WO'R v EH* [1996] 2 IR 248, and O'Driscoll, 'The Rights of Unmarried Fathers' [1999] 2 *IJFL* 18.)

Within these confines, however, the courts have acknowledged that to be a family enjoying rights under Articles 41 and 42 of the Constitution, a household need not necessarily conform to the stereotype of 'father, mother and children'. It would appear, for instance, that a married couple without children still constitutes a family for the purposes of Article 41 (*Murray v Ireland* [1985] ILRM 542, *per* Costello J at 546). Similar considerations apply to widowed persons and their children (*per* Sullivan CJ in *In re Frost, Infants* [1947] IR 3 at 28) and even, presumably, to orphaned siblings (whose parents had been married prior to their deaths). All of these families, despite their bereavements, continue to enjoy the family rights guaranteed by the Constitution. Similarly, a family headed by persons who, though married, have separated due to irreconcilable differences, nonetheless retains its privileged constitutional status (*TF v Ireland* [1995] IR 321). It is no small irony that such a family, even in the throes of marital breakdown, will be accorded full family rights under Article 41, while its non-marital but happy and stable contemporaries will not.

The rights guaranteed by Article 41 are recognised as belonging not to individual members of the family but rather to the family unit as a whole. An individual on behalf of the family may invoke them but, as Costello J notes in *Murray v Ireland* [1985] ILRM 542 at 547 they 'belong to the institution in itself as distinct from the personal rights which each individual member might enjoy by virtue of membership of the family'.

Article 41 lacks a child focus. It fails to recognise the child as a juristic person with individual rights. This is in no small measure attributable to the principle of parental autonomy created by Article 41 of the Constitution. This establishes a private realm of family life, which the State can enter only in the exceptional circumstances detailed in Article 42.5 of the Constitution. Article 42 provides as follows:

> '(1) *The state acknowledges that the primary and natural educator of the child is the family and guarantees to respect the inalienable right and duty of parents to provide, according to their means, for the religious and moral, intellectual, physical and social education of their children* . . .
>
> (2) *In exceptional cases, where the parents for physical or moral reasons fail in their duty towards their children, the state, as guardian of the common good, by appropriate means shall endeavour to supply the place of the parents, but always with due regard for the natural and imprescriptible rights of the child.*'

Clearly, this provides that only in exceptional cases, where parents, for physical or moral reasons, fail in their duty towards their children, can the State as guardian of the common good endeavour to supply the place of the parents. The very elevated evidential threshold for state intervention was clearly demonstrated by the case of *North Western Health Board v HW* [2001] 3 IR 622. The case concerned the refusal of a child's parents to allow a diagnostic phenylketonuria (PKU) test to be conducted on their child. The test involved the taking of a sample of blood by way of a heel-prick, and had been proven to reduce the incidence in Ireland of a number of serious childhood illnesses. The performance of the test was thus, as Murphy J (at 729) admitted, 'beyond debate in medical terms, unquestionably in the best interests of the infant'. 'Unwise and disturbing' (*ibid* at 741) as the parents' decision appeared, the Supreme Court felt that the autonomy of the parents prevented the State from ensuring that the child received the medical treatment which an overarching concern for his welfare would require. The individual judges furnished a variety of examples of situations in which they would regard state intervention as justified. Murray CJ, for example, spoke of an immediate and fundamental threat to the capacity of the child to continue to function as a human person, deriving from an exceptional dereliction of parental duty. The threshold for state intervention was, if anything, raised by the recent decision of the Supreme Court in *N v HSE* [2006] IESC 60. The Court in that case emphasised that the constitutional presumption in favour of parental autonomy could only be rebutted where a failure of parental duty had actually been established.

The Irish Constitution is unique in that whereas most other Western constitutions have a public/private divide, the family unit in Ireland has autonomy over and above that of the individual members of the family. In fact, the individual rights of the constituent members of the family are both directed and determined by the family as an entity in itself. Consequently, membership of the constitutional family in Ireland subordinates the rights of the individual members. This is true specifically of the rights of children and manifests itself glaringly in Supreme Court judgments on the issue.

Focusing on Article 42 of the Constitution, it is true to say that this in fact has more to do with the family than it does with the substantive right to education and, in many respects, is an addendum and subordinate to Article 41. It deals with education in a wider sense than scholastic education. When it refers to education, it is alluding to the upbringing of the child, which it holds not only to be a right but a duty of parents. This article reinforces the decision-making autonomy of the family. This can be observed on examining the intellectual structure of Article 42, which assigns a strong sense of priority to parental autonomy.

Article 42.5 of the Constitution is of particular importance in that it addresses the complete inability of parents to provide for their children's education. It has been interpreted as not being confined to a failure by the parents of a child to provide education for him/her, but extends in exceptional circumstances, to failure in other duties necessary to satisfy the personal rights of the child. This interpretation supports the assertion previously made that the right to education in Article 42 is a mere extension of the concept of 'the family' in Article 41.

Looking at Articles 41 and 42 of the Constitution in unison, it is clear that they render the rights of married parents in relation to their children 'inalienable'. Article 41 of the Constitution alludes to the inalienable and imprescriptible rights of the family. Article 42 refers to the rights and duties of married parents. Only if the circumstances allow the constitutional caveat on inalienability, contained in Article 42.5 of the Constitution, to be satisfied is there then scope for the legal supplantation of the rights of the married parents.

Section 3 of the Guardianship of Infants Act, 1964 makes it abundantly clear that in considering an application relating to the guardianship, custody or upbringing of a child, the court must have regard to the welfare of the child. This, the section states, is 'the first and paramount consideration'. The Supreme Court, however, has determined that the welfare of a child must, unless there are exceptional circumstances or other overriding factors, be considered to be best served by its remaining as part of its marital family. This was dictated, the Court considered in a number of cases, by the constitutional preference for the marital family exhibited in Article 41.3 of the Constitution and the requirement therein that it be protected from attack. (See, for example, *Re JH (An Infant)* [1985] IR 375, *North Western Health Board v HW and CW* [2001] 3 IR 622 and *N v HSE* [2006] IESC 60.) There is an uneasy tension between the provisions of Articles 41 and 42 of the Constitution and the welfare principle outlined in section 3 of the Guardianship of Infants Act, 1964.

The apparent contradiction between Articles 41 and 42 of the Constitution and the principle of the welfare of the child in section 3 of the Guardianship of Infants Act, 1964 has been correctly reconciled by the judiciary by holding that the welfare of the child is to be found within the confines of the Constitution (*North Western Health Board v HW and CW* [2001] 3 IR 635 and *N v HSE* [2006] IESC 60. See, however, *Southern Health Board v CH* [1996] 1 IR 231, 238 where O'Flaherty J observed, in a case concerning the admissibility of a videotaped interview containing allegations of parental abuse, that: 'it is easy to comprehend that the child's welfare must always be of far graver concern to the court. We must, as judges, always harken to the constitutional command which mandates, as prime consideration, the interests of the child in any legal proceedings.') This is a negative definition of welfare insofar as it impacts on the child. The focus is not on actively promoting the welfare interests of the child, but merely with ensuring that these are not seriously impaired. This approach is attributable to the wording of Articles 41 and 42 of the Irish Constitution of 1937.

On 3 November 2006, the Irish government announced its intention to hold a Constitutional referendum on children's rights. Subsequently, on 19 February 2007, the Twenty-Eighth Amendment of the Constitution Bill, 2007 (SI 14/2007) was published. The proposed scope of the amendment relates to:

- a recognition of the natural and imprescriptible rights of children

- the protection of the best interests of children in proceedings concerning custody, guardianship or access

- the protection of the best interests of children in the context of the care and adoption systems

- the protection of children in the criminal justice system.

At the time of writing this chapter, the proposed amendment had yet to be put to the Irish people. If passed, it will allow for a more appropriate balance to be struck between the autonomy of the family and the rights of the child. It will not, however, allow for a 'brave new world' in which the State always knows best.

9.3 International Obligations

9.3.1 INTRODUCTION

Internationally, the traditional nuclear family is becoming an endangered species. Notwithstanding this, the designation of the family as a private realm in Article 41 of the Constitution, which is virtually impenetrable, still endures in Ireland today as can been seen from the Supreme Court cases of *McK v Information Commissioner* [2006] IESC 2 and *N v HSE* [2006] IESC 60. In the face of such a restrictive interpretation of the 'family', litigants have sought redress under international law through international human rights treaties. However, our dualist approach to international law makes international human rights treaties binding on the State, though not on the courts, as such treaties have not been incorporated into Irish law. (Most of the other Member States of the Council of Europe adopt a monist approach to international law, where international law is automatically applicable in domestic law, without the need for any implementing legislation.) This has now changed, to a limited extent, with the incorporation of the European Convention on Human Rights and Fundamental Freedoms (ECHR) into domestic law (see **chapter 5**).

9.3.2 UN CONVENTION ON THE RIGHTS OF THE CHILD 1989

Ireland ratified the UN Convention on the Rights of the Child 1989 without reservation on 21 September 1992. Again, by virtue of Ireland's dualist nature, the provisions do not form part of domestic law. The Convention recognises children's rights in its widest sense. Article 3 of the Convention states, *inter alia*:

'*1. In all actions concerning children, whether undertaken by public or private social welfare institutions, courts of law, administrative authorities or legislative bodies, the best interest of the child shall be a primary consideration.*

2. *State parties undertake to ensure the child such protection and care as is necessary for his or her well-being, taking into account the rights and duties of his or her parents, legal guardians, or other individuals legally responsible for him or her, and, to this end, shall take all appropriate legislative and administrative measures.'*

While this Article requires only that the children's interests be *a* primary consideration, not *the* primary consideration, it must also be read alongside the series of explicit rights which the Convention protects. These include: 'the inherent right to life' (Article 6); 'the right from birth to a name, the right to acquire a nationality and, as far as possible, the right to know and be cared for by his or her parents' (Article 7); 'the right of the child to preserve his or her identity, including nationality' (Article 8); 'the right of the child who is separated from one or both parents to maintain personal relations and direct contact with both parents on a regular basis, except if it is contrary to the child's best interests' (Article 9(3)); 'the right (of a child who has the capacity to form his or her own views) to express those views freely in all matters affecting the child, the views of the child being given due weight in accordance with the age and maturity of the child' (Article 12); 'the right to freedom of expression' (Article 13); 'the right of the child to freedom of thought, conscience and religion' (Article 14(1)); 'the right of the child to freedom of association and to freedom of peaceful assembly' (Article 15); 'the right to the protection of the law against arbitrary or unlawful interference with the child's privacy, family home or correspondence and unlawful attacks on the child's honour and reputation' (Article 16); 'the right of every child to a standard of living adequate for the child's physical, mental, spiritual, moral and social development' (Article 27); 'the right of the child to education' (Article 28); and 'the right of every child alleged as, accused of, or recognised as having infringed the penal law to be treated in a manner consistent with the promotion of the child's sense of dignity and worth' (Article 40). Taking cognisance of the foregoing rights, and in particular Article 12 of the UN Convention on the Rights of the Child 1989, it can be seen that the UN Convention on the Rights of the Child 1989, is soundly based on a defensible concept of children's rights. The law in Ireland, however, falls far short of such a concept.

9.3.2.1   Participation

The primary foothold for the separate representation of children in international child law can be found in Article 12 of the United Nations Convention on the Rights of the Child 1989, which provides that:

'1. *State parties shall assure to the child who is capable of forming his or her own views the right to express those views freely in all matters affecting the child, the views of the child being given due weight in accordance with the age and maturity of the child.*

2. *For this purpose, the child shall in particular be provided the opportunity to be heard in any judicial and administrative proceedings affecting the child, either directly, or through a representative or an appropriate body, in a manner consistent with the procedural rules of national law.'*

Article 9 of the same Convention provides for the participation by children in separation and divorce processes:

'1. *State parties shall ensure that a child shall not be separated from his or her parents against his or her will, except when competent authorities subject to judicial review determine, in accordance with applicable law and procedures, that such separation is necessary for the best interests of the child. Such determination may be necessary in a particular case such as one involving abuse or neglect of the child by the parents, or one where parents are living separately and a decision must be made as to the child's place of residence.*

2. *In any proceedings pursuant to paragraph 1 of the present article, all interested parties shall be given an opportunity to participate in the proceedings and make their views known.'*

The failure of the State to bring into force s 28 of the Guardianship of Infants Act, 1964 amounts to a breach of Article 9 of the 1989 Convention. The positive effect of child participation in the separation and divorce process is detailed in the work of the developmental psychology expert E. Singer (Singer, 'Kinderen als morele personen: Argumenten vanuit een ontwikkelings-psychologisch perspectief', in Van Nijnatten and Sevenhuijsen (eds), *Dubbelleven; Nieuwe perspectieven voor kinderen na echtscheiding*, Thela Thesis, 2001, Amsterdam, 31–40).

9.3.3 EUROPEAN CONVENTION ON THE EXERCISE OF CHILDREN'S RIGHTS 1996

Ireland has signed but not ratified the European Convention on the Exercise of Children's Rights 1996. (European Treaty Series No. 160. The European Convention on the Exercise of Children's Rights was opened for signature at Strasbourg on 25 January 1996. It came into force on 1 July 2000 following ratification by Greece (11 September 1997), Poland (28 November 1997) and Slovenia (28 March 2000) in accordance with Article 21(3) of the 1996 Convention.) In some respects, it is of more limited application than its 1989 counterpart. It focuses predominantly on procedural rather than substantive rights, the emphasis being on such matters as the right of children to participation in, and information about, cases that concern their welfare. For example, Article 5 of the 1996 Convention states:

> 'Parties shall consider granting children additional procedural rights in relation to proceedings before a judicial authority offering them, in particular:
> (a) the right to apply to be assisted by an appropriate person of their choice in order to help them express their views
> (b) the right to apply themselves, or through other persons or bodies, for the appointment of a separate representative, in appropriate cases a lawyer
> (c) the right to appoint their own representative
> (d) the right to exercise some or all of the rights of parties to such proceedings.'

Clearly, the foregoing provisions are aimed primarily at children of sufficient age and maturity to understand the matters under scrutiny. That said, in appropriate cases, a child should have a person to help to express his or her views. Articles 4 and 9 of the European Convention on the Exercise of Children's Rights provide for the appointment of such a special representative. The absence of a facility for children in Ireland to articulate their views, where a case is settled in advance of the hearing, is a serious problem.

9.4 European Convention on Human Rights and Fundamental Freedoms

9.4.1 INTRODUCTION

Of special significance in discussing our international obligations are the relevant provisions of the European Convention on Human Rights and Fundamental Freedoms (ECHR), which have been incorporated into Irish law by way of statute (see **chapters 4** and **5**). As a result of incorporation, the provisions of the ECHR have become part of our domestic law. It is now possible to take proceedings in the Irish courts alleging a breach of the ECHR. Previously, to assert any rights under the ECHR, an injured party had first to exhaust all domestic remedies before bringing the case to the European Court of Human Rights (ECt.HR) in Strasbourg with the costs and delays associated with that process.

There is little doubt that inconsistencies will arise between Irish family law and practice and the standards required by the ECHR. That said, the significance of this development has been overstated in the arena of Irish family law. The indirect or interpretative mode of incorporation preserves the domestic primacy of the Constitution (see s 2 of the European Convention on Human Rights Act, 2003 and *J.McD v P.L and B.M* unreported, Supreme Court, December 10, 2009). Consequently, Article 41 of the Constitution will continue to act as an impediment to the effective implementation of the legal entitlements of individuals under the ECHR. In particular, incorporation of the ECHR at sub-constitutional level will ensure that child rights remain subordinate to parental rights. (If there is a conflict between a provision of the Constitution and the ECHR, the Constitution prevails.) Therefore, in the family law arena, there will continue to be cases where a remedy for a breach of a ECHR right cannot be procured in the Irish courts, with the only avenue at the disposal of such litigants being an application to the Strasbourg Court.

9.4.2 EUROPEAN CONVENTION ON HUMAN RIGHTS ACT, 2003

The European Convention on Human Rights Act, 2003 (2003 Act) was signed by the President on 30 June 2003 and came into force on 31 December 2003. Section 1 of the 2003 Act provides that Articles 2–14 of the ECHR and Protocols 1, 4, 6 and 7 are to be incorporated into Irish law (see **chapter 5**).

A number of issues emerge from a consideration of the provisions of the 2003 Act insofar as they impact on family and child law. The most significant is the fact that no provision has been made for legal aid in the Act, a right established under Articles 6 and 8 ECHR (see *Airey v Ireland* (1979–80) 2 EHRR 305).

9.4.2.1 The Régime

Section 2 of the 2003 Act requires the Irish courts to interpret Irish law in a manner compatible with the State's obligations under the ECHR, 'in so far as is possible'. All courts are now obliged to interpret and apply any statutory provision or rule of law in accordance with the ECHR and take judicial notice of the decisions of the institutions of the ECHR. Where this is not possible and where no other legal remedy is adequate and available, the superior courts may make declarations of incompatibility in relation to legislation and awards of damages (and other remedies) against '*organs of the State*' who behave in a manner contrary to the State's obligations under the ECHR.

Every organ of the State, pursuant to s 3(1) of the 2003 Act, is required to perform its functions in a manner compatible with the ECHR. The definition of '*organ of the State*' specifically excludes the courts. (It does however appear to include the Health Service Executive.) Section 3(2) of the 2003 Act states:

'3.–(2) *A person who has suffered injury, loss or damage as a result of a contravention may, if no other remedy in damages is available, institute proceedings to recover damages in respect of the contravention in the High Court (or, subject to subsection (3) [This subsection deals with jurisdiction limitations.], in the Circuit Court) and the Court may award to the person such damages (if any) as it considers appropriate.*'

The effect of this provision is that if a person has suffered injury, loss or damage as a result of a breach of s 3(1), he may take an action for damages but only if no other remedy in damages is available. It excludes proceedings taken in the District Court. This is a matter of particular concern in the child law area, as the District Court has principal jurisdiction for proceedings instituted under the Child Care Act, 1991. Section 3(5) of the Act states that proceedings for violation of an ECHR right must be brought within one year of the contravention. This one year period may be extended by a court order if the court considers it appropriate to do so in the interests of justice.

Section 4 of the 2003 Act requires a court to take judicial notice of both the ECHR provisions and the decisions of the institutions of the ECHR. It further requires a court to *'take due account of the principles laid down by decisions'* of the institutions of the ECHR when applying the ECHR provisions.

Section 5 of the 2003 Act provides that where the High Court, or the Supreme Court on appeal, rules that there is an incompatibility between domestic law and the Convention, a declaration of incompatibility may be granted by that court. It should, however, be noted that demonstrating that no other legal remedy is *'adequate or available'* is a condition precedent to invoking this section. Further, legal aid is not available to the applicant seeking a declaration of incompatibility. Where the courts issue a declaration of incompatibility, it is a matter for the government to consider the steps to be taken to remedy the incompatibility as such a declaration will not, for constitutional reasons, affect the validity, enforcement or continuing operation of the national law in question. Section 5(4) creates a new compensatory scheme for a person who has been granted a declaration of incompatibility by the courts. Such a person may apply to the government for payment of *ex gratia* compensation in respect of any injury, loss or damage he/she may have suffered as a result of the incompatibility. This section has been criticised for failing to provide a mechanism whereby the level of compensation awarded can be appealed.

Section 6 of the 2003 Act provides that, before a court decides whether to make a declaration of incompatibility, the Attorney General must be given notice of the proceedings in accordance with the rules of court. In summary, the remedies available to a litigant under the 2003 Act are confined to a declaration of incompatibility (and possible *ex gratia* compensation) and an action for damages against an 'organ of the State' (ie the Health Service Executive). It should also be noted that the 2003 Act is not retroactive (see *Dublin City Council v Fennell* [2005] 1 IR 604).

9.4.2.2   The District Court

Sections 2 and 4 of the 2003 Act apply in the District Court. Consequently, decisions of the ECt.HR are now relevant in public and private law cases dealt with in this Court. The District Court must also interpret legislation in a manner harmonious with the State's obligations under the ECHR. This, it must do, however, *'in so far as is possible'* and *'subject to the rules of law relating to interpretation and application'*. No remedy is available in the District Court for breach of a ECHR right. District Court issues likely to be informed by ECt.HR jurisprudence include placing children in care, access issues in respect of children placed in care, the representation of children in proceedings and expert reports in cases involving children.

9.5   Family Law and the European Convention on Human Rights

9.5.1   FAMILY LIFE

One cannot avoid noting the enormous potential of the ECHR to protect and promote the rights of individuals. Article 8(1) ECHR guarantees as a basic right, the right to respect for private and family life, home and correspondence. Article 8(2) sets out the limits of permissible interference with the enjoyment of these rights by the State. The ECHR (unlike the Irish Constitution) makes no distinction between the family life of a marital and non-marital family. (See *Marckx v Belgium* (1979–80) 2 EHRR 330, *Johnston v Ireland* (1987) 9 EHRR 203 and *Keegan v Ireland* (1994) 18 EHRR 341. See also *Berrehab v The Netherlands* (1989) 11 EHRR 322 where the ECt.HR held that the traditional family relationship between a divorced man and his marital child did not cease to exist on the separation or divorce of the parents; *Boyle v UK* (1995) 19 EHRR 179 where family life was held to exist between an uncle and a nephew; *Kroon v The Netherlands* (1994) 19 EHRR 263 where the relationship between a man and a child conceived during an extra-marital affair, which amounted to a long-term relationship wherein the parties had four children by the time of the application, constituted a family within the meaning of Article 8 of the ECHR; and *Boughanemi v France*, ECt.HR 24 April 1996, Reports of Judgments and Decisions 1996.II, 594, para 35 where family life was held to exist where the father could show a close relationship to the child. A further instructive case is *Elsholz v Germany*, Application No. 25735/94, 13 July 2000.)

Family life constitutes not only relations between parents and their children, but also extends to grandparents and grandchildren (*Marckx v Belgium* (1979–80) 2 EHRR 330). For other relationships, it is necessary to produce evidence of a real and close family tie.

In summary, the existence of family life is a question of fact and degree (*X, Y and Z v UK* [1997] 2 FLR 892). Family life, for example, has been held by the ECt.HR to include the relationship between an adopted child and adoptive parents (*X v France* (1982) 5 EHRR 302). Similarly, for a foster parent and a foster child, although the Court has noted that the content of family life may depend on the nature of the fostering arrangement (*Gaskin v UK* (1990) 12 EHRR 36, para 49; *X v Switzerland*, Application No. 8257/78, 10 July 1978; and *Rieme v Sweden* (1992) 16 EHRR 155). The position of a non-marital father lacking a legal filiation link (through marriage or recognition) was considered in *RS Yousef v The Netherlands* [2003] 1 FLR 210. In *Haas v The Netherlands* Application No. 36983/97, judgment of 13 January 2004, however, the ECt.HR refused to acknowledge the existence of family life based on 'blood tie' alone where the purpose of the application was merely to secure inheritance rights.

In *ESKI v Austria* Application No. 21949/03, judgment of 25 January 2007, the applicant challenged the Austrian Courts' decision to grant permission to adopt his daughter without his consent. The issue was considered under Article 8 ECHR. Under Austrian domestic law only in exceptional circumstances will a court overrule the refusal of consent by the parent of a child. In the present case, the applicant had acted as the child's father only in the first months of her life and had discontinued maintenance payments for the child five years prior to the adoption being granted. The ECt.HR held that there had been no violation of Article 8 ECHR. It noted, in particular, the fact that the Austrian District Court granted the adoption order only after having heard the child, then aged nine and a half, who stated that she considered her adoptive father as her father and supported the adoption application.

In *Dudgeon v United Kingdom* (1982) 4 EHRR 149 and *Norris v Ireland* (1991) 13 EHRR 186, the ECt.HR described sexual life as the most intimate aspect of a person's private life for the purposes of Article 8 ECHR (see also *X v UK* (1997) 24 EHRR 143). The ECt.HR has not, however, been prepared to extend the concept of 'family life' to include a same-sex relationship.

It can be seen that the protection to be offered to the *de facto* family as defined within the jurisprudence of the ECt.HR is varied and a wide margin of appreciation is allowed to the contracting parties. More than in any other area of law, there is great potential for conflict between the Irish domestic concept of the family and concepts set down by the ECt.HR.

9.5.2   SAME-SEX UNIONS

In *Dudgeon v UK* ((1982) 4 EHRR 149) and *Norris v Ireland* ((1991) 13 EHRR 186), the ECt.HR described sexual life as the most intimate aspect of a person's private life for the purposes of Article 8 ECHR. The ECt.HR has not, however, been prepared to extend the concept of 'family life' to include a same-sex relationship.

In *Kerkhoven, Hinke & Hinke v The Netherlands*, the European Commission on Human Rights held that a stable relationship between two women and a child born to one of them (by donor insemination) did not amount to family life within the meaning of Article 8 ECHR (See also *X v UK* (1997) 24 EHRR 143). It should also be noted that within the EU system, the Court of First Instance in Case T-264/97 *D and Sweden v Council of Ministers* [1998] ECR II-01, citing C-249/96 *Grant v Southwest Trains* [1998] ECR I-621, held that, though the ECt.HR had extended privacy to protect private homosexual relations, the European Commission on Human Rights had stated that the right to respect for 'family life' did not extend to homosexual relations. On appeal in Cases C-122 and 125/99 *D and Sweden v Council of Ministers* [2001] ECR I-4319, the ECJ emphasised the distinction between registered partnerships and traditional marriage. Since those decisions, Article 13 EC, now Article 19 TFEU provides a legal basis for the EU to take action to combat discrimination on the grounds of sexual orientation (see **chapter 11**).

In *Frette v France*, the ECt.HR held that it was not incompatible with the ECHR to exclude a single, homosexual male applicant from the adoption eligibility process on the grounds of his sexuality ([2003] 2 FLR 9). The Court stated:

> 'If account is taken of the broad margin of appreciation to be left to States in this area and the need to protect children's best interests to achieve the desired balance, the refusal to authorise **adoption** did not infringe the principle of proportionality.'

The ECt.HR seemed to depart from this approach in *EB v France* (Judgment of January 22, 2008, Application No. 43546/02). This case concerned France's refusal of the female's application for authorisation to adopt on the grounds of her sexual orientation. The ECt.HR, reading Article 8 ECHR in conjunction with Article 14 ECHR stated the position as follows:

> 'Where sexual orientation is in issue, there is a need for particularly convincing and weighty reasons to justify difference in treatment regarding rights falling within Article 8.'

It can be seen from the foregoing that the protection to be offered to the child in the *de facto* family as defined within the jurisprudence of the ECt.HR is varied, and there is a wide margin of appreciation allowed to contracting states. More than in any other area of law, the development of conflict is likely between the Irish domestic concept of the family and concepts set down by the ECt.HR.

9.5.3   THE RIGHT TO LIFE

Article 2 ECHR provides for the right to life (see **chapter 10**). Much of the case-law on the right to life is concerned with the involvement of the State in the loss of human life. Article 2 has also been invoked in cases dealing with the killing of alleged terrorists, the right to die, abortion, reproduction, euthanasia and mercy killing (for a discussion on the right to life under Article 2, see Mathieu, *The Right to Life*, Council of Europe Publishing, April 2006). Article 2(2) places an obligation on the State to put in place effective legal rules and procedures to ensure the right to life is not violated. Thus, the ECt.HR has interpreted Article 2 as imposing a positive obligation on states not only to refrain from taking lives but also to safeguard life in circumstances where life is threatened by both private parties and state parties. In the United Kingdom, the ECHR was considered in *Re A (children)* ([2000] EWCA Civ 254). This case concerned an operation to separate two conjoined twins, which was opposed by their parents. The right to life under Article 2 was a prominent issue as the operation had the potential of killing one or both twins. The Court of Appeal decided that the operation ought to proceed, having considered the arguments in relation to the right to life. This case illustrates the relevance of the ECHR to aspects of child law. It remains to be seen how the Irish courts will apply the ECHR, in a similar case, following its incorporation into Irish law.

Article 2 of the ECHR has also been used in cases involving frozen embryos (see **10.5.1**). These cases have arisen in both this jurisdiction and the United Kingdom. They concern the right of a woman to have frozen embryos implanted in circumstances where the genetic fathers have not consented to the implantation. Amongst the arguments raised for the implantation was an argument of the right to life of the embryos. In a case in the United Kingdom, the applicant, Natalie Evans was a 35-year-old woman who was left infertile following medical treatment for cancer. She had six frozen embryos that had been fertilised by her partner in 2001. The English courts decided that there was no right to implant the embryos. The case was brought to the ECt.HR (*Evans v United Kingdom*, Application No. 6339/05; (2006) 43 EHRR 21), where in its judgment the Court agreed with the judgment of the English courts. The Lower Chamber stated that consent was required from both parties in order for the embryos to be implanted. In terms of the right to life issue under Article 2 ECHR, the Grand Chamber held that the issue of when the right to life began came within the margin of appreciation of the State concerned. It was considered that under English law an embryo did not have independent rights and as such could not claim, or have claimed on its behalf a right to life under Article 2 ECHR.

The Irish Supreme Court has also considered a similar case recently; *MR v TR* [2009] IESC 82, see **10.5.1**. This case concerned a couple living in Dublin, who attended the Sims Clinic in Rathmines in 2001 for fertility treatment. Using IVF the couple had a child in 2002 and retained three surplus embryos in the clinic with a view to having them implanted at a later time. However, the couple separated and the High Court was asked to consider, when the right to life begins under Irish law. Counsel for the wife argued that under the 1983 amendment to the Constitution, the state was required to vindicate the right to life of the embryos, and that the embryo was tantamount to an 'unborn'. The 1983 amendment to the Constitution stated as follows: 'The state acknowledges the right to life of the unborn and, with due regard to the equal right to life of the mother, guarantees in its laws to respect, and, as far as practicable, by its laws to defend and vindicate that right'. However, in this case it was argued by the State (who contested the application) and the father that the constitutional protection did not extend to the embryos. In the High Court, McGovern J in *MR v TR* [2006] IEHC 359 ruled that the husband did not give implied consent to the implantation. The Supreme Court upheld the decision of the High Court.

9.5.4   LEGAL AID

In *Airey v Ireland* (1979–80) 2 EHRR 305, the ECt.HR held that Article 6 of the ECHR imposed obligations upon a state which may only be discharged by providing legal representation. (See also *Dombo Beheer BV v Netherlands* (1994) 18 EHRR 213, *P, C and S v UK* (2002) 35 EHRR 1075 and *Steel and Morris v UK* Application No. 68416/01, judgment of 15 February 2005.) This decision does not create a right to free legal aid in all civil cases, but rather imposes a duty upon the State to act, which depends upon the nature of the rights under consideration. (Interestingly, Ireland entered a reservation in respect of legal aid on 3 September 1953. A reservation gives a state certain immunity from challenge on ECHR grounds.) It is likely that the requirement to provide free legal aid will arise more frequently in relation to children than to adults.

9.5.5   THE RIGHT TO PARTICIPATE IN LEGAL PROCEEDINGS

Articles 6 and 8 ECHR afford certain procedural safeguards applicable in court proceedings in a contracting state. The right of the individual to participate in legal proceedings is one of those procedural safeguards, a conclusion underlined by the ECt.HR in *T v UK* (Application

No. 24724/94, judgment of 16 December 1999) and *V v UK* (Application No. 24888/94, judgment of 16 December 1999). Both cases concerned whether two eleven-year-old boys who were tried for murder in an adult court had received a fair trial within the meaning of Article 6 ECHR. The cases turned on whether the boys had participated effectively in their own criminal trial and the Court held in the circumstances that they had not. The provision of separate and impartial representation to children was, in these cases, deemed to be essential to the conduct of certain criminal proceedings involving children. Considering the far-reaching nature of many public law proceedings involving children, a similar approach is likely in relation to applications by the health service executive for orders for care or supervision of a child and perhaps even in civil proceedings generally. Failure to hear children, aged four and six years, was a feature of the decision in *Kutzner v Germany* (Application No. 46544/99, judgment of 26 February, 2002), even though expert evidence was obtained by the court in that case prior to its decision to take the children into care. In *C v Finland*, however, where the Supreme Court of Finland placed exclusive weight on the children's views, the ECt.HR concluded that there had been a breach of the applicant father's Article 8 rights (judgment of May 9, 2006).

At best the child's right in Ireland to representation in court applications affecting him or her is discretionary. The net result of such discretion is a chaotic system of representation for children with significant variations as to the operation of the provision of representation throughout the State. The provisions for the separate representation of children in Irish public and private law proceedings are primarily for the children themselves and the entitlement accrued to them under the ECHR, not as some kind of dispensation.

9.5.6 DELAY

The issue of delay was considered in the context of an alleged breach of Article 6 ECHR in *Philis v Greece (No. 2)* (1998) 25 EHRR 417 where at para 35 the ECt.HR stated:

> 'The Court reiterates at the outset that the reasonableness of the length of proceedings must be assessed in the light of the particular circumstances of the case and having regard to the criteria laid down in its case law, in particular the complexity of the case and the conduct of the applicant and the relevant authorities.' (See also König v Germany (1979–80) 2 EHRR 170 and The Law Society of Ireland v Malocco [2005] IESC 5.)

The prospects of a fair hearing may be diminished by significant delay in family law proceedings. In *Eastern Health Board v MK and MK*, [1999] 2 IR 99; [1999] 2 ILRM 321, Denham J expressed her concern at the considerable delay (three years) which had occurred in that case:

> 'Time is of the essence in child custody cases. Childhood exists for only a short and finite time. Custody and care arrangements of themselves create dynamics which have a profound effect on children and their families. The long-term effects can be immense. Consequently, I voice my unease at the length of time, the delay, which exists between the judgment of the High Court and the appeal.'

Delay may result in a breach of Articles 6 or 8 ECHR or, as in *W v UK* ((1988) 10 EHRR 29 at 65), of both. Article 7 of the European Convention on the Exercise of Children's Rights, 1996 requires that:

> '[I]n proceedings affecting a child the judicial authority shall act speedily to avoid any unnecessary delay and procedures shall be available to ensure that its decisions are rapidly enforced.'

Mindful that 'justice delayed' is often 'justice denied', or at least diminished, the jurisprudence of the ECt.HR has tended to lean towards requiring that the national authorities display special diligence in expediting proceedings involving children. Indeed, in *H v UK* (1988) 10 EHRR 95, the ECt.HR stated that exceptional diligence is required where the maxim 'justice delayed is justice denied' is fully applicable. This might arise where custody and access proceedings are initiated by parents of children in the care of the Health Service Executive as such proceedings are decisive for the parents' future relations with their children and have a 'particular quality of irreversibility'. In *Koudelka v Czech Republic,* Application No. 1633/05, judgment of 20 July 2006, the ECt.HR made particular reference to the need for a sufficiently prompt and systematic treatment of cases so as to avoid drift. Similarly, in *Siemianowski v Poland*, Application No. 45972/99, judgment of 6 September 2005, the ECt.HR held that the overall length of the access proceedings exceeded a 'reasonable time' and thereby breached Article 6(1) ECHR as the domestic courts allowed the matter of access and its enforcement to drift. The ECt.HR in *H v UK* alluded to delay such that the elapse of time has the effect of determining the issue. (See also *Pini and Bertani and Manera and Atripaldi v Romania*, Application 78028/01, judgment of 22 June 2004.) Denham J expressed a similar view in *M(E), ex parte v M(J)* 9 July 2003, Supreme Court (unreported), a Hague Convention case (ie child abduction case) where time is of the essence. In *Monory v Romania and Hungary*, Application No. 71099/01, judgment of 5 April, 2005, the applicant alleged that the Romanian authorities had failed to take sufficient steps to find his child and have her returned to Hungary, following his wife's wrongful retention of his child in Romania. Both parents had joint custody in respect of the child, according to Hungarian law. In failing to ensure the swift return of his child, the ECt.HR held that there had been a breach of Article 8 ECHR. (The proceedings were instituted by the applicant on 20 January 1999 and were concluded by the courts on 2 February 2000. See also *HN v Poland*, Application No. 77710/01, judgment of 13 September 2005 and *Karadzic v Croatia*, Application No. 35030/04, judgment of 15 December 2005, which both concerned child abductions and the failure of competent authorities to take sufficient steps to find the children and have them returned.)

In *Nuutinen v Finland* (ECt.HR, 27 June 2000) the ECt.HR held that Article 6 ECHR had been violated by custody and access proceedings which had lasted for five years and five months. Moreover, in *Hansen v Turkey*, Application No. 36141/97, judgment of 23 September 2003, the ECt.HR held that proceedings relating to the granting of custody and access, including the execution of the decision at the end of such proceedings, required urgent handling, as the passage of time had the potential to have irremediable consequences for relations between a child and the non-custodial parent. In *Monory v Romania and Hungary*, Application No. 71099/01, judgment of 5 April, 2005, the ECt.HR held that divorce and child custody proceedings of nearly four years and nine months was excessive and breached Article 6 ECHR in that it failed to meet the 'reasonable time' requirement.

The current delay in the procurement and completion of s 20 reports in Ireland and the difficulties encountered in retaining guardians *ad litem* must surely fall to be considered in this context. If it transpires that a child is seriously neglected or ill treated due to a delay in the procurement of a s 20 report, for example, a breach of Article 3 ECHR may also arise (see *Z and D v UK*, Application No. 29392/95, Comm Rep 10 September 1999). In *Glaser v UK* (ECt.HR, 19 September 2000) the ECt.HR stated that it is essential that custody and access cases be dealt with speedily. The ECt.HR ruled that neither the volume of work nor shortage of resources will justify excessive delay.

9.5.7 RIGHT TO A FAIR TRIAL

One of the procedural safeguards afforded by the ECHR is the right to a fair trial (see *V v UK*, Application No. 24888/94, 16 December 1999). Article 6(1) provides:

> *'In the determination of his civil rights and obligations or of any criminal charge against him, everyone is entitled to a fair and public hearing within a reasonable time by an independent and impartial tribunal established by law.' (See also Barbera, Messegue and Jabardo v Spain (2000) 11 ECHR 360.)*

In *Ruiz-Mateos v Spain* (1993) 16 EHRR 505 the ECt.HR stated that 'as a matter of general principle the right to a fair adversarial trial means the opportunity to have knowledge of and comment on the observations filed or evidence adduced by the other party'. The three central requirements of a fair trial are:

(a)   a hearing in the presence of the parties;

(b)   all evidence should be produced to the parties; and

(c)   there should be an opportunity to challenge evidence, including the right to cross-examine witnesses (*X v Austria*, Application No. 5362/72, (1972) 42 CD 145).

In children's cases, however, the Court has determined that some relaxation of the composition of a typical court and its procedures may be required. (See *McMichael v UK* (1995) 20 EHRR 205, though in that case the failure to disclose social reports to the applicants amounted to a violation of Article 6(1) ECHR. Also *L v UK* [2000] 2 FLR 322 ECHR where a breach of Article 6(1) ECHR was held in respect of the provision of documents at case conferences when not all participants see them. This case also considered the obtaining of information from Adoption Agencies and Local Authorities.)

The right to a fair trial mirrors, of course, the explicit obligations under Article 6 ECHR, but it is also arguably a part of the procedural safeguards in Article 8. The inextricable link between the rights expressed in Article 6 and the inherent safeguards of Article 8 is underlined by the decision in *Keegan v Ireland* (1994) 18 EHRR 342. In that case, involving primarily the question of a non-marital father's right to be consulted in relation to the adoption of his child, the Court held that the father's rights under Articles 6 and 8 ECHR had been violated. The Court (at p 362, para 51 in particular) noted that:

> '[t]he fact that Irish law permitted the secret placement of the child for adoption without the applicant's knowledge or consent, leading to the bonding of the child with the proposed adopters and to the subsequent making of an adoption order, amounted to an interference with his right to respect for family life.'

Article 8 ECHR was applicable, the ECt.HR emphasised, despite the fact that the natural parents of the child were never married to each other. For two years prior to the making of the adoption order, the mother and father had been living in a stable relationship and that essentially, formed a family for ECHR purposes. Alluding to Article 6 ECHR, the ECt.HR held that the father's right to 'a fair and public hearing by an independent and impartial tribunal' had also been violated. Effectively, the father had 'no rights under Irish law' to challenge the decision to place his child for adoption either before the Adoption Board or before the courts. In summary, he had 'no standing in the adoption procedure generally' (*ibid* at 364). The applicant was awarded £ 12,000 in pecuniary and non-pecuniary loss and approximately £ 38,000 in respect of his domestic and Strasbourg legal costs and expenses. The Adoption Act, 1998, in amending the Adoption Act, 1952, has now introduced consultation procedures for natural fathers in the adoption process and also details the circumstances when such procedures need to be applied.

9.5.8   PUBLIC HEARING

In general, Irish law is committed to the administration of justice in public. This principle is guaranteed by the Constitution. Article 34(1) of Constitution states:

> '*Justice shall be administered in courts established by law by judges, and, save in such special and limited cases as may be prescribed by law, shall be administered in public.*'

By way of exception to this general principle, however, family law cases and cases involving children are among the categories of cases which may by law be shielded from such public and media scrutiny. In general, the public and the media are not admitted to family proceedings. The Courts (Supplemental Provisions) Act, 1961 provides that justice may be administered otherwise than in public in specified circumstances. Section 45(1) of the 1961 Act states:

> '*Justice may be administered otherwise than in public in any of the following cases:*
> (a) *applications of an urgent nature for relief by way of habeas corpus, bail, prohibition or injunction;*
> (b) *matrimonial causes and matters;*
> (c) *lunacy and minor matters;*
> (d) *proceedings involving the disclosure of a secret manufacturing process.*'

Individual family law statutes provide that the 'in camera rule' is mandatory in most family law matters. (See s 34 of the Judicial Separation and Family Law Reform Act, 1989; s 38(5) of the Family Law (Divorce) Act, 1996; s 25(1) and (2) of the Family Law (Maintenance of Spouses and Children) Act, 1976; s 29 of the Child Care Act, 1991; s 38(6) of the Family Law Act, 1995; and s 16(1) of the Domestic Violence Act, 1996. There is no mandatory provision in the Guardianship of Infants Act, 1964 or Family Home Protection Act, 1976. That said, the discretionary provision of s 45 of the 1961 Act applies to such applications.)

Of special significance in discussing the 'in camera rule' is Article 6 ECHR. In *Werner v Austria* (judgment of 24 November 1997) the ECt.HR stated that 'the holding of court hearings in public constitutes a fundamental principle enshrined in paragraph 1 of Article 6', save where there is 'a pressing social need' and the reasons advanced for the restriction are 'relevant and sufficient'. The right to a public hearing mirrors, of course, the explicit obligations under Article 6 ECHR, but it is also a right that arises under the guarantee of freedom of expression enshrined in Article 10 ECHR.

The decision of the ECt.HR in *B and P v UK* (judgment of 24 April 2001) states that a rigid interpretation of a mandatory 'in camera rule' may be in breach of the ECHR if it is disproportionate. This case related to two fathers who wanted their residence applications concerning their sons to be heard in public, with a public pronouncement of the judgment. They pleaded breach of Articles 6 and 10 ECHR. The ECt.HR noted the existence of a judicial discretion in English domestic law to hear Children Act proceedings in public, if merited by the special features of the case. As both cases were routine and 'run of the mill' in their nature, the hearings 'in camera' did not give rise to a violation of Article 6(1) of the ECHR. Neither was there a breach of Article 10 ECHR on the ground that the fathers could not share information revealed in the cases with others, as the restrictions imposed were to protect the rights of others, to prevent the disclosure of information received in confidence and to maintain the authority of the judiciary. The restriction of disclosure was proportionate to these aims. In the Irish context, the absolute and mandatory nature of the 'in camera rule' in the 1989 and 1996 Acts is clearly inconsistent with the requirements of Article 6(1) ECHR. This shortcoming was addressed in the Civil Liability and Courts Act, 2004, which came into operation on 31 March 2005. Section 40 of the Act allows barristers, solicitors and such other persons as may be specified in Regulations (see Civil Liability and Courts Act, 2004 (s 40(3)) Regulations, 2005 SI 337/2005) to attend family law proceedings for the purposes of preparing a report on the proceedings. It provides that the 'in camera' rule shall not operate to prevent the preparation by those persons and publication of a report of proceedings or the publication of the decision of the Court in such proceedings, provided that the report or decision does not contain any information which would enable the parties to the proceedings or any child to which the proceedings relate to be identified.

Section 3 of the Child Care (Amendment) Act, 2007, which amends s 29 of the Child Care Act, 1991, facilitates limited reporting of proceedings involving the protection of children in emergency situations, care proceedings and children in the care of the Health Service Executive.

Reform of the *'in camera* rule' is necessary but involves a sensitive balancing act between the right to privacy and the right to a fair, transparent and accountable system of justice.

The Civil Liability and Courts Act, 2004, attempts to achieve this balance.

9.5.9   THE RIGHT TO MARRY

The right to marry is guaranteed by Article 12 ECHR:

> *'Men and women of marriageable age have the right to marry and to found a family, according to the national laws governing the exercise of this right.'*

In the past, this right has been held to refer to a traditional marriage between a heterosexual couple. Particular difficulty has arisen in the case of a person who is transsexual, especially where such a person has undergone gender reassignment surgery. The ECt.HR initially rejected the proposition that the failure to recognise such gender reassignment was a breach of Article 12 ECHR (see, for example, *Rees v UK* (1987) 9 EHRR 56 and *Cossey v UK* (1991) 13 EHRR 622). More recent cases, however, indicate a growing recognition of the right to marry as a member of the sex with whom one psychologically identifies (provided that the party has undergone a 'sex change'). In *Christine Goodwin v UK* (Application No. 28957/95, [2002] 2 FLR 487) the ECt.HR, in a unanimous decision, held that the United Kingdom was in breach of Articles 8 and 12 ECHR by refusing to allow a post-operative male-to-female transsexual the right to marry under any circumstances. The ECt.HR justified its departure from the *ratio* in *Rees* and *Cossey* in the following manner:

> *'Reviewing the situation in 2002, the Court observes that Article 12 secures the fundamental right of a man and woman to marry and to found a family. There have been major social changes in the institution of marriage since the adoption of the Convention as well as dramatic changes brought about by developments in medicine and science in the field of transsexuality. While it is for the Contracting State to determine inter alia the conditions under which a person claiming legal recognition as a transsexual establishes that gender re-assignment has been properly effected or under which past marriages cease to be valid and the formalities applicable to future marriages (including, for example, the information to be furnished to intended spouses), the Court finds no justification for barring the transsexual from enjoying the right to marry under any circumstances.'*
> (See also *I v UK*, Application No. 25680/94, [2002] 2 FLR 518.)

The unanimous decision of the ECt.HR in the *Goodwin* case is interesting in the Irish context in that it was issued in the same week as the rejection by the High Court of the application by Dr Lydia Annice Foy to have her birth certificate amended to reflect the fact that, though registered at birth as male, she had undergone gender-reassignment procedures to allow her to appear as a woman. (See *Foy v The Registrar of Births, Deaths and Marriages*, McKechnie J, 9 July 2002, High Court (unreported). In June 2010, the State agreed to change the domestic law to reflect the decision in the *Goodwin* case.

9.5.10   DISCRIMINATION

Article 14 ECHR, the right not to be discriminated against, has been less effective than some of the other ECHR provisions in that it can only be pleaded in conjunction with another Article in the ECHR. (This is likely to change when Protocol 14 ECHR comes into force). Article 14 states:

> *'The enjoyment of the rights and freedoms set forth in the Convention shall be secured without discrimination on any ground, such as sex, race, colour, language, religion, political or other opinion, national or social origin, associated with a national minority, property, birth or other status.'*

It has, on occasion, been used to challenge the substantive outcome of child custody/access disputes (see *Keegan v Ireland* (1994) 18 EHRR 342 and *Hoffman v Austria* (1994) 17 EHRR 293). Article 14 ECHR was unsuccessfully pleaded alongside Article 8 ECHR in *Frette v France*, Application No. 36515/97, judgment of 26 February 2002, in a case where the ECt.HR held that a ban on same-sex adoption did not violate Article 14.

In the case of *Hoffman v Austria*, the ECt.HR found a violation of Article 14 ECHR as the legislation under consideration provided a blanket ban on awarding custody to a person who had changed his/her religion (see also *Salgueiro da Silva Mouta v Portugal* (2001) 31 EHRR 1055, which directly follows the *Hoffman* case). It should be noted that the non-discrimination protocol (Protocol 12) has not yet been ratified by Ireland.

9.6 Child Law and the European Convention on Human Rights

9.6.1 INTRODUCTION

The civil and political rights enshrined in the ECHR emphasise individual and familial freedom and autonomy and protection from excessive state interference. The ECHR is not child focused as such in the same way as the United Nations Convention on the Rights of the Child 1989. It does not recognise children as a special group requiring particular protection because of their inherent vulnerability in a world of adults. The rights contained in the ECHR are as available to children as to adults, however, and there is an increasing awareness that the ECHR has potential as an important resource in the promotion of child rights. While it must be acknowledged that only a small body of ECHR case-law deals with cases from the perspective of the child, it has been utilised very effectively to protect children within their family life with their parents.

9.6.2 CARE ORDER

The right to family life cannot be interfered with, unless such interference is in accordance with law and has an aim or aims that is or are legitimate (Article 8(2) ECHR). The interference must also be shown to be 'necessary in a democratic society'. As a core principle, then, the ECHR requires that the contracting parties refrain from arbitrary interference in the lives of individuals in the State. Where the State intervenes in the life of a family, for instance by taking a child into care, the State must show that its intervention is in accordance with the law, for the furtherance of a legitimate aim or aims and necessary in a democratic society. The ECt.HR in *K and T v Finland* (2003) 36 EHRR 255 stated:

> '[A] fair balance has to be struck between the interests of the child in remaining in public care and those of the parent in being reunited with the child. In carrying out this balancing exercise, the Court will attach particular importance to the best interests of the child, which may override those of the parent. In particular, the parent cannot be entitled under Article 8 of the Convention to have such measures taken as would harm the child's health and development.'

In the aforementioned case against Finland, the ECt.HR held that as the care order was not the only option available to the local authority in that case for securing the children's protection, the reasons used to justify it were insufficient and amounted to a violation of Article 8 ECHR (*K and T v Finland, ibid*):

> '[T]he taking of a new-born baby into public care at the moment of its birth is an extremely harsh measure. There must be extraordinary compelling reasons before a baby can be physically

after implantation. Therefore an unborn under Article 40.3.3 is established after an embryo is implanted.

The concept of unborn envisages a state of being born, the potential to be born, the capacity to be born, which occurs only after the embryo has been implanted in the uterus of a mother.

This analysis may be put in a slightly different form. The right to life of the unborn is not stated as an absolute right in Article 40.3.3. Rather, it is subject to the due regard to the right to life of the mother. The right to life of the mother is not stated as an absolute right either. Article 40.3.3 refers to a situation where these two lives are connected and a balance may have to be sought between the two lives. Thus the physical situation must exist to require such a balancing act. No such connection exists between the plaintiff and the three surplus embryos now frozen and stored at the Clinic. There is no such connection between the lives of the mother and the embryos at the moment. The relationship which might require the consideration of the right to life of the unborn and the equal right of the mother does not arise in the circumstances.

This connection, relationship, between the embryos and the mother does not arise until after implantation has occurred. After the implantation of an embryo the relationship between the embryo and the mother changes. The mother has carriage of the embryos, becomes pregnant, and the embryo enters a state of "unborn". At that time an attachment begins between the two lives. It is that attachment which gives rise to the relationship addressed in Article 40.3.3.

The words of Article 40.3.3 refer to a situation where the rights of the mother and the unborn are engaged. This occurs after implantation. Thus Article 40.3.3 does not apply to pre-implantation embryos.'

It is clear from the work of the CAHR, the Report of the Irish Council for Bioethics (*Ethical, Scientific and Legal Issues Concerning Stem Cell Research Opinion*, 2008) and now a pronouncement from the Supreme Court, that this is undoubtedly an area that requires careful legislative review and regulation and this was emphasised by the Supreme Court, Hardiman J, observing that:

'There has been a marked reluctance on the part of the legislature actually to legislate on these issues: the court simply draws attention to this. That is all it can do. That is what McCarthy J. did, apparently in vain, in the *X* case eighteen years ago. But the Court does so as seriously and as urgently as it can.

The issue is all the more urgent because, of course, scientific developments in the area of embryology and the culturing of stem cells will not stand still. It has been very recently suggested that it may shortly be possible to develop human sperm from such cells. If the legislature does not address such issues, Ireland may become by default an unregulated environment for practices which may prove controversial or, at least, to give rise to a need for regulation.'

Fennelly J also stated that:

'... I join Hardiman J. in expressing concern at the total absence of any form of statutory regulation of in vitro fertilisation in Ireland. It is disturbing, to use no stronger word, that some four years after publication of the Report of the Commission on Assisted Human Reproduction, no legislative proposal has even been formulated. Counsel for the Attorney General argued before us that there is no law or public policy regarding the protection of frozen embryos, in short that they have no legal status. As I interpret these submissions, the organs of the State have no present intention to propose any legislation. It is obvious that this is extremely difficult and sensitive subject-matter ... Nonetheless, it cannot be denied that the fertilisation of the ovum brings into existence, outside the womb, the essential unique components of a potential new individual human person. I agree . . . that the frozen embryo is entitled to respect. This is the least that can be said. Arguably there may be a constitutional obligation on the State to give concrete form to that respect.'

10.6 The 'X' Case

On the issue of the right to life of the unborn, the judiciary were faced with what 'must surely qualify as the most controversial case ever to come before an Irish court' (Hogan and Whyte, *JM Kelly: The Irish Constitution*, 3rd edn, 1994, Butterworths, 796). In *Attorney General v X* [1992] 1 IR 1, or the 'X' case as it came to be known, the courts were faced with a dilemma in which they had to attempt to interpret a constitutional provision which equates 'two rights which, on those rare occasions when they come into conflict, cannot be reconciled' (Hogan and Whyte, 802). The defendant was a 14-year-old girl who had been raped and had become pregnant. The High Court had granted an injunction prohibiting the defendant from leaving the State for the purposes of obtaining an abortion. She however, had stated that if she had to go through the pregnancy, she would commit suicide. The Supreme Court decided that in certain limited circumstances an abortion would be permitted. Finlay CJ stated at 53:

'. . . the proper test to be applied is that if it is established as a matter of probability that there is a real and substantial risk to the life, as distinct from the health, of the mother, which can only be avoided by the termination of her pregnancy, such termination is permissible, having regard to the true interpretation of Art 40, s.3(3) of the Constitution.'

As the law now stands an abortion may be permissible in this jurisdiction in certain circumstances. Such an abortion will only be permissible if there is a real and substantial risk to the life of the mother which only a termination could avoid. Such a risk includes the risk of suicide by the mother.

Allied to this issue, were the issues of individuals being permitted to travel for the purposes of undergoing a termination and the dissemination of information relating to abortion.

10.7 The Thirteenth Amendment: The 'Travel Amendment'

In the *X* case, the Supreme Court had difficulties in relation to the issue of travel for the purpose of undergoing a termination. The matter has now been resolved by virtue of the Thirteenth Amendment to the Constitution, which amended Article 40.3.3 by adding:

'*This subsection shall not limit freedom to travel between the State and another state.*'

In *A & B v Eastern Health Board & C* [1998] 1 ILRM 460, the High Court explored this amendment in the context of a minor who also, as a result of rape, had become pregnant. The Eastern Health Board, which had taken the girl into care had applied to the District Court for orders allowing it to take the girl abroad for an abortion and to make all necessary arrangements for the abortion. In a judicial review application relating to the interim care order under the Child Care Act, 1991, the High Court examined the Thirteenth Amendment, Geoghegan J stating as follows:

'This amendment is framed in negative terms and must, in my view, be interpreted in the historical context in which it was inserted. There was, I think, a widespread feeling in the country that a repetition of *The Attorney General v X* [1992] 1 I R 1, should not occur in that nobody should be injuncted from actually travelling out of the country for the purpose of an abortion. It must be remembered that three out of the five judges of the Supreme Court took the view that in an appropriate case a travel injunction could be granted. It was in that context, therefore that the amendment was made and I do not think it was ever intended to give some new substantial right. Rather, it was intended to prevent injunctions against travel or having an abortion abroad. A court of law, in considering the welfare of an Irish child in Ireland and considering whether on health grounds a termination of pregnancy was necessary, must, I believe, be confined to considering the grounds for termination which would be lawful under the Irish Constitution and cannot make a direction authorising travel to another jurisdiction for a different kind of abortion. The amended Constitution does not now confer a right to abortion outside of Ireland. It merely prevents injunctions against travelling for that purpose ... the fact that there may be different views as to the importance of the constitutional right to travel does not in my view affect the issue of whether the District Court under the Child Care Act, 1991, can actually exercise a jurisdiction authorising travel for a particular purpose, namely, for an abortion in circumstances where the proposed abortion would not be allowed under Irish law. I think that the court would be prevented from doing so by the terms of the right to life of the unborn expressed in the Constitution and as the Supreme Court have held, unaffected by "the travel amendment".'

The Court made it clear that a court would not have any jurisdiction to authorise travel for the purpose of obtaining an abortion outside the grounds of the *X* case, since the amendment was drafted in negative terms—ie an individual could not be injuncted from travelling to another country, but a court would not have the jurisdiction to authorise travel to another country for an abortion beyond the grounds envisaged in the *X* case.

The issue of travel in the context of the unborn child arose again in 2007 in what is referred to as the *D v Health Service Executive (HSE)* case or the *Miss D* case. Unfortunately, at the time of writing no circulated judgment of this case was available and the following comments are based on press reports of the matter. The matter concerned a 17-year-old girl who was the subject of an interim care order. She became pregnant and upon medical tests it was realised that the child in utero was suffering from anencephaly with no chance of surviving more than some days after birth. Miss D wished to travel for an abortion to the United Kingdom. As Miss D was in care, the HSE contended that a direction from the District Court was required under the Child Care Act, 1991 to decide whether or not it would be lawful for Miss D to travel for an abortion. The High Court was told that Judge Brennan in the District Court had refused an order allowing Miss D to travel for an abortion as it would amount to a failure by him to vindicate the right to life of the unborn and would be improper and unlawful. The High Court had to consider two sets of judicial review proceedings: (a) to decide whether Miss D was entitled to an order restraining the HSE from preventing her from travelling for an abortion, and (b) a challenge by the HSE to the decision by District Court Judge Brennan refusing to grant the HSE an order allowing the girl to travel to the United Kingdom. The HSE argued that a District Court order was necessary before the girl could travel. However, all the other parties contended that no such court order was necessary and that the district judge was wrong to refuse that order. The Attorney General argued that there was no law under which the girl may be prevented from travelling to the United Kingdom and the fact the girl was the subject of an interim care order would not permit her right to travel to be impinged upon.

McKechnie J, on 9 May 2007, in the High Court stated that Miss D's right to travel could not be interfered with. The press, reporting his ruling stated that:

'Mr Justice Liam McKechnie said he "firmly and unequivocally" held the view that there was no law or constitutional impediment preventing the girl ... travelling for the purpose of terminating her pregnancy.' ('Court rules "Miss D" can travel to UK for abortion', *The Irish Times* 10 May 2007.)

The press also reported that the High Court stated that:

'...there was no law or provision of the Child Care Act which restrained a child in care from travelling for an abortion or which would support the HSE's claim that District Court permission was required for travel. Miss D's right to travel for an abortion was unaffected by Article 40.3.3 (the right to life) of the Constitution...Mr Justice McKechnie took the...view, that the right to travel took precedence over any rights conferred on the unborn by Article 40.3.3.' ('High Court rules that girl can travel for abortion', *The Irish Times*, 10 May 2007.)

10.8 The Fourteenth Amendment: The Provision of Information

From the time of the Eighth Amendment, the courts had been concerned with the matter of the advertising of information relating to abortion services. The Irish courts in *The Attorney General (SPUC) v Open Door Counselling Ltd* [1988] IR 593; *SPUC v Coogan* [1989] IR 734; *SPUC v Grogan* [1989] IR 753 seemed relatively content to restrict such information. However, in Case C-159/90 *SPUC v Grogan* [1991] ECR I-4685, the European Court of Justice (ECJ) ruled that there was a right to advertise abortion services lawfully available in another EC State once it was for economic profit. The position was clarified by the addition of the Fourteenth Amendment to the Constitution, which states at Article 40.3.3:

'*This subsection shall not limit freedom to obtain or make available, in the State, subject to such conditions as may be laid down by law, information relating to services lawfully available in another state.*'

The conditions laid down by law are contained in the Regulation of Information (Services Outside the State for the Termination of Pregnancies) Act, 1995, which the Supreme Court in *Re Article 26 and the Regulation of Information (Services Outside the State for the Termination of Pregnancies) Bill, 1995* [1995] 1 IR 1 found was not repugnant to the Constitution. The Act provides for the provision of non-directive information in relation to terminations, which does not promote or advocate it and where such information relates to lawful abortions in the State in which they are carried out.

10.9 The Proposed Twenty-Fifth Amendment: Restricting the Parameters of the '*X*' Case

Those unhappy with the decision in the *X* case felt particularly aggrieved by the fact that suicide as distinct from medical complications which arise in cases of pregnancy could be regarded as a factor that could be regarded as a real and substantial risk to the life of the mother. Government efforts to evaluate the aftermath of the *X* case by means of the report of the Constitutional Review Group in 1996 and a substantial initiative which resulted in an All-Party Oireachtas Committee on the Constitution producing a large document entitled the *Fifth Progress Report: Abortion* (Dublin, 2000) led the government to draft a proposed Amendment to the Constitution contained in the Twenty-Fifth Amendment of the Constitution (Protection of Human Life in Pregnancy) Bill, 2001 which stated at s 1(2):

'...abortion does not include the carrying out of a medical procedure by a medical practitioner at an approved place in the course of which or as a result of which unborn human life is ended where that procedure is, in the reasonable opinion of the practitioner, necessary to prevent a real and substantial risk of loss of the woman's life other than by self-destruction.'

A majority of those who voted in the referendum rejected the proposal to introduce this Bill and the law remains as set out in the *X* case.

10.10 Implications for Healthcare Professionals

Sections 58 and 59 of the Offences Against the Person Act, 1861 prohibit the administering of drugs or the use of instruments to procure abortion or the supplying of drugs or instruments to procure abortion.

After the *X* case, the Medical Council made its policy clear in the Medical Council's *A Guide to Ethical Conduct and Behaviour* (5th edn, 1998, Medical Council, Dublin) para 26.5 of which states:

> 'The deliberate and intentional destruction of the unborn child is professional misconduct. Should a child in utero suffer or lose its life as a side effect of standard medical treatment of the mother, then it is not unethical. Refusal by a doctor to treat a woman with a serious illness because she is pregnant would be grounds for complaint and could be considered to be professional misconduct.'

This clearly did not take into account the ruling of the *X* case, but rather remained in line with traditional medical opinion that should the child in utero, by no action on the part of the medical practitioner, lose its life due to standard medical procedure, then that was not unethical. This is of course a classic invocation of the doctrine of double effect. The Guidelines did not touch on the issue of the *X* case. In effect, a medical practitioner, who carried out an abortion if it came within the ambit of the *X* case grounds, notwithstanding the ruling of the Supreme Court, could still have faced a charge of professional misconduct. This did not ever happen and was unlikely to happen, since under the provisions of the Medical Practitioners' Act, 1978, a practitioner found guilty of professional misconduct by the Medical Council has a right of appeal to the High Court. It is unlikely that the High Court would uphold a charge of professional misconduct by the Medical Council when such conduct would be covered by the Supreme Court judgment. Nevertheless, the medical profession were unhappy that their guidelines left them in an ethically uncomfortable predicament.

The Medical Council, after much debate, published its first amendment to its fifth edition in December 2001, which practitioners received in 2002. The amendment replaced the previous Guidelines above and now states:

> 'The Council recognises that termination of pregnancy can occur when there is a real and substantial risk to the life of the mother and subscribes to the views expressed in Part 2 of the written submission of the Institute of Obstetricians and Gynaecologists to the All-Party Oireachtas Committee....'

Part 2, however, only states that rare complications do sometimes occur when therapeutic intervention is required when there is no prospect of survival of the baby and where failure to intervene could cause death to mother and baby. The paragraph goes on to state:

> 'We consider that there is a fundamental difference between abortion carried out with the intention of taking the life of the baby, for example for social reasons, and with the unavoidable death of the baby resulting from essential treatment to protect the life of the mother.'

These Guidelines are now contained at para 24.6 of the *Guide to Ethical Conduct and Behaviour* (6th edn, 2004, Medical Council, Dublin).

Effectively, the Guidelines seek to come to a compromise between the *X* case (by adjusting the words of the Guidelines to adopt the words of the Supreme Court in the *X* case) and the Council's views. The effect of this amendment remains to be seen. However, it seems that the lack of complete clarity might still result in a doctor defending himself against a charge for professional misconduct even though his/her actions come within the current status of the law. It is:

(a) likely that the court will be involved in any such decisions for the foreseeable future; and

(b) unlikely that a Medical Council's finding of misconduct (once such conduct is within the parameters of the *X* case) would stand on appeal to the High Court, if such court finds that the conduct was indeed within the realms of the *X* case.

The 2009 and latest edition of the Guide is updated and now states as follows (at 21):

'21.1 Abortion is illegal in Ireland except where there is a real and substantial risk to the life (as distinct from the health) of the mother. Under current legal precedent, this exception includes where there is a clear and substantial risk to the life of the mother arising from a threat of suicide. You should undertake a full assessment of any such risk in light of the clinical research on this issue.

21.2 It is lawful to provide information in Ireland about abortions abroad, subject to strict conditions. It is not lawful to encourage or advocate an abortion in individual cases.

21.3 You have a duty to provide care, support and follow-up services for women who have an abortion abroad.

21.4 In current obstetrical practice, rare complications can arise where therapeutic intervention (including termination of a pregnancy) is required at a stage when, due to extreme immaturity of the baby, there may be little or no hope of the baby surviving. In these exceptional circumstances, it may be necessary to intervene to terminate the pregnancy to protect the life of the mother, while making every effort to preserve the life of the baby.'

In light of the decisions of the High Court and the Supreme Court in *MR v TR Walsh* [2006] IEHC 359 and [2009] IESC 82 (discussed above at **10.5.1** and see **9.5.3**), the status of the embryo in vitro seems to lack constitutional protection (at the time of writing).

Paragraph 24.1 of the Guidelines state:

'The creation of new forms of life for experimental purposes or the deliberate and intentional destruction of in vitro human life already formed is professional misconduct.'

Whilst the Medical Council Guidelines are limited in their application to medical practitioners and as stated by McGovern J in the *MR v TR* case:

'These ethical guidelines do not have the force of law and offer only such limited protection as derives from the fear on the part of a doctor that he might be found guilty of professional misconduct with all the professional consequences that might follow.'

The High Court went on to state that:

'The fact that something is not prohibited by the law does not of itself mean that it is morally acceptable to carry out that act. There may be many people who, because of their moral or religious outlook regard the process of IVF as unacceptable even though it is permitted by the law. There are others who see this a great advance in medical science giving the opportunity to infertile couples to have children. In issues such as this there may well be a divide between Church and State, and between one religion and another. It is not for the Courts to weigh the views of one religion against another, or to choose between one moral view point and another. All are entitled to equal respect provided they are not subversive of the law, and provided there are no public policy reasons requiring the Courts to intervene. Moral responsibility exists even in the absence of law and arises out of the freedom of choice of the individual. People have many different ideas of morality. Society is made up of people of various religious traditions and none. If the law is to enforce morality then whose morality is it to enforce? The function of the Courts is to apply the law, which are the rules and regulations that govern society. Where these rules and regulations are to be found in articles of the Constitution they are approved of by the people, and where they are to be found in legislation they are passed by the Houses of the Oireachtas. Laws should, and generally do, reflect society's values and will be influenced by them. But at the end of the day it is the duty of the Courts to implement and apply the law, not morality.'

Thus, even though the Guidelines may have no force in law, medical practitioners should take them into account in their practices.

In similar factual circumstances, in the case of *Evans v United Kingdom* (Application No. 6339/05, (2006) 43 EHRR, see **9.5.3**), the applicant wished to have embryos implanted for which consent had initially existed prior to her relationship breaking down. Her partner thereafter did not wish to become a father. The applicant's case failed at first instance and therafter in the Court of Appeal in the United Kingdom. The House of Lords refused leave to appeal and she also failed in the European Court of Human Rights when the Court, in relation to the issue of Article 2 stated that:

'The applicant complained that the provisions of English law requiring the embryos to be destroyed once J withdrew his consent to their continued storage violated the embryos' right to life, contrary to Article 2 of the Convention, which reads as follows: "1. Everyone's right to life shall be protected by law. . . ."

The Court recalls, however, that in *Vo v. France* [GC], no. 53924/00, 82, ECHR 2004-. . . it held that, in the absence of any European consensus on the scientific and legal definition of the beginning of life, the issue of when the right to life begins comes within the margin of appreciation which the Court generally considers that States should enjoy in this sphere. Under English law, as was made clear by the domestic courts in the present applicant's case (see paras 16 and 21 above), an embryo does not have independent rights or interests and cannot claim—or have claimed on its behalf—a right to life under Article 2.

There has not, accordingly, been a violation of that provision in the present case.'

10.11 Implications of Foetal Protection for Maternal Autonomy

In other common law jurisdictions, in a situation where a 'maternal conflict' occurs, for example, where a competent adult woman does not wish to receive medical treatment (a common example being caesarean section) and that non-treatment will result in the death of her child in utero, the rights of the woman have been held to be paramount. In the UK case of *Re MB* (1987) 8 Med LR 217, 224 the Court of Appeal clarified English law on this controversial issue:

'. . . we are . . . sure that however desirable it may be for the mother to be delivered of a live and healthy baby, on this aspect of the appeal it is not a strictly relevant consideration. If therefore the competent mother refuses to have the medical intervention, the doctors may not lawfully do more than attempt to persuade her. If that persuasion is unsuccessful, there are no further steps towards medical intervention to be taken. We recognise that the effect of these conclusions is that there will be situations in which the child may die or may be seriously handicapped because the mother said no and the obstetrician was not able to take the necessary steps to avoid the death or handicap. The mother may indeed later regret the outcome, but the alternative would be an unwarranted invasion of the right of the woman to make the decision.'

This rationale was reconfirmed in the case of *St George's Healthcare NHS Trust v S; R v Collins, ex parte S* [1998] 3 WLR 936 where Judge LJ stated:

'In our judgment while pregnancy increases the personal responsibilities of a woman it does not diminish her entitlement to decide whether or not to undergo medical treatment. Although human, and protected by the law in a number of different ways...an unborn child is not a separate person from its mother. Its need for medical assistance does not prevail over her rights. She is entitled not to be forced to submit to an invasion of her body against her will, whether her own life or that of her unborn child depends on it. Her right is not reduced or diminished merely because her decision to exercise it may appear morally repugnant.... Of themselves the perceived needs of the foetus did not provide the necessary justification.'

In the United States, this is also the case as was made clear in the case of *Re AC* (1990) 573 A 20l 1235, where the Court of Appeals stated:

'We hold that in virtually all cases the question of what is to be done is to be decided by the patient—the pregnant woman—on behalf of herself and the foetus. If the patient is incompetent or otherwise unable to give an informed consent, to a proposed course of medical treatment, then her decision must be ascertained through the procedure known as substituted judgment.'

In Ireland, whilst the issue remains to be tested, it does not seem that these stances could represent the law. In *Attorney General v X* [1992] ILRM 401, 422, Hederman J stated:

'...the termination of pregnancy other than a natural one has a legal and social dimension and requires a special responsibility on the part of the State...Therefore no recognition of a mother's right of self-determination can be given priority over the protection of the unborn life. The creation of a new life, involving as it does pregnancy, birth and raising the child, necessarily involves some restriction of a mother's freedom but the alternative is the destruction of the unborn life. The termination of pregnancy is not like a visit to the doctor to cure an illness. The State must, in principle, act in accordance with the mother's duty to carry out the pregnancy.'

It is quite clear that an Irish court would not give a woman the overriding power of self-determination when a foetus can be saved and it does not represent a real and substantial risk to the life of the mother. In Ireland, it seems that if a mother wished to refuse a caesarean section, which if not carried out would result in the death of the foetus, she would probably be compelled to have this treatment, unless it carried a real and substantial risk to her life as opposed to just her health. In effect and reality, such treatment would have to be forced on the woman and here her rights to bodily integrity would be compromised in favour of the right to life of the foetus.

By virtue of a recent case, the issue of the balance of rights has again come to the fore. In a case that is being referred to as the *Coombe Hospital v K* case, an adult woman of sound mind who had just given birth, refused consent to a blood transfusion on the basis that she was a Jehovah's Witness. This was the first time such a situation had presented itself before the Irish courts.

In the past, the courts in this jurisdiction had made it clear that refusal of treatment in an adult of sound mind had to be respected, even where it lead to the death of that individual. Thus in the case of *In Re a Ward of Court* [1996] 2 IR 79, 129, it was stated by O'Flaherty J that:

'... consent to medical treatment is required in the case of a competent person (cf. *Walsh v. Family Planning Services Ltd.* [1992] 1 IR 496) and, as a corollary, there is an absolute right in a competent person to refuse medical treatment even if it leads to death ...'

In the *K* case (for which it should be noted no reported judgment exists and what is known of the application is what was reported in the press), the hospital sought a declaration from the High Court that it be allowed to administer treatment to the woman admitting that she was compos mentis.

The press report stated the following:

'Mr Justice Henry Abbott ruled that doctors must intervene in the interests of the child. The judge said he accepted Ms K was compos mentis and if brought to court on a stretcher she would oppose the application.

But he told the court he felt it necessary to override her religious beliefs on the grounds that her baby boy had no other relatives, or guardians, that were known of in the state.

Mr Justice Abbott said the interests of the child were paramount and that he must err on the side of preserving life.' ('Hospital Ordered to Give Jehovah's Witness Transfusion', *The Irish Times*, 21 September 2006.)

The Court here, it seems, balanced the right of an adult to refuse medical treatment in favour of the right of either the welfare of the child and/or of preserving its life. The impact of this judicial stance is uncertain.

Again, it must be emphasised that it is uncertain on what basis this balance of rights was carried out and it is not known whether the life of the child was or would have been in any actual danger. In other cases, as discussed previously, the law will compromise constitutional rights in favour of preserving and protecting the right to life. On the seeming facts of this case, it is difficult to see where the danger to the life of the child was if the mother's refusal had been respected. See Sheikh, 'Medico-Legal Issues and Patient Autonomy—Here Yesterday, Gone Tomorrow?' (editorial) (2006) 12 *MLJI* 2, 54.

The matter was finally decided in full by Laffoy J, in *Fitzpatrick v K & the AG*, April 25, 2008, High Court (unreported). However, on the point in question of the balancing of rights, the issue of the child's life being in danger by virtue of there being no-one to look after the child became moot—as it became apparent that the father of the child was in fact present in the jurisdiction. The High Court decided that 'Although the Hospital personnel were misled by Ms. K on this point for the duration of her stay in the Hospital, the baby's father was in the State and, indeed, visited the Hospital both before and after the baby's birth. Therefore, as regards the plaintiffs' claim, the balancing of rights question is wholly hypothetical and should not be decided.'

10.12 Implications for Refugee Law

10.12.1 THE UNBORN CHILD

The position of the rights of the unborn child have not been examined in relation to whether such rights could apply to a non-national. Various views have been expressed by the courts in relation to the application of fundamental rights to non-citizens. Whilst none can be said to have given any definitive view on this matter in the past, the decision of the High Court in *Makumbi v Minister for Justice, Equality and Law Reform* [2005] IEHC 403 (see **10.12.2**) is important in this regard.

The High Court and, on appeal, the Supreme Court have recently touched on the matter in *Baby O v Minister for Justice, Equality and Law Reform* [2002] 2 IR I69. (At the time of writing the High Court decision remains uncirculated and this report has come from a newspaper article, 'High Court Challenge by Nigerian Woman Is Dismissed', *The Irish Times*, 19 January 2002.) The facts pertained to a pregnant Nigerian national who had failed in an asylum application and who was to be deported. In November 2001, the woman obtained an order preventing deportation on a number of grounds the underlying basis of which was her pregnancy. The rights to birthright and the right to life of the unborn were invoked by the applicant. In the High Court, Smyth J seemed to distinguish this case from the *X* case, since the woman in the *X* case was a national whereas in this case, the woman was not. Also, the Court seems to have stated that the birthright provided for in Article 2 of the Constitution is an entitlement of a person born in Ireland. In relation to Article 40.3.3, the Court stated that in the absence of any adverse medical decision, the right to life was not an issue in the case and a threat to the life of the unborn had not been proffered. Keane CJ, in the Supreme Court, agreed and stated that the issue of termination of the unborn was irrelevant since the State was not seeking to terminate the pregnancy. Keane CJ stated that had the applicant arrived with a young child that would not affect the decision to deport and neither would the decision to deport differ in the case of a pregnant woman. He stated at page 182 that:

'The passage from Article 40.3.3 on which counsel relied, as explained by the judgments of the majority in this Court in *Attorney General v. X* [1992] 1 I.R. 1, was intended to prevent the legalisation of abortion either by legislation or judicial decision within the State, except where there was a real and substantial risk to the life of the mother which could only be avoided by the termination of the pregnancy. In this case, neither the State nor any of its organs was seeking to terminate the second applicant's pregnancy and the fact that the standard of ante or post-natal care available to her in Nigeria was less than would be available to her in this country was entirely irrelevant to the legality of her deportation. If the second applicant had arrived in this country accompanied by a young infant, and both of them had been refused refugee status and ordered to be deported, the life expectation of the infant, and for that matter the second applicant herself, might have been less. That would plainly not be a ground for interfering with the deportation. If the State's right to deport persons who have been refused refugee status and who have no legal right to remain in this country were thus circumscribed, it would be, in a great range of cases, virtually negated. It is obvious that the rights of the born in this context, cannot be less than those of the unborn'.

10.12.2 TRANSFER ORDERS

In the case of *Makumbi v Minister for Justice, Equality and Law Reform* [2005] IEHC 403 the issue of the right to life recognised by Bunreacht na hÉireann and Article 2 ECHR fell to be considered by the High Court in the context of a transfer order made in respect of an asylum seeker. The applicant, a national of Uganda, was the subject of a transfer order pursuant to Article 7 of the Refugee Act 1996 (Section 22) Order 2003 (SI 423/2003) requiring the applicant to leave the State and go to the United Kingdom pursuant to the provisions of Council Regulations (EC) No. 343/2003 (discussed at **15.2.4.1**). The applicant applied by way of judicial review for a number of reliefs all of which were directed to preventing the transfer of the applicant to the United Kingdom and requiring that the respondent determine the applicant's request to have her claim for asylum processed in Ireland. The application was on the basis of evidence that the applicant suffered from clinical depression and had a history of attempts to take her own life which danger would present itself if the transfer were to go ahead. A notice of opposition was delivered on behalf of the respondent in which it is contended *inter alia* that the respondent was obliged to give effect to the transfer order and has no discretion or power not to implement the transfer order or to revoke it or to consider the application to have the applicant's claim for asylum determined in this jurisdiction. Finlay Geoghegan J stated that:

> 'At issue in this application is perhaps the most fundamental of such human rights, the right to life expressly recognised by the Constitution in Article 40.3.2.

> Hence, even if the applicant is a person who is not now entitled to be in the State, the respondent in exercising the power or duty to implement the Transfer Order is obliged to uphold her right to life as guaranteed by Article 40.3.2. A constitutional interpretation of the powers which the respondent may confer on himself by s.22 of the Act of 1996 necessitates an implicit power not to implement a transfer order where the protection of the life of the person to whom it applies so requires. There is nothing in the wording of the 2003 Order which precludes such an implicit power. Hence, it appears to me that Article 7 of the 2003 Order must be construed as including not only an implicit power and duty to implement a transfer order but also an implicit power or discretion not to implement the transfer order, where the respect or protection of the right to life of a person to whom it relates so requires.

> Counsel for the applicant also relied upon Article 2 of the European Convention on Human Rights and Sections 2 and 3 of the European Convention on Human Rights Act, 2003. Section 2 of the Act of 2003 requires this Court in interpreting and applying any statutory provisions (which includes a statutory instrument) to do so in a manner compatible with the State's obligations under the Convention provisions. This is subject to the rules of law relating to interpretation and application. Under s.3 of the Act of 2003 the respondent is obliged to perform his functions under the 2003 Order and Act of 1996 in a manner compatible with the State's obligations under the Convention provisions. I am satisfied that it would not be in breach of any rule of interpretation to construe the powers and/or duties of the respondent in relation to the implementation of a transfer order under the 2003 Order as including a discretion not to implement a transfer order where to do so would be in breach of the State's obligations under Article 2 of the [ECHR].'

10.12.3 EXTRADITION AND THE RIGHT TO LIFE

In the case of *Minister for Justice v SMR* [2008] 2 IR 242 (at 254–255), the Supreme Court whilst recognising a positive obligation on a state under Article 2(1) to take appropriate steps to safeguard the lives of those within its jurisdiction, stated that in this case, that the mere possibility that stress associated with the surrender of an applicant under a European arrest warrant could precipitate acute coronary disease was not sufficient for a court to prohibit a trial so as to protect an applicant's constitutional right to bodily integrity. Something much more definite by way of threat to life was required.

10.13 The Right to Life and the Gravely Ill

The courts in Ireland have not yet been called upon to deal with the issue of the right to life in relation to the 'malformed neonate' or those just born who are very seriously ill. The Irish courts have, of course, examined the range of medico-legal and constitutional dilemmas that would arise in such cases as the *Ward* case. It is quite likely that the law as analysed and set down in the *Ward* case would apply in some degree to most such cases.

In these cases, the courts have granted permission to allow patients to die a natural death, where it was considered that any other option was not in the patient's best interests. With the very seriously malformed neonate (*Re C (a minor)* [1989] 2 All ER 782, and *In Re J (a minor)* [1990] 3 All ER 930), the PVS patient (*Airedale NHS Trust v Bland* [1993] 1 All ER 821), the near-PVS patient and patients in very low awareness states (*Re R (Adult: Medical Treatment)* [1996] 2 FLR 99) the courts have sanctioned actions to withdraw medical treatment, such that these patients' lives were allowed to 'come to an end peacefully and with dignity' (*Re C (a minor)* [1989] 2 All ER 782, *per* Lord Donaldson of Lymington MR).

10.13.1 THE MALFORMED NEONATE

The courts in the United Kingdom have been called upon to opine on a number of controversial issues, which dealt with the right to life at the early stages of life.

In *Re C* [1989] 2 All ER 782, an infant was born with a condition (congenital hydrocephalus) which had caused irreparable brain damage. The brain structure was severely and poorly formed and there was no chance of the child having a meaningful lifespan. The question then to be asked was whether the infant should receive 'treatment appropriate to a non-handicapped child' or treatment 'appropriate to her condition', subject to the fact that, as the court stated *per* Lord Donaldson of Lymington MR (at 783), 'Baby C is dying and nothing the court can do, nothing that the doctors can do and nothing known to medical science can alter that fact.'

At this point, the judge referred back to the *dicta* of Ward J, the trial judge, who directed that it was foremost in the best interests of the child that 'the hospital authority . . . be at liberty to allow her life to come to an end peacefully and with dignity.'

His reason for this direction was, as he stated (at 787), that he was:

'. . . quite satisfied that the damage is severe and irreparable. Insofar as I can assess the quality of life, which as a test in itself raised [as] many questions as it can answer, I adjudge that any quality of life has already been denied to this child because it cannot flow from a brain incapable of even limited intellectual function. Inasmuch as one judges, as I do, intellectual function to be a hallmark of our humanity, her functioning on that level is negligible if it exists at all. Coupled with her total physical handicap, the quality of her life will be demonstrably awful and intolerable . . . . Asking myself what capacity she has to interact mentally, socially, physically, I answer none. This is her permanent condition.'

Soon after this case, the same Court developed the rationale laid down in *Re C* in its landmark decision of *Re J (a minor)* [1990] 3 All ER 930. J was born very prematurely, suffering irreparable brain damage. The medical evidence showed that he was likely to develop serious spastic quadriplegia, be blind, deaf and unlikely to ever be able to speak or develop even limited intellectual abilities, but would probably feel pain to the same extent as any normal baby, since pain was such a basic response. His life expectancy was uncertain, but he was expected to die before late adolescence. He had been ventilated twice before for long periods, a procedure which was both hazardous and painful. However, he was neither dying nor on the point of dying. The question thus arose that if he suffered a further collapse, should he be re-ventilated? The trial judge stated that he should be given antibiotics in the case of infection, but should not be re-ventilated, unless the doctors thought otherwise. The case was appealed.

In dismissing the appeal, all three judges made important comments as to the status quo of the law. Lord Donaldson of Lymington, examining when to consent to a procedure to prolong the life of a patient stated (at 938):

'As this court recognised in *Re B*, account has to be taken of the pain and suffering and the quality of life which the child will experience if life is prolonged. Account has also to be taken of the pain and suffering involved in the proposed treatment itself.'

The Court, asserting its belief in the sanctity of human life, stated:

'We all believe in and assert the sanctity of human life ... even very severely handicapped people find a quality of life rewarding which to the unhandicapped may seem manifestly intolerable. People have an amazing adaptability. But in the end there will be cases in which the answer must be that it is not in the interests of the child to subject it to treatment which will cause increased suffering and produce no commensurate benefit, giving fullest possible weight to the child's and mankind's desire to survive ...'

Balcome LJ rejected the 'absolute' submission, which states that the Court must respect the sanctity of life, regardless of any other considerations. He stated (at 942):

'In my judgment there is no warrant, either on principle or authority, for the absolute submission. There is only the one test: that the interests of the ward are paramount ... I say that there should be no such rule because it could in certain circumstances be inimical to the interests of the ward that there should be such a requirement: to preserve life at all costs, whatever the quality of life to be preserved, and however distressing to the ward may be the nature of the treatment necessary to preserve life, may not be in the interests of the ward.'

Taylor LJ, in agreeing with the other two judges, stated (at 945):

'The court's high respect for the sanctity of human life imposes a strong presumption in favour of taking all steps capable of preserving it, save in exceptional circumstances. The problem is to define those circumstances ... I am of the view that there must be extreme cases in which the court is entitled to say: "The life which this treatment would prolong would be so cruel as to be intolerable." If for example, a child was so damaged as to have negligible use of its faculties and the only way of preserving its life was by the continuous administration of extremely painful treatment such that the child either would be in continuous agony or would have to be sedated continuously as to have no conscious life at all .... In those circumstances ... I consider the court is entitled in the best interest of the child to say that deliberate steps should not be taken artificially to prolong its miserable life span .... I consider that the correct approach is for the court to judge the quality of life the child would have to endure if given the treatment and decide whether in all the circumstances such a life would be so inflicted as to be intolerable to that child. ... the test must be whether the child in question, if capable of exercising sound judgment, would consider the life intolerable .... The circumstances to be considered would, in appropriate cases, include the degree of existing disability and any additional suffering or aggravation of the disability which the treatment itself would superimpose.'

Subsequently, in *Airedale NHS Trust v Bland* [1993] 1 All ER 821, 870 *per* Lord Goff, the House of Lords agreed with this reasoning.

It is clear, according to this line of reasoning, that the common law, while acknowledging the sanctity and the right to life (now in the United Kingdom by virtue of the Human Rights Act, 1998 which incorporates Article 2 ECHR, protecting the right to life, into its national law). See also the recent conjoined twins case: *Re A (children) (conjoined twins: surgical separation)* [2000] 4 All ER 961 generally and at 1016–18 *per* Ward LJ recognises that there is a threshold below which the maintenance of life may be so intolerable that the court will allow such a life not to be prolonged. It is interesting to note the courts' fluctuating criteria. In *Re C*, the Court emphasised the importance of 'intellectual function', mental, physical and social interaction and the fact that in this case the infant was dying. In *Re J*, it mattered not whether the individual involved was dying or on the point of death but whether the quality of life would be full of pain and suffering, intolerable, and a life where the use of the patient's faculties were negligible. Clearly, the degree of pain and mental impairment played an important part in the decisions. It could be said that in such cases the rights of bodily integrity outweighed the right to life.

10.13.2 PATIENTS LACKING AWARENESS AND IN STATES OF MINIMAL AND LOW AWARENESS

In the case of *Airedale NHS Trust v Bland* [1993] 1 All ER 821, where a young patient who suffered a severe crushed chest injury following the events of the Hillsborough disaster and lapsed into a PVS, the question of the withdrawal of artificial nutrition and hydration from an insensate patient came to be considered by the English courts.

From the outset, the House of Lords stated emphatically *per* Bingham MR (at 334):

'There are certain important principles relevant to this case which both parties accept.

(1) A Profound respect for the sanctity of human life is embedded in our law and moral philosophy...

The Court *per* Butler-Sloss LJ (at 344) went on to state that in this case 'there is a conflict between the principle of self-determination... and another basic principle of our society, the preservation of life'.

Lord Goff (at 367) (and *per* Lord Musthill at 395) citing various articles from various international codes including Article 2 *ECHR* stated:

'Here, the fundamental principle is the principle of the sanctity of life... But this principle, fundamental though it is, is not absolute.'

The House of Lords, looking at the totality of the treatment given and to the principles of self-autonomy and dignity (*per* Hoffman LJ at 351) and looking at the factors of:

(a)   the reality of irrecoverability to a sapient state;

(b)   the fact that there was no cure or improvement;

(c)   the treatment was invasive; and

(d)   was non-therapeutic/non-beneficial

held that the withdrawal of artificial nutrition and hydration was lawful and in the best interests of the patient.

The Irish courts also had an opportunity to examine the issue in the case of *In the Matter of a Ward of Court* [1995] 2 ILRM 401 where the adult patient was in a 'near-PVS', but was neither dead nor dying. Her condition was described by the High Court as follows:

'Over two decades ago the ward, who was then 22 years old, underwent a minor gynaecological operation under general anaesthetic. During the procedure she suffered three cardiac arrests resulting in anoxic brain damage of a very serious nature. Since that catastrophe the ward has been completely dependent on others, requiring total nursing care. She is spastic as a result of the brain damage. Both arms and hands are contracted. Both legs and feet are extended. Her jaws are clenched and because she had a tendency to bite the insides of her cheeks and her tongue, her back teeth have been capped to prevent the front teeth from fully closing. She cannot swallow. She cannot speak. She is incontinent... The ward is, of course, bedridden. She is in a condition which is nearly, but not quite, what in modern times has become known as persistent or permanent vegetative state (PVS).... In the present case the ward's heart and lungs function normally. Assuming that she is adequately furnished with nutrition and hydration (nourishment), her digestive system operates normally as do her bodily functions, although bowel movements require some assistance, but as she cannot swallow and as her teeth are spastically clenched together, she cannot receive nourishment in the normal way and as already stated, is and has had to be tube-fed since the catastrophe. Assuming that she continues to be nourished by tube, she could live for many years but of course she might also die in the short term if she developed some infection such as pneumonia, unless it were treated aggressively with antibiotics. The ward has no capacity for speech or for communicating. A speech therapist failed to elicit any means of communication. She has a minimal capacity to recognise, for example, the long established nursing staff and to react to strangers by showing distress. She also follows or tracks people with her eyes and reacts to noise, although the latter is mainly, if not indeed, wholly reflex from the brain stem and a large element of reflex eye tracking is also present in the former which, however, also has some minimal purposive content . . . I am satisfied that although the ward is not fully PVS, she is very nearly so and such cognitive capacity as she possesses is extremely minimal. A fully PVS person cannot feel pain and has no capacity for pleasure or displeasure even though they may groan or grimace or cry, especially in response to painful stimuli, nor have they any realisation whatever of their tragic situation. This is probably the ward's state but if such minimal cognition as she has includes an inkling of her catastrophic condition, then I am satisfied that that would be a terrible torment to her and her situation would be worse than if she were fully PVS there is no prospect whatsoever of any improvement in the condition of the ward.'

Echoing the words of other courts in relation to the limit of the right to life, the Supreme Court stated *per* Denham J at (457):

'The requirement to defend and vindicate the life is a requirement "as far as practicable", it is not an absolute. Life itself is not an absolute.'

In relation to the right to life, Hamilton CJ stated (at 426):

'As the process of dying is part, and an ultimate, inevitable consequence, of life, the right to life necessarily implies the right to have nature take its course and to die a natural death and, unless the individual concerned so wishes, not to have life artificially maintained by the provision of nourishment by abnormal artificial means, which have no curative effect and which is intended merely to prolong life.'

Denham J stated:

'The primary constitutional concept is to protect life within the community. The State has an interest in the moral aspect of society—for the common good. But, balanced against that is the person's right to life—which encompasses a right to die naturally and in the privacy of the family and with minimum suffering.'

The Supreme Court, allowed withdrawal of artificial nutrition and hydration stating *per* Hamilton CJ at 429 that it '. . . was intrusive and burdensome and of no curative effect . . . .'

The effect of this decision was to analyse and place the right to life not only in balance with other rights, such that the right to bodily integrity could outweigh the absolute right to life, but also to state that the right to die a natural death was in fact, very much a part of the right to life itself.

If such a case were to arise again, it would fall to be considered in light of Articles 2 and 3 ECHR following the incorporation of the ECHR into Irish law.

In the English case of *An NHS Trust v M; An NHS Trust v H* [2001] 2 FLR 367, declarations were sought to withdraw artificial nutrition and hydration in relation to two patients both of whom were in a PVS. In granting the declarations sought the Court found that withdrawal of artificial nutrition and hydration would be in the patients' best interests, and would not breach the rights of the patients under the ECHR. A person in a PVS was alive, and therefore entitled to the protection of Article 2, the right to life, which concerned a negative obligation on the State not to deprive anyone of life intentionally, and a positive obligation to protect the right to life. However, a responsible decision by a medical team not to provide treatment could not amount to intentional deprivation of life within Article 2, and therefore did not fall within the negative obligation imposed by Article 2 to refrain from taking life intentionally. While the positive obligation imposed a duty to give life-sustaining treatment in circumstances in which, according to responsible medical opinion, such treatment was in the best interests of the patient it did not impose an absolute obligation to treat if such treatment would be futile.

Butler-Sloss P stated (at 378):

'Article 2 therefore imposes a positive obligation to give life-sustaining treatment in circumstances where, according to responsible medical opinion, such treatment is in the best interests of the patient but does not impose an absolute obligation to treat if such treatment would be futile.'

In relation to the application of Article 3 ECHR, the Court stated (at 381):

'On the assumption that Art 3 requires to be considered, I am satisfied that the proposed withdrawal of treatment from these two patients has been thoroughly and anxiously considered by a number of experts in the field of PVS patients and is in accordance with the practice of a responsible body of medical opinion. The withdrawal is for a benign purpose in accordance with the best interests of the patients not to continue life-saving treatment it is legitimate and appropriate that the residual treatment to be continued until death. I am, moreover, satisfied that Art 3 requires the victim to be aware of the inhuman and degrading treatment which he or she is experiencing or at least to be in a state of physical or mental suffering. An insensate patient suffering from permanent vegetative state has no feelings and no comprehension of the treatment accorded to him or her. Article 3 does not in my judgment apply to these two cases.'

Recently, in *Burke v General Medical Council* [2005] EWCA Civ 1003, the United Kingdom Court of Appeal dealt with a situation in which Leslie Burke suffered from a congenital degenerative brain condition known as spinocerebellar ataxia, which currently confined him to a wheelchair. His condition was described in judgment:

'This is a progressively degenerative condition that follows a similar course to multiple sclerosis. He was diagnosed in 1982. He suffers very serious physical disabilities but has retained his mental competence and capacity. He has gradually lost the use of his legs and is now virtually wholly dependent on a wheelchair for mobility. He has uncoordinated movements and his condition also affects his speech, but his mental ability is not impaired. By reason of his condition there will come a time when the claimant will be entirely dependent on others for his care and indeed for his very survival. In particular he will lose the ability to swallow and will require ANH by tube to survive.'

Mr Burke's concerns were that he wanted to be fed and provided with appropriate hydration until he died of natural causes. He did not want ANH to be withdrawn. He did not want to die of thirst. He did not want a decision to be taken by doctors that his life is no longer worth living. He was concerned that the GMC Guidelines seemed to allow those eventualities possibly to occur.

At first instance the reliefs he sought were that:

(a) the withholding or withdrawal of artificial nutrition and hydration, leading to death by starvation or thirst, would be a breach of Mr Burke's rights under Articles 2, 3 and 8 and would be unlawful under domestic law;

(b) where a competent patient requests or where an incompetent patient has, prior to becoming incompetent, made it clear that they would wish to receive artificial nutrition and hydration, the withholding or withdrawal of artificial nutrition and hydration, leading to death by starvation or thirst, would be a breach of their rights under Articles 2, 3 or 8 and would be unlawful under domestic law;

(c) the refusal of artificial nutrition and hydration to an incompetent patient would be a breach of Article 2 unless providing such artificial nutrition and hydration would amount to degrading treatment contrary to Article 3;

(d) the Guidance...is unlawful in so far as it fails to safeguard the rights of patients under Articles 2, 3 and 8;

(e) paragraph 81 of the Guidance...is unlawful as it is incompatible with Articles 2, 3 and 8 and domestic law.

The respondent succeeded at first instance; however, the matter was appealed by the appellant and the appeal was allowed on the basis that Mr Burke's concerns were unfounded since the law was clear that:

'No such difficulty arises, however, in the situation that has caused Mr Burke concern, that of the competent patient who, regardless of the pain, suffering or indignity of his condition, makes it plain that he wishes to be kept alive. No authority lends the slightest countenance to the suggestion that the duty on the doctors to take reasonable steps to keep the patient alive in such circumstances may not persist. Indeed, it seems to us that for a doctor deliberately to interrupt life-prolonging treatment in the face of a competent patient's expressed wish to be kept alive, with the intention of thereby terminating the patient's life, would leave the doctor with no answer to a charge of murder.' (Per Phillips MR, [2006] 1 QB 273 at 297).

In *Burke v the United Kingdom* (Application No. I9807/06), the ECt.HR found against the applicant, stating that:

'The Court is satisfied that the presumption of domestic law is strongly in favour of prolonging life where possible, which accords with the spirit of the Convention (see also its findings as to the compatibility of domestic law with Article 2 in *Glass v. the United Kingdom*, no. 61827/00, § 75, ECHR 2004-II). It is apparent that, in the situation apprehended by the applicant in the final stages of his illness, a doctor would be obliged to take account of the applicant's previously expressed wishes and those of the persons close to him, as well as the opinions of other medical personnel and, if there was any conflict or doubt as to the applicant's best interests, then to approach a court. This does not, in the Court's view, disclose any lack of due respect for the crucial rights invoked by the applicant. Nor does the Court consider that any issue arises under Articles 2 and 3, or under Article 8, in that the applicant cannot pre-determine the administration of specific treatment in future unknown circumstances. The Court finds therefore that the applicant cannot claim to be a victim of any failure by the State to protect his rights under Articles 2, 3 or 8 of the Convention. It follows that this part of the application is manifestly illfounded within the meaning of Article 35 §§ 3 and 4 of the Convention.'

As can be seen from the above examination, the right to life exists and is invoked at various different times and stages of life itself. The right, while ranking as the highest in the hierarchy of rights, and from which all other rights stem, is not absolute, and when invoked by those who rely on them, the courts will engage in a careful exercise of balance to ensure that above and beyond all other things, the constitutional dignity of an individual is protected. It could be said that this right, which Denham J recognised (at 466 in *Ward*) as 'an unspecified right' is perhaps greater than the sum of all of the rights and in many respects is what the courts in one manner or another are seeking to protect.

10.14 International Obligations: The European Convention for the Protection of Human Rights and Fundamental Freedoms

10.14.1 THE RIGHT TO LIFE

A number of international treaties now provide Articles that deal with the right to life and what may be deemed the protection of bodily integrity. The European Court of Human Rights (ECt.HR) has dealt with the rights to life and bodily integrity in various ways. Because of the high eminence afforded to the right to life in Irish law, it is doubtful that the incorporation of the European Convention on Human Rights (ECHR) adds any particularly new dimension to the right itself except that it applies to citizens and non-citizens.

10.14.2 THE EUROPEAN CONVENTION FOR THE PROTECTION OF HUMAN RIGHTS AND FUNDAMENTAL FREEDOMS

Article 2 ECHR states that:

'1. *Everyone's right to life shall be protected by law. No one shall be deprived of his life intentionally save in the execution of a sentence of a court following his conviction of a crime for which this penalty is provided by law.*
2. *Deprivation of life shall not be regarded as inflicted in contravention of this article when it results from the use of force which is no more than absolutely necessary:*
   (a)   in defence of any person from unlawful violence;
   (b)   in order to effect a lawful arrest or to prevent the escape of a person lawfully detained;
   (c)   in action lawfully taken for the purpose of quelling a riot or insurrection'.

In *McCann v United Kingdom* (1996) 21 EHHR 97, the ECt.HR stated:

'It must also be borne in mind that, as a provision (art. 2) which not only safeguards the right to life but sets out the circumstances when the deprivation of life may be justified, Article 2 (art. 2) ranks as one of the most fundamental provisions in the Convention . . . it also enshrines one of the basic values of the democratic societies making up the Council of Europe . . . . As such, its provisions must be strictly construed.'

This has been reiterated very recently in *McKerr v United Kingdom* (4 May 2001, ECt.HR).

Recently, the ECt.HR made it clear that the right to life did not extend to the right to die. The court in the case of *Pretty v United Kingdom* (29 April 2002, ECt.HR) stated:

'The Court's case-law accords pre-eminence to Article 2 as one of the most fundamental provisions of the Convention . . . . It safeguards the right to life, without which enjoyment of any of the other rights and freedoms in the Convention is rendered nugatory . . . . The text of Article 2 expressly regulates the deliberate or intended use of lethal force by State agents. It has been interpreted however as covering not only intentional killing but also the situations where it is permitted to "use force" which may result, as an unintended outcome, in the deprivation of life . . . . The Court has further held that the first sentence of Article 2 § 1 enjoins the State not only to refrain from the intentional and unlawful taking of life, but also to take appropriate steps to safeguard the lives of those within its jurisdiction . . . . This obligation extends beyond a primary duty to secure the right to life by putting in place effective criminal-law provisions to deter the commission of offences against the person backed up by law-enforcement machinery for the prevention, suppression and sanctioning of breaches of such provisions; it may also imply in certain well-defined circumstances a positive obligation on the authorities to take preventive operational measures to protect an individual whose life is at risk from the criminal acts of another individual.... More recently, in the case of *Keenan v. the United Kingdom*, Article 2 was found to apply to the situation of a mentally ill prisoner who disclosed signs of being a suicide risk.... The consistent emphasis in all the cases before the Court has been the obligation of the State to protect life. The Court is not persuaded that "the right to life" guaranteed in Article 2 can be interpreted as involving a negative aspect.... To the extent that these aspects are recognised as so fundamental to the human condition that they require protection from State interference, they may be reflected in the rights guaranteed by other Articles of the Convention, or in other international human rights instruments. Article 2 cannot, without a distortion of language, be interpreted as conferring the diametrically opposite right, namely a right to die; nor can it create a right to self-determination in the sense of conferring on an individual the entitlement to choose death rather than life. The Court accordingly finds that no right to die, whether at the hands of a third person or with the assistance of a public authority, can be derived from Article 2 of the Convention. The Court finds that there has been no violation of Article 2 of the Convention.'

10.14.2.1 The duty to investigate the circumstances of a death

The ECt.HR has also considered the obligation to investigate the circumstances of certain deaths in the context of Article 2 ECHR. In the case of *McShane v United Kingdom* (2002) 35 EHRR 23 it was claimed that an RUC armoured personnel carrier advanced towards a hoarding. Dermot McShane fell underneath the hoarding and was killed. It was alleged that he was killed by the security forces and that there was no effective investigation into his death, invoking Article 2. In this regard, the ECt.HR outlined what it regarded as being the general principles regarding a proper investigation and stated that:

'Article 2, which safeguards the right to life and sets out the circumstances when deprivation of life may be justified, ranks as one of the most fundamental provisions in the Convention, to which in peacetime no derogation is permitted under Article 15. Together with Article 3, it also enshrines one of the basic values of the democratic societies making up the Council of Europe. The circumstances in which deprivation of life may be justified must therefore be strictly construed. The object and purpose of the Convention as an instrument for the protection of individual human beings also requires that Article 2 be interpreted and applied so as to make its safeguards practical and effective....

In the light of the importance of the protection afforded by Article 2, the Court must subject deprivations of life to the most careful scrutiny, taking into consideration not only the actions of State agents but also all the surrounding circumstances. Where the events in issue lie wholly, or in large part, within the exclusive knowledge of the authorities, as for example in the case of persons within their control in custody, strong presumptions of fact will arise in respect of injuries and death which occur. Indeed, the burden of proof may be regarded as resting on the authorities to provide a satisfactory and convincing explanation....

The text of Article 2, read as a whole, demonstrates that it covers not only intentional killing but also the situations where it is permitted to "use force" which may result, as an unintended outcome, in the deprivation of life. The deliberate or intended use of lethal force is only one factor however to be taken into account in assessing its necessity. Any use of force must be no more than "absolutely necessary" for the achievement of one or more of the purposes set out in sub-paragraphs (a) to (c). This term indicates that a stricter and more compelling test of necessity must be employed from that normally applicable when determining whether State action is "necessary in a democratic society" under paragraphs 2 of Articles 8 to 11 of the Convention.

Consequently, the force used must be strictly proportionate to the achievement of the permitted aims . . . .

The obligation to protect the right to life under Article 2 of the Convention, read in conjunction with the State's general duty under Article 1 of the Convention to "secure to everyone within [its] jurisdiction the rights and freedoms defined in [the] Convention", also requires by implication that there should be some form of effective official investigation when individuals have been killed as a result of the use of force . . . The essential purpose of such investigation is to secure the effective implementation of the domestic laws which protect the right to life and, in those cases involving State agents or bodies, to ensure their accountability for deaths occurring under their responsibility. What form of investigation will achieve those purposes may vary in different circumstances. However, whatever mode is employed, the authorities must act of their own motion, once the matter has come to their attention. They cannot leave it to the initiative of the next of kin either to lodge a formal complaint or to take responsibility for the conduct of any investigative procedures . . . .

For an investigation into alleged unlawful killing by State agents to be effective, it may generally be regarded as necessary for the persons responsible for and carrying out the investigation to be independent from those implicated in the events . . . . This means not only a lack of hierarchical or institutional connection but also a practical independence . . .

The investigation must also be effective in the sense that it is capable of leading to a determination of whether the force used in such cases was or was not justified in the circumstances . . . and to the identification and punishment of those responsible . . . . This is not an obligation of result, but of means. The authorities must have taken the reasonable steps available to them to secure the evidence concerning the incident, including inter alia eye witness testimony, forensic evidence and, where appropriate, an autopsy which provides a complete and accurate record of injury and an objective analysis of clinical findings, including the cause of death . . . Any deficiency in the investigation which undermines its ability to establish the cause of death or the person or persons responsible will risk falling foul of this standard.

A requirement of promptness and reasonable expedition is implicit in this context . . . . It must be accepted that there may be obstacles or difficulties which prevent progress in an investigation in a particular situation. However, a prompt response by the authorities in investigating a use of lethal force may generally be regarded as essential in maintaining public confidence in their adherence to the rule of law and in preventing any appearance of collusion in or tolerance of unlawful acts.

For the same reasons, there must be a sufficient element of public scrutiny of the investigation or its results to secure accountability in practice as well as in theory. The degree of public scrutiny required may well vary from case to case. In all cases, however, the next-of-kin of the victim must be involved in the procedure to the extent necessary to safeguard his or her legitimate interests . . . .'

On the basis of these principles, the Court concluded that:

'. . . there was a lack of independence of the police officers investigating the incident from the officers implicated in the incident;

the police investigation showed a lack of expedition;

the soldier who drove the APC which fatally injured Dermot McShane could not be required to attend the inquest as a witness;

the inquest procedure did not allow any verdict or findings which could play an effective role in securing a prosecution in respect of any criminal offence which may have been disclosed;

the non-disclosure of witness statements and other relevant documents contributed to long adjournments in the proceedings;

the inquest proceedings have not commenced promptly.

The Court finds that there has been a failure to comply with the procedural obligation imposed by Article 2 of the Convention and that there has been, in this respect, a violation of that provision.'

In *R (Amin) v Home Secretary* [2003] 3 WLR 1169, the deceased had been killed by a cell mate whilst in prison. Judicial review of a decision by the government not to hold a public inquiry into the death was sought. At first instance ([2001] EWHC 719), the applicant succeeded. The Court on that occasion ruled that the refusal to hold a public inquiry was a breach of Article 2 ECHR, stating:

'an independent public investigation with the family legally represented, provided with the relevant material and able to cross-examine the principal witnesses, must be held to satisfy the obligations imposed by article 2 of the European Convention on Human Rights.'

On appeal ([2003] QB 581), the decision was overturned and a further appeal was made to the House of Lords. The House of Lords agreed with the initial decision and overturned the Court of Appeal. In doing so, the Court, *per* Lord Bingham of Cornhill, (at 1185), of the right to life and the State's duties in relation to it, stated:

'A profound respect for the sanctity of human life underpins the common law as it underpins the jurisprudence under articles 1 and 2 of the Convention. This means that a state must not unlawfully take life and must take appropriate legislative and administrative steps to protect it. But the duty does not stop there. The state owes a particular duty to those involuntarily in its custody. As Anand J succinctly put it in *Nilabati Behera v State of Orissa* (1993) 2 SCC 746, 767: "There is a great responsibility on the police or prison authorities to ensure that the citizen in its custody is not deprived of his right to life." Such persons must be protected against violence or abuse at the hands of state agents. They must be protected against self-harm: *Reeves v Comr of Police of the Metropolis* [2000] 1 AC 360. Reasonable care must be taken to safeguard their lives and persons against the risk of avoidable harm.

The state's duty to investigate is secondary to the duties not to take life unlawfully and to protect life, in the sense that it only arises where a death has occurred or life-threatening injuries have occurred: *Menson v United Kingdom* (Application No. 47916/99) 6 May 2003 (unreported), 13. It can fairly be described as procedural. But in any case where a death has occurred in custody it is not a minor or unimportant duty. In this country, as noted in paragraph 16 above, effect has been given to that duty for centuries by requiring such deaths to be publicly investigated before an independent judicial tribunal with an opportunity for relatives of the deceased to participate. The purposes of such an investigation are clear: to ensure so far as possible that the full facts are brought to light; that culpable and discreditable conduct is exposed and brought to public notice; that suspicion of deliberate wrongdoing (if unjustified) is allayed; that dangerous practices and procedures are rectified; and that those who have lost their relative may at least have the satisfaction of knowing that lessons learned from his death may save the lives of others.'

In the case of *R (Plymouth CC) v HM Coroner* [2005] 2 FLR 1279, the Coroner decided to expand the scope of its investigation in relation to the death of a child who died in the care of his mother but whose circumstances had been well known to the child protection services. The coroner ruled that his investigation should not be limited to the events during the last two days of the child's life, but should extend to the role played by the child protection agencies, including the local authority, during the child's life, and specifically to whether, by act or omission, they had contributed to his death. The coroner based this decision on his conclusion that he had a duty to hold a broadened inquest under the Human Rights Act, 1998 (the UK legislation incorporating the ECHR), holding that the statutory protection agencies had, or might have, failed to protect the child's right to life, and that the State's duty to investigate such a failure was not discharged by any other investigation which was being conducted, or could be conducted. His decision was quashed. The Court stated that whilst the Coroner had been right to hold that it was his duty to consider whether there was or might have been a breach by the State of its protective duty towards the baby under Article 2 of the European Convention for the Protection of Human Rights and Fundamental Freedoms 1950, the right to life, and that a breach will be found if it is established that the authorities did not do all that could be reasonably expected of them to avoid a real and immediate risk to life of which they have or ought to have knowledge, nevertheless, the evidence did not establish that there was a real and immediate risk to the child's life and thus no question was raised under Article 2 for the Coroner and his jury to investigate. The trigger for the investigative duty under Article 2 was not activated.

Although the decision was quashed, in his judgment Wilson J stated (at 1297), the State's duty in relation to investigation:

'Article 2 of the European Convention . . . imposes three distinct duties on the State:

(a) A negative duty, namely a duty not by its agents intentionally to take a person's life save in the circumstances specified in the article. The facts in *McCann v United Kingdom* (1996) 21 EHRR 97, namely the fatal shooting by soldiers of suspected terrorists in Gibraltar, therefore gave rise to a breach of this duty in that none of the specified circumstances existed.

(b) A positive duty, namely to take all reasonable steps to protect a person's right to life under the article. In some situations this duty (the protective duty) requires the State to do more than effectively to operate a criminal justice system designed to deter the taking of life. One example is that the State is required to take all reasonable care to protect the life of a person involuntarily in its custody: per Lord Bingham of Cornhill in *R (Amin) v Secretary of State for the Home Department* [2003] UKHL 51, [2004] 1 AC 653, [2004] UKHRR 75, at [30]. Another example is that the State is required to seek to protect a person from death as a result of incompetent medical treatment or care by its effective operation of a system of professional and other regulation: *Calvelli and Ciglio v Italy* (Application No. 32967/96), 17 January 2002 (unreported) at [49].

(c) A second positive duty, collateral to the first, namely the investigative duty. Article 2 requires the State to furnish an appropriate investigation into the cause of a death which has been, or may have been, caused or contributed to, whether by a violation of such domestic laws, criminal and civil, as protect the right to life, or by a breach of the State's protective duty under Art 2: see *Edwards v United Kingdom* (2002) 35 EHRR 487 at [69]. In *R (Khan) v Secretary of State for Health* [2003] EWCA Civ 1129, [2004] 1 WLR 971 at [67(3)] the Court of Appeal observed: "The procedural obligation introduced by Art 2 has three interlocking aims: to minimise the risk of future like deaths; to give the beginnings of justice to the bereaved; and to assuage the anxieties of the public".'

It can be seen that the State is obliged, when death occurs in certain circumstances to effectively and properly investigate the death in order for Article 2 ECHR and its procedural aspects to be fulfilled.

10.14.3 THE DEATH PENALTY

The Sixth Protocol of the ECHR concerning the abolition of the death penalty states at Article 1: '*The death penalty shall be abolished. No-one shall be condemned to such penalty or executed.*'

The Criminal Justice Act, 1990 abolished the death penalty in Ireland, s 1 stating that

'No person shall suffer death for any offence.'

Subsequent to this Act, an amendment to the Constitution was passed, in 2001, which resulted in the Constitution Act, 2001, which inserted Article 15.5.2. This states that:

'The Oireachtas shall not enact any law providing for the imposition of the death penalty.'

Article 2 of the ECHR regarding the death penalty in time of war states:

'A State may make provision in its law for the death penalty in respect of acts committed in time of war or of imminent threat of war; such penalty shall be applied only in the instances laid down in the law and in accordance with its provisions. The State shall communicate to the Secretary General of the Council of Europe the relevant provisions of that law.'

It should be noted that the status quo of a nation's death penalty will have ramifications for the issue of extradition law (see the *Soering* case below). In Ireland, the Extradition Act, 1965 at s 19 states that:

'Extradition shall not be granted for an offence which is punishable by death under the law of the requesting country but is of a category for which the death penalty is not provided for by the law of the State or is not generally carried out unless the requesting country gives such assurance as the Minister considers sufficient that the death penalty will not be carried out.'

10.15 European Law Obligations

It seems that the European Court of Justice (ECJ) has not yet had to consider the rights to life but the right to integrity of the person was considered in Case 377/98 *Netherlands v European Parliament and Council* [2001] ECR I-7079 (see **10.16.3**). The EU Charter of Fundamental Rights (see **8.10**) reflecting the terms of the ECHR, states at Article 2:

'1. Everyone has the right to life.
2. No one shall be condemned to the death penalty, or executed'.

10.16 The Right to Bodily Integrity

10.16.1 AN UNENUMERATED RIGHT IN IRISH CONSTITUTIONAL LAW

This unenumerated right will be explained in terms of an individual's right to be protected against violation by the State and by private individuals (eg in medical treatment). This was the first unenumerated right to be recognised by the Irish courts. In *Ryan v Attorney General* [1965] IR 294, the plaintiff sought to allege that the State's fluoridation of water endangered her and her family's health.

In the High Court, Kenny J stated:

'I think that the personal rights which may be involved to invalidate legislation are not confined to those specified in Article 40 but include all those rights which result from the Christian and democratic nature of the State. It is however, a jurisdiction to be exercised with caution. None of the personal rights of the citizen are unlimited.'

THE RIGHT TO LIFE AND THE RIGHT TO BODILY INTEGRITY

The Court went on to state:

'In my opinion, one of the personal rights of the citizen protected by the general guarantee is the right to bodily integrity. I understand the right to bodily integrity to mean that no mutilation of the body or any of its members may be carried out on any citizen under authority of the law except for the good of the whole body and that no process which is or may, as a matter of probability, be dangerous or harmful to the life or health of the citizens or any of them may be imposed (in the sense of being made compulsory) by an Act of the Oireachtas.'

The Supreme Court upheld this finding.

The scope of this right is vast in terms of the protection of one's health by the State and others, but like every other right, it is not absolute. In *McGee v Attorney General* [1974] IR 284, the Supreme Court held that the plaintiff's right to bodily integrity was breached in effect, as Walsh J put it, the plaintiff had 'a right to be assisted in her efforts to avoid putting her life in jeopardy.'

In *The State (C) v Frawley* [1976] IR 365, it was alleged that a prisoner who was suffering from a mental condition, which caused him *inter alia* to swallow metal objects, should be released on the grounds that his bodily integrity was not being protected by the State. This was rejected by Finlay P (at 373) who stated that there could not be 'an obligation to provide for prisoners in general the best medical treatment . . .' nor a duty to 'build, equip and staff . . .' the specialised unit of the prison. However, Finlay P (at 372) did state of the right that he could not see any:

'. . . reason why the principle should not also operate to prevent an act or an omission of the Executive which, without justification, would expose the health of a person to risk or danger.'

In *The State (Richardson) v The Governor of Mountjoy Prison* [1980] ILRM 82, the Court accepted the evidence of a woman prisoner in relation to lax standards of hygiene and stated that the State had failed in its duty to protect the applicant's health.

As has been examined, the right to bodily integrity has been relied on in relation to an individual's right to refuse medical treatment and in balancing such a right with the artificial maintenance of life in the *Ward* case. The right to bodily integrity operates to ensure that the State fulfils its duty not to endanger the health of its citizens but the right also operates to ensure that individuals' rights are not breached within a private sphere. The right will also fall to be considered in the light of Article 3 ECHR. There is no doubt that certainly, in the sphere of healthcare, this right is likely to appear many times, as a topic of review before the courts, in future when attempts are made to impose medical treatment on individuals when medical professionals believe it is in the individual's best interests. The right may also be invoked along with the right to life and with the many other unenumerated rights now outlined by the courts in the gravely-ill cases and indeed in cases where the healthcare sector seeks to argue the inability to provide health by virtue of a scarcity of resources. What is almost inevitable is that these rights, whilst now somewhat explored, have much to offer by way of future judicial interpretation and application.

10.16.2 THE EUROPEAN CONVENTION FOR THE PROTECTION OF FUNDAMENTAL RIGHTS AND FREEDOMS

Article 3 on the 'Prohibition of torture' states:

'No one shall be subjected to torture or to inhuman or degrading treatment or punishment.'

Article 3 has been utilised in a number of settings. The difference between the three terms torture, inhuman or degrading treatment lies in 'a difference in the intensity of the suffering inflicted' (*Ireland v United Kingdom* (1980) 2 EHRR 25). In relation to torture in the arena of police custody, in the *Ireland v United Kingdom* decision, 'interrogation in depth' techniques (namely, deprivation of sleep, food and drink, subjection to noise and hooding) were inhuman or degrading treatment but not torture. In *Aksoy v Turkey* (1997) 23 EHRR 553, electrocution of a detainee was described by the Court as 'of such a serious and cruel nature that it can only be described as torture'.

In *Herczegfalvy v Finland* (1993) 15 EHRR 437, it was not inhuman or degrading treatment to force-treat and feed a hunger-striking prisoner with a history of psychiatric problems since 'a measure which is a therapeutic necessity cannot be regarded as inhuman or degrading'.

Such pronouncements have important ramifications for those providing healthcare and in situations where decisions in relation to forceful restraints of patients may be made. Any such decision to do so must consider whether a 'therapeutic necessity' exists.

The decision of the House of Lords in *R (Munjaz) v Mersey Care NHS Trust* [2005] 3 WLR 793 concerned a long-term psychiatric patient compulsorily detained under the Mental Treatment Acts at a high security hospital. He was placed in seclusion for continuous lengthy periods. The hospital's seclusion procedure departed from the Code of Practice in a number of respects but particularly in providing for less frequent medical reviews for all long-term secluded patients. The patient was secluded for lengthy periods. He claimed judicial review challenging the hospital's failure to amend its procedure and properly to review his seclusion. He contended that the use of seclusion that was unnecessary or that continued for longer than necessary breached his rights under Article 3 of the Convention for the Protection of Human Rights and Fundamental Freedoms.

The Court dismissed the appeal and held that the policy was not in breach of Article 3. Lord Hope (at 823) stated in relation to Article 3 that:

> 'The European court has repeatedly said that ill-treatment must attain a minimum level of severity if it is to fall within the scope of the expression "inhuman or degrading treatment" . . . This standard is to be judged in the light of the circumstances, as the court has held that in order for an arrest or detention in connection with court proceedings to be degrading within the meaning of the article it must be of a special level and it must in any event be different from the usual degree of humiliation that is inherent in arrest or detention. . . . It has also made clear that, while the absolute prohibition is not capable of modification on grounds of proportionality, issues of proportionality will arise where a positive obligation is implied as where positive obligations arise they are not absolute. In *Osman v United Kingdom* (1998) 29 EHRR 245, 305 . . . the court recognised that such obligations must be interpreted in a way which does not impose an impossible or disproportionate burden on the authorities. Nevertheless, as the court said in *Z v United Kingdom* (2001) 34 EHRR 97, 131 . . . States must take measures to provide effective protection of vulnerable persons, and these must include reasonable steps to prevent ill-treatment of which the authorities had or ought to have had knowledge.'

The UN Convention against Torture and Other Cruel Inhuman or Degrading Treatment or Punishment (1984) describes torture as 'any act by which severe pain or suffering, whether physical or mental, is intentionally inflicted . . .'.

Another important point to consider is that of contracting states extraditing or deporting individuals to a non-contracting state where a breach of Article 3 may occur. It has been held by the ECt.HR that such an action may breach the Convention when if an individual is extradited, there is a 'real risk of being subjected to torture or to inhuman or degrading treatment or punishment in the requesting country' and where there are substantial grounds to show this (*Soering v United Kingdom* (1989) 11 EHRR 439).

A similar bar from deportation may be a consideration in refugee law under the principle of non-refoulement (see **15.3.1**).

10.16.3 THE CHARTER OF FUNDAMENTAL RIGHTS OF THE EUROPEAN UNION, 2000

A Charter of Fundamental Rights for the EU was solemnly proclaimed at the Inter-Governmental Conference (IGC) in Nice in December 2000 (OJ C364/01 18 December 2000). The text of the Charter was adapted with a view to making it legally binding and this adapted version of the Charter was solemnly proclaimed by the three political institutions of the EU (the European Parliament, the Council and the Commission) on 12 December 2007 (OJ C303/01 14 February 2007) (see **8.1** and **8.10**). Post the Treaty of Lisbon, Article 6(1) TEU affords the Charter the same legal status as the Treaties (Treaty on European Union and Treaty on the Functioning of the European Union (a consolidated text of these Treaties post Lisbon is published at OJ C115/01 9 May 2008), meaning that since the entry into force of the Treaty of Lisbon on 1 December 2009, the Charter is legally binding (see **8.1** and **8.4**).

Article 3 of the Charter, entitled 'Right to the integrity of the person' provides:

> '1. *Everyone has the right to respect for his or her physical and mental integrity.*
> 2. *In the fields of medicine and biology, the following must be respected in particular:*
>   – *the free and informed consent of the person concerned, according to the procedures laid down by law,*
>   – *the prohibition of eugenic practices, in particular those aiming at the selection of persons,*
>   – *the prohibition on making the human body and its parts as such a source of financial gain,*
>   – *the prohibition of the reproductive cloning of human beings.'*

In Case 377/98 *Netherlands v European Parliament and Council* [2001] ECR I-7079, the ECJ confirmed that a fundamental right to human integrity is part of EU law and encompasses, in the context of medicine and biology, the free and informed consent of the donor and the recipient. This case is now referred to in the Explanations to the Charter, to which pursuant to Article 6(1) TEU post-Lisbon, there is to be 'due regard' in interpreting the provisions of the Charter (see **8.1**).

The rights in Article 3 of the EU Charter are a reaffirmation of the provisions of the Convention on Human Rights and Biomedicine (ETS 164 and additional Protocol ETS 168).

Thus, at international level, whilst the protection of the right to life is similar to national protection, the right to 'integrity' is wide-ranging and encompasses protections ranging from protection against torture and non-refoulement of asylum seekers to informed consent in medicine and a prohibition on reproductive human cloning. The rights to bodily integrity are ripe for further exploration by our courts.

Article 4, entitled 'Prohibition of torture and inhuman or degrading treatment or punishment', states *'No one shall be subjected to torture or to inhuman or degrading treatment or punishment.'*

10.17 Conclusion

At national and international level, the right to life is regarded as the most fundamental right in the hierarchy of human rights. It is not however, an absolute right, and the courts will balance it by taking into account other rights such as the developing right of human dignity. In addition to this balance, states cannot ignore their procedural obligations connected with the right to life such as the duty to properly investigate death in appropriate circumstances. This may have important ramifications for Coroners to ensure a more thorough investigation into the cause of death where a duty to do so is triggered.

With advances in medical technology in areas of reproduction, genetics and end of life care the right to life will no doubt continue to be considered by the courts as has been seen in the recent cases of *MR v TR, Walsh and others* [2009] IESC 82 and *Pretty v United Kingdom* (ECt.HR, 29 April 2002). Constitutional lawyers need to remain aware of developments in international jurisprudence when formulating arguments and advice in cases where the right to life will be carefully balanced and proportioned to ensure that what is achieved in every case is a respect for the human person by way of protecting and balancing their rights to life and bodily integrity.

CHAPTER 11

EQUALITY

11.1 Introduction

This chapter begins by exploring the concept of equality as there are different perceptions of what the right to equality or equal treatment means. In this jurisdiction, protections for the right are sourced from a number of bases: EU law, Bunreacht na hÉireann, domestic legislation and various international treaties. The guarantee of equality will be examined in these various spheres. It is worth noting at the outset that much of our domestic protection of the right to equality stems from the implementation here of EU law, as it is now, and because of the hierarchies of law in operation this is an important consideration.

11.2 Competing Ideas of Equality

The right to equality is one of the more difficult human rights to conceptualise, meaning different things to different people. It is an idea that carries as much political significance as legal challenge and is applicable to such diverse conceptual and practical subjects as the exercise of civil rights and the distribution of resources. The right has been mentioned in all basic human rights instruments, both national and international, since the French Revolution.

Early formulations made the idea applicable to civil and political rights and, in that sense, it was sometimes said that the right to equality did not guarantee any right in particular, but guaranteed to all that which was available. The right was usually expressed as the notion of equality before the law, which in reality demanded that states did not put any person above the law. This liberal conception of equality was perversely ascendant even in times when slavery was legal and wives were regarded as their husband's property. In fact, the task of defining equality is one of the more elusive philosophical objectives and competing theories differ widely in the values articulated and in the means proposed to achieve equality. Some of the most fundamental ideological debates have revolved around competing notions of economic equality, with left wing politics favouring more substantive redistributative economic policies and neo-liberal politicians preferring the application of the marketplace's rules to all, without special intervention. At this broad level, the arguments on equality are bound up with a range of other factors that shape public choices and values.

Debates concerning equality are not confined to economics and go to the philosophical and, ultimately legal, content of the idea. On one analysis, the right may be seen as equality of treatment, which underlies the legal notion of equality before the law, ie that all persons are entitled to the application of the same rules. This formal notion of equality has had a particular importance in the application and enforcement of laws. Allowing for the fact that personal characteristics vary, it led to the Aristotelian idea of treating like alike, but differences differently. This model of equality is perhaps the most widely accepted in the judicial and legal context and can be seen in the formulation in Article 40.1 of the 1937 Constitution, which provides:

> 'All citizens shall, as human persons, be held equal before the law. This shall not be held to mean that the State shall not in its enactments have due regard to differences of capacity, physical and moral, and of social function.'

Such uniformity of treatment may seem appealing, but without a recognition that innate characteristics or circumstance can affect one's effective participation in society, this goal may be empty. To guarantee equal access to the law does not mean that all can have access equally, particularly if a person cannot afford legal representation. It also raises problems of comparison to determine who are alike and for what purpose. More fundamentally, formal equal treatment protection cannot guarantee any better treatment because to treat all similarly characterised persons equally corresponds badly with the rationale and crucially cannot redress long-standing inequalities.

This exclusion was felt by certain persons most often excluded, especially in employment. While the initial impetus to introduce equality laws came from women's groups, racial minorities, including Travellers and the disabled, have also championed ideological change to the notion of equality. Initially, the focus was on equality of outcome, which sought to guarantee a certain equal result and not just uniform treatment. The aim goes beyond procedural fairness to secure substantive changes in conditions. For example, imposing a requirement for all potential employees to have a third level qualification will exclude those unable to go to college, just as a requirement to work full-time may exclude women who remain the primary caregivers for young children.

To overcome these structural inequalities, there has been some focus on measures of positive action to increase the representation of traditionally marginalised groups in various sectors of society, most notably the workplace. Theorists who favour this approach are committed to the aim of equality of outcome, not just equality of opportunity. Such special measures are typically justified by reference to ongoing or structural differentials in the participation of disadvantaged minorities and groups. Generally, Irish law has eschewed such measures, though there are some exceptions. Examples in law include the reservation of a certain number of places for each gender on state boards and positive duties to make reasonable accommodation for persons with disabilities.

These measures have on occasion proved controversial, attracting the criticism that they sacrifice individual ability to a Utopian ideal. Often criticised as unwieldy State attempts to restructure the marketplace, such measures are sometimes, often superficially, themselves condemned for failing to treat persons equally. The theory most often espoused by such critics and others seeking a middle ground between formal equality and equality of outcome is that of equality of opportunity, whereby certain protections are designed to ensure an equality of starting point, but that the personal characteristics determine the finish, particularly in the marketplace. This approach can itself be questioned because it in no way guarantees that everyone can compete equally for resources in that marketplace.

11.3   Equality Laws in Ireland

In many ways, the manner in which the right to equality is treated in Irish law reflects the different ideals of equality as set out above. The Constitution has been used to prevent invidious or capricious discrimination by the State, though criticised for being too weak and focused on formal equality. More particularly, specific laws requiring equality in the workplace were introduced in the 1970s. The Anti-Discrimination (Pay) Act, 1974, and the Employment Equality Act, 1977, were the first pieces of legislation on the matter in Ireland. These Acts, rooted in the directives from the then EEC, later EC, banned discrimination on the grounds of sex and marital status. They have since been repealed and replaced by the Employment Equality Act, 1998, which adds seven other protected categories to the list and introduced some measures enabling positive action. The 1998 Act applies to employment only but the Equal Status Act, 2000, bans discrimination in the provision of goods and services and in other non-employment situations. Both of these latter statutes were amended by the Equality Act, 2004.

These laws demonstrate a particular feature of modern equality law whereby specific characteristics are protected, chosen from traditionally discriminated against groups. There are nine such characteristics in the main legislation and a comparative categorical approach is used in that claiming discrimination means claiming to be a member of a class that is treated less favourably than others outside that class. Claiming discrimination, eg as a disabled person, necessarily involves proving different but less favourable treatment from others without that disability. It is difficult to escape such an approach when dealing with equality rights. The basic idea is to make these characteristics factors to be ignored or specially provided for when considering the availability of employment or goods and services. In that way equality is achieved, not because everyone is treated the same, but because certain characteristics are protected. To be successful, a claimant must not only show less favourable treatment but also that that treatment was as a result of his or her connection to a protected characteristic. In that regard, it may be more accurate to describe Irish legislation as being anti-discrimination law rather than equality law.

The theoretical approach adopted by Irish legislation is generally that of formal equality, in that less favourable treatment of an individual is outlawed if that treatment is based on the protected characteristic, though no special treatment of the characteristic is mandated. There are a number of specific rules that add to this formal approach and go to a version of substantive equality. Some positive action is permitted by Irish legislation, eg s 14(b) of the Equal Status Act, 2000, permits positive measures to cater for persons with special needs. Similarly, discrimination on the disability ground is recognised in domestic legislation as occurring where a person's disability is not reasonably accommodated. Finally, the banning of indirect discrimination outlaws seemingly neutral rules that have an adverse effect on certain groups.

11.4   A Note on the Hierarchies of Law

Given that the right to equality does not guarantee any specifically tangible entitlement or service (as opposed, for example, to the right to liberty or freedom of expression), it is peculiarly susceptible to being outweighed by more substantive considerations. This is associated with the traditional reluctance of the judiciary to engage with social and economic rights, seeing such matters as being the preserve of other branches of the State, especially the executive. The right to equality has often been seen in contrast to, and as being trumped by, substantive rights, particularly property rights, and by economic factors.

Perhaps the most famous example of such a clash was in *Re Article 26 and the Employment Equality Bill 1996* [1997] 2 IR 321. This proposed a requirement that employers make reasonable accommodation for disabled employees unless this caused undue hardship. The Supreme Court held that the Bill was unconstitutional as it was felt that obliging employers to bear the costs involved was an infringement of their property rights. In the redrafted legislation, which became the 1998 Act, the duty to make provision was limited to accommodation involving no more than a nominal cost.

Because of the involvement of the EU in equality rights, a new level was added to the hierarchy. Sex discrimination has always been a concern of the EU and is now a fundamental part of the treaties. Because of the paramount status of EU law in Ireland, no domestic law can trump its provisions. The EU has continued to develop its role in anti-discrimination law. EU law now imposes obligations to prevent discrimination on the grounds of race, religion or belief, age, sexual orientation and disability. Given the EU basis for these grounds, there has been some strengthening of the anti-discrimination measures in our law, most particularly concerning disability discrimination. In this latter case amendment has already led to change from the former 'nominal cost' exception to one more favourable to disabled persons.

11.5   International Law

There is a wealth of references to the notion of equality in international human rights conventions. In the Universal Declaration of Human Rights and the International Covenant on Civil and Political Rights, the equality guarantees are recognised as central to the delivery of the other protected rights to individuals. However, equality was not seen as a right in itself guaranteeing substantive improvement in conditions for individuals. At this international level, there were competing theories of rights in that the former Eastern Bloc countries preferred a focus on substantive economic and social rights, which came to be protected in the International Covenant on Economic, Social and Cultural Rights.

There have also been a number of specific conventions designed to promote equality with respect to particular groups. Foremost among these are the Convention on the Elimination of Discrimination against Women (often called CEDAW) and the Convention on the Elimination of Racial Discrimination (called CERD). These conventions, while not being as enforceable as domestic or EC law, can be important as they are evidence of the public policy of the State and can be used to campaign for change.

11.6   European Convention on Human Rights

As one of the most successful human rights treaties ever signed and one that can be enforced against the State, the ECHR's statements on equality will have a particular importance. Similar to the other international treaties, equality is guaranteed in terms of the delivery of the other rights under the convention. Article 14 provides:

> *'The enjoyment of the rights and freedoms set forth in this Convention shall be secured without discrimination on any ground such as sex, race, colour, language, religion, political or other opinion, national or social origin, association with a national minority, property, birth or other status.'*

Such a formal view of equality renders the right contingent on other rights for activation. A claimant must seek some substantive redress and show that there was discrimination against him or her on the ground of one of the protected categories. In *Belgian Linguistics (No. 2)* (1979) EHRR 252, the European Court of Human Rights (ECt.HR) stated that Article 14 operated as if it were an integral part of each of the Articles laying down rights and freedoms. In that case, the Court also stated that under Article 14 the principle of equal treatment would be breached if a distinction was drawn between persons which had no objective and rational justification or where the means employed was unreasonably disproportionate to the aim of the measure.

11.7   European Union Law

For matters within the competence of the European Union, EU law enjoys the paramount status of constitutional law in each Member State, thereby guaranteeing that its provisions trump any other conflicting law; see Article 29.4 of Bunreacht na hÉireann. That has proved useful in the development of equality legislation and will continue to do so as the competence of the EU develops. Given the weak nature of the right to equality in the Constitution, many who favour the strengthening of equality law look to EU developments.

Because the original aim of the EU was to create a common market within Member States, it is not surprising that the Treaty of Rome outlawed discrimination on the grounds of nationality. This is now contained in Article 18 of the Treaty on the Functioning of the European Union ('TFEU') which states that any discrimination on the ground of nationality shall be prohibited.

The TFEU now gives competence to the EU in relation to discrimination issues. Article 19 TFEU permits the Council, acting unanimously and with the consent of the European Parliament, to take appropriate action to combat discrimination based on sex, racial or ethnic origin, religion or belief, disability, age or sexual orientation.

Aside from nationality, EU law was traditionally concerned only with sex and marital status as grounds for protection against discrimination. The roots of EU equality law lie in the creation of the common market. France, which had developed measures to outlaw sex discrimination, was concerned that it would be at a competitive disadvantage if other states were not obliged to introduce similar rules. Thus, former Article 119, later Article 141 of the EC Treaty, now Article 157 TFEU guaranteed the principle of equal pay for equal work on the ground of sex. In the landmark case of *Defrenne v Sabena* [1976] ECR 455, the European Court of Justice (ECJ) held that the right was directly effective. It also suggested that the provision formed part of the social objectives of the then EEC. This has now been bolstered by the inclusion of gender discrimination in Article 19 TFEU. The general definition of discrimination as adopted by the ECJ is that 'discrimination involves the application of different rules to comparable situations, or the application of the same rules to different situations' (see Case C-342/93 *Gillespie v Northern Health and Social Services Board* [1996] ECR I-475).

Council Directive 75/117/EEC, the Equal Pay Directive, was designed to implement this principle of equal pay more fully. Council Directive 76/207/EEC followed, which broadened the application of sex discrimination law to more general employment concerns, including working conditions and the recruitment process. These directives were first implemented into Irish law by the Anti-Discrimination (Pay) Act, 1974, and the Employment Equality Act, 1977, respectively and are now enforced through the Employment Equality Act, 1998. The particular rules are dealt with when considering in the Employment Equality Act, 1998, though it must be noted that the decisions of the ECJ on the interpretation of the Treaty and directives are binding on Irish administrative and judicial authorities charged with the implementation of the rules.

Following an increased competency as a result of Treaty changes, the Council of Ministers adopted Directive 2000/43/EC of 29 June 2000, the Race Directive, which outlaws discrimination on the ground of racial and ethnic origin in employment and in the provision of goods and services. This is the first EC equality Directive that goes beyond the workplace. A second directive, called the Framework Directive 2000/78/EC of 27 November 2000, was adopted to ban discrimination in employment on the grounds of religion or belief, age, sexual orientation and disability. The Equality Act, 2004 was enacted to introduce changes necessitated by these two directives.

More recently, the Gender and Services Directive 2004/113/EC of 13 December 2004 extends the principle of equal treatment between men and women to the access to and supply of goods and services. This was already part of Irish law, but some additional necessary changes to national law were introduced by Part 14 of the Civil Law (Miscellaneous Provisions) Act, 2008.

The substantive law on the right to equality shall be examined under the following headings, though other topics of relevance will be dealt with later when dealing with domestic legislation.

11.7.1   EQUAL PAY

The notion of equal pay for equal work was fundamental to the Treaty of Rome and led to the enactment of the first specific piece of anti-discrimination law in Ireland, the Anti-Discrimination (Pay) Act, 1974. Article 141(1) of the EC Treaty provided that '[e]ach member state shall ensure that the principle of equal pay for male and female workers for equal work or work of equal value is applied.' For these purposes, pay is defined as meaning the ordinary or basic minimum wage or salary or other commission, whether in cash or in kind, which the worker receives directly or indirectly in respect of his employment from his employer. These provisions are now contained in Article 157 TFEU.

Since the enactment of the Race and Framework Directives, EU law on equal pay applies to the grounds of race, religion or belief, age, sexual orientation and disability in addition to that of sex. It is expected that the development of these new grounds of non-discrimination will mirror those relating to sex discrimination heretofore. The ECJ has given the concept of 'pay' a broad meaning and in *Garland v British Rail* [1982] ECR 359, the ECJ held that travel concessions for employees after retirement constituted pay. The fact that there was no specific entitlement to the concession in the contract of employment was held not to be relevant as the benefit was referable to the employment, which was all the Treaty required. Contributions by employers to occupational pension schemes, whether internal to the enterprise or contracted out, have also been recognised as constituting pay, see *Barber v Guardian Royal Exchange* [1990] ECR I-1889. (The difficulties arising from occupational pension schemes led to the adoption of specific rules for pensions.)

A decision on whether work is equal or equal in value is for national authorities. In *Murphy v Bord Telecom Eireann* [1988] ECR 673, the ECJ stated that there is an entitlement to equal pay where a worker carries out work of greater value to that of her comparator.

Differences in pay have also been condemned as being indirectly discriminatory by the ECJ. In *Enderby v Frenchay Health Authority* [1993] ECR I-5535 a speech therapist sought to compare herself with a male pharmacist in circumstances where most speech therapists were female and most pharmacists were male, who were paid at a higher rate. The ECJ held that where statistics show that pay differentials are based on a grading that is polarised on gender grounds, a *prima facie* case of discrimination is made out and it is for the employer to show that there are objective reasons unrelated to sex for the difference in pay.

The ECJ has adopted an approach based on the shifting burden of proof in relation to taking equal pay cases. Where an enterprise operates a pay system that disadvantages one sex and is wholly lacking in transparency, it is for the employer to prove that the pay practice is not discriminatory; see *Danfoss* [1989] IRLR 532.

11.7.2 EQUAL TREATMENT

The phrase 'equal treatment' refers to aspects of equality law in employment situations other than equal pay. Before the Treaty of Amsterdam amended the EC Treaty, the sole basis for these rules was Council Directive 76/207/EEC, which covered only gender equality. The core of this Directive was expressed in Article 2(1) which provides:

> 'For the purposes of the following provisions, the principle of equal treatment shall mean that there shall be no discrimination whatsoever on grounds of sex either directly or indirectly by reference in particular to marital or family status.'

Article 157(3) TFEU now places a legal obligation on the EU to adopt measures to ensure this principle of equal treatment of men and women in employment. Being mentioned specifically in the Treaty ensures that such equality is a fundamental aim of the EU.

Article 3 of Directive 76/207/EEC specifies that the principle of equal treatment applies to access to employment, Article 4 makes it applicable to vocational training and Article 5 to conditions of work and dismissals. While the specific rules on equal treatment are discussed below, the approach of the ECJ, which is binding on national authorities, sets the parameters of our law so cannot be overlooked.

Since the enactment of the Race and Framework Directives, EU law on equal treatment also covers the grounds of race, religion or belief, age, sexual orientation and disability. Being phrased in a similar manner to the Gender Equality Directive 76/207/EEC decisions under the earlier directive are important precedents.

One of the areas where the ECJ has been active relates to pregnancy discrimination. In the case of Case C-177/88 *Dekker v Stichting Vermingscentrum voor Jong Volwassenen (VJV—Centrum Plus)* [1990] ECR I-3941 the ECJ held that the refusal to employ a woman because she was pregnant was direct sex discrimination, contrary to Article 3, as only women can suffer such discrimination. That led to another important finding that, because of the uniqueness, there was no need for a male comparator. It was also held that financial loss incurred by an employer because of hiring a pregnant woman could not be an excuse for discrimination.

Following this, the ECJ decided the case of Case C-32/93 *Webb v EMO Air Cargo (UK) Ltd* [1994] ECR I-3567. Ms Webb was employed to replace an employee on maternity leave but to remain permanently with the company. Soon after beginning work she informed her employer of her pregnancy. She was dismissed. The employer sought to justify the dismissal by stating that a man would be similarly treated if he were also unavailable for the work he was hired to undertake.

Holding for Ms Webb in an important decision, the ECJ rejected any comparison between a pregnant woman and a sick man. Drawing on the rules contained in the Pregnancy Directive, the Court stated that EC law protections for pregnant workers could not be circumvented by arguments based on the essential presence of an employee at work.

In reaching its decision, the ECJ relied on the fact the Ms Webb was employed in a permanent capacity. This led to much debate as to whether the protections also applied to a pregnant employee employed on a fixed-term contract. The ECJ resolved this issue in favour of the protection of pregnant women in the cases of Case C-438/99 *Jimenez Melgar v Ayuntamiento de Los Barrios* [2001] ECR I-6915 and C-109/00 *Tele Danmark A/S v HK* [2001] ECR I-6993.

The ECJ has also held that less favourable treatment on the ground of a pregnancy-related illness is also unlawful gender discrimination. In *Hertz v Aldi marked K/S* [1991] IRLR 31, the ECJ stated that the dismissal of a pregnant woman for absences caused by a pregnancy-related illness during the period of maternity leave was unlawful direct discrimination on the ground of gender. However, after the maternity leave ceases, an ill woman is not protected, even if the illness has its origin in pregnancy or confinement. In Case C-394/96 *Brown v Rentokill* [1998] ECR I-4185, the ECJ held that dismissal at any time during pregnancy because of absences caused by a pregnancy-related illness was unlawful. It should be noted that dismissals for such absences after the maternity leave ends might, depending on the circumstances, be unlawful discrimination on a standard comparison with male workers.

These cases are applied by domestic adjudicators when considering gender discrimination by reasons of dismissal during or because of pregnancy. In deciding whether a dismissal was discriminatory, the Labour Court has taken a strict approach. In *Emmerdale Ltd v A Worker* (EED-025; 30 May 2002), the Court stated that an employer should have given serious consideration to a work-share arrangement where the pregnant employee desired fewer hours on medical grounds. In that case, the employer advertised the pregnant employee's position the day after she informed them of her pregnancy and a posited defence that this was to replace the employee when she was on maternity leave was rejected as the advertisement seriously undermined the employee's position and led to a loss of trust and confidence in her employers, which justified her resignation.

In *Parcourt Ltd v A Worker* (EED-0211; 15 November 2002), the claimant was held to have been dismissed because of her pregnancy. The employee had taken leave because of a pregnancy-related illness. The employer knew of her pregnancy but claimed that it was not informed of the illness and concluded that she had abandoned her employment. The Court stated that the employer should have been alert to the fact that the absence was pregnancy-related and held that a prudent employer would attempt to ascertain the facts of a situation. Both of these cases impose clear duties on employers to ensure that well regarded pregnant employees are secure in their situation at work and that an employer cannot let a pregnant employee drift away from work.

There are relatively few ECJ decisions on the new directives as yet. In C-144/04 *Mangold v Helm* [2005] ECR 22–31 the ECJ held that a German law which permitted, with minor restrictions, fixed term contracts for persons aged over fifty-two was in breach of the Framework Directive. Those workers over fifty-two affected by the provision would suffer from their exclusion from stable employment. The ECJ stated that: 'The principle of non-discrimination on grounds of age must thus be regarded as a general principle of Community law.'

More recently, the ECJ has taken a less rigid approach on age discrimination. Case C-229/08 *Colin Wolf v Stadt Frankfurt am Main*, 12 January 2010 concerned an upper age limit of 30 for the employment of certain firemen and Case C-341/08 *Domnica Petersen*, 12 January 2010 concerned an age limit for a panel of dentists. In both rulings the ECJ held that age discrimination was permitted, if done for the right reasons, such as when it is required by the nature of the job or if it is necessary for the protection of health or if it is justified by a legitimate aim, including employment policy, labour market and vocational training objectives. In the *Domenica Petersen* case, an upper age limit of 68 for entry to a certain panel of dentists was not permitted because dentists who reached that age, but were not on the panel, could continue to practise. A general age-limit imposed on all dentists in practice was permissible where its aim was to share out employment opportunities among the generations in the profession of panel dentist, if, taking into account the situation in the labour market concerned, the measure was appropriate and necessary for achieving that aim.

In Case C-13/05 *Chacón Navas v Eurest Colectividades SA* [2007] All ER (EC) 59, the ECJ held that a person who was dismissed solely by reason of illness did not fall within the definition of disability under the Framework Directive. The phrase 'disability' was not defined in the directive, and was to be given an autonomous Community meaning. The Court stated (at paras 43 and 45) that:

'Directive 2000/78 aims to combat certain types of discrimination as regards employment and occupation. In that context, the concept of "disability" must be understood as referring to a limitation which results in particular from physical, mental or psychological impairments and which hinders the participation of the person concerned in professional life…The importance which the Community legislature attaches to measures for adapting the workplace to the disability demonstrates that it envisaged situations in which participation in professional life is hindered over a long period of time. In order for the limitation to fall within the concept of "disability", it must therefore be probable that it will last for a long time.'

And at para 46:

'There is nothing in Directive 2000/78 to suggest that workers are protected by the prohibition of discrimination on grounds of disability as soon as they develop any type of sickness.'

In Case C-303/06 *Coleman v Attridge Law* [2008] IRLR 722 the ECJ clarified that the notion of discrimination by association formed part of EU law, and in particular the Framework Directive when it held that the Directive must be interpreted as meaning that the prohibition of direct discrimination was not limited to people who are themselves disabled. The ECJ ruled that where an employer treated an employee who was not himself disabled less favourably than another employee and it was established that the less favourable treatment was based on the disability of his child, whose care is provided primarily by that employee, that treatment was contrary to the prohibition of direct discrimination laid down by Article 2(2)(a).

The ECJ in Case C-54/07 *Centrum Voor Gelijkheid Van Kancn v Ferma Feryn NV*, 10 July 2008 established an important principle that racial discrimination can be considered and prosecuted by a national authority in the absence of a specific person who was the victim of such racial discrimination. In this case, a director of the respondent Firma Feryn N.V. made a public statement to the effect that his undertaking was looking to recruit fitters, but that it could not employ immigrants because its customers were reluctant to give them access to their private residence for the period of work.

The ECJ accepted that the fact that an employer declared publicly that it will not recruit employees that were of certain ethnic or racial origin was something that was clearly likely to strongly dissuade certain candidates from submitting their application and therefore it hindered their access to the labour market, and thus constituted direct discrimination in respect of recruitment within the meaning of the Race Directive. The ECJ held that the existence of such discrimination is not dependent on the identification of a complainant who claims to have been the victim. The ECJ went on hold that national institutions, such as the Equality Authority, could bring actions in these cases against the discriminator.

11.7.3   INDIRECT DISCRIMINATION

In developing the principles of discrimination the ECJ has always made a distinction between direct and indirect discrimination and this has now become a standard feature of anti-discrimination law. Direct discrimination occurs when a person is treated less favourably because he or she possesses a protected characteristic, eg because she is a woman. Indirect discrimination, sometimes called adverse effect discrimination, focuses on the effects of what are not ostensibly discriminatory rules. The ECJ had applied the principles of direct and indirect discrimination for both the equal pay provisions and the equal treatment rules.

The leading case regarding equal pay is *Bilka-Kaufhaus v Weber von Hartz* [1986] 2 *CMLR* 701. This concerned an employer's refusal to make pension contributions to part-time employees, on the basis that it was in its financial interest to discourage part-time employment. The ECJ reasoned that where such an exclusion adversely affected a much greater number of women than men it was unlawful unless an employer could show that the rule was based on objectively justifiable factors unrelated to sex. The Court continued and said that if it was found that the justification proffered (a) met a genuine need of the enterprise, (b) was suitable for attaining the objective pursued by the enterprise and (c) was necessary for that purpose, then the rule would not be discriminatory, even though it had a disparate impact. (This shows that, unlike in cases of direct gender discrimination, there is a defence to indirect discrimination.)

The application of indirect discrimination substantially broadens the scope of EC anti-discrimination rules and permits an analysis of the effects of an otherwise neutral provision. Both the Employment Equality Act, 1998, and the Equal Status Act, 2000, both as amended by the Equality Act, 2004, which introduced some changes in this regard, have provisions that incorporate similar rules into Irish law.

The leading Irish case on indirect discrimination is the Supreme Court decision in *Nathan v Bailey Gibson* [1998] 2 IR 162. The Court set out the terms of indirect discrimination by saying that a requirement relating to employment which is not an essential requirement for such employment and in respect of which the proportion of persons of one sex or (as the case may be) of a different marital status but of the same sex able to comply is a substantially higher number may amount to indirect discrimination. The Court said that in such a case it was sufficient for a worker:

> 'to show that the practice complained of bears significantly more heavily on the complainant's sex than on members of the other sex. At that stage the complainant had established a *prima facie* case of discrimination and the onus of proof shifts to the employer to show that the practice complained of is based on objectively verifiable factors which have no relation to the complainant's sex.'

11.7.4 POSITIVE ACTION

As part of their efforts to promote equality, some Member States introduced measures of positive action, or affirmative action as it is sometimes called, to counteract the effect of historical or structural inequalities. Given that such rules are discriminatory in their operation, there has always been controversy regarding their legality. The Equal Treatment Directive contains a provision, Article 2(4), which permits some measures to promote such equality.

After some wavering (see C-450/93 *Kalanke v Freie Hansestadt Bremen* [1995] ECR I-3051), the ECJ in Case C-409/95 *Marschall v Land Nordrhein-Westfalen* [1997] ECR I-6363 sanctioned a law whereby women were to be appointed to a post where, after a fair competition, they were equal with a male candidate. The law was saved because of an exception whereby women would not get priority if there were specific reasons why an individual male ought to get it. The ECJ justified the rule by reference to historical factors and stereotypes against women, which, it stated, meant that the fact that a man and a woman ended up equal following a competition did not mean they had the same chances.

The legitimacy of such positive action measures was further strengthened by the Treaty of Amsterdam which incorporated a new Article 141(4) into the EC Treaty to permit States to adopt measures *'providing for specific advantages in order to make it easier for the under-represented sex to pursue a vocational activity or to prevent or compensate for disadvantages in professional careers'*.

11.7.5 PREGNANCY AND MATERNITY

In addition to the anti-discriminatory aspects of pregnancy, the EC has also adopted other measures to protect pregnant women and women on maternity leave. These rules come from the Pregnancy and Maternity Directive 92/85/EEC. The Directive goes beyond the formal equal treatment approach of equality law by introducing specific benefits to pregnant women and women on maternity leave. Many of the provisions of the Directive relate to the protection of the health of such women, but Articles 8 to 11 protect their employment rights, eg the right not to be sacked during pregnancy and maternity leave. This Directive also introduced the right to maternity leave and the right to return to work after that time. The provisions of the Directive have been transposed into Irish law by the Unfair Dismissals Acts, 1977 to 2005, and the Maternity Protection Act, 1994, as amended.

11.7.6 SOCIAL SECURITY

The Social Security Directive 79/7 implements the principle of equal treatment between men and women in the field of social welfare. The Directive is aimed at legislation that creates social welfare entitlements for workers. It only applies to certain benefits. Article 3(1) sets out the type of scheme covered as:

'(a) Statutory schemes which provide protection against the following risks:
Sickness; invalidity; old age; accidents at work and occupational diseases; unemployment;

(b) social assistance, in so far as it is intended to supplement or replace the schemes referred to in (a).'

The Directive bans direct and indirect discrimination on the ground of sex and indirect discrimination on the basis of marital and family status. Article 4 of the Directive is one of the more important provisions as it provides that there shall be no discrimination in relation to the scope of the schemes and the conditions of access thereto; the obligation to contribute and the calculation of contributions and the calculation of social welfare benefits.

11.8 Bunreacht na hÉireann 1937

Equality appears in the Constitution under the heading 'Fundamental Rights' and is contained in Article 40.1. The addressee of the right is the State which is prevented from engaging in what is often called invidious discrimination. However, the right is one of the weaker of the fundamental rights. The terms of Article 40.1 amount to a guarantee of equality before the law, not equality as such, and it is designed to ensure that the laws of the State are enforced and apply to all equally.

The protection that stems from Article 40.1 was seen as limited to the essential attributes of human personality, and not persons in other capacities. This severely limited the scope of the protection provided. In one of the most famous explanations of this idea, Walsh J in *Quinn's Supermarket v Attorney General* [1972] IR 1 said:

'The provision is not a guarantee of absolute equality for all citizens in all circumstances, but it is a guarantee of equality as human persons and...is a guarantee related to their dignity as a human beings and a guarantee against any inequalities grounded on an assumption...that some individual...by reason of their human attributes or their ethnic or racial, social or religious background, are to be treated as the inferior or superior of other individuals in the community.'

In their analysis of Article 40.1, Hogan and Whyte question whether the human personality doctrine still reflects the actual approach of the judiciary (Hogan and Whyte, *JM Kelly: The Irish Constitution*, 4th edn, 2003, Butterworths, ch 7.2). The doctrine never applied to cases concerning the administration of justice nor democratic processes. In recent times the judiciary have been willing to discuss a wider principle of equality as a concept that tempers the exercise of power. In *McKenna v An Taoiseach (No. 2)* [1995] 2 IR 10, public financing of one side of a referendum campaign was ruled unconstitutional on the basis that neither side in a democratic exercise should be unequally favoured by government.

Article 40.1 is not a guarantee that all persons shall be treated identically, as Walsh J made clear in *State (Nicolaou) v An Bord Uchtala* [1966] IR 567:

> 'Article 40.1 is not to be read as a guarantee or undertaking that all citizens shall be treated by that law as equal for all purposes, but rather as an acknowledgement of the human equality of all citizens.'

This approach gets support from the wording of Article 40.1, which in the second sentence, often called the proviso, allows certain differences to be taken into consideration. Even if there is a differential treatment by the State, it may be justified if it corresponds with some difference of capacity or social function. This was used in the *Nicolaou* case to deny equal treatment to unmarried fathers, as the Court felt there was such a difference in social function between them and their married counterparts.

In fact there have been relatively few cases where the courts have ruled some State provision unconstitutional on the equality ground. This is in part accounted for by the reluctance to expand the scope of the equality provision, and in part by the preference to develop substantive rights.

In *O'G v Attorney General* [1985] ILRM 61, a widower challenged a rule in the Adoption Act, 1952 that required him to have another child in his custody before an adoption order could be made in his favour. No such requirement was placed on widows. The State sought to defend the law on the basis of differential function between the two, but the courts rejected this, with McMahon J stating he was satisfied that the law was:

> 'founded on an idea of difference in capacity between men and women which has no foundation in fact and . . . is therefore an unwarranted denial of human equality'.

Where the State does make distinctions between groups for the purpose of differential treatment on the ground of different function or capacity, it must not be excessive in the manner in which the distinction is made. In other words, when a statute uses what might be called a suspect classification, the rules adopted must serve a legitimate legislative purpose and the classification must be rationally related to that purpose. *An Blascaod Mór Teo v Commissioners of Public Works (No. 3)* [2000] 1 IR 1 concerned a law imposing compulsory purchase of land, except lands owned by certain persons including descendants of owners/occupiers from a certain date. In declaring the provision invalid Barrington J said (at 19) of the requirement that:

> 'It is hard to see what legitimate legislative purpose it fulfils. It is based on a principle—that of pedigree—which appears to have no place . . . in a democratic society committed to the principle of equality. This fact alone makes the classification suspect. This court agrees . . . that a constitution should be pedigree blind just as it should be colour blind or gender blind except when those issues are relevant to a legitimate legislative purpose.'

The weakness of the constitutional guarantee of equality can be seen cases such as *Dennehy v Minister for Social Welfare*, Barron J, 26 July 1984, High Court (unreported), where a man claimed that the lack of an equivalent payment to men of a deserted wives' allowance was unconstitutional. The claim failed as it was felt that there was a difference of function between men and women. A challenge to a similar welfare provision the lone parents' allowance, which received a less favourable rate of payment than deserted wives' allowance was turned down by both the High Court and the Supreme Court in *Lowth v Minister for Social Welfare* [1998] 4 IR 321. The male plaintiff clamed such differential treatment was unlawfully discriminatory on the ground of sex. The reasons for these decisions lie in the statement of O'Hanlon J in *Madigan v Attorney General* [1986] ILRM 136, where he said:

> 'It has been well recognised ... that tax laws are in a category of their own, and that very considerable latitude must be allowed to the legislature in the enormously complex task of organising and directing the financial affairs of the State.'

It appears that these, and other, considerations, can easily trump the right to equality.

Those other considerations include other provisions of the Constitution. *O'B v S* [1984] IR 316 concerned a rule of interpretation which had the effect of excluding children born outside marriage from succeeding to the intestate estate of their father under the Succession Act, 1965. The Act was challenged for breaching the child's right to equality with other children, but the Supreme Court refused the claim. In doing so the Court stated that this seemingly suspect provision was saved from unconstitutionality because of the protection given to the family based on marriage by Article 41, which justified discrimination against a child born outside marriage. (As a footnote, this case went to the European Court of Human Rights and was settled when the State agreed to change the law, which it did in the Status of Children Act, 1987. This also demonstrates how international human rights treaties can be effective.)

11.9   Domestic Legislation

The Employment Equality Act, 1998 and the Equal Status Act, 2000, both substantially amended by the Equality Act, 2004, are the two statutes that particularise anti-discrimination laws within Ireland. The 1998 Act, as amended, is the principal domestic code dealing with equal treatment at work, while the 2000 Act, as amended, caters for situations outside the workplace.

11.9.1   THE EMPLOYMENT EQUALITY ACT, 1998

When it was introduced, the Employment Equality Act, 1998 extended the grounds of employment-related discrimination beyond the previous bases of sex and marital status. Those two grounds were the only bases for seeking equality under the Anti-Discrimination (Pay) Act, 1974, and the Employment Equality Act, 1977. The 1998 Act replaced those and put in place a comprehensive list of discriminatory grounds to include, among others: gender, marital status, disability, and family status. There were certain problems with the two former statutes that necessitated reform, not least the limited nature of discriminatory grounds, but also some other matters, including the absence of a definition of sexual harassment.

Amendments to the 1998 Act were necessitated by changes in EC law introduced in the Race and Framework Directives.

The 1998 Act, as amended, is a comprehensive code for dealing with discrimination and harassment in the workplace and one that provides its own enforcement mechanisms, mainly through the Office of the Director of the Equality Tribunal, formerly called the Director of Equality Investigations. It ought to be noted that the Act is not retrospective and only discrimination occurring after its entry into force is covered.

11.9.1.1 The discriminatory grounds

Nine discriminatory grounds are contained in the statute. Gender discrimination is treated separately under the Act and is stronger in effect than the rules applicable to the other grounds, which reflects its origin as the first such protected ground in EC law. As with most equality provisions there is a comparative approach used in that claiming discrimination means claiming to be a member of a class that is treated less favourably than others along preordained lines. Claiming discrimination, eg as a disabled person, necessarily involves showing different treatment from others without that disability or with a different disability.

The nine grounds upon which discrimination is banned are, in a comparative sense:

(a) the gender ground, ie one is a woman and the other is a man;

(b) the marital status ground, ie they are of different marital status and 'marital status' means being single, married, separated, divorced or widowed;

(c) the family status ground, ie one has family status and the other does not;

(d) they are of different sexual orientation, which is defined as having a heterosexual, homosexual or bisexual orientation;

(e) one has a different religious belief from the other or that one has a religious belief and the other has not, with 'religious belief' being defined as including a religious background or outlook;

(f) that they are of different ages (for the purposes of age discrimination, discrimination is banned for those above the maximum age at which a person is statutorily obliged to attend school);

(g) that one is a person with a disability and the other either is not, or is a person with a different disability;

(h) that they are of different race, colour, nationality or ethnic or national origins;

(i) that one is a member of the Traveller community and the other is not (referred to as 'the Traveller community ground').

In this context, family status is defined in the statute as having responsibility as a parent:

(a) or as a person *in loco parentis* in relation to a person who has not attained the age of eighteen years; or

(b) or the resident primary carer in relation to a person of, or over, eighteen with a disability which is of such a nature as to give rise to the need for care or support on a continuing, regular or frequent basis.

Disability is defined broadly as:

(a) the total or partial absence of a person's bodily or mental functions, including the absence of a part of a person's body;

(b) the presence in the body of organisms causing, or likely to cause, chronic disease or illness;

(c) the malfunction, malformation or disfigurement of a part of a person's body;

(d) a condition or malfunction which results in a person learning differently from a person without the condition or malfunction; or

(e) a condition, illness or disease which affects a person's thought processes, perception of reality, emotions or judgment or which results in disturbed behaviour and shall be taken to include a disability which exists at present, or which previously existed but no longer exists or which may exist in the future or which is imputed to a person.

The Act deals with discrimination in different ways. Firstly, there are general provisions on discrimination. Part III contains specific provisions relating to discrimination between men and women, while Part IV deals with discrimination on the other grounds. Part V established the Equality Authority, Part VI established Equality Reviews and Action Plans and Part VII deals with remedies and enforcement.

11.9.1.2 Discrimination generally

Discrimination, as defined in s 6, exists where one person is treated less favourably than another is, has been or would be treated. The Act covers not just discrimination in relation to pay, but also other terms and conditions of employment. Its purpose is to equalise the employment playing field, but not necessarily to improve the quality of the field as such (other than ensuring the worthy aim of a discrimination-free workplace).

The general discrimination prohibition is set out in s 8(1) and provides that in relation to:

- access to employment

- conditions of employment

- training or experience for or in relation to employment

- promotion or regrading or

- classification of posts

an employer shall not discriminate against an employee or prospective employee and a provider of agency work shall not discriminate against an agency worker. (It should be noted that, throughout the Act, agency workers can only use other agency workers as comparators for discrimination.)

Section 8 also provides that an employer shall not, in relation to employees or employment, have rules or instructions which would result in discrimination against an employee or class of employee in relation to any of the matters specified in points (b) to (e) above or otherwise apply or operate a practice which results, or would be likely to result, in any such discrimination.

In relation to access to employment, eg a job specification, the interview or the criteria for employment, specific rules are provided and the employer will be guilty of discrimination if he or she discriminates in any arrangements made for the purpose of deciding to whom employment should be offered, or by specifying, in respect of one person or class of persons, entry requirements for employment that are not specified in respect of other persons or classes of persons, where the circumstances in which both such persons or classes would be employed are not materially different. (If there are material differences in the circumstances of employment, different specifications can be made.)

Other non-exhaustive but specified discriminations include where the employer does not offer or afford to an employee or prospective employee the same

- terms of employment (other than pay and pensions)

- working conditions and

- treatment in relation to overtime, shift work, short time, transfers, lay-offs, redundancies, dismissals and disciplinary measures

as the employer offers or affords to another person or class of persons, where the circumstances in which both such persons or classes are, or would be, employed are not materially different.

Other provisions include those in s 10 that ban discriminatory job advertisements. This was found to have been breached in *The Equality Authority v Ryanair* [2001] ELR 107 where a job advertisement stated that the respondent needed a 'young and dynamic professional' and that 'the ideal candidate will be young, dynamic....' The respondent was found to have discriminated on the ground of age.

Section 11, which covers employment agencies, provides that they cannot discriminate against persons who seek to use the services of the agency to obtain employment (unless the employer in question could lawfully discriminate for that job). Section 12 concerns the provision of vocational training and outlaws discrimination in respect of how courses are offered, by refusing or omitting access to the course or generally, in the manner in which the course is provided. Professional bodies that control the entry to or carrying on of a profession or occupation cannot discriminate in relation to membership of the body or other benefits.

Section 13 covers membership of and admission to professional or trade organisations, or organisations that control entry to a trade or profession, and provides that such bodies shall not discriminate against a person in relation to membership of that body or any benefits, other than pension rights, provided by it or in relation to entry to, or the carrying on of, that profession, vocation or occupation. Section 13A, as inserted by the Equality Act, 2004, clarified that the provisions of the Act apply to partnerships.

The basis for non-discrimination continues for as long as the employee is willing and able to do the job in question, though care should be taken to ensure that the bases for the incapability or unwillingness are not themselves based on a discrimination, such as making the employment impossible by imposing conditions which themselves are unlawful. The relevant provision in the Act is s 16 and reads in part:

> '(1) Nothing in this Act shall be construed as requiring any person to recruit or promote an individual ... if the individual—
>
> (a) will not undertake ... the duties attached to that position or will not accept ... the conditions under which those duties are, or may be required to be, performed, or
>
> (b) is not ... fully competent and available to undertake, and fully capable of undertaking, the duties attached to that position, having regard to the conditions under which those duties are, or may be required to be, performed.'

In effect, the employer has a defence to a claim for discrimination if the employee or potential employee would not be able to do the job. In extension, s 16(3) protects disabled employees by creating an employer's obligation of reasonable accommodation and by treating such employees as capable of undertaking the work if some was provided (see below).

11.9.1.3 Provisions between men and women

Part III of the Act continues the old areas of discrimination in a new context. This Part is mostly a re-enactment of the law as it applied under the 1974 and 1977 Acts in relation to sex. Both of those were based originally on Directive 75/117/EEC and Directive 76/207/EEC and the provisions of the new Act are also so based, which preserves continuity and the jurisdiction of the ECJ. There are two main concerns in this Part. The first concerns the entitlement to equal pay and the second caters for indirect discrimination.

The Act implies a mandatory equal pay clause into all contracts of employment, which is given a broad meaning in this part and includes some contracts for services. Common to all equal pay claims, there are a number of conditions to be established. Firstly, both the employee and the comparator must work for the same or an associated employer. They must both be employed on 'like work', a phrase defined in s 7, and covers situations where they both do the same work, or similar work or work of equal value for an employer or associated employer.

The concept of indirect discrimination has been explicitly extended to cover equal pay claims in s 19(4), which was amended by the Equality Act, 2004. Indirect discrimination is now defined as occurring where an apparently neutral provision puts persons of a particular gender at a particular disadvantage in respect of remuneration compared with other employees of their employer. The provision in question is unlawful unless it was objectively justified by a legitimate aim and the means of achieving the aim are appropriate and necessary. In the case of a breach the person disadvantaged shall be treated as satisfying, or not (as the case may be), the provision, whichever results in higher pay.

One recognised example of such indirect discrimination concerns part-time employees. Such workers are often paid less than their full-time counterparts and are often predominantly female. Such was the case in *St. Patrick's College, Maynooth v 19 Female Employees* (EP4/84) and, as it was held that working full-time was not an essential requirement unrelated to sex, the pay practice was held to be discriminatory.

Different rates of pay that are not based on any discriminatory ground are permitted. In the past there have been a few generally recognised exceptions. These include 'red-circling', which occurs where an employee is retained on an individually preferential rate of pay, collective bargaining and market forces.

Section 21 concerns direct discrimination, other than pay, and implies an equality clause into all contracts of employment that will override any express contractual stipulation to equalise the positions of the claimant and his or her comparator. The equalisation is by raising the standard of the discriminated person to that of the advantaged person, thus raising the overall standards. The clause does not operate if the difference of treatment is genuinely based on grounds other than gender (and of course discrimination on other grounds will be covered by a similar provision in Part IV of the Act). If the employer claims this, the burden of proof may shift to him or her to prove it.

Cases on non-pay discrimination cover many aspects of the employment relationship, from hiring to firing. Questions at interview, such as asking a woman who will look after her children, have been held to be discriminatory as they would not be asked of a man; see *Gough v St. Mary's Credit Union* (EE15/2000). This also applies to statements made outside the formal interview; see *Rodmell v TCD* (EE31/2000) where the claimant was identified as a 'lady electrician'.

In *Rotunda Hospital v Gleeson* (DEE-003/2000, 18 April 2000), the claimant was discriminated against on the ground of gender in relation to the appointment to the post of consultant obstetrician/gynaecologist. The Labour Court noted that unfavourable comments had been made during the interview that identified the claimant by her sex, a male-dominated interview panel was used and that the claimant was more qualified for the post than the appointed male. The Court awarded the claimant £50,000, one of the highest awards made.

Indirect discrimination on grounds other than pay is covered by s 22, which was amended by the Equality Act, 2004, and now provides:

> '(1)(a) *Indirect discrimination occurs where an apparently neutral provision puts persons of a particular gender . . . at a particular disadvantage in respect of any matter other than remuneration compared with other employees of their employer.*
>
> (b) *Where paragraph (a) applies, the employer shall be treated for the purposes of this Act as discriminating against each of the persons referred to . . . unless the provision is objectively justified by a legitimate aim and the means of achieving that aim are appropriate and necessary.'*

In assessing the disparate impact a provision has, a statistical or numerical analysis is often used. In *Wilson v The Adelaide and Meath Hospital* (DEC-E2002–025) a female ward attendant applied for the post of permanent porter. A requirement for the post was to have previous experience as a porter. In considering a claim that the requirement constituted indirect discrimination, the equality officer held that the appropriate pool of people within which to analyse the claim were the thirteen interviewees, made up of nine males and four females. All four females and one male could not fulfil the requirement of experience. The practice disadvantaged 100% of females but only 11% of males, which was held to be 'substantially higher' within the meaning of s 22. The onus fell on the respondent to justify the requirement, which in this case it was unable to do.

11.9.1.4 Harassment and sexual harassment

Prior to the enactment of the Equality Act, 2004, sexual harassment and harassment on other grounds were treated separately. The 2004 Act enacted a new s 14A which provides a more uniform code for all forms of harassment. Before the 1998 Act, sexual harassment had no statutory definition and was dealt with as discrimination and in consequence was treated as being unlawful on that basis. In *A Garage Proprietor v A Worker* (EE2/1985) the Labour Court stated that 'freedom from sexual harassment is a condition of work which an employee of either sex is entitled to expect'. Although commentators were generally pleased with the manner in which the Labour Court dealt with sexual harassment, specific provision was necessary, as well as provision for other forms of harassment. In addition, there were issues relating to the vicarious liability of employers for sexual and other harassment, which stemmed from the absence of a statutory definition.

That definition now states:

> 14A. (1)   'For the purposes of this Act, where—
>
>   (a)   an employee (in this section referred to as 'the victim') is harassed or sexually harassed either at a place where the employee is employed (in this section referred to as 'the workplace') or otherwise in the course of his or her employment by a person who is—
>
>   (i)   employed at that place or by the same employer,
>
>   (ii)   the victim's employer, or
>
>   (iii)   a client, customer or other business contact of the victim's employer and the circumstances of the harassment are such that the employer ought reasonably to have taken steps to prevent it,
>
>   or
>
>   (b)   without prejudice to the generality of paragraph (a)
>
>   (i)   such harassment has occurred, and
>
>   (ii)   either—
>
>   (I)   the victim is treated differently in the workplace or otherwise in the course of his or her employment by reason of rejecting or accepting the harassment,
>
>   or
>
>   (II)   it could reasonably be anticipated that he or she would be so treated,
>
>   the harassment or sexual harassment constitutes discrimination by the victim's employer in relation to the victim's conditions of employment.'

References to harassment are defined as including a reference to any form of unwanted conduct related to any of the discriminatory grounds, and references to sexual harassment are to any form of unwanted verbal, non-verbal or physical conduct of a sexual nature, being conduct which in either case has the purpose or effect of violating a person's dignity and creating an intimidating, hostile, degrading, humiliating or offensive environment for the person. It is further provided that such unwanted conduct may consist of acts, requests, spoken words, gestures or the production, display or circulation of written words, pictures or other material.

The harassment must occur in the workplace (and note the coverage of environmental harassment) or otherwise during the course of employment for the employer to be liable. There is a defence for employers under s 14A(2) if they took reasonable steps to prevent the conduct and, where it has occurred, reverse its effects.

11.9.1.5 Discrimination on other grounds

Part IV covers discrimination on the other eight grounds. In many ways, the provisions here mirror those in Part III in that there are bans on direct and indirect discrimination in relation to pay and other matters. The methods of enforcement are also similar in that the mechanism of contract modification is used. In this part, the claimant and comparator are called 'C' and 'D' respectively, which makes the statute difficult to read. Thus, if the claimant 'C' is married then 'D' will be single, widowed or divorced; if 'C' is disabled, 'D' will not be or will have a different disability.

The right to equal pay on grounds other than sex is covered by s 29, which covers both direct and indirect discrimination. An amended s 29(4) provides that the same definition of indirect discrimination applies to the other protected grounds as applies in gender cases pursuant to s 19(4), as amended, since the enactment of the Equality Act, 2004. In *Langan v C-Town Ltd* (DEC-E2003–010) a claim for equal pay was successful where it was found that a worker who was 19 years younger than his comparator performed like work.

Section 30 concerns direct discrimination, other than pay, and implies an equality clause that will override any express contractual stipulation to equalise the positions of the claimant and the comparator. Section 31 deals with indirect discrimination on the non-gender grounds. Again, since the enactment of the Equality Act, 2004, the provisions for indirect discrimination are identical to those concerning gender discrimination in s 22(1) and (1A), as amended.

One development of note concerns foreign employees. Both the Equality Tribunal and the Labour Court have held that foreign workers may need some special treatment in order to ensure equal rights at work; see *A Company v a Worker* (DET-EED024) and *Campbell Catering Ltd v Rasaq* (DET-ED048). In *Rasaq* the Labour Court stated:

> 'It is clear that many non-national workers encounter special difficulties in employment arising from a lack of knowledge concerning statutory and contractual employment rights together with differences of language and culture. In the case of disciplinary proceedings, employers have a positive duty to ensure that all workers fully understand what is alleged against them, the gravity of the alleged misconduct and their right to mount a full defence, including the right to representation. Special measures may be necessary in the case of non-national workers to ensure that this obligation is fulfilled and that the accused worker fully appreciates the gravity of the situation and is given appropriate facilitates and guidance in making a defence. In such cases, applying the same procedural standards to a non-national workers as would be applied to an Irish national could amount to the application of the same rules to different situations and could in itself amount to discrimination.'

11.9.1.6 Reasonable accommodation for disabled workers

Section 16 of the Act introduces an important special provision for disabled workers. This is a recognition that such workers may require material changes to the workplace and to the manner in which work is structured to ensure they are capable of undertaking the task. Without such a provision, the general terms of s 16 that relate to an employee's competence to work could operate against disabled workers.

It is provided that, for the purposes of the Act, a person who has a disability shall not be regarded as other than fully competent to undertake, and fully capable of undertaking, any duties if, with the assistance of special treatment or facilities, such person would be fully competent to undertake, and be fully capable of undertaking, those duties. More importantly, the Act imposes an obligation on employers to do all that is reasonable to accommodate the needs of a person who has a disability by providing such special treatment or facilities.

The amount of such provision was limited as s 16 used to provide: 'A refusal or failure to provide for special treatment or facilities . . . shall not be deemed reasonable unless such provision would give rise to a cost, other than a nominal cost, to the employer.' This was known as the 'nominal cost' exception and operated to restrict the provision of special treatment. The Bill as originally formulated had proposed a cost exception based on undue hardship, but that was deemed unconstitutional by the Supreme Court in *Re Article 26 and the Employment Equality Bill 1996* [1997] 2 IR 321.

The Framework Directive has changed the law in this area as a result of which more onerous duties can now be placed on employers in respect of accommodating their disabled workers within the meaning of the Directive; see Case C-13/05 *Chacón Navas v Eurest Colectividades* (above at **11.7.2**).

Section 16 (3), as amended by the Equality Act, 2004, now provides:

'(a) *For the purposes of this Act a person who has a disability is fully competent to undertake, and fully capable of undertaking, any duties if the person would be so fully competent and capable on reasonable accommodation (in this subsection referred to as 'appropriate measures') being provided by the person's employer.*

(b) *The employer shall take appropriate measures, where needed in a particular case, to enable a person who has a disability—*
   (i) *to have access to employment,*
   (ii) *to participate or advance in employment, or*
   (iii) *to undergo training,*
   unless the measures would impose a disproportionate burden on the employer.

(c) *In determining whether the measures would impose such a burden account shall be taken, in particular, of—*
   (i) *the financial and other costs entailed,*
   (ii) *the scale and financial resources of the employer's business, and*
   (iii) *the possibility of obtaining public funding or other assistance.'*

Section 16(4) as amended provides a definition of 'appropriate measures' for this purpose that:

'(a) *means effective and practical measures, where needed in a particular case, to adapt the employer's place of business to the disability concerned,*

(b) *without prejudice to the generality of paragraph (a), includes the adaptation of premises and equipment, patterns of working time, distribution of tasks or the provision of training or integration resources, but*

(c) *does not include any treatment, facility or thing that the person might ordinarily or reasonably provide for himself or herself.'*

From early case-law under the Act, it was clear that an employer must explore the options available to accommodate the needs of a disabled employee and that discrimination is committed by such a failure; see *Kehoe v Convertec Ltd* (DEC-E—2001–034). In *A Computer Component Company v A Worker* (EED-013/2001), the Labour Court was dealing with a case of discriminatory dismissal where the employee was dismissed because of her epilepsy. The respondent defended the action by claiming that the employee was, because of her disability, not fully competent and capable of performing her duties, and that her need could not have been accommodated. However, the Court held that if the employer concluded that she could not do her job, it had done so precipitously as it did not undertake, nor did it even consider undertaking, any safety assessment to assess any danger level from her disability or how to ameliorate any such danger. The Court stated, in finding for the claimant, that:

'On the evidence, the Court does not accept that the respondent could reasonably and objectively have come to the conclusion that the complainant was not fully competent or capable of performing the duties of her employment. Even if the respondent did reach such a conclusion, it is abundantly clear that it did not give the slightest consideration to providing the complainant with reasonable special facilities which would accommodate her needs and so overcome any difficulty which she or the respondent might otherwise experience.'

In *An Employee v A Local Authority* (DEC-E2002/4) the equality officer held that in assessing the size of a nominal cost, all employers are not to be treated in an identical fashion. It would appear that more will be expected of large employers.

While these decisions are still valid precedents, the law has now developed such that future decisions will reflect the higher obligation regarding substantive provision of opportunities to disabled workers.

The Labour Court has recently taken a stricter line when investigating complaints of discrimination. Recent decisions regarding perceptions of the abilities of disabled workers on whether discrimination must be the main feature behind an adverse decision and positive obligations to foreign workers demonstrate the manner in which anti-discrimination concepts are developing.

In *An Employee v A Government Department* [2006] ELR 224 the Court stated in relation to disability discrimination:

'The requirement to establish that there was no discrimination whatsoever means that the court must be alert to the possibility that a person with a disability may suffer discrimination not because they are disabled *per se*, but because they are perceived, because of their disability, to be less capable or less dependable than a person without a disability. The court must always be alert to the possibility of unconscious or inadvertent discrimination and mere denials of a discriminatory motive, in the absence of independent corroboration, must be approached with caution.'

In *Nevins, Murphy, Flood v Portroe Stevedores* [2005] ELR 282 the Labour Court adopting *dicta* from the case of *Nagarajan v London Regional Transport* [1998] IRLR 573 stated:

'It must be borne in mind that the prescribed reason need not be the sole or even the principal reason for the conduct impugned; it is enough that it is a contributing cause in the sense of being a *"significant influence."*'

In *A Complainant v An Employer* (DEC-E2008-068) the complainant, who was deaf, applied for a job as a Graphic Designer. He was offered an interview the next day, but could not undertake it as he needed time to organise an interpreter to be present. He requested a deferment, but this was refused on the basis that the interviewer was only available on one day. It was argued that as the complainant was offered an interview on the same terms as other candidates there was no discrimination. The Equality Officer found that the respondent's refusal constituted less favourable treatment when a reasonable deferral would have allowed the complainant to take part in the interview and have a real opportunity to access the employment. It could not show that the interviewer was unavailable in the period around the interview date.

11.9.1.7 Positive action

Section 24 of the Act, as amended, contains some provisions catering for positive discrimination, but is merely permissive of steps to promote equal opportunities between men and women and does not demand any measures in particular. In effect, it permits an employer to take positive steps to remove existing inequalities which affect women's opportunities at work. Section 26(1) permits treatment which confers benefits on women in connection with breast-feeding and maternity or adoption.

In relation to the non-gender grounds, some positive action is permitted by s 33, as amended. Measures to prevent or compensate for disadvantages linked to any of the discriminatory grounds are permitted as are measures to facilitate their integration into the workplace. It is specifically provided that measures may protect the health and safety of disabled workers.

11.9.1.8 Exceptions

The Act contains exceptions that permit some discrimination. In relation to the gender ground, s 25, as amended, permits certain discrimination where a person's gender amounts to a genuine and determining occupational qualification for the post in question and the objective is legitimate and the requirement proportionate.

The exceptions for the non-gender grounds are contained in s 34. Section 34(1), which applies to the eight non-gender grounds, permits an employer to provide a benefit to:

(a) an employee in respect of events related to members of the employee's family or any description of those members;

(b) or in respect of a person as a member of an employee's family;

(c) an employee on or by reference to an event occasioning a change in the marital status of the employee; or

(d) an employee who has family status, intended directly to provide or assist in the provision, during working hours, of care for a person for whom the employee has responsibility.

While these rules have been lauded as helping to engender a family-orientated workplace, they may have some serious downsides, foremost among which is caused by the marriage-based definition of family in the Act. It would appear that benefits given to a spouse do not have to be given to a cohabitee, despite being *prima facie* discriminatory on the grounds of marital status. In fact, this rolls back the law as such discrimination was banned under the old law. In *Eagle Star Insurance Co v A Worker* [1998] ELR 306, a scheme whereby staff and their spouses received discounted insurance was found to discriminate against a cohabitating employee. Under the 1998 Act, it is unclear whether a similar rule would be unlawful as it may be permitted by the exception.

Section 34(3), as amended provides that for the purposes of occupational schemes such as sick pay or redundancy, but not pensions, it shall not be discriminatory on the age ground for an employer to fix ages for admission to or benefit from a scheme, and other related matters.

It is also provided in s 34(4) that it shall not constitute discrimination on the age ground to fix different ages for the retirement (whether voluntarily or compulsorily) of employees or any class or description of employees. Section 34(5) states that it shall not constitute discrimination on the age ground to set a maximum age for recruitment which takes account of:

(a) any cost or period of time involved in training a recruit to a standard at which the recruit will be effective in that job; and

(b) the need for there to be a reasonable period of time prior to retirement age during which the recruit will be effective in that job.

Section 34(7) provides that it shall not constitute discrimination on the age ground for an employer to provide for different persons different rates of remuneration or different terms and conditions of employment if the difference is based on their relative seniority (or length of service) in a particular post or employment.

These age provisions have caused concern as it seems that what the Act gives with one hand, it takes away with the other. It also perpetuates notions that the elderly should not be retrained as they might not stay long enough in the employment for the employer to benefit. Of course, the legal regime does not itself facilitate workers who do in fact wish to work beyond retirement age. The same is true for disabled persons. However, clear actuarial or other evidence is required before those subsections can operate to the detriment of the aged or disabled and it would follow that it is for the employer to provide and prove that.

Disabled workers face more difficulties from s 35 with regard to equal pay. The pay provision allows a difference in pay if disabled workers cannot work the same hours or do the same amount of work because of the disability but without reference to different number of hours. The ethos would again appear to view the disabled worker as having a lower work ability.

Finally, s 37(1) allows a religious, educational or medical institution to preserve its ethos, as it will not be taken to discriminate by preferring one employee over another where reasonable to protect that ethos. The section itself is very unclear as to when this exception applies and as to its scope and fears have been expressed that it could allow discrimination. The section appears to be a kind of a statutory replication of the decision in the case of *Flynn v Power* [1985] ILRM 336, where an unmarried teacher was sacked while pregnant. The school was run by a Roman Catholic order which had demanded, before the applicant became pregnant, that she terminate her extra-marital relationship. The High Court held that this did not constitute dismissal on the grounds of pregnancy, but was because the applicant's behaviour was a rejection of the school's religious tenets.

Section 37(2), as amended, permits a difference of treatment on the non-gender grounds where the characteristic in question constitutes a genuine and determining occupational requirement and the objective is legitimate and the requirement proportionate.

11.9.1.9 The Equality Authority

Part V establishes the Equality Authority which takes over from the former Employment Equality Agency. Its functions are to work towards eliminating discrimination in employment, promote equality of opportunity and provide information to the public on the workings of this and other Acts. The Authority is empowered to draw up codes of practice for the promotion of equality and ending discrimination. A code can be approved by the Minister and if this is done it becomes admissible in evidence in proceedings under the Act and 'shall be taken into account in determining' the issue. The Authority has published such a code of practice on Sexual Harassment and Harassment (SI 78/2002), which outlines how employers should deal with such complaints.

The Authority gives general advice on discrimination law and can sponsor cases under discrimination law, which in effect means that it can give legal representation to claimants. The Authority can also conduct inquiries into certain matters and employ others for that purpose, once a term of reference has been set. This shows the proactive nature of the Authority's role. The inquiry is given information-gathering powers in relation to the investigation, which can result in reports and recommendations being made. If a breach of the Act is found during the investigation the Authority can serve a non-discrimination notice, calling on the employer etc to cease the matter in question. The Authority must hear representations made by the employer, who can also appeal to the Labour Court against the findings. The notices can be enforced by High Court or Circuit Court injunction. Failure to comply with the notice is a criminal offence.

11.9.1.10 Remedies

Redress under the statute is dealt with in Part VII. In s 75 the Act establishes a Director of the Equality Tribunal, formerly called the Director of Equality Investigations. Complaints of discrimination at work are made to the Director. Hearings will take place before an equality officer appointed by the Director. The forum is now called the Equality Tribunal. As a result of changes introduced by the Equality Act, 2004, cases of dismissal on a discriminatory ground can now be referred to the Equality Tribunal, whereas they formerly had to be referred to the Labour Court. Gender discrimination cases may be taken to the Circuit Court, where it should be noted there is no monetary limit on awards.

In pursuing claims, the claimant is given a right to information from the respondent, though some exceptions are allowed regarding confidential information. In particular, no information can be given concerning a particular individual without his or her consent, which will be important in equal pay claims. Claims that a person was discriminated against on more than one ground can be dealt with together.

A limitation period of six months applies to making a complaint, other than equal pay claims, from the date of the most recent occurrence of the act of discrimination, which can be extended to one year in exceptional circumstances on the application of a complainant. There is a specific provision which eases the operation of the time limit in cases where there has been some material misrepresentation by a respondent.

Under s 79(3A), as inserted by the Equality Act 2004, the Director may hold a preliminary hearing into certain matters, including compliance with statutory requirement regarding referrals and whether the complainant is an employee. The Director has a power under s 77A, as inserted, to dismiss frivolous, vexatious or misconceived claims.

When a case is referred, mediation may be offered, but this will not occur where either the claimant or respondent objects. In that case, the Equality Tribunal shall, if a complainant applies for continuance within 28 days of a non-resolution notice, investigate the case and hear all interested persons. At the conclusion, the Tribunal shall make a decision. Equal pay claims in the Circuit Court can involve the Director who may be asked by the Court to nominate an equality officer to investigate.

The Director can order redress—in equal pay claims arrears for three years or from the date employment began, if sooner. The Director can also make an order for equal treatment or for compensation for the effects of discrimination. The Circuit Court can make similar orders. To comply with European law, there is no cap on the jurisdiction of the Circuit Court in claims based on gender discrimination. Otherwise, there is a cap of 104 weeks' pay. In cases where the claimant is not in receipt of pay from the respondent the limit is €12,697.38 (formerly £10,000.)

A decision of the Director can be appealed to the Labour Court. A further appeal lies on a point of law to the High Court. If an employer fails to comply with a decision or determination an application can be brought to the Circuit Court to order compliance. This also applies to mediated settlements.

In *Minister for Justice, Equality and Law Reform v The Equality Tribunal* [2009] IEHC 72 the High Court ruled that the Equality Tribunal did not have jurisdiction to investigate a claim of discrimination based on rules that are set out in a statutory instrument where the effect of the challenge was to declare that the rule was unlawful. It held that, unless permitted by the Employment Equality Acts, this was a function for the High Court.

11.9.1.11 Victimisation

Because of fears that persons who assert their rights under this Act may be penalised for so doing, the Act bans victimisation. Victimisation is defined in s 74(2), as amended, as occurring:

'where dismissal or other adverse treatment of an employee by his or her employer occurs as a reaction to—

(a) a complaint of discrimination made by the employee to the employer,

(b) any proceedings by a complainant,

(c) an employee having represented or otherwise supported a complainant,

(d) the work of an employee having been compared with that of another employee for any of the purposes of this Act or any enactment repealed by this Act,

(e) an employee having been a witness in any proceedings under this Act or the Equal Status Act 2000 or any such repealed enactment,

(f) an employee having opposed by lawful means an act which is unlawful under this Act or the said Act of 2000 or which was unlawful under any such repealed enactment, or

(g) an employee having given notice of an intention to take any of the actions mentioned in the preceding paragraphs.'

11.9.1.12 Evidential matters

The courts have long recognised the problems of gathering evidence in discrimination cases. Browne-Wilkinson LJ in *Glasgow City Council v Zafar* [1998] 2 All ER 953, 958 stated that complaints of racial discrimination:

'... present special problems of proof for complainants since those who discriminate on the grounds of race or gender do not in general advertise their prejudices: indeed they may not even be aware of them.'

This demonstrates what is often said in discrimination cases, that it is the result of a policy or rule that is at issue, not the motive of the alleged discriminator. Neill LJ in *King v Great Britain-China Centre* [1992] ICR 516 stated (at 528–9):

'(2) It is important to bear in mind that it is unusual to find direct evidence of racial discrimination. Few employers would be prepared to admit such discrimination even to themselves. In some cases the discrimination will not be ill intentioned but merely based on an assumption that "he or she would not have fitted in".

(3) The outcome of the case will therefore usually depend on what inferences it is proper to draw from the primary facts found by the tribunal. These inferences can include, in appropriate cases, any inferences that it is just and equitable to draw ... from an evasive or equivocal reply to a questionnaire.

(4) Though there will be some cases where, for example, the non-selection of the applicant for a post or for promotion is clearly not on racial grounds, a finding of discrimination and a finding of a difference in race will often point to the possibility of racial discrimination. In such circumstances the tribunal will look to the employer for an explanation. If no explanation is then put forward or if the tribunal considers the explanation to be inadequate or unsatisfactory it will be legitimate for the tribunal to infer that the discrimination was on racial grounds.'

Both decisions were quoted with approval by Quirke J in *Davis v DIT*, 23 June 2000, High Court (unreported). The Labour Court has also accepted that these principles were applicable to all claims of discrimination in *Ntoko v Citibank* [2004] ELR 116. That case also clarified that in cases where no actual comparator was available, a complainant could use a hypothetical comparator to prove his or her claim for discrimination.

In the past there were some special evidential burden rules in gender discrimination cases involving the operation of the shifting burden of proof. This had long been a rule applied by Irish decision-makers, and later by the ECJ. The relevant rules are now applicable to all claims of unlawful discrimination through s 85A of the 1998 Act, as inserted by the Equality Act 2004. Under the new statutory provisions where a complainant can establish facts from which discrimination may be presumed, it shall be for the employer to prove the contrary. This is a statutory replication of burden of proof obligations created by both the Race and the Framework Directives. The rules will operate in a similar fashion to that described in older cases, eg in *Mitchell v SHB* (DEE-011, 15 February 2001) the Labour Court explained the burden of proof as follows:

> 'This indicates that a claimant must prove, on the balance of probabilities, the primary facts on which they rely in seeking to raise a presumption of unlawful discrimination. It is only if those primary facts are established to the satisfaction of the Court, and they are regarded by the Court as being of sufficient significance to raise a presumption of discrimination, that the onus shifts to the respondent to prove that there was no infringement of the principle of equal treatment.'

Before the insertion of s 85A, it was said that a claimant must show a *prima facie* case of discrimination, at which point the burden of proof shifts to the respondent to prove there was no discrimination. *Prima facie* evidence was defined by an equality officer in *Dublin Corp v Gibney* (EE5/1986) as: 'evidence which in the absence of any credible contradictory evidence by the employer would lead any reasonable person to conclude that discrimination had occurred'. This is a broadly similar approach to the manner in which a presumption is raised under s 85A and is still used in some cases.

11.10   The Equal Status Act, 2000

The Equal Status Act, 2000, as amended by the Equality Act, 2004, is an attempt to combat discrimination in contexts other than the employment relationship on the same nine grounds as the 1998 Act. Generally, it bans discrimination in the provision of goods and services and accommodation and education to the general public. In this Act three forms of discrimination are banned.

Section 3 defines discrimination generally, with the basic form being where, on any of the protected grounds, which exists at present or previously existed or which may exist in the future or which is imputed to a person, a person is treated less favourably than another is, has been or would be treated. This broad definition enables historic features to be taken into account, though only acts of discrimination that occur after the legislation came into force in October 2000 can form the basis of a claim. For example, if someone used to possess a protected characteristic and is treated less favourably because of that, such discrimination is unlawful if the less favourable treatment occurs after the operation of the Act.

A second form of discrimination arises where a person associated with another is treated less favourably because of that association, where similar treatment of the other person would amount to discrimination. Discrimination by association is an important matter for a law of this nature to cover as the nature of discrimination is to base exclusion on matters of irrelevance. The exact nature of association is a matter that should be clarified, but a standard definition would limit the concept to availing of a service together with a person with the characteristic. This would be a conservative approach and a broader meaning should be considered to ensure proper protection.

The final definition of discrimination caters for indirect discrimination and occurs where an apparently neutral provision puts a person in possession of a relevant characteristic at a particular disadvantage compared with other persons, unless the provision is objectively justified by a legitimate aim and the means of achieving that aim are appropriate and necessary.

The inclusion of indirect discrimination is vital because discrimination often occurs in covert ways, as service providers are unlikely to directly discriminate, especially when they learn of the consequences of so doing. The ban on indirect discrimination means that supposedly neutral criteria cannot be used to cloak what in reality amounts to unlawful unequal treatment. For a bar to have a requirement of living in a house would amount to indirect discrimination on the Traveller community ground as substantially more non-Travellers can comply with it and it would appear difficult to justify it as a reasonable requirement for being provided with a service otherwise available to the 'general public'.

11.10.1 ACTIVITIES COVERED

One of the central provisions of the Equal Status Act, contained in s 5, is to ban discrimination in the disposal of goods or the provision of services that are available to the public generally or a section of the public. It is irrelevant that the service or goods are given for consideration or not. The State is not specifically included in the definition of service provider and this was a cause for criticism among interested groups, but the law will cover the State regardless. Service is defined more particularly, but without prejudice to generality, as access to and the use of any place; facilities for banking, insurance, loans, etc, entertainment, cultural activities and transport; services provided by a club and professional or trade services.

For the first time in Irish law a business cannot refuse to serve a person simply because he or she falls into one of the categories. A black person cannot be refused service on the basis of being black nor a woman because she is a woman. In this regard, the nature of the law must be understood. It is not a demand that everyone in a protected class be served at all times, but just that they be treated the same as anyone else in relation to that service. To the extent that the provision of any service is discriminatory of someone else who cannot thereby avail of the service the Act will require an equality of discrimination.

In *O'Reilly v Q Bar* [2003] ELR 35, a 72-year-old was discriminated against on the ground of age when he was refused admission to a bar that catered predominantly for younger persons. In *Gallagher v Merlin's Night Club* (DEC-S2002–133), the claimant was successful in a gender discrimination case where he was refused admission to a nightclub because he was wearing sandals. A woman in the claimant's company was admitted while wearing similar sandals and the claimant was told by a doorman that women were permitted to wear sandals in the club.

In *Maughan v The Glimmerman* (DEC-S2001–020) a blanket ban on children being present on a licensed premises with their parents was found to be discriminatory of those parents on the basis of their family status.

As a result of changes introduced by Part 4 of the Intoxicating Liquor Act, 2003, all claims for discrimination against licensed premises are now referred to the District Court. That Act also permits a measure of age discrimination in pubs, in that a policy of not serving persons below a specified age is permitted as long as the policy is displayed on the premises and is implemented in good faith.

There are some exceptions in s 5(2) where this principle of equal treatment is abrogated. Differences on the gender ground in relation to services of an aesthetic or cosmetic nature where the services require physical contact are excluded. For example, a women's hairdresser need not serve men and vice versa. Other permissible differences of treatment include that in relation to the provision of pensions, insurance policies and other matters related to the assessment of risk, where there is clear actuarial evidence to justify the difference, disposals of goods by will or gift and there is also an exception relating to sporting events. Age requirements for a person to be an adoptive or foster parent are specifically excluded as are cultural performances where persons can be treated differently on gender, age and disability for reasons of authenticity. While the list of exceptions is long they appear necessary as otherwise some peculiar consequences would follow. Indeed this reflects the true notion of equality of treating similar things the same but differences differently.

Section 6 deals with the provision of accommodation and provides that nobody shall discriminate in the disposal of any estate or interest in premises or in providing accommodation or any services relating thereto. This does not apply to disposals by gift or will. Neither does it apply to the provision of accommodation by a person in a part of their home (other than a self-contained unit) or where the provision of accommodation affects the person's private or family life. Grounds of privacy in relation to accommodation of one gender only is also included as an exemption. Landlords will have to be particularly careful to ensure that only objective factors are used to decide to whom to let premises. For example, in the past many pregnant women have had difficulties securing rented accommodation. Discrimination on that basis is now unlawful.

The admission and access to courses of education are covered by s 7, which also bans discrimination in relation to the punishment and sanction of students. This is a welcome addition to the notion of service provision and demonstrates the broad nature of the Act in the remit of activities covered. Again, some discrimination is permitted, eg if a non-third-level establishment admits students of one gender only then it is not unlawful to exclude members of the opposite gender, and schools which promote religious values are entitled to prefer students of that religion, so long as a refusal to admit a student is essential to maintain the ethos of the school. This latter test is very stringent, as it will be difficult to prove that the exclusion of a potential student is essential for the ethos in question. Other equality related obligations are placed on universities by s 36 of the Universities Act, 1997.

Section 8 of the Act deals with discriminating clubs and outlaws discrimination, which in this regard is defined as having a rule, policy or practice which discriminates against a member or applicant for membership, or where a person involved in management so discriminates. Specific instances such as refusing membership and providing differential terms and conditions of membership are mentioned as examples of discrimination. By covering not just rules and policies, but extending the provisions to practices, clubs that operate subtle forms of making certain persons unwelcome are in danger of breaching the law. Section 9 allows certain clubs to discriminate, for example if its purpose is to provide for a particular gender, religion, age, nationality or national origin. In *Equality Authority v Portmarnock Golf Club* [2009] IESC 73 the Supreme Court held a golf club which restricted membership to one gender was permitted by s 9.

The sanction against discriminating clubs is somewhat different to those generally under the Act. When a club is accused, by an individual or the Equality Authority, of discrimination the matter goes to the District Court for determination and if found to be discriminating, no certificate of registration can issue or be renewed under the Registration of Clubs Acts, 1904 to 1995, in other words the club will lose its drink licence. This is a proper sanction as such a licence is a benefit given by the State and there is no reason to allow it continue to benefit a discriminating club. It appears that other remedies under the Act can also be pursued by persons discriminated against.

11.10.2 REASONABLE ACCOMMODATION FOR THE DISABLED

One group that requires more than just formal equality is the disabled. Often, because of the disability, such persons need special provision to ensure their right to full participation in society. In this regard, ss 17, 18 and 19 cater for public transport and the disabled. Section 17 permits the Minister to make regulations to ensure that new road and rail passenger vehicles are equipped so as to be readily accessible to, and usable by, persons with a disability. Section 18 applies similar rules to bus and rail stations, while s 19 provides that local authorities shall provide dipped footpaths near pedestrian crossings, etc to facilitate disabled users. The Act does not extend its provisions to taxis and hackneys.

Throughout the Act, there are provisions that allow some special rules for promoting special interests of certain groups. Without such an express rule, special provision might itself be discriminatory, and in effect they allow for the unequal treatment of some groups, including the disabled. However, these provisions do not demand special treatment. For disabled people, s 4 is of crucial importance in this regard by providing that failure by a service provider to do all that is reasonable to accommodate a disabled person by providing special treatment or facilities, if without such it would be impossible or unduly difficult for a disabled person to avail of the service, amounts to discrimination under the Act. Section 4(2) says that a failure to provide special treatment will not be reasonable unless the provision would give rise to a cost, other than a nominal cost, to the service provider.

In *Roche v Alabaster Associates Ltd* [2002] ELR 343, a visually impaired person was refused permission to bring his guide dog into a pub. The respondent claimed that this was due to food hygiene regulations. The equality officer held that the respondent knew of the disability, did not do all that was reasonable to accommodate the needs of the claimant and that the food hygiene regulations did not compel the dog's exclusion. The pub was ordered to pay the maximum compensation under the Act to the claimant.

11.10.3 MISCELLANEOUS

Sexual and other harassment has been recognised as a serious problem in the workplace, but it may also happen in other environments. Section 12 of the Act, as amended by the Equality Act 2004, outlaws both of these. Sexual harassment occurs where one person subjects the victim to any form of unwanted verbal, non-verbal or physical conduct of a sexual nature. Harassment is similarly defined as regards the other discriminatory grounds. These are broad definitions that mirror those under the Employment Equality Act, 1998, as amended. For instance it covers not just direct sexual harassment, but also environmental harassment, eg where a club is decked with lewd pictures of naked women.

Mention should also be made of s 15, reputedly introduced at the behest of publicans. The section provides, for greater certainty, that nothing requires a service provider to provide service in circumstances which would lead a reasonable individual to the belief, on grounds other than the discriminatory grounds, that the provision of services would create a substantial risk of criminal or disorderly conduct or behaviour or damage to property.

Section 15(2) provides that actions taken in good faith by a liquor licence holder for the sole purpose of complying with the Licensing Acts, 1833 to 1999 shall not amount to discrimination. In *Maughan v The Glimmerman* (DEC-S2001–020), the claimant was refused service in a bar, which attempted to rely on this provision in its defence. The equality officer held that the respondent could not do so in circumstances where it had no previous knowledge of the claimant or his associates so a refusal could not have been made 'in good faith' for fear of breach of the licensing Acts. In *Conroy v Costello* (DEC-S2001–014), it was held that: 'In order to take an action in good faith it has to be free of any discriminatory motivation.' In *Collins v Drogheda Lodge Pub* (DEC-S2002–097/100), it was held that the issue of good faith was to be judged subjectively.

11.10.4 ENFORCEMENT

The enforcement procedures under the Act are similar to those under the Employment Equality Act and the same offices are to be used. The Equality Authority and the Director of the Equality Tribunal have a role in all Irish anti-discrimination cases.

In *Doherty v South Dublin County Council* (No. 2) [2007] 2 IR 696, it was held that rights arising under the Equal Status Act can only be enforced through the mechanisms as provided for in the Act and that no separate cause of action was created.

A person who claims to have suffered prohibited conduct must first raise the matter with the service provider within two months (in exceptional cases this time can be extended by a further two months by the Director of the Equality Tribunal). If the claimant gets an unsatisfactory response or if there is no response after one month, he or she can refer the case to the Director within six months of the incident, which can be extended in exceptional cases. The complainant must be the person who suffered the discrimination. The Equality Authority can also refer cases to the Director, where the conduct is of a general nature or where the person who suffered discrimination would not reasonably be expected to take a case. Many of the powers of the Director in investigating complaints are similar to those under the Employment Equality Act, 1998, as amended.

As noted above, claims of discrimination against pubs are now referred to the District Court; see Part 4 of the Intoxicating Liquor Act, 2003.

It should also be noted that equality officers have adopted the shifting burden of proof in making decisions under the Act in a similar manner to that employed to the non-gender grounds under the 1998 Act. In several cases, it has been stated that a claimant must prove three matters to establish a *prima facie* case of discrimination and thereby shift the burden of proof to the respondent. These are:

(a) membership of a discriminatory ground;

(b) evidence of specific treatment of the claimant by the respondent;

(c) evidence that the treatment received by the claimant was less favourable than the treatment someone not covered by that ground did or would have received in similar circumstances.

The Director is given wide powers of investigation under the Act and if satisfied that the claim is made out, can order damages up to the District Court limit, €6,348.69 (£5,000). The Director can also order that specified persons take a certain course of action designed to stop the discriminatory activity. An appeal lies from the determination of the Director to the Circuit Court, and from there to the High Court on a point of law. A decision of the Director can be enforced by the Circuit Court where a person fails to comply with it.

CHAPTER 12

DUE PROCESS AND THE RIGHT TO A FAIR TRIAL

12.1   Introduction

For many years, the rights of citizens suspected or accused of criminal offences were protected by Article 38.1 of the Constitution, which provides that *'no person shall be tried on any criminal charge save in due course of law'*. The Irish courts were able to draw, in particular, on the jurisprudence of the 'due process' guarantees of the US courts, while developing their own lines of authority.

The most trenchant expression of the concept in Irish jurisprudence is to be found in *Conroy v Attorney General* [1965] IR 411, where Kenny J observed that the phrase

'"due process of law" was adopted by those who drafted the Fifth Amendment of the Constitution of the United States of America which prevents any person being deprived of life, liberty or property without due process of law. I think that section 1 of (Article 38) gives a constitutional right to every person to be tried in accordance with the law and in accordance with due course or due process of law...'

In its nature difficult to define, the idea was expanded upon in *State (Healy) v Donoghue* [1976] IR 325 by Gannon J as 'a phrase of very wide import which includes...the application of basic principles of justice which are inherent in the proper course of the exercise of the judicial function...'

However, in the period immediately after the Second World War, significant additional sources for the protection of rights became available in the two great political documents, the (United Nations) International Covenant on Civil and Political Rights (the Covenant) and the European Convention on Human Rights and Fundamental Freedoms (the ECHR).

The relevant provisions of the Irish Constitution are examined in this chapter. The Covenant is used relatively little in this jurisdiction and its provisions are in most instances almost identical to those of the ECHR. The ECHR has been the subject of considerable interest in recent times, as a result of Ireland's incorporation of the ECHR arising from international obligations under the Good Friday Agreement (see **5.3**). The precise relationship between the Constitution and the ECHR is currently in flux. This is partly due to the very recent incorporation by way of the European Convention on Human Rights Act, 2003, but also to the apparent conflict between, on the one hand, the traditional Irish juristic approach to constitutional sovereignty and, on the other, the role of the European Court of Human Rights (ECt.HR) as, in effect, a court of final appeal on certain constitutional issues. In a nutshell, 'while the Convention applies *to* Ireland, it does not apply *within* Ireland' (O'Connell, 'Ireland', in Blackburn and Polakiewicz (eds), *Fundamental Rights in Europe: The ECHR and its Member States, 1952–2000*, 2001, OUP, 423, 425).

The Supreme Court has repeatedly rejected the notion of direct applicability of ECHR law, particularly if a case is being made that the Irish and ECHR jurisprudence are in conflict and the ECHR should prevail, as for example in *Norris v AG* [1984] IR 36. Here, the applicant was challenging the validity of criminal laws, which forbade certain homosexual acts, even between consenting adults in private, an argument which had already been accepted by the Strasbourg Court in *Dudgeon v UK* (1982) 4 EHRR 149. In the Supreme Court, the argument that the Court should take on board the *Dudgeon* judgment was dismissed by the Court, in clear terms. Henchy J remarked (at 68) that '[the European] Convention...although it has by its terms a binding force on the Government...as one of its signatories, forms no part of the domestic law of this State'.

The European Convention on Human Rights Act, 2003, provides only (at s 2(1)) that courts shall, in so far as possible, interpret the laws of the State in a manner compatible with the state's obligations under the ECHR provisions, that judicial notice shall be taken of ECHR provisions and jurisprudence (at s 4), and that the High or Supreme Courts may make a 'Declaration of Incompatibility' as between the state's laws and the ECHR (at s 5). But the *Norris* position remains unaffected, and the operation of the 'Declaration of Incompatibility' leaves untouched the offending law, and in any event is only to come into play where no other legal remedy 'is adequate and available' (s 5(1)).

This point was well illustrated in a series of challenges to s 62 of the Housing Act, 1966, as amended, where declarations of incompatibility were granted by the High Court (see, for example, *Donegan v Dublin County Council* [2008] IEHC 288). Despite clear signals from the High Court, s 62 remains in force, unamended, notwithstanding its gross shortcomings, and a succession of findings of incompatibility with both Articles 6 and 8 of the Convention, and with Article 40 of the Constitution (see the remarks of O'Neill J in *Dublin City Council v Gallagher* [2008] IEHC 354 and see **5.7**).

Further developments in relation to direct applicability are likely to arise due to the European Union proposals to legislate for a Charter of Fundamental Rights. This is dealt with in more detail at **12.7**.

12.2   Sources of the Available Protections

12.2.1   THE IRISH CONSTITUTION

Articles 34 to 37 provide in general for the administration of justice by the Courts. Article 38.1 is the key provision in relation to criminal charges, underpinned by Article 40.4.1, prohibiting detention save in accordance with law.

Article 38 provides:

> '1. *No person shall be tried on any criminal charge save in due course of law.*
> 2. *Minor offences may be tried by courts of summary jurisdiction.*
> 3. *1° Special courts may be established by law for the trial of offences in cases where it may be determined in accordance with such law that the ordinary courts are inadequate to secure the effective administration of justice and the preservation of public peace and order.*
> *2° The constitution, powers, jurisdiction and procedure of such special courts shall be prescribed by law.*
> 4. *1° Military tribunals may be established for the trial of offences against military law alleged to have been committed by persons while subject to military law and also to deal with a state of war or armed rebellion.*

> 2° *A member of the Defence Forces not on active service shall not be tried by any court-martial or other military tribunal for an offence cognisable by the civil courts unless such offence is within the jurisdiction of any court-martial or other military tribunal under any law for the enforcement of military discipline.*
>
> 5. *Save in the case of the trial of offences under section 2, section 3, or section 4 of this article, no person shall be tried on any criminal charge without a jury.*
>
> 6. *The provisions of Articles 34 and 35 of this Constitution shall not apply to any court or tribunal set up under section 3 or section 4 of this Article.'*

Article 40 provides, *inter alia*:

> '1. *All citizens shall, as human persons, be held equal before the law* . . .
>
> 3. 1° *The State guarantees in its laws to respect, and, as far as practicable, by its laws to defend and vindicate the personal rights of the citizen* . . .
>
> 4. 1° *No citizen shall be deprived of his personal liberty save in accordance with law* . . .'

12.2.2 THE EUROPEAN CONVENTION ON HUMAN RIGHTS AND FUNDAMENTAL FREEDOMS

The essential aspects, from the point of view of this chapter, are those contained in Articles 6 and 7 and the provisions of the Seventh Protocol, already signed, and soon to be ratified by Ireland.

Article 6 provides:

> '*Right to a fair trial:*
>
> 1. *In the determination of his civil rights and obligations or of any criminal charge against him, everyone is entitled to a fair and public hearing within a reasonable time by an independent and impartial tribunal established by law. Judgment shall be pronounced publicly, but the press and public may be excluded from all or part of the trial in the interests of morals, public order or national security in a democratic society, where the interests of juveniles or the protection of the private life of the parties so require, or to the extent strictly necessary in the opinion of the court in special circumstances where publicity would prejudice the interests of justice.*
>
> 2. *Everyone charged with a criminal offence shall be presumed innocent until proved guilty according to law.*
>
> 3. *Everyone charged with a criminal offence has the following minimum rights:*
>
>   (a) *to be informed promptly, in a language which he understands, and in detail, of the nature and cause of the accusation against him;*
>
>   (b) *to have adequate time and facilities for the preparation of his defence;*
>
>   (c) *to defend himself in person or through legal assistance of his own choosing or, if he has not sufficient means to pay for legal assistance, to be given it free when the interests of justice so require;*
>
>   (d) *to examine or have examined witnesses against him and to obtain the attendance and examination of witnesses on his behalf under the same conditions as witnesses against him;*
>
>   (e) *to have the free assistance of an interpreter if he cannot understand or speak the language used in court.'*

Article 7 provides:

> '*No punishment without law.*
>
> 1. *No one shall be held guilty of any criminal offence on account of any act or omission which did not constitute a criminal offence under national or international law at the time when it was committed. Nor shall a heavier penalty be imposed than the one which was applicable at the time the criminal offence was committed.*

2. *This Article shall not prejudice the trial and punishment of any person for any act or omission which, at the time when it was committed, was criminal according to the general principles of law recognised by civilised nations.'*

Insofar as it is relevant to this chapter, the Seventh Protocol provides as follows:

'Article 2—Right of appeal in criminal matters
1. *Everyone convicted of a criminal offence by a tribunal shall have the right to have his conviction or sentence reviewed by a higher tribunal. The exercise of this right, including the grounds on which it may be exercised, shall be governed by law.*
2. *This right may be subject to exceptions in regard to offences of a minor character, as prescribed by law, or in cases in which the person concerned was tried in the first instance by the highest tribunal or was convicted following an appeal against acquittal.*

Article 3—Compensation for wrongful conviction
When a person has by a final decision been convicted of a criminal offence and when subsequently his conviction has been reversed, or he has been pardoned, on the ground that a new or newly discovered fact shows conclusively that there has been a miscarriage of justice, the person who has suffered punishment as a result of such conviction shall be compensated according to the law or the practice of the State concerned, unless it is proved that the non-disclosure of the unknown fact in time is wholly or partly attributable to him.

Article 4—Right not to be tried or punished twice
1. *No one shall be liable to be tried or punished again in criminal proceedings under the jurisdiction of the same State for an offence for which he has already been finally acquitted or convicted in accordance with the law and penal procedure of that State.*
2. *The provisions of the preceding paragraph shall not prevent the reopening of the case in accordance with the law and penal procedure of the State concerned, if there is evidence of new or newly-discovered facts, or if there has been a fundamental defect in the previous proceedings, which could affect the outcome of the case.*
3. *No derogation from this Article shall be made under Article 15 of the Convention.'*

12.2.3 THE CONSTITUTION AND THE ECHR

The broad thrust of both the ECHR and the Constitution is similar, but the ECHR jurisprudence is both wider and more detailed in scope than the Irish equivalent. This is hardly surprising, given that all of the major western European countries have subscribed to the ECHR for many years, and have contributed law, lawyers and judges to the collective resolution of human rights issues for a generation, with an acknowledgement of the special character of human rights legislation, which calls for a generous approach to interpretation.

Both Irish and ECHR jurisprudence has tended, perhaps not surprisingly, to focus mainly on the 'due process' formalities of criminal procedure and trials, but it is clear from the authorities that the guarantees extend, as appropriate, to civil matters. In *Airey v Ireland* (1979–80) 2 EHRR 305, for example, the ECt.HR, sitting at Strasbourg, imposed on Ireland an obligation to institute a system of civil legal aid for separation proceedings, its absence being found by the ECt.HR as an interference with the applicant's right of effective access to the courts.

The Irish Supreme Court, while in many ways not an especially conservative institution, has suffered from the traditional restrictions placed on, or assumed by, judges in the common law tradition. In contrast, the ECHR jurisprudence is constantly developing and, unlike the traditional common law approach, the court is not bound by previous decisions. As a living instrument, which must be interpreted in the light of present day conditions, the ECHR has evolved significantly, particularly as regards the appearance of fairness in the administration of justice. In *Airey v Ireland*, the case referred to above, which effectively imposed a civil legal aid system on Ireland, it was said that the ECHR 'is intended to guarantee not rights that are theoretical and illusory but rights that are practical and effective.'

Many of the 'rights' conferred by the ECHR also contain limitations (see, for example, Articles 8 to 11). Any interference with rights must be justified by the State in the context of the permissible restrictions contained in each Article. The onus will be on the State to show that the restrictions were, firstly, appropriately prescribed by law, and secondly, necessary in a democratic society. Exceptions to the rights 'must be narrowly interpreted' (*Sunday Times v UK* (1980) 2 EHRR 245).

Both of the Strasbourg institutions, that is the Court and the now-abolished Commission, as well as a number of common law countries, have to a greater extent than Ireland, acknowledged a guiding principle of human rights law interpretation, such as is suitable to give to individuals the full measure of the fundamental rights and freedoms referred to therein. New Zealand courts, for example, have long acknowledged that human rights legislation has a 'special character' which calls for a 'broad and purposive approach to construction' (*R v Goodwin (No.1)* [1993] 2 NZL 153).

A further yardstick, the principle of proportionality, which the court considers in assessing the validity of any restriction of rights, involves balancing the demands of the community and the protection of the fundamental rights of individuals. Article 18 further prohibits states applying permissible restrictions to purposes outside those prescribed by the Convention. There is a margin of appreciation, that is, in the field of social and moral policy each state has or may have different standards, which will inform how states deal with particular issues of a human rights nature.

Domestic courts, which are signatories to the Convention, and which are considering questions that have arisen in relation to asserted ECHR Rights, are required to take into account decisions of the Strasbourg Court and the Commission, but the Irish Supreme Court, for technically sound reasons, has refused consistently to afford Convention law what observers would describe as full weight (see O'Connell, 'Ireland', in Blackburn and Polakiewicz (eds), *Fundamental Rights in Europe: The ECHR and its Member States 1952–2000*, 2001, OUP, 423).

Among the general principles previously established by the Court and Commission are those that the Convention 'is an instrument designed to maintain and promote the ideals and values of a democratic society'. Critical features of such a society are 'pluralism, tolerance and broadmindedness' and 'respect for the rule of law' (see *Dudgeon v UK* (1982) 4 EHRR 149).

12.3 Specific Due Process Protections

12.3.1 WHAT PROCEEDINGS ARE PROTECTED?

The whole of Article 6 refers to the determination of criminal charges, but Article 6(1) also applies to civil rights and obligations. Put simply, Article 6(1) entitles everyone to a fair and public hearing within a reasonable time by an independent and impartial tribunal established by law. The Court has traditionally interpreted this Article broadly on the grounds that it is of fundamental importance to the operation of democracy. When assessing if the rights of an applicant have been protected, the Court will have regard to the proceedings as a whole, including any appeal, and the extent to which such appeal may have corrected defects in the first instance proceedings (*Edwards v UK* (1993) 15 EHRR 417). Considering that the right to the fair administration of justice holds such a prominent place, the restrictive interpretation of Article 6(1) would not correspond to the aim and purpose of that provision (*Delcourt v Belgium* (1979) 1 EHRR 355).

When considering if any 'proceedings' are civil or criminal, the ECHR takes an 'autonomous approach'. It will disregard any categorisation of a matter as civil by the State, if the nature of the alleged offence and the severity of any penalty imply that the matter should properly be regarded as criminal. This is similar to the Irish approach, as exemplified in *Melling v O'Mathghamhna* [1962] IR 1—the real question to be determined is whether at the conclusion of the proceedings, there is a punitive sanction.

Although criminal proceedings receive special and distinct due process protection under Article 38 of the Constitution, this is only to be expected given the special role of the State in the prosecution of criminal offences against individuals. However, Articles 34, 35 and 36 make clear the determination of the Irish state to provide for an independent and impartial judiciary, administering justice in public in all cases, civil and criminal.

12.3.2   EQUALITY OF ARMS

'Equality of arms' is the most important principle of Article 6 as developed by the case-law. It postulates the idea that each party to a proceeding should have equal opportunity to present a side of the case and that neither should enjoy any substantial advantage over his opponent. Obviously, the right to legal representation in appropriate cases flows from this requirement. One of the most important Irish human rights cases, which is the authority for a number of human rights entitlements, arises from this issue. In *State (Healy) v Donoghue* [1976] IR 325, the Supreme Court formally acknowledged the right to legal assistance, and in the case under consideration, the right to state-funded legal aid, as being central to the concept of due course of law and a fair trial.

Although *State (Healy) v Donoghue* concerned itself with the defence entitlements in criminal proceedings, it had long been argued that the right to state-funded representation went much further than that, a view which was vindicated in *Magee v Farrell* [2005] IEHC 388). Relying entirely on constitutional grounds, as the complaint pre-dated the incorporation of the ECHR, Gilligan J held that the applicant was entitled to legal aid for the purpose of being represented at the inquest into her son's death which occurred in Garda (police) custody.

In a very recent case, the Supreme Court considered what was required to be provided by the State, by way of legal representation, to ensure 'parity of representation', which the Court, in its judgment, was at pains to stress was not synonymous with 'equality of arms'. *Carmody v Minister for Justice, Equality and Law Reform* [2009] IESC 71 concerned a challenge, on both Constitutional and ECHR grounds, to the provisions of the Criminal Justice (Legal Aid) Act, 1962, s 2(1), which provided for legal aid only by a solicitor in the District Court (see **5.7**). The Prosecution were represented by solicitor and counsel, in what was an admittedly complex and unusual case. The applicant, Mr Carmody, argued that this placed him in an inferior position in relation to his defence, and argued that the Act was bad in that it failed to provide for representation by counsel in any case, no matter how complicated. The Court, in a preliminary procedural ruling, decided that where Constitution and ECHR challenges were raised, a court should deal first with the constitutional question.

In deciding the point at issue, the Court placed heavy reliance on *Healy v Donoghue* (above). The Court declined to strike down the Act, but granted the applicant, on very narrow grounds, and in a judgment mainly expressed in the negative, a remedy—that he should be entitled to apply for representation by counsel, and have that application determined, prior to the case against him continuing. Necessarily, of course, some form of legislative change will be required to meet the ruling of the court.

What Casey (*Constitutional Law in Ireland*, 3rd edn, 2000, Round Hall, Sweet and Maxwell, 517) describes as 'the general overarching criterion of fairness' is the touchstone of Irish authorities in this area. Bearing in mind the overall discretion of trial judges, such discretion must be exercised 'within constitutional parameters' and in the light of overall fairness. Obviously, such a concept cannot be exhaustively defined, but in, for example, *DPP v Doyle* [1994] 2 IR 286, the Supreme Court found an obligation on the prosecution to disclose statements to the defence in summary trials of indictable offences, if the interests of justice demand it.

The ECt.HR has already held that it would be a breach of the principle where an expert witness appointed by the defence is not accorded the same facilities as one appointed by the prosecution (*Bonisch v Austria* (1987) 9 EHRR 191). Similar principles oblige prosecuting and investigating authorities to disclose any material in their possession which may assist the accused in exonerating himself or which may undermine the credibility of a prosecution witness (*Jespers v Belgium* (1981) 27 DR 61).

In *JF v DPP* [2005] IESC 24 a prosecution was prohibited when the complainant in a sexual assault case refused to undergo examination (in relation to the delay in making a complaint) by the defence psychologist, while simultaneously the DPP wished to adduce evidence from the State-appointed psychologist as to the reasons for the delay as outlined to him by the complainant. The Court found that the situation violated both Irish constitutional and ECHR principles.

12.3.3   EVIDENCE AND FAIR TRIAL PROCEDURES

Broadly speaking, the rules of evidence are a matter for each contracting state, although the ECt.HR will exceptionally examine whether the proceedings as a whole were fair or assess the weight of the evidence before a national court. Perhaps surprisingly, the Court has held that Article 6 does not necessarily require the exclusion of illegally obtained evidence. This contrasts with states that operate a strict 'exclusionary rule', which *prima facie* rules out evidence obtained in consequence of breaches of rights.

The Supreme Court has dealt with this issue by establishing two categories of rights capable of being infringed in the collection of evidence, legal rights and constitutional rights. The two are not always readily distinguishable. In broad terms, the courts will incline away from admitting evidence obtained in breach of a constitutional right, save in 'extraordinary excusing circumstances' (*People (AG) v O'Brien* [1965] IR 142). Where evidence is obtained in breach of a mere legal right, such evidence shall be admissible 'unless the Court in its discretion excludes it' (*per* the Supreme Court in *DPP v McMahon* [1986] IR 393).

A review of the exclusionary rule, by a rare seven judge Supreme Court, may be pending. Depending on the outcome of the court's deliberations on a preliminary point, the court may move to a reconsideration of the rule in the second stage of *DPP v Cash* [2007] IEHC 108, heard at first instance by Charleton J in the High Court, and at the time of going to print, adjourned in the Supreme Court. A careful analysis of the authorities in the High Court led Charleton J to the conclusion that the time was right for such a review.

12.3.4   PREJUDICIAL PUBLICITY

Particularly if a case is to be tried by a jury, 'a virulent press campaign against the accused' is capable of violating the right to a fair trial (*X v Austria* 11 CD 31 1963). However, the Court will take account of the fact that some comment by the press on a trial involving a matter of public interest is inevitable and will also consider what steps the judge has taken to counter the effect of the prejudice in his charge to the jury.

The Irish judges have been very slow to prohibit cases from proceeding, because of adverse pre-trial publicity. In particular, in *Z v DPP* [1994] 2 IR 476, concerning the trial of the alleged rapist of a young girl who had been at the centre of the *Attorney General v X* [1992] 1 IR 1 case which had attracted enormous national and international publicity, the Supreme Court permitted the trial to proceed subject to appropriate safeguards in the form of warnings to the jury. However, a temporary stay was afforded the defendant, a former Taoiseach, in *DPP v Haughey (No. 2)* [2001] IR 162, for similar reasons, while the applicant in *Magee v O'Dea* [1994] 1 IR 500 succeeded in avoiding extradition to the United Kingdom because of adverse publicity in that jurisdiction.

12.3.5 REASONS FOR A DECISION

It is a basic requirement of a fair trial in both civil and criminal cases that courts should give reasons for their judgments. Common law decisions such as *Breen v Amalgamated Engineering Union* [1971] 2 QB 175 have been given ready acceptance in Ireland in such cases as *Kinahan v Minister for Justice, Equality and Law Reform*, 21 February 2001, Supreme Court (unreported). In *McAlister v Minister for Justice, Equality and Law Reform* [2003] 1 ILRM 161, Finnegan P stated that 'it is important that justice should be seen to be done and this will very often require that a person affected by a decision should know why that particular decision has been taken....' This does not apply to jury trials.

Where a submission to the court in the course of a trial would, if accepted, be decisive of the outcome of the case, it must be specifically and expressly addressed in a ruling by the Court (*Hiro Bilani v Spain* (1995) 19 EHRR 566).

12.3.6 THE RIGHT TO A PUBLIC HEARING

The fundamental entitlement to a hearing in public is designed to protect litigants from 'the administration of justice in secret with no public scrutiny' and to maintain public confidence in the courts and in the administration of justice (*Pretto v Italy* (1984) 6 EHRR 182). For these reasons, only in exceptional circumstances can the press be excluded. This provision is mirrored in Article 34.1 of the Constitution, providing as it does for justice to 'be administered in public'. Article 34.1 actually limits this proviso to allow for private sittings of the courts in circumstances prescribed by law, but those categories of cases which are so heard in private, mainly involving family law, tend to be heard out of the public gaze by general consent.

12.3.7 THE ENTITLEMENT TO TRIAL WITHIN A REASONABLE TIME

Of particular interest in Ireland is the right to trial within a reasonable time. There are frequent complaints from litigants, the media and indeed many of the judges about the delays in getting cases on for trial in the higher criminal courts in particular. Deriving, again, in part from *State (Healy) v Donoghue* [1976] IR 325 where it was described as 'the right to trial with reasonable expedition', the question has repeatedly been brought before the appellate courts over the last 20 or so years. One issue which has been addressed is the right to early trial of summary offences.

Many appellate decisions have dealt with this question, and the leading authority now is *DPP v Byrne* [2005] 2 IR 310 where Peart J in the High Court reviewed and considered the authorities, introduced the concept of 'system delay', fixed the State, blameworthy or not with full responsibility for delays within the prosecutorial and court systems, and obliged the prosecution to explain any such delays prior to a case continuing for hearing. The High Court held that the right to a trial in accordance with the law, which included the right to an expeditious trial, was independent of the right to a fair trial.

The other major issue, which has frequently arisen, is the circumstances in which prosecutions should be prohibited where the alleged offences were committed many years ago. Here, the reason for the delay has generally been the absence of any complaint for a number of years, occasionally decades. The early leading authority was *B v DPP* [1997] 3 IR 140, where the trial of alleged offences between 20 and 30 years old was allowed to continue, notwithstanding the Supreme Court finding '...an inordinate delay...' in the making of the complaint. The Court found as highly relevant the fact that the alleged perpetrator was in a dominant position vis-à-vis the complainants, who felt unable to report the allegations of sexual abuse until many years later. This led the Court to emphasise the community's right to proceed with the prosecution.

However, in *O'C v DPP* [2000] 3 IR 87, another case dealing with sexual offences, the Court prohibited a case of similar age, on the basis that evidence which was, or may have been, available to the defence had the complaint been promptly made, and which might have helped to refute it, was by virtue of the delay no longer available.

Many years, and appellate cases later, the Supreme Court, in *H v DPP* [2006] IESC 55, reviewed all of the relevant jurisprudence in this area, and gave a definitive pronouncement of the position. The Court held that, in general, there was no necessity to hold an enquiry into the reasons for the delay in making the complaint. The issue, the Court held, was whether the delay had resulted in prejudice to an accused so as to give rise to a real or serious risk of an unfair trial, acknowledging that there may be 'wholly exceptional circumstances' where it would be unjust or unfair to put the accused on trial. Within a few months, in *MG v DPP* [2007] IESC 4, the Supreme Court indeed found such exceptional circumstances, where it was evident that the complainant had persistently attempted to blackmail the alleged perpetrator of sexual abuse. The Court prohibited the trial on the basis that the complainant had used the threat of proceedings and publicity as a means for extracting private pecuniary gain. *Per* Fennelly J:

> 'This is an unprecedented situation. If the Appellant's case were to be considered as one based on delay alone or on prosecutorial behaviour alone, it would not succeed. However, I am of opinion that this Court should be slow to permit the criminal courts to be used as an instrument of blackmail. This is a matter of public policy. In most cases, improper demands by a witness would not provide a basis for halting a prosecution. However, the sole witness in respect of each alleged offence has consistently sought to use the threat of exposure to criminal prosecution, and thus the courts themselves, as a means of extracting private pecuniary benefit.

> I believe that this exceptional element means that it would be wrong and unjust to put the Appellant on trial on any of the charges.'

In a European context, the entitlement to trial within a reasonable time is intended to prevent a person charged from remaining 'too long in a state of uncertainty about his fate' (*Stogmuller v Austria* (1979) 1 EHRR 155). The reasonable time guarantee runs from the time an individual is charged. What constitutes a 'reasonable time' is extremely flexible and there are no absolute time limits set by the ECHR or by ECt.HR jurisprudence. A more rigorous standard theoretically applies when the defendant is in custody.

A good example of this approach was *Barry v Ireland* (Application No. 18273/2004, judgment of December 15, 2005—see **4.6**), where an elderly doctor had sought remedies, in the domestic courts, relating to criminal complaints against him, including an application for prohibition based on delay. After over six years, he failed in his action. However, the delays within the system in the domestic courts, including lengthy periods awaiting reserved judgments, were such as to entitle him to a declaration by the ECt.HR that his entitlement to trial within a reasonable time had been violated.

ECt.HR law also makes the State responsible for delays attributable either to the prosecution or the court but suggests that understandable delays may arise from complex cases including numerous defendants or charges or where unusually difficult legal issues arise. It remains an unfortunate fact of legal life that delays, and cases involving the alleged effect of delays, continue both to bedevil the legal system, and to exercise the minds of the appellate judiciary. For a helpful and extensive exposition of the issues, see the judgment of Kearns J, in the Supreme Court in *McFarlane v DPP* [2008] IESC 7. The facts of that case led to an application which is currently pending before the ECt.HR.

12.3.8 'BY AN INDEPENDENT TRIBUNAL'

Trial 'by an independent tribunal' is a fundamental tenet of human rights law. It is recognised in Article 6 ECHR, providing as it does for trial, either civil or criminal, by an independent and impartial tribunal established by law, in the Irish Constitution, as aforementioned (see **12.3.1** above), and in common law principles of natural justice, all of which contribute to this cornerstone of any legal system. In the leading Irish case, *People (AG) v Singer* [1975] IR 408, the foreman of the jury in a fraud trial had been a minor victim of the fraud. The conviction, not surprisingly, was set aside. As to the ECt.HR, in *Hauschildt v Denmark* (1990) 12 EHRR 266, the Court observed that:

> '...even appearances may be of a certain importance...what is at stake is public confidence in the courts...accordingly, any judge in respect of whom there is a legitimate reason to fear a lack of impartiality must withdraw....'

12.3.9 THE PROTECTION AGAINST SELF-INCRIMINATION AND THE RIGHT TO SILENCE

The common law principle of the protection against self-incrimination and the right to silence receives its most profound endorsement in the Fifth Amendment of the US Constitution. In Ireland, the Supreme Court held the right to be not only a common law right but also a constitutional right, which might, however, be validly limited by legislation (*O'Leary v AG* [1995] 1 IR 254).

There has, indeed, been a series of statutory encroachments, including the Criminal Justice Act, 1984, the Criminal Justice (Drug Trafficking) Act, 1998 and the Offences Against the State (Amendment) Act, 1998 and more recently in the Criminal Justice Act, 2007, and the Criminal Justice (Amendment) Act, 2009, both of the latter passing into law against a backdrop of significant controversy, all of which provide for adverse inferences to be drawn against a suspect who declines to answer questions while being questioned in Garda custody. In *Rock v Ireland* [1997] 3 IR 484, the Supreme Court affirmed a 'proportionality test', balancing the suspect's right to avoid self-incrimination with the State's right to protect life, person and the property of citizens. It is significant in the judgment that the inferences that may be drawn could not themselves form the basis for a conviction but were merely capable of corroborating other evidence. A similar approach has been maintained by the ECt.HR, in such cases as *Murray v UK* (1996) 22 EHRR 29.

A similar issue arose in a different form in the *Quinn v Ireland* (Application No. 36887/1997) and *Heaney & McGuinness v Ireland* (Application No. 34720/1997) cases. In both cases, the suspects had refused to answer questions when being questioned under s 52 of the Offences Against the State Act, 1939, such a refusal constituting an offence in itself. The Supreme Court upheld the legislation as constitutionally valid, relying on the entitlement of the community to have crime properly investigated and/or detected.

The ECt.HR took a different view, holding that 'the right not to incriminate oneself, in particular, presupposes that the prosecution in a criminal case seeks to prove their case against the accused without resort to evidence by obtained methods of coercion or oppression in defiance of the will of the accused'.

Yet another related issue was considered in the Irish courts in *In Re National Irish Bank* [1999] 1 ILRM 321, concerning ss 10 and 18 of the Companies Act, 1990. Here, officials of the Bank were compelled to answer questions under s 10, failure to do so being a criminal offence. Section 18 went on to provide that answers given under penalty by virtue of s 10 could then be used as evidence in a criminal prosecution of the same individual under s 18. Relying on the 'balancing of rights' argument, the Supreme Court found that bank officials could not invoke the privilege against self-incrimination to refuse to answer questions put under s 10. The separate, but obviously related, question, as to the admissibility of any s 10 admissions in any subsequent trial for an offence under s 18 was, in effect, reserved to a future trial judge, with a reminder from the Supreme Court that admissions could only be admitted against an accused if they were shown to be voluntary. This is presumably a difficult task for the prosecution if answers were extracted under threat of penalty at the time of the making of the s 10 demand.

Similar UK legislation was impugned as a breach of Article 6 ECHR in *Saunders v UK* (1997) 23 EHRR 313. The Court found a violation of Article 6. In the case itself, a senior company executive was compelled by one government agency to furnish information about the way in which the company conducted its business, which resulted in him incriminating himself. The government then turned the information obtained over to prosecuting authorities to be used in criminal proceedings subsequently brought against him. In the domestic courts, he failed in his argument that the admissions should not be used against him. He appealed to the ECt.HR, where he was successful. The Court has generally considered that the right to silence and the right not to incriminate oneself are universally recognised international standards lying at the heart of the idea of fair procedures. The right to a fair trial in a criminal case includes 'the right of anyone charged with a criminal offence . . . to remain silent and not to contribute to incriminating himself' (*Funke v France* (1993) 16 EHRR 297). In the *Saunders* case, the Court held that the privilege against self-incrimination was 'closely linked' to the 'presumption of innocence'.

However, different considerations have been held by the Court to apply to laws permitting the drawing of adverse inferences from the silence of suspects under interrogation who subsequently become accused at trial (see *Murray v UK* above). This is consistent with the Supreme Court's approach as considered above.

Following conviction in the (non-jury) Special Criminal Court on a charge of murder, there is, pending before the Court of Criminal Appeal, a case which may develop the law on inferences in this jurisdiction to a clearer extent than hitherto (*DPP v Gerard Macken*, unreported). *Macken* was a rare first-instance exposition of 'inferences' provisions (in this case, the 2007 Criminal Justice Act), being given a substantial airing as part of the prosecution case. It is notable that the ECt.HR continues to emphasise both the right to remain silent and to early access to legal advice for suspects, as foundation stones of due process in criminal cases. This, despite the ruling in *Murray* (above), is likely to provide difficulties for Ireland, at some point, and possibly in the *Macken* case in the long run, bearing in mind particularly the State's continuing refusal to provide for legal advice throughout questioning in the Garda station (see the *Lavery* case, at **12.4.2** below). For an interesting recent insight into the ECt.HR's thinking, see *Pishchalnikov v Russia*, Application No. 7025/2004, judgment of 24 September 2009.

12.3.10 THE PRESUMPTION OF INNOCENCE

An absolute minimum requirement of the common law systems, the presumption of innocence, is another fundamental guarantee of Article 6 ECHR. In the ECHR jurisprudence, it applies only to persons who are charged and has no application at the time of investigation into alleged offences. However, provided that the overall burden of proof of guilt remains on the prosecution, Article 6(2) does not prohibit rules, which transfer aspects of the burden of proof to the accused and presumptions of law or fact operating against the accused are permitted. However, such rules, either shifting the burden of proof or applying presumptions against the accused, must 'be confined within reasonable limits' (*Salabiaku v France* (1988) 13 EHRR 379).

In Irish constitutional law, the existence of the right to the presumption of innocence has been stated. Deriving from the US Constitution, it received endorsement relatively late in Irish law, in *People (AG) v O'Callaghan* [1966] IR 501, but has frequently been repeated since then in judicial pronouncements. As in the ECt.HR, the Irish courts have permitted some limited evidential encroachments on the presumption, which are admitted in the relevant cases as shifting an evidential burden on to the accused (see for example *Hardy v Ireland*, 18 March 1993, Supreme Court (unreported)). The Supreme Court has justified its approach by emphasising that at all times, the legal burden of proof remains with the prosecution.

12.4   Specific Guarantees to Ensure Fairness in Criminal Trials Provided by the ECHR

Specific guarantees to ensure fairness in criminal trials are of the utmost importance and are contained in Article 6(3) and the Seventh Protocol. Most, if not all of these are mirrored by Irish constitutional provisions.

12.4.1   THE RIGHT TO KNOW THE DETAILS OF THE CHARGE

An accused person has a right to be informed of the charge against him, in a language he understands, and in detail. This principle is concerned with what the accused must be told at the time of charge, rather than with the disclosure of evidence in the course of the preparation for the trial itself (*Brozicek v Italy* (1990) 12 EHRR 371).

In a more recent case, also originating in Italy, an accused person, tried entirely in absentia, was held to have his Article 6 rights violated, notwithstanding the appointment of a lawyer to represent his interests. The accused was never advised of the charges against him, nor of the evidence, never had any contact with his lawyers, and never had any participation in the trial. He was blameless in this regard, as he was never traced by the authorities at any stage of the investigation (*Sejdovic v Italy*, Application No. 56581/2000, judgment of 1 March 2006).

12.4.2   THE RIGHT TO REPRESENTATION AND TO LEGAL AID

The accused must be given adequate time and facilities for the preparation of a defence. Obviously, the adequacy of the time allowed will depend upon the complexity of the case. The Court has seen it as fundamental that a defence lawyer must be appointed in sufficient time to allow the case to be properly prepared (*X and Y v Austria* [1978] 12 DR 160). The requirement to afford adequate facilities for the preparation of the defence case obliges the State to adopt such measures as will place the defence on an equal footing with the prosecution (*Jespers v Belgium* (1981) 27 DR 61).

Article 6(3)(c) provides an accused with the right to represent himself in person or should he wish it, through legal assistance of his own choosing. It also provides that an accused may have legal assistance provided free of charge, if the interests of justice require it and he does not have sufficient means to pay for a lawyer. This is part of the 'equality of arms' set of rights discussed briefly above. States may however, place 'reasonable restrictions' on the right of an accused to counsel of his choice, although as a general rule, the accused's choice of lawyer should be respected (*Goddi v Italy* (1984) 6 EHRR 457). There must be good reason for excluding a lawyer from the court, such as a breach of professional ethics.

Irish constitutional law appears to go further. In *State (Freeman) v Connellan* [1986] IR 433, a judge in the District Court refused to assign the applicant the legal aid solicitor of his own choosing. The High Court held that the applicant could only be refused the solicitor of choice if 'there is good and sufficient reason why the applicant should be deprived of . . . (the solicitor's . . .) services.' In order that the requirements of Article 6(3)(c) are met, representation provided by the State must be effective. The State will not generally be responsible for the inadequacies of a legal aid lawyer, but the authorities may be required to intervene where 'the failure to provide effective representation is manifest' and it has been brought to their attention. A lawyer appointed by the Court against the express wish of the accused will, generally, be 'incompatible with the notion of a fair trial . . . if it lacks relevant and sufficient justification . . .' (*Croissant v Germany* (1993) 16 EHRR 135).

In one specific instance however, Article 6 sits uneasily with the current state of the law in Ireland. *Lavery v The Member in Charge, Carrickmacross Garda Station* [1999] 2 IR 390, following on from a similar approach in *DPP v Pringle* (1981) 2 Frewen 57, expressly removed the entitlement for a solicitor to be present throughout detention or even during interviews in the investigative stages of a case. The Supreme Court may unwittingly have underestimated the significance, in terms of an investigation, of this period of detention. That significance was underlined in *DPP v Buck* [2002] 2 IR 268 where a suspect was arrested on a Sunday afternoon and requested a solicitor. Notwithstanding the difficulties in getting access to a solicitor, the suspect was questioned for a substantial period of time by relays of Gardaí before getting access to a solicitor. The Supreme Court found no violation of the applicant's constitutional rights, placing substantial reliance on the trial judge's findings that there were no conscious and deliberate violations of the applicant's right of access to a solicitor. The trial judge also found, and it was held to be significant, that there was no causative link between any breach of the applicant's constitutional rights and the making of the incriminating admissions.

Article 6(3)(c) ECHR has also been interpreted as requiring confidentiality of communications between detained persons and their lawyers, the ECt.HR citing such confidentiality as 'one of the basic requirements of a fair trial in a democratic society' (*S v Switzerland* (1992) 14 EHRR 670).

The vexed question of 'adequacy of counsel', a major plank of appeal in the United States, particularly in death penalty cases, is now starting to emerge in Europe, and indeed in Ireland. In the cases of *DPP v Paul Lynch* (CCA 27/7/1999) and *DPP v John Bartley* (unreported), the Court of Criminal Appeal opened the door for the proposition that an inadequately, or badly, represented accused may, as part of the appeal process, be entitled to have their convictions set aside and a retrial ordered. (On the facts of the two cases, Lynch's appeal failed and Bartley's succeeded.) However, the ECt.HR may be prepared to impose a heavier burden on states. In *Sannino v Italy* (Application No. 30961/03, judgment of 27 April 2006), the domestic Court had assigned counsel to represent the accused. The lawyer had been absent from Court for a number of hearings, had not called defence witnesses, and 'had not the slightest knowledge of the case . . .' Although the accused had made no contemporaneous complaint, the Court found that 'given the patent shortcomings of the assigned counsel, it had been incumbent on the authorities to intervene', and found that the accused's Article 6 rights had been violated.

12.4.3 THE RIGHT TO CONFRONT PROSECUTION WITNESSES

Controversy in the area of the right to confront prosecution witnesses has tended to revolve around questions of hearsay and anonymity of witnesses. Broadly, hearsay evidence is not admissible, but the Strasbourg Court has allowed some flexibility in the admissibility of ordinarily prohibited hearsay evidence, where it is based on a statutory provision, which is accompanied by safeguards (see for example *Trivedi v UK* Application No. 31700/96, 27 May 1977). However, the Court will incline away from approving rules of evidence, which do not permit, at some stage, cross-examination (*Kostovski v Netherlands* (1989) 12 EHRR 434).

The Court has held that ordinarily witnesses should not remain anonymous, as ignorance of their identity may deprive the defence of particulars that would enable them to demonstrate that the witness is prejudiced, hostile or unreliable. However, in exceptional circumstances, arrangements to preserve the anonymity of a witness could in principle be justified if there was an identifiable threat to the life or physical safety of the witness. Although such evidence is admissible in restrictive circumstances, the evidence should still be treated with 'extreme care' and a conviction should not be based 'solely or to a decisive extent' on evidence given anonymously (*Doorsen v Netherlands* (1996) 22 EHRR 330).

Clearly, the ECt.HR will treat each case in this field on its merits. Two contrasting recent cases illustrate the point. In *Sapunarescu v Germany* (Application No. 22007/03, decision of 11 September 2006), an informer in a drugs case testified by written statement, and was also cross-examined by written question and answer at the trial. Clearly, the position was some way short of the ideal. The State argued that the informer's identity should not be disclosed for fear of reprisals. The accused was also alleged to have confessed, and the informer issue was to establish a defence of agent provocateur, a defence which, it seems, was not without substance. However the Court found that the conduct of the case by the domestic Court, taken as a whole, did not violate the applicant's Article 6 rights. By contrast, the Court inclined the other way in *Krasniki v Czech Republic* (Application No. 51277/99, judgment of 28 February 2006), also a drugs case, where one witness for the prosecution testified anonymously, and a second, absent entirely from the trial, had her written statement admitted into evidence. The conviction was based solely on the evidence of the two witnesses. The ECt.HR held that, absent convincing explanations for the alleged fear of reprisals and the reasons for granting anonymity, taken with the fact that the questionable evidence had been decisive in the finding of the domestic court, had violated the applicant's rights and his appeal succeeded.

Ireland has stuck fairly resolutely to the hearsay rule, allowing, in the main, only the accepted common law exceptions. This is a regular feature of jurisdictions where the courtroom tradition of oral examination of witnesses and legal argument predominates. As to the anonymity of witnesses, this is extremely rare in Ireland. Recent legislation has provided for the taking of evidence by video-link, mainly in cases alleging sexual offences against young victims, but this is solely to remove the complainant from the oppressive atmosphere of the court and the witness is available for cross-examination in the ordinary way.

12.4.4 THE RIGHT TO FREE INTERPRETATION

The right to free interpretation is of increasing importance as the population of non-nationals residing in Ireland is growing. It is clearly an essential part of any system of justice that parties to the proceedings should be able to follow and properly participate in, those proceedings, if necessary through an interpreter. However the Supreme Court was proactive in its determination on this issue at an early stage, describing the right as 'one of the fundamental principles of the administration of . . . justice . . .', and to disregard it would mean that any conviction obtained in breach 'could not possibly stand in any court of law . . .' (*State (Buchan) v Coyne* 70 ILTR 185).

Likewise, Article 6(3)(e) ECHR provides that the accused has the right to the free assistance of an interpreter if he cannot understand or speak the language used in court. This is part of the state's obligation to run its judicial system fairly. The right is unqualified. A charged or convicted person cannot therefore be ordered to pay the costs of an interpreter. Although there is no recorded instance of an assertion of this right in civil proceedings, identical considerations will presumably apply, whether a case is taken in the Irish courts or the Strasbourg Court, as to the entitlement of a litigant to free interpretation services in appropriate cases.

12.4.5 THE PROSECUTION'S DUTY OF DISCLOSURE

In the context of ECt.HR jurisprudence, there is much overlap between the specific guarantees of Article 6(3) ECHR and the principles of 'equality of arms'. An issue gaining increasing importance in Ireland, the duty of disclosure imposed on the prosecution, has already been adjudicated upon by the Commission in *Jespers v Belgium* (1981) 27 DR 61 (see **12.3.2** above). Here, it was decided that the authorities, whether investigating or prosecuting, must disclose to the defence any material in their possession, or to which they could gain access, which may assist the accused in exonerating himself or in obtaining a lighter sentence. This was extended in *Edwards v UK* (1993) 15 EHRR 417 to include material that might be of assistance in undermining the credibility of a prosecution witness.

Recent Irish cases appear wholeheartedly to embrace the ECt.HR European standard. In *Braddish v DPP* [2001] 3 IR 127, Hardiman J prohibited a retrial from taking place when it emerged that a videotape purporting to have recorded a robbery in which the accused could be identified as a participant had in fact been returned to its owner, who had subsequently erased it. The prosecution were relying, instead, on a disputed confession statement. The Court reviewed the common law authorities and found that the Gardaí had a right to seize and preserve evidence, but that right carried with it the obligation to preserve and disclose to the defence all evidence obtained, whether or not helpful to the State's case. The Court referred to the 'unique investigative role . . . [of the Gardaí] . . .' and imposed a duty 'to seek out and preserve all evidence having a bearing or potential bearing on the issue of guilt or innocence . . .'

The Supreme Court appears to have extended this principle in *Dunne v DPP* [2002] 2 IR 305. Fennelly J, after reviewing the authorities extensively, found as 'the underlying principle . . .' that the accused should receive 'a fair trial'. In the course of evidence in the lower courts, it was unresolved as to whether a videotape of a robbery had either ever existed, or alternatively, had ever been handed to the Gardaí. The Court felt bound to resolve the issues in favour of the accused and Fennelly J observed that this approach, based as it was on *Braddish* (above) might seem a 'very significant new step in the law', imposing, as it did, a positive duty on the Gardaí, to collect evidence which has a potential bearing on the trial, with the possible sanction of a prohibition if they failed to comply with that duty.

Dunne and *Braddish* would appear to represent the height of this strand of jurisprudence, and more recent cases suggest a dilution of the heavy burden on the investigating authorities. In *Scully v DPP* [2005] 2 ILRM 203 the Supreme Court refused relief to an applicant who complained that a potentially exculpatory videotape had been disposed of by the investigators, on the grounds, *inter alia*, that he had neither sought the videotape out at an early time, nor moved his application for judicial review sufficiently promptly. It was, however, a significant feature of the case that the relevance of the videotape was purely theoretical and unproven, and indeed most likely of no evidential value. In *McKeown v Judges of Dublin District Court* [2003] IESC 26 these issues were further discussed and McCracken J concluded that the issue was not whether the Gardaí's failure, negligent or innocent, was to be deemed faulty, but whether that failure had prejudiced the accused's right to a fair trial.

The passage of the Criminal Justice (Surveillance) Act, 2009, a new departure in the State, by way of an attempt to legitimise the long-standing practice of covert surveillance, is worthy of note at this stage. The Act itself is clearly an attempt to bring Ireland into conformity with its Article 8 obligations, as hitherto there has been no comprehensive law governing 'bugging', and other practices, although criminal justice professionals have long been aware of their existence. Having said that, there is clearly a major potential difficulty for the parties in relation to disclosure in criminal trials. Section 15 of the Act, in what is likely to be an extraordinarily complex minefield for lawyers and judges, prohibits disclosure of even the existence of a surveillance authorisation, except by court order. Section 15(2) prohibits the Court from ordering disclosure when to do so 'would create a material risk' to, *inter alia*, the security of the State, or the ability of the State to protect witnesses, including their identities. Bearing in mind the obvious tension between the rights of an accused in criminal proceedings, and the desire of the authorities to protect, say, a Garda informer, it is difficult to see how these issues can be resolved satisfactorily. The Supreme Court, in *DPP v McKevitt* [2008] IESC 51, examined this issue in relation to material withheld (possibly) from the defence by the security services of third party states, concluding that there had, in all of the circumstances, including assurances as to relevance given to the trial court by prosecuting counsel, been no breach of the accused's entitlements. Whether the Strasbourg Court would take the same view is open to question. They in fact canvassed similar issues in an English case, *A and others v UK*, Application No. 3455/05, [2009] EHRR 301. Examining a complicated system for adjudicating on whether material adverse to the applicants should be disclosed or not, the ECt.HR ruled that the real test was whether or not the applicants and their advisers had been appraised of the allegations against them to a sufficient extent to be able to refute them. While no doubt a well-intentioned attempt to bridge the gap between asserted considerations of national security, on the one hand, and the ability to mount a proper defence on the other, the reality is that compromises are made in this area when states assert to courts that the direst consequences must inevitably follow an adverse ruling. It will be interesting to track the operation of the Irish surveillance legislation in due course.

12.5 Rights Arising on the Conclusion of Criminal Proceedings

12.5.1 THE RIGHT TO REVIEW A CRIMINAL CONVICTION OR SENTENCE

The right to review of a criminal conviction or sentence is guaranteed by Article 2 of the Seventh Protocol ECHR subject only to exceptions in regard to offences of a minor character, as prescribed by law or to cases in which the person concerned was tried in the first instance by the highest tribunal or was convicted following an appeal against an acquittal.

The Irish judicial system provides comprehensive access to appeals. From the District Court, there is a full appeal, on law or fact, as of right, in every case. In all other courts, the right of appeal is limited to issues of law and the court of first instance is effectively the finder of fact.

12.5.2 DOUBLE JEOPARDY

An obscure provision in Article 4(2) of the Seventh Protocol ECHR challenges the fundamental and seemingly immovably established principle of the common law, the prohibition on double jeopardy. Simply stated, a person once acquitted at trial of criminal offences could historically in the common law jurisdictions never be retried. Article 4(2) of the Seventh Protocol ECHR permits an exception to that situation '*if there is evidence of new or newly discovered facts, or if there has been a fundamental defect in the previous proceedings which could affect the outcome of the case*'. There is as yet no recorded instance of the operation of this section.

In fact, even in the common law jurisdictions, this is not as immutable a principle as is commonly believed, and a series of Supreme Court decisions has left open the possibility of retrials for 'acquitted' accused, even, in appropriate cases, where an accused has been acquitted by a jury. (See, for example, *DPP v O'Shea* [1982] IR 384, for contrasting judicial views of this topic. O'Higgins CJ and Henchy J took very different views of the matter, the former leaving open the idea that an acquitted accused might be susceptible to retrial, the latter roundly condemning the notion.)

There has now been a very significant development in the United Kingdom in this area, which will presumably be the subject of a challenge to Strasbourg at some stage. By virtue of the Criminal Justice Act 2003, ss 79–97, a previously acquitted accused can be retried for an offence in respect of which they have previously been acquitted, provided that the Court of Appeal is satisfied that there is 'new and compelling evidence' as to the guilt of the person previously acquitted, and that the 'interests of justice' require a further trial. The DPP must apply to the Court of Appeal to quash the original acquittal, prior to the new prosecution commencing. The first case under the new Act was the celebrated case of William Dunlop, convicted on 11 September 2006 of the murder of Julie Hogg in 1989, having been acquitted in 1991 (see Scott, 'Two Stabs at Justice' (2006) *Law Gazette*, www.lawgazette.co.uk/features, 9 November 2006).

12.6 Freedom from Retrospective Criminal Legislation

Article 7 ECHR seeks to prohibit the retroactive application of criminal law resulting in a conviction or the imposition of a criminal penalty. It seeks to avoid the penalisation of conduct which was not criminal at the time when the relevant act occurred.

However, a major exception, contained in Article 7(2) ECHR, is intended to allow the application of national and international legislation enacted during and after the Second World War to punish war crimes and other lesser offences. This exception, when created, was intended to allow the application of national and international legislation enacted expressly to deal with such offences as it became clear that such offences had occurred and that there was no specific legislation to deal with offences which had attracted universal abhorrence.

Article 15.5 of the Irish Constitution expressly prohibits retrospective criminal legislation. It is difficult to envisage a change in this position.

Court was not unanimous in its decision and it is unlikely that a newspaper here would, under existing Irish defamation law, be afforded such scope as the burden of proving the truthfulness of the statements of fact published rests at all stage with the defendants.

Other decisions of the ECt.HR on accuracy of matters of fact are *Fressoz v France* (1999) 5 BHRC 654, *Thorgeirson v Iceland* (1992) 14 EHRR 843, *Selisto v Finland* (2006) 42 EHRR 144 and *Cumpona and Mazare v Romania* (2005) 41 EHRR 200.

13.7   The Irish Experience of Article 10 ECHR

As we have seen, the Irish courts have, in a number of cases, recognised the importance of the ECHR and have had regard to its provisions. The Irish courts have also, even prior to incorporation, shown a certain willingness to consider the case-law on the interpretation and implementation of the ECHR. How then has the right to freedom of expression, as guaranteed by Article 10, impacted upon Irish law?

13.7.1   JURIES AND DAMAGES IN DEFAMATION CASES

The primary method by which the Irish courts can vindicate the good name of a person who has been defamed is by awarding damages. The majority of defamation cases are heard by a jury in the High Court. The jury determines both liability and quantum. Until very recently, they decided the level of any award with only very limited guidance from the trial judge. Under s 31 of the Defamation Act 2009, the judge must now give directions to the jury on damages but the legislation does not specify what nature or form those directions are to take.

13.7.2   *DE ROSSA V INDEPENDENT NEWSPAPERS*

In July 1997, the former government minister, Proinsias de Rossa, received damages of IR £300,000 (€380,921) for a libel in the *Sunday Independent*. The newspaper appealed on quantum only, arguing that the award was excessive and disproportionate to any damage done to Mr de Rossa's reputation.

Importantly, the *Sunday Independent* sought to challenge the then system under Irish law whereby juries determine not only whether an article is libellous but also the size of the award without any realistic guidance by the trial judge.

The newspaper relied on UK and European case-law, on Article 10 ECHR and, in particular, a decision of the ECt.HR in *Tolstoy Miloslavsky v UK* (1995) 20 EHRR 442. In that case, the Court considered a defamation award of £1.5m. It stressed that these damages had been awarded by a jury which had received no specific guidelines relating to its assessment of damages. The Court concluded that:

> 'Having regard to the size of the award in the appellant's case in conjunction with the lack of adequate and effective safeguards at the relevant time against a disproportionately large award, the court finds that there has been a violation of the applicant's rights under Article 10 of the Convention.'

In the event, the Supreme Court in *De Rossa v Independent Newspapers* [1999] 4 IR 432 (by a four-to-one majority) felt that, given the serious nature of the libel of Mr de Rossa, the jury were 'justified in going to the top of the bracket' and that the award was 'not disproportionate to the injury' suffered by Mr de Rossa. In the majority decision, the Chief Justice stated that the law must reflect a due balancing of the constitutional right to freedom of expression and the constitutional protection of every citizen's good name. He said that the obligations arising from the provisions of the Constitution and the ECHR were met by the existing law of the State which provided that the award must always be reasonable and fair and bear a due correspondence with the injuries suffered, with the requirement that if it was disproportionately high, it would be set aside on appeal.

13.7.3   EUROPEAN COURT OF HUMAN RIGHTS DECISION

The *Sunday Independent* newspaper challenged the decision of the Supreme Court before the ECt.HR.

The State relied on the latitude given Ireland by the 'margin of appreciation' and stressed the difference in the size of the award against Independent Newspapers and that made in *Tolstoy Miloslavsky*.

Independent Newspapers argued that the circumstances of *de Rossa* could not realistically be separated from those in *Tolstoy Miloslavsky*.

By a six-to-one majority (Barreto J dissenting), the ECt.HR in *Independent News and Media plc v Ireland* (2006) 42 EHRR 1024 (see **4.6**) preferred the State's arguments. The essential question was whether, having regard to the size of the award, there were adequate and effective domestic safeguards, at first instance and on appeal, against disproportionate awards. The Court stressed that a 'State remains free to choose the measures which it considers best adopted to address domestically the Convention matter at issue'.

The majority judges also stressed the supervisory role of the appellate court in ensuring that the principle of proportionality was upheld. Allied to the margin of appreciation this meant that there was no violation of Article 10 ECHR.

13.7.4   *O'BRIEN V MGN* **AND** *LEECH V INDEPENDENT NEWSPAPERS*

The disinclination of the Irish courts to countenance the introduction of a ceiling on libel damages in Ireland was also stressed in the decision of the Supreme Court in *O'Brien v Mirror Group Newspapers* [2001] 1 IR 1. However, perhaps with an eye towards Strasbourg, the Court determined that an award of IR £250,000 (€317,434) to a well-known Irish businessman, who the *Irish Mirror* suggested had bribed a politician, was excessive and awarded a retrial. A practical infirmity in the Court's balancing approach in the absence of a ceiling is shown by the fact that the second jury gave Mr O'Brien damages of €750,000, many times greater than the first award. That award was then appealed by the newspaper and the case settled.

The inclusion of a provision in the Defamation Act, 2009 (s 13) stressing that the Supreme Court may substitute its view on damages for that of a jury, rather than ordering a re-trial, is an effort to prevent such 'yo-yo' litigation, with cases bouncing between the High and Supreme Courts until the jury reach the 'correct' verdict. This also appears to be an effort to keep Irish defamation law compliant with the ECHR.

Further, an award of €1.872 million to a public relations consultant, Mrs Monica Leech, by a jury in June 2009 over suggestions that she had received government contracts because she had an affair with a government minister will put further pressure on the Supreme Court to keep Irish law in line with the ECHR. This award is much closer to that in *Tolstoy Miloslavsky v UK* (1995) EHRR 442 (see **13.7.2**), so the precedent in *Independent News and Media plc v Ireland* (2006) 42 EHRR 1024 (see **12.7.3** and **4.6**) may not apply.

13.8   The Right to Privacy

The right to privacy is explicitly recognised in Article 8 ECHR and is an unenumerated right protected by Article 40.3° of the Irish Constitution. There have been relatively few Irish decisions on the sometimes conflicting rights of free expression enjoyed by the media and of privacy.

However the incorporation of the ECHR into Irish and UK law has lead to an increase in successful privacy claims. In 2005, there was a significant decision of the ECt.HR on this topic, which has been elaborated on in subsequent decisions. The impact of these decisions is being felt on domestic law in the UK and Ireland. Indeed it has been argued, with some force, that, while the incorporation of the ECHR into Irish law had been predicted to give added protection to the principle of freedom of expression, in reality it has been the right to privacy that has been the real beneficiary of this. (See Patrick Dillon-Malone BL, 'Freedom of Expression, Privacy and the Media' in Kilkelly, U. (ed) *ECHR and Irish Law*, 2nd edn, 2009, Jordans.)

13.8.1   CELEBRITY WEDDINGS AND A PRINCE'S THOUGHTS

On 18 November 2000, the celebrity couple Michael Douglas and Catherine Zeta-Jones married in New York. *OK!* magazine paid approximately £1m for exclusive rights to cover the wedding. Shortly before publication, however, a rival magazine, *Hello!*, began printing an edition containing unauthorised photographs of the nuptials. Douglas and Zeta-Jones successfully sued for damages. The awards were small. The couple were awarded £14,600 in total, including £3,750 for the emotional hurt caused by *Hello!* Zeta-Jones had told the Court that she felt 'devastated' and 'violated' when she discovered 'unflattering' paparazzi pictures had been taken. Nonetheless, it is telling, in one of the first cases of its type, that the UK courts felt it appropriate to protect two well-known public figures, who by their own admission were in the business of selling strictly controlled insights into their private life (*Douglas and Zeta-Jones v Hello!* [2005] EWCA Civ 595).

In 2006, Prince Charles sued the *Mail on Sunday* for breach of confidence. The claim centred on eight handwritten journals containing the Prince's 'private and personal thoughts' of overseas tours, parts of which were published by the newspaper. In *Prince of Wales v Associated Newspapers* [2006] EWHC 522 (Ch), Blackburne J said it was necessary to answer two questions in order to decide the case: (1) did the Prince have a reasonable expectation of privacy? and (2) how should his right to privacy under Article 8 ECHR be balanced against the newspaper's right to freedom of expression under Article 10 ECHR? While the Prince's journals had been circulated to family members, close friends and advisers, they were still private. Further, while the Prince had spoken out publicly on many issues, Blackburne J felt that this did not remove the cloak of privacy covering the journals. 'Were it otherwise,' he said, 'no politician could ever have any reasonable expectation of privacy in a private diary in which he expresses political views.'

An expectation of privacy having been established, the judge then considered the competing Article 10 rights. He reiterated that what is in the public interest should not be confused with what is interesting to the public. The contribution the journals made to public debate or to informing the electorate was minimal. The Prince's rights therefore trumped those of the *Mail on Sunday*.

The Court of Appeal upheld Blackburne J's decision: *Associated Newspapers v The Prince of Wales* [2007] 3 WLR 194. While laying stress on the fact that the journals had been leaked to the *Mail on Sunday* by a palace employee in breach of his duty of confidentiality, the Court reiterated that the significance of the interference with the Prince's Article 8 rights outweighed those of the newspaper under Article 10.

13.8.2 CELEBRITY ADDICTIONS AND FOIBLES

In February 2001, the *Daily Mirror* reported that Naomi Campbell was receiving treatment at Narcotics Anonymous for drug addiction. Campbell was also surreptitiously photographed leaving a meeting. She issued proceedings claiming, among other things, that the publication breached her rights under Article 8 ECHR. The case reached the House of Lords and is reported at *Campbell v MGN* [2004] AC 457.

The information disclosed by the paper was divided into five categories:

(i)   The fact that Ms Campbell was a drug addict;

(ii) The fact that she was receiving treatment;

(iii) The fact that she was receiving treatment at Narcotics Anonymous;

(iv) The details of the treatment—for how long, how frequently and what times of the day she had been receiving it, the nature of it and the extent of her commitment; and

(v)   The photograph of her leaving the meeting with other addicts.

Campbell had previously lied in public, claiming that she did not use drugs. In doing so, she sought to distinguish herself from other well-known figures in the fashion industry. Because of this, Campbell was not entitled to protection for categories (i) and (ii).

However, by a three-to-two majority, the House of Lords decided that the publication of material falling within categories (iii) to (v) was a breach of confidence and an infringement of the supermodel's rights under Article 8 ECHR.

One of the majority Judges in the House of Lords, Lord Hope, said that, had it not been for the publication of the photograph, he might have found for the *Mirror*. The other majority Judges, Lady Hale and Lord Carswell, said that the article wrongly went beyond simply stating that Campbell was receiving therapy—to which she could not object—and intruded into what had some of the characteristics of medical treatment. Lady Hale ruled that the need for treatment for drug addicts was more important than the right of the public to know about it. 'People trying to recover from drug addiction need considerable dedication and commitment, along with constant reinforcement from those around them' she said.

The Lords decided that the *Mirror* could reveal the need for and the fact of the medical treatment but not its details. But what details were revealed? Simply that Campbell had been receiving treatment for three months, often twice a day and that, despite her fortune, she was 'just another addict trying to put her life back together'. It is hard to disagree with Lord Nicholls in his dissenting judgment:

> 'Disclosure that Ms Campbell had opted for this form of treatment was not a disclosure of any more significance than saying a person who has fractured a limb has his limb in plaster or that a person suffering from cancer is undergoing a course of chemotherapy... The brief reference to the way she was being treated at the meeting did no more than spell out and apply to Ms Campbell common knowledge of how Narcotics Anonymous meetings are conducted'.

Nonetheless, the case shows the level of protection that Article 8 can give to an even outwardly unsympathetic claimant.

The *Campbell* decision was applied by the Court of Appeal in *Murray v Big Pictures (UK) Ltd* [2008] 3 WLR 1360. This case involved a photograph of the infant son of Mrs Joanne Murray, aka JK Rowling of Harry Potter fame. The photograph, taken covertly using a long lens, showed the child being pushed in a buggy by his father with his mother alongside. The Court asked whether a toddler in a pushchair had a reasonable expectation of privacy in the sense that a reasonable person, in his position would feel that the photograph should not be published. The Court decided that he had, and that his 'private recreation was intended to be enjoyed in the company of family and friends and that, on the test employed in *Von Hannover v Germany* [2005] 40 EHRR 1, see **13.8.3**), publicity of such activities is intrusive and can adversely affect the exercise of such social activities.' The decision maintained the position that a photograph taken in a public place and published without consent will not of itself engage Article 8. However, the courts will consider the circumstances of each case and how a reasonable person would feel at the prospect of their photograph being exploited commercially.

A later case from 2008 is perhaps more notable for its profile than its establishment of any new legal principle. Max Mosley is the son of Britain's 1930s fascist leader and a leading figure in motor racing. *The News of the World* said he had engaged in a sado-masochistic sex session with prostitutes which had Nazi and anti-Semitic overtones. Mr Mosley argued that the activities were entirely private.

Eady J found that there was no evidence that what took place was, as the paper's headline claimed, a 'sick Nazi orgy' or that Mr Mosley had engaged in anti-Semitic activity. Consequently, the newspaper's defence that the publication was in the public interest, particularly because of Mr Mosley's parentage and position, had little merit. Eady J stressed that, in these circumstances, there was nothing 'landmark' in his decision but that it simply involved the application of established principles to the facts. He did however stress that if the sex session had had a Nazi or anti-Semitic theme, his decision could have been different because 'there could be a public interest in that being revealed at least to those in the FIA (formula one motor racing's governing body) to whom (Mr Mosley) is accountable. He has to deal with many people of all races and religions and has spoken out against racism in the sport. If he really were behaving in the way that I have just described, that would, for many people, call seriously into question his suitability for his FIA role. It would be information which people arguably should have the opportunity to know and evaluate' (*Mosley v News Group Newspapers* [2008] EWHC 1777, paras 122–123).

Whether Judge Eady's views as quoted above are wholly in line with the case-law of the ECt.HR, to which we now turn, is a moot point but, on a first analysis, his views seem more liberal than those emanating from Strasbourg.

13.8.3 *VON HANNOVER V GERMANY*

The ECt.HR delivered an important decision on privacy and on Article 10 ECHR in *Von Hannover v Germany* [2005] 40 EHRR 1. The applicant is perhaps better known as Princess Caroline of Monaco. Three German magazines—*Bunte, Neue Post* and *Freizeit Review*—published photographs which showed the Princess skiing, horse-riding, sitting in a café and playing tennis with her husband, Prince Ernst-August of Hannover. Some of the pictures included Princess Caroline's children. The photographs were all taken in public places.

The ECt.HR said that publication of the photographs had violated the Princess's right to privacy. 'Every person, however well known, must be able to enjoy a legitimate hope for the protection of . . . their private life', the Court said. 'The general public did not have a legitimate interest in knowing Caroline von Hannover's whereabouts or how she behaved generally in her private life.'

The Court overturned a German ruling, which said that, as a public figure, Princess Caroline had to accept being photographed in public. This was the so-called 'doorstep' defence. Broadly, when the family physically crossed the threshold of their home, they entered a public world.

This decision was directly applied in the UK in *Murray v Big Pictures (UK) Ltd* [2008] 3 WLR 1360, see **13.8.2**).

13.8.4   ECT.HR AND 'IMAGE RIGHTS'

Recent decisions of the ECt.HR appear to reveal an ever-widening interpretation of Article 8. In *Reklos and Davourlis v Greece* (Application No. 1234/05, judgment of 15 January 2009) the Court found an unjustified infringement of Article 8 where a newborn baby had been photographed in a private hospital without parental consent. The images were simple portrait photographs taken as part of a commercial photography service operated by the hospital. There was no suggestion of publication; they were simply taken and retained. The Court said that 'private life is a broad concept not susceptible to exhaustive definition'. In what could be viewed as a step towards a recognition of an image right, the Court stated at:

> 'A person's image constitutes one of the chief attributes of his or her personality, as it reveals the person's unique characteristics and distinguishes the person from his or her peers. The right to protection of one's image is thus one of the essential components of personal development and presupposes the right to control the use of that image. Whilst in most cases the right to control such use involves the possibility for an individual to refuse publication of his or her image, it also covers the individual's right to object to the recording, conversion and reproduction of the image by another person.'

In parallel, the ECt.HR also appears to be moving the bar higher for any countervailing public interest argument. In *Egeland and Hanseid v Norway* (Application No. 34438/04, judgment of 16 April 2009) a Norwegian newspaper was convicted and fined for publishing photographs of a high profile murderer being led away from court shortly after her conviction. Despite the fact that the photographs were taken in a public place and related to an important public event, the murderer's rights had been infringed. The ECt.HR stressed that she had not consented to the photographs, that they showed her in a 'state of strong emotion' and that 'the interests in resisting publication of the photographs outweighed those of the press in informing the public on a matter of public concern'.

13.8.5   IRISH DECISIONS ON ARTICLE 8 ECHR AND PRIVACY

Different criteria are applied by both domestic courts and the ECt.HR between applications for prior restraint and *ex post facto* determinations of the balancing exercise between Article 10 and competing rights. This divergence is reflected in recent Irish decisions involving privacy and the mass media.

In *Kennedy & Arnold v Ireland* [1988] ILRM 472, see **13.2**, damages were awarded to two journalists for the deliberate, conscious and unjustifiable electronic eavesdropping by the State on their private telephone conversations.

A more recent case involving state agencies is *Gray v Minister for Justice* [2007] IEHC 52. Here members of An Garda Síochána had disclosed to the press the fact that the claimant's nephew, a convicted rapist, was staying in their home. Quirke J. decided that this information was confidential and sensitive and its disclosure was negligent and unlawful. He did, however, appear to view the claim as primarily one in negligence and the breach of the plaintiff's privacy a consequence of that negligence rather than a stand-alone claim.

An unusual decision, but one of the first to involve the trial of a breach of privacy claim against a non-state agency, is *Sinnott v Nationalist & Leinster Times* (31 July 2008,

High Court (unreported)). A Carlow GAA player was photographed taking part in an inter-county game at Croke Park. A photograph of him, in which his genitalia could be seen, was published in the *Carlow Nationalist*. The newspaper said the publication was a mistake. However, Budd J. considered that there had been a deliberate and conscious breach of privacy, notwithstanding the fact that the incident recorded in the photograph had happened in front of thousands of spectators.

Of greater significance is the High Court decision in *Herrity v Associated Newspapers* [2008] IEHC 249 (see **13.8.7**). The defendant newspaper had published a series of articles which contained extracts of telephone conversations between the plaintiff and a Catholic priest, with whom she was in a relationship. The Court found that these conversations had been recorded without her knowledge by a private investigator employed by her estranged husband. In her decision, Dunne J stressed that the conversations had been recorded and published in breach of s 98 of the Postal and Telecommunications Services Act, 1983, as amended. This prohibits the interception of telephone calls and the publication of their contents.

The High Court rejected the newspaper's argument that actions for breach of the constitutional right to privacy were limited to cases against state agencies. Dunne J awarded damages, including punitive damages, of €90,000.

The newspaper sought to rely upon its right to freedom of expression and the public interest in its story to justify publication. However, both arguments failed, largely because of how the extracts of the conversations were obtained. Dunne J. said: 'I cannot see how anyone can assert a right to freedom of expression to publish transcripts of private telephone conversations where the legislature has expressly prohibited the interception of telecommunications messages'.

As the publication complained of occurred before the coming into effect of the European Convention on Human Rights Act, 2003, Dunne J did not feel it necessary to comment on the provisions of the ECHR. She relied upon the claimant's constitutional right to privacy. She did however, sound a note of caution on the respective strengths of the constitutional rights of privacy and freedom of expression:

> 'There is a hierarchy of constitutional rights and, as a general proposition, I think that cases in which the right to privacy will prevail over the right to freedom of expression may well be few and far between'.

13.8.6 IRISH DECISIONS ON PRIOR RESTRAINT

While a decision at interlocutory stage, *Maguire v Drury* [1995] 1ILRM 108 is perhaps a high watermark for the press. In a case with strong echoes of *Herrity v Associated Newspapers* [2008] IEHC 249, see **13.8.5**, a newspaper sought to publish an interview with a man whose wife had an extra-marital affair with a Catholic priest. She asked the court to stop publication because of the damage it would cause their children. O'Hanlon J refused the application, quoting, with approval from the judgment of Hoffmann LJ in the Court of Appeal in England in the decision of *R v Central Independent Television plc*, 9 February 1994, who stated:

> 'The motives which impel judges to assume a power to balance freedom of speech against other interests are almost always understandable and humane in the facts of the particular case before them. Newspapers are sometimes irresponsible and their motives in a market economy cannot be expected to be unalloyed by considerations of commercial advantage. Publication may cause needless pain, distress and damage to individuals or harm to other aspects of the public interest. But a freedom which is restricted to what judges think to be responsible or in the public interest is no freedom.

Freedom means the right to publish things which government and judges, however well motivated, think should not be published. It means the right to say things which "right thinking people" regard as dangerous or irresponsible.'

Another significant pre-publication application was *Cogley v Radio Telifís Éireann (RTE)* [2005] 2 ILRM 529. The owners of Leas Cross Nursing Home sought to injunct the broadcast of an RTE 'Prime Time Investigates' programme which made very serious allegations about the manner in which the home was operated over a significant period of time.

An experienced care worker was engaged by RTE to take up a job at Leas Cross. He was equipped with a concealed camera so he could record what he observed. The owners claimed that the secret filming and its broadcast would breach their constitutional and ECHR rights to privacy.

Clarke J distinguished between a right of privacy in the underlying information whose disclosure it is sought to prevent and one which does not extend to that underlying information but where it is contended that the methods by which the information has been obtained amount to a breach of privacy. Differing considerations would apply, most particularly at an interlocutory stage. The right to privacy of the owners of Leas Cross fell into the second of these categories.

The High Court decided that the issues raised by the programme were of very significant public interest—particularly the standard of care at the home and whether it was adequately regulated. The rights enjoyed by the owners of Leas Cross could not preclude this from being broadcast. However, 'the manner in which secret filming occurred . . . [gave] rise to more significant questions'.

Despite this, Clarke J determined that if the accusations in the programme were borne out to be correct then any breach of privacy involved in obtaining confidential information by surreptitious means would give rise to small, or even nominal, damages, which damages would be an adequate remedy. He therefore refused the injunction sought.

The decision has been hailed as a victory for freedom of expression. However, the judgment contains traps for the media.

First, Clarke J went out of his way to stress that his decision should not be seen as supporting any general proposition that the ends of newsgathering justify the means. He was mindful that 'it is all too easy to dress up very many issues with an exaggerated or unreal public dimension'. Second, when looking at the respective rights to privacy and freedom of expression, he said:

'I would wish to emphasise that the balancing exercise which I have found the Court must engage in is not one which would arise at all in circumstances where the underlying information sought to be disclosed was of a significantly private nature and where there was no, or no significant, legitimate public interest in its disclosure. In such a case (for example where the information intended to be disclosed concerned the private life of a public individual in circumstances where there was no significant public interest of a legitimate variety in the material involved) it would be seem to me that the normal criteria for the grant of an interlocutory injunction should be applied.'

13.8.7 BALANCE

The difficulty of achieving the correct balance between the rights protected by Articles 8 and 10 ECHR is shown by the conflicting approaches taken in recent cases in Ireland and England. The *Von Hannover* decision reflects what in the past has been the greater protection given by the European civil law jurisdictions to the right to privacy than by their common law counterparts. It is difficult to see how the decision of the ECt.HR in

Egeland and Hanseid v Norway (Application No. 34438/04, judgment of 16 April 2009, see **13.8.4**) would have been made in an Irish or UK court and it will be interesting to see if persons convicted of serious crimes will seek to bring a similar case here.

It is often difficult to see where precisely the balance between Article 8 and Article 10 lies—as the tortuous history of Naomi Campbell's case shows. She won in the High Court, lost in the Court of Appeal but succeeded, by a three-to-two majority, in the House of Lords. As the editor of the defeated newspaper ruefully pointed out, of the nine judges who heard the case, five had found in favour of the *Mirror* but of the four who did not, three were, unfortunately for him, in the House of Lords. Would the decision in the Irish High Court in *Herrity v Associated Newspapers* [2008] IEHC 249 (see **13.8.5**) have been different if the newspaper had merely reported on the fact of Mrs Herrity's relationship with a priest, without revealing extracts of their telephone conversations? How the common law courts grapple with this balancing exercise is one of the greatest challenges facing them when interpreting and enforcing the ECHR.

13.9 Freedom to Receive Information

Article 10 cannot be used to derive a general right of access to information. In *Guerra v Italy* (1998) 26 EHRR 357, the ECt.HR stated unequivocally that the freedom to receive information essentially prohibited a government from restricting a person from receiving information that others wished to impart. However, it did not impose on the authorities in that case the obligation to collect and distribute information about the health risks to the local community from a nearby factory.

In *Open Door and Dublin Well Woman v Ireland* (1992) 15 EHRR 244, there was a violation of Article 10 where a court injunction prevented the provision of information services concerning abortion by the applicant counsellors. The Court found the ban disproportionate; it was absolute, the counselling given was neutral and the information was lawfully available elsewhere in Ireland or by contact outside in a less supervised manner. This imposed a risk to those women who sought abortion at a later stage and who did not receive counselling or proper aftercare.

13.10 Article 2 ECHR: The Right to Life

Article 2 ECHR guarantees the most basic human right, the right to life (see **chapter 10**). Perhaps surprisingly, this Article has already had an impact on the media's right to free expression in the United Kingdom. Article 2 states:

> 'Everyone's right to life shall be protected by law. No one shall be deprived of his life intentionally save in the execution of a sentence of a court following his conviction of a crime for which this penalty is provided by law.'

The murder of James Bulger by Jon Venables and Robert Thompson on 12 February 1993 was an horrific crime that caused much public outrage and attracted international media attention. At the end of the murder trial, the judge determined, notwithstanding the youth of the accused, that they could be named and their images shown by the media. During the period of their detention, however, injunctions were put in place which restricted the information which the media were entitled to publish. Those injunctions came to an end when Venables and Thompson reached the age of 18. They then applied to the President of the Queen's Bench Division in the United Kingdom for injunctions preventing their identification for the rest of their lives. They were supported in their applications by the Home Office. Venables and Thompson had received death threats and the authorities proposed to give them new identities upon their release. Notwithstanding resistance by lawyers for the print media, the injunctions were granted and made final after a full trial.

The President of the Queen's Bench Division, Dame Elizabeth Butler-Sloss, determined that Venables and Thompson were 'uniquely notorious' and would be for the rest of their lives at serious risk of attacks from members of the public, as well as from relatives and friends of the murdered child. As she put it in *Venables and Thompson v Newsgroup Newspapers and Others* [2001] EWHC QB 32:

> 'If any section of the media decided to give information leading to the identification of either young man, such publication would put his life at risk. In the exceptional circumstances of this case and applying English domestic law and the right to life enshrined in Article 2 of the European Convention, I have come to the conclusion that I am compelled to take steps in the almost unique circumstances of this case to protect their lives and wellbeing.'

While recognising the enormous importance of freedom of expression, she nonetheless granted an open-ended injunction for the rest of the lives of Venables and Thompson.

Similar protection was afforded to Maxine Carr, the girlfriend of Ian Huntley who was convicted of murdering two young girls in Soham in August 2002. The Order was granted, in an unreported decision, by Eady J on 24 February 2005. It was the first permanent ban to protect someone who was not involved in a killing.

13.11 Protection of Journalists' Sources

A question of some importance to freedom of expression is the confidentiality of journalistic sources. The European Court has considered such confidentiality to be a necessary precondition for press freedom protected by Article 10.

In *Goodwin v UK* (1996) 22 EHRR 123, the Court considered whether an order requiring a journalist to disclose his source contravened Article 10. In finding that it did, a majority of the Court stated:

> 'Protection of journalistic sources is one of the basic conditions for press freedom, as is reflected in the laws and professional codes of conduct in a number of contracting states and is affirmed in several international instruments on journalistic freedom. Without such protection, sources may be deterred from assisting the press in informing the public on matters of public interest. As a result, the vital public watchdog role of the press may be undermined and the ability of the press to provide accurate and reliable information may be adversely affected. Having regard to the importance of protection of journalistic sources for press freedom in a democratic society and the potentially chilling effect an order of source disclosure has on the exercise of that freedom, such a measure cannot be compatible with Article 10 of the Convention unless it is justified by an overriding requirement in the public interest.'

In Mr Goodwin's case, there was no such overriding requirement in the public interest.

This decision would appear to fly in the face of Irish law as enunciated in *Re Kevin O'Kelly* (1972) 108 ILTR 97 which held that journalists had no greater or lesser right to refuse to disclose confidential information than any other citizen. However, in an unreported case in the Dublin Circuit Court in early 1996 (*Nicola Gallagher v Garda Representative Association*), both counsel for the Attorney General and the presiding Judge, Carroll J, accepted that a journalist could only be asked to reveal a confidential source when it was both necessary and relevant for the administration of justice. This was a considerable change from the position of the authorities in 1972, consequent upon Article 10 ECHR and European case-law on it.

That change was copperfastened by the decision of a Divisional High Court and of the Supreme Court in *Mahon & Ors v Keena and Kennedy* [2007] IEHC 348 and [2009] IESC 64. While the outcome of the balancing exercise differed between the Courts, both gave a strong affirmation of the importance of confidential sources as a necessary pre-condition for press freedom and the chilling effect on Article 10 rights if journalists were obliged to reveal those sources. Both Courts quoted with approval the above extract from the decision of the ECt.HR in *Goodwin v UK* (1996) 22 EHRR 123.

13.12   Freedom of Expression in the EU

13.12.1   INTRODUCTION

In addition to the Irish Constitution and the ECHR, the right to freedom of expression is recognised and protected at a third level, that is, within European Union law (see **chapter 8**).

While a basic Charter governing fundamental rights in the European Union (see **8.1** and **8.10**) has only recently been given legal status and there are relatively few decisions on the topic, the treatment of fundamental rights by the ECJ is expected to develop as greater opportunities arise to invoke the right of freedom of expression before it.

The situations in which freedom of expression have been considered by the ECJ are very different to those under the ECHR. The ECJ deals with matters of public law and regulation, reflective of the Union's economic foundations and objectives.

13.12.2   RECOGNITION OF FREEDOM OF EXPRESSION UNDER EU LAW

13.12.2.1   General: the nature of fundamental rights

The recognition of fundamental rights within EC law has largely resulted from judicial activism. The original treaties made no provision for rights for individuals other than those economic rights necessary to achieve the objectives of the common market, such as the right to provide and receive services within the common market (Articles 49–55 EC Treaty; see also Joined Cases 286/82 and 26/83 *Luisi and Carbone v Ministero del Tesoro* [1984] 1 ECR 377) and to establish a business in another Member State (Article 43 EC). Whereas all EU Member States are parties to the ECHR, the EU itself, prior to the Treaty of Lisbon, did not have the requisite power to accede to the ECHR (*Opinion 2/94* [1996] ECR I-1759 and see **8.5**).

The constitutional traditions of the Member States and the ECHR have been the main sources for the ECJ in recognising and protecting fundamental rights, as general principles of EC law. This movement was later enshrined in Article 6 TEU (ex Article F) (see **chapter 8**).

13.12.2.2   Freedom of expression

Measures likely to restrict EC rights such as the freedom to provide services must be interpreted in the light of general legal principles and in particular of fundamental rights. This was determined in a series of decisions starting with Case 29/69 *Stauder v City of Ulm*

[1969] ECR 419 and finding best expression in Case 4/73 *Nold v Commission* [1974] ECR 491 and Case 5/88 *Wachauf* [1989] ECR 2609.

As it is guaranteed by the ECHR, freedom of expression is one of the rights in the light of which the ECJ or national court must appraise any measure restricting EU rights. This was recognised implicitly in Joined Cases 43 and 63/82 *VBVB/VBBB v Commission* [1984] ECR 19 (although the applicants' submission failed on the facts) and made explicit in Case C-260/89 *Elliniki Radiophona Tiléorassi* [1991] ECR I-2925 (*ERT*) where the ECJ stated (para 44) as follows:

> 'It is for the national court, and if necessary, the Court of Justice, to appraise the application of those provisions having regard to all the rules of Community law, including freedom of expression, as embodied in Article 10 of the European Convention on Human Rights, as a general principle of law the observance of which is ensured by the Court.'

However, the protection of freedom of expression under EU law extends only to matters of EU competence, that is, to the institutions of the European Union and to Member States when implementing EC law.

In Joined Cases 60 and 61/84 *Cinéthèque v Fédération Nationale des Cinémas Français* [1985] ECR 2605, the ECJ was asked to examine the compatibility with EC law and, in particular, with freedom of expression, of French legislation which imposed an interval between the exploitation of movies in cinemas and on video. The ECJ found that Article 30 EC (later Article 28 EC and post-Lisbon Article 34 TFEU), which prohibits measures with equivalent effect to quantitative restrictions on imports, did not apply. The French statute covered all video cassettes, whether imported or domestically produced, and was proportionate to the objective sought, viz. to encourage cinema production. Accordingly, the ECJ declined to examine the impact of freedom of expression in an area falling within the jurisdiction of the national legislator.

Likewise, in Case C-159/90 *SPUC v Grogan* [1991] ECR I-4685, the ECJ decided that although Irish students, in distributing information regarding abortion services available in the United Kingdom, were exercising their right to freedom of expression, the lack of an economic link between them and the service providers removed them from the scope of EC law. Accordingly, any limitation on their freedom of expression fell to be determined in accordance with national rules.

These cases illustrate that freedom of expression is rarely considered by the ECJ as a stand-alone right. To come within the jurisdiction of the ECJ, a link with EC law—usually an economic link—must be shown.

13.12.3 CASE-LAW OF THE EUROPEAN COURT OF JUSTICE

Many of the ECJ's decisions touching on freedom of expression centre on regulatory matters.

13.12.3.1 Broadcasting

As Case C-260/89 *ERT* [1991] ECR I-2925, discussed above, shows, broadcasting is heavily regulated in most Member States. ERT, the exclusive franchisee for radio and television in Greece, sought to prevent the broadcasting of television programmes by a rival television station. The defendant claimed that the grant of a television monopoly by the Greek government infringed EC rules on competition and its fundamental rights, including freedom of expression. In response to a preliminary reference from the national court, the ECJ declared that national provisions restricting the freedom to provide services were only justified if they were compatible with fundamental rights—in this instance, with freedom of expression.

Measures designed to promote media diversity have been found by the ECJ to conform to Community law and the promotion of freedom of expression: Case C-353/89 *Commission v Netherlands* [1991] ECR I-4069; Case C-23/93 *TV10 SA v Commissariaat voor de Media* [1994] ECR I-4795. These cases concerned a Dutch law requiring domestic broadcasters to allocate airtime on national radio and television to associations representing different social, cultural, religious or philosophical views. In the first case, the ECJ found that the derogation from Article 59 EC was permissible, insofar as the law in question was intended to establish a pluralist and non-commercial broadcasting system, as part of a cultural policy to safeguard the freedom of expression of various groups in the Netherlands. In *TV10*, a broadcaster established in Luxembourg contested its treatment as a domestic undertaking for the purposes of the Act. The Dutch authorities determined that the company had been established in Luxembourg merely to avoid the obligations imposed on domestic undertakings. Its day-to-day management was in the hands of Dutch nationals, its target audience was the Dutch public and its advertisements were made in the Netherlands. The ECJ rejected submissions that the authorities' decision breached the applicant's right of freedom of expression under Article 10 ECHR. In doing so, it referred to its earlier finding that the maintenance of freedom of expression was the very thing which the legislation sought to guarantee.

The importance of ensuring the proportionality of measures restricting freedom of expression was highlighted in another case regarding broadcasting: Case C-245/01 *RTL Television v NLR* [2003] ECR I-1. In this case, the ECJ found that restrictions placed on advertising breaks during films broadcast on television did not unduly restrict the broadcasters' freedom of expression as these related only to the frequency of breaks and not to their timing or the content of the advertising. The Court found that the restrictions could be justified as they aimed to protect consumers against excessive advertising and to protect their interest in having access to quality programmes.

13.12.3.2 Publishing

Unsurprisingly, the need for press diversity is viewed by the ECJ as crucial to freedom of expression.

The subject was first broached in Joined Cases 43 and 63/82 *VBVB/VBBB* [1984] ECR 19, discussed above. The European Commission had struck down a system of resale price maintenance in publishing. The applicants challenged this decision before the ECJ. They claimed that the system encouraged the publication of a multiplicity of titles and ensured the availability of works of minority interest. The Commission's actions in restricting the system would make publishing dependent on state subsidies and would fetter freedom of expression. Works of minority interest would no longer be published and the loss of a multiplicity of publications would detrimentally affect free speech. The ECJ recognised the importance of the right to freedom of expression throughout the EU. However, it rejected the applicant's argument on the grounds that they had failed to establish a real link between resale price maintenance and freedom of expression. The Commission had acted to ensure freedom of trade between Member States and the normal conditions of competition would apply. The ability of publishers and distributors to trade would be unaffected by the Commission's decision so freedom of expression was not affected.

The fullest discussion of the freedom of expression in this context is in Case C-368/95 *Familiapress* [1997] ECR I-3689. Austrian law on unfair competition prohibited the sale of certain periodicals containing competitions and promotions. It was hoped to protect small publications unable to offer significant prizes. A company from Germany—where no such provision exists—claimed this was an improper restriction on the free movement of goods. The ECJ's examination of freedom of expression centred on Austria's public policy justification for derogation from its treaty obligations, primarily its claims that the law was intended to safeguard press diversity. The Court referred to its decision in Case C-353/89 *Commission v Netherlands* [1991] ECR 1–4069, where the maintenance of press diversity was recognised as a noble aim. It also observed that Article 10(2) ECHR permitted derogations from freedom of expression to maintain press diversity, provided such derogations were prescribed by law and necessary in a democratic society. Accordingly, it was for the national court to determine whether a prohibition was proportionate to the aim of maintaining press diversity and whether that objective could be attained by less restrictive measures, on the basis of a study of the national press market.

The limits of the right to free expression, as set out in Article 10(2) ECHR, were discussed in a slightly different context in Case C-219/91 *Ter Voort* [1992] ECR I-5485. Here the ECJ held that Directive 65/65/EEC, which instituted a national licensing system for medicinal products, did not restrict the freedom of expression of third parties publishing information ascribing therapeutic effects to those products. The applicant had ascribed medicinal properties to tea produced and distributed by another company. Such publication did not bring the products within the scope of the Directive and so could not infringe the publication rights of persons unconnected with the manufacturer or seller of the product. The ECJ went on to state that even where the freedom of expression of a third party *connected* with the manufacturer/seller of the product (and thus subject to the provisions of the Directive) could be regarded as limited by the Directive, 'it should be borne in mind that the inherent requirements of the exercise of that freedom must be judged against the requirements of the objective of the protection of public health pursued by Directive 65/65' (para 38).

Finally, the conflicting interests of freedom of expression in publication over the Internet and the right to privacy and the protection of personal data were considered by the ECJ in Case C-101/01 *Bodil Lindqvist* [2003] ECR I-12971.

13.12.3.3 Freedom of expression and officials of the European Union

The importance of freedom of expression, journalistic integrity and independence from the institutions of the European Union was recognised in Case 100/88 *Oyowe and Traore v Commission* [1989] ECR 4285. The Commission had refused to appoint the applicants, journalists with a Community-funded publication on Africa-Caribbean-Pacific ('ACP') States, as Community officials on the grounds, *inter alia*, that the journalists' work would be incompatible with the duty of allegiance owed by officials under the Staff Regulations. The ECJ found against the Commission. It stated that:

'the duty of allegiance to the Communities imposed on officials in the Staff Regulations cannot be interpreted in such a way as to conflict with freedom of expression, a fundamental right which the Court must ensure is respected in Community law, which is particularly important in cases, such as the present, concerning journalists whose primary duty is to write in complete independence of the views of either the ACP States or the Commission' (para 16).

This does not mean that all restrictions on the freedom of expression of officials of the Communities are contrary to EC law: see Joined Cases T-34 and 163/96 *Connolly v Commission* [1999] ECR II-463. The ECJ held that a requirement that Community officials obtain prior authorisation for the publication of certain articles was justified on the basis that (i) it reflected a legitimate objective that texts dealing with the activities of the Community should not adversely affect its interests or reputation; and (ii) it was not disproportionate to this objective, as prior authorisation was only required where the publication was connected to the activities of the Community and could only be withheld if the publication was likely to jeopardise the interests of the Community.

The ECJ held in the later case of Case C-340/P *Commission v Cwik* [2001] ECR I-10269 that, where permission to publish an article is refused, the official is entitled to be given the reasons for such refusal. Furthermore, the mere fact that the official intends to publish an article expressing an opinion differing from the position adopted by the institution is not sufficient to show that it is liable to prejudice the interests of the Communities. To accept such a proposition, and on these grounds restrict freedom of expression, would be to negate the purpose of that fundamental right.

13.12.4 FUTURE DEVELOPMENTS

As with the ECHR, freedom of expression under EC law is not absolute. It may be used as a balance to other rights—eg in assessing whether derogations to trade laws are acceptable—and in turn may be subject to the exercise of other rights and policy requirements. In this context, proportionality is the ultimate arbiter: *Familiapress; Connolly*, and Case C-112/00 *Schmidberger v Austria* [2003] ECR I-5659.

The decisions of the ECJ have, to date, been less sophisticated and nuanced than those of the ECt.HR or the Irish courts. However, there are indications that this could change. The right has been pleaded more frequently in recent years, reflecting its growing familiarity within the legal order: see Case C-235/92 *Montecatini v Commission* [1999] ECR I-4539. Further, there have been two significant constitutional developments.

First, the 'treatification' of human rights has introduced the possibility of sanctions against Member States that fail to observe and protect those rights. Article 7 TEU (introduced by the Treaty of Amsterdam) provides a mechanism whereby a majority of Member States can impose sanctions for the persistent disregard of fundamental rights by a Member State. Indeed, a perceived failure to guarantee freedom of expression was one of the grounds on which the 14 Member States decided to impose sanctions on Austria when the controversial Freedom Party, led by Jörg Haider, entered a coalition government in 2000. (The sanctions were withdrawn when a study of Austria's behaviour concluded that they were unjustified.)

Second, the right to freedom of expression is guaranteed by Article 11 of the Charter of Fundamental Rights of the European Union, proclaimed at Nice in December 2000 (OJ 2000/C364/01 18 December 2000) and by an adapted version of the Charter solemnly proclaimed by the three political institutions of the EU on 12 December 2007 (OJ C303/01 14 February, 2007) (see **8.1** and **8.10**). Post the Treaty of Lisbon, Article 6(1) TEU affords the Charter the same legal status as the Treaties meaning that since the entry into force of the Treaty of Lisbon on 1 December 2009, the Charter is legally binding (see **8.1** and **8.4**).

Article 11 of the Charter provides:

> *'1.   Everyone has the right to freedom of expression. This right shall include freedom to hold opinions and to receive and impart information and ideas without interference by public authority and regardless of frontiers.*
> *2.   The freedom and pluralism of the media shall be respected.'*

It is notable that the Charter, which is addressed to the institutions of the EU and to Member States when implementing European Union law, adopts the language of Article 10(1) ECHR and reflects the jurisprudence of the ECJ, on the need to protect media diversity.

In addition, Article 52 of the Charter provides that insofar as the enumerated rights correspond to rights guaranteed by the ECHR, the meaning and scope of those rights shall be the same as those laid down in the Convention, although EU law may provide more extensive protection. How this will operate in practice will depend to a large extent on the status of the Charter, but it is hoped that it will help resolve the thorny problems of jurisdiction sidestepped by the ECJ in accepting the contents of the ECHR, not as binding, but as general principles of EC law.

13.13 Conclusion

While the extent of the impact of Article 10 on freedom of expression has yet to be fully determined by the Irish courts, there is already a considerable body of European case-law which, it can be properly anticipated, will have an impact here. While in many cases, the Irish constitutional and common law protection of freedom of expression coincides with European jurisprudence, there are areas where it is considerably less liberal and changes are likely.

A common theme of Irish and European jurisprudence, even within the presently less developed case-law of the ECJ enforcing European Community law, is the need to balance the right of freedom of expression with conflicting rights. It is not, and cannot be, an absolute right. Yet it is central to a properly functioning democracy. The concepts of balance and proportionality allow for considerable discretion and give scope for judicial activism or retrenchment. With increasingly quick worldwide communication, the challenges for Irish and European judges have never been greater. How they respond to them will determine not just the effectiveness of Article 10, but possibly of the ECHR itself.

CHAPTER 14

LIBERTY

14.1 Introduction

The concept of liberty has legal and philosophical dimensions. In political philosophy, discussions of liberty have been at the centre of debate from at least the time of the enlightenment. Ideas propagated from that time have fed into our notions of what a legal conceptualisation of the right to liberty should encapsulate. The classic statement of liberalism was made by John Stuart Mill who, in *On Liberty*, described a situation whereby every person was entitled to the maximum freedom consistent with the liberty of others. In this debate the concept of liberty is sought as against the State.

This formal aspect of liberty is otherwise contrasted with more Marxist notions which tended to concentrate not on the confines of freedom to act, but on actual ability of a person so to act in accordance with his wishes, and in turn how those ought to be controlled in the common good. This also shows how notions of liberty are bound up not just with political ideologies, but with beliefs regarding economics and the nature of public decision-making.

The modern notion of liberty as a fundamental legal norm also began at the time of the enlightenment. This may best encapsulated in the French idea of *liberté, égalité, fraternité*, or that of the American Declaration of Independence with its aim of securing life, liberty and the pursuit of happiness.

For lawyers, the right to liberty has tended to be a more formal concept concerning physical restraint, sometimes called personal liberty. Wider aspects of the freedoms guaranteed by other conceptualisations of liberty are protected by other rights. The legal right to liberty has always involved a challenge to the power of the State to detain and restrain citizens, whatever the wider conceptualisation of liberty and freedom then fashionable in society. One could picture a political prisoner imprisoned for opposing authoritarianism. A more commonplace example is a criminal incarceration following conviction, but deprivations of the right are triggered in a stop-and-search situation and other civil detentions. As a right, liberty has been at the centre of all major right-recognising legal documents from the time of the enlightenment and is a core civil and political right. The basic notion is that individuals should not be subjected to arbitrary or capricious detention.

The Irish Constitution includes a right to liberty in Article 40.4, which provides:

'*1°.   No citizen shall be deprived of his personal liberty save in accordance with law.*'

Therefore even at constitutional level it is clear that there can be lawful deprivations of liberty. Much of the case-law in this area focuses on these exceptions where deprivation of liberty is permissible at law and on the procedural and legal safeguards of the individual deprived of such a basic right.

The Constitution also established a very particular mechanism giving practical effect to this right which permits, and sometimes demands, a judicial inquiry to ensure that detention is lawful. This is correctly called an inquiry under Article 40.4, but is colloquially known as an application for *habeas corpus*, discussed below at **14.4**.

The right is also protected in the Universal Declaration on Human Rights, the International Covenant on Civil and Political Rights, the European Convention on Human Rights and other instruments.

The right to liberty has received renewed focus in the light of an increase in the powers of detention following the enactment of anti-terrorist legislation in many countries following the events of 11 September 2001. In Ireland, the right has also been the subject of debate with the introduction of criminal justice measures designed to fight drug-related gangland crime.

14.2 The Constitutional Protection of The Right to Liberty

The right to liberty is protected in the 'Fundamental Rights' section of Bunreacht na hÉireann, 1937. The addressee of the right is the State. If a private citizen abuses a person's right to liberty that may amount to wrongful imprisonment, which is both a criminal offence and a tort.

The constitutional guarantee protecting the right to liberty has evolved since 1937. The right's protection was at first curtailed by the interpretation given to the meaning of the phrase *'in accordance with law'*. Initially, this was interpreted in a formal manner such that a deprivation sanctioned by a law properly enacted was constitutionally permissible. This positivist approach could be seen at work in *Re Article 26 and the Offences Against The State (Amendment) Bill, 1940* [1940] IR 470 which involved a challenge to provisions allowing internment. Sullivan CJ in the Supreme Court stated at 482:

> 'The phrase "in accordance with law" is used in several Articles of the Constitution, and we are of opinion that it means in accordance with the law as it exists at the time when the particular Article is invoked and sought to be applied. In this Article, it means the law as it exists at the time when the legality of the detention arises for determination. A person in custody is detained in accordance with law if he is detained in accordance with the provisions of a statute duly passed by the Oireachtas; subject always to the qualification that such provisions are not repugnant to the Constitution or to any provision thereof.

> Accordingly, in our opinion, this Article cannot be relied upon for the purpose of establishing the proposition that the Bill is repugnant to the Constitution—such repugnancy must be established by reference to some other provision of the Constitution.'

This approach would have seriously curtailed the effectiveness of Article 40.4, and may have reduced it to a guarantee of liberty merely against improperly enacted curtailments, without reference to the fundamental underlying legality of the detention. This approach would not have protected citizens against an arbitrary detention once it was based on a formally valid law.

The courts ultimately rejected the positivist approach in favour of one that evaluates a curtailment of the right to liberty by reference to a more fundamental notion of legal validity. This first occurred in *The People (AG) v O'Callaghan* [1966] IR 501, which concerned the conditions on which bail could be refused. The Supreme Court signalled that deprivations of liberty specified in the Offences Against the State Act, 1939 were permissible only because the stringent conditions laid down for its operation, including a government declaration that the powers were necessary to secure public peace and order. This demonstrated that notwithstanding that the Act was a validly enacted law, it needed further constitutional justification not to fall foul of the right to liberty.

This new approach was copperfastened in *King v AG* [1981] IR 233 where provisions of the Vagrancy Act, 1824, which criminalised a person who was a 'reputed thief', were struck down as unconstitutional. Henchy J in the Supreme Court stated at 257:

> 'it violates the guarantee in Article 40, s. 4, sub-s. 1, that no citizen shall be deprived of personal liberty save in accordance with law—which means without stooping to methods which ignore the fundamental norms of the legal order postulated by the Constitution...'

A law such as the Vagrancy Act could only be struck down because the saver given to deprivations of liberty is benchmarked against fundamental constitutional principles. This is vital to effectiveness as otherwise only the fact of law, not the content, would be considered.

Some commentators detected a roll-back of the protection of the right to liberty in the case of *A v The Governor of Arbour Hill Prison* ([2006] 4 IR 8). This involved a challenge to a continuing detention of a person convicted under a law declared unconstitutional shortly before. In *C.C. v Ireland* ([2006] 4 IR 1) s 1 of the Criminal Law (Amendment) Act, 1935, which created the offence of unlawful carnal knowledge with a girl under the age of 15, was found to be unconstitutional as it did not permit a defence of reasonable mistake as to the girl's age. As a result of the unconstitutionality the applicant, who was imprisoned for the offence which now no longer existed, claimed that there was no valid law justifying his continued detention. Murray CJ stated, in the *A* case on p. 130:

> 'Absolute retroactivity based solely on the notion of an Act being void *ab initio* so as to render any previous final judicial decisions null would lead the Constitution to have dysfunctional effects in the administration of justice...The application of a principle of absolute retroactivity consequent upon the unconstitutionality of an Act in the field of criminal law would render null and of no effect final verdicts or decisions affected by an Act which at the time had been presumed or acknowledged to be constitutional and otherwise had been fairly tried. Such unqualified retroactivity would be a denial of justice to the victims of crime and offend against fundamental and just interests of society.'

The Supreme Court does not seem to have interpreted the Constitution as requiring a continuing lawfulness of detention, which may be required under the European Convention on Human Rights (see below). The judgment suggests that a conviction is lawful once valid when imposed, and imprisonment of foot of such a conviction remains valid despite the absence of a continuing basis for it.

More recently, the High Court considered the imprisonment of debtors pursuant to s 6 of the Enforcement of Court Orders Act, 1940. The section operated in a manner that in effect imprisoned not only those who would not pay, but also those who could not pay their debts. In *McCann v Monaghan District Judges* [2009] IEHC 276 Laffoy J noted in determining the section to be unconstitutional, that:

> 'Having in place an effective statutory scheme for enforcement of contractual obligations, including the payment of debt, is unquestionably a reasonable and legitimate objective in the interests of the common good in a democratic society. The means by which effectiveness is achieved may reasonably necessitate affording a creditor a remedy which entitles him or her to seek to have a debtor imprisoned, but such means will constitute an infringement of the debtor's right to personal liberty guaranteed by Article 40.4.1 unless they pass the proportionality test.'

The guarantee of liberty is applicable to all deprivations of liberty from the details of the enacted law upon which incarcerations is based, to the legality of detention in an individual case before the court and thus to the exercise of the power of detention. This latter has many facets from powers of arrest to conditions of incarceration, its purpose, and civil detentions.

14.3 Deprivations of Liberty

There are many examples of detentions sanctioned by Irish law. Many relate to criminal matters, but some are imposed for the welfare of the detainee. All of these detentions must be lawful in that the law creating the power of detention must be valid and the detention in each individual case must follow the law.

14.3.1 CRIMINAL INVESTIGATIONS

Deprivations of liberty are relatively commonplace in the exercise of law enforcement by the State. These range from powers to investigate crimes and to stop and search suspects, to powers of arrest and of detention. All of these must be justified by common law, statute or EC law, and, must not otherwise breach constitutional rights.

The State has an obligation to detect and prevent crimes, which in turn has led to the recognition of a common law power to stop persons suspected of committing a crime to investigate the matter and to operate random road blocks for that end; see *DPP (Stratford) v Fagan* [1994] 3 IR 265. There are also numerous statutory powers to stop and search, an example being the power of search under s 23 of the Misuse of Drugs Act, 1977, as amended, which permitted a policeman to search a person and if he considered it necessary for the purpose, detain the person for such time as was reasonably necessary for making the search. The Supreme Court rejected a challenge to this power in *O'Callaghan v Ireland* [1994] 1 IR 555. In upholding the power the Supreme Court referenced the authority of the Oireachtas to reconcile the exercise of personal rights with the claims of the common good. That was the case here given the real threat from drugs, thus the power was a legitimate and proportionate deprivation of liberty. The Court also noted that a person detained for search but not arrested has the same rights as an arrested person, *per* Finlay CJ (at 563):

> 'A person lawfully in the custody of the Garda Síochána for either of these purposes will have appropriate rights concerning access to legal advice, freedom from harassment, interrogation or assault, and all the other rights that are appropriate to an arrested person.'

14.3.2 POWERS OF ARREST

The State also has wide powers of arrest. In effect these are powers to stop and detain a person. At common law arrest was solely for the purpose of bringing a person before a court for charging and did not as such form part of the criminal investigative régime. Rather it was one of a number of means of instituting criminal proceedings, which can also be done by summons and warrant. The power to detain after arrest is a separate matter, now provided for by statute. An arresting officer can use reasonable force in effecting the arrest, under s 19 of the Non Fatal Offences Against the Person Act, 1997. The question as to whether the arrest is lawful shall be determined according to the circumstances as the person using the force believed them to be. On the other hand, a person may reasonably physically resist an unlawful restraint on his or her liberty, including an attempted unlawful arrest. This may be a delicate balance as resisting a lawful arrest is itself an offence, and may constitute an assault and battery.

The issue of whether a person is or is not under arrest is one of fact. While a deprivation of liberty is a necessary component, it may not be sufficient and there is no precise definition of an arrest. In any case the issue for a court is whether a deprivation of liberty is lawful; see *Dunne v Clinton* [1930] IR 366, discussed below at **14.3.3**. In *DPP v McCreesh* [1992] 2 IR 239, Hederman J stated (at 250):

> 'An arrest consists in or involves the seizure or touching of a person's body accompanied by a form of words which indicate to that person that he is under restraint. Whilst the older cases held that words alone would not suffice to constitute an arrest, nowadays words alone *may* amount to an arrest if, in the circumstances, they are calculated to bring, and do bring, to the person's notice that he was under restraint and he submitted to the compulsion—see *e.g. Alderson v. Booth* [1969] 2 Q.B. 216.'

In order to constitute a valid arrest the courts have stated that the person must be informed that he is under a restraint and must know of the reason for the arrest. The courts have also said that the onus is on the arrested person to prove that he did not know the reason for the arrest, which in effect means that if he knows the reason, even though not so informed by the policeman, the arrest is valid. Otherwise, the police are under a duty to inform of the ground of arrest, particularly when asked.

It should be noted that Article 5(2) ECHR provides:

> '2.   Everyone who is arrested shall be informed promptly, in a language which he understands, of the reasons for his arrest and of any charge against him.'

An arrest can be effected on foot of a court warrant. There are also many statute-based powers of arrest without warrant. Specific examples include the Offences Against the State Act, 1939, or the Misuse of Drugs Act, 1977, which provide powers of arrest for specific offences. The conditions specified in the particular statute for the exercise of the power must be complied with. Such a condition commonly demands the arresting officer to have a reasonable suspicion or belief that a certain offence has been committed.

The general power to arrest is now contained in s 4 of the Criminal Law Act, 1997, which replaced the common law powers. This power of arrest applies to an arrestable offence, which is one carrying a potential penalty of upwards of five years imprisonment and provides:

> '(1)   Subject to subsections (4) and (5), any person may arrest without warrant anyone who is or whom he or she, with reasonable cause, suspects to be in the act of committing an arrestable offence.
>
> (2)   Subject to subsections (4) and (5), where an arrestable offence has been committed, any person may arrest without warrant anyone who is or whom he or she, with reasonable cause, suspects to be guilty of the offence.
>
> (3)   Where a member of the Garda Síochána, with reasonable cause, suspects that an arrestable offence has been committed, he or she may arrest without warrant anyone whom the member, with reasonable cause, suspects to be guilty of the offence.
>
> (4)   An arrest other than by a member of the Garda Síochána may only be effected by a person under subsection (1) or (2) where he or she, with reasonable cause, suspects that the person to be arrested by him or her would otherwise attempt to avoid, or is avoiding, arrest by a member of the Garda Síochána.
>
> (5)   A person who is arrested pursuant to this section by a person other than a member of the Garda Síochána shall be transferred into the custody of the Garda Síochána as soon as practicable.

(6)   This section shall not affect the operation of any enactment restricting the institution of proceedings for an offence or prejudice any power of arrest conferred by law apart from this section.'

Again, these powers are for the purpose of ensuring the attendance of an accused at court, and not for the purpose of detention to facilitate interrogation, although many recent statutes contain such power of detention for that purpose. All powers of arrest must be exercised for their correct purpose, otherwise the arrest may be rendered unlawful if there is a conscious and deliberate violation of the right to liberty; *State (Trimbole) v Governor of Mountjoy Prison* [1985] IR 550. This could have a serious impact on the admissibility in court of evidence gathered subsequent to an unlawful detention.

Thus it is unlawful to exercise a power of arrest as a device to bring a person into custody to be questioned on another issue. Both the arrest and subsequent detention would be rendered unlawful. In *State (Bowes) v Fitzpatrick* [1978] ILRM 195 the accused was arrested for malicious damage to a knife found at a murder scene. The arrest was really for the purpose for investigating the murder and as there was no interest whatsoever in prosecuting for the malicious damage the arrest was invalid.

14.3.3   INFORMAL DETENTION

In the past, before wider powers of detention were introduced, persons were often said to be helping the police with their inquiries, a euphemism for being questioned prior to a possible arrest. The courts, which sometimes tacitly accepted evidence-gathering questioning after arrest, have not recognised any halfway house between arrest and detention. In *Dunne v Clinton* [1930] IR 366 the plaintiffs sued for false imprisonment when they had been told they were 'detained'. They had initially gone voluntarily to the police station and had not been arrested. The High Court, *per* Hanna J said (at 372):

'In law there can be no half-way house between the liberty of the subject, unfettered by restraint, and an arrest. If a person under suspicion voluntarily agrees to go to a police station to be questioned, his liberty is not interfered with, as he can change his mind at any time. If, having been examined, he is asked, and voluntarily agrees, to remain in the barracks until some investigation is made, he is still a free subject, and can leave at any time. But a practice has grown up of "detention", as distinct from arrest. It is, in effect, keeping a suspect in custody, perhaps under as comfortable circumstances as the barracks will permit, without making any definite charge against him, and with the intimation in some form of words or gesture that he is under restraint, and will not be allowed to leave. As, in my opinion, there could be no such thing as notional liberty, this so-called detention amounts to arrest, and the suspect has in law been arrested and in custody during the period of his detention.'

The Court therefore treated the restriction of the plaintiffs as in law a detention, as it was a total restraint of their liberty imposed on them by the action of the police. As they has not been taken as then required before a peace commissioner the detention was unlawful.

The courts will therefore treat such informally detailed persons as being under *de facto* arrest, which triggers safeguards regarding their rights. In *People (DPP) v O'Loughlin* [1979] IR 85 O'Higgins CJ in the Court of Criminal Appeal said (at 91):

' "Holding for questioning" and "taking into custody" and "detaining" are merely different ways of describing the act of depriving a man of his liberty. To do such without lawful authority is an open defiance of Article 40, s. 4, sub-s. 1, of the Constitution.'

From the above it is clear that a person can be voluntarily in custody giving information, so long as that position is clear. Matters change when he becomes a suspect. As Walsh said in his book on *Criminal Procedure* (2002, Round Hall, 4–08):

'It follows...that where a person has come to a Garda station voluntarily, he must be formally arrested as soon as a member of the Garda Siochana makes up his or her mind to detain him.'

If the detention continues it will become unlawful.

14.3.4   DETENTION PENDING TRIAL

There is a general obligation upon the police to bring a person arrested under warrant to a District Court to deal with the offence concerned. There is a similar obligation to bring a person before the District Court as soon as practicable after being charged in the case of an arrest without warrant (see s 15 of the Criminal Justice Act, 1951, as amended). As noted above, if there is an unreasonable delay in bringing a person to court the detention may become unlawful.

The general power of detention after arrest is designed to secure attendance at court. An arrested person can be granted station bail, with or without recognisance from him and/or a surety. For more serious offences, the District Court can decide whether to remand the accused in custody or on bail. This is generally a decision for the District Court, or if refused, or in the case of more serious offences such as murder, for the High Court. Other courts also have some bail granting jurisdiction in cases before them.

Generally, courts are concerned where an accused but untried person is remanded in custody as an innocent person is incarcerated and may be caused hardship by such imprisonment. This has led to a presumption in favour of granting bail rather than remanding an accused in custody. The Supreme Court has stated that an accused should be given bail unless the opposing party shows reasons for not so doing.

The grounds upon which bail could be refused were first established by the Supreme Court in the case of *The People (AG) v O'Callaghan* [1966] IR 501, where Walsh J said (at 516–17):

'In this country it would be quite contrary to the concept of personal liberty enshrined in the Constitution that any person should be punished in respect of any matter upon which he has not been convicted or that in any circumstances he should be deprived of his liberty upon only the belief that he will commit offences if left at liberty, save in the most extraordinary circumstances....'

This was a clear statement against the notion of preventative detention, ie detention based on the suspicion that a person would commit further offences if released on bail. The Court did recognise that there were grounds for the refusal of bail. These were the likelihood of the accused not attending at trial, the seriousness of the charge and potential punishment and the likelihood of interference with evidence or witnesses.

This restrictive approach eventually led to calls for reform, calls that were eventually enacted in a constitutional amendment to Article 41.4.6° which provides that:

'*Provision may be made by law for the refusal of bail by a court to a person charged with a serious offence where it is reasonably considered necessary to prevent the commission of a serious offence by that person.*'

This in turn led to the enactment of the Bail Act, 1997 which implemented the changes. This provided, at s 2(2), that for serious offences, ie those with a penalty of more than five years imprisonment, the considerations for bail were:

'(a)   *the nature and degree of seriousness of the offence with which the accused person is charged and the sentence likely to be imposed on conviction,*
(b)   *the nature and degree of seriousness of the offence apprehended and the sentence likely to be imposed on conviction,*

    (c)   *the nature and strength of the evidence in support of the charge,*

    (d)   *any conviction of the accused person for an offence committed while he or she was on bail,*

    (e)   *any previous convictions of the accused person including any conviction the subject of an appeal (which has neither been determined nor withdrawn) to a court,*

    (f)   *any other offence in respect of which the accused person is charged and is awaiting trial.'*

Section 2(1) provides:

'Where an application for bail is made by a person charged with a serious offence, a court may refuse the application if the court is satisfied that such refusal is reasonably considered necessary to prevent the commission of a serious offence by that person.'

The Act also specified the terms and procedures upon which bail can be granted which were added to by the Criminal Justice Act, 2007.

14.3.5   DETENTION PENDING CHARGE

At common law there was no power of post-arrest detention, which undoubtedly caused difficulties in investigating crimes. Starting with anti-terrorist measures, but extending slowly beyond such matters, there are a number of statutes that give a power of detention following arrest and before charge. These measures are seen by many as erosions of civil liberties.

Possibly one of the best-known powers of detention is that contained in s 39 of the Offences Against the State Act, 1939, as amended. This allows for an initial detention in a police station or prison or other place for 24 hours, to be extended by another 24 hours where an officer not below the rank of Chief Superintendent so directs. There is a further provision permitting a District Court application to permit a further 24 hours detention. This power of detention is for the purpose of investigating the alleged commission of a crime by the person arrested; see *People (DPP) v Quilligan* [1987] ILRM 606. This Act is designed to cover a range of offences related to terrorist-type activities.

The first general power of post-arrest detention was created by s 4 of the Criminal Justice Act, 1984, as amended. This permits a policeman to detain a person whom he has reasonable cause to suspect has committed certain serious offences where that is necessary for the proper investigation of the offence. The initial detention is for six hours from the time of the arrest, but that can be extended to 12 hours under certain conditions. A further amendment introduced by s 9 of the Criminal Justice Act, 2006, permits a further 12 hours detention.

Anti-drug trafficking legalisation also contains provision for extended detention, possibly up to seven days. Section 50 of the Criminal Justice Act, 2007, as amended by the Criminal Justice (Amendment) Act, 2009, introduced extended detention for certain serious crimes relating to organised crimes. The detention can, on full application, be up to seven days. If it becomes clear that the there are no longer reasonable grounds for believing that a detention is necessary for the proper investigation of the offence the person is to be released from custody forthwith.

14.3.6   LONG-TERM DETENTION (IMPRISONMENT)

Persons can be held by court warrant for long periods following their conviction by a competent court, following a fair trial. There is limited scope for challenging such detentions separate from challenging the conviction or sentence. It is generally accepted that an otherwise lawful detention in prison could be vitiated by poor prison conditions, but as Hogan and Whyte (*JM Kelly: The Irish Constitution*, 4th edn, 2003, para 7.4.25) note, there is no example of a successful case in point. The argument stems from the proposition that while many of a detainee's constitutional rights are abrogated during a valid detention, many others remain intact, including those relating to bodily integrity and freedom from inhuman or degrading treatment. Similarly, while technical flaws in orders or detention warrants may create an illegal detention, not every technical flaw will vitiate an otherwise valid detention.

14.3.7 DEPRIVATIONS OF LIBERTY OTHERWISE THAN IN THE CONTEXT OF A CRIMINAL INVESTIGATION/PROSECUTION

The law also permits detentions in situations other than as a punishment for having committed a crime. There are commonly two bases for these. The first is welfare-based, ie where a person is detained for what is perceived to be their own good. An example is commitment to a psychiatric hospital. The second base tends to be public order. This is commonly utilised against persons with no entitlement to be in the State, though some other condition must also be satisfied. The detention of certain immigrants and asylum seekers is an example (see **15.2.5.4**, **15.2.5.5** and **15.4.9**).

14.3.8 DETENTION PURSUANT TO THE MENTAL HEALTH ACT

Persons with mental disorders have been subject to civil detention, sometimes called commitment, in psychiatric hospitals. The power was initially contained in the Mental Treatment Act, 1945, as amended. That statute provided for a number of different kinds of detention depending upon the condition of the patient. The procedure was purely a civil one and involved a reception order being made by a doctor following an examination. There was no independent review of the detention by a quasi-judicial tribunal. This was upheld by the Supreme Court in *In re Philip Clarke* [1950] IR 235, where it was said by O'Byrne J (at 247–8) that:

> 'The impugned legislation is of a paternal character, clearly intended for the care and custody of persons suspected to be suffering from mental infirmity and for the safety and well-being of the public generally. The existence of mental infirmity is too widespread to be overlooked, and was, no doubt, present to the minds of the draughtsmen when it was proclaimed in Art. 40, 1, of the Constitution that, though all citizens, as human beings, are to be held equal before the law, the State may, nevertheless, in its enactments, have due regard to differences of capacity, physical and moral, and of social function. We do not see how the common good would be promoted or the dignity and freedom of the individual assured by allowing persons, alleged to be suffering from such infirmity, to remain at large to the possible danger of themselves and others.

> The section is carefully drafted so as to ensure that the person, alleged to be of unsound mind, shall be brought before, and examined by, responsible medical officers with the least possible delay. This seems to us to satisfy every reasonable requirement, and we have not been satisfied, and do not consider that the Constitution requires, that there should be a judicial inquiry or determination before such a person can be placed and detained in a mental hospital.'

Thus the constitution permitted a form of preventative detention in this type of case. While that seems to be the last word on the constitutional aspect, it was clear that the absence of automatic independent periodic review was a breach of the ECHR, see below at **14.5**. It should also be noted that the constitutional *habeas corpus* application was often used to challenge such detentions.

The Mental Health Act, 2001, came into force in 2006 and has replaced the provisions regarding the commitment of patients formerly contained in the Mental Treatment Act, 1945, as amended. This Act permits the detention of a person with a mental disorder, as defined in the Act. The procedure allows an involuntary admission recommendation to be made by a doctor. This recommendation lasts for seven days. The person is then brought, sometimes by the police, to the psychiatric hospital, called an approved centre under the Act. It is the consultant psychiatrist at that hospital who makes a further examination and, where appropriate, the actual admission order under s 14 of the Act that justifies the detention. This admission order permits the admission, detention and treatment of a patient for 21 days. The order then expires unless it is renewed.

The initial renewal order, made by a consultant psychiatrist, will last for a maximum of three months. That can itself be renewed for a further period of six months, and thereafter for periods of up to a year on each renewal. The initial admission order and all renewal extensions must be reviewed by the Mental Health Tribunal (the Tribunal) within 21 days of being made, and there is an appeal to the Circuit Court from the decision of the Tribunal.

This Tribunal is a three-member body established under the Act to independently review the admission order. The patient is entitled to legal representation before the Tribunal, and this is provided through the Mental Health Commission. If the Tribunal considers that the patient is not suffering from a mental disorder it must order his or her discharge. However, the admission order can be upheld by the Tribunal even if there was some flaw in the procedures, so long as the failure does not affect the substance of the order and does not cause an injustice (see s 18(1)).

In a challenge taken to a detention under these new procedures in *O'D v Kennedy and others* [2007] 3 IR 689 Charleton J said (at 15):

> 'These provisions are exacting and complex. They were designed, however, by the Oireachtas in order to replace the situation whereby it was potentially possible for a person to be certified and detained in a mental hospital and then forgotten. The need for periodic review and renewal, and the independent examination of these conditions is not a mere bureaucratic layer grafted on to the previous law for the treatment of those who are seriously ill and a danger to themselves and others: it is an essential component of the duty of society to maintain the balance between the protection of its interests and the rights of those who are apparently mentally ill.'

However, Charleton J also considered s 18(1) and held that even where there were technical defects in the admission order, such could be cured by a subsequent validation of the admission order by the Tribunal. He continued that the High Court has a more limited role in assessing the validity on a *habeas corpus* application, in that it can only consider the lawfulness of a detention at a particular point in time, and stated (at 705):

> 'I would expressly hold that if at a time when the High Court considers an application for habeas corpus, a period of unlawful detention has been cured validly by a decision of the Mental Health Tribunal under s.18(1) of the Mental Health Act, 2001 that the remedy is no longer available.'

14.3.9 DETENTION OF CHILDREN WITH SPECIAL NEEDS

Children taken into care under the ordinary provisions of the Child Care Act, 1991 can be placed in residential homes. However, this did not provide for the secure detention of children who were out of control. The gap was filled by the High Court, which used its inherent jurisdiction over children to order secure detention; see eg *FN v Minister for Health* [1995] 1 IR 409. Before that decision, children were sometimes 'criminalised', ie charged with offences so that courts could have jurisdiction to order their detention.

The courts have since recognised that they can detain children without the need to convict them of an offence. This is usually in special care units, but on occasion can be in prison,

the European Convention on Human Rights Act, 2003 (see **chapter 5**), and the Criminal Justice (United Nations Convention Against Torture) Act, 2000. The right to asylum is now enshrined in the Charter of Fundamental Rights (see **15.2.4** below on EU law). International human rights instruments are of great assistance in the interpretation of refugee law, and identifying what constitutes persecutory treatment.

15.2.4   EU LAW

Article 78 of the Treaty on the Functioning of the European Union (TFEU) (a consolidated text of the Treaty on European Union and the TFEU, formerly the EC Treaty, post Lisbon are published at OJ C115/01 9 May 2008) (ex Article 63, points 1 and 2, and 64(2) EC Treaty) provides that:

'The Union shall develop a common policy on asylum, subsidiary protection and temporary protection with a view to offering appropriate status to any third-country national requiring international protection and ensuring compliance with the principle of non-refoulement. *This policy must be in accordance with the Geneva Convention of 28 July 1951 and the Protocol of 31 January 1967 relating to the status of refugees, and other relevant treaties.'*

EU asylum legislation now has a legal basis in Title V (ex Title IV) of Part Three TFEU. Pursuant to Article 1 of Protocol (No 21) on The Position of The United Kingdom and Ireland in Respect of the Area of Freedom, Security and Justice, and subject to an option to take part in the adoption of any proposed measures, Ireland does not take part in the adoption of measures pursuant to Title V. A similar protocol applied to the UK and Ireland in respect of ex Title IV measures prior to the Treaty of Lisbon.

The Treaty of Amsterdam 1997 committed the EU to establishing a common area of freedom, security and justice. The political mandate and overall policy agenda progressing this common area has been provided by a series of five-year programmes: 'The Tampere Programme' 1999–2004, 'The Hague Programme' 2005–2009, and now 'The Stockholm Programme' 2010–2014. Under what was then Article 63(1) of the Treaty Establishing the European Community, the Council was obliged to adopt measures on asylum, in accordance with the 1951 Convention and the 1967 Protocol, in respect, *inter alia*, of the following:

- criteria and mechanisms for determining which Member State is responsible for considering an application for asylum submitted by a national of a third-country in one of the Member States

- minimum standards on the reception of asylum seekers in Member States

- minimum standards with respect to the qualification of nationals of third-countries as refugees

- minimum standards on procedures in Member States for granting or withdrawing refugee status

- minimum standards for giving temporary protection to displaced persons from third-countries who cannot return to their country of origin and for persons who otherwise need international protection.

The requisite measures have been adopted in the following legal instruments, these being the legal instruments comprising the core of EU international protection and refugee law:

- Council Regulation (EC) 343/2003 of 18 February 2003 establishing the criteria and mechanisms for determining the Member State responsible for examining an asylum application lodged in one of the Member States by a third-country national ('the Dublin Regulation')

INTERNATIONAL PROTECTION AND REFUGEE LAW

- Council Directive 2003/9/EC of 27 January 2003 laying down minimum standards for the reception of asylum seekers ('The Reception Directive')

- Council Directive 2004/83/EC of 29 April 2004 on minimum standards for the qualification and status of third-country nationals or stateless persons as refugees or as persons who otherwise need international protection and the content of the protection granted ('The Qualification Directive')

- Council Directive 2005/85/EC of 1 December 2005 on minimum standards on procedures in Member States for granting and withdrawing refugee status ('The Procedures Directive')

- Council Directive 2001/55/EC of 20 July 2001 on minimum standards for giving temporary protection in the event of a mass influx of displaced persons and on measures promoting a balance of efforts between Member States in receiving such persons and bearing the consequences thereof ('The Temporary Protection Directive').

Ireland has chosen to take part in all of these instruments, except for Council Directive 2003/9/EC on reception conditions. Council Regulations are binding and directly applicable, take effect without the need for further enactment, and may be relied upon by individuals before domestic courts. Directives are binding as to the result to be achieved, but they allow the State discretion as to the means of implementation, whether by legislation or administrative action. Indeed, mechanical transposition of a directive by legislative action at national level is not always necessary if existing laws already provide for the objectives to be achieved (see the observations of the High Court in relation to Directive 2005/85/EC in *Dokie & Ajibiola v Refugee Applications Commissioner & Ors*, 19 January 2010, High Court (unreported) at para 9).

The Treaty of Lisbon requires the development of a common European asylum policy with a view to offering appropriate status to any third-country national requiring international protection, and ensuring compliance with the principle of *non-refoulement*. To this end, under Article 78 TFEU (ex Article 63, points 1 and 2, and 64(2) EC Treaty) the Parliament and the Council are obliged to adopt measures on asylum, in accordance with the 1951 Convention and the 1967 Protocol for a common European asylum system comprising, *inter alia*:

(a) *a uniform status of asylum for nationals of third-countries, valid throughout the Union;*

(b) *a uniform status of subsidiary protection for nationals of third- countries who, without obtaining European asylum, are in need of international protection;*

(c) *a common system of temporary protection for displaced persons in the event of a massive inflow;*

(d) *common procedures for the granting and withdrawing of uniform asylum or subsidiary protection status;*

(e) *criteria and mechanisms for determining which Member State is responsible for considering an application for asylum or subsidiary protection;*

(f) *standards concerning the conditions for the reception of applicants for asylum or subsidiary protection;*

(g) *partnership and cooperation with third-countries for the purpose of managing inflows of people applying for asylum or subsidiary or temporary protection.*

The core legislative instruments of the EU asylum *acquis* are currently being recast. With the entry into force of the Treaty of Lisbon asylum-related matters, instead of requiring unanimity among the Member States, will be adopted by qualified majority voting in the Council and the co-decision procedures with the Parliament. Most legislative initiatives under the Stockholm Programme will apply to Ireland only if the State 'opts in'.

If a conflict arises between EU law and the law of a Member State, EU law takes precedence, and the law of the Member State is ignored. This is known as the principle of supremacy or primacy of EU law. See Case 6/64 *Costa v ENEL* [1964] ECR 585. Article 29 of the Constitution of Ireland establishes the supremacy of EU law in Ireland (see **2.4** and **2.4.2**).

Prior to the Treaty of Lisbon, the European Court of Justice (ECJ) did not have the same competency in relation to asylum and other matters in the area of freedom, security and justice as it did in other areas. In particular, Article 234 of the Treaty Establishing the European Community allowed any court or tribunal to refer questions relating to the interpretation of EU law to the ECJ for a preliminary ruling, but this was restricted in relation to asylum, and other Title V (ex Title IV) matters. Now, however, the TFEU allows preliminary references from any court or tribunal to the ECJ on matters relating to asylum (see Article 267 TFEU).

As a result of the Treaty of Lisbon, Article 6(1) TFEU provides that the Charter of Fundamental Rights is binding on the Member States, with the concomitant effects of putting the right to asylum into a binding human rights instrument for the first time, and establishing the right to asylum and the principle of *non-refoulement* as general principles of EU law. Article 18 of the Charter provides for the right to asylum as follows:

> 'The right to asylum shall be guaranteed with due respect for the rules of the Geneva Convention of 28 July 1951 and the Protocol of 31 January 1967 relating to the status of refugees and in accordance with the Treaty on European Union and the Treaty on the Functioning of the European Union ... '

Article 19 of the Treaty prohibits *refoulement*:

> 'no one may be removed, expelled or extradited to a State where there is a serious risk that he or she would be subjected to the death penalty, torture or other inhuman or degrading treatment or punishment.'

The Charter is directly legally binding on all European institutions, offices and agencies as well as Member States when implementing EU law (see **8.10**).

15.2.4.1 Council Regulation (EC) 343/2003 ('The Dublin Regulation')

Council Regulation (EC) 343/2003 establishes the criteria and mechanisms for determining the Member State responsible for examining an asylum application lodged in one of the Member States by a third-country national. The Regulation is directly applicable, but has been given domestic effect through s 22 of the Refugee Act, 1996 (as amended), and the Refugee Act, 1996 (Section 22) Order, 2003 (SI 423/2003). It provides a system to determine the Member State responsible for determining an applicant's refugee status, and allows for the transfer of an asylum applicant in one state to another participating state deemed responsible for examining the applicant's asylum claim. The Regulation provides a set of hierarchical criteria to determine the Member State responsible for examining a claim:

(a) The Member State where an unaccompanied minor applicant has a family member legally present.

(b) The Member State where an applicant has a family member resident as a refugee.

(c) The Member State where an applicant has a family member awaiting a first-instance asylum decision.

(d) The Member State that issued an applicant with a residence document.

(e) The Member State entered irregularly by an applicant.

(f) The Member State that allowed an applicant to enter without a visa.

(g) The Member State where an applicant applied for asylum in an international transit area.

(h) The Member State where the first asylum application was lodged.

    (i)   The Member State responsible for the largest number of an applicant's family members, where the above criteria would result in the family being separated.

The Member State responsible for examining an application is obliged to 'take charge' of an asylum seeker who has lodged an application in a different Member State and complete the examination of the asylum application. Similarly, the Member State responsible is obliged to 'take back' an applicant whose application is under examination and who is in another Member State without permission, an applicant who has withdrawn the first application and made an application in another Member State, and an applicant whose application it has rejected. Transfer of an applicant to the Member State responsible is generally required to take place within six months of acceptance of the take-charge request.

15.2.4.2   Council Directive 2003/9/EC ('The Reception Directive')

Member States participating in Council Directive 2003/9/EC were required to ensure their domestic legislation complied with the Directive from 6 February 2005. Ireland, however, is not participating in the adoption of the Directive pursuant to the Protocol on the position of the United Kingdom and Ireland annexed to the TEU and to the Treaty establishing the European Community by the Treaty of Amsterdam. The Directive sets out minimum standards of reception conditions for applicants for asylum in Member States in order to ensure that they will have a dignified standard of living, and to afford them comparable living conditions in all Member States. The Directive also seeks to limit secondary movements of asylum seekers who might be influenced by a variety of reception conditions in the Member States. The Directive provides asylum seekers with certain rights, including the right to freedom of movement within the territory of the host Member State, the right to maintain family unity, the right of minors to education, the right to work, the right to conditions sufficient to ensure a standard of living adequate for the health of applicants and capable of ensuring their subsistence, and the right to emergency health care and essential treatment of illness.

15.2.4.3   Council Directive 2004/83/EC ('The Qualification Directive')

Member States were required to bring into force domestic legislation necessary to comply with Council Directive 2004/83/EC by 10 October 2006. Ireland 'opted-in' to the Directive pursuant to Article 3 of the Protocol on the position of the United Kingdom and Ireland by way of a notification dated 13 February 2002. The Directive is currently given domestic effect by the European Communities (Eligibility for Protection) Regulations, 2006 (SI 518/2006). The Directive establishes minimum standards for the qualification of third-country nationals and stateless persons as refugees or beneficiaries of subsidiary protection, the minimum levels of rights and benefits attached to the protection granted, and the benefits to be enjoyed by those given protection and their family members. Member States can apply more favourable standards.

15.2.4.4   Council Directive 2005/85/EC ('The Procedures Directive')

The Member States were required to have domestic legislation in place complying with Council Directive 2005/85/EC by 1 December 2007, and it applies to applications for asylum lodged in the Member States after that date. The Immigration, Residence and Protection Bill, 2010 proposes new legislative provisions to give effect to the Directive. The European Commission has decided to iniate proceedings in the European Court of Justice against Ireland for its failure to fully implement the Directive. The purpose of the Directive is to establish minimum standards for procedures within EU Member States for granting and withdrawing refugee status. The Directive is divided into chapters dealing with general provisions, basic principles and guarantees, procedures at first instance, procedures for withdrawal of refugee status, and appeals procedures. The Directive provides asylum seekers with certain rights and guarantees, including the right to access the procedure, the right to remain in the Member State pending examination of an asylum application, and the right to an effective remedy.

15.2.4.5   Council Directive 2001/55/EC ('The Temporary Protection Directive')

Member States were required to ensure domestic legislation complied with Council Directive 2001/55/EC from 31 December 2002. Ireland originally opted not to participate in the adoption of this Directive, but subsequently requested that it take part, and by the Decision 2003/690/EC of 2 October 2003, the Directive was deemed to apply to Ireland. The Immigration, Residence and Protection Bill, 2010 proposes compliant provisions. The Directive establishes minimum standards for granting temporary protection and rights for people who need such protection. It defines temporary protection as:

> 'a procedure of exceptional character to provide, in the event of a mass influx or imminent mass influx of displaced persons from third countries who are unable to return to their country of origin, immediate and temporary protection to such persons, in particular if there is also a risk that the asylum system will be unable to process this influx without adverse effects for its efficient operation, in the interests of the persons concerned and other persons requesting protection.'

15.2.5   IRISH LEGISLATION

15.2.5.1   The Refugee Act, 1996

The Refugee Act, 1996 (as amended), sets out core aspects of the current law governing the processing of applications for refugee status in Ireland. The principal purpose of the Act is to give statutory effect to the State's obligations under the 1951 Convention and the 1967 Protocol. Although the act pre-dates Council Directive 2004/83/EC, it is the legislation that, in conjunction with the European Communities (Eligibility for Protection) Regulations, 2006 (SI 518/2006), is relied upon to comply with that Directive. The Act, as amended, provided for the independent Refugee Applications Commissioner (the Commissioner) and Refugee Appeals Tribunal (the Tribunal). The Act implements the definition of a refugee and, substantially, the exclusion clauses from the 1951 Convention. It provides for the prohibition of *refoulement*, and that applicants for asylum shall be given leave to enter and remain in the State. The Act also sets out the rights of declared refugees.

15.2.5.2   The Immigration Act, 1999

The Immigration Act, 1999 made many amendments to the Refugee Act, 1996 including setting out the powers of authorised officers and immigration officers, and replacing the Appeal Board with the Refugee Appeals Tribunal.

15.2.5.3   The Illegal Immigrants (Trafficking) Act, 2000

Section 5 of the Illegal Immigrants (Trafficking) Act, 2000 provides that certain decisions made in the asylum process, including decisions of the Commissioner and the Tribunal, and the Minister's decision whether to declare an applicant a refugee, cannot be questioned other than by way of judicial review. The Act provides for more stringent rules in relation to judicial review than those set out in Order 84 of the Rules of the Superior Courts.

15.2.5.4   The Immigration Act, 2003

The Immigration Act, 2003 amended the Refugee Act, 1996 substantially, providing, *inter alia*, for the following:

* Fingerprinting of asylum seekers
* Increased periods of detention for asylum applicants

- Increased duty to co-operate placed on the applicant

- Mandatory credibility considerations

- Safe countries of origin

- Prioritisation directions

- Special accelerated procedures at appeal stage

- Tribunal Chairperson's discretion not to publish decisions that in his or her opinion are not of legal importance

15.2.5.5 The Refugee Act, 1996 (Section 22) Order, 2003 (SI 423/2003)

This Order puts in place arrangements to give effect to Council Regulation (EC) 343/2003. The Order contains provisions allowing for the detention of asylum applicants pending their transfer to another Member State.

15.2.5.6 European Communities (Eligibility for Protection) Regulations, 2006 (SI 518/2006)

The European Communities (Eligibility for Protection) Regulations, 2006 (SI 518/2006) are intended to give effect to Council Directive 2004/83/EC, which came into force in October 2006 and which provides, *inter alia*, for a system of subsidiary protection. The Irish Regulations transpose the Directive's criteria for eligibility for subsidiary protection and contain provisions relating to assessment criteria in the decision-making process of the Commissioner and the Tribunal in respect of refugee status determination.

15.2.5.7 Proposed legislative reform

The Immigration, Residence and Protection Bill, 2010 proposes a reformed system for processing applications for protection, and proposes to repeal, *inter alia*, the Refugee Act, 1996, the Immigration Acts, 1999, 2003, and 2004, s 5 of the Illegal Immigrants (Trafficking) Act, 2000, and the European Communities (Eligibility for Protection) Regulations, 2006 (SI 518/2006). The Bill proposes a shift to a single determination procedure for protection claims: applicants would be required to set out all of the grounds on which they wish to remain in the State at the outset of the claim, and all matters would be examined together. The Bill is drafted in order to transpose into Irish law Council Directive 2005/85 EC, which has required domestic legislative compliance since 1 December 2007, and to integrate the provisions of the European Communities (Eligibility for Protection) Regulations, 2006 into primary legislation.

15.2.6 ACADEMIC TEXTS

Leading texts on refugee law include Guy Goodwin-Gill's *The Refugee in International Law;* James Hathaway's *The Law of Refugee Status; Asylum Law and Practice* by Mark Symes and Peter Jorro and *The Status of Refugees in International Law* by Atle Grahl Madson. Both Hathaway's and Goodwin-Gill's texts have been cited with approval by the Irish High Court. A leading periodical is the *International Journal of Refugee Law*. The *Refugee Law Reader* is an online reader on refugee law containing primary documents and academic literature.

The *Michigan Guidelines* are published from time to time on various aspects of refugee law, and as a result of conferences held by leading international refugee lawyers to consider specific matters of refugee law. There are currently Michigan Guidelines on the concept of the causal nexus in the Convention's refugee definition, internal flight, well-founded fear, the concept of a safe third-country, and the right to work for refugees and asylum seekers. The Guidelines have been cited with approval in international jurisprudence.

15.3   Principles of International Protection Law

15.3.1   THE PRINCIPLE OF *NON-REFOULEMENT*

Article 21(1) of Council Directive 2004/83/EC states that Member States shall respect the principle of *non-refoulement* in accordance with their international obligations. Article 33 of the 1951 Convention contains a prohibition of expulsion or return. The UN Convention Against Torture also contains a requirement of *non-refoulement*.

Section 5 of the Refugee Act, 1996 provides:

> *'(1)   A person shall not be expelled from the State or returned in any manner whatsoever to the frontiers of territories where, in the opinion of the Minister, the life or freedom of that person would be threatened on account of his or her race, religion, nationality, membership of a particular social group or political opinion.*
>
> *(2)   Without prejudice to the generality of subsection (1), a person's freedom shall be regarded as being threatened if, inter alia, in the opinion of the Minister, the person is likely to be subject to a serious assault (including a serious assault of a sexual nature).'*

In his judgment in *Meadows v The Minister for Justice, Equality and Law Reform*, 21 January 2010, Supreme Court (unreported), Murray CJ clarified the Minister's obligations in relation to his power to deport a person who has advanced a claim for international protection:

> 'In cases where there is no claim or factual material put forward to suggest that a deportation order would expose the deportee to any of the risks referred to in s 5 then no issue as regards refoulement arises and the decision of the Minister with regard to s 5 considerations is a mere formality and the rationale of the decision will be self evident.
>
> On the other hand if such material has been presented to him by or on behalf of the proposed deportee, as the case here, the Minister must specifically address that issue and form an opinion. Views or conclusions on such issues may have already been arrived at by officers who considered a proposed deportee's application for asylum at the initial or appeal stages, and their conclusions or views may be before the Minister but it remains at this stage for the Minister and the Minister alone in the light of all the material before him to form an opinion in accordance with s 5 as to the nature of the risk, if any, to which a proposed deportee might be exposed. This position is underscored by the fact that s 3 envisages that a proposed deportee be given an opportunity to make submissions directly to the Minister on his proposal to make a deportation order at that stage. The fact that certain decisions have been made by officers at an earlier stage in the course of the application for refugee status does not absolve him from making that decision himself.'

Murray CJ with specific reference to a decision in respect of the principle of *non- refoulement* under s 5 of the Refugee Act, 1996, further stated that administrative decisions affecting the rights and obligations of persons should at least disclose the essential rationale on foot of which the decision is taken, and that the rationale should be patent from the terms of the decision or capable of being inferred from its terms and its context. Murray CJ stated that if the criteria for judicial review set out in *O'Keefe v An Bord Pleanála* (1993) 1 IR 39 and *The State (Keegan) v Stardust Victims' Compensation Tribunal* [1986] IR 642 are to be effectively deployed, even in circumstances where the application of the principle of proportionality does not arise, at the very least the rationale underlying the decision regarding *refoulement* under s 5 of the Refugee Act 1996 must be discernible expressly or inferentially.

15.3.2   THE LAW OF REFUGEE STATUS

Section 2 of the Refugee Act, 1996 states as follows:

'In this Act ''a refugee'' means a person who, owing to a well founded fear of being persecuted for reasons of race, religion, nationality, membership of a particular social group or political opinion, is outside the country of his or her nationality and is unable or, owing to such fear, is unwilling to avail himself or herself of the protection of that country; or who, not having a nationality and being outside the country of his or her former habitual residence, is unable or, owing to such fear, is unwilling to return to it, but does not include a person who—

> *(a)   is receiving from organs or agencies of the United Nations (other than the High Commissioner) protection or assistance,*
>
> *(b)   is recognised by the competent authorities of the country in which he or she has taken residence as having the rights and obligations which are attached to the possession of the nationality of that country,*
>
> *(c)   there are serious grounds for considering that he or she—*
>
> > *(i)   has committed a crime against peace, a war crime, or a crime against humanity, as defined in the international instruments drawn up to make provision in respect of such crimes,*
> >
> > *(ii)   has committed a serious non-political crime outside the State prior to his or her arrival in the State, or*
> >
> > *(iii) has been guilty of acts contrary to the purposes and principles of the United Nations.'*

Article 2(c) of Council Directive 2004/83/EC states:

'''refugee'' means a third country national who, owing to a well-founded fear of being persecuted for reasons of race, religion, nationality, political opinion or membership of a particular social group, is outside the country of nationality and is unable or, owing to such fear, is unwilling to avail himself or herself of the protection of that country, or a stateless person, who, being outside of the country of former habitual residence for the same reasons as mentioned above, is unable or, owing to such fear, unwilling to return to it, and to whom Article 12 does not apply' [Article 12 deals with exclusion and is discussed below]

The elements of the definition may be distilled as follows:

- Well-founded fear

- Persecution

- Reasons

- Outside country of nationality or habitual residence

- Failure of state protection

- Exclusion from refugee status

- Cessation of refugee status

15.3.2.1   Well-founded fear

An applicant for asylum must have a well-founded fear of persecution to be declared as a refugee. Article 4(4) of Council Directive 2004/83/EC states:

'The fact that an applicant has already been subject to persecution or serious harm or to direct threats of such persecution or such harm, is a serious indication of the applicant's well-founded fear of persecution or real risk of suffering serious harm, unless there are good reasons to consider that such persecution or serious harm will not be repeated.'

Regulation 5(2) of the European Communities (Eligibility for Protection) Regulations, 2006 states:

'The fact that a protection applicant has already been subject to persecution or serious harm, or to direct threats of such persecution or such harm, shall be regarded as a serious indication of the applicant's well-founded fear of persecution or real risk of suffering serious harm, unless there are good reasons to consider that such persecution or serious harm will not be repeated, but compelling reasons arising out of previous persecution or serious harm alone may nevertheless warrant a determination that the applicant is eligible for protection.'

In *MST & Ors v The Minister for Justice, Equality and Law Reform*, 4 December 2009, High Court (unreported) [2009] IEHC 529 the Court found that the additional wording in the final clause of Regulation 5(2) was permitted by Recital 8 and Article 3 of the Directive which allow Member States to introduce or maintain more favourable standards so long as those standards are compatible with the Directive. In *Rostas v The Refugee Appeals Tribunal*, High Court, 31 July 2003 (unreported) Gilligan J stated that an applicant who has suffered past persecution is entitled to a legal presumption of a well-founded fear of future persecution, and that the presumption may be rebutted by showing a change in the conditions in the country of origin in the context of an individualised analysis.

The *Michigan Guidelines on Well Founded Fear* state at para 4 that:

'the protection of the Refugee Convention is not predicated on the existence of ''fear'' in the sense of trepidation. It requires instead the demonstration of ''fear'' understood as a forward-looking expectation of risk. Once fear so conceived is voiced by the act of seeking protection, it falls to the state party assessing refugee status to determine whether that expectation is borne out by the actual circumstances of the case. If it is, then the applicant's fear (that is, his or her expectation) of being persecuted should be adjudged well-founded.'

Refugee *sur place* claims are explicitly recognised under Regulation 6 of the 2006 Regulations:

'(1) A well-founded fear of being persecuted or a real risk of suffering serious harm may be based on events which have taken place since the protection applicant left his or her country of origin.

(2) A well-founded fear of being persecuted or a real risk of suffering serious harm may be based on activities which have been engaged in by the protection applicant since he or she left his or her country of origin, in particular where the protection decision-maker is satisfied that the activities relied upon constitute the expression and continuation of convictions or orientations held by the protection applicant in the country of origin.'

15.3.2.2   Persecution

Regulation 9(1) of the European Communities (Eligibility for Protection) Regulations, 2006 provides that acts of persecution for the purposes of s 2 of the Refugee Act, 1996 must:

'(a) be sufficiently serious by their nature or repetition as to constitute a severe violation of basic human rights, in particular the rights from which derogation cannot be made under Article 15(2) of the European Convention for the Protection of Human Rights and Fundamental Freedoms; or

(b) be an accumulation of various measures, including violations of human rights which is sufficiently severe as to affect an individual in a similar manner as mentioned in subparagraph (a).'

Regulation 9(2) sets out that persecution can take the form of:

'(a) acts of physical or mental violence, including acts of sexual violence;

371

(b) *legal, administrative, police, and/or judicial measures which are in themselves discriminatory or which are implemented in a discriminatory manner;*

(c) *prosecution or punishment, which is disproportionate or discriminatory;*

(d) *denial of judicial redress resulting in a disproportionate or discriminatory punishment;*

(e) *prosecution or punishment for refusal to perform military service in a conflict, where performing military service would include crimes or acts falling under the exclusion clauses as set out in section 2(c) of the 1996 Act;*

(f) *acts of a gender-specific or child-specific nature.'*

In *Rostas v Refugee Appeals Tribunal*, 31 July 2003, High Court (unreported), Gilligan J stated that persecution consists in serious and sustained or systematic violation of fundamental human rights, civil, political, social or economic, together with an absence or failure of state protection, including where such a situation results from the cumulative effect of various measures of discrimination.

Paragraph 51 of the UNHCR Handbook states that it may be inferred from the principle of *non-refoulement* in Article 33 of the 1951 Convention that a threat to life or freedom on account of race, religion, nationality, political opinion or membership of a particular social group is always persecution. The Handbook states that other serious violations of human rights—for the same reasons—would also constitute persecution. Paragraph 52 of the Handbook states that whether other prejudicial actions or threats amount to persecution will depend on the circumstances of each case, including evaluation of the opinions and feelings of the person concerned. Paragraph 53 of the Handbook states that an applicant may have been subjected to various discriminatory measures, in some cases combined with other adverse factors, that may justify a claim to well-founded fear of persecution on 'cumulative grounds'.

Paragraph 54 of the Handbook states that it is only in certain circumstances that discrimination will amount to persecution, for example where measures of discrimination lead to consequences of a substantially prejudicial nature for the person concerned. Paragraph 55 of the Handbook states that where measures of discrimination are, in themselves, not of a serious character, they may nevertheless give rise to a reasonable fear of persecution if they produce, in the mind of the person concerned, a feeling of apprehension and insecurity as regards his future existence.

Persecution of an applicant's close family may constitute persecution for the purposes of the Convention. In *Shen v Canada* [2004] 1 FCR D-23, the Federal Court of Canada held that the persecution of an infant child could constitute persecution of a parent.

A good starting place for understanding persecution is to consider the basic rights recognised by states in international human rights instruments. The table below (adapted from a presentation by Prof. James Hathaway) lays out the rights protected by the Universal Declaration of Human Rights (UDHR), the International Covenant on Economic, Social, and Cultural Rights (ICESCR), the International Covenant on Civil and Political Rights (ICCPR) and the European Convention on Human Rights (ECHR). Professor Hathaway writes: 'The types of harm to be protected against include the breach of any right within the first category, a discriminatory or non-emergency abrogation of a right within the second category, or the failure to implement a right within the third category which is either discriminatory or not grounded in the absolute lack of resources' (*The Law of Refugee Status*, p. 112). For further information about how this chart should be used, see Chapter 4 of *The Law of Refugee Status* and also Professor Hathaway's article 'The Relationship Between Human Rights and Refugee Law: What Refugee Law Judges Can Contribute,' in IARLJ, *The Realities of Refugee Determination on the Eve of a New Millennium: The Role of the Judiciary* 80–90 (1999).

TABLE 1: Identifying persecution: rights recognised by states in some international human rights instruments.

RIGHT	ECHR	UDHR	ICESR	ICCPR
LEVEL 1				
Life	2	3		6
Torture	3	5		7
Slavery	4	4		8
Ex post facto pros.	6, 7	11(2)		15
Recog. As person		6		16
Thought, religion	9	18		18
LEVEL 2				
Arb. Arrest/detention	5	9		9, 10
Fair crim. Proced.	7	10,11		14
Privacy	8	12, 25	10	17, 23
Internal movement		13		12(1)
Leave and return		13		12(2–4)
Opin./Expt/ass/assn	10	18–20		19–22
Trade union mem.	11	20	8	22
Partake in govt.		21		25(a)
Public employ't		21		25(c)
Vote genuine elec.		21		25(b)
LEVEL 3				
Work		23	6	
Just cond. Emply't		23	7	
Food/cloth/housing		23	11(1)	
Medical care		25	12	
Social security		22	9	
Basic education		26	13–14	
Cultural express.		27	15	
LEVEL 4				
Private property		17		
Unemploy. Protec.		23		

(Table produced here by kind permission of Prof. James Hathaway.)

15.3.2.3 Reasons

The persecution feared by an applicant must have some connection to his/her race, religion, nationality, membership of a particular social group, or political opinion. The reason for persecution may be connected to either the instigators of the feared persecution, or to a State's failure to protect. The House of Lords case of *Islam and Shah v Secretary of State for the Home Department* [1999] 2 All ER 545 involved Pakistani women who feared they would be beaten by their husbands and subjected to false allegations of adultery. While the agents of persecution were not necessarily motivated by a convention ground, Pakistan was found to have refused to protect the applicants because they were women, thus satisfying the convention nexus of 'membership of a particular social group'.

Article 10(2) of Council Directive 2004/83/EC states that when assessing if an applicant has a well-founded fear of being persecuted it is immaterial whether the applicant actually possesses the racial, religious, national, social or political characteristic that attracts the persecution, provided that such a characteristic is attributed to the applicant by the actor of persecution.

Race

Article 10(1)(a) of Council Directive 2004/83/EC provides that the concept of race shall in particular include considerations of colour, descent, or membership of a particular ethnic group.

Religion

Article 10(1)(b) of Council Directive 2004/83/EC provides that the concept of religion shall in particular include the holding of theistic, non-theistic and atheistic beliefs, the participation in, or abstention from, formal worship in private or in public, either alone or in community with others, other religious acts or expressions of view, or forms of personal or communal conduct based on or mandated by any religious belief. In *RYT v Minister for Justice, Equality and Law Reform*, 23 January 2007, High Court (unreported) Herbert J stated that in considering evidence regarding persecution on the ground of religion, a decision-maker must not substitute their own view of an applicant's religious activities for a consideration of the probable view of those activities likely to be taken by the authorities in the applicant's country of origin in light of the evidence.

Nationality

Article 10(1)(c) of Council Directive 2004/83/EC provides that the concept of nationality shall not be confined to citizenship or lack thereof but shall in particular include membership of a group determined by its cultural, ethnic, or linguistic identity, common geographical or political origins or its relationship with the population of another state. James Hathaway in *The Law of Refugee Status*, outlines that the nationality category may apply to:

- Resident internationally unprotected people

- People denied full citizenship in their own state

- Victims of 'ascribed nationality'

- Residents of previously sovereign areas

- People whose nationality may be understood in a sociological sense.

Particular social group

Article 10(1)(d) of Council Directive 2004/83/EC provides as follows:

'a group shall be considered to form a particular social group where in particular:

members of that group share an innate characteristic, or a common background that cannot be changed, or share a characteristic or belief that is so fundamental to identity or conscience that a person should not be forced to renounce it, and
that group has a distinct identity in the relevant country, because it is perceived as being different by the surrounding society;

depending on the circumstances in the country of origin, a particular social group might include a group based on a common characteristic of sexual orientation. Sexual orientation cannot be understood to include acts considered to be criminal in accordance with national law of the Member States: Gender related aspects might be considered, without by themselves alone creating a presumption for the applicability of this Article'.

Section 1 of the Refugee Act, 1996 states that membership of a particular social group includes membership of a trade union and also includes membership of a group of persons whose defining characteristic is their belonging to the female or the male sex or having a particular sexual orientation.

Many social groups have been recognised in international case-law. Kirby J's litany in *Applicant A v Minister for Immigration and Ethnic Affairs* (1997) 190 CLR 225 is apposite:

'Members of particular social groups include members of the nobility of a former Eastern European Kingdom; members of the landed gentry in pre-communist Romania; farmers in areas of military operations in El Salvador; a former funeral director and his wife engaged in the private sector in pre-communist Poland; a woman from Trinidad subject to spousal abuse over 15 years; homosexual and bisexual men and women in countries where their sexual conduct, even with adults and in private; is illegal; dispossessed landlords who have abandoned their claim to property after revolution, but are still subject to stigma; unmarried women in a Moslem country without the protection of a male relative living in that country; members of the Tamil minority fleeing from Sri Lanka; young males who have evaded or deserted from compulsory military service in countries engaged in active military operations condemned by the international community; members of stigmatised professional groups and trade unions; soldiers of the army of the former regime in South Vietnam; Roman Catholics and ethnic Chinese fleeing from Vietnam; and freemasons escaping from Cuba.'

In *Msengi v Minister for Justice, Equality and Law Reform*, 1 December 2006, High Court (unreported) the Court found that HIV positive women in South Africa may constitute a particular social group. The House of Lords in *Islam and Shah v Secretary of State for the Home Department* [1999] 2 All ER 545 held that the category 'particular social group' includes whatever groups might be regarded as coming within the anti-discriminatory objectives of the 1951 Convention. The House of Lords found that what identifies a particular social group is its possession of a common immutable characteristic that is beyond the power of the individual to change, except at the cost of renunciation of fundamental human rights. La Forest J in *Canada (AG) v Ward* [1993] 2 SCR 689 held that social groups include (1) groups defined by an innate, immutable characteristic, (2) groups defined by past voluntary status where this experience cannot be changed, and (3) existing groups defined by volition so long as the purpose of the group is so fundamental to human dignity that they ought not to be required to abandon it.

In *The Law of Refugee Status*, James Hathaway identifies five interpretive approaches to the concept of particular social group:

(1) The Clarification Approach. This view holds that the ground of particular social group was a signal to define the other four grounds generously, ie, that this fifth ground embellished the others rather than being a substantive category.

(2) Particular Social Group as a Catch-All. This view holds that the category is a catch-all for any types of persecution that might arise.

(3) The Intuitive Approach. This supposes that a decision-maker will recognise a particular social group when faced with one.

(4) The Social Perception Test. This view posits that there must be some characteristic of the group other than persecution or common fear, and that the characteristic must set the group apart.

(5) *Ejusdem Generis*. This doctrine holds that general words used in an enumeration with specific words should be construed in a manner consistent with the specific words. In *Savchenkov v Secretary of State for the Home Department* [1996] Imm AR 28 it was said that the other Convention reasons reflected a civil or political status, and that membership of a particular social group should be interpreted *ejusdem generis*.

Political opinion

Article 10(1)(e) of Council Directive 2004/83/EC provides that the concept of political opinion shall in particular include the holding of an opinion, thought or belief on a matter related to the potential actors of persecution ... and to their policies or methods, whether or not that opinion, thought or belief has been acted upon by the applicant.

15.3.2.4 Outside country of nationality or habitual residence

To be a refugee, an applicant for international protection must be outside their country of nationality or, in the case of stateless persons, the country in which they were habitually resident. So long as an individual remains within the boundaries of his or her state, even though they may be persecuted, he or she cannot be a refugee. It is important to determine the application in respect of the correct country of nationality. In *Gioshvilli v The Minister for Justice, Equality and Law Reform*, 31 January, High Court (unreported) the applicant, a Georgian national, left Georgia to live in Russia, a country of which he was not a national. The Court held that in considering the claim in relation to Russia only, the decision-maker erred in law as consideration of the claim related to a country in respect of which the applicant could not claim nationality.

Asylum applicants without a nationality (ie, stateless persons) but with a fear of persecution in their country of former habitual residence come within the refugee definition in s 2 of the Refugee Act, 1996. Similarly, Regulation 2 of the European Communities (Eligibility for Protection) Regulations, 2006 defines 'country of origin' as meaning the country or countries of nationality or, for stateless persons, of former habitual residence.

Paragraph 101 of the UNHCR Handbook states that in the case of stateless refugees, the 'country of nationality' is replaced by the 'country of his former habitual residence', and rather than showing that the applicant is unwilling to avail themselves of the protection of that country, he or she must simply show that he or she is unwilling to return to it, and that seeking the protection of the State of former habitual residence does not arise.

In *Revenko v Secretary of State for the Home Department* (2001) 1 QB 601 the Court held, *inter alia*, that statelessness *per se* does not confer refugee status, and that a well-founded current fear of persecution on Convention grounds must be demonstrated. In *AD v Refugee Appeals Tribunal & Min for Justice* [2009] IEHC 326, 17 July 2009, High Court (unreported), the High Court considered the applicant's contention that s 2 of the Refugee Act, 1996 should be read literally in the case of a stateless person, who would therefore not have to show a fear of persecution on Convention grounds. The Court rejected the applicant's argument and approved the decision in *Revenko*, stating that to do otherwise would mean that stateless persons would be treated more favourably than applicants with nationality status. The Court stated that the drafting history, as well as the majority of academics and the comparative jurisprudence did not support the contrary view, and held that for stateless persons to fall within the refugee definition they must also show a well-founded fear of persecution for a Convention reason.

15.3.2.5 Failure of state protection

An asylum seeker cannot be in need of protection abroad if he or she has protection at home. Article 7 of Council Directive 2004/83/EC states that protection can be provided by the State, or parties or organisations, including international organisations, controlling the State or a substantial part of the territory of the State. In Joined Cases C-175/08, C-176/08, C-178/08 and C-179/08 *Abdulla and Ors v Germany*, 2 March 2010, the European Court of Justice (ECJ) stated that the actors of protection referred to in Article 7(1)(b) of the Directive may comprise international organisations controlling the State or a substantial part of the territory of the State, including by means of the presence of a multinational force in that territory.

If it is established that meaningful national protection is available to an asylum seeker, a fear of persecution cannot exist. Regulation 2 of the European Communities (Eligibility for Protection) Regulations, 2006 provides that:

> '*protection against persecution or serious harm shall be regarded as being generally provided where reasonable steps are taken by a state or parties or organisations, including international organisations, controlling a state or a substantial part of the territory of that state to prevent the persecution or suffering of serious harm, inter alia, by operating an effective legal system for the detection, prosecution and punishment of acts constituting persecution or serious harm, where the applicant has access to such protection.*'

Regulation 8 of the 2006 Regulations provides that for the purpose of assessing whether an international organisation controls a state or a substantial part of its territory and provides protection against persecution or serious harm, the protection decision-maker shall take into account any guidance which may be provided in relevant Council Acts.

The asylum seeker must show that he or she is unable or, owing to their fear, unwilling to avail of state protection from the feared persecution. Where an applicant for asylum has not sought state protection, the decision-maker must consider whether the applicant's evidence and the country of origin information is sufficient to rebut the presumption of state protection (*DK v Refugee Appeals Tribunal & Anor*, 5 May 2006, High Court (unreported)). The High Court has stated that a reference to an isolated example of state protection is insufficient to justify a finding of adequate state action, and that the test is whether the country of origin concerned provides reasonable protection in practical terms (*VI v Minister for Justice, Equality and Law Reform*, 10 May 2005, High Court (unreported)).

'Internal protection' or 'internal flight', is said to arise as a possible alternative to refugee protection where effective protection is not possible in one part of the country of origin, but is possible in another part of the same country. Regulation 7(1) of the 2006 Regulations provides that as part of the assessment of the protection needs of an applicant, a determination that an applicant is not in need of protection can be made if 'the applicant can reasonably be expected to stay in a part of his country of origin where there is no well founded fear of being persecuted or real risk of suffering serious harm'. The decision-maker in making such an examination shall have regard to 'the general circumstances prevailing in that part of the country and to the personal circumstances of the applicant'.

The High Court has found it to be arguable that a decision on internal flight must comply with the UNHCR guidelines on the matter, and that a decision-maker must consider whether it would be reasonable in the circumstances for a claimant to relocate in the manner suggested (*VNI & Ors v Refugee Appeals Tribunal & Anor*, 24 June 2005, High Court (unreported)).

Leave was granted in the case of *MM v Refugee Appeals Tribunal & Ors*, 11 November 2009, High Court (unreported) on the grounds that the Tribunal had erred in law in respect of Article 7 of the Directive in failing to identify a part of the country as a site for relocation, and in failing to conduct the necessary inquiries to verify whether it was a place where the applicant could be reasonably expected to stay without fear of being persecuted or a real risk of suffering serious harm. Similarly, in *SBE v Refugee Appeals Tribunal & Min for Justice* [2009] IEHC 479, 28 October 2009, High Court (unreported) leave was granted to judicially review the decision of the Tribunal in part on the basis that it was a substantial argument that the contested decision was in breach of the obligations imposed by Regulation 7 in finding that internal relocation in Nigeria was available to the applicant in circumstances where the issue received no attention or investigation before the Commissioner, and the Tribunal did not identify a specific part of Nigeria as a prospective site for such relocation.

15.3.2.6 Exclusion from refugee status

Section 2 of the Refugee Act, 1996 substantially transposes the exclusion clauses from the 1951 Geneva Convention relating to the Status of Refugees:

> '[A refugee] ... *does not include a person who—*
>
> (a) *is receiving from organs or agencies of the United Nations (other than the High Commissioner) protection or assistance,*
> (b) *is recognised by the competent authorities of the country in which he or she has taken residence as having the rights and obligations which are attached to the possession of the nationality of that country,*
> (c) *there are serious grounds for considering that he or she—*
>> (i) *has committed a crime against peace, a war crime, or a crime against humanity, as defined in the international instruments drawn up to make provision in respect of such crimes,*
>> (ii) *has committed a serious non-political crime outside the State prior to his or her arrival in the State, or*
>> (iii) *has been guilty of acts contrary to the purposes and principles of the United Nations.'*

It should be noted, however, that Article 1D of the 1951 Convention has not been fully incorporated into Irish law. Article 1D states:

> *'This Convention shall not apply to persons who are at present receiving from organs or agencies of the United Nations other than the United Nations High Commissioner for Refugees protection or assistance.*
>
> *When such protection or assistance has ceased for any reason, without the position of such persons being definitively settled in accordance with the relevant resolutions adopted by the General Assembly of the United Nations, these persons shall ipso facto be entitled to the benefits of this Convention.'*

It is also noteworthy that s 2(c) of the 1996 Act provides an applicant is excluded from being a refugee where there are serious grounds for considering that he or she participated in the commission of the acts or crimes mentioned in s 2(c) of the Act, while Regulation 12 of the European Communities (Eligibility for Protection) Regulations, 2006, transposing Article 12 of Council Directive 2004/83/EC, provides that an applicant is excluded from being a refugee if he or she has instigated or otherwise participated in the commission of the acts or crimes mentioned in s 2(c) of the 1996 Act.

The Grand Chamber of the Court of Justice of the EU ruled in case C-31/09 *Bolbol v Bevándorlási és Állampolgársági Hivatal*, 17 June 2010, that 'for the purposes of the first sentence of Article 12(1)(a) of Council Directive 2004/83/EC, a person receives protection or assistance from an agency of the United Nations other than UNHCR when that person has actually availed himself of that protection or assistance'.

15.3.2.7 Cessation and revocation of refugee status

The legislative basis for revocations is set out in s 21 of the Refugee Act, 1996 (as amended), which includes provisions essentially transposing the cessation clauses from Article 1C of the 1951 Convention:

'(1) Subject to subsection (2), if the Minister is satisfied that a person to whom a declaration has been given—

(a) has voluntarily re-availed himself or herself of the protection of the country of his or her nationality,

(b) having lost his or her nationality, has voluntarily re-acquired it,

(c) has acquired a new nationality (other than the nationality of the State) and enjoys the protection of the country of his or her new nationality,

(d) has voluntarily re-established himself or herself in the country which he or she left or outside which he or she remained owing to fear of persecution,

(e) can no longer, because the circumstances in connection with which he or she has been recognised as a refugee have ceased to exist, continue to refuse to avail himself or herself of the protection of the country of his or her nationality,

(f) being a person who has no nationality is, because the circumstances in connection with which he or she has been recognised as a refugee have ceased to exist, able to return to the country of his or her former habitual residence,

(g) is a person whose presence in the State poses a threat to national security or public policy ('ordre public'), or

(h) is a person to whom a declaration has been given on the basis of information furnished to the Commissioner or, as the case may be, the Tribunal which was false or misleading in a material particular,

the Minister may, if he or she considers it appropriate to do so, revoke the declaration.'

Pursuant to s 17(2)(a) of the Refugee Act, 1996 if the Minister for Justice and Law Reform considers that in the interest of national security or public policy it is necessary to do so, he may order in writing that the rights accruing to a declared refugee do not apply, and may require the person to leave the State.

Regulation 11(1) of the European Communities (Eligibility for Protection) Regulations, 2006 provides the Minister with a power to refuse to grant or renew or to revoke a declaration of refugee status where there are reasonable grounds for regarding the applicant as a danger to the security of the State, or where the person, having been convicted by a final judgment of a particularly serious crime, constitutes a danger to the community of the State. Regulation 11(2) of the 2006 Regulations provides that where a person to whom a declaration has already been given misrepresented or omitted facts (including through the use of false documents) and this was decisive in granting the declaration, or where a person to whom a declaration was given should have been excluded, the Minister may revoke or refuse to renew the declaration.

Section 17(4) of the Refugee Act, 1996 provides that the Minister shall not give a declaration to a refugee who has been recognised as a refugee under the Geneva Convention by a state other than the State and who has been granted asylum in that State and whose reason for leaving or not returning to that State and for seeking a declaration in the State does not relate to a fear of persecution in that State.

15.3.3 THE LAW OF SUBSIDIARY PROTECTION

15.3.3.1 Persons eligible for subsidiary protection

Regulation 2(1) of the European Communities (Eligibility for Protection) Regulations 2006 provides that 'person eligible for subsidiary protection' means a person—

'(a) who is not a national of a Member State,

(b) who does not qualify as a refugee,

(c) in respect of whom substantial grounds have been shown for believing that the person concerned, if returned to his or her country of origin, would face a real risk of suffering serious harm as defined in these regulations,

(d) to whom regulation 13 of these regulations does not apply, and

(e) is unable, or, owing to such risk, unwilling to avail himself or herself of the protection of that country'

Regulation 2(1) also defines serious harm as consisting of (a) the death penalty or execution, (b) torture or inhuman or degrading treatment or punishment, or (c) serious and individual threat to a civilian's life or person by reason of indiscriminate violence in situations of armed conflict. In relation to subsidiary protection, there is no requirement that an applicant show a nexus to a ground in the 1951 Convention, as required in refugee law.

In Case C-465/07 *Elgafaji v Staatssecretaris van Justitie* [2009] WLR (D) 59 the Dutch Council of State asked the ECJ whether Article 15(c) must be interpreted as meaning that the existence of a serious and individual threat to the life or person of an applicant was subject to the condition that the applicant adduce evidence that he would be specifically targeted by reason of factors particular to his circumstances. The ECJ compared the three types of serious harm set out in Article 15 and noted that Article 15(c) covered a more general risk of harm as compared with Article 15(a) and (b). The court further noted that there were three features of Article 15(c): (i) that it referred more generally to a threat, (ii) that that threat was inherent in a general situation of armed conflict and (iii) that the threat is described as indiscriminate. The ECJ stated that in that context the word 'individual' must be understood as covering harm to civilians irrespective of their identity. The Court stated that the provision must nevertheless be subject to a coherent interpretation in relation to the other two situations referred to in Article 15, and must therefore be interpreted by close reference to individualisation. In that regard, the Court held that the more an applicant is able to show that he is specifically targeted by reason of factors specific to his personal circumstances, the lower the level of indiscriminate violence required for him to be eligible for subsidiary protection. The Court added that two factors may be taken into account: the geographical scope of the situation of indiscriminate violence and the actual destination of the applicant if he is returned, and the existence of any serious indication of real risk.

In its *Statement on Subsidiary Protection under the EC Qualification Directive for People Threatened by Indiscriminate Violence*, the UNHCR states:

'*Article 15(c) should be construed as a basis for the grant of subsidiary protection to persons, including former combatants, at risk from indiscriminate violence in broadly-defined situations of armed conflict. The requirement for an "individual" threat should not be interpreted in an excessively narrow manner, but rather as requiring that the risk faced by the individual claimant is real, and not remote, in his or her individual circumstances.*'

In *NH v Minister for Justice* [2008] 4 IR 452 the Court found that Council Directive 2004/83/EC imposed higher standards than those previously in operation in respect of the obligations on the Minister for Justice to ensure that people in need of international protection are not *refouled*. In particular, the Court found that the definition of torture that the Minister had to consider prior to the transposition of the Directive was narrower than that contained in Article 15 of the Directive, and that the limitation in the protection from *refoulement* of s 5(1) of thc Refugee Act, 1996, that the threat be on account of an applicant's race, religion, nationality, membership of a particular social group or political opinion, was not present in Article 15 of the Directive. The Court stated that it did not appear that consideration of the *non-refoulement* provision in s 5 of the Refugee Act, 1996 would result in the Minister having considered in every case matters that he was now obliged to consider under Article 15.

In *FN v The Minister for Justice* [2009] 1 IR 88, Charleton J stated that the primary focus in an application for subsidiary protection is any risk the appellant alleges he or she would be subject to upon return to his or her country of origin considered in light of the situation at hand in terms of peacefulness and the functionality of ordinary protection in that state. The Court also stated that, in relation to 'serious harm', the regulations focus on attacks or threats by human agency and that matters such as health and welfare were not within the remit of subsidiary protection.

15.3.3.2 Exclusion from and cessation of subsidiary protection

Regulation 13 of the European Communities (Eligibility for Protection) Regulations, 2006 provides for exclusion from subsidiary protection:

'(1) A person is excluded from being eligible for subsidiary protection where there are serious reasons for considering that he or she—
(a) has committed a crime against peace, a war crime, or a crime against humanity, as defined in the international instruments drawn up to make provision in respect of such crimes;
(b) has committed a serious crime;
(c) has been guilty of acts contrary to the purposes and principles of the United Nations as set out in the Preamble and Articles 1 and 2 of the Charter of the United Nations; or
(d) constitutes a danger to the community or to the security of the State.
(2) Paragraph (1) applies also to persons who instigate or otherwise participate in the commission of the crimes or acts mentioned therein.
(3) A person may be excluded from being eligible for subsidiary protection if he or she has, prior to his or her admission to the State, committed one or more crimes, outside the scope of paragraph (1), which would be punishable by imprisonment had they been committed in the State, and left his or her country of origin solely in order to avoid sanctions resulting from these crimes.'

Regulation 14 of the European Communities (Eligibility for Protection) Regulations, 2006 provides for revocation of or refusal to renew subsidiary protection:

'(1) The Minister shall revoke or refuse to renew a permission granted to a person under Regulation 4 where—
(a) subject to paragraph (2), the circumstances which led to the granting of the permission have ceased to exist or have changed to such a degree that protection is no longer required;
(b) the person should have been or is excluded from being a person eligible for subsidiary protection under Regulation 13(1) or (2); or
(c) misrepresentation or omission of facts, whether or not including the use of false documents, by the person were decisive for the granting of subsidiary protection status.
(2) In determining whether paragraph (1)(a) applies, the Minister shall have regard to whether the change of circumstances referred to in that provision is of such a significant and

Tribunal to direct in writing any person whose evidence is required by the Tribunal to attend before the Tribunal, and s 16(12) provides that any witness whose evidence has been or is to be given before the Tribunal is entitled to the same privileges and immunities as a witness in a court. Section 16(14) provides that hearings before the Tribunal are conducted in private, although a representative of the UNHCR may attend as an observer pursuant to s 16(15).

A hearing usually begins with the Tribunal Member explaining the Tribunal's role to the applicant. The applicant then presents her evidence, after which the presenting officer may ask questions of the applicant. The applicant's legal representative and the presenting officer may also make submissions. The Tribunal Member may ask questions at any time. Pursuant to s 16(6) of the 1996 Act the Tribunal may request the Commissioner to make such further inquiries and to furnish the Tribunal with such further information as the Tribunal considers necessary within such period as may be specified by the Tribunal.

Having heard the evidence, the Tribunal will consider the matter and issue a decision to the applicant and his or her solicitor if one is on record. If the decision is to set aside the Commissioner's recommendation, the Minister is obliged under s 17(1) of the 1996 Act to declare the appellant to be a refugee, subject to considerations of national security or public policy. There is no appeal from a decision of the Tribunal affirming the Commissioner's recommendation, after which the Minister typically notifies the failed appellant that he or she proposes to make a deportation order in his or her case and explaining his or her options.

Article 39(1) of Council Directive 2005/85/EC requires Member States to ensure that applicants for asylum have the right to an effective remedy before a court or tribunal against certain decisions including decisions taken on their application for asylum. In *Dokie & Ajibiola v Refugee Applications Commissioner & Ors*, 19 January 2010, High Court (unreported), the Court, in a judgment granting leave, noted that there is an apparent dichotomy between the appeal function attributed to the Tribunal prior to the Minister's determination of applications pursuant to s 17 of the Refugee Act, 1996 and the requirement of Article 39 of the Directive that the Member States provide an effective remedy before a court or Tribunal against the first instance determination of asylum applications. As noted above, the substantive decision in *Dokie* has been reserved at the time of writing.

15.4.6 THE MINISTER'S DECLARATION

If the Refugee Applications Commissioner or, on appeal, the Refugee Appeals Tribunal recommends to the Minister that an applicant should be given a declaration as a refugee, s 17(1)(a) of the Refugee Act 1996 (as amended) obliges the Minister for Justice and Law Reform to give that applicant a statement in writing declaring that the applicant is a refugee. Section 17(1)(b) provides that in any other case the Minister may refuse to give the applicant a declaration. Under s 17(5), where the Minister decides to refuse a declaration, he or she is obliged to send the applicant a notice in writing stating that—

(a) *his or her application for a declaration has been refused,*
(b) *the period of entitlement of the applicant to remain in the State under section 9 has expired, and*
(c) *the Minister may make an order under section 3 of the Immigration Act, 1999, requiring the applicant to leave the State . . . .*

Section 3(1) of the Immigration Act, 1999 allows the Minister, subject to the prohibition of *refoulement*, to require, by order, a non national to leave the State and to remain thereafter out of the State. Section 3(2)(f) provides that an order under s 3(1) may be made in respect of a person whose application for asylum the Minister has refused.

Regulation 4(1)(a) of the Regulations provides that a notification of a proposal under s 3(3) of the Immigration Act, 1999 shall include a statement that, where a person to whom s 3(2)(f) of that Act applies considers that he or she is a person eligible for subsidiary protection, he or she may, in addition to making representations under s 3(3)(b) of that Act, make an application for subsidiary protection to the Minister within the 15 day period referred to in the notification.

Under s 17(6) of the Refugee Act, 1996 the Minister may, at his or her discretion, grant permission in writing to a person who has withdrawn his or her application or to whom the Minister has refused to give a declaration to remain in the State for such period and subject to such conditions as the Minister may specify in writing. The Minister may amend or revoke any order under s 17 pursuant to s17(9).

15.4.7 FRESH ASYLUM APPLICATIONS

Article 32 of Council Directive 2005/85/EC provides for subsequent applications for asylum. Article 32(3) provides that a subsequent application for asylum shall be subject first to a preliminary examination as to whether, after the withdrawal of the previous application or after a decision has been taken in respect of the previous decision, new elements or findings relating to the examination of whether he/she qualifies as a refugee by virtue of Directive 2004/83/EC have arisen or have been presented by the applicant. Under Article 32(4), if, following the preliminary examination, new elements or findings arise or are presented by the applicant which significantly add to the likelihood of the applicant qualifying as a refugee by virtue of Directive 2004/83/EC, the application shall be further examined in conformity with Chapter II of the Council Directive. Article 32(6) provides that Member States may decide to further examine the application only if the applicant concerned was, through no fault of his/her own, incapable of asserting the new elements or findings in the previous procedure, in particular by exercising his/her right to an effective remedy pursuant to Article 39 of the Council Directive.

An applicant whose asylum application has been refused by the Minister for Justice and Law Reform can request that the Minister, at his discretion, allow him or her to make a further application for a declaration under s 17(7) of the Refugee Act, 1996. In *COI v The Minister for Justice, Equality and Law Reform*, 2 March 2007, High Court (unreported), a case predating operation of Council Directive 2005/85/EC, the Court held that in dealing with applications for the Minister's consent to make a fresh application for asylum pursuant to s 17(7) of the Refugee Act, 1996 (as amended), the Minister is obliged to act fairly and in accordance with the principles of natural justice, and cannot act arbitrarily, and that an applicant is entitled to go to the relevant bodies established under the asylum legislation to make a further application for asylum where there is fresh evidence that another claim has been successful on essentially the same facts. The Court posited that the correct test was whether there was a reasonable prospect of a favourable view being taken by the Commissioner with regard to the new information.

15.4.8 SUBSIDIARY PROTECTION PROCEDURE

Ireland does not currently have a single procedure for international protection. Such a process is proposed by the Immigration, Residence and Protection Bill, 2010. Under the current regime, in order to apply for subsidiary protection, an applicant must first have applied for, and have been refused, refugee status. The Minister for Justice and Law Reform considers applications for subsidiary protection pursuant to Regulation 4(3) of the European Communities (Eligibility for Protection) Regulations, 2006. In the event that the Minister decides that the applicant is not a person eligible for subsidiary protection, refuses the application, the Minister will then proceed to consider whether or not to make the deportation order, and will consider matters pursuant to s 3 of the Immigration Act, 1999 (as amended). Consideration of subsidiary protection precedes consideration of whether to make a deportation order. There is no appeal from a negative subsidiary protection decision, and there is no legal provision to suspend removal pending determination of an application.

Prior to the coming into operation of the European Communities (Eligibility for Protection) Regulations, 2006 (SI 518/2006) on 10 October 2006, failed asylum seekers who sought international protection could generally only seek to avoid *refoulement* by making representations against the making of a deportation order. The Minister initially refused to accept applications for subsidiary protection in respect of people who had been issued before 10 October 2006 with deportation orders. In the Joined Cases of *NH v The Minister for Justice [2008] 4 IR 452*, applicants who had been refused declarations of refugee status, and who were the subjects of deportation orders issued before 10 October 2006, applied for subsidiary protection under the new legislative scheme, contending that they had an automatic right to apply for subsidiary protection pursuant to Council Directive 2004/83/EC. The Minister was of the view that their applications were invalid and had to be refused as their deportation orders pre-dated the transposition of the Directive, and asserted that he had no discretion to consider the applications. The Court held that while people who did not have a deportation order made against them as of 10 October 2006 had an automatic right to apply for subsidiary protection, Regulation 4(2) of the 2006 Regulations gave the Minister a discretion to consider applications for subsidiary protection from applicants already issued with a deportation order where such applicants identify relevant altered circumstances.

Pursuant to Regulation 17(1) of the European Communities (Eligibility for Protection) Regulations, 2006, a person who has been approved for subsidiary protection shall be granted permission to remain in the State for three years. That permission shall be renewable unless compelling reasons of national security or public order otherwise require. Pursuant to Regulation 14(1) the Minister for Justice and Law Reform shall revoke or refuse to renew a permission granted to a person where:

'(a) subject to paragraph (2), the circumstances which led to the granting of the permission have ceased to exist or have changed to such a degree that protection is no longer required;

(b) the person should have been or is excluded from being a person eligible for subsidiary protection under Regulation 13(1) or (2); or

(c) misrepresentation or omission of facts, whether or not including the use of false documents, by the person were decisive for the granting of subsidiary protection status.'

In determining whether a change of circumstances pursuant to regulation 14(1)(a) applies, the Minister shall have regard to whether the change of circumstances referred to in that provision is of such a significant and non-temporary nature that the person granted subsidiary protection no longer faces a real risk of serious harm (Regulation 14(2)). Pursuant to Regulation 14(3) the Minister may revoke or refuse to renew a permission granted where the person concerned should have been excluded from being eligible for subsidiary protection in accordance with regulation 13(3). An opportunity will be given in such cases for the person in question to make representations to the Minister pursuant to s 3 of the Immigration Act, 1999. Regulation 17(2) provides that the permission to remain granted to people in need of subsidiary protection 'shall be renewable, unless compelling reasons of national security or public order (*ordre public*), otherwise require'.

15.4.9 LEAVE TO REMAIN

The procedures relating to leave to remain are dealt with in more depth elsewhere in this text (see **16.4.2.4**). Failed applicants for asylum who make representations against deportation may be granted temporary permission to remain in the State for *non-refoulement* (see

15.3.1) or humanitarian reasons, and that while this mechanism falls outside the asylum process, it nonetheless may act as a international protection status.

Any person who is refused a declaration of refugee status will receive from the Ministerial Decisions Unit of the Department of Justice and Law Reform a notice that the Minister proposes to make a deportation order in respect of him or her under section 3 of the Immigration Act, 1999. As well as informing the applicant of his or her right to apply for subsidiary protection at this time, the Minister will inform the person who has been refused a declaration of refugee status: (i) that the Minister is proposing to deport the applicant, and will, consider representations pursuant to section 3 of the Immigration Act, 1999 (as amended) as to why a deportation order should not be made; (ii) that the applicant may leave the jurisdiction voluntarily; and (iii) that the applicant can consent to a deportation order. Applicants are requested to furnish any representations within 15 working days of the date of the notice.

Following the consideration of any such application, including consideration of any representations, any issues relating to the person's country of origin, a consideration of the position of the applicant *vis-à-vis* section 5 of the Refugee Act, 1996 (as amended) on the prohibition of *refoulement*, section 4 of the Criminal Justice (UN Convention against Torture) Act, 2000 and taking into account rights under the European Convention on Human Rights and the Irish Constitution, where appropriate, the Minister for Justice and Law Reform decides whether the applicant should become the subject of a deportation order or if, instead, he should grant him or her temporary leave to remain in the State.

Where a decision is made to grant leave to remain in the State, this decision is conveyed in writing to the successful applicant and to his/her legal representative, if they are on record. This communication advises the successful applicant of the conditions attaching to his or her permission to remain in the State, the circumstances under which this permission can be revoked, the means by which they can become registered in the State, and the process involved in applying for the renewal of the permission to remain. This communication does not advise the successful applicant of the specific reasons for the grant of leave to remain. Accordingly, a recipient of leave tor remain will not know whether the reason for the grant of leave to remain relates to a *non-refoulement* and international protection claim, where applicable, or only to other matters.

15.4.10 ADMINISTRATIVE ARRANGEMENTS FOR VICTIMS OF HUMAN TRAFFICKING

Procedures dealing with human trafficking are dealt with elsewhere in this text (see **16.6.5**). It is sufficient to note here that 'Administrative Immigration Arrangements for the Protection of Victims of Human Trafficking' published by the Department of Justice on 13 November 2008 sets out the arrangements for both a sixty-days recovery and reflection period for victims of trafficking, and a temporary residence permission. Although the arrangements are stated to be for the protection of victims of trafficking, they are predicated on assistance in the context of Garda investigations, rather than on protection as such, and do not create any entitlement to long term residency or protection in the State.

Permission to remain lawfully in the State for a period of sixty days (i.e., the recovery and reflection period) is granted to a person 'who has been identified by a member of the Garda Síochána not below the rank of Superintendant in GNIB as a suspected victim of human trafficking'. The recovery and reflection period is to allow the person:

(a) time to recover

(b) to escape the influence of the alleged perpetrators of the trafficking, and

(c) to take an informed decision as to whether to assist Gardai or other relevant authorities in relation to any investigation or prosecution arising in relation to the alleged trafficking.

The granting of the recovery and reflection period does not of itself create any entitlement for the person to assert a right to reside in the State when the period expires.

The Minister for Justice and Law Reform will grant a temporary residence permission valid for six months where he or she is satisfied that:

(a) the person has severed all relations with the alleged perpetrators of the trafficking, and

(b) it is necessary for the purposes of allowing the suspected victim to continue to assist the Garda Síochána or other relevant authorities in relation to an investigation or prosecution arising in relation to the trafficking.

The granting of temporary residence permission does not create of itself any right to long-term or permanent residence.

The Criminal Law (Human Trafficking) Act, 2008 gives effect to, *inter alia*, the EU Framework Decision on Combating Trafficking in Human Beings (for the purpose of labour and sexual exploitation) and the EU Framework Decision on Combating the Sexual Exploitation of Children and Child Pornography. The Act does not, however, deal with the protection of victims of trafficking. The regulatory impact analysis states that the then Bill was solely concerned with the criminal law response to trafficking, and that the protection of victims of trafficking would be dealt with administratively. The Immigration, Residence and Protection Bill, 2010 proposes to put the administrative arrangements outlined above on a legislative footing.

15.4.11 DETENTION

15.4.11.1 Detention of asylum applicants

Article 18(1) of Council Directive 2005/85/EC states that Member States shall not hold a person in detention for the sole reason that he/she is an applicant for asylum. Section 9(8) of the Refugee Act, 1996 (as amended) provides that an immigration officer or a member of an Garda Síochána may detain an applicant, if they suspect with reasonable cause, that he or she:

'(a) poses a threat to national security or public order in the State,
(b) has committed a serious non-political crime outside the State,
(c) has not made reasonable efforts to establish his or her true identity,
(d) intends to avoid removal from the State in the event of his or her application for asylum being transferred to a convention country pursuant to section 22 [or a safe third country (within the meaning of that section).]
(e) intends to leave the State and enter another state without lawful authority, or
(f) without reasonable cause his destroyed his or her identity or travel documents or is in possession of forged identity documents.'

Section 9(8) does not apply to persons under the age of 18. Pursuant to ss 10(1)(c) and (f) of the 1996 Act a detained person shall be informed by the immigration officer without delay, where possible in a language he or she understands, that he or she is entitled to consult a solicitor and is entitled to the assistance of an interpreter for the purposes of such a consultation.

Section 9(8) is not a criminal law provision. As it is considered a civil matter, legal aid is provided by solicitors from the Refugee Legal Service. A solicitor's role in this context is to oppose the Garda application to detain his or her client pursuant to s 9(8) in the District Court. The Garda swears an information that sets out the background of the case and basis for detention. A further information will usually be sworn for any subsequent Court applications for renewal of detention.

A person detained pursuant to s 9(8) must be brought before a judge of the District Court as soon as practicable. Where the Court is satisfied that a reasonable cause exists pursuant to the relevant section, the Court may commit the person to a place of detention for a period not exceeding 21 days from the time of her detention, after which period the applicant must be again brought before the District Court for a fresh application, or released. In *SN v Governor of Cloverhill Prison* [2005] IEHC 471, 14 April 2005, High Court (unreported) the Court held that a District Court Judge must set out clearly the evidential basis for detention pursuant to s 9(8) of the Refugee Act, 1996.

The Judge may also grant conditional release pursuant to s 9(9)(b)(ii). The conditions of release may be varied on application by either party pursuant to s 9(9)(d). A person who fails to comply with a condition imposed may be detained and again brought before a Judge of the District Court. There is no statutory limit on the number of times an application pursuant to s 9(8) may be made in relation to an applicant. There is no appeal to the Circuit Court from a District Court Judge's decision to detain an applicant pursuant to this Section.

In the event that at any time during the period of detention an immigration officer or Garda forms the opinion that none of the paragraphs of s 9(8) apply, the applicant shall be brought before a Judge of the District Court and, if satisfied, the Judge shall release the person from detention, pursuant to s 9(9)(c).

The Refugee Act, 1996 (Places and Conditions of Detention Regulations 2000 (SI No. 344 of 2000) provides details on the right of access to a solicitor for persons detained in Garda Stations. Further to these Regulations, a detainee should not be brought before a court or removed from the State without having first had the opportunity, at his/her request, to consult with a solicitor.

15.4.11.2 Detention pending transfer under the Dublin Regulation

Section 22(1)(b) of the Refugee Act, 1996 (as amended) allows the Minister to make such orders as appear to him or her to be necessary or expedient for the purpose of giving effect to Council Regulation (EC) 343/2003. Section 22(1) provides, *inter alia*, that without prejudice to the generality of subsection (1), an order under this section may—

'(i)   *specify the measures to be taken for the purpose of the removal of a person whose application has been transferred to a convention country or a safe third country from the State to that convention country or safe third country including, where necessary, the temporary detention or restraint of the person, and*

(j)   *provide for the temporary detention (for a period not exceeding 48 hours) of a person who, having arrived in the State directly from a convention country or a safe third country, makes an application for asylum until a decision on the matters at paragraph (a) has been made.'*

As noted above, the Refugee Act, 1996 (Section 22) Order, 2003 (SI No. 423 of 2003) is the principle statutory instrument giving effect to the Council Regulation, and Article 7(5) of the Order provides that a person to whom a notice of the making of a transfer has been issued may without further notice be arrested and detained for the purpose of ensuring his or her departure from the State in accordance with the transfer order. The transfer order must already have been made and the notification issued in order to activate this provision. Where a person detained institutes court proceedings challenging the validity of the transfer order, an application may be made to determine whether the person shall continue to be detained or be released. The Court may attach conditions to release as it considers appropriate, including requiring the person to reside or remain at a particular place, requiring them to report at specific intervals and to surrender any passport or document. On occasion it arises that an applicant who is detained pursuant to s 9(8) of the Act is subsequently the subject of a transfer order. In those circumstances, the Gardaí may decide not to apply for a further period of detention pursuant to s 9(8) but instead to allow release under this section but subsequently detain the person pursuant to Refugee Act 1996 (Section 22) Order, 2003 for the purpose of effecting transfer to another Member State.

15.4.11.3 Detention of non-Irish nationals generally

Section 12 of the Immigration Act 2003 provides:

'*(1)* *Every non-national shall produce on demand, unless he or she gives a satisfactory explanation of the circumstances which prevent him or her from so doing—*

(a) a valid passport or other equivalent document, issued by or on behalf of an authority recognised by the Government, which establishes his or her identity and nationality, and

(b) in case he or she is registered or deemed to be registered under this Act, his or her registration certificate.

(2) A non-national who contravenes this section shall be guilty of an offence.'

15.4.12 JUDICIAL REVIEW

The procedures that apply to judicial review of most decisions made within the asylum and international protection processes differ from those that apply to administrative decisions typically under Order 84 of the Rules of the Superior Courts. Under s 5(2) of the Illegal Immigrants (Trafficking) Act, 2000, an application for leave to apply for judicial review of specified decisions in the asylum process, (a) must be made within 14 days of the impugned decision, (b) must be made on notice to the Minister for Justice and Law Reform, (c) require substantial grounds, and (d) can only be appealed to the Supreme Court where the High Court certifies that its own decision involves a point of law of exceptional public importance, and that it is in the public interest that an appeal should be taken. The decisions subject to s 5(2) of the 2000 Act are:

- Notification of a proposal to deport under ss 3(3)(a) and 3(3)(b)(ii) Immigration Act, 2002

- Deportation order made under s 3(1) Immigration Act, 2002

- Refusal of permission to land made under the Aliens Order, 1946 or s 4(3) of the Immigration Act, 2004

- Exclusion order under s 4 of the Immigration Act, 1999

- Refusal of refugee status by or on behalf of the Minister

- Recommendation requiring the Commissioner/Tribunal to accord priority to certain classes of applications under s 12 of the Refugee Act, 1996 (as amended)

- Recommendation of the Commissioner that an applicant should not be declared a refugee under s 13 of the Refugee Act, 1996 (as amended)

- Decision of the Tribunal under s 16 of the Refugee Act, 1996 (as amended) affirming the Commissioner's recommendation that an applicant should not be declared a refugee

- Determination of the Commissioner/Tribunal re the Dublin Regulation under s 22 of the Refugee Act, 1996 (as amended)

- Refusal of a declaration of refugee status by the Minister under s 17 of the Refugee Act, 1996 (as amended)

- Orders re Dublin Convention/Regulation 343/2003 under s 22 of the Refugee Act, 1996 (as amended)

- Decision of the Tribunal re appeal of an ancillary Dublin Convention/Regulation 343/2003 order under s 22(4)(b) of the Refugee Act, 1996 (as amended)

- Decisions to revoke a declaration of refugee status by the Minister under s 21 of the Refugee Act, 1996 (as amended).

The extent to which the recommendation of the Refugee Applications Commissioner is susceptible to review has been the subject of several recent decisions of the Superior Courts. In *Kayode v The Refugee Applications Commissioner*, 28 January 2009, Supreme Court (unreported) the applicant sought an order of *certiorari* of the decision of the authorised officer of the Commissioner on the basis that the decision was unreasonable in that insufficient regard was had to the fact that the applicant's mother was a refugee and her case was closely similar to that of the applicant. The trial judge at the judicial review hearing refused to quash the decision of the Commissioner by way of *certiorari*, but granted leave to appeal his decision having certified that the decision involved a point of law of exceptional public importance.

The Supreme Court held that the trial judge was entitled in law to exercise his discretion to refuse the application and hold that the appeal to the Tribunal was a more appropriate remedy, where the issue raised by the applicant principally, but not exclusively, related to the quality of the decision. The Court stated that whether an order for *certiorari* should be made depends on the consideration of the factors referred to by Denham J in *Stefan v The Minister for Justice* [2001] 4 IR 203, those factors being, (a) the existence of an alternative remedy, (b) the conduct of the applicant, (c) the merits of the application, (d) the consequences to the applicant if an order of *certiorari* is not granted, and (e) the degree of fairness of procedures. The Court also stated that the following statement of O'Higgins CJ in *The State (Abenglen Properties Ltd) v Dublin Corporation* [1984] IR 381 was an important statement of the law:

> '...there may be cases where the decision exhibits an error of law and a perfectly simple appeal can rectify the complaint, or where administrative legislation provides adequate appeal machinery which is particularly suitable for dealing with errors in the application of the code in question. In such cases, while retaining or with the power to quash, a Court should be slow to do so unless satisfied that, for some particular reason, the appeal or alternative remedy is not adequate.'

The Court found that while the claimed breach of fair procedures in *Stefan* (a failure to translate a key document) was self evidently a serious matter, the basis on which the appellant in *Kayode* claimed a want of fair procedures was the claim that the Commissioner did not take sufficient account of the fact that the appellant's mother had been granted refugee status, and that what weight ought to be attached to the mother's case was a matter for the Commissioner.

In *JM v Refugee Appeals Commissioner & Anor* [2009] IEHC 352, 29 July 2009, High Court (unreported) the applicant was successful in his application for *certiorari* because the core reason for the negative recommendation was a finding that the applicant was entitled to acquire nationality in a country other than his country of feared persecution, in circumstances where the authorised officer had not questioned the applicant sufficiently to ascertain if this option was in fact open to him. The Court held that the process by which the Commissioner reached his decision was capable of having continuing adverse effects on the applicant in the course of the appeal (eg, the applicant would not have had the benefit of an oral hearing) and was satisfied that the defects could not be cured on appeal. The Court stated that to determine whether *certiorari* should lie against the Commissioner it must be determined if there has been a fundamental flaw or illegality such that a rehearing upon appeal before the Tribunal would be an inadequate remedy.

In *NAA v Refugee Applications Commissioner & Ors* [2007] IEHC 54, 23 February 2007, High Court (unreported) the High Court held that decisions of the Refugee Applications Commissioner do not merge with those of the Tribunal. Consequently, where an appeal has been determined an applicant will usually be unable to challenge the Commissioner's decision, unless there are special circumstances.

The ordinary rules of judicial review apply in accordance with Order 84 of the Superior Court Rules to applications for review in respect of any decisions in the process not covered by s 5(2) of the 2000 Act (eg, the Minister's decision in respect of subsidiary protection).

15.4.13 TREATMENT OF MINORS IN THE ASYLUM PROCESS

EU Council Resolution of 26 June 1997 on unaccompanied minors who are nationals of third-countries provides that an allowance should be made for an unaccompanied minor's age, maturity and mental development, and for the fact that he or she may have limited knowledge of conditions in the country of origin'. Council Directive 2004/83/EC mandates the best interest of the child should be a primary consideration of Member States when implementing the Directive. Article 30 of the Directive sets out specific provisions relating to unaccompanied minors following the grant of refugee or subsidiary protection status.

Article 17(7) of Council Directive 2005/85/EC provides that the 'best interests of the child shall be a primary consideration for Member States when implementing this Article' and sets out guarantees for unaccompanied minors, including provision for a representative for the unaccompanied minor (subject to certain exceptions), that any interview with an unaccompanied minor should be conducted by a person who has the necessary knowledge of the special needs of minors, and provision (subject to specific conditions) for the medical examination of a minor to determine age.

In domestic legislation, s 8(5)(a) of the Refugee Act, 1996 (as amended) states that:

> 'where it appears to an immigration officer or an authorised officer that a child under the age of 18 years, who has either arrived at the frontiers of the State or has entered the State, is not in the custody of any person, the officer shall, as soon as practicable, so inform the Health Service Executive and thereupon the provisions of the Child Care Act 1991 shall apply in relation to the child.'

Section 8(5)(b) authorises the Health Service Executive to decide whether or not an application for a declaration of refugee status should be made. The Refugee Act does not define what constitutes a separated child. The UNHCR has developed guidelines and policies in relation to best international practice in dealing with unaccompanied minors. The United Nations Convention on the Rights of the Child 1989 sets out internationally accepted principles governing the rights of children. This Convention was ratified by Ireland but has yet to be incorporated into domestic law. In the High Court judgment of *AN & Ors v Minister for Justice, Equality and Law Reform & Anor*, 18 October 2007, Supreme Court (unreported) the Court noted that 'The provisions of the Refugee Act, 1996 must be construed, and its operation applied by the authorities in accordance with the Convention on the Rights of the Child which has been ratified by Ireland.'

The Separated Children in Europe Programme (SCEP) defines separated children as:

> 'Under 18 years of age who are outside their country of origin and separated from both parents or their previous/legal customary primary caregiver . . . they may be victims of trafficking for sexual or other exploitation, or they may have travelled to Europe to escape conditions of serious deprivation.'

The term 'not in the custody of any person' in s 8(5)(a) of the Refugee Act, 1996 (as amended) would appear to envisage a narrower definition than that defined by the UNHCR guidelines. The Health Service Executive can and does in practice reunite minors with adult relatives who are not their legal guardians. Once this happens the minors are no longer the responsibility of the unaccompanied minors unit within the HSE. The decision whether an asylum application should be made on behalf of the minor then rests with the adult relative.

A report from the Law Society recommended that a uniform definition of unaccompanied minor and separated child should be adopted in legislation to reflect the broader international definition. The difficulty with the current lack of clarity regarding the definition of a minor means that in practice children are united with adults or relatives who are not their legal guardians within the meaning of the Guardianship of Infants Act, 1964, and such children are potentially excluded from protection.

The first report of the Special Rapporteur on Children from November 2007 recommended that the SCEP definition of 'separated children' be adopted in Irish legislation along with the introduction of broad protections for such children. This recommendation has not been adopted. The Immigration Residence and Protection Bill, 2010 proposes changes to the law. Head 28 of the Bill as published in July 2010 proposes that: 'Where ... it appears to an immigration officer that a foreign national under the age of 18 years ... is not accompanied or is not to be accompanied by a person of or over that age who is taking responsibility for the foreign national, the officer shall, as soon as practicable, notify the Health Service Executive of that fact ... '

There is no provision in current or proposed domestic legislation for an immigration officer to assess the suitability of the adult claiming responsibility, or to consider the best interests of the child. Neither is there any provision in current legislation to allow an application to the court for direction akin to that under s 45 of the Child Care Act, 1991 or to seek to have a Guardian *ad litem* appointed. If concerns arise about the suitability of the adult accompanying the child, there is no provision to seek that a DNA test be conducted to ensure they are related if this has been asserted.

The Committee on the Rights of the Child General Comment No 6 notes at para 33 that:

> 'States are required to create the underlying legal framework and to take necessary measures to secure proper representation of an unaccompanied or separated child's best interests. Therefore, States should appoint a guardian or adviser as soon as the unaccompanied or separated child is identified and maintain such guardianship arrangements until the child has either reached the age of majority or has permanently left the territory and/or the jurisdiction of the State ... '

In clarifying that the guardian or adviser should have the necessary expertise, the General Comment states: 'Agencies or individuals whose interests could potentially be in conflict with those of the child's should not be eligible for guardianship.' It goes on to state that: 'In cases where a child is accompanied by a non-family adult or caretaker, suitability for guardianship must be scrutinized more closely.' The General Comment recommends that review mechanisms should be introduced and the quality of guardianship monitored 'to ensure the best interests of the child are being represented throughout the decision-making process and, in particular, to prevent abuse'.

The UN Committee on the Rights of the Child issued a recommendation to Ireland that children

> 'be provided with the opportunity to be heard in any judicial and administrative proceedings affecting them, and that due weight be given to those views in accordance with the age and maturity of the child, including the use of independent representations (guardian ad litem) provided for under the Child Care Act of 1991, in particular cases where children are separated from their parents.'

15.5   Rights of Persons with International Protection

15.5.1   THE RIGHTS OF REFUGEES

Council Directive 2004 83/EC sets out the rights of refugees in respect of residence permits, travel documents, freedom of movement, access to employment, access to education, social welfare, health care, accommodation, and integration.

Domestically, the rights accruing to a declared refugee are mainly set out in ss 3 and 18 of the Refugee Act, 1996 (as amended). Section 3 provides that a refugee shall generally have the same rights and privileges as citizens, and enumerates particular rights in respect of the right to reside in the State, to employment, medical care, social welfare, travel, access to the courts, freedom of religion and religious education of children, and access to trade unions.

Section 3(2)(a)(iii) of the 1996 Act provides that a declared refugee is entitled to reside in the State and to have the same rights of travel in or to or from the State as an Irish citizen. Section 4(1) of the 1996 Act provides that pursuant to an application in writing, and on payment of a fee, the Minister for Justice and Law Reform shall issue to a refugee in relation to whom a declaration is in force a travel document identifying the holder thereof as a person to whom a declaration has been given, subject to s 4(2) of the 1996 Act, which provides that the Minister may refuse to issue such a document in the interest of public security or public policy.

Section 3(2)(a)(ii) of the 1996 Act provides that a declared refugee shall be entitled to receive the same medical care and services and the same social welfare benefits as those to which Irish citizens are entitled. Social welfare benefits are defined as including any payment or services provided for in or under the Social Welfare Acts, the Health Acts, 1947 to 1994, and the Housing Acts, 1966 to 1992. Pursuant to ss 3(1) and 3(2)(a)(i) of the 1996 Act, a refugee in respect of whom a declaration is in force is entitled to seek and enter employment, to carry on any business, trade or profession, and to have access to education and training in the State in the like manner and to the like extent in all respects as an Irish citizen. Section 3(2)(a)(vi) further provides that a declared refugee shall have the right to form and be a member of associations and trade unions in the like manner and to the like extent in all respects as an Irish citizen.

Section 18 of the Refugee Act, 1996 (as amended) provides that a refugee may apply for permission to be granted to a member of his or her family to enter and reside in the State. The Minister for Justice and Law Reform is obliged to grant permission to a member of the family of the refugee (ie spouse, parent (if the applicant is under 18 years old), or unmarried child (under 18 years)). The Minister has discretion to grant permission to enter and reside in the State to a dependent member of the family of a refugee (who may be a child, parent, brother, sister grandparent, grandchild, ward or guardian of the refugee), provided that person is dependent on the refugee or suffering from a mental or physical disability to such an extent that they cannot maintain him/herself fully. The Minister refers the application to the Commissioner for investigation under the Refugee Act, 1996, and on completion of the investigation, the Commissioner submits a report to the Minister for a decision. Where the Minister grants permission to enter and reside to a member of the family or dependent member of the family of a refugee, the individual is entitled to such rights and privileges as are specified in s 3 of the Refugee Act, 1996 for such a period as the refugee is entitled to remain in the State.

Under s 15(1) of the Irish Nationality and Citizenship Act, 1956 (as amended), the Minister for Justice and Law Reform may grant an application for naturalisation if he or she is satisfied that an applicant satisfies certain 'conditions for naturalisation'. The Minister has discretion under s 16 of the 1956 Act, as amended, to grant naturalisation to certain categories of applicant, including refugees, where the conditions for naturalisation are not satisfied. Typically, a non-Irish national is entitled to apply for citizenship after five years of lawful residence in Ireland, and must also establish that they are in good standing, intend in good faith to continue to reside in the State after naturalisation, and undertake an oath of fidelity to the nation and loyalty to the State. The five-year residency requirement, and the other conditions of naturalisation can be waived at the Minister's discretion in the case of refugees. The fees in relation to naturalisation are also waived for refugees.

Pursuant to s 24(2) a programme refugee is be entitled to the same rights and privileges as Convention refugees in the State during the time he or she is permitted to remain. Programme refugees are not expressly entitled to apply for family reunification pursuant to s 18 of the Refugee Act, 1996 (as amended), but the Minister for Justice and Law Reform has accepted and processed such applications. The length of authorisation given to a programme refugee to reside in the State is at the discretion of the Minister. Their residence permits may be renewed at the discretion and at such intervals as may be requested by the Minister.

15.5.2 THE RIGHTS OF PERSONS WITH SUBSIDIARY PROTECTION

Under Regulation 19(1)(c) of the European Communities (Eligibility for Protection) Regulations, 2006, people granted subsidiary protection are entitled to the same medical care, services and social benefits as an Irish citizen. This is more favourable than the minimum guarantee provided by Article 27(2) of Council Directive 2005/85EC. Under Regulation 19(1)(b) persons who are granted subsidiary protection are also entitled to seek and enter employment, to carry on any business, trade or profession in the State in the like manner and to the like extent in all respects as an Irish citizen. Again, this is more favourable than the minimum guarantee of Article 26(3) of Council Directive 2005/85/EC. Persons with subsidiary protection are also entitled to have access to education and training in the State in the like manner and to the like extent in all respects as an Irish citizen.

Under Regulation 19(1)(a) persons granted subsidiary protection 'shall be entitled to the same rights of travel in or to or from the State, other than to his country of origin, as those to which Irish citizens are entitled'. Regulation 18(1) provides that on application in writing, and subject to payment of any necessary fee, the Minister for Justice and Law Reform shall issue the applicant with a travel document, although the Minister may, for reasons of national security or public order (*ordre public*), refuse to issue a travel document (Regulation 18(2)).

Under Regulation 16(1) a person who has been found eligible for subsidiary protection and has received a determination to that effect may apply to the Minister for Justice and Law Reform for permission to be granted to a member of his or her family to enter and to reside in the State. The Regulations' provisions in this regard are similar to those in s 18 of the Refugee Act, 1996 (as amended) vis-à-vis Convention refugees. Under the Regulations, the Minister is obliged to investigate, or cause to be investigated, such an application to determine the relationship between the applicant and the person who is the subject of the application and that person's domestic circumstances. If the Minister is satisfied that the person who is the subject of the application is a member of the family of the applicant, the Minister is obliged to grant permission in writing to the person to enter and reside in the State. A 'member of the family' may be either

'(i)   *where the applicant is married, his or her spouse (provided that the marriage is subsisting on the date of the application under to paragraph (1)),*

(ii)   *where the applicant is, on the date of the application under paragraph (1), under the age of 18 years and is not married, his or her parents, or*

(iii)   *a child of the applicant who, on the date of the application under to paragraph (1), is under the age of 18 years and is not married.*

The Regulations also provide that the Minister may grant permission to a dependent member of the family of an applicant to enter and reside in the State. A 'dependent member of the family', in relation to an applicant, means any grandparent, parent, brother, sister, child, grandchild, ward or guardian of the applicant who is wholly or mainly dependent on the applicant or is suffering from a mental or physical incapacity to such extent that it is not reasonable to expect him or her to maintain himself or herself fully. The Minister may refuse to grant permission to enter and reside to a person in the interest of national security or public policy, or where the person the subject of the application is or would be excluded from refugee or subsidiary protection status.

Unlike the special provision in respect of refugees, there is no legislative provision giving the Minister for Justice and Law Reform discretion to waive conditions of naturalisation in respect of people who are granted subsidiary protection. Accordingly, a person who has been granted subsidiary protection may apply for citizenship only after fulfilling the naturalisation condition of being resident in the State for five years or more.

15.5.3 THE RIGHTS OF PERSONS WITH LEAVE TO REMAIN

The rights of persons granted leave to remain are not legislated for, and persons granted leave to remain for *non-refoulement* reasons will not necessarily be afforded different rights from those granted leave to remain for discretionary reasons. The rights granted to a person with leave to remain vary dependent on their circumstances. Some, but not all, grantees are entitled to work. The duration of leave to remain in the State and applications for renewal are subject to ministerial discretion. Persons granted leave to remain have no statutory entitlement to be granted family reunification. Grantees are entitled to access to third level education in the same manner as citizens. Persons granted leave to remain must be legally resident in the State for five years before they are eligible to apply for citizenship pursuant to the Irish Nationality and Citizenship Act, 1956 (as amended).

15.5.4 THE RIGHTS OF VICTIMS OF HUMAN TRAFFICKING

The rights of victims of human trafficking who are granted temporary permission to remain in the State are not legislated for. The 'Administrative Immigration Arrangements for the Protection of Protection of Victims of Human Trafficking' published by the Department of Justice, Equality and Law Reform on 13 November 2008 state that a person who has been granted a recovery and reflection period will not be the subject of removal proceedings for as long as his or her recovery and reflection period remains valid. Neither the grant of the recovery and reflection period nor a temporary residence permission, of themselves, create any entitlement for the person to assert any further right to reside in the State or permanent residence.

15.5.5 THE HABITUAL RESIDENCE CONDITION IN RESPECT OF SOCIAL WELFARE BENEFITS

To qualify for social welfare benefits, a person must satisfy a 'Habitual Residence Condition', introduced to ensure that only persons who have been living in Ireland for a certain period of time can qualify for benefits. Five factors set out in s 246(3)(4) of the Social Welfare Consolidation Act, 2005 (as amended) are taken into consideration to determine whether a person satisfies the requirement:

> '(a) the length and continuity of residence in the State or in any other particular country;
> (b) the length and purpose of any absence from the State;
> (c) the nature and pattern of the person's employment;

(d)   the person's main centre of interest;

(e)   the future intentions of the person concerned as they appear from all the circumstances.

Amendments to s 246(4)(5) of the Social Welfare Consolidation Act, 2005 introduced the additional qualification that a person who does not have a right to reside in the State shall not be regarded as being habitually resident in the State. Persons with refugee status, programme refugee status, subsidiary protection, and leave to remain in accordance with ss 4 or 5 of the Immigration Act, 2004, among others, are taken to have a right to reside in the State for the purpose of the Act. Section 246 of Act (as amended) provides that those with, *inter alia*, refugee status, programme refugee status, subsidiary protection, or leave to remain under the Immigration Act 2004 shall not be regarded as being habitually resident in the State for any period before the date on which the relevant declaration or permission was given. Article 28 of Council Directive 2004/83/EC provides minimum standards in respect of social welfare benefits as follows:

'1.   *Member States shall ensure that beneficiaries of refugee or subsidiary protection status receive, in the Member State that has granted such statuses, the necessary social assistance, as provided to nationals of that Member State.*

2.   *By exception to the general rule laid down in paragraph 1, Member States may limit social assistance granted to beneficiaries of subsidiary protection status to core benefits which will then be provided at the same levels and under the same eligibility conditions as nationals.*

15.6   Conclusion

The rights of those seeking, and in receipt of, international protection in the State are derived from international and EU law. The 1951 Convention Relating to the Status of Refugees remains the international standard for refugee protection. This is recognised by Recital 3 of Council Directive 2004/83/EC which states that the 1951 Convention and its 1967 Protocol provide the cornerstone of the international legal regime for the protection of refugees. The Convention and its Protocol were initially given effect though the Refugee Act, 1996. The EU asylum *acquis* also requires domestic compliance, to the extent that Ireland has opted into it.

The importance of EU law in this area will be clear from the prominence given to EU legislation in this chapter. The Charter of Fundamental Rights of the European Union now establishes the right to asylum as a general principle of EU law. Refugee and protection law, however, is a politically sensitive area and so remains subject to continued change and evolution. The political mandate and overall policy agenda is now derived from the Stockholm Programme, rather than exclusively from Irish domestic concerns, and is now directed at a common European asylum system. The legislative framework of asylum law is now the EU asylum *acquis*. The efficacy of the Court of Justice of the European Union as judicial arbiter in asylum matters is clear in light of the Treaty of Lisbon.

The domestic law framework, set out in the Refugee Act, 1996, the Immigration Acts 1999-2004, the Illegal Immigrants Act, 2000 and the European Community (Eligibility for Protection) Regulations, 2006 (S.I. No. 518 of 2006), which partially transposed Council Directive 2004/83/EC ('the Qualification Directive) into Irish law, controls the procedures for administration of the determination procedure in respect of international protection. The Immigration, Residence, and Protection Bill, 2010 contains the most important proposed overhaul of the area since the Refugee Act, 1996 was enacted. The Bill is drafted to transpose Council Directive 2005/85/EC ('the Procedures Directive'), and integrate the provisions of the European Community (Eligibility for Protection) Regulations, 2006, into primary legislation. The Bill as drafted also seeks to introduce a single procedure for applicants for international protection. Whilst this proposed legislative reform is important, many of the changes brought about by EU legislation already require domestic compliance due to the supremacy of EU law.

The Irish case law referred to in this chapter arises from applications for judicial review and, while some such case law yields important interpretation of refugee law, judicial review typically focuses on the decision-making process, rather than the merits of cases. The Refugee Appeals Tribunal, which deals substantively with refugee appeals in relation to both facts and law does not generally make its decisions publicly available, having published only a few of its decisions. Accordingly, in order to find judicial interpretation of substantive refugee law, practitioners and decision-makers must often look to jurisprudence from other jurisdictions.

This chapter can only skim the surface of a very extensive and expanding area of law. Refugee lawyers will need to read further, and will need to be aware not only of refugee and international human rights case law, but of the principles of EU law, and the case law of the European Court of Justice, and in relation to areas beyond asylum law. Refugee law is clearly not as discrete an area as might have previously been thought. The confluence of refugee law and many other areas of law, whether immigration law, employment law, criminal law, family law, or child law has become ever clearer as modern Irish refugee law evolves.

CHAPTER 16

IMMIGRATION AND CITIZENSHIP LAW

16.1 Introduction

Irish domestic immigration law, the subject of this chapter, regulates the entry and residence of *'foreign nationals'*, generally defined as persons who are neither Irish nor European Union (EU)/European Economic Area (EEA) nationals. Traditionally, the legislation also refers to 'aliens' and 'non-nationals'.

Entry and residence of nationals of the European Union (EU) and their family members, on the other hand, are regulated in Ireland by the European Communities (Free Movement of Persons) Regulations 2006 and 2008 (SI 656/2006 and SI 310/2008), implementing Directive 2004/38/EC on the right of citizens of the Union and their family members to move and reside freely within the territory of the Member States. The European Communities (Aliens) Regulations, 1977 (SI 393/1977) and the European Communities (Right of Residence for Non-Economically Active Persons) Regulations, 1997 (SI 57/1997) regulate the entry and residence of EEA nationals who are not covered by Directive 2004/38/EC.

> 'Part of the motivation behind the establishment of a common market was to ensure the integration of the European people. Without free movement of workers, the internal labour market within the EU would remain inconsistent, with areas of unemployment and low wages and other areas of high wages and labour shortages and no means of ensuring that workers could migrate from one area to another'. (Law Society of Ireland, *European Law*, 3rd edn, 2008, OUP 20–46).

To date, immigration into Ireland has been the subject of a large variety of legislative measures, starting with the Aliens Act, 1935 and the Aliens Orders, 1946 and 1975. Parts of the 1935 Act and the Orders made thereunder have been declared unconstitutional following legal challenges in the case of *DPP & Anor v Leontjava* [2004] IESC 37, largely reversing an earlier High Court judgment regarding the unconstitutionality of s 5(1) of the Aliens Act, 1935 and s 2 of the Immigration Act 1999, and in the case of *Laurentiu v Minister for Justice, Equality and Law Reform* [1999] IESC 47, resulting in legislation which now largely replaces the Act and its Orders.

The principal acts regulating entry and residence in the State today are the Immigration Act, 1999, the Immigration Act, 2003 and the Immigration Act, 2004 with multiple regulations having been passed thereunder, regulating matters such as visa requirements, fees and places of detention as well as the prescribed form of deportation orders. The Illegal Immigrants (Trafficking) Act, 2000 created an offence of facilitating *'the entry into the State of a person whom [the person concerned] knows or has reasonable cause to believe to be an illegal immigrant or a person who intends to seek asylum'*. The Act also introduced significant changes to the way in which immigration and asylum related decisions can be challenged (see also **chapter 15**).

The State has the power to control the entry, the residency, and the exit, of foreign nationals. As stated in the case of *Pok Sun Shum v Ireland* [1986] ILRM 593:

'(i)n relation to the permission to remain in the State, it seems (. . .) that the State, through its Ministry for Justice, must have very wide powers in the interest of the common good to control aliens, their entry into the State, their departure and their activities within the State'.

However, it is clear that the executive power regarding the control of the entry and residence of foreign nationals in the State must be exercised in a manner which is consistent with and not in breach of the constitutionally protected rights of persons and that the Minister in his actions is constrained by the provisions of s 3 of the European Convention on Human Rights Act, 2003 (see **chapter 5**).

The acquisition of Irish citizenship is regulated by the Irish Nationality and Citizenship Act, 1956 as most recently amended, following the Citizenship Referendum in June 2004. The constitutional amendment passed at that time had the effect that persons born on the island of Ireland no longer have a constitutional right to be Irish citizens, unless, at the time of their birth, one of their parents is an Irish citizen or is entitled to be an Irish citizen. The Irish Nationality and Citizenship Act, 2004, which came into force on 1 January 2005, now governs how other people born in Ireland may become Irish citizens (see **16.5.3.1** below).

16.2 Entry

16.2.1 VISA APPLICATIONS AND VISA APPEALS

Visas are defined in s 1 of the Immigration Act, 2003 as:

'an endorsement made on a passport or travel document other than an Irish passport or Irish travel document for the purposes of indicating that the holder thereof is authorised to land in the State subject to any other conditions of landing being fulfilled'.

Currently, the granting and refusal of visas to foreign nationals intending to come to Ireland on a visit or for a longer term is not regulated by statute. However, a number of issues relating to visa applications are the subject of Visa Orders made by the Minister for Justice and Law Reform pursuant to s 17 of the Immigration Act, 2004.

As set out by Clark J in the recent case of *RMR and BH v The Minister for Justice, Equality and Law Reform and the Attorney General* [2009] IEHC 279:

'it is clear that the Minister is under no legal obligation to grant a visa—the grant or refusal of visas is entirely within his discretion and it is for the visa applicant to convince the Minister that he or she should be granted a visa. Government policy determines which foreign nationals require visas to visit or transit the State and whether they can work in the State. The inherent executive power and responsibility of the Government to formulate immigration policy is supplemented by statutory provisions including the Aliens Act 1935 and the Immigration Acts 1999, 2003 and 2004. There is at present no statutory framework for issuing visas.'

Reform of the law in this area is currently under way and it is envisaged that a statutory basis for issuing and revoking visa applications together with definitions of various entry and transit visas will form part of future legislation.

The majority of foreign nationals intending to come to Ireland on a visit or more long-term require an entry visa. Schedule 1 of the Immigration Act, 2004 (Visas) No. 2 Order, 2009 (SI 453/2009) lists those countries whose nationals currently do not require a visa to enter Ireland. Those exempted from the visa requirement include nationals of the EEA and Switzerland as well as certain countries including for example the United States of America, Canada, New Zealand, Australia, Taiwan, Brazil and South Africa.

Furthermore, the Order provides that holders of a valid Convention travel document (see **chapter 15**) issued by certain listed Member States of the EEA or by Switzerland, do not require a visa to enter the State where the intended purpose of the travel to the State by the holder of such a travel document is solely for a visit of up to a maximum period of three months. Others exempt from the requirement are holders of a valid permanent residence card issued under Regulation 16 of the European Communities (Free Movement of Persons) (No. 2) Regulations 2006 (SI 656/2006) (see **16.3**), or of a valid residence card issued under Regulation 7 of the Regulations.

Only certain nationalities require a transit visa for the purpose of passing through Ireland. These are listed in Schedule 2 of the above named Order and include, for example Afghanistan, Cuba, Iraq and Nigeria. A transit visa, which is defined in s 1 of the Immigration Act, 2003 as:

> 'an endorsement made on a passport or travel document other than an Irish passport or Irish travel document for the purposes of indicating that the holder thereof is authorised to arrive at a port in the State for purposes of passing through the port in order to travel to another state subject to any other conditions of arrival being fulfilled',

does not permit the holder to leave the port or airport at which he or she arrived; it is granted for the purpose of transit to an onward destination and granted on condition that the person concerned holds a valid entry visa for his or her final destination, if required.

Depending on the country of residence of the visa applicant, an application for a visa can be made either online or directly at an Irish embassy or consulate.

In accordance with the relevant administrative procedures, the following minimum documentation is required for all visa applications:

- a completed visa application personally signed by the applicant

- consent of both parents for children under the age of 18 travelling alone

- consent of one parent/evidence of sole custody where the child is travelling with the other parent

- valid passport

- evidence of financial self-sufficiency for the duration of stay in Ireland

- details of any other family members presently in Ireland, or any other EU Member State

- details of any previous visa applications for Ireland

- details of visa refusals for any other country.

Further documentation is required under the various categories of visas, for example a visa application for an international student will have to include: evidence of enrolment in a privately funded course involving at least 15 hours of organised daytime tuition each week, evidence of payment of the requisite fee to the college, evidence of academic ability and English language skills to follow the chosen course, evidence of immediate access to at least €7,000 for each year of studies, and evidence of private medical insurance. Furthermore, students applying for an entry visa to come to Ireland must be able to account for any gaps in their educational history and must provide evidence of their intention to return to their country of permanent residence following completion of their studies in Ireland.

Visa required nationals who are legally resident in Ireland require a re-entry visa if they leave the State with the intention of re-entry within the period of validity of their current permission to be in the State.

In the case of a visa refusal, the applicant can appeal the decision in writing by way of written submission to a Visa Appeals Officer. Depending on the location of the visa applicant, appeals will have to be submitted to the Department of Justice and Law Reform or to an Appeal Officer within the relevant Irish embassy. Although there is no statutory time limit for the submission of an appeal, appellants are advised by the Department to lodge appeals within two months from the date of refusal. In order to obtain the reasons for the refusal of their visa application, applicants have to consult the Visa Decisions Page on the website of the Irish Naturalisation and Immigration Service, using their visa reference number, which is issued once the visa application is first lodged. Should a visa appeal be successful, the decision will be reversed on the Visa Decisions Page. Unsuccessful applicants receive a decision in writing from the Visa Appeals Officer. There is no further remedy available at that point other than a possible application for Judicial Review in the High Court.

16.2.2   LEAVE TO LAND, REFUSAL OF ENTRY AND REMOVAL

The possession of a visa does not guarantee entry to the State. Pursuant to s 4 of the Immigration Act, 2004, an immigration officer at the port of entry has the authority to grant or deny admission, and to decide on the duration a person may remain in the State as well as any conditions attached to the stay.

In accordance with s 4(2) of the Immigration Act, 2004, foreign nationals arriving by air or sea from a place outside the State, have the obligation to present themselves to an immigration officer and to apply for permission to land or be in the State. Section 4(5) of the Act applies in relation to foreign nationals arriving in the State by land from Northern Ireland and creates an obligation not to remain for longer than one month without permission to land or be in the State. However, foreign nationals arriving in the State by land from Northern Ireland, who wish to engage in employment, business or a profession within the State, have the obligation to *'report in person to the registration officer for the place in which* [they intend] *to reside, produce to the officer a valid passport or other equivalent document, (. . .), which establishes* [their] *identity and nationality, and furnish such information as the officer may reasonably require regarding the purpose of* [their] *arrival (. . .)'*, within seven days of entering the State (s 4(5)(c)).

Section 4(3), which is equally applicable to persons arriving by air, sea or land, provides that an immigration officer may refuse to give permission to land or be in the State if the officer is satisfied:

'(a)   *that the non-national is not in a position to support himself or herself and any accompanying dependants;*

(b)   *that the non-national intends to take up employment in the State, but is not in possession of a valid employment permit (within the meaning of the Employment Permits Act 2003);*

(c)   *that the non-national suffers from a condition set out in the First Schedule;*

(d)   *that the non-national has been convicted (whether in the State or elsewhere) of an offence that may be punished under the law of the place of conviction by imprisonment for a period of one year or by a more severe penalty;*

(e)   *that the non-national, not being exempt, by virtue of an order under section 17, from the requirement to have an Irish visa, is not the holder of a valid Irish visa;*

(f)   *that the non-national is the subject of—*

(i)   *a deportation order (within the meaning of the Act of 1999),*

(ii)   *an exclusion order (within the meaning of that Act), or*

(iii)   *a determination by the Minister that it is conducive to the public good that he or she remain outside the State;*

(g)   *that the non-national is not in possession of a valid passport or other equivalent document, issued by or on behalf of an authority recognised by the Government, which establishes his or her identity and nationality;*

> (h)   that the non-national—
>
>   (i)   intends to travel (whether immediately or not) to Great Britain or Northern Ireland, and
>
>   (ii)   would not qualify for admission to Great Britain or Northern Ireland if he or she arrived there from a place other than the State;
>
> (i)   that the non-national, having arrived in the State in the course of employment as a seaman, has remained in the State without the leave of an immigration officer after the departure of the ship in which he or she so arrived;
>
> (j)   that the non-national's entry into, or presence in, the State could pose a threat to national security or be contrary to public policy;
>
> (k)   that there is reason to believe that the non-national intends to enter the State for purposes other than those expressed by the non-national'.

While there is an obligation to provide reasons for the refusal of permission to land or be in the State in writing, the decision of an immigration officer in this regard is not subject to an appeal. A person seeking to challenge the refusal to permit them to enter the State would have to resort to judicial review proceedings before the High Court.

A foreign national is liable to removal from the State pursuant to s 5(1) of the Immigration Act, 2003, if he or she has been refused leave to land, or, coming from any place outside the State other than Great Britain or Northern Ireland, has landed in the State except without the leave of an immigration officer or of the Minister, in contravention of Article 5(1) of the Aliens Order, 1946, or has landed at an unapproved port, in contravention of Article 6 of the Aliens Order, 1946, or is deemed to have been refused leave to land in accordance with the Aliens Order, 1946, in so far as an immigration officer or a member of the Garda Síochána, with reasonable cause, suspects that he or she has been unlawfully in the State for a continuous period of less than three months.

In the case of *Gulyas & Anor v The Minister for Justice, Equality and Law Reform* [2001] 3 IR 216, Carroll J held that a decision to refuse leave to land, in this case to a Hungarian national seeking leave to enter and be in the State for the purpose of a visit to her former employers with whom she had developed a friendship, which was based on a mistake of fact regarding the financial resources available to Ms Gulyas during her visit, was 'at variance with reason and common sense' and that therefore there had been a 'lack of fair procedures' in relation to the decision to refuse leave to land.

The Minister has the power to remove persons who have been refused leave to land. However, s 5(1) of the Immigration Act, 2003 restricts this power to persons *'whom an immigration officer or a member of An Garda Síochána, with reasonable cause, suspects has been unlawfully in the State for a continuous period of less than 3 months'*.

The High Court confirmed in the case of *K v Minister for Justice, Equality and Law Reform* [2008] IEHC 35 that even in a case where there would have been a power to refuse permission to land as contained in s 4 of the Immigration Act, 2004, at the time of the person's arrival, s 5(1) of the Immigration Act, 2003 does not allow the person to be removed from the State without a formal deportation procedure under s 3 of the Immigration Act, 1999 (see **16.6.1** below) in a situation where he or she has spent more than three months in the State since his or her arrival.

16.2.3   POWERS OF SEARCH, ARREST AND DETENTION

In accordance with s 7(3)(a) of the Immigration Act, 2004:

> *'any non-national landing or embarking at any place in the State shall, on being required so to do by an immigration officer or a member of the Garda Síochána, make a declaration as to whether or not he or she is carrying or conveying any documents and, if so required, shall produce them to the officer or member'.*

Section 7(3)(b) further provides that:

> 'the officer or member may search any such non-national and any luggage belonging to him or her or under his or her control with a view to ascertaining whether the non-national is carrying or conveying any documents and may examine and detain, for such time as he or she may think proper for the purpose of such examination, any documents so produced or found on the search'.

And pursuant to s 13 of the Immigration Act, 2004:

> 'a member of An Garda Síochána may arrest without warrant a person whom he or she reasonably suspects to have committed an offence under this Act (other than Section 10) or Section 2(1) of the Employment Permits Act 2003'

for example for the failure to produce on demand, a valid passport or other equivalent document, and in case the person concerned is registered or deemed to be registered under the Act, his or her registration certificate (s 12).

However, as established by O'Neill J in the case of *Olafusi v Governor of Cloverhill Prison* [2009] IEHC 558, 'the criminal justice process cannot be used or adapted to facilitate the ascertainment of the identity of such a person'. This case concerned a foreign national who had been arrested and charged with offences contrary to ss 12(1)(a) and (2) and s 13 of the Immigration Act, 2004 for failure to produce evidence of his identity and nationality and for failure to provide a satisfactory explanation of the circumstances that prevented him from doing so. In this case, the District Court judge had refused a guilty plea because of a concern as to the true identity of the person concerned. O'Neill J held in this case that:

> '(w)here such a person offers a plea of guilty the Court must, in the absence of appropriate exceptional circumstances, proceed to sentence. Insofar as there are difficulties encountered in establishing the identity of persons, this is a matter to be resolved by the immigration authorities and the Gardaí'.

He further observed that '(i)n this regard (...) there are statutory provisions which provide for the detention of such persons quite apart from the criminal process, (...)'.

Similarly, s 5(2) of the Immigration Act, 2003 authorises an immigration officer or a member of An Garda Síochána to arrest and detain:

> *(a)* a non-national to whom leave to land has been refused under Article 5(2) of the Aliens Order 1946 (No. 395/1946),
>
> *(b)* a non-national who has failed to comply with Article 5(1) of the Order [landing without leave of an immigration officer],
>
> *(c)* a non-national who has entered the State [elsewhere than at an approved port] in contravention of Article 6 of the Order,
>
> *(d)* a non-national deemed to be a person to whom leave to land has been refused under the Order,
>
> *(e)* a non-national who has failed to comply with Section 4(2) of the Immigration Act 2004 [the duty to present himself or herself to an immigration officer and apply for permission to land or be in the State],
>
> *(f)* a non-national who has been refused a permission [to land or be in the State] under Section 4(3) of that Act,
>
> *(g)* a non-national who is in the State in contravention of Section 5(1) of that Act [presence in the State other than in accordance with the terms of any permission given],
>
> *(h)* a non-national who has landed in the State [elsewhere than at an approved port] in contravention of Section 6(1) of that Act.'

However, in accordance with s 5(3) of the Act, a person whom an immigration officer or a member of the Garda Síochána with reasonable cause, suspects to have been unlawfully in the State for a continuous period of less than three months and who has been arrested and detained pursuant to s 5(2) may only be detained until such time as he or she is removed from the State.

return travel costs without recourse to the Member State's social assistance system and he or she must have sickness insurance for all the risks normally covered for nationals of the Member State. The maximum duration of a hosting agreement is five years.

Following signature of a valid hosting agreement the researcher must be admitted into the Member State subject to the presentation of a valid travel document, the hosting agreement and, where applicable, presentation of a statement of financial responsibility issued by the research organization. Furthermore, the researcher must not be considered to pose a threat to public policy, public security or public health.

16.3.3.4 Permission to remain following notification of intention to deport

Before making a deportation order, the Minister for Justice and Law Reform has the obligation to notify the person concerned, pursuant to s 3(3) of the Immigration Act, 1999 of his or her intention to make such order. It is then open to the person concerned to make representations in writing to the Minister, within fifteen working days of sending him or her the notification, to leave the State before the Minister decides the matter, or to consent to the making of a deportation order.

The making of representations pursuant to s 3(3)(b) of the Immigration Act, 1999 are generally referred to as an 'application for permission to remain on humanitarian grounds'. However, matters which the Minister is obliged to take into account pursuant to s 3(6) of the Act include a wide range of considerations:

(a) the age of the person

(b) the duration of residence in the State of the person

(c) the family and domestic circumstances of the person

(d) the nature of the person's connection with the State (if any)

(e) the employment (including self-employment) record of the person

(f) the employment (including self-employment) prospects of the person

(g) the character and conduct of the person both within and (where relevant and ascertainable) outside the State (including any criminal convictions)

(h) humanitarian considerations

(i) any representations duly made by or on behalf of the person

(j) the common good

(k) considerations of national security and public policy.

The Supreme Court held in the case of *Bode (A Minor) v Minister for Justice, Equality & Law Reform & Ors* [2007] IESC 62 that the so-called 'Section 3 Process' is 'a statutory scheme providing that the Minister, in considering the situation of foreign nationals, shall have regard to a wide range of issues when making a decision (...). Constitutional and Convention rights are appropriately considered at that stage'.

In the later judgments of *Oguekwe v Minister for Justice Equality and Law Reform* [2008] IESC 25 and *Dimbo v Minister for Justice Equality and Law Reform* [2008] IESC 26, regarding the details of the considerations to be made prior to the issuing of a deportation order, Denham J set out a 'non exhaustive list of matters which may assist, and which relate to, the position of an Irish born child whose parents may be considered for a deportation order'. These matters are discussed further at **16.6** below.

Where the Minister, following consideration of representations made by or on behalf of a person threatened with deportation, decides not to make a deportation order, the person concerned is generally given permission to remain in the State on the basis of the powers vested in the Minister by s 4(1) of the Immigration Act, 2004.

16.4   Family Reunification

There are no statutory provisions in Irish legislation which regulate the entry and residence of foreign nationals for the purpose of the reunification or establishment of families with the exception of s 18 of the Refugee Act, which regulates the reunification of persons granted refugee status with certain family members who have remained outside the State and the right to enter and reside in Ireland of EEA nationals and their family members as regulated in the European Communities (Aliens) Regulations, 1977 (SI 393/1977), the European Communities (Right of Residence of Non-Economically Active Persons) Regulations, 1997 and the European Communities (Free Movement of Persons) Regulations, 2006 and 2008 in regard to EEA nationals and their family members (see Law Society of Ireland, *European Law*, 4th edn, 2008, OUP, 20–46).

The granting of permission to enter and remain in the State to family members of Irish nationals and lawfully resident foreign nationals remains at the discretion of the Minister for Justice and Law Reform implemented through administrative procedures published on the website of the Irish Naturalisation and Immigration Service (INIS).

In relation to applications affecting families, the High Court has acknowledged as a general principle that:

> '(i)t has been the norm to consider the rights of all the members of what is presented as the constituent parts of the applicant's family. This is quite evident from a number of decided cases before our courts and where the necessary consideration of the relevant files revealed that the Minister does have regard to the effect of a deportation on those members of the family left behind as well as the effect on the family member being deported' (Clark J in *A v Minister for Justice, Equality and Law Reform* [2009] IEHC 245).

16.4.1   REFUGEE FAMILY REUNIFICATION

In accordance with s 18 of the Refugee Act, 1996 (as amended), a person who has received a declaration pursuant to s 17(1) of the Refugee Act (as amended) that he or she is a refugee, may apply to the Minister for Justice and Law Reform for permission to be granted to a member of his or her family to enter and to reside in the State.

A 'member of the family' is defined in the s 18(3)(b) of the Act as:

> *(i)   in case the refugee is married, his or her spouse (provided that the marriage is subsisting on the date of the refugee's application [for family reunification])*
>
> *(ii)   in case the refugee is, on the date of his or her application [for family reunification], under the age of 18 years and is not married, his or her parents*
>
> *(iii)   a child of the refugee who, on the date of the refugee's application [for family reunification], is under the age of 18 years and is not married'.*

Subject to national security and public policy concerns, the Minister shall grant permission in writing to the family member to enter and reside in the State.

At the discretion of the Minister, 'dependent family members' which are defined in s 18(4)(b) of the Act as:

> *'any grandparent, parent, brother, sister, child, grandchild, ward or guardian of the refugee who is depending on the refugee or who is dependent on the refugee or is suffering from a mental or*

physical disability to such an extent that it is not reasonable for him or her to maintain himself or herself fully',

may also be granted permission to enter and reside in the State.

Once granted permission to enter and be in the State, family members and dependent family members will be entitled to the same rights and privileges as the refugee, as set out in s 3 of the Refugee Act, 1996 (as amended) for such period as the refugee is entitled to remain in the State, including:

(i) to seek and enter employment, to carry on any business, trade or profession and to have access to education and training in the State in the like manner and to the like extent in all respects as an Irish citizen

(ii) to receive, upon and subject to the terms and conditions applicable to Irish citizens, the same medical care and services and the same social welfare benefits as those to which Irish citizens are entitled

(iii) subject to national security and public policy: (I) to reside in the State, and (II) to the same rights of travel in or to or from the State as those to which Irish citizens are entitled

(iv) the same freedom to practise his or her religion and the same freedom as regards the religious education of his or her child as an Irish citizen

(v) access to the courts in the like manner and to the like extent in all respects as an Irish citizen, and

(vi) the right to form and be a member of associations and trade unions in the like manner and to the like extent in all respects as an Irish citizen.

Procedurally, an application for refugee family reunification must be submitted in writing to the Department of Justice and Law Reform. The application is then forwarded to the Office of the Refugee Applications Commissioner (ORAC) for examination as required under s 18 of the Refugee Act, 1996 (as amended). When the examination is completed, the Commissioner will prepare and forward a report to the Department of Justice and Law Reform, where a decision will be made.

Upon receipt of a positive decision, a visa application will have to be submitted by or on behalf of the family member or dependent family member concerned in so far as they are visa required nationals (see **16.2.1** above).

While it is possible to appeal a negative visa decision, there is no appeals mechanism through which a refusal of family reunification pursuant to s 18 of the Refugee Act, 1996 (as amended) could be challenged. The only available remedy is an application for judicial review to the High Court which was recognised in the case of *T v The Minister for Justice, Equality and Law Reform* [2008] IEHC 361:

'family reunification is not only a way of bringing families back together, but it is also essential to facilitate the integration of third-country nationals into the State (...). Refugees finding themselves alone in a foreign country which has admitted them, traumatised by the events that brought them there, more than ever need the society and support of their immediate family. Every effort must be made to ensure such reunification occurs as quickly as possible'.

In this case, which involved a delay of more than four years in relation to making a decision on a family reunification application submitted by a recognised refugee from Ghana in respect of his four children, Hedigan J referred to the earlier cases of *Awe v The Minister for Justice, Equality and Law Reform* [2006] IEHC 6, *Iatan and Others v The Minister for Justice, Equality and Law Reform & Ors* [2006] IEHC 30 and *KM and GD v The Minister for Justice, Equality and Law Reform* [2007] IEHC 234, and held that:

'(t)he requirements of constitutional justice dictate that an applicant seeking administrative relief, whether in the immigration context or otherwise, is entitled to a decision within a reasonable time. The applicant in the present case applied for family reunification in June, 2003 and did not receive a decision until August, 2007; there was, therefore, a delay of over 4 years. This is a most unsatisfactory state of affairs. Bearing this in mind, the Court is of the view that the fact that it is open to the applicant to make a fresh application for family reunification does not provide an answer to the applicant's difficulties. According to information provided on the website of the Irish Naturalisation and Immigration Service (INIS), "(t)he average time processing for Family Reunification applications is 24 months (as at January 2008)". Thus, if the applicant was to submit a fresh application, each of his children would have reached the age of majority by the time a decision was reached'.

16.4.2   FAMILY REUNIFICATION FOR IRISH NATIONALS

As outlined above, there is currently no statutory scheme setting out the rights and entitlements of Irish nationals to be joined by or to live with foreign national family members in the State. Such applications are currently being made by spouses and non-marital partners of Irish nationals, as well as by foreign nationals who are parents of Irish citizen children and by the foreign national parents of adults who are naturalised Irish citizens.

The website of the Irish Naturalisation and Immigration Service (INIS) provides details in relation to some of the applications that may be made in respect of spouses and non-marital partners of Irish nationals. However, information regarding dependents of the ascending or descending line and information regarding foreign national parents seeking to enter and/or remain in the State on the basis of their family relationship with an Irish national child is not provided.

16.4.2.1   Spouse of an Irish National

Marriage to an Irish national does not confer an automatic right of residence in the State. A foreign national who wishes to reside in the State on the basis of their marriage to an Irish national must make an application for permission to remain in the State and the granting of such permission is at the discretion of the Minister for Justice and Law Reform. It is generally accepted, as set out in the case of *R (Mahmood) v Secretary of State for the Home Department* [2001] 1 WLR 840 that:

'(1)   A State has a right under international law to control the entry of non-nationals into its territory, subject always to its treaty obligations.

(2)   Article 8 does not impose on a State any general obligation to respect the choice of residence of a married couple.

(3)   Removal or exclusion of one family member from a State where other members of the family are lawfully resident will not necessarily infringe Article 8 provided that there are no insurmountable obstacles to the family living together in the country of origin of the family member excluded, even where this involves a degree of hardship for some or all members of the family.

(4)   Article 8 is likely to be violated by the expulsion of a member of a family that has been long established in a State if the circumstances are such that it is not reasonable to expect the other members of the family to follow that member expelled.

(5)   Knowledge on the part of one spouse at the time of marriage that rights of residence of the other were precarious militates against a finding that an order excluding the latter spouse violates Article 8.

(6)   Whether interference with family rights is justified in the interests of controlling immigration will depend on (i) the facts of the particular case and (ii) the circumstances prevailing in the State whose action is impugned'.

In an interpretation of the jurisprudence of the European Court of Human Rights (ECt.HR), Dunne J noted the following principles in the case of *S & Ors v MJELR* [2007] IEHC 398:

'1.   Family can include the relationship between an adult child and his parents (see for example *Boughanemi v France* [1996] 22 E.H.R.R. 228).

2.   Family life may also include siblings, adult or minor (see Boughanemi and *Olsson v Sweden* [1989] 11 E.H.R.R. 259).

3.   The relationship between a parent and an adult child does not necessarily constitute family life without evidence of further elements of dependency involving more than the normal, emotional ties. (See *Advic v United Kingdom* [1995] 20 E.H.R.R, C.D. 125).

4.   The existence or not of family life falling within the scope of Article 8 depends on a number of factors and the circumstances of each case'.

However, in so far as there are no concerns that the marriage of an Irish national to a foreign national is a so-called 'marriage of convenience', i.e. a marriage contracted for the sole purpose of enabling the person concerned to enter or reside in Ireland, residence permits are generally granted to spouses of Irish nationals who are currently legally in the State on production of the following documentation to the Garda National Immigration Bureau (GNIB): original marriage certificate, original passports and evidence of joint address.

Spouses of Irish nationals who do not have current permission to remain in the State must make a written application to the Irish Naturalisation and Immigration Service, enclosing documentation regarding the spouse's/partner's immigration history in this State, his or her current legal status, the original marriage certificate, detailed information regarding the couple's relationship history and the context in which their marriage took place as well as evidence of joint address in Ireland, original passports and birth certificates, divorce papers (if applicable) and other supporting documentation, for example photographs.

Where a foreign national spouse of an Irish national is the subject of a deportation order, it is possible to make an application pursuant to s 3(11) of the Immigration Act, 1999 for the revocation of same, on the basis of the couple's change of circumstances (see also **16.6** below). However, as set out by Fennelly J in the case of *Cirpaci (nee McCormack) v The Minister for Justice, Equality and Law Reform* [2005] IESC 42, matters such as a previous unsuccessful asylum application, the evasion of deportation and the immediate commencement of moves to be readmitted to the State following marriage to an Irish national without subsequent cohabitation for an appreciable time 'are all matters of legitimate concern for the State'. In dismissing the appeal to the Supreme Court in this case, Fennelly J added that:

'as the European Court has repeatedly said, a State is not bound to respect the choice of residence made by married couples. It is relevant to bear in mind that the Appellants were aware of the husband's unfavourable immigration history when they entered into their marriage'.

Applications for residence permits made by spouses of Irish nationals can take up to 12 months to process. It seems from the case-law of the Irish High Court that a processing time of 12 months is the maximum time which can be considered reasonable. As Edwards J set out in the case of *M v The Minister for Justice, Equality and Law Reform* [2007] IEHC 234, a period of 11 months from the date of application to the receipt of a decision:

'is certainly sub optimal and close to the limits of what is reasonable. (. . .). However, (. . .), I do not believe that the degree of delay is presently such that it could be characterised as being unreasonable and/or unconscionable. If the applicant were kept waiting for a decision longer than 12 months I would have no hesitation in finding the delay to be unreasonable and, being unjustifiable notwithstanding any scarcity of resources, unconscionable'.

In relation to the delay of 11 months, Edwards J did not consider 'that the degree of delay in the case to date, such as it is, has so prejudiced the applicants as to breach their rights under Article 41 of the Constitution, and under Article 8 of the aforementioned Convention'.

In most cases, the foreign national spouse of an Irish national is granted permission to remain in the State with permission to work and/enter set up a business without the need for an employment or business permit. The permission granted will generally be valid for an initial period of five years en par with the permission granted to spouses of EEA nationals resident and working in the State (see Law Society of Ireland, *European Law*, 4th edn, 2008, OUP, 20–46).

Unlike in the case of spouses of EEA nationals resident in the State on the basis of their free movement rights, there are no rights of retention of residence in the event of death, separation or divorce, even in situations involving domestic violence, and successful applicants do not have a statutory right to family reunification with other family members.

However, pursuant to s 4(7) of the Immigration Act, 2004, the Minister for Justice and Law Reform does have discretion to extend and vary the permission to remain granted to family members of Irish nationals following the breakdown of a family relationship. And based on the powers vested in him by s 4(1) of the Immigration Act, 2004, the Minister may also grant permission to enter and remain in the State to the spouse's other third-country family members.

The reverse discrimination in relation to family reunification with third-country national family members of EU nationals who have not exercised free movement rights when compared to those who have moved from one EU Member State to another is recognised as an issue throughout the EU. To date, the ECJ has consistently held that the freedoms guaranteed by the EC Treaty do not apply in 'purely internal situations'. However, the ECJ, now the Court of Justice of the European Union, has acknowledged that:

'(. . .) citizenship of the Union, established by Article 8 of the EC Treaty [now Article 20 TFEU] is not intended to extend the scope ratione materiae of the Treaty also to internal situations which have links with Community law. Any discrimination which nationals of a Member State may suffer under the law of that State fall within the scope of that law and must therefore be dealt with within the framework of the internal legal system of that State' (C-64/96 and C-65/96 *Land Nordrhein-Westfalen v Kari Uecker and Vera Jacquet v Land Nordrhein-Westfalen* [1997] ECR I-03171).

The absence of a statutory entitlement to family reunification for Irish nationals may be in breach of Article 8 in conjunction with Article 14 ECHR. However, to date the High Court has not acknowledged the existence of discrimination in this regard and has therefore failed to provide a view on whether the difference in treatment of Irish nationals is in accordance with law and proportionate, as required by Article 14. In the case of *M & Ors v MJELR* [2009] IEHC 500, Edwards J held that:

'it is fundamental to the notion of discrimination that you have two persons who are in an equivalent situation and that one is treated differently from the other, not withstanding this equivalence. In this case [a case concerning a naturalised Irish national seeking permission to have her mother reside with her as a dependent family member in the ascending line en par with the provisions of Article 2(2)(d) of Directive 2004/38/EC] however, the court is satisfied that the first named applicant's situation is not equivalent to that of a non-Irish EU worker who travels to Ireland to take up a job and brings her non-EU national mother with her to reside in Ireland'.

He further found that:

'(I)n the case of the non-Irish worker that person has specifically invoked her freedom of movement rights under the EU Treaties, and the provisions of Directive 38/2004/EC. By comparison, the first named applicant a naturalised Irish person is entitled as of right to work here and does not need to invoke or rely upon any Treaty right, or the provisions of any Directive'.

And he concluded that therefore 'her situation is not equivalent to the situation of a non-Irish EU national exercising her free movement rights'.

In a further judgment rejecting reverse discrimination arguments, Cooke J stated that:

'(I)t is well settled case-law that the Community law principle of unlawful discriminatory treatment is to the effect that discrimination is unlawful where, without objective justification, like situations are treated differently, or different situations are treated as if they were the same. (Case 13/63 *Italy v Commission* [1963] ECR 165)'.

He held that the child involved in this case:

'is in exactly the same position in relation to the exercise of the directive rights as the national of any other Member State residing in his own member state of nationality. His rights are less than those of a child of non-Irish nationality, but only if that child has established residence in Ireland'.

And he concluded that '(T)his is not a like situation' (see *O v Minister for Justice, Equality and Law Reform* [2009] IEHC 531).

16.4.2.2   De Facto relationship with an Irish National

In accordance with the administrative procedures published on the website of the Irish Naturalisation and Immigration Service, foreign nationals who wish to enter or remain in the State on the basis of a non-marital relationship with an Irish national must be in a position to provide evidence of a durable attested relationship of at least two years.

A residence permit may be granted at the discretion of the Minister for Justice and Law Reform upon submission of an application in writing which is accompanied by evidence of identity and nationality of both parties, evidence of finances of both parties, and evidence of relationship of at least two years duration (ie tenancy agreement, utility bills, bank statements, etc).

Subject to the immigration status of the foreign national, permission to remain may be granted. This permission will exempt the foreign national from employment permit requirements as well as business permit requirements. However, where the foreign national partner was previously in the State without permission, he or she may be granted permission to remain as a dependant for an initial period of one year.

16.4.2.3   Dependent relatives of Irish nationals

Unlike EEA nationals resident in the State on the basis of their free movement rights, Irish nationals do not have a statutory entitlement to be joined in the State by dependent relatives in the ascending or descending lines. And unlike in respect of dependent relatives of persons granted refugee status in the State, Irish law does not make specific reference to the statutory and executive discretion of the Minister for Justice and Law Reform to grant permission to enter and remain in the State to dependent relatives of Irish nationals.

The ECt.HR recognised in the case of *Marckx v Belgium* (1979–80) 2 EHRR 330 that 'family life within the meaning of Article 8, includes at least the ties between near relatives, for instance, those between grandparents and grandchildren'.

In the case of *O v The Minister for Justice, Equality and Law Reform* [2008] IEHC 80, a case concerning an application for the revocation of a deportation order made by the grandmother of two Irish citizen children born in 2002, who had entered the State in July 2002 together with her two daughters, their respective partners and one small child, Clark J recognised, in principle, the inclusion of a grandmother as part of the family as protected by Article 8 of the ECHR. He held that:

'(t)he first applicant's position as the mother of an adult family group with whom she has lived for upwards of four years is facing rupture by the Minister's decision to uphold his order for deportation. I believe the applicant should be permitted to argue that the refusal to revoke her deportation order may not have been a decision arrived at following proper consideration of the competing interests of maintaining an orderly immigration process and the interest of respecting family life. (. . .)'.

16.4.2.4 Parents and other family members of Irish citizen children

Again, there is no statutory entitlement for Irish citizen children to be joined by parents or other family members in the State. Following the judgment of the High Court in the case of *Fajujonu v Minister for Justice* [1987] IEHC 2, there was a general policy under which parents of Irish citizen children were usually granted permission to remain in the State. It has been reported that approximately 10,500 foreign nationals were granted leave to remain in the State, on the basis of parentage of an Irish born child, between 1996 and February, 2003. However, following the judgments in *Lobe and Osayande v Minister for Justice, Equality and Law Reform* [2003] IESC 3, this policy was suspended. In these two Joined Cases, the Supreme Court re-confirmed that a foreign national parent of an Irish born child did not have an automatic entitlement to remain in the State with the child. Following the Supreme Court decision in these cases, applications for residency made solely on the basis of parentage of an Irish citizen child were no longer being processed and instead, many of the 11,493 parents who had outstanding applications at the time, were issued with notifications of intention to deport pursuant to s 3(3) of the Immigration Act, 1999. From January to March 2005, parents of Irish citizen children were given the opportunity to apply for permission to remain in the State under the so-called 'IBC/05 Scheme' on condition that they had been continuously resident in Ireland since the birth of their child, that they had not been involved in criminal activity and that the parent concerned was taking a role in the upbringing of the child.

In the case of *Bode (A Minor) v Minister for Justice, Equality & Law Reform & Ors* [2007] IESC 62, in allowing an appeal against the earlier decision of Finlay Geoghegan J in *Bode & Ors v Minister for Justice, Equality & Law Reform & Ors* [2006] IEHC 341, the Supreme Court clarified further that:

'(t)he IBC/05 Scheme was a scheme established by the Minister, exercising executive power, to deal administratively with a unique group of foreign nationals in a generous manner, on general principles. The parameters of the scheme were set out clearly, (. . .).

At no stage was it intended that within the ambit of the scheme the Minister would consider, or did the Minister consider, Constitutional or Convention rights of the applicants. Thus the terms of the pleadings and of the appeal relating to the Constitutional and Convention rights of the applicants were misconceived and premature. Applicants who were not successful in their application under the IBC/05 Scheme remain in the same position as they had been before their application.'

Keane CJ outlined further that:

'(t)he Oireachtas has established a statutory scheme providing that the Minister, in considering the situation of foreign nationals, shall have regard to a wide range of issues when making a decision under Section 3 of the Immigration Act 1999, as amended. Constitutional and Convention rights are appropriately considered at that stage. If there is a change of circumstances then an application may be made to the Minister to consider further matters under Section 3(11) Immigration Act, 1999, as amended'.

However, the Supreme Court has since clarified in the cases of *Oguekwe v Minister for Justice Equality and Law Reform* [2008] IESC 25 and *Dimbo v Minister for Justice Equality and Law Reform* [2008] IESC 26 that:

'the decision making process should identify a substantial reason which requires the deportation of a foreign national parent of an Irish born citizen. The test is whether a substantial reason has been identified requiring a deportation order. (...). (...) the Minister is required to make a reasonable and proportionate decision'.

More recently, the High Court has had further opportunity to define the basis on which a parent of an Irish citizen may be deported from the State and in particular whether the absence of 'insurmountable obstacles' to the family of the deportee, including the Irish citizen child involved, moving with him to his country of origin would render the deportation permissible under Article 8 ECHR. In the case of *Alli v Minister for Justice, Equality & Law Reform* (2 December 2009, High Court (unreported)), Clarke J summarised his findings as follows:

'Having considered the arguments on both sides the Court has concluded that the Minister did not err in law in asking the question whether there were any "insurmountable obstacles" to the family moving with Mr Alli to Nigeria and continuing family life there with him. The posing of that question is well established in the ECtHR jurisprudence on Article 8 and is unaffected by recent U.K. judgments. Its relevance is reaffirmed by the Supreme Court's judgment in *Oguekwe*. An evaluation of whether there are any insurmountable obstacles to the family moving with the deportee incorporates an evaluation of the reasonableness of expecting that family to move'.

He continued to hold that:

'(h)aving identified that there were no insurmountable obstacles to the family following Mr Alli to Nigeria and following a fact-specific consideration of the applicants' circumstances, the Minister identified the following "substantial reason" for the deportation of Mr Alli: "there is no less restrictive process available which would achieve the legitimate aim of the State to maintain control of its own borders and operate a regulated system for control, processing and monitoring of non-national persons in the State"'.

The Court was therefore 'satisfied that in all the circumstances and on the basis in particular of the judgment of the Supreme Court in *A.O. and D.L.*, this constitutes a "substantial reason associated with the common good" which requires the deportation'. According to the Court, (t)he judgment in *Oguekwe* requires that the Minister weighs the applicants' constitutional and Convention rights against the rights of the State and reaches a reasonable and proportionate decision. Bearing in mind that the rights of the applicants and their family members which, though of considerable importance, are not absolute and can be outweighed, the Court was satisfied that in the circumstances of this case, these requirements were met and that the Minister reached a reasonable and proportionate decision (see also **16.6** Departure below).

16.4.3 FAMILY REUNIFICATION FOR MIGRANT WORKERS AND SCIENTIFIC RESEARCHERS

The administrative procedures published on the website of the Irish Naturalisation and Immigration Service provide for the family reunification of certain migrant workers. However, there is no statutory right to family reunification for this category of migrants and decisions are made at the discretion of the Minister for Justice and Law Reform pursuant to s 4 of the Immigration Act, 2004.

In accordance with the procedures, applications for family reunification may be made in respect of family members of 'qualifying sponsors'. Qualifying sponsors are defined as foreign nationals who have a valid employment permit and have been in employment for at least 12 months prior to the date of application. It is a requirement that the sponsor is in full-time employment on the date of application and has an income above the threshold which would qualify the family for payment under the Family Income Supplement (FIS) Scheme administered by the Department of Social and Family Affairs.

In order for family reunification to be granted, the spouses are obliged to provide a marriage certificate and, if the marriage took place after the qualifying sponsor took up residence in Ireland, evidence of the relationship must be provided. Where a marriage was contracted by proxy, the spouses are generally required to submit a declaration from the Irish courts under s 29 of the Family Law Act, 1995, to confirm that the marriage is recognised in Ireland.

Where the applicant is the dependent child (under 18 years) of a qualifying sponsor, evidence of the family relationship such as a birth certificate and adoption papers must be provided. Furthermore, written consent from the other parent or evidence of sole custody in the form of a court order is required where children travel alone to join a parent working in Ireland. Sponsors and their dependent children may be required to present DNA evidence, obtained at their own expense and certified to the satisfaction of the Minister, in support of their claims to be related.

Green Card holders (see **16.3.2.2**) and scientific researchers (see **16.3.3.3**) on the other hand may be accompanied by their spouses and dependent children when they first arrive in Ireland. Alternatively, spouses and dependants may join them later subject to normal immigration rules.

The administrative procedures also provide for non-marital partners of legally resident foreign nationals to join their partners in Ireland and subject to the immigration status of the foreign national applicant, permission to remain may be granted. Applicants are required to submit the following documentation: copies of current passports of both parties, evidence of finances of both parties, evidence of relationship of at least four years duration (ie tenancy agreement, utility bills, bank statements, etc), history of activities of both parties in the State.

Family members of foreign national workers, Green Card holders and scientific researchers are not exempt from employment permit requirements.

However, in accordance with Article 7 of Decision No. 1/80 of the Association Council of 19 September 1980 on the development of the Association between the European Economic Community (EEC) and Turkey,

> *'the members of the family of a Turkish worker duly registered as belonging to the labour force of a Member State, who have been authorised to join him or her shall be entitled, subject to the priority to be given to workers of Member States of the Community, to respond to any offer of employment after they have been legally resident for at least three years in that Member State and shall enjoy free access to any paid employment of their choice provided they have been legally resident there for at least five years'.*

Furthermore,

> *'children of Turkish workers who have completed a course of vocational training in the host country may respond to any offer of employment there, irrespective of the length of time they have been resident in that Member State, provided one of their parents has been legally employed in the Member State concerned for at least three years'.*

Additionally, Article 9 of Decision No. 1/80 provides that:

'Turkish children residing legally in a Member State of the Community with their parents who are or have been legally employed in that Member State, shall be admitted to courses of general education, apprenticeship and vocational training under the same educational entry qualifications as the children of nationals of that Member State. They may in that Member State be eligible to benefit from the advantages provided for under the national legislation in this area'.

16.5   Long-term Residence and Citizenship

16.5.1   LONG-TERM RESIDENCE

Currently, the granting of long-term residence is regulated through administrative procedures published on the website of the Irish Naturalisation and Immigration Service. However, it is the Government's intention to provide a statutory basis for this scheme in forthcoming legislation in this area.

A long-term residence permit is a residence permit which is valid for five years and which may be renewed at the discretion of the Minister for Justice and Law Reform. It is not a permanent status.

Those eligible to apply for long-term residence are persons who have been legally resident in the State for over five years or more, i.e. a minimum of 60 consecutive months, on the basis of employment permits or under the work visa/work authorisation scheme. In this regard, it is important to note that in the calculation of the reckonable period of residence, only time spent in the State legally and while on employment permit conditions is taken into account; any gaps in a person's period of legal residence may lead to his or her application being refused. Successful applicants will be granted permission to remain on Stamp 4 conditions which will allow them to enter employment or set up a business without the need for an employment or business permission.

The dependants of an applicant for long-term residence, who have themselves been legally resident in the State for five years or more may also apply for long-term residence. However, the granting of long-term residence to dependent family members will not exempt them from the employment permit requirement.

It is the stated aim of the Government that the current administrative arrangements will provide a pathway to long-term residence for 'Green Card' holders after two years and that this will be put on statutory footing as part of future legislation in this area. Pending the introduction of new legislation, 'Green Card' holders are not required to apply for the renewal of their 'Green Card' but, provided they have complied with their previous immigration and employment permit conditions and are of 'good character', a Stamp 4 permission of one year's duration will be issued following the expiry of their current 'Green Card'.

In order to make an application for long-term residence, the following documentation must be submitted: copy of employment permits or work visas/work authorisations, copy of the applicant's current GNIB Certificate of Registration, a copy of the applicant's passport(s) including all endorsements.

Following approval of an application a fee of €500 is payable to the Department of Justice and Law Reform in accordance with the Long Term Residency (Fees) Regulations, 2009 made pursuant to the Minister's powers under ss 19(1)(a) and 20 of the Immigration Act, 2004.

16.5.2 PERMISSION TO REMAIN WITHOUT CONDITION AS TO TIME AND WITHOUT CONDITION

16.5.2.1 Permission without condition as to time

In accordance with the administrative procedures published on the website of the Irish Naturalisation and Immigration Service, non-EEA nationals who have lived in Ireland for at least eight years and who are of 'good character' may be permitted to remain in Ireland without condition as to time. International students, temporary registered doctors, trainee accountants, intra company transferees and spouses or dependants of an intra company transferees do not qualify for this permission. Persons granted this permission are permitted to enter employment or self-employment without the need for an employment permit or business permission.

16.5.2.2 Permission to remain without condition

A Stamp 6 permit may be issued in respect of an Irish national with dual citizenship who wants his or her entitlement to remain in Ireland to be endorsed on their foreign passport. This stamp certifies that the holder of the passport is permitted to remain in Ireland without condition.

Those qualifying for this permit include persons who have acquired Irish citizenship through their parents, through a grandparent, through naturalisation or post-nuptial citizenship.

16.5.3 CITIZENSHIP

Irish citizenship is based on Article 9 of the Constitution which, while providing that: *'any person who was a citizen of Saorstát Éireann immediately before the coming into operation of this Constitution shall become and be a citizen of Ireland'*, provides further that *'(t)he future acquisition and loss of Irish nationality and citizenship shall be determined in accordance with law'*. Furthermore, in accordance with Article 9.3 *'(n)o person may be excluded from Irish nationality and citizenship by reason of the sex of such person'*.

The Laws governing citizenship in Ireland are set out in the Irish Nationality and Citizenship Act, 1956 as amended by the Irish Nationality and Citizenship Act, 1986, the Irish Nationality and Citizenship Act, 1994, the Irish Nationality and Citizenship Act, 2001 and, most recently, the Irish Nationality and Citizenship Act, 2004.

In accordance with s 29 of the Irish Nationality and Citizenship Act, 1956 as amended, *'an Irish citizen, wherever born shall be entitled to all the rights and privileges conferred by the terms of any enactment on persons born in the State'*.

16.5.3.1 Citizenship by birth

Subject to s 6A of the Irish Nationality and Citizenship Act, 1956 as amended, every person born in the island of Ireland is an Irish citizen.

Following the amendment of the Act through the Irish Nationality and Citizenship Act, 2004, s 6A now provides that:

'a person born in the island of Ireland shall not be entitled to be an Irish citizen unless a parent of that person has, during the period of 4 years immediately preceding the person's birth, been resident in the island of Ireland for a period of not less than 3 years or periods the aggregate of which is not less than 3 years'.

However, this provision does not apply to persons born before 1 January 2005, persons born in the island of Ireland to an Irish parent or a parent who was entitled to be an Irish citizen, to a parent of British nationality or to a parent who at the time of the person's birth was entitled to reside in the State or in Northern Ireland without conditions as to time. The provision also does not apply to persons neither of whose parents was an Irish citizen, entitled to be an Irish citizen, a British citizen or a person entitled to reside in the State or in Northern Ireland without condition as to time in a situation where at least one of the parents was at the time of his or her birth entitled to diplomatic immunity in the State.

For the purpose of s 6A a period of residence that is in contravention of s 5(1) of the Immigration Act, 2004, in other words, a period during which the parent concerned was present in the State without permission and a period of residence for the purpose of education or study as well as any period of residence for the purpose of the making of an application pursuant to s 9(2) of the Refugee Act, 1996 (as amended) shall not be reckonable. This means in practice that children born to parents who were not permitted to remain in the State at the time of the child's birth, children born to students and children born to persons who are in the process of applying for refugee status cannot acquire citizenship by birth even where their parents had been resident in Ireland for three years or more prior to the child's birth.

Furthermore, '(a) person born in an Irish ship or an Irish aircraft wherever it may be is deemed to be born in the island of Ireland' (s 13 of the Act).

16.5.3.2   Citizenship by descent

In accordance with s 7(1) of the Irish Nationality and Citizenship Act, 1956 (as amended), 'a person is an Irish citizen from birth if at the time of his or her birth either parent was an Irish citizen or would, if alive, have been an Irish citizen'.

However, a person born outside the island of Ireland to a parent who was also born outside the island of Ireland is not entitled to Irish citizenship unless the parent from whom he or she derives citizenship is at the time of that person's birth registered in the Foreign Births Register, in accordance with s 27 of the Act, or the parent concerned was at the time of his or her birth abroad in the public service.

16.5.4   CITIZENSHIP OF FOUNDLINGS AND ADOPTED CHILDREN

Section 10 of the Irish Nationality and Citizenship Act, 1956 (as amended) provides that 'every deserted newborn child first found in the State shall, unless the contrary is proven, be deemed to have been born in the island of Ireland to parents at least one of whom is an Irish citizen'.

And in accordance with s 11 of the Act:

'upon an adoption order being made under the Adoption Act 1952, in a case in which the adopter or, where the adoption is by a married couple, either spouse is an Irish citizen, the adopted child, if not already an Irish citizen, shall be an Irish citizen'.

16.5.5   NATURALISATION

Pursuant to s 14 of the Irish Nationality and Citizenship Act, 1956 as amended 'Irish citizenship may be conferred to a non-national by means of a certificate of naturalisation granted by the Minister'.

The conditions for the issuing of a certificate of naturalisation are that the applicant:

'(a)   (i) is of full age, or (ii) is a minor born in the State
(b)   is of good character
(c)   has had a period of one year's continuous residence in the State immediately before the date of the application and, during the eight years immediately preceding that period, has had a total residence in the State amounting to four years
(d)   intends in good faith to continue to reside in the State after naturalisation, and
(e)   has made, either before a Justice of the District Court in open court or in such manner as the Minister, for special reasons, allows, a declaration in the prescribed manner, of fidelity to the nation and loyalty to the State'.

It is important to note that decisions on applications for naturalisation pursuant to s 15 are made at the 'absolute discretion' of the Minister for Justice and Law Reform.

While the High Court has confirmed in the recent case of *H v Minister for Justice, Equality and Law Reform* [2009] IEHC 78, concerning a Chinese national who had come to Ireland as a programme refugee in 2000, that 'the Minister enjoys an absolute discretion' and that '(i)t is also quite clear that an applicant for naturalisation has no right or entitlement to a particular outcome'. The Court considered the fact that two of the applicant's sons had convictions for road traffic matters, and the fact that one son was facing a charge in respect of a crime of violence, to be an irrelevant consideration. In granting an order quashing the Minister's decision, Edwards J stressed that:

'it is offensive to all notions of justice that a person can be prejudiced on account of his or her family associations, in circumstances where the person concerned is of acknowledged good character. We cannot help the families we are born into, anymore than a child can help it as to who his parents are'.

On the question of the meaning of 'good character' Cooke J held in the case of *B v Minister for Justice, Equality and Law Reform* [2009] IEHC 449, a case concerning a person with refugee status whose application for naturalisation had been refused on the basis that he had come to the adverse attention of An Garda Síochána and was therefore not considered of sufficient character to be granted citizenship, that '(i)t is for the Minister to determine what criteria fall to be considered in assessing whether the condition as to "good character" is met'.

Reckonable periods of residence for the purpose of an application for naturalisation exclude any time spent in the State in contravention of s 5(1) of the Immigration Act, 2004, in other words periods in which the person concerned was present in the State without permission. A period of residence for the purpose of education or study or a period of residence for the purpose of the making of an application pursuant to s 9(2) of the Refugee Act, 1996 (as amended) are also not reckonable for the purpose of an application for naturalisation.

The exclusion of time spent in the State as an asylum seeker was confirmed by Peart J as 'completely logical and fair' in the case of *Robert v Minister for Justice, Equality and Law Reform*, 2 November 2004, High Court (unreported) as cited in Quinn, *Handbook on Immigration and Asylum in Ireland 2007*, (2008) ESRI, 238–9.

In certain cases, the Minister may, in his absolute discretion, dispense with some or all of the conditions of naturalisation. In accordance with s 16(1) of the Irish Nationality and Citizenship Act, 1956, these include situations:

'(a)   where the applicant is of Irish descent or Irish associations;
(b)   where the applicant is a parent or guardian acting on behalf of a minor of Irish descent or Irish associations;
(c)   where the applicant is a naturalised Irish citizen acting on behalf of a minor child of the applicant;

(. . .)

(f)   *where the applicant is or has been resident abroad in the public service;*

(g)   *where the applicant is a person who is a refugee within the meaning of the United Nations Convention relating to the Status of Refugees of the 28th day of July 1951 and the Protocol Relating to the Status of Refugees of the 31st day of January 1967 or is a Stateless person within the meaning of the United Nations Convention relating to the Status of Stateless Persons of the 28th day of September 1954'.*

For example, applications made by persons with refugee status are routinely accepted for consideration three years after the granting of refugee status.

Section 16(2) of the Act further defines the meaning of *'Irish associations'* as a relation by *'blood, affinity or adoption to a person who is an Irish citizen or entitled to be an Irish citizen'*. The Irish courts have yet to clarify whether a sibling of an Irish citizen child may apply or have made on his or her behalf an application to the Minister seeking to have conditions for naturalisation dispensed with in their cases on the basis of their blood connection to their Irish citizen brother or sister.

In accordance with s 17 of the Act, an application for naturalisation must be in the *'prescribed form'*. The relevant forms can be found on the website of the Irish Naturalisation and Immigration Service and currently include three types of forms: 'Form 8 for applications for naturalisation as an Irish citizen', 'Form 9 for applications for a certificate of naturalisation for a minor' and 'Form 10 for an application for a certificate of naturalisation for a minor of Irish descent'.

16.5.5.1   Naturalisation of spouses of Irish nationals and post-nuptial citizenship

In accordance with s 15A of the Irish Nationality and Citizenship Act, 1956, the Minister for Justice and Law Reform:

> *'may, in his or her absolute discretion, grant an application for a certificate of naturalisation to the non-national spouse of an Irish citizen if satisfied that the applicant*
>
> *(a)   is of full age,*
>
> *(b)   is of good character,*
>
> *(c)   is married to that citizen for a period of not less than 3 years,*
>
> *(d)   is in a marriage recognised under the laws of the State as subsisting,*
>
> *(e)   and that citizen are living together as husband and wife and that citizen submits to the Minister an affidavit in the prescribed form to that effect,*
>
> *(f)   had immediately before the date of the application a period of one year's continuous residence in the island of Ireland,*
>
> *(g)   had, during the 4 years immediately preceding that period, a total residence in the island of Ireland amounting to 2 years,*
>
> *(h)   intends in good faith to continue to reside in the island of Ireland after naturalisation, and*
>
> *(i)   has made, either before a judge of the District Court in open court or in such manner as the Minister, for special reasons, allows, a declaration in the prescribed manner, of fidelity to the nation and loyalty to the State'.*

Prior to 29 November 2005 spouses of Irish nationals who had married their Irish citizen spouses before 30 November 2002 were in a position, after three years of marriage to lodge a declaration, accepting Irish citizenship. There was no requirement that the couple reside on the island of Ireland.

16.5.5.2   Refusal of naturalisation

Where an application for naturalisation is refused, the applicant is not automatically entitled to the reasons for the refusal and the Act does not provide a mechanism through which a decision to refuse naturalisation can be challenged. In fact, Kelly J held in *Parshuram Mishra v The Minister for Justice, Ireland and The Attorney General* [1996] 1 IR 189, that 'it is clear that there is no obligation imposed by the Act on the Minister to give reasons for her decision'. However, he did go on to consider that 'an implicit entitlement to reasons may arise where a right of appeal exists from the decision and the reasons may be required so as to enable the affected individual to exercise that right in an effective way. Indeed, there may well be circumstances where even without a right of appeal natural justice or fairness may require that reasons be given'.

Several cases regarding the provision of reasons for the refusal of applications for naturalisation have subsequently proceeded to the Information Commissioner who held in the case of *X v Department of Justice, Equality and Law Reform* [2005] IEIC 7 that:

> 'there is no inconsistency in the furnishing by the Minister of a statement of reasons pursuant to Section 18 of the [Freedom of Information] Act [1997 as amended], and the discretion vested in the Minister by the 1956 Act as amended'.

With this decision, she clarified that despite the absolute discretion of the Minister to grant an application for a certificate of naturalisation, decisions under the Irish Nationality and Citizenship Act, 1956 are 'affected by section 18(1) unless otherwise excluded by reference to the general provisions of section 18(2)'.

In a subsequent decision regarding *Mr X v Department of Justice, Equality and Law Reform* [2006] IEIC 3, the Information Commissioner accepted that the Department was 'entitled to refuse to provide [Mr X] with a statement of reasons under section 18(2) of the [Freedom of Information] Act'. Section 18(2) of that Act provides that nothing in the section is to be taken as requiring either:

> '(a)   the giving to a person of information contained in an exempt record, or (b) the disclosure of the existence or non-existence of a record if the non-disclosure of its existence or non-existence is required by this Act'.

The only remedy available for the challenging of a refusal to grant a certificate of naturalisation is an application for the judicial review of the matter to the High Court. In *B v Minister for Justice, Equality and Law Reform* [2009] IEHC 449, Cooke J clarified that:

> 'Section 15 [of the Irish Nationality and Citizenship Act 1956 as amended] provides that when the Minister is satisfied that an applicant fulfils the naturalisation conditions he may nevertheless refuse to grant the certificate in his absolute discretion'

and that:

> '(I)n such event the Court cannot act as a court of appeal from the decision and while the Minister's discretion is not an unfettered one, the Court cannot interfere so long as it has been exercised by the Minister in accordance with the powers granted under the section and has been exercised fairly and in accordance with the principles of natural justice'.

In the words of Cooke J, referring to the case of *Pok Sun Shun v Ireland* [1986] ILRM 593:

> '(i)t is only where it is shown that the Minister has failed in some way to carry out the legal requirements of the section or failed to act fairly that the Court has power to review the decision (see the judgment at 596)'.

16.5.5.3   Revocation and loss of citizenship

In accordance with s 19(1) of the Irish Nationality and Citizenship Act, 1956,

> 'the Minister may revoke a certificate of naturalisation if he is satisfied:
> (a)   that the issue of the certificate was procured by fraud, misrepresentation whether innocent or fraudulent, or concealment of material facts or circumstances, or

(b) *that the person to whom it was granted has, by any overt act, shown himself to have failed in his duty of fidelity to the nation and loyalty to the State, or*

(c) *that (except in the case of a certificate of naturalisation which is issued to a person of Irish descent or associations) the person to whom it is granted has been ordinarily resident outside the State or, in the case of an application for a certificate of naturalisation granted under section 15A, resident outside the island of Ireland (otherwise than in the public service) for a continuous period of seven years and without reasonable excuse has not during that period registered annually in the prescribed manner his name and a declaration of his intention to retain Irish citizenship with an Irish diplomatic mission or consular office or with the Minister, or*

(d) *that the person to whom it is granted is also, under the law of a country at war with the State, a citizen of that country, or*

(e) *that the person to whom it is granted has by any voluntary act other than marriage acquired another citizenship'.*

The constitutionality of s 19(1)(b) has been described as 'highly questionable' on the basis of 'the drastic nature of revocation of citizenship and the consequent question whether anyone other than a judge in a court could order it and partly because the criterion here set up is so vague that it invites an unpredictable, subjective application of a kind hostile to the concept of 'due process' or 'due course of law' (Hogan & Whyte, *JM Kelly: The Irish Constitution*, 4th edn, 2006, Tottel Publishing, p 166). Under the Act, notice of intention to revoke citizenship must be provided in accordance with s 19(2) of the Act and the person concerned may apply to the Minister for an inquiry as to the reasons for the revocation and the case must be referred to a 'Committee of Inquiry' which reports its findings to the Minister.

In the case of *Kelly v Ireland* [1996] 2 ILRM 364, the High Court dealt with a case concerning an order made by the Minister for Foreign Affairs impounding the passport of a woman who had been issued with an Irish passport following her marriage to an Irish citizen in the UK in 1984 as well as an order declaring her not to be an Irish citizen. It was alleged by the Irish authorities that Mrs Kelly had already been married at the time she entered into the marriage with Mr Kelly. However, Barron J held in this case that the applicant was entitled to the relief sought, and in particular to the declaration that she is an Irish citizen on the basis that 'it is necessary where a bigamous marriage is alleged that the first marriage is strictly proved'. He clarified also that 'the onus was on the respondents to establish that the marriage was a sham because the parties did not participate in the ceremony in order to become man and wife, but to prevent the applicant from being deported'. He went on to hold that '(t)his onus had not been discharged' in this particular case.

Citizenship may be lost in accordance with s 21 of the Act following the renunciation of citizenship by *an Irish citizen of full age who is or is about to become a citizen of another country and for that reason desires to renounce citizenship'.* For this purpose, a 'declaration of alienage' may be lodged in the prescribed manner by a person who is ordinarily resident outside the State. The declaration becomes effective at the time of lodgement if the person concerned already has the citizenship of another country or after the time of lodgement, upon becoming a citizen of another country. However, during a time of war, as defined in Article 28.3.3 of the Constitution, a declaration of alienage may only be made with the consent of the Minister for Justice and Law Reform.

16.5.6 PASSPORT APPLICATIONS AND CERTIFICATES OF NATIONALITY

Pursuant to s 6(1) of the Passport Act, 2008, *'a person who is an Irish citizen and is, subject to this Act, thereby entitled to be issued with a passport, may apply in that behalf to the Minister'* [for

Foreign Affairs]. A person whose application for a passport has been refused is entitled to the reasons for the refusal and may appeal the decision pursuant to s 19 of the Act, subject to the provisions of the Passport (Appeals) Regulations, 2008 (SI 413/2008).

Additionally, a person who is an Irish citizen by birth or descent can apply for a certificate of nationality stating that he or she is, at the date of the certificate, an Irish citizen (ss 28 and 28A of the Irish Nationality and Citizenship Act, 1956).

16.6 Departure

16.6.1 DEPORTATION

Subject to the prohibition of *refoulement* within the meaning of s 5 of the Refugee Act and s 4 of the Criminal Justice (UN Convention Against Torture) Act, 2000, *'the Minister* [for Justice and Law Reform] *may by order require a non-national to leave the State within such period as may be specified in the order and remain thereafter out of the State'* (see **chapter 15**).

An order pursuant to s 3(1) of the Immigration Act, 1999 may be made in respect of:

'(a) *a person who has served or is serving a term of imprisonment imposed on him or her by a court in the State,*

(b) *a person whose deportation has been recommended by a court in the State before which such person was indicted for or charged with any crime or offence,*

(c) *a person who has been required to leave the State under Regulation 14 of the European Communities (Aliens) Regulations, 1977 (S.I. No. 393 of 1977),*

(d) *a person to whom Regulation 19 of the European Communities (Right of Residence for Non-Economically Active Persons) Regulations, 1997 (S.I. No. 57 of 1997) applies,*

(e) *a person whose application for asylum has been transferred to a convention country for examination pursuant to section 22 of the Refugee Act, 1996,*

(f) *a person whose application for asylum has been refused by the Minister,*

(g) *a person to whom leave to land in the State has been refused,*

(h) *a person who, in the opinion of the Minister, has contravened a restriction or condition imposed on him or her in respect of landing in or entering into or leave to stay in the State,*

(i) *a person whose deportation would, in the opinion of the Minister, be conducive to the common good'.*

Before making a deportation order in respect of a person, the Minister is required to notify him or her in writing of the proposal to make such an order and the reasons for it. In this regard, the Supreme Court confirmed in the case of *P v Minister for Justice, Equality and Law Reform* [2001] IESC 107 that 'the provisions of Section 3(3)(a) are mandatory, to be complied with literally, and incapable of waiver or estoppel'.

Section 3(3)(b) of the Act provides that a person who has been so notified may, within 15 working days from the sending of the notification, make representations in writing to the Minister and the Minister is obliged to take into account any representations made by or on behalf of the person before making a decision whether to deport. Furthermore, the person concerned is entitled to receive a decision in writing and the reasons for it, where necessary and possible in a language that he or she understands. However, no appeal lies against a subsequent decision to issue a deportation order.

Furthermore, in accordance with s 3(4) of the Act, a notification of the Minister's proposal to deport a person must include:

'(a) *a statement that the person concerned may make representations in writing to the Minister within 15 working days of the sending to him or her of the notification,*

(b) *a statement that the person may leave the State before the Minister decides the matter and shall require the person to so inform the Minister in writing and to furnish the Minister with information concerning his or her arrangements for leaving,*

(c) *a statement that the person may consent to the making of the deportation order within 15 working days of the sending to him or her of the notification and that the Minister shall thereupon arrange for the removal of the person from the State as soon as practicable, and*

(d) *any other information which the Minister considers appropriate in the circumstances'.*

It must be noted however, that s 3(3) does not apply to a person who has consented in writing to the making of a deportation order, provided that the Minister is satisfied that he or she understands the consequences of such consent, or to a person who is outside the State. Furthermore, notification pursuant to s 3(3) need not be given to persons who have been required to leave the State under Regulation 14 of the European Communities (Aliens) Regulations, 1977, to persons to whom Regulation 19 of the European Communities (Right of Residence for Non-Economically Active Persons) Regulations, 1997 applies or to persons whose application for asylum has been transferred to another country for examination pursuant to s 22 of the Refugee Act, 1996 under the 'Dublin Convention' (see **chapter 15**). Separate procedures, set out in the relevant statutes, apply in respect of these categories of migrants (s 3(5)).

Finally, s 3(6) of the Act requires the Minister for Justice and Law Reform, in determining whether to make a deportation order in relation to a person, to have regard to:

'(a) *the age of the person;*

(b) *the duration of residence in the State of the person;*

(c) *the family and domestic circumstances of the person;*

(d) *the nature of the person's connection with the State, if any;*

(e) *the employment (including self-employment) record of the person;*

(f) *the employment (including self-employment) prospects of the person;*

(g) *the character and conduct of the person both within and (where relevant and ascertainable) outside the State (including any criminal convictions);*

(h) *humanitarian considerations;*

(i) *any representations duly made by or on behalf of the person;*

(j) *the common good; and*

(k) *considerations of national security and public policy, so far as they appear or are known to the Minister.*

In the judgments of *Oguekwe v Minister for Justice Equality and Law Reform* [2008] IESC 25 and *Dimbo v Minister for Justice Equality and Law Reform* [2008] IESC 26, regarding the details of the considerations to be made prior to the issuing of a deportation order, Denham J set out a very useful 'non exhaustive list of matters which may assist, and which relate to, the position of an Irish born child whose parents may be considered for a deportation order'. Accordingly,

'(1) *The Minister should consider the circumstances of each case by due inquiry in a fair and proper manner as to the facts and factors affecting the family.*

(2) *Save for exceptional cases, the Minister is not required to inquire into matters other than those which have been sent to him by and on behalf of applicants and which are on the file of the department. The Minister is not required to inquire outside the documents furnished by and on behalf of the applicants, except in exceptional circumstances.*

(3) *In a case, such as this, the relevant factual matrix includes the facts relating to the personal rights, of the Irish born citizen child, and of the family unit.*

(4) *The facts to be considered include those expressly referred to in the relevant statutory scheme, which in this case is the Act of 1999, being:-*

''(a) *the age of the person/s;*

(b) *the duration of residence in the State of the person/s;*

(c)   *the family and domestic circumstances of the person/s;*

(d)   *the nature of the person's/persons' connection with the State (if any);*

(e)   *the employment (including self-employment) record of the person/s;*

(f)   *the employment (including self-employment) prospects of the person/s;*

(g)   *the character and conduct of the person/persons both within and (where relevant and ascertainable) outside the State (including any criminal convictions);*

(h)   *humanitarian considerations;*

(i)   *any representations duly made by or on behalf of the person/persons;*

(j)   *the common good; and*

(k)   *considerations of national security and public policy;*
        so far as they appear or are known to the Minister.

(5)   *The Minister should consider the potential interference with rights of the applicants. This will include consideration of the nature and history of the family unit.*

(6)   *The Minister should consider expressly the Constitutional rights, including the personal rights, of the Irish born child. These rights include the right of the Irish born child to:-*

(a)   *reside in the State,*

(b)   *be reared and educated with due regard to his welfare,*

(c)   *the society, care and company of his parents; and*

(d)   *protection of the family, pursuant to Article 41,*

The Minister should deal expressly with the rights of the child in any decision. Specific reference to the position of an Irish born child of a foreign national parent is required in decisions and documents relating to any decision to deport such foreign national parent.

(7)   *The Minister should consider the Convention rights of the applicants, including those of the Irish born child. These rights overlap to some extent, and may be considered together with the Constitutional rights.*

(8)   *Neither Constitution nor Convention rights of the applicants are absolute. All rights require to be considered in the context of the factual matrix of the case.*

(9)   *The Minister is not obliged to respect the choice of residence of a married couple.*

(10)   *The State's rights require also to be considered. The State has the right to control the entry, presence, and exit of foreign nationals, subject to the Constitution and to international agreements. Thus the State may consider issues of national security, public policy, the integrity of the Immigration Scheme, its consistency and fairness to persons and to the State. Fundamentally, also, the Minister should consider the common good, embracing both statutory and Constitutional principles, and the principles of the Convention in the European context.*

(11)   *The Minister should weigh the factors and principles in a fair and just manner to achieve a reasonable and proportionate decision. While the Irish born child has the right to reside in the State, there may be a substantial reason, associated with the common good, for the Minister to make an order to deport a foreign national who is a parent of an Irish born child, even though the necessary consequence is that in order to remain a family unit the Irish born child must leave the State. However, the decision should not be disproportionate to the ends sought to be achieved.*

(12)   *The Minister should consider whether in all the circumstances of the case there is a substantial reason associated with the common good which required the deportation of the foreign national parent.*

In such circumstances the Minister should take into consideration the personal circumstances of the Irish born child and the foreign national parents including, in this case, whether it would be reasonable to expect family members to follow the third named applicant to Nigeria.

(13)   *The Minister should be satisfied that there is a substantial reason for deporting a foreign national parent, that the deportation is not disproportionate to the ends sought to be achieved, and that the order of deportation is a necessary measure for the purpose of achieving the common good.*

(14)   The Minister should also take into account the common good and policy considerations which would lead to similar decisions in other cases.

(15)   There should be a substantial reason given for making an order of deportation of a parent of an Irish born child'.

The question remains in how far the above criteria are to be universally applied at least in situations where the rights of families as protected by the Articles 41 and 42 of the Constitution as well as by Article 8 ECHR would be affected by a decision to deport a member of the family.

In this regard, Charleton J held in *O v Minister for Justice, Equality and Law Reform* [2009] IEHC 1236, a case concerning a 22-year-old Nigerian woman seeking to remain in Ireland as part of a family unit together with her legally resident Nigerian mother and her two much younger sisters who were Irish citizens, that:

'it is a serious matter to interfere with the family rights that arise as between an Irish child and the foreign parent of that Irish child'. He specified that: '(i)n that specific circumstance, the rights that will be interfered with by the deportation of a nurturing mother or caring father are those in favour of that child being educated and nurtured in this State as an Irish person by his or her parents. It must be carefully considered by the Minister that the deportation of a non-Irish parent will often inevitably result in the Irish child being brought away as well and thus effectively losing all that membership of this nation involves and, in the case of those countries that do not allow joint nationality, their Irish citizenship as well'.

However, he did not accept

'that the analysis conducted by the Supreme Court in *Oguekwe* is capable of being extended, save in the most exceptional circumstances, involving perhaps the death of a mother or genuinely nurturing father or very serious disability of an Irish child, circumstances where the family naturally looks to its own for nurture, to aunts, uncles, grandparents, siblings or cousins'. And he concluded that '(w)ere I to hold otherwise, it would involve an extension of the law beyond the precise tests set down by the Supreme Court in *Oguekwe*. These are specifically geared to an analysis of a decision to deport either parent of an Irish child'.

In an earlier interpretation of the Supreme Court judgment in *Oguekwe*, in the case of *Yang & Ors v Minister for Justice Equality and Law Reform* (13 February 2009, High Court (unreported)), Charleton J set out by way of *ex tempore* judgment that in this case, involving the deportation of the father of an Irish citizen child whose mother, the partner of Mr Yang, was legally resident in the State with the child, that 'a completely wrong test of insurmountable obstacle to the family living together in the country of origin' in the decision to issue a deportation order in respect of Mr Yang, had replaced 'what was the very careful reasoning of Denham J whereby she not only included reason but also included proportion in that regard'.

The meaning of the phrases 'proportionate', 'insurmountable obstacles' and 'substantial reason' were clarified in the more recent judgment of Clark J in the case of *Alli [a minor] & Anor v MJELR* [2009] IEHC 595. The Court gave the following synopsis of its finding in this case at the end of the judgment (see para 97–101):

'Having considered the arguments on both sides the Court has concluded that the Minister did not err in law in asking the question whether there were any "insurmountable obstacles" to the family moving with Mr Alli to Nigeria and continuing family life there with him. (. . .). An evaluation of whether there are any insurmountable obstacles to the family moving with the deportee incorporates an evaluation of the reasonableness of expecting that family to move.

Having identified that there were no insurmountable obstacles to the family following Mr Alli to Nigeria and following a fact-specific consideration of the applicants' circumstances, the Minister identified the following "substantial reason" for the deportation of Mr Alli: *"there is no less restrictive process available which would achieve the legitimate aim of the State to maintain control of its own borders and operate a regulated system for control, processing and monitoring of non-national persons in the State"*; the Court is satisfied that in all the circumstances and on the basis in particular of the judgment of the Supreme Court in *A.O. and D.L.*, this constitutes a "substantial reason associated with the common good" which requires the deportation'.

Clark J concluded that '(t)he judgment in *Oguekwe* requires that the Minister weighs the applicants' constitutional and Convention rights against the rights of the State and reaches a reasonable and proportionate decision. Bearing in mind that the rights of the applicants and their family members which, though of considerable importance, are not absolute and can be outweighed, the Court is satisfied that in the circumstances of this case, these requirements were met and that the Minister reached a reasonable and proportionate decision'.

16.6.2 ARREST AND DETENTION

A person who is subject to a deportation order made under s 3 of the Immigration Act, 1999 may be detained in accordance with the provisions of the Act for the purpose of ensuring his or her deportation from the State.

Other purposes of detention are defined in s 5 of the Immigration Act, 1999 which allows for the detention of a person in respect of whom a deportation order is in force and where an immigration officer or member of An Garda Síochána with reasonable cause suspects that he or she:

'(a) *has failed to comply with any provision of the order or with a requirement in a notice under section 3(3)(b)(ii),*

(b) *intends to leave the State and enter another state without lawful authority,*

(c) *has destroyed his or her identity documents or is in possession of forged identity documents, or*

(d) *intends to avoid removal from the State'.*

Reviewing the Supreme Court decision in *Re The Illegal Immigrants (Trafficking) Bill 1999* [2000] 2 IR 360, Finlay Geoghegan J concluded in the case of *O (BF) v Governor of Dóchas Centre* [2003] IEHC 622 that 'the power of detention under [s] 5(1) of the Act of 1999 is exercisable only for the purpose of ensuring deportation'. In this regard, she also considered the earlier judgment in the case of *East Donegal Co-Operative v Attorney General* [1970] IR 317 in which it was held that:

'the relevant executive authority must be vigilant to ensure that the detention be brought to an end if, having regard to new circumstances or discovery of new facts or for some other reason, it is no longer necessary. This should be done independently of any application in that regard by the person concerned'.

Having regard to the considerations in the latter case, Finlay Geoghegan J held in the *O (BF)* case in relation to pre-deportation detention that:

'there must be as a precondition to the valid exercise of the power, [to detain] a concluded intention to deport the applicant concerned. (. . .). Until such time as there is a definite or concluded intention to deport the person in question, it cannot be said that detention is necessary for the purpose of ensuring deportation'.

However, even where an injunction restraining deportation has been granted, detention may continue. Denham J for the Supreme Court clarified in the case of *Arisukwu v Minister for Justice, Equality and Law Reform* [2006] IESC 13 that:

'(t)he executive at all relevant times maintained an intent to deport, as it was entitled to do, but the intent was held subject to a court order. Thus the separation of powers, between the executive and the courts, was preserved and honoured. The courts have the power to judicially review the procedures and this duty was not impinged upon by the continuing intent [to deport] (subject to court order) of the executive.'

The places in which a person against whom a deportation order is in force may be detained are prescribed in the Immigration Act 1999 (Deportation) Regulations, 2005 (SI 55/2005).

Section 5(6)(a) of the Act restricts the period of detention permitted to eight weeks in aggregate. However, certain periods shall be excluded from the calculation of the period of detention. These include for example, periods during which the person concerned is remanded in custody pending criminal trial or serving a term of imprisonment and, if a foreign national seeks to challenge the decision to deport him or her, the period from the institution of any court proceedings until their final determination.

16.6.3   EXCLUSION

Pursuant to s 3(1) of the Immigration Act, 1999, *'the Minister may by order require any non-national specified in the order to leave the State within such period as may be specified in the order and to remain thereafter out of the State'*. In other words, a deportation order also becomes an exclusion order of indefinite duration.

The standard form for a deportation order is set out in the Immigration Act 1999 (Deportation) Regulations, 2005 (SI 55/2005) and includes an obligation to remain out of the State. An option to delete or amend this aspect of a deportation order in the prescribed form is not provided.

16.6.4   REVOCATION OF DEPORTATION ORDERS

It is possible to apply for the revocation of a deportation order under s 3(11) of the Immigration Act, 1999. Such an application can be made at any time before the actual enforcement of the order or thereafter by a person who is outside the State and is seeking readmission to the State. However, in contrast to s 3(6) of the Act, s 3(11) does not set out the procedure for the making of an application or the matters that the Minister must take into account when deciding whether or not to revoke an order.

The case of *F(P) & Anor v Minister for Justice, Equality and Law Reform* [2005] IEHC 9, decided by Ryan J on 26 January 2005, concerned an application for the revocation of a deportation order made in respect of a Romanian national who was the spouse of an Irish national with whom she had cohabited prior to her deportation from the State and with whom she had subsequently spent some time in Romania before applying to have the order revoked pursuant to s 3(11) of the Act.

In this case, the High Court first rejected the notion that the Minister's refusal to revoke the order was disproportionate on the basis that:

'a refusal of the application, (. . .), cannot be condemned on the ground of proportionality because the legitimate interests of the State in this area are an adequate justification for the power to exclude a person who is not entitled to be in the State. A person who has been lawfully deported cannot contend that a refusal to reverse the earlier valid decision is *ipso facto* disproportionate'.

However, Ryan J went on to quash the Minister's decision to refuse the revocation of the deportation order on the grounds of irrationality. He held that:

'(...) the reason advanced in this case for rejecting the application is not logically connected to the discretion being exercised. Another way of putting that is to say that the decision maker took into account irrelevant material. I think however that it goes further than that. He addressed himself to an issue and made a factual conclusion in respect of a situation which had been almost entirely brought about by the deportation and which was in no way related to any concern that could legitimately or reasonably or logically have been present to his mind'.

16.6.5 LEGAL REMEDIES

As outlined throughout this chapter, the administrative procedures regarding the entry and residence of foreign nationals in the State do not generally provide a right to appeal. Where such right exists, the appeal lies with an appeals officer who is an officer of the Minister for Justice and Law Reform in the same way as the original decision-maker. Ireland, unlike the UK, does not have an administrative tribunal which deals with asylum as well as immigration and citizenship appeals.

Where foreign nationals and their Irish family members seek to challenge immigration and citizenship related decisions, the only available legal remedy at present is a judicial review in the High Court.

In this regard s 5 of the Illegal Immigrants (Trafficking) Act, 2000, as amended, provides in relation to certain immigration related decisions that the validity of:

- a notification of intention to deport under s 3(3)(a) of the Immigration Act1999

- a notification providing reasons for the decision to deport following representations made under s 3(3)(b) of the Immigration Act, 1999

- a deportation order under s 3(1) of the Immigration Act, 1999

- a refusal under Article 5 of the Aliens (Amendment) (No. 2) Order, 1999 (SI 24/ 1999)

- an exclusion order under s 4 of the Immigration Act, 1999

- a decision to refuse permission to enter or be in the State

- a decision to refuse the extension or variation of permission to be in the State

shall not be questioned otherwise than by way of an application for judicial review under Order 84 of the Rules of the Superior Courts (SI 15/1986).

An application for leave to apply for judicial review under Order 84 must be made within 14 days from the date on which the person concerned was notified of the decision, determination, recommendation, refusal or making of the Order concerned unless the High Court considers that there is good and sufficient reason for extending the period within which the application shall be made.

Furthermore an application for the judicial review of any of the above listed decisions must be made by motion on notice to the Minister for Justice and Law Reform and any other person specified for that purpose by order of the High Court.

Introducing a somewhat higher threshold than for ordinary judicial review applications, s 5 further requires that leave to apply for judicial review *'shall not be granted unless the High Court is satisfied that there are substantial grounds for contending that the decision, determination, recommendation, refusal or order is invalid or ought to be quashed'*.

Section 5(3)(a) of the Illegal Immigrants (Trafficking) Act, 2000 also restricts access to the Supreme Court for applicants seeking to challenge the High Court's refusal to grant leave by providing that:

> *(t)he determination of the High Court of an application for leave to apply for judicial review as aforesaid or of an application for such judicial review shall be final and no appeal shall lie from the decision of the High Court to the Supreme Court in either case except with the leave of the High Court which leave shall only be granted where the High Court certifies that its decision involves a point of law of exceptional public importance and that it is desirable in the public interest that an appeal should be taken to the Supreme Court'.*

The only exemption from the requirement to obtain a certificate from the High Court is made in relation to cases involving a question as to the validity of any law having regard to the provisions of the Constitution (s 5(3)(b)).

Furthermore, in the case of *Cosma v Minister for Justice, Equality and Law Reform* [2006] IESC 44, the Supreme Court granted a declaration confirming that an application for the revocation of a deportation order pursuant to s 3(11) of the Immigration Act, 1999 is not governed by s 5 of the Illegal Immigrants (Trafficking) Act, 2000 and that therefore the applicant in that case did not require a certificate from a High Court judge in order to institute an appeal before the Supreme Court and has an unfettered right to appeal an order of the High Court.

It is also possible to apply to the High Court for an injunction restraining the Minister for Justice and Law Reform, for example, from enforcing a deportation order while its validity is being tested through judicial review proceedings.

Dealing with an application for an injunction restraining the deportation of a Nigerian national father of an Irish citizen child in circumstances where the deportation order regarding the applicant had been made in ignorance of the impending birth of the child and in a situation where, consequently, the Minister 'did not have the factual information which would have been necessary for him to reach a decision which was proportionate and fair in all of the circumstances', Irvine J granted an injunction in the case of *E v MJELR* [2008] IEHC 68. Quoting from the decision of McCracken J who had held in *Cosma v Minister for Justice, Equality and Law Reform* [2006] IESC 44 that it was difficult to envisage the circumstances that might demand the making of such an order but that '(i)t might conceivably be exercised when a previously unknown fact comes to light, being a fact which was unknown at the time of making of the deportation order', Irvine J was satisfied that the *E* case was 'precisely the type of case that merits the granting of an injunction given that the purpose of the within proceedings is to seek to vindicate and protect the applicant's constitutional rights to the care and support of his natural father'. He concluded that:

> '(i)n these special circumstances (. . .) the Court should, if so asked, seek to maintain the status quo in the light of the applicant's constitutional rights to the care and support of his natural father until the respondent has revisited the application of [the father] under s. 3(11) of the Act'.

In any event, before a deportation order can be enforced, the statutory 14 day time limit for the institution of judicial review proceedings provided for in s 5(2)(a) of the Illegal Immigrants (Trafficking) Act, 2000 has to have passed. As outlined by Geoghegan J in the case of *Adebayo v Commissioner of An Garda Síochána* [2006] IESC 8:

> '(i)f there is a time limit provided by the Act to enable them to challenge such an event, it does not seem to be a sensible interpretation of the Act to suggest that, notwithstanding the exercise of the statutory entitlement to apply for leave for judicial review requiring no extension of time, they may nevertheless be spirited out of the country. On any reasonable and purposive interpretation of the Act that cannot be so.'

He went on to summarise his view that:

> 'no deportation may be implemented during the currency of the fourteen day period and that if in fact an application for leave is brought within that period no deportation

order may be implemented until the court determines the application for leave and only then if the court does not order otherwise upon the granting of leave. Having regard to the very nature of this legislation and its intent it would seem likely that a court properly exercising its discretion would normally grant the stay or the injunction as the case might be if leave was being given'.

However, the consequence of the judgment is not that a stay of the deportation order or an injunction is automatically granted in conjunction with the granting of leave. A separate application remains necessary in this regard.

16.6.6 VOLUNTARY RETURN AND CONSENT TO DEPORTATION ORDERS

As outlined above, where the Minister for Justice and Law Reform proposes to make a deportation order, the options to be given to the person concerned must include leaving the State 'before the Minister decides the matter' (s 3(4)(b) of the Immigration Act, 1999) or 'consenting to the making of the deportation order within 15 working days of the sending to him or her of the notification' (s 3(4)(c) of the Immigration Act, 1999).

Where a person consents in writing to the making of a deportation order, the Minister has the obligation to arrange for the removal of the person 'as soon as practicable'. However, where a person, who has consented to the making of a deportation order, is not deported within three months of the making of the order, the order will no longer be effective (s 3(8) of the Immigration Act, 1999).

16.7 Conclusion

The impending reform of legislation in this area continues to represent an ideal opportunity to comprehensively amend outdated and inadequate immigration legislation. However, draft legislation published in July 2010 in the form of the Immigration, Residence and Protection Bill, 2010 fails to set out clear rules regarding the rights and obligations of migrants seeking to come to Ireland. Instead, the Bill provided a legal skeleton, containing procedural rules which the Minister for Justice and Law Reform then has the power to 'flesh out' by making immigration regulations. As a result, the rules setting out the basis for migrants to enter and remain in the State, the conditions on which such permission will be granted and what entitlements migrants may or may not have while in the State, will be left to secondary legislation. Draft regulations have not been published to date and it is therefore unclear what areas they will cover. However, given the current lack of clarity and published guidelines on the criteria or issues to be considered by immigration officers determining matters on behalf of the Minister, the publication of clear criteria, alongside draft legislation, would have to be welcomed. Clearly spelling out migrants' entitlements and obligations will help prevent the difficulties they, and those charged with administering and enforcing immigration legislation, currently face, including delays in obtaining decisions and inconsistencies in decision-making.

FURTHER READING

CHAPTER 1

Alston, (ed) *The EU and Human Rights*, 1999, Oxford University Press.

Alston and Steiner, *International Human Rights in Context*, 2000, New York: Oxford University Press.

Baderin and McCorquodale, *Economic, Social and Cultural Rights in Action*, 2007, Oxford University Press.

Brownlie, *Basic Documents on Human Rights*, 4th edn, 2002, Oxford University Press.

Campbell *et al*, *Protecting Human Rights*, 2003, Oxford University Press.

Halstead, *Unlocking Human Rights*, 2009, Hodder Education.

Ishay, *The History of Human Rights*, 2004, University of California Press.

Mahoney, *The Challenge of Human Rights*, 2007, Blackwell.

Marks *et al*, *International Human Rights Lexicon*, 2005, Oxford University Press.

Nickel, *Making Sense of Human Rights*, 2007, Blackwell.

Provost, *International Human Rights and Humanitarian Law*, 2002, Cambridge University Press.

Smith, *The Essentials of Human Rights*, 2005, Hodder Arnold.

Smith, *Textbook on International Human Rights*, 2005, Oxford University Press.

Steiner and Alston, *International Human Rights in Context*, 3rd edn, 2007, Oxford University Press.

Woodiwiss, *Human Rights*, 2005, Routledge.

CHAPTER 2

Aziz, 'Sovereignty Lost, Sovereignty Regained? The European Integration Project and the Bundesverfassungsgericht', Robert Schuman Centre Working Paper, EUI 2001/3.

Brownlie, *Principles of Public International Law*, 5th edn, 1998, Oxford University Press.

Byrne and McCutcheon, *The Irish Legal System*, 3rd edn, 1996, Butterworths.

Casey, *Constitutional Law*, 2nd edn, 1992, Sweet and Maxwell.

Charter of Fundamental Rights of the EU (OJ C303/02 14 December 2007).

Collins, *European Community Law in the United Kingdom*, 4th edn, 2001, Butterworths.

Craig and de Búrca (eds), *The Evolution of EU Law*, 1999, Oxford University Press.

Craig and de Búrca, *EU Law: Text, Cases and Materials*, 3rd edn, 2003, Oxford University Press.

Craig and de Búrca, *EU Law: Text, Cases and Materials*, 4th edn, 2008, Oxford University Press.

INDEX

INDEX

INDEX

INDEX